EUROPEAN UNION LAW

Dimiter Bhyangov

European Union Law

Documents

Edited by

Professor Dr. Frank Emmert, LL.M.

C.H. Beck
München

KLUWER LAW INTERNATIONAL
THE HAGUE - LONDON - BOSTON

Published by Kluwer Law International
P.O. Box 85889
2508 CN The Hague, The Netherlands

Sold and distributed in Germany by
Verlag C.H. Beck
Postfach 400340
80703 München, Germany

Sold and distributed in North, Central and South America
by Kluwer Law International
675 Massachusetts Avenue
Cambridge, MA 021139, USA

Sold and distributed in all other countries by
Kluwer Law International
Distribution Centre
P.O. Box 322
3300 AH Dordrecht, The Netherlands.

A C.I.P. Catalogue record for this book is available from the Library of Congress

Printed on acid-free paper

ISBN 3-406-46130-1 (Beck)
ISBN 90 411 1302 9 (Kluwer) (PB)
ISBN 90 411 1312 6 (Kluwer) (HB)

© 1999 Kluwer Law International

Kluwer Law International incorporates the publishing programmes of Graham & Trotman Ltd, Kluwer Law and Taxation Publishers and Martinus Nijhoff Publishers.

TABLE OF CONTENTS

FOUR: HUMAN RIGHTS AND CIVIL LIBERTIES

FIVE: ECONOMIC FREEDOMS IN THE INTERNAL MARKET

Free Movement of Goods

Free Movement of Persons

The Freedom to Provide Services and the Freedom of Establishment

SIX: EUROPEAN UNION COMPETITION POLICY

Cartels and Abuses of Dominant Positions

Block Exemption Regulations

Labour Law and Social Policy

INTRODUCTION

The purpose of the present volume is to provide advanced students of European integration and all those working with European Union law in practice with a compact collection of the most important primary and secondary sources of this law, a quick reference guide, a desk-copy for rapid and frequent consultation.

This collection has a number of advantages over compilations which were previously available. First of all, it includes many documents relating to the institutions of the EU and their decisionmaking processes. Sources of law, such as the Rules of Procedure of Parliament, Council and Commission are useful not only to the student who is trying to understand the work of these institutions but also to the practitioner who wants to check the formal legality of an act of one of these institutions. Barristers will appreciate the Statutes of the Court of Justice, the Rules of Procedure of both Courts of the EU, as well as additional documents, such as the official advice for lawyers preparing written pleadings for the Court of First Instance, and the Ombudsman Decision.

Secondly, all regulations and directives, as well as most other documents, are reproduced with their preambles. In particular the preambles of the secondary sources provide useful information, since it is here that the institutions dispose of their duty of motivating their legislative activity. These passages are thus important for the interpretation of the operative parts of the legal rules.

Thirdly, all documents are printed with article headlines. Since Community law is not exactly userfriendly in this respect, most headlines have been added by the editors. Those additions, as well as all other modifications of the official wording of the legal rules, are indicated by [brackets] and intended for the better understanding of the texts.

Ease of access to the law is further enhanced in this volume by carefully designed tables of contents, one general and several specific for the longer documents, as well as a professional index to key words and expressions.

The documents themselves, were generally obtained directly from the institutions in electronic format, namely by downloading from the official web-site of the EU, and in one case of the Council of Europe. Where documents have been amended subsequent to their adoption, these amendments have been incorporated into the text. All documents are thus "consolidated".

Wherever possible, the law has been updated to the 30th of June 1999. Subsequent amendments and important new legislation will be incorporated in new editions of this volume. Users are advised, wherever this is necessary, to check the up-to-dateness of any specific piece of legislation via the web-site of the EU at http://europa.eu.int/index.htm. After choosing a language, visitors to this web-site are welcomed by a choice of items. In the upper right hand corner, under "Abc", they will find buttons for "official documents" and "legal texts". The latter leads to the web-site of EurLex and thus to the official primary and secondary legal materials. When selecting "Community legislation in force", users gain free access to a database of some 16.000 legislative and administrative measures of the EU and can check each one of them for its validity and any recent amendments. Usually, the text of amendments can be obtained directly from this web-site free of charge some six weeks after adoption.

The other part of the EU web-site which is of particular interest to lawyers is the section entitled "Institutions", which opens doors to all kinds of preparatory acts, green and white papers, Commission Notices, etc.

On condition that the present volume is well received by the readership, the editor and the publisher are planning to develop a whole range of books with documents, cases, and commentary, covering the law of the European Union, but also other areas of international law, such as the law of the World Trade Organisation, international human rights, public international law, etc.

As editor of the present volume, I would like to thank my assistants Ms. Erelin Kikas, Mr. Valdis Levkans, Ms. Triin Liim, and Ms. Katrin Oder for their invaluable help in the compilation and preparation of the documents for publication. Needless to say, the responsibility for any weaknesses and mistakes remains mine alone.

Readers are invited to direct comments and suggestions for the improvement of subsequent editions directly to me at the following address:

Prof. Dr. Frank Emmert, LL.M.
Dean of the Law School
Concordia International University Estonia
Kaluri tee 3, Haabneeme, Viimsi vald
EE-74001 Harjumaa, Estonia
Tel. +372-2-790 529
Fax +372-2-790 216
e-mail FrankEmmert@ciue.edu.ee

Tallinn, July 1999

ONE: THE FOUNDATIONS OF AN "EVER CLOSER UNION"

Treaty on European Union (Consolidated Version)

Table of Contents

HIS MAJESTY THE KING OF THE BELGIANS, HER MAJESTY THE QUEEN OF
DENMARK, THE PRESIDENT OF THE FEDERAL REPUBLIC OF GERMANY, THE
PRESIDENT OF THE HELLENIC REPUBLIC, HIS MAJESTY THE KING OF SPAIN,
THE PRESIDENT OF THE FRENCH REPUBLIC, THE PRESIDENT OF IRELAND,
THE PRESIDENT OF THE ITALIAN REPUBLIC, HIS ROYAL HIGHNESS THE
GRAND DUKE OF LUXEMBOURG, HER MAJESTY THE QUEEN OF THE NE-
THERLANDS, THE PRESIDENT OF THE PORTUGUESE REPUBLIC, HER MA-
JESTY THE QUEEN OF THE UNITED KINGDOM OF GREAT BRITAIN AND NOR-
THERN IRELAND,

RESOLVED to mark a new stage in the process of European integration undertaken
with the establishment of the European Communities,
RECALLING the historic importance of the ending of the division of the European
continent and the need to create firm bases for the construction of the future Europe,

CONFIRMING their attachment to the principles of liberty, democracy and respect for human rights and fundamental freedoms and of the rule of law,

CONFIRMING their attachment to fundamental social rights as defined in the European Social Charter signed at Turin on 18 October 1961 and in the 1989 Community Charter of the Fundamental Social Rights of Workers,

DESIRING to deepen the solidarity between their peoples while respecting their history, their culture and their traditions,

DESIRING to enhance further the democratic and efficient functioning of the institutions so as to enable them better to carry out, within a single institutional framework, the tasks entrusted to them,

RESOLVED to achieve the strengthening and the convergence of their economies and to establish an economic and monetary union including, in accordance with the provisions of this Treaty, a single and stable currency,

DETERMINED to promote economic and social progress for their peoples, taking into account the principle of sustainable development and within the context of the accomplishment of the internal market and of reinforced cohesion and environmental protection, and to implement policies ensuring that advances in economic integration are accompanied by parallel progress in other fields,

RESOLVED to establish a citizenship common to nationals of their countries,

RESOLVED to implement a common foreign and security policy including the progressive framing of a common defence policy, which might lead to a common defence in accordance with the provisions of Article 17, thereby reinforcing the European identity and its independence in order to promote peace, security and progress in Europe and in the world,

RESOLVED to facilitate the free movement of persons, while ensuring the safety and security of their peoples, by establishing an area of freedom, security and justice, in accordance with the provisions of this Treaty,

RESOLVED to continue the process of creating an ever closer union among the peoples of Europe, in which decisions are taken as closely as possible to the citizen in accordance with the principle of subsidiarity,

IN VIEW of further steps to be taken in order to advance European integration,

HAVE DECIDED to establish a European Union and to this end have designated as their Plenipotentiaries ...

WHO, having exchanged their full powers, found in good and due form, have agreed as follows.

TITLE I
COMMON PROVISIONS

Article 1 (ex Article A) [Founding a European Union]

By this Treaty, the HIGH CONTRACTING PARTIES establish among themselves a EUROPEAN UNION, hereinafter called "the Union".

This Treaty marks a new stage in the process of creating an ever closer union among the peoples of Europe, in which decisions are taken as openly as possible and as closely as possible to the citizen.

The Union shall be founded on the European Communities, supplemented by the policies and forms of cooperation established by this Treaty. Its task shall be to organise, in a manner demonstrating consistency and solidarity, relations between the Member States and between their peoples.

Article 2 (ex Article B) [Objectives of the Union]

The Union shall set itself the following objectives:

— to promote economic and social progress and a high level of employment and to achieve balanced and sustainable development, in particular through the creation of an area without internal frontiers, through the strengthening of economic and social cohesion and through the establishment of economic and monetary union, ultimately including a single currency in accordance with the provisions of this Treaty;

— to assert its identity on the international scene, in particular through the implementation of a common foreign and security policy including the progressive framing of a common defence policy, which might lead to a common defence, in accordance with the provisions of Article 17;

— to strengthen the protection of the rights and interests of the nationals of its Member States through the introduction of a citizenship of the Union;

— to maintain and develop the Union as an area of freedom, security and justice, in which the free movement of persons is assured in conjunction with appropriate measures with respect to external border controls, asylum, immigration and the prevention and combatting of crime;

— to maintain in full the *acquis communautaire* and build on it with a view to considering to what extent the policies and forms of cooperation introduced by this Treaty may need to be revised with the aim of ensuring the effectiveness of the mechanisms and the institutions of the Community.

The objectives of the Union shall be achieved as provided in this Treaty and in accordance with the conditions and the timetable set out therein while respecting the principle of subsidiarity as defined in Article 5 of the Treaty establishing the European Community.

Article 3 (ex Article C) [Coherence and Consistency of the Union]

The Union shall be served by a single institutional framework which shall ensure the consistency and the continuity of the activities carried out in order to attain its objectives while respecting and building upon the *acquis communautaire*.

The Union shall in particular ensure the consistency of its external activities as a whole in the context of its external relations, security, economic and development policies. The Council and the Commission shall be responsible for ensuring such consistency and shall cooperate to this end. They shall ensure the implementation of these policies, each in accordance with its respective powers.

Article 4 (ex Article D) [The European Council]

The European Council shall provide the Union with the necessary impetus for its development and shall define the general political guidelines thereof.

The European Council shall bring together the Heads of State or Government of the Member States and the President of the Commission. They shall be assisted by the Ministers for Foreign Affairs of the Member States and by a Member of the Commission. The European Council shall meet at least twice a year, under the chairmanship of the Head of State or Government of the Member State which holds the Presidency of the Council.

The European Council shall submit to the European Parliament a report after each of its meetings and a yearly written report on the progress achieved by the Union.

Article 5 (ex Article E) [The Principle of Enumerated Powers]

The European Parliament, the Council, the Commission, the Court of Justice and the Court of Auditors shall exercise their powers under the conditions and for the purposes provided for, on the one hand, by the provisions of the Treaties establishing the European Communities and of the subsequent Treaties and Acts modifying and supplementing them and, on the other hand, by the other provisions of this Treaty.

Article 6 (ex Article F) [Common Principles of the Union, Respect for the National Identity of the Member States and Individual Human Rights]

1.   The Union is founded on the principles of liberty, democracy, respect for human rights and fundamental freedoms, and the rule of law, principles which are common to the Member States.
2.   The Union shall respect fundamental rights, as guaranteed by the European Convention for the Protection of Human Rights and Fundamental Freedoms signed in Rome on 4 November 1950 and as they result from the constitutional traditions common to the Member States, as general principles of Community law.
3.   The Union shall respect the national identities of its Member States.
4.   The Union shall provide itself with the means necessary to attain its objectives and carry through its policies.

Article 7 (ex Article F.1) [Sanctions for Cases of Serious and Persistent Breaches of the Common Principles]

1.   The Council, meeting in the composition of the Heads of State or Government and acting by unanimity on a proposal by one third of the Member States or by the Commission and after obtaining the assent of the European Parliament, may determine the existence of a serious and persistent breach by a Member State of principles mentioned in Article 6(1), after inviting the government of the Member State in question to submit its observations.
2.   Where such a determination has been made, the Council, acting by a qualified majority, may decide to suspend certain of the rights deriving from the application of this Treaty to the Member State in question, including the voting rights of the representative of the government of that Member State in the Council. In doing so, the Council shall take into account the possible consequences of such a suspension on the rights and obligations of natural and legal persons.
     The obligations of the Member State in question under this Treaty shall in any case continue to be binding on that State.
3.   The Council, acting by a qualified majority, may decide subsequently to vary or revoke measures taken under paragraph 2 in response to changes in the situation which led to their being imposed.
4.   For the purposes of this Article, the Council shall act without taking into account the vote of the representative of the government of the Member State in question. Abstentions by members present in person or represented shall not prevent the adoption of decisions referred to in paragraph 1. A qualified majority shall be defined as the same proportion of the weighted votes of the members of the Council concerned as laid down in Article 205(2) of the Treaty establishing the European Community.
     This paragraph shall also apply in the event of voting rights being suspended pursuant to paragraph 2.
5.   For the purposes of this Article, the European Parliament shall act by a two-thirds majority of the votes cast, representing a majority of its members.

TITLE II
PROVISIONS AMENDING THE TREATY ESTABLISHING THE EUROPEAN ECONOMIC COMMUNITY WITH A VIEW TO ESTABLISHING THE EUROPEAN COMMUNITY

Article 8 (ex Article G) [From the Economic Community to the European Community]
The Treaty establishing the European Economic Community shall be amended in accordance with the provisions of this Article in order to establish a European Community.
A.   - Throughout the Treaty:
The term "European Economic Community" shall be replaced by the term "European Community".
B.   ...
[the amendments have been incorporated into the text of the EEC Treaty; the text reproduced on pp. 19 et seq. is thus the EC Treaty as amended by the Maastricht and Amsterdam Treaties]

TITLE III
PROVISIONS AMENDING THE TREATY ESTABLISHING THE EUROPEAN COAL AND STEEL COMMUNITY

Article 9 (ex Article H)
The Treaty establishing the European Coal and Steel Community shall be amended in accordance with the provisions of this Article. [...]

TITLE IV
PROVISIONS AMENDING THE TREATY ESTABLISHING THE EUROPEAN ATOMIC ENERGY COMMUNITY

Article 10 (ex Article I)
The Treaty establishing the European Atomic Energy Community shall be amended in accordance with the provisions of this Article. [...]

TITLE V
PROVISIONS ON A COMMON FOREIGN AND SECURITY POLICY

Article 11 (ex Article J.1) [Objectives of the CFSP]
1.   The Union shall define and implement a common foreign and security policy covering all areas of foreign and security policy, the objectives of which shall be:
—   to safeguard the common values, fundamental interests, independence and integrity of the Union in conformity with the principles of the United Nations Charter;
—   to strengthen the security of the Union in all ways;
—   to preserve peace and strengthen international security, in accordance with the principles of the United Nations Charter, as well as the principles of the Helsinki Final Act and the objectives of the Paris Charter, including those on external borders;
—   to promote international cooperation;
—   to develop and consolidate democracy and the rule of law, and respect for human rights and fundamental freedoms.
2.   The Member States shall support the Union's external and security policy actively and unreservedly in a spirit of loyalty and mutual solidarity.

The Member States shall work together to enhance and develop their mutual political solidarity. They shall refrain from any action which is contrary to the interests of the Union or likely to impair its effectiveness as a cohesive force in international relations.

The Council shall ensure that these principles are complied with.

Article 12 (ex Article J.2) [Instruments Available to the Union]
The Union shall pursue the objectives set out in Article 11 by:
— defining the principles of and general guidelines for the common foreign and security policy;
— deciding on common strategies;
— adopting joint actions;
— adopting common positions;
— strengthening systematic cooperation between Member States in the conduct of policy.

Article 13 (ex Article J.3) [Principles and General Guidelines, Common Strategies]
1. The European Council shall define the principles of and general guidelines for the common foreign and security policy, including for matters with defence implications.
2. The European Council shall decide on common strategies to be implemented by the Union in areas where the Member States have important interests in common.

Common strategies shall set out their objectives, duration and the means to be made available by the Union and the Member States.
3. The Council shall take the decisions necessary for defining and implementing the common foreign and security policy on the basis of the general guidelines defined by the European Council.

The Council shall recommend common strategies to the European Council and shall implement them, in particular by adopting joint actions and common positions. The Council shall ensure the unity, consistency and effectiveness of action by the Union.

Article 14 (ex Article J.4) [Adoption of Joint Actions]
1. The Council shall adopt joint actions. Joint actions shall address specific situations where operational action by the Union is deemed to be required. They shall lay down their objectives, scope, the means to be made available to the Union, if necessary their duration, and the conditions for their implementation.
2. If there is a change in circumstances having a substantial effect on a question subject to joint action, the Council shall review the principles and objectives of that action and take the necessary decisions. As long as the Council has not acted, the joint action shall stand.
3. Joint actions shall commit the Member States in the positions they adopt and in the conduct of their activity.
4. The Council may request the Commission to submit to it any appropriate proposals relating to the common foreign and security policy to ensure the implementation of a joint action.
5. Whenever there is any plan to adopt a national position or take national action pursuant to a joint action, information shall be provided in time to allow, if necessary, for prior consultations within the Council. The obligation to provide prior information shall not apply to measures which are merely a national transposition of Council decisions.
6. In cases of imperative need arising from changes in the situation and failing a Council decision, Member States may take the necessary measures as a matter of

urgency having regard to the general objectives of the joint action. The Member State concerned shall inform the Council immediately of any such measures.

7. Should there be any major difficulties in implementing a joint action, a Member State shall refer them to the Council which shall discuss them and seek appropriate solutions. Such solutions shall not run counter to the objectives of the joint action or impair its effectiveness.

Article 15 (ex Article J.5) [Adoption of Common Positions]

The Council shall adopt common positions. Common positions shall define the approach of the Union to a particular matter of a geographical or thematic nature. Member States shall ensure that their national policies conform to the common positions.

Article 16 (ex Article J.6) [Collaboration Between Member States and Union]

Member States shall inform and consult one another within the Council on any matter of foreign and security policy of general interest in order to ensure that the Union's influence is exerted as effectively as possible by means of concerted and convergent action.

Article 17 (ex Article J.7) [Security and Defence]

1. The common foreign and security policy shall include all questions relating to the security of the Union, including the progressive framing of a common defence policy, in accordance with the second subparagraph, which might lead to a common defence, should the European Council so decide. It shall in that case recommend to the Member States the adoption of such a decision in accordance with their respective constitutional requirements.

The Western European Union (WEU) is an integral part of the development of the Union providing the Union with access to an operational capability notably in the context of paragraph 2. It supports the Union in framing the defence aspects of the common foreign and security policy as set out in this Article. The Union shall accordingly foster closer institutional relations with the WEU with a view to the possibility of the integration of the WEU into the Union, should the European Council so decide. It shall in that case recommend to the Member States the adoption of such a decision in accordance with their respective constitutional requirements.

The policy of the Union in accordance with this Article shall not prejudice the specific character of the security and defence policy of certain Member States and shall respect the obligations of certain Member States, which see their common defence realised in the North Atlantic Treaty Organisation (NATO), under the North Atlantic Treaty and be compatible with the common security and defence policy established within that framework.

The progressive framing of a common defence policy will be supported, as Member States consider appropriate, by cooperation between them in the field of armaments.

2. Questions referred to in this Article shall include humanitarian and rescue tasks, peacekeeping tasks and tasks of combat forces in crisis management, including peacemaking.

3. The Union will avail itself of the WEU to elaborate and implement decisions and actions of the Union which have defence implications.

The competence of the European Council to establish guidelines in accordance with Article 13 shall also obtain in respect of the WEU for those matters for which the Union avails itself of the WEU.

When the Union avails itself of the WEU to elaborate and implement decisions of the Union on the tasks referred to in paragraph 2 all Member States of the Union shall be entitled to participate fully in the tasks in question. The Council, in agreement with the institutions of the WEU, shall adopt the necessary practical arrangements to allow all Member States contributing to the tasks in question to participate fully and on an equal footing in planning and decision-taking in the WEU.

Decisions having defence implications dealt with under this paragraph shall be taken without prejudice to the policies and obligations referred to in paragraph 1, third subparagraph.

4. The provisions of this Article shall not prevent the development of closer cooperation between two or more Member States on a bilateral level, in the framework of the WEU and the Atlantic Alliance, provided such cooperation does not run counter to or impede that provided for in this Title.

5. With a view to furthering the objectives of this Article, the provisions of this Article will be reviewed in accordance with Article 48.

Article 18 (ex Article J.8) [Powers of the Presidency, the Secretary-General of the Council, the Commission and the Council]

1. The Presidency shall represent the Union in matters coming within the common foreign and security policy.

2. The Presidency shall be responsible for the implementation of decisions taken under this Title; in that capacity it shall in principle express the position of the Union in international organisations and international conferences.

3. The Presidency shall be assisted by the Secretary-General of the Council who shall exercise the function of High Representative for the common foreign and security policy.

4. The Commission shall be fully associated in the tasks referred to in paragraphs 1 and 2. The Presidency shall be assisted in those tasks if need be by the next Member State to hold the Presidency.

5. The Council may, whenever it deems it necessary, appoint a special representative with a mandate in relation to particular policy issues.

Article 19 (ex Article J.9) [Coordinated Action in International Organizations and Conferences]

1. Member States shall coordinate their action in international organisations and at international conferences. They shall uphold the common positions in such form.

In international organisations and at international conferences where not all the Member States participate, those which do take part shall uphold the common positions.

2. Without prejudice to paragraph 1 and Article 14(3), Member States represented in international organisations or international conferences where not all the Member States participate shall keep the latter informed of any matter of common interest.

Member States which are also members of the United Nations Security Council will concert and keep the other Member States fully informed. Member States which are permanent members of the Security Council will, in the execution of their functions, ensure the defence of the positions and the interests of the Union, without prejudice to their responsibilities under the provisions of the United Nations Charter.

Article 20 (ex Article J.10) [Cooperation of Diplomatic and Consular Missions and Representatives]

The diplomatic and consular missions of the Member States and the Commission Delegations in third countries and international conferences, and their representations to international organisations, shall cooperate in ensuring that the common positions and joint actions adopted by the Council are complied with and implemented.

They shall step up cooperation by exchanging information, carrying out joint assessments and contributing to the implementation of the provisions referred to in Article 20 of the Treaty establishing the European Community.

Article 21 (ex Article J.11) [Consultation of Parliament]

The Presidency shall consult the European Parliament on the main aspects and the basic choices of the common foreign and security policy and shall ensure that the views of the European Parliament are duly taken into consideration. The European Parliament shall be kept regularly informed by the Presidency and the Commission of the development of the Union's foreign and security policy.

The European Parliament may ask questions of the Council or make recommendations to it. It shall hold an annual debate on progress in implementing the common foreign and security policy.

Article 22 (ex Article J.12) [Initiation of Procedures]

1. Any Member State or the Commission may refer to the Council any question relating to the common foreign and security policy and may submit proposals to the Council.
2. In cases requiring a rapid decision, the Presidency, of its own motion, or at the request of the Commission or a Member State, shall convene an extraordinary Council meeting within forty-eight hours or, in an emergency, within a shorter period.

Article 23 (ex Article J.13) [Decision making and Voting]

1. Decisions under this Title shall be taken by the Council acting unanimously. Abstentions by members present in person or represented shall not prevent the adoption of such decisions.

When abstaining in a vote, any member of the Council may qualify its abstention by making a formal declaration under the present subparagraph. In that case, it shall not be obliged to apply the decision, but shall accept that the decision commits the Union. In a spirit of mutual solidarity, the Member State concerned shall refrain from any action likely to conflict with or impede Union action based on that decision and the other Member States shall respect its position. If the members of the Council qualifying their abstention in this way represent more than one third of the votes weighted in accordance with Article 205(2) of the Treaty establishing the European Community, the decision shall not be adopted.
2. By derogation from the provisions of paragraph 1, the Council shall act by qualified majority:
— when adopting joint actions, common positions or taking any other decision on the basis of a common strategy;
— when adopting any decision implementing a joint action or a common position.
If a member of the Council declares that, for important and stated reasons of national policy, it intends to oppose the adoption of a decision to be taken by qualified majority, a vote shall not be taken. The Council may, acting by a qualified majority, request that the matter be referred to the European Council for decision by unanimity.

The votes of the members of the Council shall be weighted in accordance with Article 205(2) of the Treaty establishing the European Community. For their adoption, decisions shall require at least 62 votes in favour, cast by at least 10 members.

This paragraph shall not apply to decisions having military or defence implications.
3. For procedural questions, the Council shall act by a majority of its members.

Article 24 (ex Article J.14) [Negotiation and Ratification of International Agreements]

When it is necessary to conclude an agreement with one or more States or international organisations in implementation of this Title, the Council, acting unanimously, may authorise the Presidency, assisted by the Commission as appropriate, to open negotiations to that effect. Such agreements shall be concluded by the Council acting unanimously on a recommendation from the Presidency. No agreement shall be binding on a Member State whose representative in the Council states that it has to comply with the requirements of its own constitutional procedure; the other members of the Council may agree that the agreement shall apply provisionally to them.

The provisions of this Article shall also apply to matters falling under Title VI.

Article 25 (ex Article J.15) [The Political Committee]

Without prejudice to Article 207 of the Treaty establishing the European Community, a Political Committee shall monitor the international situation in the areas covered by the common foreign and security policy and contribute to the definition of policies by delivering opinions to the Council at the request of the Council or on its own initiative. It shall also monitor the implementation of agreed policies, without prejudice to the responsibility of the Presidency and the Commission.

Article 26 (ex Article J.16) [The Secretary-General of the Council as High Representative for the CFSP]

The Secretary-General of the Council, High Representative for the common foreign and security policy, shall assist the Council in matters coming within the scope of the common foreign and security policy, in particular through contributing to the formulation, preparation and implementation of policy decisions, and, when appropriate and acting on behalf of the Council at the request of the Presidency, through conducting political dialogue with third parties.

Article 27 (ex Article J.17) [Involvement of the European Commission]

The Commission shall be fully associated with the work carried out in the common foreign and security policy field.

Article 28 (ex Article J.18) [Institutional and Budgetary Provisions]

1.   Articles 189, 190, 196 to 199, 203, 204, 206 to 209, 213 to 219, 255 and 290 of the Treaty establishing the European Community shall apply to the provisions relating to the areas referred to in this Title.

2.   Administrative expenditure which the provisions relating to the areas referred to in this Title entail for the institutions shall be charged to the budget of the European Communities.

3.   Operational expenditure to which the implementation of those provisions gives rise shall also be charged to the budget of the European Communities, except for such expenditure arising from operations having military or defence implications and cases where the Council acting unanimously decides otherwise.

In cases where expenditure is not charged to the budget of the European Communities it shall be charged to the Member States in accordance with the gross national product scale, unless the Council acting unanimously decides otherwise. As for expenditure arising from operations having military or defence implications, Member States whose representatives in the Council have made a formal declaration under Article 23(1), second subparagraph, shall not be obliged to contribute to the financing thereof.

4.   The budgetary procedure laid down in the Treaty establishing the European Community shall apply to the expenditure charged to the budget of the European Communities.

TITLE VI
PROVISIONS ON POLICE AND JUDICIAL COOPERATION IN CRIMINAL MATTERS

Article 29 (ex Article K.1) [Area of Freedom, Security and Justice: Objectives and Means]

Without prejudice to the powers of the European Community, the Union's objective shall be to provide citizens with a high level of safety within an area of freedom, security and justice by developing common action among the Member States in the fields of police and judicial cooperation in criminal matters and by preventing and combatting racism and xenophobia.

That objective shall be achieved by preventing and combatting crime, organised or otherwise, in particular terrorism, trafficking in persons and offences against children, illicit drug trafficking and illicit arms trafficking, corruption and fraud, through:
— closer cooperation between police forces, customs authorities and other competent authorities in the Member States, both directly and through the European Police Office (Europol), in accordance with the provisions of Articles 30 and 32;
— closer cooperation between judicial and other competent authorities of the Member States in accordance with the provisions of Articles 31(a) to (d) and 32;
— approximation, where necessary, of rules on criminal matters in the Member States, in accordance with the provisions of Article 31(e).

Article 30 (ex Article K.2) [Common Action in Police Cooperation; Europol]
1.   Common action in the field of police cooperation shall include:
(a)   operational cooperation between the competent authorities, including the police, customs and other specialised law enforcement services of the Member States in relation to the prevention, detection and investigation of criminal offences;
(b)   the collection, storage, processing, analysis and exchange of relevant information, including information held by law enforcement services on reports on suspicious financial transactions, in particular through Europol, subject to appropriate provisions on the protection of personal data;
(c)   cooperation and joint initiatives in training, the exchange of liaison officers, secondments, the use of equipment, and forensic research;
(d)   the common evaluation of particular investigative techniques in relation to the detection of serious forms of organised crime.
2.   The Council shall promote cooperation through Europol and shall in particular, within a period of five years after the date of entry into force of the Treaty of Amsterdam:
(a)   enable Europol to facilitate and support the preparation, and to encourage the coordination and carrying out, of specific investigative actions by the competent authorities of the Member States, including operational actions of joint teams comprising representatives of Europol in a support capacity;
(b)   adopt measures allowing Europol to ask the competent authorities of the Member States to conduct and coordinate their investigations in specific cases and to develop specific expertise which may be put at the disposal of Member States to assist them in investigating cases of organised crime;
(c)   promote liaison arrangements between prosecuting/investigating officials specialising in the fight against organised crime in close cooperation with Europol;
(d)   establish a research, documentation and statistical network on cross-border crime.

Article 31 (ex Article K.3) [Common Action on Judicial Cooperation in Criminal Matters]
Common action on judicial cooperation in criminal matters shall include:
(a) facilitating and accelerating cooperation between competent ministries and judicial or equivalent authorities of the Member States in relation to proceedings and the enforcement of decisions;
(b) facilitating extradition between Member States;
(c) ensuring compatibility in rules applicable in the Member States, as may be necessary to improve such cooperation;
(d) preventing conflicts of jurisdiction between Member States;
(e) progressively adopting measures establishing minimum rules relating to the constituent elements of criminal acts and to penalties in the fields of organised crime, terrorism and illicit drug trafficking.

Article 32 (ex Article K.4) [Police Operation in Other Member States]
The Council shall lay down the conditions and limitations under which the competent authorities referred to in Articles 30 and 31 may operate in the territory of another Member State in liaison and in agreement with the authorities of that State.

Article 33 (ex Article K.5) [Member State´s Domaine Réservé]
This Title shall not affect the exercise of the responsibilities incumbent upon Member States with regard to the maintenance of law and order and the safeguarding of internal security.

Article 34 (ex Article K.6) [Collaboration Between Member States and Union; Decision Making and Voting]
1. In the areas referred to in this Title, Member States shall inform and consult one another within the Council with a view to coordinating their action. To that end, they shall establish collaboration between the relevant departments of their administrations.
2. The Council shall take measures and promote cooperation, using the appropriate form and procedures as set out in this Title, contributing to the pursuit of the objectives of the Union. To that end, acting unanimously on the initiative of any Member State or of the Commission, the Council may:
(a) adopt common positions defining the approach of the Union to a particular matter;
(b) adopt framework decisions for the purpose of approximation of the laws and regulations of the Member States. Framework decisions shall be binding upon the Member States as to the result to be achieved but shall leave to the national authorities the choice of form and methods. They shall not entail direct effect;
(c) adopt decisions for any other purpose consistent with the objectives of this Title, excluding any approximation of the laws and regulations of the Member States. These decisions shall be binding and shall not entail direct effect; the Council, acting by a qualified majority, shall adopt measures necessary to implement those decisions at the level of the Union;
(d) establish conventions which it shall recommend to the Member States for adoption in accordance with their respective constitutional requirements. Member States shall begin the procedures applicable within a time limit to be set by the Council.
    Unless they provide otherwise, conventions shall, once adopted by at least half of the Member States, enter into force for those Member States. Measures implementing conventions shall be adopted within the Council by a majority of two-thirds of the Contracting Parties.
3. Where the Council is required to act by a qualified majority, the votes of its members shall be weighted as laid down in Article 205(2) of the Treaty establishing the

European Community, and for their adoption acts of the Council shall require at least 62 votes in favour, cast by at least 10 members.
4.   For procedural questions, the Council shall act by a majority of its members.

Article 35 (ex Article K.7) [Jurisdiction of the Court of Justice]
1.   The Court of Justice of the European Communities shall have jurisdiction, subject to the conditions laid down in this Article, to give preliminary rulings on the validity and interpretation of framework decisions and decisions, on the interpretation of conventions established under this Title and on the validity and interpretation of the measures implementing them.
2.   By a declaration made at the time of signature of the Treaty of Amsterdam or at any time thereafter, any Member State shall be able to accept the jurisdiction of the Court of Justice to give preliminary rulings as specified in paragraph 1.
3.   A Member State making a declaration pursuant to paragraph 2 shall specify that either:
(a)   any court or tribunal of that State against whose decisions there is no judicial remedy under national law may request the Court of Justice to give a preliminary ruling on a question raised in a case pending before it and concerning the validity or interpretation of an act referred to in paragraph 1 if that court or tribunal considers that a decision on the question is necessary to enable it to give judgment, or
(b)   any court or tribunal of that State may request the Court of Justice to give a preliminary ruling on a question raised in a case pending before it and concerning the validity or interpretation of an act referred to in paragraph 1 if that court or tribunal considers that a decision on the question is necessary to enable it to give judgment.
4.   Any Member State, whether or not it has made a declaration pursuant to paragraph 2, shall be entitled to submit statements of case or written observations to the Court in cases which arise under paragraph 1.
5.   The Court of Justice shall have no jurisdiction to review the validity or proportionality of operations carried out by the police or other law enforcement services of a Member State or the exercise of the responsibilities incumbent upon Member States with regard to the maintenance of law and order and the safeguarding of internal security.
6.   The Court of Justice shall have jurisdiction to review the legality of framework decisions and decisions in actions brought by a Member State or the Commission on grounds of lack of competence, infringement of an essential procedural requirement, infringement of this Treaty or of any rule of law relating to its application, or misuse of powers. The proceedings provided for in this paragraph shall be instituted within two months of the publication of the measure.
7.   The Court of Justice shall have jurisdiction to rule on any dispute between Member States regarding the interpretation or the application of acts adopted under Article 34(2) whenever such dispute cannot be settled by the Council within six months of its being referred to the Council by one of its members. The Court shall also have jurisdiction to rule on any dispute between Member States and the Commission regarding the interpretation or the application of conventions established under Article 34(2)(d).

Article 36 (ex Article K.8) [The Coordinating Committee]
1.   A Coordinating Committee shall be set up consisting of senior officials. In addition to its coordinating role, it shall be the task of the Committee to:
—   give opinions for the attention of the Council, either at the Council's request or on its own initiative;

— contribute, without prejudice to Article 207 of the Treaty establishing the European Community, to the preparation of the Council's discussions in the areas referred to in Article 29.
2.   The Commission shall be fully associated with the work in the areas referred to in this Title.

Article 37 (ex Article K.9) [Common Positions in International Organizations and Conferences]

Within international organisations and at international conferences in which they take part, Member States shall defend the common positions adopted under the provisions of this Title.
Articles 18 and 19 shall apply as appropriate to matters falling under this Title.

Article 38 (ex Article K.10) [Negotiation and Ratification of International Agreements]

Agreements referred to in Article 24 may cover matters falling under this Title.

Article 39 (ex Article K.11) [Consultation of Parliament]

1.   The Council shall consult the European Parliament before adopting any measure referred to in Article 34(2)(b), (c) and (d). The European Parliament shall deliver its opinion within a time-limit which the Council may lay down, which shall not be less than three months. In the absence of an opinion within that time-limit, the Council may act.
2.   The Presidency and the Commission shall regularly inform the European Parliament of discussions in the areas covered by this Title.
3.   The European Parliament may ask questions of the Council or make recommendations to it. Each year, it shall hold a debate on the progress made in the areas referred to in this Title.

Article 40 (ex Article K.12) [Closer Cooperation Between Certain Member States]

1.   Member States which intend to establish closer cooperation between themselves may be authorised, subject to Articles 43 and 44, to make use of the institutions, procedures and mechanisms laid down by the Treaties provided that the cooperation proposed:
(a) respects the powers of the European Community, and the objectives laid down by this Title;
(b) has the aim of enabling the Union to develop more rapidly into an area of freedom, security and justice.
2.   The authorisation referred to in paragraph 1 shall be granted by the Council, acting by a qualified majority at the request of the Member States concerned and after inviting the Commission to present its opinion; the request shall also be forwarded to the European Parliament.
If a member of the Council declares that, for important and stated reasons of national policy, it intends to oppose the granting of an authorisation by qualified majority, a vote shall not be taken. The Council may, acting by a qualified majority, request that the matter be referred to the European Council for decision by unanimity.
The votes of the members of the Council shall be weighted in accordance with Article 205(2) of the Treaty establishing the European Community. For their adoption, decisions shall require at least 62 votes in favour, cast by at least 10 members.
3.   Any Member State which wishes to become a party to cooperation set up in accordance with this Article shall notify its intention to the Council and to the Commission, which shall give an opinion to the Council within three months of receipt of that notification, possibly accompanied by a recommendation for such specific arrangements as it may deem necessary for that Member State to become a party to the

cooperation in question. Within four months of the date of that notification, the Council shall decide on the request and on such specific arrangements as it may deem necessary. The decision shall be deemed to be taken unless the Council, acting by a qualified majority, decides to hold it in abeyance; in this case, the Council shall state the reasons for its decision and set a deadline for re-examining it. For the purposes of this paragraph, the Council shall act under the conditions set out in Article 44.
4.   The provisions of Articles 29 to 41 shall apply to the closer cooperation provided for by this Article, save as otherwise provided for in this Article and in Articles 43 and 44.
    The provisions of the Treaty establishing the European Community concerning the powers of the Court of Justice of the European Communities and the exercise of those powers shall apply to paragraphs 1, 2 and 3.
5.   This Article is without prejudice to the provisions of the Protocol integrating the Schengen *acquis* into the framework of the European Union.

Article 41 (ex Article K.13) [Institutional and Budgetary Provisions]
1.   Articles 189, 190, 195, 196 to 199, 203, 204, 205(3), 206 to 209, 213 to 219, 255 and 290 of the Treaty establishing the European Community shall apply to the provisions relating to the areas referred to in this Title.
2.   Administrative expenditure which the provisions relating to the areas referred to in this Title entail for the institutions shall be charged to the budget of the European Communities.
3.   Operational expenditure to which the implementation of those provisions gives rise shall also be charged to the budget of the European Communities, except where the Council acting unanimously decides otherwise. In cases where expenditure is not charged to the budget of the European Communities it shall be charged to the Member States in accordance with the gross national product scale, unless the Council acting unanimously decides otherwise.
4.   The budgetary procedure laid down in the Treaty establishing the European Community shall apply to the expenditure charged to the budget of the European Communities.

Article 42 (ex Article K.14) [Transfer of Areas into the First Pillar]
The Council, acting unanimously on the initiative of the Commission or a Member State, and after consulting the European Parliament, may decide that action in areas referred to in Article 29 shall fall under Title IV of the Treaty establishing the European Community, and at the same time determine the relevant voting conditions relating to it. It shall recommend the Member States to adopt that decision in accordance with their respective constitutional requirements.

TITLE VII (EX TITLE VIA)
PROVISIONS ON CLOSER COOPERATION

Article 43 (ex Article K.15) [Conditions for Closer Cooperation Between Certain Member States]
1.   Member States which intend to establish closer cooperation between themselves may make use of the institutions, procedures and mechanisms laid down by this Treaty and the Treaty establishing the European Community provided that the cooperation:
(a) is aimed at furthering the objectives of the Union and at protecting and serving its interests;
(b) respects the principles of the said Treaties and the single institutional framework of the Union;

(c) is only used as a last resort, where the objectives of the said Treaties could not be attained by applying the relevant procedures laid down therein;
(d) concerns at least a majority of Member States;
(e) does not affect the "acquis communautaire" and the measures adopted under the other provisions of the said Treaties;
(f) does not affect the competences, rights, obligations and interests of those Member States which do not participate therein;
(g) is open to all Member States and allows them to become parties to the cooperation at any time, provided that they comply with the basic decision and with the decisions taken within that framework;
(h) complies with the specific additional criteria laid down in Article 11 of the Treaty establishing the European Community and Article 40 of this Treaty, depending on the area concerned, and is authorised by the Council in accordance with the procedures laid down therein.
2. Member States shall apply, as far as they are concerned, the acts and decisions adopted for the implementation of the cooperation in which they participate. Member States not participating in such cooperation shall not impede the implementation thereof by the participating Member States.

Article 44 (ex Article K.16) [Decision Making and Voting]
1. For the purposes of the adoption of the acts and decisions necessary for the implementation of the cooperation referred to in Article 43, the relevant institutional provisions of this Treaty and of the Treaty establishing the European Community shall apply. However, while all members of the Council shall be able to take part in the deliberations, only those representing participating Member States shall take part in the adoption of decisions. The qualified majority shall be defined as the same proportion of the weighted votes of the members of the Council concerned as laid down in Article 205(2) of the Treaty establishing the European Community. Unanimity shall be constituted by only those Council members concerned.
2. Expenditure resulting from implementation of the cooperation, other than administrative costs entailed for the institutions, shall be borne by the participating Member States, unless the Council, acting unanimously, decides otherwise.

Article 45 (ex Article K.17) [Information of Parliament]
The Council and the Commission shall regularly inform the European Parliament of the development of closer cooperation established on the basis of this Title.

TITLE VIII (EX TITLE VII)
FINAL PROVISIONS

Article 46 (ex Article L) [Limited Jurisdiction of the Court of Justice]
The provisions of the Treaty establishing the European Community, the Treaty establishing the European Coal and Steel Community and the Treaty establishing the European Atomic Energy Community concerning the powers of the Court of Justice of the European Communities and the exercise of those powers shall apply only to the following provisions of this Treaty:
(a) provisions amending the Treaty establishing the European Economic Community with a view to establishing the European Community, the Treaty establishing the European Coal and Steel Community and the Treaty establishing the European Atomic Energy Community;
(b) provisions of Title VI, under the conditions provided for by Article 35;

(c) provisions of Title VII, under the conditions provided for by Article 11 of the Treaty establishing the European Community and Article 40 of this Treaty;
(d) Article 6(2) with regard to action of the institutions, insofar as the Court has jurisdiction under the Treaties establishing the European Communities and under this Treaty;
(e) Articles 46 to 53.

Article 47 (ex Article M) [Application of the Community Treaties]

Subject to the provisions amending the Treaty establishing the European Economic Community with a view to establishing the European Community, the Treaty establishing the European Coal and Steel Community and the Treaty establishing the European Atomic Energy Community, and to these final provisions, nothing in this Treaty shall affect the Treaties establishing the European Communities or the subsequent Treaties and Acts modifying or supplementing them.

Article 48 (ex Article N) [Procedure for Amendment of the Treaties]

The government of any Member State or the Commission may submit to the Council proposals for the amendment of the Treaties on which the Union is founded.

If the Council, after consulting the European Parliament and, where appropriate, the Commission, delivers an opinion in favour of calling a conference of representatives of the governments of the Member States, the conference shall be convened by the President of the Council for the purpose of determining by common accord the amendments to be made to those Treaties. The European Central Bank shall also be consulted in the case of institutional changes in the monetary area.

The amendments shall enter into force after being ratified by all the Member States in accordance with their respective constitutional requirements.

Article 49 (ex Article O) [Admission of New Member States]

Any European State which respects the principles set out in Article 6(1) may apply to become a member of the Union. It shall address its application to the Council, which shall act unanimously after consulting the Commission and after receiving the assent of the European Parliament, which shall act by an absolute majority of its component members.

The conditions of admission and the adjustments to the Treaties on which the Union is founded which such admission entails shall be the subject of an agreement between the Member States and the applicant State. This agreement shall be submitted for ratification by all the contracting States in accordance with their respective constitutional requirements.

Article 50 (ex Article P) [Repealing Certain Provisions of the Merger Treaty and the SEA]

1. Articles 2 to 7 and 10 to 19 of the Treaty establishing a Single Council and a Single Commission of the European Communities, signed in Brussels on 8 April 1965, are hereby repealed.
2. Article 2, Article 3(2) and Title III of the Single European Act signed in Luxembourg on 17 February 1986 and in The Hague on 28 February 1986 are hereby repealed.

Article 51 (ex Article Q) [Unlimited Duration]

This Treaty is concluded for an unlimited period.

Article 52 (ex Article R) [Ratification and Entry into Force]
1.   This Treaty shall be ratified by the High Contracting Parties in accordance with their respective constitutional requirements. The instruments of ratification shall be deposited with the Government of the Italian Republic.
2.   This Treaty shall enter into force on 1 January 1993, provided that all the instruments of ratification have been deposited, or, failing that, on the first day of the month following the deposit of the instrument of ratification by the last signatory State to take this step.

Article 53 (ex Article S) [Authentic Language Versions]
This Treaty, drawn up in a single original in the Danish, Dutch, English, French, German, Greek, Irish, Italian, Portuguese and Spanish languages, the texts in each of these languages being equally authentic, shall be deposited in the archives of the government of the Italian Republic, which will transmit a certified copy to each of the governments of the other signatory States.
Pursuant to the Accession Treaty of 1994, the Finnish and Swedish versions of this Treaty shall also be authentic.

In witness whereof the undersigned Plenipotentiaries have signed this Treaty.
Done at Maastricht on the seventh day of February in the year one thousand nine hundred and ninety-two.

European Community Treaty (Consolidated Version)

Table of Contents

HIS MAJESTY THE KING OF THE BELGIANS, THE PRESIDENT OF THE FEDERAL REPUBLIC OF GERMANY, THE PRESIDENT OF THE FRENCH REPUBLIC, THE PRESIDENT OF THE ITALIAN REPUBLIC, HER ROYAL HIGHNESS THE GRAND DUCHESS OF LUXEMBOURG, HER MAJESTY THE QUEEN OF THE NETHER-LANDS,[1]

DETERMINED to lay the foundations of an ever closer union among the peoples of Europe,
RESOLVED to ensure the economic and social progress of their countries by common action to eliminate the barriers which divide Europe,
AFFIRMING as the essential objective of their efforts the constant improvements of the living and working conditions of their peoples,
RECOGNISING that the removal of existing obstacles calls for concerted action in order to guarantee steady expansion, balanced trade and fair competition,
ANXIOUS to strengthen the unity of their economies and to ensure their harmonious development by reducing the differences existing between the various regions and the backwardness of the less-favoured regions,
DESIRING to contribute, by means of a common commercial policy, to the progressive abolition of restrictions on international trade,
INTENDING to confirm the solidarity which binds Europe and the overseas countries and desiring to ensure the development of their prosperity, in accordance with the principles of the Charter of the United Nations,
RESOLVED by thus pooling their resources to preserve and strengthen peace and liberty, and calling upon the other peoples of Europe who share their ideal to join in their efforts,
DETERMINED to promote the development of the highest possible level of knowledge for their peoples through a wide access to education and through its continuous updating,
HAVE DECIDED to create a EUROPEAN COMMUNITY and to this end have designated as their Plenipotentiaries: [...]
WHO, having exchanged their full powers, found in good and due form, have agreed as follows.

---

1   The Kingdom of Denmark, the Hellenic Republic, the Kingdom of Spain, Ireland, the Republic of Austria, the Portuguese Republic, the Republic of Finland, the Kingdom of Sweden and the United Kingdom of Great Britain and Northern Ireland have since become members of the European Community.

PART ONE
PRINCIPLES

Article 1 (ex Article 1) [Founding the European Community]
By this Treaty, the HIGH CONTRACTING PARTIES establish among themselves a
EUROPEAN COMMUNITY.

Article 2 (ex Article 2) [General Tasks of the European Community]
The Community shall have as its task, by establishing a common market and an
economic and monetary union and by implementing common policies or activities
referred to in Articles 3 and 4, to promote throughout the Community a harmonious,
balanced and sustainable development of economic activities, a high level of employment and of social protection, equality between men and women, sustainable and non-
inflationary growth, a high degree of competitiveness and convergence of economic
performance, a high level of protection and improvement of the quality of the environment, the raising of the standard of living and quality of life, and economic and social
cohesion and solidarity among Member States.

Article 3 (ex Article 3) [Specific Objectives of the European Community]
1.   For the purposes set out in Article 2, the activities of the Community shall include,
as provided in this Treaty and in accordance with the timetable set out therein:
(a) the prohibition, as between Member States, of customs duties and quantitative re-
       strictions on the import and export of goods, and of all other measures having
       equivalent effect;
(b) a common commercial policy;
(c) an internal market characterised by the abolition, as between Member States, of
       obstacles to the free movement of goods, persons, services and capital;
(d) measures concerning the entry and movement of persons as provided for in Title
       IV;
(e) a common policy in the sphere of agriculture and fisheries;
(f)   a common policy in the sphere of transport;
(g) a system ensuring that competition in the internal market is not distorted;
(h) the approximation of the laws of Member States to the extent required for the
       functioning of the common market;
(i)   the promotion of coordination between employment policies of the Member States
       with a view to enhancing their effectiveness by developing a coordinated strategy
       for employment;
(j)   a policy in the social sphere comprising a European Social Fund;
(k) the strengthening of economic and social cohesion;
(l)   a policy in the sphere of the environment;
(m) the strengthening of the competitiveness of Community industry;
(n) the promotion of research and technological development;
(o) encouragement for the establishment and development of trans-European net-
       works;
(p) a contribution to the attainment of a high level of health protection;
(q) a contribution to education and training of quality and to the flowering of the cul-
       tures of the Member States;
(r)   a policy in the sphere of development cooperation;
(s) the association of the overseas countries and territories in order to increase trade
       and promote jointly economic and social development;
(t)   a contribution to the strengthening of consumer protection;
(u) measures in the spheres of energy, civil protection and tourism.

2.   In all the activities referred to in this Article, the Community shall aim to eliminate inequalities, and to promote equality, between men and women.

Article 4 (ex Article 3a) [Economic Policy and Monetary Union]
1.   For the purposes set out in Article 2, the activities of the Member States and the Community shall include, as provided in this Treaty and in accordance with the time-table set out therein, the adoption of an economic policy which is based on the close coordination of Member States' economic policies, on the internal market and on the definition of common objectives, and conducted in accordance with the principle of an open market economy with free competition.
2.   Concurrently with the foregoing, and as provided in this Treaty and in accordance with the timetable and the procedures set out therein, these activities shall include the irrevocable fixing of exchange rates leading to the introduction of a single currency, the ECU, and the definition and conduct of a single monetary policy and exchange-rate policy the primary objective of both of which shall be to maintain price stability and, without prejudice to this objective, to support the general economic policies in the Community, in accordance with the principle of an open market economy with free competition.
3.   These activities of the Member States and the Community shall entail compliance with the following guiding principles: stable prices, sound public finances and monetary conditions and a sustainable balance of payments.

Article 5 (ex Article 3b) [Enumerated Powers, Subsidiarity, Proportionality]
The Community shall act within the limits of the powers conferred upon it by this Treaty and of the objectives assigned to it therein.

In areas which do not fall within its exclusive competence, the Community shall take action, in accordance with the principle of subsidiarity, only if and insofar as the objectives of the proposed action cannot be sufficiently achieved by the Member States and can therefore, by reason of the scale or effects of the proposed action, be better achieved by the Community.

Any action by the Community shall not go beyond what is necessary to achieve the objectives of this Treaty.

Article 6 (ex Article 3c) [Environmental Protection to be Integrated in all Policies and Activities]
Environmental protection requirements must be integrated into the definition and imple-mentation of the Community policies and activities referred to in Article 3, in particular with a view to promoting sustainable development.

Article 7 (ex Article 4) [Institutions of the European Community]
1.   The tasks entrusted to the Community shall be carried out by the following institutions:
—   a EUROPEAN PARLIAMENT,
—   a COUNCIL,
—   a COMMISSION,
—   a COURT OF JUSTICE,
—   a COURT OF AUDITORS.
Each institution shall act within the limits of the powers conferred upon it by this Treaty.
2.   The Council and the Commission shall be assisted by an Economic and Social Committee and a Committee of the Regions acting in an advisory capacity.

Article 8 (ex Article 4a) [Institutions of Monetary Union]

A European System of Central Banks (hereinafter referred to as "ESCB") and a European Central Bank (hereinafter referred to as "ECB") shall be established in accordance with the procedures laid down in this Treaty; they shall act within the limits of the powers conferred upon them by this Treaty and by the Statute of the ESCB and of the ECB (hereinafter referred to as "Statute of the ESCB") annexed thereto.

Article 9 (ex Article 4b) [The European Investment Bank]

A European Investment Bank is hereby established, which shall act within the limits of the powers conferred upon it by this Treaty and the Statute annexed thereto.

Article 10 (ex Article 5) [Mutual Loyalty]

Member States shall take all appropriate measures, whether general or particular, to ensure fulfilment of the obligations arising out of this Treaty or resulting from action taken by the institutions of the Community. They shall facilitate the achievement of the Community's tasks.

They shall abstain from any measure which could jeopardise the attainment of the objectives of this Treaty.

Article 11 (ex Article 5a) [Closer Cooperation Between Certain Member States]

1.   Member States which intend to establish closer cooperation between themselves may be authorised, subject to Articles 43 and 44 of the Treaty on European Union, to make use of the institutions, procedures and mechanisms laid down by this Treaty, provided that the cooperation proposed:
(a) does not concern areas which fall within the exclusive competence of the Community;
(b) does not affect Community policies, actions or programmes;
(c) does not concern the citizenship of the Union or discriminate between nationals of Member States;
(d) remains within the limits of the powers conferred upon the Community by this Treaty; and
(e) does not constitute a discrimination or a restriction of trade between Member States and does not distort the conditions of competition between the latter.

2.   The authorisation referred to in paragraph 1 shall be granted by the Council, acting by a qualified majority on a proposal from the Commission and after consulting the European Parliament.

If a member of the Council declares that, for important and stated reasons of national policy, it intends to oppose the granting of an authorisation by qualified majority, a vote shall not be taken. The Council may, acting by a qualified majority, request that the matter be referred to the Council, meeting in the composition of the Heads of State or Government, for decision by unanimity.

Member States which intend to establish closer cooperation as referred to in paragraph 1 may address a request to the Commission, which may submit a proposal to the Council to that effect. In the event of the Commission not submitting a proposal, it shall inform the Member States concerned of the reasons for not doing so.

3.   Any Member State which wishes to become a party to cooperation set up in accordance with this Article shall notify its intention to the Council and to the Commission, which shall give an opinion to the Council within three months of receipt of that notification. Within four months of the date of that notification, the Commission shall decide on it and on such specific arrangements as it may deem necessary.

4.   The acts and decisions necessary for the implementation of cooperation activities shall be subject to all the relevant provisions of this Treaty, save as otherwise provided for in this Article and in Articles 43 and 44 of the Treaty on European Union.
5.   This Article is without prejudice to the provisions of the Protocol integrating the Schengen *acquis* into the framework of the European Union.

Article 12 (ex Article 6) [No Discrimination on the Basis of Nationality]
Within the scope of application of this Treaty, and without prejudice to any special provisions contained therein, any discrimination on grounds of nationality shall be prohibited.
   The Council, acting in accordance with the procedure referred to in Article 251, may adopt rules designed to prohibit such discrimination.

Article 13 (ex Article 6a) [Community Action to Combat Discrimination]
Without prejudice to the other provisions of this Treaty and within the limits of the powers conferred by it upon the Community, the Council, acting unanimously on a proposal from the Commission and after consulting the European Parliament, may take appropriate action to combat discrimination based on sex, racial or ethnic origin, religion or belief, disability, age or sexual orientation.

Article 14 (ex Article 7a) [The Internal Market]
1.   The Community shall adopt measures with the aim of progressively establishing the internal market over a period expiring on 31 December 1992, in accordance with the provisions of this Article and of Articles 15, 26, 47(2), 49, 80, 93 and 95 and without prejudice to the other provisions of this Treaty.
2.   The internal market shall comprise an area without internal frontiers in which the free movement of goods, persons, services and capital is ensured in accordance with the provisions of this Treaty.
3.   The Council, acting by a qualified majority on a proposal from the Commission, shall determine the guidelines and conditions necessary to ensure balanced progress in all the sectors concerned.

Article 15 (ex Article 7c) [Derogations on the Way Towards the Internal Market]
When drawing up its proposals with a view to achieving the objectives set out in Article 14, the Commission shall take into account the extent of the effort that certain economies showing differences in development will have to sustain during the period of establishment of the internal market and it may propose appropriate provisions.
   If these provisions take the form of derogations, they must be of a temporary nature and must cause the least possible disturbance to the functioning of the common market.

Article 16 (ex Article 7d) [Derogations for Services of General Economic Interest]
Without prejudice to Articles 73, 86 and 87, and given the place occupied by services of general economic interest in the shared values of the Union as well as their role in promoting social and territorial cohesion, the Community and the Member States, each within their respective powers and within the scope of application of this Treaty, shall take care that such services operate on the basis of principles and conditions which enable them to fulfil their missions.

PART TWO
CITIZENSHIP OF THE UNION

Article 17 (ex Article 8) [Citizenship of the Union]
1.   Citizenship of the Union is hereby established. Every person holding the nationality of a Member State shall be a citizen of the Union. Citizenship of the Union shall complement and not replace national citizenship.
2.   Citizens of the Union shall enjoy the rights conferred by this Treaty and shall be subject to the duties imposed thereby.

Article 18 (ex Article 8a) [Freedom of Movement and Choice of Residence]
1.   Every citizen of the Union shall have the right to move and reside freely within the territory of the Member States, subject to the limitations and conditions laid down in this Treaty and by the measures adopted to give it effect.
2.   The Council may adopt provisions with a view to facilitating the exercise of the rights referred to in paragraph 1; save as otherwise provided in this Treaty, the Council shall act in accordance with the procedure referred to in Article 251. The Council shall act unanimously throughout this procedure.

Article 19 (ex Article 8b) [Municipal and European Elections]
1.   Every citizen of the Union residing in a Member State of which he is not a national shall have the right to vote and to stand as a candidate at municipal elections in the Member State in which he resides, under the same conditions as nationals of that State. This right shall be exercised subject to detailed arrangements adopted by the Council, acting unanimously on a proposal from the Commission and after consulting the European Parliament; these arrangements may provide for derogations where warranted by problems specific to a Member State.
2.   Without prejudice to Article 190(4) and to the provisions adopted for its implementation, every citizen of the Union residing in a Member State of which he is not a national shall have the right to vote and to stand as a candidate in elections to the European Parliament in the Member State in which he resides, under the same conditions as nationals of that State. This right shall be exercised subject to detailed arrangements adopted by the Council, acting unanimously on a proposal from the Commission and after consulting the European Parliament; these arrangements may provide for derogations where warranted by problems specific to a Member State.

Article 20 (ex Article 8c) [Diplomatic and Consular Protection]
Every citizen of the Union shall, in the territory of a third country in which the Member State of which he is a national is not represented, be entitled to protection by the diplomatic or consular authorities of any Member State, on the same conditions as the nationals of that State. Member States shall establish the necessary rules among themselves and start the international negotiations required to secure this protection.

Article 21 (ex Article 8d) [Petitions to the European Parliament; the Ombudsperson]
Every citizen of the Union shall have the right to petition the European Parliament in accordance with Article 194.
Every citizen of the Union may apply to the Ombudsman established in accordance with Article 195.
Every citizen of the Union may write to any of the institutions or bodies referred to in this Article or in Article 7 in one of the languages mentioned in Article 314 and have an answer in the same language.

Article 22 (ex Article 8e) [Evolution of Citizenship Rights]
The Commission shall report to the European Parliament, to the Council and to the Economic and Social Committee every three years on the application of the provisions of this Part. This report shall take account of the development of the Union.
On this basis, and without prejudice to the other provisions of this Treaty, the Council, acting unanimously on a proposal from the Commission and after consulting the European Parliament, may adopt provisions to strengthen or to add to the rights laid down in this Part, which it shall recommend to the Member States for adoption in accordance with their respective constitutional requirements.

PART THREE
COMMUNITY POLICIES
TITLE I
FREE MOVEMENT OF GOODS

Article 23 (ex Article 9) [Establishing the Customs Union]
1.   The Community shall be based upon a customs union which shall cover all trade in goods and which shall involve the prohibition between Member States of customs duties on imports and exports and of all charges having equivalent effect, and the adoption of a common customs tariff in their relations with third countries.
2.   The provisions of Article 25 and of Chapter 2 of this Title shall apply to products originating in Member States and to products coming from third countries which are in free circulation in Member States.

Article 24 (ex Article 10) [Third Country Products in Free Circulation in the Internal Market]
Products coming from a third country shall be considered to be in free circulation in a Member State if the import formalities have been complied with and any customs duties or charges having equivalent effect which are payable have been levied in that Member State, and if they have not benefited from a total or partial drawback of such duties or charges.

Chapter 1 The Customs Union

Article 25 (ex Article 12) [Prohibition of Import Duties and Charges Having Equivalent Effect]
Customs duties on imports and exports and charges having equivalent effect shall be prohibited between Member States. This prohibition shall also apply to customs duties of a fiscal nature.

Article 26 (ex Article 28) [Decision making on the Common Customs Tariff]
Common Customs Tariff duties shall be fixed by the Council acting by a qualified majority on a proposal from the Commission.

Article 27 (ex Article 29) [Guidelines for the Commission]
In carrying out the tasks entrusted to it under this Chapter the Commission shall be guided by:
(a) the need to promote trade between Member States and third countries;
(b) developments in conditions of competition within the Community insofar as they lead to an improvement in the competitive capacity of undertakings;
(c) the requirements of the Community as regards the supply of raw materials and semi-finished goods; in this connection the Commission shall take care to avoid

distorting conditions of competition between Member States in respect of finished goods;
(d) the need to avoid serious disturbances in the economies of Member States and to ensure rational development of production and an expansion of consumption within the Community.

Chapter 2 Prohibition of Quantitative Restrictions Between Member States

Article 28 (ex Article 30) [Prohibition of Quantitative Import Restrictions and Measures Having Equivalent Effect]
Quantitative restrictions on imports and all measures having equivalent effect shall be prohibited between Member States.

Article 29 (ex Article 34) [Prohibition of Quantitative Export Restrictions and Measures Having Equivalent Effect]
Quantitative restrictions on exports, and all measures having equivalent effect, shall be prohibited between Member States.

Article 30 (ex Article 36) [Justifications for Remaining Quantitative Restrictions and Measures Having Equivalent Effect]
The provisions of Articles 28 and 29 shall not preclude prohibitions or restrictions on imports, exports or goods in transit justified on grounds of public morality, public policy or public security; the protection of health and life of humans, animals or plants; the protection of national treasures possessing artistic, historic or archaeological value; or the protection of industrial and commercial property. Such prohibitions or restrictions shall not, however, constitute a means of arbitrary discrimination or a disguised restriction on trade between Member States.

Article 31 (ex Article 37) [State Monopolies of a Commercial Character]
1.   Member States shall adjust any State monopolies of a commercial character so as to ensure that no discrimination regarding the conditions under which goods are procured and marketed exists between nationals of Member States.
     The provisions of this Article shall apply to any body through which a Member State, in law or in fact, either directly or indirectly supervises, determines or appreciably influences imports or exports between Member States. These provisions shall likewise apply to monopolies delegated by the State to others.
2.   Member States shall refrain from introducing any new measure which is contrary to the principles laid down in paragraph 1 or which restricts the scope of the Articles dealing with the prohibition of customs duties and quantitative restrictions between Member States.
3.   If a State monopoly of a commercial character has rules which are designed to make it easier to dispose of agricultural products or obtain for them the best return, steps should be taken in applying the rules contained in this Article to ensure equivalent safeguards for the employment and standard of living of the producers concerned.

TITLE II
AGRICULTURE

Article 32 (ex Article 38) [The Internal Market for Agricultural Products]
1.   The common market shall extend to agriculture and trade in agricultural products. "Agricultural products" means the products of the soil, of stock farming and of fisheries and products of first-stage processing directly related to these products.
2.   Save as otherwise provided in Articles 33 to 38, the rules laid down for the establishment of the common market shall apply to agricultural products.
3.   The products subject to the provisions of Articles 33 to 38 are listed in Annex I to this Treaty.
4.   The operation and development of the common market for agricultural products must be accompanied by the establishment of a common agricultural policy.

Article 33 (ex Article 39) [Objectives of the Common Agricultural Policy]
1.   The objectives of the common agricultural policy shall be:
(a) to increase agricultural productivity by promoting technical progress and by ensuring the rational development of agricultural production and the optimum utilisation of the factors of production, in particular labour;
(b) thus to ensure a fair standard of living for the agricultural community, in particular by increasing the individual earnings of persons engaged in agriculture;
(c) to stabilise markets;
(d) to assure the availability of supplies;
(e) to ensure that supplies reach consumers at reasonable prices.
2.   In working out the common agricultural policy and the special methods for its application, account shall be taken of:
(a) the particular nature of agricultural activity, which results from the social structure of agriculture and from structural and natural disparities between the various agricultural regions;
(b) the need to effect the appropriate adjustments by degrees;
(c) the fact that in the Member States agriculture constitutes a sector closely linked with the economy as a whole.

Article 34 (ex Article 40) [Progressive Establishment of the
Common Agricultural Policy]
1.   In order to attain the objectives set out in Article 33, a common organisation of agricultural markets shall be established.
This organisation shall take one of the following forms, depending on the product concerned:
(a) common rules on competition;
(b) compulsory coordination of the various national market organisations;
(c) a European market organisation.
2.   The common organisation established in accordance with paragraph 1 may include all measures required to attain the objectives set out in Article 33, in particular regulation of prices, aids for the production and marketing of the various products, storage and carryover arrangements and common machinery for stabilising imports or exports.
The common organisation shall be limited to pursuit of the objectives set out in Article 33 and shall exclude any discrimination between producers or consumers within the Community.
Any common price policy shall be based on common criteria and uniform methods of calculation.

3. In order to enable the common organisation referred to in paragraph 1 to attain its objectives, one or more agricultural guidance and guarantee funds may be set up.

Article 35 (ex Article 41) [Coordinated and Joint Training and Marketing]
To enable the objectives set out in Article 33 to be attained, provision may be made within the framework of the common agricultural policy for measures such as:
(a) an effective coordination of efforts in the spheres of vocational training, of research and of the dissemination of agricultural knowledge; this may include joint financing of projects or institutions;
(b) joint measures to promote consumption of certain products.

Article 36 (ex Article 42) [Limited Applicability of Competition Rules]
The provisions of the Chapter relating to rules on competition shall apply to production of and trade in agricultural products only to the extent determined by the Council within the framework of Article 37(2) and (3) and in accordance with the procedure laid down therein, account being taken of the objectives set out in Article 33.
The Council may, in particular, authorise the granting of aid:
(a) for the protection of enterprises handicapped by structural or natural conditions;
(b) within the framework of economic development programmes.

Article 37 (ex Article 43) [Adoption of Implementing Legislation]
1. In order to evolve the broad lines of a common agricultural policy, the Commission shall, immediately this Treaty enters into force, convene a conference of the Member States with a view to making a comparison of their agricultural policies, in particular by producing a statement of their resources and needs.
2. Having taken into account the work of the Conference provided for in paragraph 1, after consulting the Economic and Social Committee and within two years of the entry into force of this Treaty, the Commission shall submit proposals for working out and implementing the common agricultural policy, including the replacement of the national organisations by one of the forms of common organisation provided for in Article 34(1), and for implementing the measures specified in this Title.
These proposals shall take account of the interdependence of the agricultural matters mentioned in this Title.
The Council shall, on a proposal from the Commission and after consulting the European Parliament, acting by a qualified majority, make regulations, issue directives, or take decisions, without prejudice to any recommendations it may also make.
3. The Council may, acting by a qualified majority and in accordance with paragraph 2, replace the national market organisations by the common organisation provided for in Article 34(1) if:
(a) the common organisation offers Member States which are opposed to this measure and which have an organisation of their own for the production in question equivalent safeguards for the employment and standard of living of the producers concerned, account being taken of the adjustments that will be possible and the specialisation that will be needed with the passage of time;
(b) such an organisation ensures conditions for trade within the Community similar to those existing in a national market.
4. If a common organisation for certain raw materials is established before a common organisation exists for the corresponding processed products, such raw materials as are used for processed products intended for export to third countries may be imported from outside the Community.

Article 38 (ex Article 46) [Countervailing Charges]
Where in a Member State a product is subject to a national market organisation or to internal rules having equivalent effect which affect the competitive position of similar production in another Member State, a countervailing charge shall be applied by Member States to imports of this product coming from the Member State where such organisation or rules exist, unless that State applies a countervailing charge on export.

The Commission shall fix the amount of these charges at the level required to redress the balance; it may also authorise other measures, the conditions and details of which it shall determine.

TITLE III
FREE MOVEMENT OF PERSONS, SERVICES AND CAPITAL
Chapter 1 Workers

Article 39 (ex Article 48) [Scope of the Free Movement of Employed Persons]
1.   Freedom of movement for workers shall be secured within the Community.
2.   Such freedom of movement shall entail the abolition of any discrimination based on nationality between workers of the Member States as regards employment, remuneration and other conditions of work and employment.
3.   It shall entail the right, subject to limitations justified on grounds of public policy, public security or public health:
(a) to accept offers of employment actually made;
(b) to move freely within the territory of Member States for this purpose;
(c) to stay in a Member State for the purpose of employment in accordance with the provisions governing the employment of nationals of that State laid down by law, regulation or administrative action;
(d) to remain in the territory of a Member State after having been employed in that State, subject to conditions which shall be embodied in implementing regulations to be drawn up by the Commission.
4.   The provisions of this Article shall not apply to employment in the public service.

Article 40 (ex Article 49) [Progressive Elimination of Restrictions]
The Council shall, acting in accordance with the procedure referred to in Article 251 and after consulting the Economic and Social Committee, issue directives or make regulations setting out the measures required to bring about freedom of movement for workers, as defined in Article 39, in particular:
(a) by ensuring close cooperation between national employment services;
(b) by abolishing those administrative procedures and practices and those qualifying periods in respect of eligibility for available employment, whether resulting from national legislation or from agreements previously concluded between Member States, the maintenance of which would form an obstacle to liberalisation of the movement of workers;
(c) by abolishing all such qualifying periods and other restrictions provided for either under national legislation or under agreements previously concluded between Member States as imposed on workers of other Member States conditions regarding the free choice of employment other than those imposed on workers of the State concerned;
(d) by setting up appropriate machinery to bring offers of employment into touch with applications for employment and to facilitate the achievement of a balance between supply and demand in the employment market in such a way as to avoid serious threats to the standard of living and level of employment in the various regions and industries.

Article 41 (ex Article 50) [Youth Exchange]

Member States shall, within the framework of a joint programme, encourage the exchange of young workers.

Article 42 (ex Article 51) [Adoption of Implementing Legislation in the Field of Social Security]

The Council shall, acting in accordance with the procedure referred to in Article 251, adopt such measures in the field of social security as are necessary to provide freedom of movement for workers; to this end, it shall make arrangements to secure for migrant workers and their dependants:

(a) aggregation, for the purpose of acquiring and retaining the right to benefit and of calculating the amount of benefit, of all periods taken into account under the laws of the several countries;

(b) payment of benefits to persons resident in the territories of Member States.

The Council shall act unanimously throughout the procedure referred to in Article 251.

Chapter 2 Right of Establishment

Article 43 (ex Article 52) [Scope of the Freedom of Establishment of Self-Employed Persons]

Within the framework of the provisions set out below, restrictions on the freedom of establishment of nationals of a Member State in the territory of another Member State shall be prohibited. Such prohibition shall also apply to restrictions on the setting-up of agencies, branches or subsidiaries by nationals of any Member State established in the territory of any Member State.

Freedom of establishment shall include the right to take up and pursue activities as self-employed persons and to set up and manage undertakings, in particular companies or firms within the meaning of the second paragraph of Article 48, under the conditions laid down for its own nationals by the law of the country where such establishment is effected, subject to the provisions of the Chapter relating to capital.

Article 44 (ex Article 54) [Progressive Elimination of Existing Restrictions]

1. In order to attain freedom of establishment as regards a particular activity, the Council, acting in accordance with the procedure referred to in Article 251 and after consulting the Economic and Social Committee, shall act by means of directives.

2. The Council and the Commission shall carry out the duties devolving upon them under the preceding provisions, in particular:

(a) by according, as a general rule, priority treatment to activities where freedom of establishment makes a particularly valuable contribution to the development of production and trade;

(b) by ensuring close cooperation between the competent authorities in the Member States in order to ascertain the particular situation within the Community of the various activities concerned;

(c) by abolishing those administrative procedures and practices, whether resulting from national legislation or from agreements previously concluded between Member States, the maintenance of which would form an obstacle to freedom of establishment;

(d) by ensuring that workers of one Member State employed in the territory of another Member State may remain in that territory for the purpose of taking up activities therein as self-employed persons, where they satisfy the conditions which they would be required to satisfy if they were entering that State at the time when they intended to take up such activities;

(e) by enabling a national of one Member State to acquire and use land and buildings situated in the territory of another Member State, insofar as this does not conflict with the principles laid down in Article 33(2);

(f) by effecting the progressive abolition of restrictions on freedom of establishment in every branch of activity under consideration, both as regards the conditions for setting up agencies, branches or subsidiaries in the territory of a Member State and as regards the subsidiaries in the territory of a Member State and as regards the conditions governing the entry of personnel belonging to the main establishment into managerial or supervisory posts in such agencies, branches or subsidiaries;

(g) by coordinating to the necessary extent the safeguards which, for the protection of the interests of members and other, are required by Member States of companies or firms within the meaning of the second paragraph of Article 48 with a view to making such safeguards equivalent throughout the Community;

(h) by satisfying themselves that the conditions of establishment are not distorted by aids granted by Member States.

Article 45 (ex Article 55) [Exceptions for the Exercise of Official Authority]
The provisions of this Chapter shall not apply, so far as any given Member State is concerned, to activities which in that State are connected, even occasionally, with the exercise of official authority.

The Council may, acting by a qualified majority on a proposal from the Commission, rule that the provisions of this Chapter shall not apply to certain activities.

Article 46 (ex Article 56) [Exceptions on Grounds of Public Policy,
Public Security or Public Health]
1.   The provisions of this Chapter and measures taken in pursuance thereof shall not prejudice the applicability of provisions laid down by law, regulation or administrative action providing for special treatment for foreign nationals on grounds of public policy, public security or public health.
2.   The Council shall, acting in accordance with the procedure referred to in Article 251, issue directives for the coordination of the abovementioned provisions.

Article 47 (ex Article 57) [Adoption of Implementing Legislation for the
Mutual Recognition of Diplomas, Qualifications, and Other Conditions of Access to
Self-Employed Professions]
1.   In order to make it easier for persons to take up and pursue activities as self-employed persons, the Council shall, acting in accordance with the procedure referred to in Article 251, issue directives for the mutual recognition of diplomas, certificates and other evidence of formal qualifications.
2.   For the same purpose, the Council shall, acting in accordance with the procedure referred to in Article 251, issue directives for the coordination of the provisions laid down by law, regulation or administrative action in Member States concerning the taking-up and pursuit of activities as self-employed persons. The Council, acting unanimously throughout the procedure referred to in Article 251, shall decide on directives the implementation of which involves in at least one Member State amendment of the existing principles laid down by law governing the professions with respect to training and conditions of access for natural persons. In other cases the Council shall act by qualified majority.

3.   In the case of the medical and allied and pharmaceutical professions, the progressive abolition of restrictions shall be dependent upon coordination of the conditions for their exercise in the various Member States.

Article 48 (ex Article 58) [Application of the Rules to Legal Persons]
Companies or firms formed in accordance with the law of a Member State and having their registered office, central administration or principal place of business within the Community shall, for the purposes of this Chapter, be treated in the same way as natural persons who are nationals of Member States.

"Companies or firms" means companies or firms constituted under civil or commercial law, including cooperative societies, and other legal persons governed by public or private law, save for those which are non-profit-making.

Chapter 3 Services

Article 49 (ex Article 59) [Progressive Elimination of Restrictions on the Freedom to Provide Services]
Within the framework of the provisions set out below, restrictions on freedom to provide services within the Community shall be prohibited in respect of nationals of Member States who are established in a State of the Community other than that of the person for whom the services are intended.

The Council may, acting by a qualified majority on a proposal from the Commission, extend the provisions of the Chapter to nationals of a third country who provide services and who are established within the Community.

Article 50 (ex Article 60) [Scope of the Freedom to Provide Services]
Services shall be considered to be "services" within the meaning of this Treaty where they are normally provided for remuneration, insofar as they are not governed by the provisions relating to freedom of movement for goods, capital and persons.

"Services" shall in particular include:
(a)   activities of an industrial character;
(b)   activities of a commercial character;
(c)   activities of craftsmen;
(d)   activities of the professions.
Without prejudice to the provisions of the Chapter relating to the right of establishment, the person providing a service may, in order to do so, temporarily pursue his activity in the State where the service is provided, under the same conditions as are imposed by that State on its own nationals.

Article 51 (ex Article 61) [Transport and Financial Services]
1.   Freedom to provide services in the field of transport shall be governed by the provisions of the Title relating to transport.
2.   The liberalisation of banking and insurance services connected with movements of capital shall be effected in step with the liberalisation of movement of capital.

Article 52 (ex Article 63) [Progressive Elimination of Existing Restrictions on Services]
1.   In order to achieve the liberalisation of a specific service, the Council shall, on a proposal from the Commission and after consulting the Economic and Social Committee and the European Parliament, issue directives acting by a qualified majority.

2. As regards the directives referred to in paragraph 1, priority shall as a general rule be given to those services which directly affect production costs or the liberalisation of which helps to promote trade in goods.

Article 53 (ex Article 64) [Accelerated Elimination of Restrictions]

The Member States declare their readiness to undertake the liberalisation of services beyond the extent required by the directives issued pursuant to Article 52(1), if their general economic situation and the situation of the economic sector concerned so permit.

To this end, the Commission shall make recommendations to the Member States concerned.

Article 54 (ex Article 65) [Prohibition of Discriminatory Measures]

As long as restrictions on freedom to provide services have not been abolished, each Member State shall apply such restrictions without distinction on grounds of nationality or residence to all persons providing services within the meaning of the first paragraph of Article 49.

Article 55 (ex Article 66) [Applicability of Articles 45 to 48 in the Field of Services]

The provisions of Articles 45 to 48 shall apply to the matters covered by this Chapter.

Chapter 4 Capital and Payments

Article 56 (ex Article 73b) [Elimination of all Restrictions in the Internal Market and in Relations to Third Countries]

1. Within the framework of the provisions set out in this Chapter, all restrictions on the movement of capital between Member States and between Member States and third countries shall be prohibited.
2. Within the framework of the provisions set out in this Chapter, all restrictions on payments between Member States and between Member States and third countries shall be prohibited.

Article 57 (ex Article 73c) [Exceptions for Direct Investment in or from Third Countries]

1. The provisions of Article 56 shall be without prejudice to the application to third countries of any restrictions which exist on 31 December 1993 under national or Community law adopted in respect of the movement of capital to or from third countries involving direct investment - including in real estate - establishment, the provision of financial services or the admission of securities to capital markets.
2. Whilst endeavouring to achieve the objective of free movement of capital between Member States and third countries to the greatest extent possible and without prejudice to the other Chapters of this Treaty, the Council may, acting by a qualified majority on a proposal from the Commission, adopt measures on the movement of capital to or from third countries involving direct investment - including investment in real estate - establishment, the provision of financial services or the admission of securities to capital markets. Unanimity shall be required for measures under this paragraph which constitute a step back in Community law as regards the liberalisation of the movement of capital to or from third countries.

Article 58 (ex Article 73d) [Exceptions for Tax Enforcement Measures; Restrictions on the Right of Establishment]

1. The provisions of Article 56 shall be without prejudice to the right of Member States:

(a) to apply the relevant provisions of their tax law which distinguish between tax-payers who are not in the same situation with regard to their place of residence or with regard to the place where their capital is invested;
(b) to take all requisite measures to prevent infringements of national law and regula-tions, in particular in the field of taxation and the prudential supervision of financial institutions, or to lay down procedures for the declaration of capital movements for purposes of administrative or statistical information, or to take measures which are justified on grounds of public policy or public security.
2.   The provisions of this Chapter shall be without prejudice to the applicability of restrictions on the right of establishment which are compatible with this Treaty.
3.   The measures and procedures referred to in paragraphs 1 and 2 shall not consti-tute a means of arbitrary discrimination or a disguised restriction on the free movement of capital and payments as defined in Article 56.

Article 59 (ex Article 73f) [Safeguard Measures]

Where, in exceptional circumstances, movements of capital to or from third countries cause, or threaten to cause, serious difficulties for the operation of economic and mo-netary union, the Council, acting by a qualified majority on a proposal from the Com-mission and after consulting the ECB, may take safeguard measures with regard to third countries for a period not exceeding six months if such measures are strictly necessary.

Article 60 (ex Article 73g) [Exceptions for Sanctions in the Framework of the Common Foreign and Security Policy]

1.   If, in the cases envisaged in Article 301, action by the Community is deemed necessary, the Council may, in accordance with the procedure provided for in Article 301, take the necessary urgent measures on the movement of capital and on pay-ments as regards the third countries concerned.
2.   Without prejudice to Article 297 and as long as the Council has not taken mea-sures pursuant to paragraph 1, a Member State may, for serious political reasons and on grounds of urgency, take unilateral measures against a third country with regard to capital movements and payments. The Commission and the other Member States shall be informed of such measures by the date of their entry into force at the latest.
     The Council may, acting by a qualified majority on a proposal from the Commis-sion, decide that the Member State concerned shall amend or abolish such measures. The President of the Council shall inform the European Parliament of any such deci-sion taken by the Council.

TITLE IV (EX TITLE IIIA)
VISAS, ASYLUM, IMMIGRATION AND OTHER POLICIES RELATED TO FREE MOVEMENT OF PERSONS

Article 61 (ex Article 73i) [Adoption of Measures on External Border Controls, Asylum, and Immigration]

In order to establish progressively an area of freedom, security and justice, the Council shall adopt:
(a) within a period of five years after the entry into force of the Treaty of Amsterdam, measures aimed at ensuring the free movement of persons in accordance with Article 14, in conjunction with directly related flanking measures with respect to external border controls, asylum and immigration, in accordance with the pro-visions of Article 62(2) and (3) and Article 63(1)(a) and (2)(a), and measures to

prevent and combat crime in accordance with the provisions of Article 31(e) of the Treaty on European Union;
(b) other measures in the fields of asylum, immigration and safeguarding the rights of nationals of third countries, in accordance with the provisions of Article 63;
(c) measures in the field of judicial cooperation in civil matters as provided for in Article 65;
(d) appropriate measures to encourage and strengthen administrative cooperation, as provided for in Article 66;
(e) measures in the field of police and judicial cooperation in criminal matters aimed at a high level of security by preventing and combatting crime within the Union in accordance with the provisions of the Treaty on European Union.

Article 62 (ex Article 73j) [Adoption of Measures on Border Controls and Visas]
The Council, acting in accordance with the procedure referred to in Article 67, shall, within a period of five years after the entry into force of the Treaty of Amsterdam, adopt:
(1) measures with a view to ensuring, in compliance with Article 14, the absence of any controls on persons, be they citizens of the Union or nationals of third countries, when crossing internal borders;
(2) measures on the crossing of the external borders of the Member States which shall establish:
    (a) standards and procedures to be followed by Member States in carrying out checks on persons at such borders;
    (b) rules on visas for intended stays of no more than three months, including:
        (i)   the list of third countries whose nationals must be in possession of visas when crossing the external borders and those whose nationals are exempt from that requirement;
        (ii)   the procedures and conditions for issuing visas by Member States;
        (iii) a uniform format for visas;
        (iv)   rules on a uniform visa;
(3) measures setting out the conditions under which nationals of third countries shall have the freedom to travel within the territory of the Member States during a period of no more than three months.

Article 63 (ex Article 73k) [Adoption of Measures on Asylum, Protection of Refugees, Immigration, and Migration]
The Council, acting in accordance with the procedure referred to in Article 67, shall, within a period of five years after the entry into force of the Treaty of Amsterdam, adopt:
(1) measures on asylum, in accordance with the Geneva Convention of 28 July 1951 and the Protocol of 31 January 1967 relating to the status of refugees and other relevant treaties, within the following areas:
    (a) criteria and mechanisms for determining which Member State is responsible for considering an application for asylum submitted by a national of a third country in one of the Member States,
    (b) minimum standards on the reception of asylum seekers in Member States,
    (c) minimum standards with respect to the qualification of nationals of third countries as refugees,
    (d) minimum standards on procedures in Member States for granting or withdrawing refugee status;
(2) measures on refugees and displaced persons within the following areas:

(a) minimum standards for giving temporary protection to displaced persons from third countries who cannot return to their country of origin and for persons who otherwise need international protection,

(b) promoting a balance of effort between Member States in receiving and bearing the consequences of receiving refugees and displaced persons;

(3) measures on immigration policy within the following areas:

(a) conditions of entry and residence, and standards on procedures for the issue by Member States of long term visas and residence permits, including those for the purpose of family reunion,

(b) illegal immigration and illegal residence, including repatriation of illegal residents;

(4) measures defining the rights and conditions under which nationals of third countries who are legally resident in a Member State may reside in other Member States.

Measures adopted by the Council pursuant to points 3 and 4 shall not prevent any Member State from maintaining or introducing in the areas concerned national provisions which are compatible with this Treaty and with international agreements.

Measures to be adopted pursuant to points 2(b), 3(a) and 4 shall not be subject to the five year period referred to above.

Article 64 (ex Article 73l) [Safeguard Clause]

1.   This Title shall not affect the exercise of the responsibilities incumbent upon Member States with regard to the maintenance of law and order and the safeguarding of internal security.

2.   In the event of one or more Member States being confronted with an emergency situation characterised by a sudden inflow of nationals of third countries and without prejudice to paragraph 1, the Council may, acting by qualified majority on a proposal from the Commission, adopt provisional measures of a duration not exceeding six months for the benefit of the Member States concerned.

Article 65 (ex Article 73m) [Judicial Cooperation in Civil Matters]

Measures in the field of judicial cooperation in civil matters having cross-border implications, to be taken in accordance with Article 67 and insofar as necessary for the proper functioning of the internal market, shall include:

(a) improving and simplifying:
— the system for cross-border service of judicial and extrajudicial documents;
— cooperation in the taking of evidence;
— the recognition and enforcement of decisions in civil and commercial cases, including decisions in extrajudicial cases;

(b) promoting the compatibility of the rules applicable in the Member States concerning the conflict of laws and of jurisdiction;

(c) eliminating obstacles to the good functioning of civil proceedings, if necessary by promoting the compatibility of the rules on civil procedure applicable in the Member States.

Article 66 (ex Article 73n) [Administrative Cooperation]

The Council, acting in accordance with the procedure referred to in Article 67, shall take measures to ensure cooperation between the relevant departments of the administrations of the Member States in the areas covered by this Title, as well as between those departments and the Commission.

Article 67 (ex Article 73o) [Decision Making and Voting]
1.   During a transitional period of five years following the entry into force of the Treaty of Amsterdam, the Council shall act unanimously on a proposal from the Commission or on the initiative of a Member State and after consulting the European Parliament.
2.   After this period of five years:
—   the Council shall act on proposals from the Commission; the Commission shall examine any request made by a Member State that it submit a proposal to the Council;
—   the Council, acting unanimously after consulting the European Parliament, shall take a decision with a view to providing for all or parts of the areas covered by this Title to be governed by the procedure referred to in Article 251 and adapting the provisions relating to the powers of the Court of Justice.
3.   By derogation from paragraphs 1 and 2, measures referred to in Article 62(2)(b) (i) and (iii) shall, from the entry into force of the Treaty of Amsterdam, be adopted by the Council acting by a qualified majority on a proposal from the Commission and after consulting the European Parliament.
4.   By derogation from paragraph 2, measures referred to in Article 62(2)(b) (ii) and (iv) shall, after a period of five years following the entry into force of the Treaty of Amsterdam, be adopted by the Council acting in accordance with the procedure referred to in Article 251.

Article 68 (ex Article 73p) [Jurisdiction of the Court of Justice]
1.   Article 234 shall apply to this Title under the following circumstances and conditions: where a question on the interpretation of this Title or on the validity or interpretation of acts of the institutions of the Community based on this Title is raised in a case pending before a court or a tribunal of a Member State against whose decisions there is no judicial remedy under national law, that court or tribunal shall, if it considers that a decision on the question is necessary to enable it to give judgment, request the Court of Justice to give a ruling thereon.
2.   In any event, the Court of Justice shall not have jurisdiction to rule on any measure or decision taken pursuant to Article 62(1) relating to the maintenance of law and order and the safeguarding of internal security.
3.   The Council, the Commission or a Member State may request the Court of Justice to give a ruling on a question of interpretation of this Title or of acts of the institutions of the Community based on this Title. The ruling given by the Court of Justice in response to such a request shall not apply to judgments of courts or tribunals of the Member States which have become res judicata.

Article 69 (ex Article 73q) [Exceptions in Protocols]
The application of this Title shall be subject to the provisions of the Protocol on the position of the United Kingdom and Ireland and to the Protocol on the position of Denmark and without prejudice to the Protocol on the application of certain aspects of Article 14 of the Treaty establishing the European Community to the United Kingdom and to Ireland.

TITLE V (EX TITLE IV)
TRANSPORT

Article 70 (ex Article 74) [Establishment of a Common Transport Policy]
The objectives of this Treaty shall, in matters governed by this Title, be pursued by Member States within the framework of a common transport policy.

Article 71 (ex Article 75) [Progressive Introduction of the Common Transport Policy]
1.   For the purpose of implementing Article 70, and taking into account the distinctive features of transport, the Council shall, acting in accordance with the procedure referred to in Article 251 and after consulting the Economic and Social Committee and the Committee of the Regions, lay down:
(a) common rules applicable to international transport to or from the territory of a Member State or passing across the territory of one or more Member States;
(b) the conditions under which non-resident carriers may operate transport services within a Member State;
(c) measures to improve transport safety;
(d) any other appropriate provisions.
2.   By way of derogation from the procedure provided for in paragraph 1, where the application of provisions concerning the principles of the regulatory system for transport would be liable to have a serious effect on the standard of living and on employment in certain areas and on the operation of transport facilities, they shall be laid down by the Council acting unanimously on a proposal from the Commission, after consulting the European Parliament and the Economic and Social Committee. In so doing, the Council shall take into account the need for adaptation to the economic development which will result from establishing the common market.

Article 72 (ex Article 76) [Prohibition of Discrimination on Grounds of Nationality]
Until the provisions referred to in Article 71(1) have been laid down, no Member State may, without the unanimous approval of the Council, make the various provisions governing the subject on 1 January 1958 or, for acceding States, the date of their accession less favourable in their direct or indirect effect on carriers of other Member States as compared with carriers who are nationals of that State.

Article 73 (ex Article 77) [State Aids in the Transport Sector]
Aids shall be compatible with this Treaty if they meet the needs of coordination of transport or if they represent reimbursement for the discharge of certain obligations inherent in the concept of a public service.

Article 74 (ex Article 78) [Transport Rates and Conditions]
Any measures taken within the framework of this Treaty in respect of transport rates and conditions shall take account of the economic circumstances of carriers.

Article 75 (ex Article 79) [Elimination of Discriminatory Prices]
1.   In the case of transport within the Community, discrimination which takes the form of carriers charging different rates and imposing different conditions for the carriage of the same goods over the same transport links on grounds of the country of origin or of destination of the goods in question shall be abolished.
2.   Paragraph 1 shall not prevent the Council from adopting other measures in pursuance of Article 71(1).
3.   The Council shall, acting by a qualified majority on a proposal from the Commission and after consulting the Economic and Social Committee, lay down rules for implementing the provisions of paragraph 1.
    The Council may in particular lay down the provisions needed to enable the institutions of the Community to secure compliance with the rule laid down in paragraph 1 and to ensure that users benefit from it to the full.
4.   The Commission shall, acting on its own initiative or on application by a Member State, investigate any cases of discrimination falling within paragraph 1 and, after con-

sulting any Member State concerned, shall take the necessary decisions within the framework of the rules laid down in accordance with the provisions of paragraph 3.

Article 76 (ex Article 80) [Prohibition of Protectionistic National Measures]
1.   The imposition by a Member State, in respect of transport operations carried out within the Community, of rates and conditions involving any element of support or protection in the interest of one or more particular undertakings or industries shall be prohibited, unless authorised by the Commission.
2.   The Commission shall, acting on its own initiative or on application by a Member State, examine the rates and conditions referred to in paragraph 1, taking account in particular of the requirements of an appropriate regional economic policy, the needs of underdeveloped areas and the problems of areas seriously affected by political circumstances on the one hand, and of the effects of such rates and conditions on competition between the different modes of transport on the other.

After consulting each Member State concerned, the Commission shall take the necessary decisions.
3.   The prohibition provided for in paragraph 1 shall not apply to tariffs fixed to meet competition.

Article 77 (ex Article 81) [Prohibition of Excessive Charges in Cross-Border Transport]
Charges or dues in respect of the crossing of frontiers which are charged by a carrier in addition to the transport rates shall not exceed a reasonable level after taking the costs actually incurred thereby into account.

Member States shall endeavour to reduce these costs progressively.

The Commission may make recommendations to Member States for the application of this Article.

Article 78 (ex Article 82) [Compensating Economic Disadvantages Caused by the Division of Germany]
The provisions of this Title shall not form an obstacle to the application of measures taken in the Federal Republic of Germany to the extent that such measures are required in order to compensate for the economic disadvantages caused by the division of Germany to the economy of certain areas of the Federal Republic affected by that division.

Article 79 (ex Article 83) [Advisory Committee on Transport]
An Advisory Committee consisting of experts designated by the governments of Member States shall be attached to the Commission. The Commission, whenever it considers it desirable, shall consult the Committee on transport matters without prejudice to the powers of the Economic and Social Committee.

Article 80 (ex Article 84) [Scope of the Common Transport Policy]
1.   The provisions of this Title shall apply to transport by rail, road and inland waterway.
2.   The Council may, acting by a qualified majority, decide whether, to what extent and by what procedure appropriate provisions may be laid down for sea and air transport.
The procedural provisions of Article 71 shall apply.

TITLE VI (EX TITLE V)
COMMON RULES ON COMPETITION, TAXATION AND APPROXIMATION OF LAWS
Chapter 1 Rules on Competition

Section 1 Rules Applying to Undertakings
Article 81 (ex Article 85) [Prohibition of Cartels]

1. The following shall be prohibited as incompatible with the common market: all agreements between undertakings, decisions by associations of undertakings and concerted practices which may affect trade between Member States and which have as their object or effect the prevention, restriction or distortion of competition within the common market, and in particular those which:
(a) directly or indirectly fix purchase or selling prices or any other trading conditions;
(b) limit or control production, markets, technical development, or investment;
(c) share markets or sources of supply;
(d) apply dissimilar conditions to equivalent transactions with other trading parties, thereby placing them at a competitive disadvantage;
(e) make the conclusion of contracts subject to acceptance by the other parties of supplementary obligations which, by their nature or according to commercial usage, have no connection with the subject of such contracts.
2. Any agreements or decisions prohibited pursuant to this Article shall be automatically void.
3. The provisions of paragraph 1 may, however, be declared inapplicable in the case of:
— any agreement or category of agreements between undertakings;
— any decision or category of decisions by associations of undertakings;
— any concerted practice or category of concerted practices,
which contributes to improving the production or distribution of goods or to promoting technical or economic progress, while allowing consumers a fair share of the resulting benefit, and which does not:
(a) impose on the undertakings concerned restrictions which are not indispensable to the attainment of these objectives;
(b) afford such undertakings the possibility of eliminating competition in respect of a substantial part of the products in question.

Article 82 (ex Article 86) [Prohibition of the Abuse of a Dominant Position]
Any abuse by one or more undertakings of a dominant position within the common market or in a substantial part of it shall be prohibited as incompatible with the common market insofar as it may affect trade between Member States.
Such abuse may, in particular, consist in:
(a) directly or indirectly imposing unfair purchase or selling prices or other unfair trading conditions;
(b) limiting production, markets or technical development to the prejudice of consumers;
(c) applying dissimilar conditions to equivalent transactions with other trading parties, thereby placing them at a competitive disadvantage;
(d) making the conclusion of contracts subject to acceptance by the other parties of supplementary obligations which, by their nature or according to commercial usage, have no connection with the subject of such contracts.

Article 83 (ex Article 87) [Implementing Measures for the Common Competition Policy]

1.   The appropriate regulations or directives to give effect to the principles set out in Articles 81 and 82 shall be laid down by the Council, acting by a qualified majority on a proposal from the Commission and after consulting the European Parliament.

2.   The regulations or directives referred to in paragraph 1 shall be designed in particular:

(a) to ensure compliance with the prohibitions laid down in Article 81(1) and in Article 82 by making provision for fines and periodic penalty payments;

(b) to lay down detailed rules for the application of Article 81(3), taking into account the need to ensure effective supervision on the one hand, and to simplify administration to the greatest possible extent on the other;

(c) to define, if need be, in the various branches of the economy, the scope of the provisions of Articles 81 and 82;

(d) to define the respective functions of the Commission and of the Court of Justice in applying the provisions laid down in this paragraph;

(e) to determine the relationship between national laws and the provisions contained in this Section or adopted pursuant to this Article.

Article 84 (ex Article 88) [Member State Competencies in the Transitional Period]

Until the entry into force of the provisions adopted in pursuance of Article 83, the authorities in Member States shall rule on the admissibility of agreements, decisions and concerted practices and on abuse of a dominant position in the common market in accordance with the law of their country and with the provisions of Article 81, in particular paragraph 3, and of Article 82.

Article 85 (ex Article 89) [Commission Competencies]

1.   Without prejudice to Article 84, the Commission shall ensure the application of the principles laid down in Articles 81 and 82. On application by a Member State or on its own initiative, and in cooperation with the competent authorities in the Member States, who shall give it their assistance, the Commission shall investigate cases of suspected infringement of these principles. If it finds that there has been an infringement, it shall propose appropriate measures to bring it to an end.

2.   If the infringement is not brought to an end, the Commission shall record such infringement of the principles in a reasoned decision. The Commission may publish its decision and authorise Member States to take the measures, the conditions and details of which it shall determine, needed to remedy the situation.

Article 86 (ex Article 90) [Public Undertakings]

1.   In the case of public undertakings and undertakings to which Member States grant special or exclusive rights, Member States shall neither enact nor maintain in force any measure contrary to the rules contained in this Treaty, in particular to those rules provided for in Article 12 and Articles 81 to 89.

2.   Undertakings entrusted with the operation of services of general economic interest or having the character of a revenue-producing monopoly shall be subject to the rules contained in this Treaty, in particular to the rules on competition, insofar as the application of such rules does not obstruct the performance, in law or in fact, of the particular tasks assigned to them. The development of trade must not be affected to such an extent as would be contrary to the interests of the Community.

3.   The Commission shall ensure the application of the provisions of this Article and shall, where necessary, address appropriate directives or decisions to Member States.

Section 2 Aids Granted by States
Article 87 (ex Article 92) [Prohibition of State Aids; Exceptions to the Prohibition]
1.   Save as otherwise provided in this Treaty, any aid granted by a Member State or through State resources in any form whatsoever which distorts or threatens to distort competition by favouring certain undertakings or the production of certain goods shall, insofar as it affects trade between Member States, be incompatible with the common market.
2.   The following shall be compatible with the common market:
(a) aid having a social character, granted to individual consumers, provided that such aid is granted without discrimination related to the origin of the products concerned;
(b) aid to make good the damage caused by natural disasters or exceptional occurrences;
(c) aid granted to the economy of certain areas of the Federal Republic of Germany affected by the division of Germany, insofar as such aid is required in order to compensate for the economic disadvantages caused by that division.
3.   The following may be considered to be compatible with the common market:
(a) aid to promote the economic development of areas where the standard of living is abnormally low or where there is serious underemployment;
(b) aid to promote the execution of an important project of common European interest or to remedy a serious disturbance in the economy of a Member State;
(c) aid to facilitate the development of certain economic activities or of certain economic areas, where such aid does not adversely affect trading conditions to an extent contrary to the common interest;
(d) aid to promote culture and heritage conservation where such aid does not affect trading conditions and competition in the Community to an extent that is contrary to the common interest;
(e) such other categories of aid as may be specified by decision of the Council acting by a qualified majority on a proposal from the Commission.

Article 88 (ex Article 93) [Notification of State Aids; Supervisory Procedure]
1.   The Commission shall, in cooperation with Member States, keep under constant review all systems of aid existing in those States. It shall propose to the latter any appropriate measures required by the progressive development or by the functioning of the common market.
2.   If, after giving notice to the parties concerned to submit their comments, the Commission finds that aid granted by a State or through State resources is not compatible with the common market having regard to Article 87, or that such aid is being misused, it shall decide that the State concerned shall abolish or alter such aid within a period of time to be determined by the Commission.
    If the State concerned does not comply with this decision within the prescribed time, the Commission or any other interested State may, in derogation from the provisions of Articles 226 and 227, refer the matter to the Court of Justice direct.
    On application by a Member State, the Council may, acting unanimously, decide that aid which that State is granting or intends to grant shall be considered to be compatible with the common market, in derogation from the provisions of Article 87 or from the regulations provided for in Article 89, if such a decision is justified by exceptional circumstances. If, as regards the aid in question, the Commission has already initiated the procedure provided for in the first subparagraph of this paragraph, the fact that the State concerned has made its application to the Council shall have the effect of suspending that procedure until the Council has made its attitude known.

If, however, the Council has not made its attitude known within three months of the said application being made, the Commission shall give its decision on the case.
3.   The Commission shall be informed, in sufficient time to enable it to submit its comments, of any plans to grant or alter aid. If it considers that any such plan is not compatible with the common market having regard to Article 87, it shall without delay initiate the procedure provided for in paragraph 2. The Member State concerned shall not put its proposed measures into effect until this procedure has resulted in a final decision.

Article 89 (ex Article 94) [Implementing Legislation]
The Council, acting by a qualified majority on a proposal from the Commission and after consulting the European Parliament, may make any appropriate regulations for the application of Articles 87 and 88 and may in particular determine the conditions in which Article 88(3) shall apply and the categories of aid exempted from this procedure.

Chapter 2 Tax Provisions

Article 90 (ex Article 95) [Prohibition of Discriminatory Internal Taxes]
No Member State shall impose, directly or indirectly, on the products of other Member States any internal taxation of any kind in excess of that imposed directly or indirectly on similar domestic products.
   Furthermore, no Member State shall impose on the products of other Member States any internal taxation of such a nature as to afford indirect protection to other products.

Article 91 (ex Article 96) [Repayment of Internal Taxes upon Exportation]
Where products are exported to the territory of any Member State, any repayment of internal taxation shall not exceed the internal taxation imposed on them whether directly or indirectly.

Article 92 (ex Article 98) [Prohibition of Export Subsidies and Countervailing Duties in Intra-Community Trade]
In the case of charges other than turnover taxes, excise duties and other forms of indirect taxation, remissions and repayments in respect of exports to other Member States may not be granted and countervailing charges in respect of imports from Member States may not be imposed unless the measures contemplated have been previously approved for a limited period by the Council acting by a qualified majority on a proposal from the Commission.

Article 93 (ex Article 99) [Implementing Legislation for the Harmonization of Indirect Taxes]
The Council shall, acting unanimously on a proposal from the Commission and after consulting the European Parliament and the Economic and Social Committee, adopt provisions for the harmonisation of legislation concerning turnover taxes, excise duties and other forms of indirect taxation to the extent that such harmonisation is necessary to ensure the establishment and the functioning of the internal market within the time-limit laid down in Article 14.

Chapter 3 Approximation of Laws

Article 94 (ex Article 100) [Approximation of National Laws via Unanimous Council Directives]
The Council shall, acting unanimously on a proposal from the Commission and after consulting the European Parliament and the Economic and Social Committee, issue directives for the approximation of such laws, regulations or administrative provisions of the Member States as directly affect the establishment or functioning of the common market.

Article 95 (ex Article 100a) [Approximation of National Laws via Measures of Council and Parliament under Article 251]
1.   By way of derogation from Article 94 and save where otherwise provided in this Treaty, the following provisions shall apply for the achievement of the objectives set out in Article 14. The Council shall, acting in accordance with the procedure referred to in Article 251 and after consulting the Economic and Social Committee, adopt the measures for the approximation of the provisions laid down by law, regulation or administrative action in Member States which have as their object the establishment and functioning of the internal market.
2.   Paragraph 1 shall not apply to fiscal provisions, to those relating to the free movement of persons nor to those relating to the rights and interests of employed persons.
3.   The Commission, in its proposals envisaged in paragraph 1 concerning health, safety, environmental protection and consumer protection, will take as a base a high level of protection, taking account in particular of any new development based on scientific facts. Within their respective powers, the European Parliament and the Council will also seek to achieve this objective.
4.   If, after the adoption by the Council or by the Commission of a harmonisation measure, a Member State deems it necessary to maintain national provisions on grounds of major needs referred to in Article 30, or relating to the protection of the environment or the working environment, it shall notify the Commission of these provisions as well as the grounds for maintaining them.
5.   Moreover, without prejudice to paragraph 4, if, after the adoption by the Council or by the Commission of a harmonisation measure, a Member State deems it necessary to introduce national provisions based on new scientific evidence relating to the protection of the environment or the working environment on grounds of a problem specific to that Member State arising after the adoption of the harmonisation measure, it shall notify the Commission of the envisaged provisions as well as the grounds for introducing them.
6.   The Commission shall, within six months of the notifications as referred to in paragraphs 4 and 5, approve or reject the national provisions involved after having verified whether or not they are a means of arbitrary discrimination or a disguised restriction on trade between Member States and whether or not they shall constitute an obstacle to the functioning of the internal market.
     In the absence of a decision by the Commission within this period the national provisions referred to in paragraphs 4 and 5 shall be deemed to have been approved.
     When justified by the complexity of the matter and in the absence of danger for human health, the Commission may notify the Member State concerned that the period referred to in this paragraph may be extended for a further period of up to six months.
7.   When, pursuant to paragraph 6, a Member State is authorised to maintain or introduce national provisions derogating from a harmonisation measure, the Commission shall immediately examine whether to propose an adaptation to that measure.

8.   When a Member State raises a specific problem on public health in a field which has been the subject of prior harmonisation measures, it shall bring it to the attention of the Commission which shall immediately examine whether to propose appropriate measures to the Council.

9.   By way of derogation from the procedure laid down in Articles 226 and 227, the Commission and any Member State may bring the matter directly before the Court of Justice if it considers that another Member State is making improper use of the powers provided for in this Article.

10. The harmonisation measures referred to above shall, in appropriate cases, include a safeguard clause authorising the Member States to take, for one or more of the non-economic reasons referred to in Article 30, provisional measures subject to a Community control procedure.

Article 96 (ex Article 101) [Elimination of National Measures Distorting Competition]

Where the Commission finds that a difference between the provisions laid down by law, regulation or administrative action in Member States is distorting the conditions of competition in the common market and that the resultant distortion needs to be eliminated, it shall consult the Member States concerned.

If such consultation does not result in an agreement eliminating the distortion in question, the Council shall, on a proposal from the Commission, acting by a qualified majority, issue the necessary directives. The Commission and the Council may take any other appropriate measures provided for in this Treaty.

Article 97 (ex Article 102) [Measures Preventing Future Distortions of Competition]

1.   Where there is a reason to fear that the adoption or amendment of a provision laid down by law, regulation or administrative action may cause distortion within the meaning of Article 96, a Member State desiring to proceed therewith shall consult the Commission. After consulting the Member States, the Commission shall recommend to the States concerned such measures as may be appropriate to avoid the distortion in question.

2.   If a State desiring to introduce or amend its own provisions does not comply with the recommendation addressed to it by the Commission, other Member States shall not be required, in pursuance of Article 96, to amend their own provisions in order to eliminate such distortion. If the Member State which has ignored the re-commendation of the Commission causes distortion detrimental only to itself, the provisions of Article 96 shall not apply.

TITLE VII (EX-TITLE VI)
ECONOMIC AND MONETARY POLICY
Chapter 1 Economic Policy

Article 98 (ex Article 102a) [An Open Market Economy with Free Competition]

Member States shall conduct their economic policies with a view to contributing to the achievement of the objectives of the Community, as defined in Article 2, and in the context of the broad guidelines referred to in Article 99(2). The Member States and the Community shall act in accordance with the principle of an open market economy with free competition, favouring an efficient allocation of resources, and in compliance with the principles set out in Article 4.

Article 99 (ex Article 103) [Coordination of Economic Policy]
1.   Member States shall regard their economic policies as a matter of common concern and shall coordinate them within the Council, in accordance with the provisions of Article 98.
2.   The Council shall, acting by a qualified majority on a recommendation from the Commission, formulate a draft for the broad guidelines of the economic policies of the Member States and of the Community, and shall report its findings to the European Council.

The European Council shall, acting on the basis of the report from the Council, discuss a conclusion on the broad guidelines of the economic policies of the Member States and of the Community.

On the basis of this conclusion, the Council shall, acting by a qualified majority, adopt a recommendation setting out these broad guidelines. The Council shall inform the European Parliament of its recommendation.
3.   In order to ensure closer coordination of economic policies and sustained convergence of the economic performances of the Member States, the Council shall, on the basis of reports submitted by the Commission, monitor economic developments in each of the Member States and in the Community as well as the consistency of economic policies with the broad guidelines referred to In paragraph 2, and regularly carry out an overall assessment.

For the purpose of this multilateral surveillance, Member States shall forward information to the Commission about important measures taken by them in the field of their economic policy and such other information as they deem necessary.
4.   Where it is established, under the procedure referred to in paragraph 3, that the economic policies of a Member State are not consistent with the broad guidelines referred to in paragraph 2 or that they risk jeopardising the proper functioning of economic and monetary union, the Council may, acting by a qualified majority on a recommendation from the Commission, make the necessary recommendations to the Member State concerned. The Council may, acting by a qualified majority on a proposal from the Commission, decide to make its recommendations public.

The President of the Council and the Commission shall report to the European Parliament on the results of multilateral surveillance. The President of the Council may be invited to appear before the competent committee of the European Parliament if the Council has made its recommendations public.
5.   The Council, acting in accordance with the procedure referred to in Article 252, may adopt detailed rules for the multilateral surveillance procedure referred to in paragraphs 3 and 4 of this Article.

Article 100 (ex Article 103a) [Council Measures in Exceptional Situations]
1.   Without prejudice to any other procedures provided for in this Treaty, the Council may, acting unanimously on a proposal from the Commission, decide upon the measures appropriate to the economic situation, in particular if severe difficulties arise in the supply of certain products.
2.   Where a Member State is in difficulties or is seriously threatened with severe difficulties caused by exceptional occurrences beyond its control, the Council may, acting unanimously on a proposal from the Commission, grant, under certain conditions, Community financial assistance to the Member State concerned. Where the severe difficulties are caused by natural disasters, the Council shall act by qualified majority. The President of the Council shall inform the European Parliament of the decision taken.

Article 101 (ex Article 104) [Prohibition of Loans by the ECB or National Central
Banks to Public Authorities]
1.   Overdraft facilities or any other type of credit facility with the ECB or with the central banks of the Member States (hereinafter referred to as "national central banks") in
favour of Community institutions or bodies, central governments, regional, local or
other public authorities, other bodies governed by public law, or public undertakings of
Member States shall be prohibited, as shall the purchase directly from them by the
ECB or national central banks of debt instruments.
2.   Paragraph 1 shall not apply to publicly owned credit institutions which, in the context of the supply of reserves by central banks, shall be given the same treatment by
national central banks and the ECB as private credit institutions.

Article 102 (ex Article 104a) [Prohibition of Privileged Access
of Public Authorities to Financial Institutions]
1.   Any measure, not based on prudential considerations, establishing privileged
access by Community institutions or bodies, central governments, regional, local or
other public authorities, other bodies governed by public law, or public undertakings of
Member States to financial institutions, shall be prohibited.
2.   The Council, acting in accordance with the procedure referred to in Article 252,
shall, before 1 January 1994, specify definitions for the application of the prohibition
referred to in paragraph 1.

Article 103 (ex Article 104b) [No Liability of the Community
for the Member States and of Member States for Each Other]
1.   The Community shall not be liable for or assume the commitments of central governments, regional, local or other public authorities, other bodies governed by public
law, or public undertakings of any Member State, without prejudice to mutual financial
guarantees for the joint execution of a specific project. A Member State shall not be
liable for or assume the commitments of central governments, regional, local or other
public authorities, other bodies governed by public law, or public undertakings of another Member State, without prejudice to mutual financial guarantees for the joint execution of a specific project.
2.   If necessary, the Council, acting in accordance with the procedure referred to in
Article 252, may specify definitions for the application of the prohibition referred to in
Article 101 and in this Article.

Article 104 (ex Article 104c) [Budgetary Discipline;
Measures in Case of Excessive Deficits]
1.   Member States shall avoid excessive government deficits.
2.   The Commission shall monitor the development of the budgetary situation and of
the stock of government debt in the Member States with a view to identifying gross
errors. In particular it shall examine compliance with budgetary discipline on the basis
of the following two criteria:
(a) whether the ratio of the planned or actual government deficit to gross domestic
     product exceeds a reference value, unless:
     —   either the ratio has declined substantially and continuously and reached a
         level that comes close to the reference value;
     —   or, alternatively, the excess over the reference value is only exceptional and
         temporary and the ratio remains close to the reference value;
(b) whether the ratio of government debt to gross domestic product exceeds a refe-
     rence value, unless the ratio is sufficiently diminishing and approaching the refe-
     rence value at a satisfactory pace.

The reference values are specified in the Protocol on the excessive deficit procedure annexed to this Treaty.

3.   If a Member State does not fulfil the requirements under one or both of these criteria, the Commission shall prepare a report. The report of the Commission shall also take into account whether the government deficit exceeds government investment expenditure and take into account all other relevant factors, including the medium-term economic and budgetary position of the Member State.

The Commission may also prepare a report if, notwithstanding the fulfilment of the requirements under the criteria, it is of the opinion that there is a risk of an excessive deficit in a Member State.

4.   The Committee provided for in Article 114 shall formulate an opinion on the report of the Commission.

5.   If the Commission considers that an excessive deficit in a Member State exists or may occur, the Commission shall address an opinion to the Council.

6.   The Council shall, acting by a qualified majority on a recommendation from the Commission, and having considered any observations which the Member State concerned may wish to make, decide after an overall assessment whether an excessive deficit exists.

7.   Where the existence of an excessive deficit is decided according to paragraph 6, the Council shall make recommendations to the Member State concerned with a view to bringing that situation to an end within a given period. Subject to the provisions of paragraph 8, these recommendations shall not be made public.

8.   Where it establishes that there has been no effective action in response to its recommendations within the period laid down, the Council may make its recommendations public.

9.   If a Member State persists in failing to put into practice the recommendations of the Council, the Council may decide to give notice to the Member State to take, within a specified time-limit, measures for the deficit reduction which is judged necessary by the Council in order to remedy the situation.

In such a case, the Council may request the Member State concerned to submit reports in accordance with a specific timetable in order to examine the adjustment efforts of that Member State.

10. The rights to bring actions provided for in Articles 226 and 227 may not be exercised within the framework of paragraphs 1 to 9 of this Article.

11. As long as a Member State fails to comply with a decision taken in accordance with paragraph 9, the Council may decide to apply or, as the case may be, intensify one or more of the following measures:

— to require the Member State concerned to publish additional information, to be specified by the Council, before issuing bonds and securities;

— to invite the European Investment Bank to reconsider its lending policy towards the Member State concerned;

— to require the Member State concerned to make a non-interest-bearing deposit of an appropriate size with the Community until the excessive deficit has, in the view of the Council, been corrected;

— to impose fines of an appropriate size.

The President of the Council shall inform the European Parliament of the decisions taken.

12. The Council shall abrogate some or all of its decisions referred to in paragraphs 6 to 9 and 11 to the extent that the excessive deficit in the Member State concerned has, in the view of the Council, been corrected. If the Council has previously made public recommendations, it shall, as soon as the decision under paragraph 8 has been

abrogated, make a public statement that an excessive deficit in the Member State concerned no longer exists.

13. When taking the decisions referred to in paragraphs 7 to 9, 11 and 12, the Council shall act on a recommendation from the Commission by a majority of two-thirds of the votes of its members weighted in accordance with Article 205(2), excluding the votes of the representative of the Member State concerned.

14. Further provisions relating to the implementation of the procedure described in this Article are set out in the Protocol on the excessive deficit procedure annexed to this Treaty.

The Council shall, acting unanimously on a proposal from the Commission and after consulting the European Parliament and the ECB, adopt the appropriate provisions which shall then replace the said Protocol.

Subject to the other provisions of this paragraph, the Council shall, before 1 January 1994, acting by a qualified majority on a proposal from the Commission and after consulting the European Parliament, lay down detailed rules and definitions for the application of the provisions of the said Protocol.

Chapter 2 Monetary Policy

Article 105 (ex Article 105) [Objectives and Tasks of the European System of Central Banks]

1. The primary objective of the ESCB shall be to maintain price stability. Without prejudice to the objective of price stability, the ESCB shall support the general economic policies in the Community with a view to contributing to the achievement of the objectives of the Community as laid down in Article 2. The ESCB shall act in accordance with the principle of an open market economy with free competition, favouring an efficient allocation of resources, and in compliance with the principles set out in Article 4.

2. The basic tasks to be carried out through the ESCB shall be:
— to define and implement the monetary policy of the Community;
— to conduct foreign exchange operations consistent with the provisions of Article 111;
— to hold and manage the official foreign reserves of the Member States;
— to promote the smooth operation of payment systems.

3. The third indent of paragraph 2 shall be without prejudice to the holding and management by the governments of Member States of foreign-exchange working balances.

4. The ECB shall be consulted:
— on any proposed Community act in its fields of competence;
— by national authorities regarding any draft legislative provision in its fields of competence, but within the limits and under the conditions set out by the Council in accordance with the procedure laid down in Article 107(6).
The ECB may submit opinions to the appropriate Community institutions or bodies or to national authorities on matters in its fields of competence.

5. The ESCB shall contribute to the smooth conduct of policies pursued by the competent authorities relating to the prudential supervision of credit institutions and the stability of the financial system.

6. The Council may, acting unanimously on a proposal from the Commission and after consulting the ECB and after receiving the assent of the European Parliament, confer upon the ECB specific tasks concerning policies relating to the prudential supervision of credit institutions and other financial institutions with the exception of insurance undertakings.

Article 106 (ex Article 105a) [Issuing of Bank Notes and Coins]

1. The ECB shall have the exclusive right to authorise the issue of banknotes within the Community. The ECB and the national central banks may issue such notes. The banknotes issued by the ECB and the national central banks shall be the only such notes to have the status of legal tender within the Community.

2. Member States may issue coins subject to approval by the ECB of the volume of the issue. The Council may, acting in accordance with the procedure referred to in Article 252 and after consulting the ECB, adopt measures to harmonise the denominations and technical specifications of all coins intended for circulation to the extent necessary to permit their smooth circulation within the Community.

Article 107 (ex Article 106) [Structure of the European Central Bank and the European System of Central Banks]

1. The ESCB shall be composed of the ECB and of the national central banks.

2. The ECB shall have legal personality.

3. The ESCB shall be governed by the decision-making bodies of the ECB which shall be the Governing Council and the Executive Board.

4. The Statute of the ESCB is laid down in a Protocol annexed to this Treaty.

5. Articles 5.1, 5.2, 5.3, 17, 18, 19.1, 22, 23, 24, 26, 32.2, 32.3, 32.4, 32.6, 33.1(a) and 36 of the Statute of the ESCB may be amended by the Council, acting either by a qualified majority on a recommendation from the ECB and after consulting the Commission or unanimously on a proposal from the Commission and after consulting the ECB. In either case, the assent of the European Parliament shall be required.

6. The Council, acting by a qualified majority either on a proposal from the Commission and after consulting the European Parliament and the ECB or on a recommendation from the ECB and after consulting the European Parliament and the Commission, shall adopt the provisions referred to in Articles 4, 5.4, 19.2, 20, 28.1, 29.2, 30.4 and 34.3 of the Statute of the ESCB.

Article 108 (ex Article 107) [Independence of the European Central Bank and of National Central Banks]

When exercising the powers and carrying out the tasks and duties conferred upon them by this Treaty and the Statute of the ESCB, neither the ECB, nor a national central bank, nor any member of their decision-making bodies shall seek or take instructions from Community institutions or bodies, from any government of a Member State or from any other body. The Community institutions and bodies and the governments of the Member States undertake to respect this principle and not to seek to influence the members of the decision-making bodies of the ECB or of the national central banks in the performance of their tasks.

Article 109 (ex Article 108) [Alignment of National Law with the Treaty and the Statute of the ESCB]

Each Member State shall ensure, at the latest at the date of the establishment of the ESCB, that its national legislation including the statutes of its national central bank is compatible with this Treaty and the Statute of the ESCB.

Article 110 (ex Article 108a) [Regulations, Decisions, Recommendations and Opinions of the ECB]

1. In order to carry out the tasks entrusted to the ESCB, the ECB shall, in accordance with the provisions of this Treaty and under the conditions laid down in the Statute of the ESCB:

— make regulations to the extent necessary to implement the tasks defined in Article 3.1, first indent, Articles 19.1, 22 and 25.2 of the Statute of the ESCB and in cases which shall be laid down in the acts of the Council referred to in Article 107(6);
— take decisions necessary for carrying out the tasks entrusted to the ESCB under this Treaty and the Statute of the ESCB;
— make recommendations and deliver opinions.
2.   A regulation shall have general application. It shall be binding in its entirety and directly applicable in all Member States.
Recommendations and opinions shall have no binding force.
A decision shall be binding in its entirety upon those to whom it is addressed.
Articles 253 to 256 shall apply to regulations and decisions adopted by the ECB.
The ECB may decide to publish its decisions, recommendations and opinions.
3.   Within the limits and under the conditions adopted by the Council under the procedure laid down in Article 107(6), the ECB shall be entitled to impose fines or periodic penalty payments on undertakings for failure to comply with obligations under its regulations and decisions.

Article 111 (ex Article 109) [Exchange Rates of the Euro in Relation to Non-EU Currencies]

1.   By way of derogation from Article 300 [ex 228], the Council may, acting unanimously on a recommendation from the ECB or from the Commission, and after consulting the ECB in an endeavour to reach a consensus consistent with the objective of price stability, after consulting the European Parliament, in accordance with the procedure in paragraph 3 for determining the arrangements, conclude formal agreements on an exchange-rate system for the ECU in relation to non-Community currencies. The Council may, acting by a qualified majority on a recommendation from the ECB or from the Commission, and after consulting the ECB in an endeavour to reach a consensus consistent with the objective of price stability, adopt, adjust or abandon the central rates of the ECU within the exchange-rate system. The President of the Council shall inform the European Parliament of the adoption, adjustment or abandonment of the ECU central rates.
2.   In the absence of an exchange-rate system in relation to one or more non-Community currencies as referred to in paragraph 1, the Council, acting by a qualified majority either on a recommendation from the Commission and after consulting the ECB or on a recommendation from the ECB, may formulate general orientations for exchange-rate policy in relation to these currencies. These general orientations shall be without prejudice to the primary objective of the ESCB to maintain price stability.
3.   By way of derogation from Article 300, where agreements concerning monetary or foreign exchange regime matters need to be negotiated by the Community with one or more States or international organisations, the Council, acting by a qualified majority on a recommendation from the Commission and after consulting the ECB, shall decide the arrangements for the negotiation and for the conclusion of such agreements. These arrangements shall ensure that the Community expresses a single position. The Commission shall be fully associated with the negotiations.
Agreements concluded in accordance with this paragraph shall be binding on the institutions of the Community, on the ECB and on Member States.
4.   Subject to paragraph 1, the Council shall, on a proposal from the Commission and after consulting the ECB, acting by a qualified majority decide on the position of the Community at international level as regards issues of particular relevance to economic and monetary union and, acting unanimously, decide its representation in compliance with the allocation of powers laid down in Articles 99 and 105.

5.   Without prejudice to Community competence and Community agreements as regards economic and monetary union, Member States may negotiate in international bodies and conclude international agreements.

Chapter 3 Institutional Provisions

Article 112 (ex Article 109a) [Organs of the European Central Bank]

1.   The Governing Council of the ECB shall comprise the members of the Executive Board of the ECB and the Governors of the national central banks.

2.   (a) The Executive Board shall comprise the President, the Vice-President and four other members.

(b)   The President, the Vice-President and the other members of the Executive Board shall be appointed from among persons of recognised standing and professional experience in monetary or banking matters by common accord of the governments of the Member States at the level of Heads of State or Government, on a recommendation from the Council, after it has consulted the European Parliament and the Governing Council of the ECB.

Their term of office shall be eight years and shall not be renewable.

Only nationals of Member States may be members of the Executive Board.

Article 113 (ex Article 109b) [Cooperation with Council and Commission]

1.   The President of the Council and a member of the Commission may participate, without having the right to vote, in meetings of the Governing Council of the ECB.

The President of the Council may submit a motion for deliberation to the Governing Council of the ECB.

2.   The President of the ECB shall be invited to participate in Council meetings when the Council is discussing matters relating to the objectives and tasks of the ESCB.

3.   The ECB shall address an annual report on the activities of the ESCB and on the monetary policy of both the previous and current year to the European Parliament, the Council and the Commission, and also to the European Council. The President of the ECB shall present this report to the Council and to the European Parliament, which may hold a general debate on that basis.

The President of the ECB and the other members of the Executive Board may, at the request of the European Parliament or on their own initiative, be heard by the competent committees of the European Parliament.

Article 114 (ex Article 109c) [The Monetary Committee and the Economic and Financial Committee]

1.   In order to promote coordination of the policies of Member States to the full extent needed for the functioning of the internal market, a Monetary Committee with advisory status is hereby set up.

It shall have the following tasks:

—   to keep under review the monetary and financial situation of the Member States and of the Community and the general payments system of the Member States and to report regularly thereon to the Council and to the Commission;

—   to deliver opinions at the request of the Council or of the Commission, or on its own initiative for submission to those institutions;

—   without prejudice to Article 207, to contribute to the preparation of the work of the Council referred to in Articles 59, 60, 99(2), (3), (4) and (5), 100, 102, 103, 104, 116(2), 117(6), 119, 120, 121(2) and 122(1);

—   to examine, at least once a year, the situation regarding the movement of capital and the freedom of payments, as they result from the application of this Treaty and of measures adopted by the Council; the examination shall cover all measures relating to capital movements and payments; the Committee shall report to the Commission and to the Council on the outcome of this examination.

The Member States and the Commission shall each appoint two members of the Monetary Committee.

2.   At the start of the third stage, an Economic and Financial Committee shall be set up. The Monetary Committee provided for in paragraph 1 shall be dissolved.

The Economic and Financial Committee shall have the following tasks:
— to deliver opinions at the request of the Council or of the Commission, or on its own initiative for submission to those institutions;
— to keep under review the economic and financial situation of the Member States and of the Community and to report regularly thereon to the Council and to the Commission, in particular on financial relations with third countries and international institutions;
— without prejudice to Article 207, to contribute to the preparation of the work of the Council referred to in Articles 59, 60, 99(2), (3), (4) and (5), 100, 102, 103, 104, 105(6), 106(2), 107(5) and (6), 111, 119, 120(2) and (3), 122(2), 123(4) and (5), and to carry out other advisory and preparatory tasks assigned to it by the Council;
— to examine, at least once a year, the situation regarding the movement of capital and the freedom of payments, as they result from the application of this Treaty and of measures adopted by the Council; the examination shall cover all measures relating to capital movements and payments; the Committee shall report to the Commission and to the Council on the outcome of this examination.

The Member States, the Commission and the ECB shall each appoint no more than two members of the Committee.

3.   The Council shall, acting by a qualified majority on a proposal from the Commission and after consulting the ECB and the Committee referred to in this Article, lay down detailed provisions concerning the composition of the Economic and Financial Committee. The President of the Council shall inform the European Parliament of such a decision.

4.   In addition to the tasks set out in paragraph 2, if and as long as there are Member States with a derogation as referred to in Articles 122 and 123, the Committee shall keep under review the monetary and financial situation and the general payments system of those Member States and report regularly thereon to the Council and to the Commission.

Article 115 (ex Article 109d) [Recommendations and Proposals by the Commission]
For matters within the scope of Articles 99(4), 104 with the exception of paragraph 14, 111, 121, 122 and 123(4) and (5), the Council or a Member State may request the Commission to make a recommendation or a proposal, as appropriate. The Commission shall examine this request and submit its conclusions to the Council without delay.

Chapter 4 Transitional Provisions

Article 116 (ex Article 109e) [First and Second Stage of Economic and Monetary Union]
1.   The second stage for achieving economic and monetary union shall begin on 1 January 1994.
2.   Before that date:
(a) each Member State shall:
— adopt, where necessary, appropriate measures to comply with the prohibitions laid down in Article 56 and in Articles 101 and 102(1);

— adopt, if necessary, with a view to permitting the assessment provided for in subparagraph (b), multiannual programmes intended to ensure the lasting convergence necessary for the achievement of economic and monetary union, in particular with regard to price stability and sound public finances;

(b) the Council shall, on the basis of a report from the Commission, assess the progress made with regard to economic and monetary convergence, in particular with regard to price stability and sound public finances, and the progress made with the implementation of Community law concerning the internal market.

3. The provisions of Articles 101, 102(1), 103(1) and 104 with the exception of paragraphs 1, 9, 11 and 14 shall apply from the beginning of the second stage. The provisions of Articles 100(2), 104(1), (9) and (11), 105, 106, 108, 111, 112, 113 and 114(2) and (4) shall apply from the beginning of the third stage.

4. In the second stage, Member States shall endeavour to avoid excessive government deficits.

5. During the second stage, each Member State shall, as appropriate, start the process leading to the independence of its central bank, in accordance with Article 109.

Article 117 (ex Article 109f) [The European Monetary Institute]

1. At the start of the second stage, a European Monetary Institute (hereinafter referred to as "EMI") shall be established and take up its duties; it shall have legal personality and be directed and managed by a Council, consisting of a President and the Governors of the national central banks, one of whom shall be Vice-President.

The President shall be appointed by common accord of the governments of the Member States at the level of Heads of State or Government, on a recommendation from the Council of the EMI, and after consulting the European Parliament and the Council. The President shall be selected from among persons of recognised standing and professional experience in monetary or banking matters. Only nationals of Member States may be President of the EMI. The Council of the EMI shall appoint the Vice-President.

The Statute of the EMI is laid down in a Protocol annexed to this Treaty.

2. The EMI shall:
— strengthen cooperation between the national central banks;
— strengthen the coordination of the monetary policies of the Member States, with the aim of ensuring price stability;
  monitor the functioning of the European Monetary System;
— hold consultations concerning issues falling within the competence of the national central banks and affecting the stability of financial institutions and markets;
— take over the tasks of the European Monetary Cooperation Fund, which shall be dissolved; the modalities of dissolution are laid down in the Statute of the EMI;
— facilitate the use of the ECU and oversee its development, including the smooth functioning of the ECU clearing system.

3. For the preparation of the third stage, the EMI shall:
— prepare the instruments and the procedures necessary for carrying out a single monetary policy in the third stage;
— promote the harmonisation, where necessary, of the rules and practices governing the collection, compilation and distribution of statistics in the areas within its field of competence;
— prepare the rules for operations to be undertaken by the national central banks within the framework of the ESCB;
— promote the efficiency of cross-border payments;
— supervise the technical preparation of ECU banknotes.

At the latest by 31 December 1996, the EMI shall specify the regulatory, organisational and logistical framework necessary for the ESCB to perform its tasks in the third stage. This framework shall be submitted for decision to the ECB at the date of its establishment.

4. The EMI, acting by a majority of two thirds of the members of its Council, may:
— formulate opinions or recommendations on the overall orientation of monetary policy and exchange-rate policy as well as on related measures introduced in each Member State;
— submit opinions or recommendations to governments and to the Council on policies which might affect the internal or external monetary situation in the Community and, in particular, the functioning of the European Monetary System;
— make recommendations to the monetary authorities of the Member States concerning the conduct of their monetary policy.

5. The EMI, acting unanimously, may decide to publish its opinions and its recommendations.

6. The EMI shall be consulted by the Council regarding any proposed Community act within its field of competence.

Within the limits and under the conditions set out by the Council, acting by a qualified majority on a proposal from the Commission and after consulting the European Parliament and the EMI, the EMI shall be consulted by the authorities of the Member States on any draft legislative provision within its field of competence.

7. The Council may, acting unanimously on a proposal from the Commission and after consulting the European Parliament and the EMI, confer upon the EMI other tasks for the preparation of the third stage.

8. Where this Treaty provides for a consultative role for the ECB, references to the ECB shall be read as referring to the EMI before the establishment of the ECB.

9. During the second stage, the term "ECB" used in Articles 230, 232, 233, 234, 237 and 288 shall be read as referring to the EMI.

Article 118 (ex Article 109g) [Currency Composition of the ECU Basket]
The currency composition of the ECU basket shall not be changed.
From the start of the third stage, the value of the ECU shall be irrevocably fixed in accordance with Article 123(4).

Article 119 (ex Article 109h) [Balance of Payment-Difficulties
of Individual Member States]
1. Where a Member State is in difficulties or is seriously threatened with difficulties as regards its balance of payments either as a result of an overall disequilibrium in its balance of payments, or as a result of the type of currency at its disposal, and where such difficulties are liable in particular to jeopardise the functioning of the common market or the progressive implementation of the common commercial policy, the Commission shall immediately investigate the position of the State in question and the action which, making use of all the means at its disposal, that State has taken or may take in accordance with the provisions of this Treaty. The Commission shall state what measures it recommends the State concerned to take.

If the action taken by a Member State and the measures suggested by the Commission do not prove sufficient to overcome the difficulties which have arisen or which threaten, the Commission shall, after consulting the Committee referred to in Article 114, recommend to the Council the granting of mutual assistance and appropriate methods therefor.

The Commission shall keep the Council regularly informed of the situation and of how it is developing.

2.   The Council, acting by a qualified majority, shall grant such mutual assistance; it shall adopt directives or decisions laying down the conditions and details of such assistance, which may take such forms as:
(a) a concerted approach to or within any other international organisations to which Member States may have recourse;
(b) measures needed to avoid deflection of trade where the State which is in difficulties maintains or reintroduces quantitative restrictions against third countries;
(c) the granting of limited credits by other Member States, subject to their agreement.
3.   If the mutual assistance recommended by the Commission is not granted by the Council or if the mutual assistance granted and the measures taken are insufficient, the Commission shall authorise the State which is in difficulties to take protective measures, the conditions and details of which the Commission shall determine.

Such authorisation may be revoked and such conditions and details may be changed by the Council acting by a qualified majority.
4.   Subject to Article 122(6), this Article shall cease to apply from the beginning of the third stage.

Article 120 (ex Article 109i) [Member State Measures Against a Sudden Crisis in the Balance of Payments]
1.   Where a sudden crisis in the balance of payments occurs and a decision within the meaning of Article 119(2) is not immediately taken, the Member State concerned may, as a precaution, take the necessary protective measures. Such measures must cause the least possible disturbance in the functioning of the common market and must not be wider in scope than is strictly necessary to remedy the sudden difficulties which have arisen.
2.   The Commission and the other Member States shall be informed of such protective measures not later than when they enter into force. The Commission may recommend to the Council the granting of mutual assistance under Article 119.
3.   After the Commission has delivered an opinion and the Committee referred to in Article 114 has been consulted, the Council may, acting by a qualified majority, decide that the State concerned shall amend, suspend or abolish the protective measures referred to above.
4.   Subject to Article 122(6), this Article shall cease to apply from the beginning of the third stage.

Article 121 (ex Article 109j) [The Convergence Criteria and the Beginning of the Third Stage]
1.   The Commission and the EMI shall report to the Council on the progress made in the fulfilment by the Member States of their obligations regarding the achievement of economic and monetary union. These reports shall include an examination of the compatibility between each Member State's national legislation, including the statutes of its national central bank, and Articles 108 and 109 of this Treaty and the Statute of the ESCB. The reports shall also examine the achievement of a high degree of sustainable convergence by reference to the fulfilment by each Member State of the following criteria:
— the achievement of a high degree of price stability; this will be apparent from a rate of inflation which is close to that of, at most, the three best performing Member States in terms of price stability;
— the sustainability of the government financial position; this will be apparent from having achieved a government budgetary position without a deficit that is excessive as determined in accordance with Article 104(6);

— the observance of the normal fluctuation margins provided for by the exchange-rate mechanism of the European Monetary System, for at least two years, without devaluing against the currency of any other Member State;
— the durability of convergence achieved by the Member State and of its participation in the exchange-rate mechanism of the European Monetary System being reflected in the long-term interest-rate levels.

The four criteria mentioned in this paragraph and the relevant periods over which they are to be respected are developed further in a Protocol annexed to this Treaty. The reports of the Commission and the EMI shall also take account of the development of the ECU, the results of the integration of markets, the situation and development of the balances of payments on current account and an examination of the development of unit labour costs and other price indices.

2. On the basis of these reports, the Council, acting by a qualified majority on a recommendation from the Commission, shall assess:
— for each Member State, whether it fulfils the necessary conditions for the adoption of a single currency;
— whether a majority of the Member States fulfil the necessary conditions for the adoption of a single currency, and recommend its findings to the Council, meeting in the composition of the Heads of State or Government. The European Parliament shall be consulted and forward its opinion to the Council, meeting in the composition of the Heads of State or Government.

3. Taking due account of the reports referred to in paragraph 1 and the opinion of the European Parliament referred to in paragraph 2, the Council, meeting in the composition of the Heads of State or Government, shall, acting by a qualified majority, not later than 31 December 1996:
— decide, on the basis of the recommendations of the Council referred to in paragraph 2, whether a majority of the Member States fulfil the necessary conditions for the adoption of a single currency;
— decide whether it is appropriate for the Community to enter the third stage, and if so:
— set the date for the beginning of the third stage.

4. If by the end of 1997 the date for the beginning of the third stage has not been set, the third stage shall start on 1 January 1999. Before 1 July 1998, the Council, meeting in the composition of the Heads of State or Government, after a repetition of the procedure provided for in paragraphs 1 and 2, with the exception of the second indent of paragraph 2, taking into account the reports referred to in paragraph 1 and the opinion of the European Parliament, shall, acting by a qualified majority and on the basis of the recommendations of the Council referred to in paragraph 2, confirm which Member States fulfil the necessary conditions for the adoption of a single currency.

Article 122 (ex Article 109k) [Member States with a Derogation]
1. If the decision has been taken to set the date in accordance with Article 121(3), the Council shall, on the basis of its recommendations referred to in Article 121(2), acting by a qualified majority on a recommendation from the Commission, decide whether any, and if so which, Member States shall have a derogation as defined in paragraph 3 of this Article. Such Member States shall in this Treaty be referred to as "Member States with a derogation".

If the Council has confirmed which Member States fulfil the necessary conditions for the adoption of a single currency, in accordance with Article 121(4), those Member States which do not fulfil the conditions shall have a derogation as defined in paragraph 3 of this Article. Such Member States shall in this Treaty be referred to as "Member States with a derogation".

2. At least once every two years, or at the request of a Member State with a derogation, the Commission and the ECB shall report to the Council in accordance with the procedure laid down in Article 121(1). After consulting the European Parliament and after discussion in the Council, meeting in the composition of the Heads of State or Government, the Council shall, acting by a qualified majority on a proposal from the Commission, decide which Member States with a derogation fulfil the necessary conditions on the basis of the criteria set out in Article 121(1), and abrogate the derogations of the Member States concerned.

3. A derogation referred to in paragraph 1 shall entail that the following Articles do not apply to the Member State concerned: Articles 104(9) and (11), 105(1), (2), (3) and (5), 106, 110, 111, and 112(2)(b). The exclusion of such a Member State and its national central bank from rights and obligations within the ESCB is laid down in Chapter IX of the Statute of the ESCB.

4. In Articles 105(1), (2) and (3), 106, 110, 111 and 112(2)(b), "Member State" shall be read as "Member States without a derogation".

5. The voting rights of Member States with a derogation shall be suspended for the Council decisions referred to in the Articles of this Treaty mentioned in paragraph 3. In that case, by way of derogation from Articles 205 and 250(1), a qualified majority shall be defined as two-thirds of the votes of the representatives of the Member States without a derogation weighted in accordance with Article 205(2), and unanimity of those Member States shall be required for an act requiring unanimity.

6. Articles 119 and 120 shall continue to apply to a Member State with a derogation.

Article 123 (ex Article 109l) [Creation of ECB, ESCB, and the Common Currency]
1. Immediately after the decision on the date for the beginning of the third stage has been taken in accordance with Article 121(3), or, as the case may be, immediately after 1 July 1998:
— the Council shall adopt the provisions referred to in Article 107(6);
— the governments of the Member States without a derogation shall appoint, in accordance with the procedure set out in Article 50 of the Statute of the ESCB, the President, the Vice-President and the other members of the Executive Board of the ECB. If there are Member States with a derogation, the number of members of the Executive Board may be smaller than provided for in Article 11.1 of the Statute of the ESCB, but in no circumstances shall it be less than four.
As soon as the Executive Board is appointed, the ESCB and the ECB shall be established and shall prepare for their full operation as described in this Treaty and the Statute of the ESCB. The full exercise of their powers shall start from the first day of the third stage.

2. As soon as the ECB is established, it shall, if necessary, take over tasks of the EMI. The EMI shall go into liquidation upon the establishment of the ECB; the modalities of liquidation are laid down in the Statute of the EMI.

3. If and as long as there are Member States with a derogation, and without prejudice to Article 107(3) of this Treaty, the General Council of the ECB referred to in Article 45 of the Statute of the ESCB shall be constituted as a third decision-making body of the ECB.

4. At the starting date of the third stage, the Council shall, acting with the unanimity of the Member States without a derogation, on a proposal from the Commission and after consulting the ECB, adopt the conversion rates at which their currencies shall be irrevocably fixed and at which irrevocably fixed rate the ECU shall be substituted for these currencies, and the ECU will become a currency in its own right. This measure shall by itself not modify the external value of the ECU. The Council shall, acting accor-

ding to the same procedure, also take the other measures necessary for the rapid introduction of the ECU as the single currency of those Member States.

5.   If it is decided, according to the procedure set out in Article 122(2), to abrogate a derogation, the Council shall, acting with the unanimity of the Member States without a derogation and the Member State concerned, on a proposal from the Commission and after consulting the ECB, adopt the rate at which the ECU shall be substituted for the currency of the Member State concerned, and take the other measures necessary for the introduction of the ECU as the single currency in the Member State concerned.

Article 124 (ex Article 109m) [Member State Exchange Rate Policies Prior to Participation in Monetary Union]

1.   Until the beginning of the third stage, each Member State shall treat its exchange-rate policy as a matter of common interest. In so doing, Member States shall take account of the experience acquired in cooperation within the framework of the European Monetary System (EMS) and in developing the ECU, and shall respect existing powers in this field.

2.   From the beginning of the third stage and for as long as a Member State has a derogation, paragraph 1 shall apply by analogy to the exchange-rate policy of that Member State.

TITLE VIII (EX TITLE VIA)
EMPLOYMENT

Article 125 (ex Article 109n) [A Coordinated Strategy for Employment]

Member States and the Community shall, in accordance with this Title, work towards developing a coordinated strategy for employment and particularly for promoting a skilled, trained and adaptable workforce and labour markets responsive to economic change with a view to achieving the objectives defined in Article 2 of the Treaty on European Union and in Article 2 of this Treaty.

Article 126 (ex Article 109o) [Obligations of the Member States]

1.   Member States, through their employment policies, shall contribute to the achievement of the objectives referred to in Article 125 in a way consistent with the broad guidelines of the economic policies of the Member States and of the Community adopted pursuant to Article 99(2).

2.   Member States, having regard to national practices related to the responsibilities of management and labour, shall regard promoting employment as a matter of common concern and shall coordinate their action in this respect within the Council, in accordance with the provisions of Article 128.

Article 127 (ex Article 109p) [Community Support for Member State Strategies]

1.   The Community shall contribute to a high level of employment by encouraging cooperation between Member States and by supporting and, if necessary, complementing their action. In doing so, the competences of the Member States shall be respected.

2.   The objective of a high level of employment shall be taken into consideration in the formulation and implementation of Community policies and activities.

Article 128 (ex Article 109q) [Guidelines for and Recommendations to Member States]

1.   The European Council shall each year consider the employment situation in the Community and adopt conclusions thereon, on the basis of a joint annual report by the Council and the Commission.

2.   On the basis of the conclusions of the European Council, the Council, acting by a qualified majority on a proposal from the Commission and after consulting the European Parliament, the Economic and Social Committee, the Committee of the Regions and the Employment Committee referred to in Article 130, shall each year draw up guidelines which the Member States shall take into account in their employment policies. These guidelines shall be consistent with the broad guidelines adopted pursuant to Article 99(2).

3.   Each Member State shall provide the Council and the Commission with an annual report on the principal measures taken to implement its employment policy in the light of the guidelines for employment as referred to in paragraph 2.

4.   The Council, on the basis of the reports referred to in paragraph 3 and having received the views of the Employment Committee, shall each year carry out an examination of the implementation of the employment policies of the Member States in the light of the guidelines for employment. The Council, acting by a qualified majority on a recommendation from the Commission, may, if it considers it appropriate in the light of that examination, make recommendations to Member States.

5.   On the basis of the results of that examination, the Council and the Commission shall make a joint annual report to the European Council on the employment situation in the Community and on the implementation of the guidelines for employment.

Article 129 (ex Article 109r) [Incentive Measures by the Community]

The Council, acting in accordance with the procedure referred to in Article 251 [ex Article 189b] and after consulting the Economic and Social Committee and the Committee of the Regions, may adopt incentive measures designed to encourage cooperation between Member States and to support their action in the field of employment through initiatives aimed at developing exchanges of information and best practices, providing comparative analysis and advice as well as promoting innovative approaches and evaluating experiences, in particular by recourse to pilot projects.

Those measures shall not include harmonisation of the laws and regulations of the Member States.

Article 130 (ex Article 109s) [The Employment Committee]

The Council, after consulting the European Parliament, shall establish an Employment Committee with advisory status to promote coordination between Member States on employment and labour market policies. The tasks of the Committee shall be:

—   to monitor the employment situation and employment policies in the Member States and the Community;

—   without prejudice to Article 207, to formulate opinions at the request of either the Council or the Commission or on its own initiative, and to contribute to the preparation of the Council proceedings referred to in Article 128. In fulfilling its mandate, the Committee shall consult management and labour. Each Member State and the Commission shall appoint two members of the Committee.

TITLE IX (EX TITLE VII)
COMMON COMMERCIAL POLICY

Article 131 (ex Article 110) [Adoption of a Common Commercial Policy]
By establishing a customs union between themselves Member States aim to contribute, in the common interest, to the harmonious development of world trade, the progressive abolition of restrictions on international trade and the lowering of customs barriers.
   The common commercial policy shall take into account the favourable effect which the abolition of customs duties between Member States may have on the increase in the competitive strength of undertakings in those States.

Article 132 (ex Article 112) [National Export Subsidies]
1.   Without prejudice to obligations undertaken by them within the framework of other international organisations, Member States shall progressively harmonise the systems whereby they grant aid for exports to third countries, to the extent necessary to ensure that competition between undertakings of the Community is not distorted.
   On a proposal from the Commission, the Council shall, acting by a qualified majority, issue any directives needed for this purpose.
2.   The preceding provisions shall not apply to such a drawback of customs duties or charges having equivalent effect nor to such a repayment of indirect taxation including turnover taxes, excise duties and other indirect taxes as is allowed when goods are exported from a Member State to a third country, insofar as such a drawback or repayment does not exceed the amount imposed, directly or indirectly, on the products exported.

Article 133 (ex Article 113) [Scope of the Common Commercial Policy;
Implementing Measures]
1.   The common commercial policy shall be based on uniform principles, particularly in regard to changes in tariff rates, the conclusion of tariff and trade agreements, the achievement of uniformity in measures of liberalisation, export policy and measures to protect trade such as those to be taken in the event of dumping or subsidies.
2.   The Commission shall submit proposals to the Council for implementing the common commercial policy.
3.   Where agreements with one or more States or international organisations need to be negotiated, the Commission shall make recommendations to the Council, which shall authorise the Commission to open the necessary negotiations.
   The Commission shall conduct these negotiations in consultation with a special committee appointed by the Council to assist the Commission in this task and within the framework of such directives as the Council may issue to it.
   The relevant provisions of Article 300 shall apply.
4.   In exercising the powers conferred upon it by this Article, the Council shall act by a qualified majority.
5.   The Council, acting unanimously on a proposal from the Commission and after consulting the European Parliament, may extend the application of paragraphs 1 to 4 to international negotiations and agreements on services and intellectual property insofar as they are not covered by these paragraphs.

Article 134 (ex Article 115) [Cooperation for the Prevention of Trade Deflection]
In order to ensure that the execution of measures of commercial policy taken in accordance with this Treaty by any Member State is not obstructed by deflection of trade, or where differences between such measures lead to economic difficulties in one or

more Member States, the Commission shall recommend the methods for the requisite cooperation between Member States. Failing this, the Commission may authorise Member States to take the necessary protective measures, the conditions and details of which it shall determine.

In case of urgency, Member States shall request authorisation to take the necessary measures themselves from the Commission, which shall take a decision as soon as possible; the Member States concerned shall then notify the measures to the other Member States. The Commission may decide at any time that the Member States concerned shall amend or abolish the measures in question.

In the selection of such measures, priority shall be given to those which cause the least disturbance of the functioning of the common market.

TITLE X (EX TITLE VIIA)
CUSTOMS COOPERATION

Article 135 (ex Article 116) [Measures for the Improvement of Cooperation Between Customs Authorities]
Within the scope of application of this Treaty, the Council, acting in accordance with the procedure referred to in Article 251 [ex Article 189b], shall take measures in order to strengthen customs cooperation between Member States and between the latter and the Commission. These measures shall not concern the application of national criminal law or the national administration of justice.

TITLE XI (EX TITLE VIII)
SOCIAL POLICY, EDUCATION, VOCATIONAL TRAINING AND YOUTH
Chapter 1 Social Provisions

Article 136 (ex Article 117) [Improvement of Working Conditions and Standards of Living]
The Community and the Member States, having in mind fundamental social rights such as those set out in the European Social Charter signed at Turin on 18 October 1961 and in the 1989 Community Charter of the Fundamental Social Rights of Workers, shall have as their objectives the promotion of employment, improved living and working conditions, so as to make possible their harmonisation while the improvement is being maintained, proper social protection, dialogue between management and labour, the development of human resources with a view to lasting high employment and the combatting of exclusion.

To this end the Community and the Member States shall implement measures which take account of the diverse forms of national practices, in particular in the field of contractual relations, and the need to maintain the competitiveness of the Community economy.

They believe that such a development will ensue not only from the functioning of the common market, which will favour the harmonisation of social systems, but also from the procedures provided for in this Treaty and from the approximation of provisions laid down by law, regulation or administrative action.

Article 137 (ex Article 118) [Community Measures; Implementation by the Member States and by Management and Labour]
1. With a view to achieving the objectives of Article 136, the Community shall support and complement the activities of the Member States in the following fields:
— improvement in particular of the working environment to protect workers' health and safety;

— working conditions;
— the information and consultation of workers;
— the integration of persons excluded from the labour market, without prejudice to Article 150;
— equality between men and women with regard to labour market opportunities and treatment at work.

2.   To this end, the Council may adopt, by means of directives, minimum requirements for gradual implementation, having regard to the conditions and technical rules obtaining in each of the Member States. Such directives shall avoid imposing administrative, financial and legal constraints in a way which would hold back the creation and development of small and medium-sized undertakings.

The Council shall act in accordance with the procedure referred to in Article 251 after consulting the Economic and Social Committee and the Committee of the Regions.

The Council, acting in accordance with the same procedure, may adopt measures designed to encourage cooperation between Member States through initiatives aimed at improving knowledge, developing exchanges of information and best practices, promoting innovative approaches and evaluating experiences in order to combat social exclusion.

3.   However, the Council shall act unanimously on a proposal from the Commission, after consulting the European Parliament, the Economic and Social Committee and the Committee of the Regions in the following areas:
— social security and social protection of workers;
— protection of workers where their employment contract is terminated;
— representation and collective defence of the interests of workers and employers, including co-determination, subject to paragraph 6;
— conditions of employment for third-country nationals legally residing in Community territory;
— financial contributions for promotion of employment and job-creation, without prejudice to the provisions relating to the Social Fund.

4.   A Member State may entrust management and labour, at their joint request, with the implementation of directives adopted pursuant to paragraphs 2 and 3.

In this case, it shall ensure that, no later than the date on which a directive must be transposed in accordance with Article 249, management and labour have introduced the necessary measures by agreement, the Member State concerned being required to take any necessary measure enabling it at any time to be in a position to guarantee the results imposed by that directive.

5.   The provisions adopted pursuant to this Article shall not prevent any Member State from maintaining or introducing more stringent protective measures compatible with this Treaty.

6.   The provisions of this Article shall not apply to pay, the right of association, the right to strike or the right to impose lock-outs.

Article 138 (ex Article 118a) [Consultation of Management and Labour]
1.   The Commission shall have the task of promoting the consultation of management and labour at Community level and shall take any relevant measure to facilitate their dialogue by ensuring balanced support for the parties.
2.   To this end, before submitting proposals in the social policy field, the Commission shall consult management and labour on the possible direction of Community action.
3.   If, after such consultation, the Commission considers Community action advisable, it shall consult management and labour on the content of the envisaged proposal.

Management and labour shall forward to the Commission an opinion or, where appropriate, a recommendation.
4.   On the occasion of such consultation, management and labour may inform the Commission of their wish to initiate the process provided for in Article 139. The duration of the procedure shall not exceed nine months, unless the management and labour concerned and the Commission decide jointly to extend it.

Article 139 (ex Article 118b) [Community Measures Implementing Agreements by Management and Labour]

1.   Should management and labour so desire, the dialogue between them at Community level may lead to contractual relations, including agreements.
2.   Agreements concluded at Community level shall be implemented either in accordance with the procedures and practices specific to management and labour and the Member States or, in matters covered by Article 137, at the joint request of the signatory parties, by a Council decision on a proposal from the Commission.
   The Council shall act by qualified majority, except where the agreement in question contains one or more provisions relating to one of the areas referred to in Article 137(3), in which case it shall act unanimously.

Article 140 (ex Article 118c) [Cooperation in Social Policy Matters]

With a view to achieving the objectives of Article 136 and without prejudice to the other provisions of this Treaty, the Commission shall encourage cooperation between the Member States and facilitate the coordination of their action in all social policy fields under this chapter, particularly in matters relating to:
— employment;
— labour law and working conditions;
— basic and advanced vocational training;
— social security;
— prevention of occupational accidents and diseases;
— occupational hygiene;
— the right of association and collective bargaining between employers and workers.
To this end, the Commission shall act in close contact with Member States by making studies, delivering opinions and arranging consultations both on problems arising at national level and on those of concern to international organisations.
   Before delivering the opinions provided for in this Article, the Commission shall consult the Economic and Social Committee.

Article 141 (ex Article 119) [Equal Pay for Men and Women]

1.   Each Member State shall ensure that the principle of equal pay for male and female workers for equal work or work of equal value is applied.
2.   For the purpose of this Article, "pay" means the ordinary basic or minimum wage or salary and any other consideration, whether in cash or in kind, which the worker receives directly or indirectly, in respect of his employment, from his employer.
   Equal pay without discrimination based on sex means:
(a) that pay for the same work at piece rates shall be calculated on the basis of the same unit of measurement;
(b) that pay for work at time rates shall be the same for the same job.
3.   The Council, acting in accordance with the procedure referred to in Article 251, and after consulting the Economic and Social Committee, shall adopt measures to ensure the application of the principle of equal opportunities and equal treatment of men and women in matters of employment and occupation, including the principle of equal pay for equal work or work of equal value.

4.   With a view to ensuring full equality in practice between men and women in working life, the principle of equal treatment shall not prevent any Member State from
maintaining or adopting measures providing for specific advantages in order to make
it easier for the under-represented sex to pursue a vocational activity or to prevent or
compensate for disadvantages in professional careers.

Article 142 (ex Article 119a) [Paid Holidays]
Member States shall endeavour to maintain the existing equivalence between paid
holiday schemes.

Article 143 (ex Article 120) [Annual Reports]
The Commission shall draw up a report each year on progress in achieving the objectives of Article 136, including the demographic situation in the Community. It shall
forward the report to the European Parliament, the Council and the Economic and
Social Committee.
    The European Parliament may invite the Commission to draw up reports on parti-
cular problems concerning the social situation.

Article 144 (ex Article 121) [Delegation of Powers to the Commission]
The Council may, acting unanimously and after consulting the Economic and Social
Committee, assign to the Commission tasks in connection with the implementation of
common measures, particularly as regards social security for the migrant workers
referred to in Articles 39 to 42.

Article 145 (ex Article 122) [Report on Social Developments]
The Commission shall include a separate chapter on social developments within the
Community in its annual report to the European Parliament.
    The European Parliament may invite the Commission to draw up reports on any
particular problems concerning social conditions.

Chapter 2 The European Social Fund

Article 146 (ex Article 123) [Establishment of the European Social Fund]
In order to improve employment opportunities for workers in the internal market and to
contribute thereby to raising the standard of living, a European Social Fund is hereby
established in accordance with the provisions set out below; it shall aim to render the
employment of workers easier and to increase their geographical and occupational
mobility within the Community, and to facilitate their adaptation to industrial changes
and to changes in production systems, in particular through vocational training and retraining.

Article 147 (ex Article 124) [Composition of the European Social Fund]
The Fund shall be administered by the Commission.
    The Commission shall be assisted in this task by a Committee presided over by
a Member of the Commission and composed of representatives of governments, trade
unions and employers' organisations.

Article 148 (ex Article 125) [Implementing Decisions]
The Council, acting in accordance with the procedure referred to in Article 251 and
after consulting the Economic and Social Committee and the Committee of the Regions, shall adopt implementing decisions relating to the European Social Fund.

Chapter 3 Education, Vocational Training and Youth

Article 149 (ex Article 126) [Community Incentives in Education]
1.   The Community shall contribute to the development of quality education by encouraging cooperation between Member States and, if necessary, by supporting and supplementing their action, while fully respecting the responsibility of the Member States for the content of teaching and the organisation of education systems and their cultural and linguistic diversity.
2.   Community action shall be aimed at:
—   developing the European dimension in education, particularly through the teaching and dissemination of the languages of the Member States;
—   encouraging mobility of students and teachers, inter alia by encouraging the academic recognition of diplomas and periods of study;
—   promoting cooperation between educational establishments;
—   developing exchanges of information and experience on issues common to the education systems of the Member States;
—   encouraging the development of youth exchanges and of exchanges of socio-educational instructors;
—   encouraging the development of distance education.
3.   The Community and the Member States shall foster cooperation with third countries and the competent international organisations In the field of education, in particular the Council of Europe.
4.   In order to contribute to the achievement of the objectives referred to in this Article, the Council:
—   acting in accordance with the procedure referred to in Article 251, after consulting the Economic and Social Committee and the Committee of the Regions, shall adopt incentive measures, excluding any harmonisation of the laws and regulations of the Member States;
—   acting by a qualified majority on a proposal from the Commission, shall adopt recommendations.

Article 150 (ex Article 127) [Community Support for Vocational Training]
1.   The Community shall implement a vocational training policy which shall support and supplement the action of the Member States, while fully respecting the responsibility of the Member States for the content and organisation of vocational training.
2.   Community action shall aim to:
—   facilitate adaptation to industrial changes, in particular through vocational training and retraining;
—   improve initial and continuing vocational training in order to facilitate vocational integration and reintegration into the labour market;
—   facilitate access to vocational training and encourage mobility of instructors and trainees and particularly young people;
—   stimulate cooperation on training between educational or training establishments and firms;
—   develop exchanges of information and experience on issues common to the training systems of the Member States.
3.   The Community and the Member States shall foster cooperation with third countries and the competent international organisations in the sphere of vocational training.
4.   The Council, acting in accordance with the procedure referred to in Article 251 and after consulting the Economic and Social Committee and the Committee of the Regions, shall adopt measures to contribute to the achievement of the objectives referred

to in this Article, excluding any harmonisation of the laws and regulations of the Member States.

TITLE XII (EX TITLE IX)
CULTURE

Article 151 (ex Article 128) [Community Incentives in the Cultural Sector]
1.   The Community shall contribute to the flowering of the cultures of the Member States, while respecting their national and regional diversity and at the same time bringing the common cultural heritage to the fore.
2.   Action by the Community shall be aimed at encouraging cooperation between Member States and, if necessary, supporting and supplementing their action in the following areas:
—   improvement of the knowledge and dissemination of the culture and history of the European peoples;
—   conservation and safeguarding of cultural heritage of European significance;
—   non-commercial cultural exchanges;
—   artistic and literary creation, including in the audiovisual sector.
3.   The Community and the Member States shall foster cooperation with third countries and the competent international organisations in the sphere of culture, in particular the Council of Europe.
4.   The Community shall take cultural aspects into account in its action under other provisions of this Treaty, in particular in order to respect and to promote the diversity of its cultures.
5.   In order to contribute to the achievement of the objectives referred to in this Article, the Council:
—   acting in accordance with the procedure referred to in Article 251 and after consulting the Committee of the Regions, shall adopt incentive measures, excluding any harmonisation of the laws and regulations of the Member States. The Council shall act unanimously throughout the procedure referred to in Article 251;
—   acting unanimously on a proposal from the Commission, shall adopt recommendations.

TITLE XIII (EX TITLE X)
PUBLIC HEALTH

Article 152 (ex Article 129) [Community Incentives in the Public Health Sector]
1.   A high level of human health protection shall be ensured in the definition and implementation of all Community policies and activities.
Community action, which shall complement national policies, shall be directed towards improving public health, preventing human illness and diseases, and obviating sources of danger to human health. Such action shall cover the fight against the major health scourges, by promoting research into their causes, their transmission and their prevention, as well as health information and education.
The Community shall complement the Member States' action in reducing drugs-related health damage, including information and prevention.
2.   The Community shall encourage cooperation between the Member States in the areas referred to in this Article and, if necessary, lend support to their action.
Member States shall, in liaison with the Commission, coordinate among themselves their policies and programmes in the areas referred to in paragraph 1. The Commission may, in close contact with the Member States, take any useful initiative to promote such coordination.

3.   The Community and the Member States shall foster cooperation with third countries and the competent international organisations in the sphere of public health.
4.   The Council, acting in accordance with the procedure referred to in Article 251 and after consulting the Economic and Social Committee and the Committee of the Regions, shall contribute to the achievement of the objectives referred to in this Article through adopting:
(a) measures setting high standards of quality and safety of organs and substances of human origin, blood and blood derivatives; these measures shall not prevent any Member State from maintaining or introducing more stringent protective measures;
(b) by way of derogation from Article 37, measures in the veterinary and phytosanitary fields which have as their direct objective the protection of public health;
(c) incentive measures designed to protect and improve human health, excluding any harmonisation of the laws and regulations of the Member States.
The Council, acting by a qualified majority on a proposal from the Commission, may also adopt recommendations for the purposes set out in this Article.
5.   Community action in the field of public health shall fully respect the responsibilities of the Member States for the organisation and delivery of health services and medical care. In particular, measures referred to in paragraph 4(a) shall not affect national provisions on the donation or medical use of organs and blood.

TITLE XIV (EX TITLE XI)
CONSUMER PROTECTION

Article 153 (ex Article 129a) [Community Measures for Consumer Protection]
1.   In order to promote the interests of consumers and to ensure a high level of consumer protection, the Community shall contribute to protecting the health, safety and economic interests of consumers, as well as to promoting their right to information, education and to organise themselves in order to safeguard their interests.
2.   Consumer protection requirements shall be taken into account in defining and implementing other Community policies and activities.
3.   The Community shall contribute to the attainment of the objectives referred to in paragraph 1 through:
(a) measures adopted pursuant to Article 95 in the context of the completion of the internal market;
(b) measures which support, supplement and monitor the policy pursued by the Member States.
4.   The Council, acting in accordance with the procedure referred to in Article 251 and after consulting the Economic and Social Committee, shall adopt the measures referred to in paragraph 3(b).
5.   Measures adopted pursuant to paragraph 4 shall not prevent any Member State from maintaining or introducing more stringent protective measures. Such measures must be compatible with this Treaty. The Commission shall be notified of them.

TITLE XV (EX TITLE XII)
TRANS-EUROPEAN NETWORKS

Article 154 (ex Article 129b) [Promotion of Trans-European Networks]
1.   To help achieve the objectives referred to in Articles 14 and 158 and to enable citizens of the Union, economic operators and regional and local communities to derive full benefit from the setting-up of an area without internal frontiers, the Community shall

contribute to the establishment and development of trans-European networks in the areas of transport, telecommunications and energy infrastructures.
2.   Within the framework of a system of open and competitive markets, action by the Community shall aim at promoting the interconnection and interoperability of national networks as well as access to such networks. It shall take account in particular of the need to link island, landlocked and peripheral regions with the central regions of the Community.

Article 155 (ex Article 129c) [Guidelines for Measures in the Sphere of Trans-European Networks]
1.   In order to achieve the objectives referred to in Article 154, the Community:
—   shall establish a series of guidelines covering the objectives, priorities and broad lines of measures envisaged in the sphere of trans-European networks; these guidelines shall identify projects of common interest;
—   shall implement any measures that may prove necessary to ensure the interoperability of the networks, in particular in the field of technical standardisation;
—   may support projects of common interest supported by Member States, which are identified in the framework of the guidelines referred to in the first indent, particularly through feasibility studies, loan guarantees or interest-rate subsidies; the Community may also contribute, through the Cohesion Fund set up pursuant to Article 161, to the financing of specific projects in Member States in the area of transport infrastructure.
The Community's activities shall take into account the potential economic viability of the projects.
2.   Member States shall, in liaison with the Commission, coordinate among themselves the policies pursued at national level which may have a significant impact on the achievement of the objectives referred to in Article 154. The Commission may, in close cooperation with the Member State, take any useful initiative to promote such coordination.
3.   The Community may decide to cooperate with third countries to promote projects of mutual interest and to ensure the interoperability of networks.

Article 156 (ex Article 129d) [Decision Making in the Sphere of Trans-European Networks]
The guidelines and other measures referred to in Article 155(1) shall be adopted by the Council, acting in accordance with the procedure referred to in Article 251 and after consulting the Economic and Social Committee and the Committee of the Regions.
    Guidelines and projects of common interest which relate to the territory of a Member State shall require the approval of the Member State concerned.

TITLE XVI (EX TITLE XIII)
INDUSTRY

Article 157 (ex Article 130) [Promotion of Industry]
1.   The Community and the Member States shall ensure that the conditions necessary for the competitiveness of the Community's industry exist.
    For that purpose, in accordance with a system of open and competitive markets, their action shall be aimed at:
—   speeding up the adjustment of industry to structural changes;
—   encouraging an environment favourable to initiative and to the development of undertakings throughout the Community, particularly small and medium-sized undertakings;

— encouraging an environment favourable to cooperation between undertakings;
— fostering better exploitation of the industrial potential of policies of innovation, research and technological development.

2.   The Member States shall consult each other in liaison with the Commission and, where necessary, shall coordinate their action. The Commission may take any useful initiative to promote such coordination.

3.   The Community shall contribute to the achievement of the objectives set out in paragraph 1 through the policies and activities it pursues under other provisions of this Treaty. The Council, acting unanimously on a proposal from the Commission, after consulting the European Parliament and the Economic and Social Committee, may decide on specific measures in support of action taken in the Member States to achieve the objectives set out in paragraph 1.

This Title shall not provide a basis for the introduction by the Community of any measure which could lead to a distortion of competition.

TITLE XVII (EX TITLE XIV)
ECONOMIC AND SOCIAL COHESION

Article 158 (ex Article 130a) [Promotion of Economic and Social Cohesion]
In order to promote its overall harmonious development, the Community shall develop and pursue its actions leading to the strengthening of its economic and social cohesion.

In particular, the Community shall aim at reducing disparities between the levels of development of the various regions and the backwardness of the least favoured regions or islands, including rural areas.

Article 159 (ex Article 130b) [Establishment of Structural Funds]
Member States shall conduct their economic policies and shall coordinate them in such a way as, in addition, to attain the objectives set out in Article 158. The formulation and implementation of the Community's policies and actions and the implementation of the internal market shall take into account the objectives set out in Article 158 and shall contribute to their achievement. The Community shall also support the achievement of these objectives by the action it takes through the Structural Funds (European Agricultural Guidance and Guarantee Fund, Guidance Section; European Social Fund; European Regional Development Fund), the European Investment Bank and the other existing financial instruments.

The Commission shall submit a report to the European Parliament, the Council, the Economic and Social Committee and the Committee of the Regions every three years on the progress made towards achieving economic and social cohesion and on the manner in which the various means provided for in this Article have contributed to it. This report shall, if necessary, be accompanied by appropriate proposals.

If specific actions prove necessary outside the Funds and without prejudice to the measures decided upon within the framework of the other Community policies, such actions may be adopted by the Council acting unanimously on a proposal from the Commission and after consulting the European Parliament, the Economic and Social Committee and the Committee of the Regions.

Article 160 (ex Article 130c) [The Regional Development Fund]
The European Regional Development Fund is intended to help to redress the main regional imbalances in the Community through participation in the development and structural adjustment of regions whose development is lagging behind and in the conversion of declining industrial regions.

Article 161 (ex Article 130d) [Decision Making Regarding the Structural Funds]
Without prejudice to Article 162, the Council, acting unanimously on a proposal from
the Commission and after obtaining the assent of the European Parliament and consulting the Economic and Social Committee and the Committee of the Regions, shall
define the tasks, priority objectives and the organisation of the Structural Funds, which
may involve grouping the Funds. The Council, acting by the same procedure, shall also
define the general rules applicable to them and the provisions necessary to ensure
their effectiveness and the coordination of the Funds with one another and with the
other existing financial instruments.

A Cohesion Fund set up by the Council in accordance with the same procedure
shall provide a financial contribution to projects in the fields of environment and trans-
European networks in the area of transport infrastructure.

Article 162 (ex Article 130e) [Implementing Decisions]
Implementing decisions relating to the European Regional Development Fund shall be
taken by the Council, acting in accordance with the procedure referred to in Article 251
and after consulting the Economic and Social Committee and the Committee of the
Regions.

With regard to the European Agricultural Guidance and Guarantee Fund, Guidance
Section, and the European Social Fund, Articles 37 and 148 respectively shall continue
to apply.

TITLE XVIII (EX TITLE XV)
RESEARCH AND TECHNOLOGICAL DEVELOPMENT

*Article 163 (ex Article 130f) [Promotion of Research and Technological
Development]*
1.   The Community shall have the objective of strengthening the scientific and technological bases of Community industry and encouraging it to become more competitive
at international level, while promoting all the research activities deemed necessary by
virtue of other Chapters of this Treaty.
2.   For this purpose the Community shall, throughout the Community, encourage undertakings, including small and medium-sized undertakings, research centres and universities in their research and technological development activities of high quality; it
shall support their efforts to cooperate with one another, aiming, notably, at enabling
undertakings to exploit the internal market potential to the full, in particular through the
opening-up of national public contracts, the definition of common standards and the
removal of legal and fiscal obstacles to that cooperation.
3.   All Community activities under this Treaty in the area of research and technological
development, including demonstration projects, shall be decided on and implemented
in accordance with the provisions of this Title.

Article 164 (ex Article 130g) [Community Measures]
In pursuing these objectives, the Community shall carry out the following activities,
complementing the activities carried out in the Member States:
(a) implementation of research, technological development and demonstration pro-
     grammes, by promoting cooperation with and between undertakings, research
     centres and universities;
(b) promotion of cooperation in the field of Community research, technological de-
     velopment and demonstration with third countries and international organisations;
(c) dissemination and optimisation of the results of activities in Community research,
     technological development and demonstration;

(d) stimulation of the training and mobility of researchers in the Community.

Article 165 (ex Article 130h) [Coordination of Community and National Measures]
1.   The Community and the Member States shall coordinate their research and technological development activities so as to ensure that national policies and Community policy are mutually consistent.
2.   In close cooperation with the Member State, the Commission may take any useful initiative to promote the coordination referred to in paragraph 1.

Article 166 (ex Article 130i) [Multi-Annual Framework Programmes]
1.   A multiannual framework programme, setting out all the activities of the Community, shall be adopted by the Council, acting in accordance with the procedure referred to in Article 251 after consulting the Economic and Social Committee.
The framework programme shall:
—   establish the scientific and technological objectives to be achieved by the activities provided for in Article 164 and fix the relevant priorities;
—   indicate the broad lines of such activities;
—   fix the maximum overall amount and the detailed rules for Community financial participation in the framework programme and the respective shares in each of the activities provided for.
2.   The framework programme shall be adapted or supplemented as the situation changes.
3.   The framework programme shall be implemented through specific programmes developed within each activity. Each specific programme shall define the detailed rules for implementing it, fix its duration and provide for the means deemed necessary. The sum of the amounts deemed necessary, fixed in the specific programmes, may not exceed the overall maximum amount fixed for the framework programme and each activity.
4.   The Council, acting by a qualified majority on a proposal from the Commission and after consulting the European Parliament and the Economic and Social Committee, shall adopt the specific programmes.

Article 167 (ex Article 130j) [Implementation of Multi-Annual Framework Programmes]
For the implementation of the multiannual framework programme the Council shall:
—   determine the rules for the participation of undertakings, research centres and universities;
—   lay down the rules governing the dissemination of research results.

Article 168 (ex Article 130k) [Supplementary Programmes in Certain Member States]
In implementing the multiannual framework programme, supplementary programmes may be decided on involving the participation of certain Member States only, which shall finance them subject to possible Community participation.
The Council shall adopt the rules applicable to supplementary programmes, particularly as regards the dissemination of knowledge and access by other Member States.

Article 169 (ex Article 130l) [Participation of the Community in National Research and Development Programmes]
In implementing the multiannual framework programme the Community may make provision, in agreement with the Member States concerned, for participation in research

and development programmes undertaken by several Member States, including participation in the structures created for the execution of those programmes.

Article 170 (ex Article 130m) [Cooperation with Third Countries]
In implementing the multiannual framework programme the Community may make provision for cooperation in Community research, technological development and demonstration with third countries or international organisations.

The detailed arrangements for such cooperation may be the subject of agreements between the Community and the third parties concerned, which shall be negotiated and concluded in accordance with Article 300.

Article 171 (ex Article 130n) [Joint Research Centres]
The Community may set up joint undertakings or any other structure necessary for the efficient execution of Community research, technological development and demonstration programmes.

Article 172 (ex Article 130o) [Implementing Measures]
The Council, acting by qualified majority on a proposal from the Commission and after consulting the European Parliament and the Economic and Social Committee, shall adopt the provisions referred to in Article 171.

The Council, acting in accordance with the procedure referred to in Article 251 and after consulting the Economic and Social Committee, shall adopt the provisions referred to in Articles 167, 168 and 169. Adoption of the supplementary programmes shall require the agreement of the Member States concerned.

Article 173 (ex Article 130p) [Annual Reports to Parliament and Council]
At the beginning of each year the Commission shall send a report to the European Parliament and the Council. The report shall include information on research and technological development activities and the dissemination of results during the previous year, and the work programme for the current year.

TITLE XIX (EX TITLE XVI)
ENVIRONMENT

Article 174 (ex Article 130r) [Objectives of the Community Policy on the Environment]
1.   Community policy on the environment shall contribute to pursuit of the following objectives:
—   preserving, protecting and improving the quality of the environment;
—   protecting human health;
—   prudent and rational utilisation of natural resources;
—   promoting measures at international level to deal with regional or worldwide environmental problems.
2.   Community policy on the environment shall aim at a high level of protection taking into account the diversity of situations in the various regions of the Community. It shall be based on the precautionary principle and on the principles that preventive action should be taken, that environmental damage should as a priority be rectified at source and that the polluter should pay.

In this context, harmonisation measures answering environmental protection requirements shall include, where appropriate, a safeguard clause allowing Member States to take provisional measures, for non-economic environmental reasons, subject to a Community inspection procedure.

3.   In preparing its policy on the environment, the Community shall take account of:
— available scientific and technical data;
— environmental conditions in the various regions of the Community;
— the potential benefits and costs of action or lack of action;
— the economic and social development of the Community as a whole and the ba-
     lanced development of its regions.
4.   Within their respective spheres of competence, the Community and the Member
States shall cooperate with third countries and with the competent international organisations. The arrangements for Community cooperation may be the subject of agreements between the Community and the third parties concerned, which shall be negotiated and concluded in accordance with Article 300.
     The previous subparagraph shall be without prejudice to Member States' compe-
tence to negotiate in international bodies and to conclude international agreements.

Article 175 (ex Article 130s) [Implementing Measures]

1.   The Council, acting in accordance with the procedure referred to in Article 251 and
after consulting the Economic and Social Committee and the Committee of the Regions, shall decide what action is to be taken by the Community in order to achieve the
objectives referred to in Article 174.
2.   By way of derogation from the decision-making procedure provided for in paragraph 1 and without prejudice to Article 95, the Council, acting unanimously on a proposal from the Commission and after consulting the European Parliament, the Economic and Social Committee and the Committee of the Regions, shall adopt:
— provisions primarily of a fiscal nature;
— measures concerning town and country planning, land use with the exception of
     waste management and measures of a general nature, and management of water
     resources;
— measures significantly affecting a Member State's choice between different energy
     sources and the general structure of its energy supply.
The Council may, under the conditions laid down in the preceding subparagraph, define those matters referred to in this paragraph on which decisions are to be taken by
a qualified majority.
3.   In other areas, general action programmes setting out priority objectives to be
attained shall be adopted by the Council, acting in accordance with the procedure
referred to in Article 251 and after consulting the Economic and Social Committee and
the Committee of the Regions.
     The Council, acting under the terms of paragraph 1 or paragraph 2 according to
the case, shall adopt the measures necessary for the implementation of these programmes.
4.   Without prejudice to certain measures of a Community nature, the Member States
shall finance and implement the environment policy.
5.   Without prejudice to the principle that the polluter should pay, if a measure based
on the provisions of paragraph 1 involves costs deemed disproportionate for the public
authorities of a Member State, the Council shall, in the act adopting that measure, lay
down appropriate provisions in the form of:
— temporary derogations, and/or
— financial support from the Cohesion Fund set up pursuant to Article 161.

Article 176 (ex Article 130t) [More Stringent National Protective Measures]

The protective measures adopted pursuant to Article 175 shall not prevent any Member State from maintaining or introducing more stringent protective measures. Such

measures must be compatible with this Treaty. They shall be notified to the Commission.

TITLE XX (EX TITLE XVII)
DEVELOPMENT COOPERATION

Article 177 (ex Article 130u) [Objectives of the Community Policy on Development Cooperation]
1.   Community policy in the sphere of development cooperation, which shall be complementary to the policies pursued by the Member States, shall foster:
—   the sustainable economic and social development of the developing countries, and more particularly the most disadvantaged among them;
—   the smooth and gradual integration of the developing countries into the world economy;
—   the campaign against poverty in the developing countries.
2.   Community policy in this area shall contribute to the general objective of developing and consolidating democracy and the rule of law, and to that of respecting human rights and fundamental freedoms.
3.   The Community and the Member States shall comply with the commitments and take account of the objectives they have approved in the context of the United Nations and other competent international organisations.

Article 178 (ex Article 130v) [Relationship to Other Community Policies]
The Community shall take account of the objectives referred to in Article 177 in the policies that it implements which are likely to affect developing countries.

Article 179 (ex Article 130w) [Implementing Measures; ACP-EEC Conventions]
1.   Without prejudice to the other provisions of this Treaty, the Council, acting in accordance with the procedure referred to in Article 251, shall adopt the measures necessary to further the objectives referred to in Article 177. Such measures may take the form of multiannual programmes.
2.   The European Investment Bank shall contribute, under the terms laid down in its Statute, to the implementation of the measures referred to in paragraph 1.
3.   The provisions of this Article shall not affect cooperation with the African, Caribbean and Pacific countries in the framework of the ACP-EC Convention.

Article 180 (ex Article 130x) [Coordination of Community and National Development Cooperation and Aid Programmes]
1.   The Community and the Member States shall coordinate their policies on development cooperation and shall consult each other on their aid programmes, including in international organisations and during international conferences. They may undertake joint action. Member States shall contribute if necessary to the implementation of Community aid programmes.
2.   The Commission may take any useful initiative to promote the coordination referred to in paragraph 1.

Article 181 (ex Article 130y) [Cooperation with Third Countries and International Organizations]
Within their respective spheres of competence, the Community and the Member States shall cooperate with third countries and with the competent international organisations. The arrangements for Community cooperation may be the subject of agreements between the Community and the third parties concerned, which shall be negotiated and concluded in accordance with Article 300.

The previous paragraph shall be without prejudice to Member States' competence to negotiate in international bodies and to conclude international agreements.

PART FOUR
ASSOCIATION OF THE OVERSEAS COUNTRIES AND TERRITORIES

Article 182 (ex Article 131) [Association of Certain Countries and Territories and its Purpose]
The Member States agree to associate with the Community the non-European countries and territories which have special relations with Denmark, France, the Netherlands and the United Kingdom. These countries and territories (hereinafter called the "countries and territories") are listed in Annex II to this Treaty.

The purpose of association shall be to promote the economic and social development of the countries and territories and to establish close economic relations between them and the Community as a whole.

In accordance with the principles set out in the Preamble to this Treaty, association shall serve primarily to further the interests and prosperity of the inhabitants of these countries and territories in order to lead them to the economic, social and cultural development to which they aspire.

Article 183 (ex Article 132) [Objectives of Association]
Association shall have the following objectives:
(1) Member States shall apply to their trade with the countries and territories the same treatment as they accord each other pursuant to this Treaty.
(2) Each country or territory shall apply to its trade with Member States and with the other countries and territories the same treatment as that which it applies to the European State with which is has special relations.
(3) The Member States shall contribute to the investments required for the progressive development of these countries and territories.
(4) For investments financed by the Community, participation in tenders and supplies shall be open on equal terms to all natural and legal persons who are nationals of a Member State or of one of the countries and territories.
(5) In relations between Member States and the countries and territories the right of establishment of nationals and companies or firms shall be regulated in accordance with the provisions and procedures laid down in the Chapter relating to the right of establishment and on a non-discriminatory basis, subject to any special provisions laid down pursuant to Article 187.

Article 184 (ex Article 133) [Elimination of Customs Duties]
1.   Customs duties on imports into the Member States of goods originating in the countries and territories shall be prohibited in conformity with the prohibition of customs duties between Member States in accordance with the provisions of this Treaty.
2.   Customs duties on imports into each country or territory from Member States or from the other countries or territories shall be prohibited in accordance with the provisions of Article 25.
3.   The countries and territories may, however, levy customs duties which meet the needs of their development and industrialisation or produce revenue for their budgets.

The duties referred to in the preceding subparagraph may not exceed the level of those imposed on imports of products from the Member State with which each country or territory has special relations.

4.   Paragraph 2 shall not apply to countries and territories which, by reason of the particular international obligations by which they are bound, already apply a non-discriminatory customs tariff.

5.   The introduction of or any change in customs duties imposed on goods imported into the countries and territories shall not, either in law or in fact, give rise to any direct or indirect discrimination between imports from the various Member States.

Article 185 (ex Article 134) [Measures Preventing Deflections of Trade]
If the level of the duties applicable to goods from a third country on entry into a country or territory is liable, when the provisions of Article 184(1) have been applied, to cause deflections of trade to the detriment of any Member State, the latter may request the Commission to propose to the other Member States the measures needed to remedy the situation.

Article 186 (ex Article 135) [Free Movement of Employees]
Subject to the provisions relating to public health, public security or public policy, freedom of movement within Member States for workers from the countries and territories, and within the countries and territories for workers from Member States, shall be governed by agreements to be concluded subsequently with the unanimous approval of Member States.

Article 187 (ex Article 136) [Implementing Measures]
The Council, acting unanimously, shall, on the basis of the experience acquired under the association of the countries and territories with the Community and of the principles set out in this Treaty, lay down provisions as regards the detailed rules and the procedure for the association of the countries and territories with the Community.

Article 188 (ex Article 136a) [Specific Provisions for Greenland]
The provisions of Articles 182 to 187 shall apply to Greenland, subject to the specific provisions for Greenland set out in the Protocol on special arrangements for Greenland, annexed to this Treaty.

PART FIVE
INSTITUTIONS OF THE COMMUNITY
TITLE I
PROVISIONS GOVERNING THE INSTITUTIONS
Chapter 1 The Institutions

Section 1 The European Parliament
Article 189 (ex Article 137) [Representation of the Peoples of the Member States]
The European Parliament, which shall consist of representatives of the peoples of the States brought together in the Community, shall exercise the powers conferred upon it by this Treaty.

The number of Members of the European Parliament shall not exceed seven hundred.

Article 190 (ex Article 138) [Elections and Composition]
1.   The representatives in the European Parliament of the peoples of the States brought together in the Community shall be elected by direct universal suffrage.

2.   The number of representatives elected in each Member State shall be as follows:

Belgium	25
Denmark	16

Germany	99
Greece	25
Spain	64
France	87
Ireland	15
Italy	87
Luxembourg	6
Netherlands	31
Austria	21
Portugal	25
Finland	16
Sweden	22
United Kingdom	87.

In the event of amendments to this paragraph, the number of representatives elected in each Member State must ensure appropriate representation of the peoples of the States brought together in the Community.

3.   Representatives shall be elected for a term of five years.

4.   The European Parliament shall draw up a proposal for elections by direct universal suffrage in accordance with a uniform procedure in all Member States or in accordance with principles common to all Member States.

The Council shall, acting unanimously after obtaining the assent of the European Parliament, which shall act by a majority of its component members, lay down the appropriate provisions, which it shall recommend to Member States for adoption in accordance with their respective constitutional requirements.

5.   The European Parliament shall, after seeking an opinion from the Commission and with the approval of the Council acting unanimously, lay down the regulations and general conditions governing the performance of the duties of its Members.

Article 191 (ex Article 138a) [Political Parties at European Level]
Political parties at European level are important as a factor for integration within the Union. They contribute to forming a European awareness and to expressing the political will of the citizens of the Union.

Article 192 (ex Article 138b) [Participation in Decision Making]
Insofar as provided in this Treaty, the European Parliament shall participate in the process leading up to the adoption of Community acts by exercising its powers under the procedures laid down in Articles 251 and 252 and by giving its assent or delivering advisory opinions.

The European Parliament may, acting by a majority of its Members, request the Commission to submit any appropriate proposal on matters on which it considers that a Community act is required for the purpose of implementing this Treaty.

Article 193 (ex Article 138c) [Committees of Inquiry]
In the course of its duties, the European Parliament may, at the request of a quarter of its Members, set up a temporary Committee of Inquiry to investigate, without prejudice to the powers conferred by this Treaty on other institutions or bodies, alleged contraventions or maladministration in the implementation of Community law, except where the alleged facts are being examined before a court and while the case is still subject to legal proceedings.

The temporary Committee of Inquiry shall cease to exist on the submission of its report.

The detailed provisions governing the exercise of the right of inquiry shall be determined by common accord of the European Parliament, the Council and the Commission.

Article 194 (ex Article 138d) [Right to Petition]

Any citizen of the Union, and any natural or legal person residing or having its registered office in a Member State, shall have the right to address, individually or in association with other citizens or persons, a petition to the European Parliament on a matter which comes within the Community's fields of activity and which affects him, her or it directly.

Article 195 (ex Article 138e) [The Ombudsperson]

1.   The European Parliament shall appoint an Ombudsman empowered to receive complaints from any citizen of the Union or any natural or legal person residing or having its registered office in a Member State concerning instances of maladministration in the activities of the Community institutions or bodies, with the exception of the Court of Justice and the Court of First Instance acting in their judicial role.

In accordance with his duties, the Ombudsman shall conduct inquiries for which he finds grounds, either on his own initiative or on the basis of complaints submitted to him direct or through a Member of the European Parliament, except where the alleged facts are or have been the subject of legal proceedings. Where the Ombudsman establishes an instance of maladministration, he shall refer the matter to the institution concerned, which shall have a period of three months in which to inform him of its views. The Ombudsman shall then forward a report to the European Parliament and the institution concerned. The person lodging the complaint shall be informed of the outcome of such inquiries.

The Ombudsman shall submit an annual report to the European Parliament on the outcome of his inquiries.

2.   The Ombudsman shall be appointed after each election of the European Parliament for the duration of its term of office. The Ombudsman shall be eligible for reappointment.

The Ombudsman may be dismissed by the Court of Justice at the request of the European Parliament if he no longer fulfils the conditions required for the performance of his duties or if he is guilty of serious misconduct.

3.   The Ombudsman shall be completely independent in the performance of his duties. In the performance of those duties he shall neither seek nor take instructions from any body. The Ombudsman may not, during his term of office, engage in any other occupation, whether gainful or not.

4.   The European Parliament shall, after seeking an opinion from the Commission and with the approval of the Council acting by a qualified majority, lay down the regulations and general conditions governing the performance of the Ombudsman's duties.

Article 196 (ex Article 139) [Parliamentary Sessions]

The European Parliament shall hold an annual session. It shall meet, without requiring to be convened, on the second Tuesday in March.

The European Parliament may meet in extraordinary session at the request of a majority of its Members or at the request of the Council or of the Commission.

Article 197 (ex Article 140) [The Presidency; Cooperation with Commission and Council]

The European Parliament shall elect its President and its officers from among its Members.

Members of the Commission may attend all meetings and shall, at their request, be heard on behalf of the Commission.

The Commission shall reply orally or in writing to questions put to it by the European Parliament or by its Members.

The Council shall be heard by the European Parliament in accordance with the conditions laid down by the Council in its Rules of Procedure.

Article 198 (ex Article 141) [Voting in Parliament]

Save as otherwise provided in this Treaty, the European Parliament shall act by an absolute majority of the votes cast.

The Rules of Procedure shall determine the quorum.

Article 199 (ex Article 142) [Rules of Procedure; Publication of Proceedings]

The European Parliament shall adopt its Rules of Procedure, acting by a majority of its Members.

The proceedings of the European Parliament shall be published in the manner laid down in its Rules of Procedure.

Article 200 (ex Article 143) [Annual General Report]

The European Parliament shall discuss in open session the annual general report submitted to it by the Commission.

Article 201 (ex Article 144) [Motion of Censure on the Activities of the Commission]

If a motion of censure on the activities of the Commission is tabled before it, the European Parliament shall not vote thereon until at least three days after the motion has been tabled and only by open vote.

If the motion of censure is carried by a two-thirds majority of the votes cast, representing a majority of the Members of the European Parliament, the Members of the Commission shall resign as a body. They shall continue to deal with current business until they are replaced in accordance with Article 214. In this case, the term of office of the Members of the Commission appointed to replace them shall expire on the date on which the term of office of the Members of the Commission obliged to resign as a body would have expired.

Section 2 The Council

Article 202 (ex Article 145) [Powers and Obligations of the Council]

To ensure that the objectives set out in this Treaty are attained the Council shall, in accordance with the provisions of this Treaty:

— ensure coordination of the general economic policies of the Member States;

— have power to take decisions;

— confer on the Commission, in the acts which the Council adopts, powers for the implementation of the rules which the Council lays down. The Council may impose certain requirements in respect of the exercise of these powers. The Council may also reserve the right, in specific cases, to exercise directly implementing powers itself. The procedures referred to above must be consonant with principles and rules to be laid down in advance by the Council, acting unanimously on a proposal from the Commission and after obtaining the Opinion of the European Parliament.

Article 203 (ex Article 146) [Composition and Presidency]
The Council shall consist of a representative of each Member State at ministerial level, authorised to commit the government of that Member State.

The office of President shall be held in turn by each Member State in the Council for a term of six months in the order decided by the Council acting unanimously.

Article 204 (ex Article 147) [Meetings]
The Council shall meet when convened by its President on his own initiative or at the request of one of its members or of the Commission.

Article 205 (ex Article 148) [Voting in the Council]
1.   Save as otherwise provided in this Treaty, the Council shall act by a majority of its members.
2.   Where the Council is required to act by a qualified majority, the votes of its members shall be weighted as follows:

Belgium	5
Denmark	3
Germany	10
Greece	5
Spain	8
France	10
Ireland	3
Italy	10
Luxembourg	2
Netherlands	5
Austria	4
Portugal	5
Finland	3
Sweden	4
United Kingdom	10.

For their adoption, acts of the Council shall require at least:
—   62 votes in favour where this Treaty requires them to be adopted on a proposal from the Commission,
—   62 votes in favour, cast by at least 10 members, in other cases.
3.   Abstentions by members present in person or represented shall not prevent the adoption by the Council of acts which require unanimity.

Article 206 (ex Article 150) [Transfer of Voting Rights]
Where a vote is taken, any member of the Council may also act on behalf of not more than one other member.

Article 207 (ex Article 151) [The Committee of Permanent Representatives
COREPER; the General Secretariat]
1.   A committee consisting of the Permanent Representatives of the Member States shall be responsible for preparing the work of the Council and for carrying out the tasks assigned to it by the Council. The Committee may adopt procedural decisions in cases provided for in the Council's Rules of Procedure.
2.   The Council shall be assisted by a General Secretariat, under the responsibility of a Secretary-General, High Representative for the common foreign and security policy,

who shall be assisted by a Deputy Secretary-General responsible for the running of the General Secretariat. The Secretary-General and the Deputy Secretary-General shall be appointed by the Council acting unanimously.

The Council shall decide on the organisation of the General Secretariat.

3. The Council shall adopt its Rules of Procedure.

For the purpose of applying Article 255(3), the Council shall elaborate in these Rules the conditions under which the public shall have access to Council documents. For the purpose of this paragraph, the Council shall define the cases in which it is to be regarded as acting in its legislative capacity, with a view to allowing greater access to documents in those cases, while at the same time preserving the effectiveness of its decision-making process. In any event, when the Council acts in its legislative capacity, the results of votes and explanations of vote as well as statements in the minutes shall be made public.

Article 208 (ex Article 152) [Proposals from the Commission]

The Council may request the Commission to undertake any studies the Council considers desirable for the attainment of the common objectives, and to submit to it any appropriate proposals.

Article 209 (ex Article 153) [Rules Governing Various Committees]

The Council shall, after receiving an opinion from the Commission, determine the rules governing the committees provided for in this Treaty.

Article 210 (ex Article 154) [Determination of Salaries, Allowances and Pensions]

The Council shall, acting by a qualified majority, determine the salaries, allowances and pensions of the President and Members of the Commission, and of the President, Judges, Advocates-General and Registrar of the Court of Justice. It shall also, again by a qualified majority, determine any payment to be made instead of remuneration.

Section 3 The Commission
Article 211 (ex Article 155) [Powers and Obligations of the Commission]

In order to ensure the proper functioning and development of the common market, the Commission shall:

— ensure that the provisions of this Treaty and the measures taken by the institutions pursuant thereto are applied;
— formulate recommendations or deliver opinions on matters dealt with in this Treaty, if it expressly so provides or if the Commission considers it necessary;
— have its own power of decision and participate in the shaping of measures taken by the Council and by the European Parliament in the manner provided for in this Treaty;
— exercise the powers conferred on it by the Council for the implementation of the rules laid down by the latter.

Article 212 (ex Article 156) [General Report]

The Commission shall publish annually, not later than one month before the opening of the session of the European Parliament, a general report on the activities of the Community.

Article 213 (ex Article 157) [Composition of the Commission]

1. The Commission shall consist of 20 Members, who shall be chosen on the grounds of their general competence and whose independence is beyond doubt.

The number of Members of the Commission may be altered by the Council, acting unanimously.

Only nationals of Member States may be Members of the Commission.

The Commission must include at least one national of each of the Member States, but may not include more than two Members having the nationality of the same State.

2.   The Members of the Commission shall, in the general interest of the Community, be completely independent in the performance of their duties.

In the performance of these duties, they shall neither seek nor take instructions from any government or from any other body. They shall refrain from any action incompatible with their duties. Each Member State undertakes to respect this principle and not to seek to influence the Members of the Commission in the performance of their tasks.

The Members of the Commission may not, during their term of office, engage in any other occupation, whether gainful or not. When entering upon their duties they shall give a solemn undertaking that, both during and after their term of office, they will respect the obligations arising therefrom and in particular their duty to behave with integrity and discretion as regards the acceptance, after they have ceased to hold office, of certain appointments or benefits. In the event of any breach of these obligations, the Court of Justice may, on application by the Council or the Commission, rule that the Member concerned be, according to the circumstances, either compulsorily retired in accordance with Article 216 or deprived of his right to a pension or other benefits in its stead.

Article 214 (ex Article 158) [Procedure of Appointment and Term of Office]

1.   The Members of the Commission shall be appointed, in accordance with the procedure referred to in paragraph 2, for a period of five years, subject, if need be, to Article 201.

Their term of office shall be renewable.

2.   The governments of the Member States shall nominate by common accord the person they intend to appoint as President of the Commission; the nomination shall be approved by the European Parliament.

The governments of the Member States shall, by common accord with the nominee for President, nominate the other persons whom they intend to appoint as Members of the Commission.

The President and the other Members of the Commission thus nominated shall be subject as a body to a vote of approval by the European Parliament. After approval by the European Parliament, the President and the other Members of the Commission shall be appointed by common accord of the governments of the Member States.

Article 215 (ex Article 159) [Retirement, Resignation, Death]

Apart from normal replacement, or death, the duties of a Member of the Commission shall end when he resigns or is compulsorily retired.

The vacancy thus caused shall be filled for the remainder of the Member's term of office by a new Member appointed by common accord of the governments of the Member States. The Council may, acting unanimously, decide that such a vacancy need not be filled.

In the event of resignation, compulsory retirement or death, the President shall be replaced for the remainder of his term of office. The procedure laid down in Article 214(2) shall be applicable for the replacement of the President.

Save in the case of compulsory retirement under Article 216, Members of the Commission shall remain in office until they have been replaced.

Article 216 (ex Article 160) [Compulsory Retirement]
If any Member of the Commission no longer fulfils the conditions required for the performance of his duties or if he has been guilty of serious misconduct, the Court of Justice may, on application by the Council or the Commission, compulsorily retire him.

Article 217 (ex Article 161) [Vice-Presidents]
The Commission may appoint a Vice-President or two Vice-Presidents from among its Members.

Article 218 (ex Article 162) [Cooperation of Commission and Council; Rules of Procedure]
1.   The Council and the Commission shall consult each other and shall settle by common accord their methods of cooperation.
2.   The Commission shall adopt its Rules of Procedure so as to ensure that both it and its departments operate in accordance with the provisions of this Treaty. It shall ensure that these rules are published.

Article 219 (ex Article 163) [Voting in the Commission]
The Commission shall work under the political guidance of its President.

The Commission shall act by a majority of the number of Members provided for in Article 213.

A meeting of the Commission shall be valid only if the number of Members laid down in its Rules of Procedure is present.

Section 4 The Court of Justice
Article 220 (ex Article 164) [Duties of the Court]
The Court of Justice shall ensure that in the interpretation and application of this Treaty the law is observed.

Article 221 (ex Article 165) [Composition and Sessions of the Court]
The Court of Justice shall consist of 15 Judges.

The Court of Justice shall sit in plenary session. It may, however, form chambers, each consisting of three, five or seven Judges, either to undertake certain preparatory inquiries or to adjudicate on particular categories of cases in accordance with rules laid down for these purposes.

The Court of Justice shall sit in plenary session when a Member State or a Community institution that is a party to the proceedings so requests.

Should the Court of Justice so request, the Council may, acting unanimously, increase the number of Judges and make the necessary adjustments to the second and third paragraphs of this Article and to the second paragraph of Article 223.

Article 222 (ex Article 166) [Advocates-General]
The Court of Justice shall be assisted by eight Advocates-General. However, a ninth Advocate-General shall be appointed as from 1 January 1995 until 6 October 2000.

It shall be the duty of the Advocate-General, acting with complete impartiality and independence, to make, in open court, reasoned submissions on cases brought before the Court of Justice, in order to assist the Court in the performance of the task assigned to it in Article 220.

Should the Court of Justice so request, the Council may, acting unanimously, increase the number of Advocates-General and make the necessary adjustments to the third paragraph of Article 223.

Article 223 (ex Article 167) [Appointments of Judges and Advocates-General]
The Judges and Advocates-General shall be chosen from persons whose independence is beyond doubt and who possess the qualifications required for appointment to the highest judicial offices in their respective countries or who are jurisconsults of recognised competence; they shall be appointed by common accord of the governments of the Member States for a term of six years.

Every three years there shall be a partial replacement of the Judges. Eight and seven Judges shall be replaced alternately.

Every three years there shall be a partial replacement of the Advocates-General. Four Advocates-General shall be replaced on each occasion.

Retiring Judges and Advocates-General shall be eligible for reappointment.

The Judges shall elect the President of the Court of Justice from among their number for a term of three years. He may be re-elected.

Article 224 (ex Article 168) [The Registrar]
The Court of Justice shall appoint its Registrar and lay down the rules governing his service.

Article 225 (ex Article 168a) [The Court of First Instance]
1.   A Court of First Instance shall be attached to the Court of Justice with jurisdiction to hear and determine at first instance, subject to a right of appeal to the Court of Justice on points of law only and in accordance with the conditions laid down by the Statute, certain classes of action or proceeding defined in accordance with the conditions laid down in paragraph 2. The Court of First Instance shall not be competent to hear and determine questions referred for a preliminary ruling under Article 234.
2.   At the request of the Court of Justice and after consulting the European Parliament and the Commission, the Council, acting unanimously, shall determine the classes of action or proceeding referred to in paragraph 1 and the composition of the Court of First Instance and shall adopt the necessary adjustments and additional provisions to the Statute of the Court of Justice. Unless the Council decides otherwise, the provisions of this Treaty relating to the Court of Justice, in particular the provisions of the Protocol on the Statute of the Court of Justice, shall apply to the Court of First Instance.
3.   The members of the Court of First Instance shall be chosen from persons whose independence is beyond doubt and who possess the ability required for appointment to judicial office; they shall be appointed by common accord of the governments of the Member States for a term of six years. The membership shall be partially renewed every three years. Retiring members shall be eligible for reappointment.
4.   The Court of First Instance shall establish its Rules of Procedure in agreement with the Court of Justice. Those rules shall require the unanimous approval of the Council.

Article 226 (ex Article 169) [Procedures of the Commission Against
Member States]
If the Commission considers that a Member State has failed to fulfil an obligation under this Treaty, it shall deliver a reasoned opinion on the matter after giving the State concerned the opportunity to submit its observations.

If the State concerned does not comply with the opinion within the period laid down by the Commission, the latter may bring the matter before the Court of Justice.

Article 227 (ex Article 170) [Procedures of the Member States Against Each Other]

A Member State which considers that another Member State has failed to fulfil an obligation under this Treaty may bring the matter before the Court of Justice.

Before a Member State brings an action against another Member State for an alleged infringement of an obligation under this Treaty, it shall bring the matter before the Commission.

The Commission shall deliver a reasoned opinion after each of the States concerned has been given the opportunity to submit its own case and its observations on the other party's case both orally and in writing.

If the Commission has not delivered an opinion within three months of the date on which the matter was brought before it, the absence of such opinion shall not prevent the matter from being brought before the Court of Justice.

Article 228 (ex Article 171) [Compliance with Article 226 and 227 Judgments]

1. If the Court of Justice finds that a Member State has failed to fulfil an obligation under this Treaty, the State shall be required to take the necessary measures to comply with the judgment of the Court of Justice.

2. If the Commission considers that the Member State concerned has not taken such measures it shall, after giving that State the opportunity to submit its observations, issue a reasoned opinion specifying the points on which the Member State concerned has not complied with the judgment of the Court of Justice.

If the Member State concerned fails to take the necessary measures to comply with the Court's judgment within the time-limit laid down by the Commission, the latter may bring the case before the Court of Justice. In so doing it shall specify the amount of the lump sum or penalty payment to be paid by the Member State concerned which it considers appropriate in the circumstances.

If the Court of Justice finds that the Member State concerned has not complied with its judgment it may impose a lump sum or penalty payment on it.

This procedure shall be without prejudice to Article 227.

Article 229 (ex Article 172) [Unlimited Jurisdiction]

Regulations adopted jointly by the European Parliament and the Council, and by the Council, pursuant to the provisions of this Treaty, may give the Court of Justice unlimited jurisdiction with regard to the penalties provided for in such regulations.

Article 230 (ex Article 173) [Procedures Against Acts of the Community]

The Court of Justice shall review the legality of acts adopted jointly by the European Parliament and the Council, of acts of the Council, of the Commission and of the ECB, other than recommendations and opinions, and of acts of the European Parliament intended to produce legal effects vis-à-vis third parties.

It shall for this purpose have jurisdiction in actions brought by a Member State, the Council or the Commission on grounds of lack of competence, infringement of an essential procedural requirement, infringement of this Treaty or of any rule of law relating to its application, or misuse of powers.

The Court of Justice shall have jurisdiction under the same conditions in actions brought by the European Parliament, by the Court of Auditors and by the ECB for the purpose of protecting their prerogatives.

Any natural or legal person may, under the same conditions, institute proceedings against a decision addressed to that person or against a decision which, although in the form of a regulation or a decision addressed to another person, is of direct and individual concern to the former.

The proceedings provided for in this Article shall be instituted within two months of the publication of the measure, or of its notification to the plaintiff, or, in the absence thereof, of the day on which it came to the knowledge of the latter, as the case may be.

Article 231 (ex Article 174) [Declaring Community Acts to be Void]
If the action is well founded, the Court of Justice shall declare the act concerned to be void.

In the case of a regulation, however, the Court of Justice shall, if it considers this necessary, state which of the effects of the regulation which it has declared void shall be considered as definitive.

Article 232 (ex Article 175) [Procedures Against the Community for Failure to Act]
Should the European Parliament, the Council or the Commission, in infringement of this Treaty, fail to act, the Member States and the other institutions of the Community may bring an action before the Court of Justice to have the infringement established.

The action shall be admissible only if the institution concerned has first been called upon to act. If, within two months of being so called upon, the institution concerned has not defined its position, the action may be brought within a further period of two months.

Any natural or legal person may, under the conditions laid down in the preceding paragraphs, complain to the Court of Justice that an institution of the Community has failed to address to that person any act other than a recommendation or an opinion.

The Court of Justice shall have jurisdiction, under the same conditions, in actions or proceedings brought by the ECB in the areas falling within the latter's field of competence and in actions or proceedings brought against the latter.

Article 233 (ex Article 176) [Compliance with Article 230 and 232 Judgments]
The institution or institutions whose act has been declared void or whose failure to act has been declared contrary to this Treaty shall be required to take the necessary measures to comply with the judgment of the Court of Justice.

This obligation shall not affect any obligation which may result from the application of the second paragraph of Article 288.

This Article shall also apply to the ECB.

Article 234 (ex Article 177) [The Preliminary Rulings Procedure]
The Court of Justice shall have jurisdiction to give preliminary rulings concerning:
(a) the interpretation of this Treaty;
(b) the validity and interpretation of acts of the institutions of the Community and of the ECB;
(c) the interpretation of the statutes of bodies established by an act of the Council, where those statutes so provide.

Where such a question is raised before any court or tribunal of a Member State, that court or tribunal may, if it considers that a decision on the question is necessary to enable it to give judgment, request the Court of Justice to give a ruling thereon.

Where any such question is raised in a case pending before a court or tribunal of a Member State against whose decisions there is no judicial remedy under national law, that court or tribunal shall bring the matter before the Court of Justice.

Article 235 (ex Article 178) [Community Liability]
The Court of Justice shall have jurisdiction in disputes relating to compensation for damage provided for in the second paragraph of Article 288.

Article 236 (ex Article 179) [Staff Cases]

The Court of Justice shall have jurisdiction in any dispute between the Community and its servants within the limits and under the conditions laid down in the Staff Regulations or the Conditions of Employment.

Article 237 (ex Article 180) [Procedures Between Member States, the EIB and the ECB]

The Court of Justice shall, within the limits hereinafter laid down, have jurisdiction in disputes concerning:

(a) the fulfilment by Member States of obligations under the Statute of the European Investment Bank. In this connection, the Board of Directors of the Bank shall enjoy the powers conferred upon the Commission by Article 226;

(b) measures adopted by the Board of Governors of the European Investment Bank. In this connection, any Member State, the Commission or the Board of Directors of the Bank may institute proceedings under the conditions laid down in Article 230;

(c) measures adopted by the Board of Directors of the European Investment Bank. Proceedings against such measures may be instituted only by Member States or by the Commission, under the conditions laid down in Article 230, and solely on the grounds of non-compliance with the procedure provided for in Article 21(2), (5), (6) and (7) of the Statute of the Bank;

(d) the fulfilment by national central banks of obligations under this Treaty and the Statute of the ESCB. In this connection the powers of the Council of the ECB in respect of national central banks shall be the same as those conferred upon the Commission in respect of Member States by Article 226. If the Court of Justice finds that a national central bank has failed to fulfil an obligation under this Treaty, that bank shall be required to take the necessary measures to comply with the judgment of the Court of Justice.

Article 238 (ex Article 181) [Procedures Based on Arbitration Clauses]

The Court of Justice shall have jurisdiction to give judgment pursuant to any arbitration clause contained in a contract concluded by or on behalf of the Community, whether that contract be governed by public or private law.

Article 239 (ex Article 182) [Procedures Based on Special Agreements]

The Court of Justice shall have jurisdiction in any dispute between Member States which relates to the subject matter of this Treaty if the dispute is submitted to it under a special agreement between the parties.

Article 240 (ex Article 183) [Presumption of Jurisdiction in Favour of National Courts]

Save where jurisdiction is conferred on the Court of Justice by this Treaty, disputes to which the Community is a party shall not on that ground be excluded from the jurisdiction of the courts or tribunals of the Member States.

Article 241 (ex Article 184) [Invoking the Inapplicability of a Regulation]

Notwithstanding the expiry of the period laid down in the fifth paragraph of Article 230, any party may, in proceedings in which a regulation adopted jointly by the European Parliament and the Council, or a regulation of the Council, of the Commission, or of the ECB is at issue, plead the grounds specified in the second paragraph of Article 230 in order to invoke before the Court of Justice the inapplicability of that regulation.

Article 242 (ex Article 185) [Suspensory Effect]

Actions brought before the Court of Justice shall not have suspensory effect. The Court of Justice may, however, if it considers that circumstances so require, order that application of the contested act be suspended.

Article 243 (ex Article 186) [Interim Measures]

The Court of Justice may in any cases before it prescribe any necessary interim measures.

Article 244 (ex Article 187) [Enforcement of Judgments]

The judgments of the Court of Justice shall be enforceable under the conditions laid down in Article 256.

Article 245 (ex Article 188) [Statute and Rules of Procedure]

The Statute of the Court of Justice is laid down in a separate Protocol.

The Council may, acting unanimously at the request of the Court of Justice and after consulting the Commission and the European Parliament, amend the provisions of Title III of the Statute.

The Court of Justice shall adopt its Rules of Procedure. These shall require the unanimous approval of the Council.

Section 5 The Court of Auditors
Article 246 (ex Article 188a) [Duties of the Court of Auditors]

The Court of Auditors shall carry out the audit.

Article 247 (ex Article 188b) [Composition and Independence]

1.   The Court of Auditors shall consist of 15 Members.
2.   The Members of the Court of Auditors shall be chosen from among persons who belong or have belonged in their respective countries to external audit bodies or who are especially qualified for this office. Their independence must be beyond doubt.
3.   The Members of the Court of Auditors shall be appointed for a term of six years by the Council, acting unanimously after consulting the European Parliament.

The Members of the Court of Auditors shall be eligible for reappointment.

They shall elect the President of the Court of Auditors from among their number for a term of three years. The President may be re-elected.
4.   The Members of the Court of Auditors shall, in the general interest of the Community, be completely independent in the performance of their duties.
In the performance of these duties, they shall neither seek nor take instructions from any government or from any other body. They shall refrain from any action incompatible with their duties.
5.   The Members of the Court of Auditors may not, during their term of office, engage in any other occupation, whether gainful or not. When entering upon their duties they shall give a solemn undertaking that, both during and after their term of office, they will respect the obligations arising therefrom and in particular their duty to behave with integrity and discretion as regards the acceptance, after they have ceased to hold office, of certain appointments or benefits.
6.   Apart from normal replacement, or death, the duties of a Member of the Court of Auditors shall end when he resigns, or is compulsorily retired by a ruling of the Court of Justice pursuant to paragraph 7.

The vacancy thus caused shall be filled for the remainder of the Member's term of office.

Save in the case of compulsory retirement, Members of the Court of Auditors shall remain in office until they have been replaced.

7.   A Member of the Court of Auditors may be deprived of his office or of his right to a pension or other benefits in its stead only if the Court of Justice, at the request of the Court of Auditors, finds that he no longer fulfils the requisite conditions or meets the obligations arising from his office.

8.   The Council, acting by a qualified majority, shall determine the conditions of employment of the President and the Members of the Court of Auditors and in particular their salaries, allowances and pensions. It shall also, by the same majority, determine any payment to be made instead of remuneration.

9.   The provisions of the Protocol on the privileges and immunities of the European Communities applicable to the Judges of the Court of Justice shall also apply to the Members of the Court of Auditors.

Article 248 (ex Article 188c) [Audit of all Accounts of the Community;
Statement of Assurance; Annual Report]

1.   The Court of Auditors shall examine the accounts of all revenue and expenditure of the Community. It shall also examine the accounts of all revenue and expenditure of all bodies set up by the Community insofar as the relevant constituent instrument does not preclude such examination.

The Court of Auditors shall provide the European Parliament and the Council with a statement of assurance as to the reliability of the accounts and the legality and regularity of the underlying transactions which shall be published in the Official Journal of the European Communities.

2.   The Court of Auditors shall examine whether all revenue has been received and all expenditure incurred in a lawful and regular manner and whether the financial management has been sound. In doing so, it shall report in particular on any cases of irregularity.

The audit of revenue shall be carried out on the basis both of the amounts established as due and the amounts actually paid to the Community.

The audit of expenditure shall be carried out on the basis both of commitments undertaken and payments made.

These audits may be carried out before the closure of accounts for the financial year in question.

3.   The audit shall be based on records and, if necessary, performed on the spot in the other institutions of the Community, on the premises of any body which manages revenue or expenditure on behalf of the Community and in the Member States, including on the premises of any natural or legal person in receipt of payments from the budget. In the Member States the audit shall be carried out in liaison with national audit bodies or, if these do not have the necessary powers, with the competent national departments. The Court of Auditors and the national audit bodies of the Member States shall cooperate in a spirit of trust while maintaining their independence. These bodies or departments shall inform the Court of Auditors whether they intend to take part in the audit.

The other institutions of the Community, any bodies managing revenue or expenditure on behalf of the Community, any natural or legal person in receipt of payments from the budget, and the national audit bodies or, if these do not have the necessary powers, the competent national departments, shall forward to the Court of Auditors, at its request, any document or information necessary to carry out its task.

In respect of the European Investment Bank's activity in managing Community expenditure and revenue, the Court's rights of access to information held by the Bank shall be governed by an agreement between the Court, the Bank and the Commission.

In the absence of an agreement, the Court shall nevertheless have access to information necessary for the audit of Community expenditure and revenue managed by the Bank.

4.   The Court of Auditors shall draw up an annual report after the close of each financial year. It shall be forwarded to the other institutions of the Community and shall be published, together with the replies of these institutions to the observations of the Court of Auditors, in the Official Journal of the European Communities.

The Court of Auditors may also, at any time, submit observations, particularly in the form of special reports, on specific questions and deliver opinions at the request of one of the other institutions of the Community.

It shall adopt its annual reports, special reports or opinions by a majority of its Members.

It shall assist the European Parliament and the Council in exercising their powers of control over the implementation of the budget.

Chapter 2 Provisions Common to Several Institutions

Article 249 (ex Article 189) [Forms of Secondary Community Law]
In order to carry out their task and in accordance with the provisions of this Treaty, the European Parliament acting jointly with the Council, the Council and the Commission shall make regulations and issue directives, take decisions, make recommendations or deliver opinions.

A regulation shall have general application. It shall be binding in its entirety and directly applicable in all Member States.

A directive shall be binding, as to the result to be achieved, upon each Member State to which it is addressed, but shall leave to the national authorities the choice of form and methods.

A decision shall be binding in its entirety upon those to whom it is addressed.

Recommendations and opinions shall have no binding force.

Article 250 (ex Article 189a) [Amendment of Commission Proposals]
1.   Where, in pursuance of this Treaty, the Council acts on a proposal from the Commission, unanimity shall be required for an act constituting an amendment to that proposal, subject to Article 251(4) and (5).
2.   As long as the Council has not acted, the Commission may alter its proposal at any time during the procedures leading to the adoption of a Community act.

Article 251 (ex Article 189b) [The Co-Decision Procedure]
1.   Where reference is made in this Treaty to this Article for the adoption of an act, the following procedure shall apply.
2.   The Commission shall submit a proposal to the European Parliament and the Council.

The Council, acting by a qualified majority after obtaining the opinion of the European Parliament,
—   if it approves all the amendments contained in the European Parliament's opinion, may adopt the proposed act thus amended;
—   if the European Parliament does not propose any amendments, may adopt the proposed act;
—   shall otherwise adopt a common position and communicate it to the European Parliament. The Council shall inform the European Parliament fully of the reasons which led it to adopt its common position. The Commission shall inform the European Parliament fully of its position.

If, within three months of such communication, the European Parliament:
(a) approves the common position or has not taken a decision, the act in question shall be deemed to have been adopted in accordance with that common position;
(b) rejects, by an absolute majority of its component members, the common position, the proposed act shall be deemed not to have been adopted;
(c) proposes amendments to the common position by an absolute majority of its component members, the amended text shall be forwarded to the Council and to the Commission, which shall deliver an opinion on those amendments.

3.   If, within three months of the matter being referred to it, the Council, acting by a qualified majority, approves all the amendments of the European Parliament, the act in question shall be deemed to have been adopted in the form of the common position thus amended; however, the Council shall act unanimously on the amendments on which the Commission has delivered a negative opinion. If the Council does not approve all the amendments, the President of the Council, in agreement with the President of the European Parliament, shall within six weeks convene a meeting of the Conciliation Committee.

4.   The Conciliation Committee, which shall be composed of the members of the Council or their representatives and an equal number of representatives of the European Parliament, shall have the task of reaching agreement on a joint text, by a qualified majority of the members of the Council or their representatives and by a majority of the representatives of the European Parliament. The Commission shall take part in the Conciliation Committee's proceedings and shall take all the necessary initiatives with a view to reconciling the positions of the European Parliament and the Council. In fulfilling this task, the Conciliation Committee shall address the common position on the basis of the amendments proposed by the European Parliament.

5.   If, within six weeks of its being convened, the Conciliation Committee approves a joint text, the European Parliament, acting by an absolute majority of the votes cast, and the Council, acting by a qualified majority, shall each have a period of six weeks from that approval in which to adopt the act in question in accordance with the joint text. If either of the two institutions fails to approve the proposed act within that period, it shall be deemed not to have been adopted.

6.   Where the Conciliation Committee does not approve a joint text, the proposed act shall be deemed not to have been adopted.

7.   The periods of three months and six weeks referred to in this Article shall be extended by a maximum of one month and two weeks respectively at the initiative of the European Parliament or the Council.

Article 252 (ex Article 189c) [The Cooperation Procedure]
Where reference is made in this Treaty to this Article for the adoption of an act, the following procedure shall apply:
(a) The Council, acting by a qualified majority on a proposal from the Commission and after obtaining the opinion of the European Parliament, shall adopt a common position.
(b) The Council's common position shall be communicated to the European Parliament. The Council and the Commission shall inform the European Parliament fully of the reasons which led the Council to adopt its common position and also of the Commission's position.

If, within three months of such communication, the European Parliament approves this common position or has not taken a decision within that period, the Council shall definitively adopt the act in question in accordance with the common position.

(c) The European Parliament may, within the period of three months referred to in point (b), by an absolute majority of its component Members, propose amendments to the Council's common position. The European Parliament may also, by the same majority, reject the Council's common position. The result of the proceedings shall be transmitted to the Council and the Commission.

If the European Parliament has rejected the Council's common position, unanimity shall be required for the Council to act on a second reading.

(d) The Commission shall, within a period of one month, re-examine the proposal on the basis of which the Council adopted its common position, by taking into account the amendments proposed by the European Parliament.

The Commission shall forward to the Council, at the same time as its re-examined proposal, the amendments of the European Parliament which it has not accepted, and shall express its opinion on them. The Council may adopt these amendments unanimously.

(e) The Council, acting by a qualified majority, shall adopt the proposal as re-examined by the Commission.

Unanimity shall be required for the Council to amend the proposal as re-examined by the Commission.

(f) In the cases referred to in points (c), (d) and (e), the Council shall be required to act within a period of three months. If no decision is taken within this period, the Commission proposal shall be deemed not to have been adopted.

(g) The periods referred to in points (b) and (f) may be extended by a maximum of one month by common accord between the Council and the European Parliament.

Article 253 (ex Article 190) [Statement of Reasons]

Regulations, directives and decisions adopted jointly by the European Parliament and the Council, and such acts adopted by the Council or the Commission, shall state the reasons on which they are based and shall refer to any proposals or opinions which were required to be obtained pursuant to this Treaty.

Article 254 (ex Article 191) [Publication and Entry into Force of Regulations, Directives and Decisions]

1. Regulations, directives and decisions adopted in accordance with the procedure referred to in Article 251 shall be signed by the President of the European Parliament and by the President of the Council and published in the Official Journal of the European Communities. They shall enter into force on the date specified in them or, in the absence thereof, on the twentieth day following that of their publication.

2. Regulations of the Council and of the Commission, as well as directives of those institutions which are addressed to all Member States, shall be published in the Official Journal of the European Communities. They shall enter into force on the date specified in them or, in the absence thereof, on the twentieth day following that of their publication.

3. Other directives, and decisions, shall be notified to those to whom they are addressed and shall take effect upon such notification.

Article 255 (ex Article 191a) [Citizens' Access to Community Documents]

1. Any citizen of the Union, and any natural or legal person residing or having its registered office in a Member State, shall have a right of access to European Parliament, Council and Commission documents, subject to the principles and the conditions to be defined in accordance with paragraphs 2 and 3.

2. General principles and limits on grounds of public or private interest governing this right of access to documents shall be determined by the Council, acting in accordance

with the procedure referred to in Article 251 within two years of the entry into force of the Treaty of Amsterdam.

3.   Each institution referred to above shall elaborate in its own Rules of Procedure specific provisions regarding access to its documents.

Article 256 (ex Article 192) [Enforcement of Decisions]

Decisions of the Council or of the Commission which impose a pecuniary obligation on persons other than States, shall be enforceable.

Enforcement shall be governed by the rules of civil procedure in force in the State in the territory of which it is carried out. The order for its enforcement shall be appended to the decision, without other formality than verification of the authenticity of the decision, by the national authority which the government of each Member State shall designate for this purpose and shall make known to the Commission and to the Court of Justice.

When these formalities have been completed on application by the party concerned, the latter may proceed to enforcement in accordance with the national law, by bringing the matter directly before the competent authority.

Enforcement may be suspended only by a decision of the Court of Justice. However, the courts of the country concerned shall have jurisdiction over complaints that enforcement is being carried out in an irregular manner.

Chapter 3 The Economic and Social Committee

Article 257 (ex Article 193) [Establishment of the Economic and Social Committee]

An Economic and Social Committee is hereby established. It shall have advisory status.

The Committee shall consist of representatives of the various categories of economic and social activity, in particular, representatives of producers, farmers, carriers, workers, dealers, craftsmen, professional occupations and representatives of the general public.

Article 258 (ex Article 194) [Appointment of Members]

The number of members of the Economic and Social Committee shall be as follows:

Belgium	12
Denmark	9
Germany	24
Greece	12
Spain	21
France	24
Ireland	9
Italy	24
Luxembourg	6
Netherlands	12
Austria	12
Portugal	12
Finland	9
Sweden	12
United Kingdom	24.

The members of the Committee shall be appointed by the Council, acting unanimously, for four years. Their appointments shall be renewable.

The members of the Committee may not be bound by any mandatory instructions.

They shall be completely independent in the performance of their duties, in the general interest of the Community.

The Council, acting by a qualified majority, shall determine the allowances of members of the Committee.

Article 259 (ex Article 195) [Appointment Procedure]

1.   For the appointment of the members of the Committee, each Member State shall provide the Council with a list containing twice as many candidates as there are seats allotted to its nationals.

The composition of the Committee shall take account of the need to ensure adequate representation of the various categories of economic and social activity.

2.   The Council shall consult the Commission. It may obtain the opinion of European bodies which are representative of the various economic and social sectors to which the activities of the Community are of concern.

Article 260 (ex Article 196) [Presidency and Rules of Procedure; Meetings]

The Committee shall elect its chairman and officers from among its members for a term of two years.

It shall adopt its Rules of Procedure.

The Committee shall be convened by its chairman at the request of the Council or of the Commission. It may also meet on its own initiative.

Article 261 (ex Article 197) [Specialized Sections and Sub-Committees]

The Committee shall include specialised sections for the principal fields covered by this Treaty.

These specialised sections shall operate within the general terms of reference of the Committee. They may not be consulted independently of the Committee.

Subcommittees may also be established within the Committee to prepare on specific questions or in specific fields, draft opinions to be submitted to the Committee for its consideration.

The Rules of Procedure shall lay down the methods of composition and the terms of reference of the specialised sections and of the subcommittees.

Article 262 (ex Article 198) [Mandatory and Optional Consultation of the Committee]

The Committee must be consulted by the Council or by the Commission where this Treaty so provides. The Committee may be consulted by these institutions in all cases in which they consider it appropriate. It may issue an opinion on its own initiative in cases in which it considers such action appropriate.

The Council or the Commission shall, if it considers it necessary, set the Committee, for the submission of its opinion, a time-limit which may not be less than one month from the date on which the chairman receives notification to this effect. Upon expiry of the time-limit, the absence of an opinion shall not prevent further action.

The opinion of the Committee and that of the specialised section, together with a record of the proceedings, shall be forwarded to the Council and to the Commission.

The Committee may be consulted by the European Parliament.

Chapter 4 The Committee of the Regions

Article 263 (ex Article 198a) [Establishment and Composition]
A Committee consisting of representatives of regional and local bodies, hereinafter referred to as "the Committee of the Regions", is hereby established with advisory status.
The number of members of the Committee of the Regions shall be as follows:

Belgium	12
Denmark	9
Germany	24
Greece	12
Spain	21
France	24
Ireland	9
Italy	24
Luxembourg	6
Netherlands	12
Austria	12
Portugal	12
Finland	9
Sweden	12
United Kingdom	24.

The members of the Committee and an equal number of alternate members shall be appointed for four years by the Council acting unanimously on proposals from the respective Member States. Their term of office shall be renewable. No member of the Committee shall at the same time be a Member of the European Parliament.

The members of the Committee may not be bound by any mandatory instructions. They shall be completely independent in the performance of their duties, in the general interest of Community.

Article 264 (ex Article 198b) [Presidency and Rules of Procedure; Meetings]
The Committee of the Regions shall elect its chairman and officers from among its members for a term of two years.

It shall adopt its Rules of Procedure.

The Committee shall be convened by its chairman at the request of the Council or of the Commission. It may also meet on its own initiative.

Article 265 (ex Article 198c) [Mandatory and Optional Consultation of the Committee]
The Committee of the Regions shall be consulted by the Council or by the Commission where this Treaty so provides and in all other cases, in particular those which concern cross-border cooperation, in which one of these two institutions considers it appropriate.

The Council or the Commission shall, if it considers it necessary, set the Committee, for the submission of its opinion, a time-limit which may not be less than one month from the date on which the chairman receives notification to this effect. Upon expiry of the time-limit, the absence of an opinion shall not prevent further action.

Where the Economic and Social Committee is consulted pursuant to Article 262, the Committee of the Regions shall be informed by the Council or the Commission of the request for an opinion. Where it considers that specific regional interests are involved, the Committee of the Regions may issue an opinion on the matter.

The Committee of the Regions may be consulted by the European Parliament. It may issue an opinion on its own initiative in cases in which it considers such action appropriate.

The opinion of the Committee, together with a record of the proceedings, shall be forwarded to the Council and to the Commission.

Chapter 5 The European Investment Bank

Article 266 (ex Article 198d) [Legal Personality; Members; Statute]
The European Investment Bank shall have legal personality.

The members of the European Investment Bank shall be the Member States.

The Statute of the European Investment Bank is laid down in a Protocol annexed to this Treaty.

Article 267 (ex Article 198e) [Duties of the European Investment Bank]
The task of the European Investment Bank shall be to contribute, by having recourse to the capital market and utilising its own resources, to the balanced and steady development of the common market in the interest of the Community. For this purpose the Bank shall, operating on a non-profit-making basis, grant loans and give guarantees which facilitate the financing of the following projects in all sectors of the economy:
(a) projects for developing less-developed regions;
(b) projects for modernising or converting undertakings or for developing fresh activities called for by the progressive establishment of the common market, where these projects are of such a size or nature that they cannot be entirely financed by the various means available in the individual Member States;
(c) projects of common interest to several Member States which are of such a size or nature that they cannot be entirely financed by the various means available in the individual Member States.
In carrying out its task, the Bank shall facilitate the financing of investment programmes in conjunction with assistance from the Structural Funds and other Community financial instruments.

TITLE II
FINANCIAL PROVISIONS

Article 268 (ex Article 199) [The Community Budget]
All items of revenue and expenditure of the Community, including those relating to the European Social Fund, shall be included in estimates to be drawn up for each financial year and shall be shown in the budget.

Administrative expenditure occasioned for the institutions by the provisions of the Treaty on European Union relating to common foreign and security policy and to co-operation in the fields of justice and home affairs shall be charged to the budget. The operational expenditure occasioned by the implementation of the said provisions may, under the conditions referred to therein, be charged to the budget.
The revenue and expenditure shown in the budget shall be in balance.

Article 269 (ex Article 201) [Own Resources of the Community]
Without prejudice to other revenue, the budget shall be financed wholly from own resources.

The Council, acting unanimously on a proposal from the Commission and after consulting the European Parliament, shall lay down provisions relating to the system of own resources of the Community, which it shall recommend to the Member States for adoption in accordance with their respective constitutional requirements.

Article 270 (ex Article 201a) [Budgetary Discipline]

With a view to maintaining budgetary discipline, the Commission shall not make any proposal for a Community act, or alter its proposals, or adopt any implementing measure which is likely to have appreciable implications for the budget without providing the assurance that that proposal or that measure is capable of being financed within the limit of the Community's own resources arising under provisions laid down by the Council pursuant to Article 269.

Article 271 (ex Article 202) [Authorization on an Annual Basis]

The expenditure shown in the budget shall be authorised for one financial year, unless the regulations made pursuant to Article 279 provide otherwise.

In accordance with conditions to be laid down pursuant to Article 279, any appropriations, other than those relating to staff expenditure, that are unexpended at the end of the financial year may be carried forward to the next financial year only.

Appropriations shall be classified under different chapters grouping items of expenditure according to their nature or purpose and subdivided, as far as may be necessary, in accordance with the regulations made pursuant to Article 279.

The expenditure of the European Parliament, the Council, the Commission and the Court of Justice shall be set out in separate parts of the budget, without prejudice to special arrangements for certain common items of expenditure.

Article 272 (ex Article 203) [Financial Year; Draft Budget; Adoption of the Final Budget]

1.   The financial year shall run from 1 January to 31 December.
2.   Each institution of the Community shall, before 1 July, draw up estimates of its expenditure. The Commission shall consolidate these estimates in a preliminary draft budget. It shall attach thereto an opinion which may contain different estimates.
The preliminary draft budget shall contain an estimate of revenue and an estimate of expenditure.
3.   The Commission shall place the preliminary draft budget before the Council not later than 1 September of the year preceding that in which the budget is to be implemented.

The Council shall consult the Commission and, where appropriate, the other institutions concerned whenever it intends to depart from the preliminary draft budget.

The Council, acting by a qualified majority, shall establish the draft budget and forward it to the European Parliament.
4.   The draft budget shall be placed before the European Parliament not later than 5 October of the year preceding that in which the budget is to be implemented.

The European Parliament shall have the right to amend the draft budget, acting by a majority of its Members, and to propose to the Council, acting by an absolute majority of the votes cast, modifications to the draft budget relating to expenditure necessarily resulting from this Treaty or from acts adopted in accordance therewith.

If, within 45 days of the draft budget being placed before it, the European Parliament has given its approval, the budget shall stand as finally adopted. If within this period the European Parliament has not amended the draft budget nor proposed any modifications thereto, the budget shall be deemed to be finally adopted.

If within this period the European Parliament has adopted amendments or proposed modifications, the draft budget together with the amendments or proposed modifications shall be forwarded to the Council.

5.   After discussing the draft budget with the Commission and, where appropriate, with the other institutions concerned, the Council shall act under the following conditions:

(a) the Council may, acting by a qualified majority, modify any of the amendments adopted by the European Parliament;

(b) with regard to the proposed modifications:
— where a modification proposed by the European Parliament does not have the effect of increasing the total amount of the expenditure of an institution, owing in particular to the fact that the increase in expenditure which it would involve would be expressly compensated by one or more proposed modifications correspondingly reducing expenditure, the Council may, acting by a qualified majority, reject the proposed modification. In the absence of a decision to reject it, the proposed modification shall stand as accepted;
— where a modification proposed by the European Parliament has the effect of increasing the total amount of the expenditure of an institution, the Council may, acting by a qualified majority, accept this proposed modification. In the absence of a decision to accept it, the proposed modification shall stand as rejected;
— where, in pursuance of one of the two preceding subparagraphs, the Council has rejected a proposed modification, it may, acting by a qualified majority, either retain the amount shown in the draft budget or fix another amount.

The draft budget shall be modified on the basis of the proposed modifications accepted by the Council.

If, within 15 days of the draft being placed before it, the Council has not modified any of the amendments adopted by the European Parliament and if the modifications proposed by the latter have been accepted, the budget shall be deemed to be finally adopted. The Council shall inform the European Parliament that it has not modified any of the amendments and that the proposed modifications have been accepted.

If within this period the Council has modified one or more of the amendments adopted by the European Parliament or if the modifications proposed by the latter have been rejected or modified, the modified draft budget shall again be forwarded to the European Parliament. The Council shall inform the European Parliament of the results of its deliberations.

6.   Within 15 days of the draft budget being placed before it, the European Parliament, which shall have been notified of the action taken on its proposed modifications, may, acting by a majority of its Members and three-fifths of the votes cast, amend or reject the modifications to its amendments made by the Council and shall adopt the budget accordingly. If within this period the European Parliament has not acted, the budget shall be deemed to be finally adopted.

7.   When the procedure provided for in this Article has been completed, the President of the European Parliament shall declare that the budget has been finally adopted.

8.   However, the European Parliament, acting by a majority of its Members and two-thirds of the votes cast, may, if there are important reasons, reject the draft budget and ask for a new draft to be submitted to it.

9.   A maximum rate of increase in relation to the expenditure of the same type to be incurred during the current year shall be fixed annually for the total expenditure other than that necessarily resulting from this Treaty or from acts adopted in accordance therewith.

The Commission shall, after consulting the Economic Policy Committee, declare what this maximum rate is as it results from:

— the trend, in terms of volume, of the gross national product within the Community;
— the average variation in the budgets of the Member States; and
— the trend of the cost of living during the preceding financial year.

The maximum rate shall be communicated, before 1 May, to all the institutions of the Community. The latter shall be required to conform to this during the budgetary procedure, subject to the provisions of the fourth and fifth subparagraphs of this paragraph.

If, in respect of expenditure other than that necessarily resulting from this Treaty or from acts adopted in accordance therewith, the actual rate of increase in the draft budget established by the Council is over half the maximum rate, the European Parliament may, exercising its right of amendment, further increase the total amount of that expenditure to a limit not exceeding half the maximum rate.

Where the European Parliament, the Council or the Commission consider that the activities of the Communities require that the rate determined according to the procedure laid down in this paragraph should be exceeded, another rate may be fixed by agreement between the Council, acting by a qualified majority, and the European Parliament, acting by a majority of its Members and three-fifths of the votes cast.

10. Each institution shall exercise the powers conferred upon it by this Article, with due regard for the provisions of the Treaty and for acts adopted in accordance therewith, in particular those relating to the Communities' own resources and to the balance between revenue and expenditure.

Article 273 (ex Article 204) [Preliminary Appropriations]

If, at the beginning of a financial year, the budget has not yet been voted, a sum equivalent to not more than one-twelfth of the budget appropriations for the preceding financial year may be spent each month in respect of any chapter or other subdivision of the budget in accordance with the provisions of the Regulations made pursuant to Article 279; this arrangement shall not, however, have the effect of placing at the disposal of the Commission appropriations in excess of one-twelfth of those provided for in the draft budget in course of preparation.

The Council may, acting by a qualified majority, provided that the other conditions laid down in the first subparagraph are observed, authorise expenditure in excess of one-twelfth.

If the decision relates to expenditure which does not necessarily result from this Treaty or from acts adopted in accordance therewith, the Council shall forward it immediately to the European Parliament; within 30 days the European Parliament, acting by a majority of its Members and three-fifths of the votes cast, may adopt a different decision on the expenditure in excess of the one-twelfth referred to in the first subparagraph. This part of the decision of the Council shall be suspended until the European Parliament has taken its decision. If within the said period the European Parliament has not taken a decision which differs from the decision of the Council, the latter shall be deemed to be finally adopted.

The decisions referred to in the second and third subparagraphs shall lay down the necessary measures relating to resources to ensure application of this Article.

Article 274 (ex Article 205) [Implementation of the Community Budget by the Commission]

The Commission shall implement the budget, in accordance with the provisions of the regulations made pursuant to Article 279, on its own responsibility and within the limits of the appropriations, having regard to the principles of sound financial management. Member States shall cooperate with the Commission to ensure that the appropriations are used in accordance with the principles of sound financial management.

The regulations shall lay down detailed rules for each institution concerning its part in effecting its own expenditure.

Within the budget, the Commission may, subject to the limits and conditions laid down in the regulations made pursuant to Article 279, transfer appropriations from one chapter to another or from one subdivision to another.

Article 275 (ex Article 205a) [Submission of Accounts to Council and Parliament]
The Commission shall submit annually to the Council and to the European Parliament the accounts of the preceding financial year relating to the implementation of the budget. The Commission shall also forward to them a financial statement of the assets and liabilities of the Community.

Article 276 (ex Article 206) [Discharge]
1.   The European Parliament, acting on a recommendation from the Council which shall act by a qualified majority, shall give a discharge to the Commission in respect of the implementation of the budget. To this end, the Council and the European Parliament in turn shall examine the accounts and the financial statement referred to in Article 275, the annual report by the Court of Auditors together with the replies of the institutions under audit to the observations of the Court of Auditors, the statement of assurance referred to in Article 248(1), second subparagraph and any relevant special reports by the Court of Auditors.
2.   Before giving a discharge to the Commission, or for any other purpose in connection with the exercise of its powers over the implementation of the budget, the European Parliament may ask to hear the Commission give evidence with regard to the execution of expenditure or the operation of financial control systems. The Commission shall submit any necessary information to the European Parliament at the latter's request.
3.   The Commission shall take all appropriate steps to act on the observations in the decisions giving discharge and on other observations by the European Parliament relating to the execution of expenditure, as well as on comments accompanying the recommendations on discharge adopted by the Council.

At the request of the European Parliament or the Council, the Commission shall report on the measures taken in the light of these observations and comments and in particular on the instructions given to the departments which are responsible for the implementation of the budget. These reports shall also be forwarded to the Court of Auditors.

Article 277 (ex Article 207) [Unit of Account; Financial Contributions
by the Member States]
The budget shall be drawn up in the unit of account determined in accordance with the provisions of the regulations made pursuant to Article 279.

Article 278 (ex Article 208) [Transfer of Currencies and Other Financial Operations]
The Commission may, provided it notifies the competent authorities of the Member States concerned, transfer into the currency of one of the Member States its holdings in the currency of another Member State, to the extent necessary to enable them to be used for purposes which come within the scope of this Treaty. The Commission shall as far as possible avoid making such transfers if it possesses cash or liquid assets in the currencies which it needs.

The Commission shall deal with each Member State through the authority designated by the State concerned. In carrying out financial operations the Commission shall employ the services of the bank of issue of the Member State concerned or of any other financial institution approved by that State.

Article 279 (ex Article 209) [Financial Regulations, Methods and Procedures]
The Council, acting unanimously on a proposal from the Commission and after consulting the European Parliament and obtaining the opinion of the Court of Auditors, shall:
(a) make Financial Regulations specifying in particular the procedure to be adopted for establishing and implementing the budget and for presenting and auditing accounts;
(b) determine the methods and procedure whereby the budget revenue provided under the arrangements relating to the Community's own resources shall be made available to the Commission, and determine the measures to be applied, if need be, to meet cash requirements;
(c) lay down rules concerning the responsibility of financial controllers, authorising officers and accounting officers, and concerning appropriate arrangements for inspection.

Article 280 (ex Article 209a) [Measures Against Fraud]
1.   The Community and the Member States shall counter fraud and any other illegal activities affecting the financial interests of the Community through measures to be taken in accordance with this Article, which shall act as a deterrent and be such as to afford effective protection in the Member States.
2.   Member States shall take the same measures to counter fraud affecting the financial interests of the Community as they take to counter fraud affecting their own financial interests.
3.   Without prejudice to other provisions of this Treaty, the Member States shall co-ordinate their action aimed at protecting the financial interests of the Community against fraud. To this end they shall organise, together with the Commission, close and regular cooperation between the competent authorities.
4.   The Council, acting in accordance with the procedure referred to in Article 251, after consulting the Court of Auditors, shall adopt the necessary measures in the fields of the prevention of and fight against fraud affecting the financial interests of the Community with a view to affording effective and equivalent protection in the Member States. These measures shall not concern the application of national criminal law or the national administration of justice.
5.   The Commission, in cooperation with Member States, shall each year submit to the European Parliament and to the Council a report on the measures taken for the implementation of this Article.

PART SIX
GENERAL AND FINAL PROVISIONS

Article 281 (ex Article 210) [Legal Personality of the Community]
The Community shall have legal personality.

Article 282 (ex Article 211) [Legal Capacity and Representation]
In each of the Member States, the Community shall enjoy the most extensive legal capacity accorded to legal persons under their laws; it may, in particular, acquire or dispose of movable and immovable property and may be a party to legal proceedings. To this end, the Community shall be represented by the Commission.

Article 283 (ex Article 212) [Staff Regulations]
The Council shall, acting by a qualified majority on a proposal from the Commission and after consulting the other institutions concerned, lay down the Staff Regulations of officials of the European Communities and the Conditions of Employment of other servants of those Communities.

Article 284 (ex Article 213) [Inquiries by the Commission]
The Commission may, within the limits and under conditions laid down by the Council in accordance with the provisions of this Treaty, collect any information and carry out any checks required for the performance of the tasks entrusted to it.

Article 285 (ex Article 213a) [Community Statistics]
1.   Without prejudice to Article 5 of the Protocol on the Statute of the European System of Central Banks and of the European Central Bank, the Council, acting in accordance with the procedure referred to in Article 251, shall adopt measures for the production of statistics where necessary for the performance of the activities of the Community.
2.   The production of Community statistics shall conform to impartiality, reliability, objectivity, scientific independence, cost-effectiveness and statistical confidentiality; it shall not entail excessive burdens on economic operators.

Article 286 (ex Article 213b) [Data Protection]
1.   From 1 January 1999, Community acts on the protection of individuals with regard to the processing of personal data and the free movement of such data shall apply to the institutions and bodies set up by, or on the basis of, this Treaty.
2.   Before the date referred to in paragraph 1, the Council, acting in accordance with the procedure referred to in Article 251, shall establish an independent supervisory body responsible for monitoring the application of such Community acts to Community institutions and bodies and shall adopt any other relevant provisions as appropriate.

Article 287 (ex Article 214) [Professional Secrecy]
The members of the institutions of the Community, the members of committees, and the officials and other servants of the Community shall be required, even after their duties have ceased, not to disclose information of the kind covered by the obligation of professional secrecy, in particular information about undertakings, their business relations or their cost components.

Article 288 (ex Article 215) [Contractual Liability;
Non-Contractual Liability; Personal Liability]
The contractual liability of the Community shall be governed by the law applicable to the contract in question.

In the case of non-contractual liability, the Community shall, in accordance with the general principles common to the laws of the Member States, make good any damage caused by its institutions or by its servants in the performance of their duties.

The preceding paragraph shall apply under the same conditions to damage caused by the ECB or by its servants in the performance of their duties.

The personal liability of its servants towards the Community shall be governed by the provisions laid down in their Staff Regulations or in the Conditions of Employment applicable to them.

Article 289 (ex Article 216) [Seat of the Institutions]
The seat of the institutions of the Community shall be determined by common accord of the Governments of the Member States.

Article 290 (ex Article 217) [Languages of the Institutions]
The rules governing the languages of the institutions of the Community shall, without prejudice to the provisions contained in the Rules of Procedure of the Court of Justice, be determined by the Council, acting unanimously.

Article 291 (ex Article 218) [Privileges and Immunities of the Community]
The Community shall enjoy in the territories of the Member States such privileges and immunities as are necessary for the performance of its tasks, under the conditions laid down in the Protocol of 8 April 1965 on the privileges and immunities of the European Communities. The same shall apply to the European Central Bank, the European Monetary Institute, and the European Investment Bank.

Article 292 (ex Article 219) [Dispute Settlement]
Member States undertake not to submit a dispute concerning the interpretation or application of this Treaty to any method of settlement other than those provided for therein.

*Article 293 (ex Article 220) [Supplementary Agreements Between Member States
for the Benefit of Their Nationals]*
Member States shall, so far as is necessary, enter into negotiations with each other with a view to securing for the benefit of their nationals:
— the protection of persons and the enjoyment and protection of rights under the same conditions as those accorded by each State to its own nationals;
— the abolition of double taxation within the Community;
— the mutual recognition of companies or firms within the meaning of the second paragraph of Article 48, the retention of legal personality in the event of transfer of their seat from one country to another, and the possibility of mergers between companies or firms governed by the laws of different countries;
— the simplification of formalities governing the reciprocal recognition and enforcement of judgments of courts or tribunals and of arbitration awards.

Article 294 (ex Article 221) [Equal Treatment for Shareholders]
Member States shall accord nationals of the other Member States the same treatment as their own nationals as regards participation in the capital of companies or firms within the meaning of Article 48, without prejudice to the application of the other provisions of this Treaty.

*Article 295 (ex Article 222) [Non-Interference with National Systems
of Property Ownership]*
This Treaty shall in no way prejudice the rules in Member States governing the system of property ownership.

*Article 296 (ex Article 223) [Safeguard Clause for Essential Interests of National
Security]*
1.   The provisions of this Treaty shall not preclude the application of the following rules:
(a) no Member State shall be obliged to supply information the disclosure of which it considers contrary to the essential interests of its security;

(b) any Member State may take such measures as it considers necessary for the protection of the essential interests of its security which are connected with the production of or trade in arms, munitions and war material; such measures shall not adversely affect the conditions of competition in the common market regarding products which are not intended for specifically military purposes.

2.   The Council may, acting unanimously on a proposal from the Commission, make changes to the list, which it drew up on 15 April 1958, of the products to which the provisions of paragraph 1(b) apply.

Article 297 (ex Article 224) [Cooperation in Situations of Serious Internal or External Disturbances]

Member States shall consult each other with a view to taking together the steps needed to prevent the functioning of the common market being affected by measures which a Member State may be called upon to take in the event of serious internal disturbances affecting the maintenance of law and order, in the event of war, serious international tension constituting a threat of war, or in order to carry out obligations it has accepted for the purpose of maintaining peace and international security.

Article 298 (ex Article 225) [Preventing Distortions of Competition]

If measures taken in the circumstances referred to in Articles 296 and 297 have the effect of distorting the conditions of competition in the common market, the Commission shall, together with the State concerned, examine how these measures can be adjusted to the rules laid down in the Treaty.

By way of derogation from the procedure laid down in Articles 226 and 227, the Commission or any Member State may bring the matter directly before the Court of Justice if it considers that another Member State is making improper use of the powers provided for in Articles 296 and 297. The Court of Justice shall give its ruling in camera.

Article 299 (ex Article 227) [Geographic Application of the Treaty]

1.   This Treaty shall apply to the Kingdom of Belgium, the Kingdom of Denmark, the Federal Republic of Germany, the Hellenic Republic, the Kingdom of Spain, the French Republic, Ireland, the Italian Republic, the Grand Duchy of Luxembourg, the Kingdom of the Netherlands, the Republic of Austria, the Portuguese Republic, the Republic of Finland, the Kingdom of Sweden and the United Kingdom of Great Britain and Northern Ireland.

2.   The provisions of this Treaty shall apply to the French overseas departments, the Azores, Madeira and the Canary Islands.

However, taking account of the structural social and economic situation of the French overseas departments, the Azores, Madeira and the Canary Islands, which is compounded by their remoteness, insularity, small size, difficult topography and climate, economic dependence on a few products, the permanence and combination of which severely restrain their development, the Council, acting by a qualified majority on a proposal from the Commission and after consulting the European Parliament, shall adopt specific measures aimed, in particular, at laying down the conditions of application of the present Treaty to those regions, including common policies.

The Council shall, when adopting the relevant measures referred to in the second subparagraph, take into account areas such as customs and trade policies, fiscal policy, free zones, agriculture and fisheries policies, conditions for supply of raw materials and essential consumer goods, State aids and conditions of access to structural funds and to horizontal Community programmes.

The Council shall adopt the measures referred to in the second subparagraph taking into account the special characteristics and constraints of the outermost regions without undermining the integrity and the coherence of the Community legal order, including the internal market and common policies.

3.   The special arrangements for association set out in Part Four of this Treaty shall apply to the overseas countries and territories listed in Annex II to this Treaty.

This Treaty shall not apply to those overseas countries and territories having special relations with the United Kingdom of Great Britain and Northern Ireland which are not included in the aforementioned list.

4.   The provisions of this Treaty shall apply to the European territories for whose external relations a Member State is responsible.

5.   The provisions of this Treaty shall apply to the Åland Islands in accordance with the provisions set out in Protocol No 2 to the Act concerning the conditions of accession of the Republic of Austria, the Republic of Finland and the Kingdom of Sweden.

6.   Notwithstanding the preceding paragraphs:

(a) this Treaty shall not apply to the Faeroe Islands;

(b) this Treaty shall not apply to the Sovereign Base Areas of the United Kingdom of Great Britain and Northern Ireland in Cyprus;

(c) this Treaty shall apply to the Channel Islands and the Isle of Man only to the extent necessary to ensure the implementation of the arrangements for those islands set out in the Treaty concerning the accession of new Member States to the European Economic Community and to the European Atomic Energy Community signed on 22 January 1972.

Article 300 (ex Article 228) [Agreements Between the Community and Third Countries or International Organizations]

1.   Where this Treaty provides for the conclusion of agreements between the Community and one or more States or international organisations, the Commission shall make recommendations to the Council, which shall authorise the Commission to open the necessary negotiations. The Commission shall conduct these negotiations in consultation with special committees appointed by the Council to assist it in this task and within the framework of such directives as the Council may issue to it.

In exercising the powers conferred upon it by this paragraph, the Council shall act by a qualified majority, except in the cases where the first subparagraph of paragraph 2 provides that the Council shall act unanimously.

2.   Subject to the powers vested in the Commission in this field, the signing, which may be accompanied by a decision on provisional application before entry into force, and the conclusion of the agreements shall be decided on by the Council, acting by a qualified majority on a proposal from the Commission. The Council shall act unanimously when the agreement covers a field for which unanimity is required for the adoption of internal rules and for the agreements referred to in Article 310.

By way of derogation from the rules laid down in paragraph 3, the same procedures shall apply for a decision to suspend the application of an agreement, and for the purpose of establishing the positions to be adopted on behalf of the Community in a body set up by an agreement based on Article 310, when that body is called upon to adopt decisions having legal effects, with the exception of decisions supplementing or amending the institutional framework of the agreement.

The European Parliament shall be immediately and fully informed on any decision under this paragraph concerning the provisional application or the suspension of agreements, or the establishment of the Community position in a body set up by an agreement based on Article 310.

3.   The Council shall conclude agreements after consulting the European Parliament, except for the agreements referred to in Article 133(3), including cases where the

agreement covers a field for which the procedure referred to in Article 251 or that referred to in Article 252 is required for the adoption of internal rules. The European Parliament shall deliver its opinion within a time-limit which the Council may lay down according to the urgency of the matter. In the absence of an opinion within that time-limit, the Council may act.

By way of derogation from the previous subparagraph, agreements referred to in Article 310, other agreements establishing a specific institutional framework by organising cooperation procedures, agreements having important budgetary implications for the Community and agreements entailing amendment of an act adopted under the procedure referred to in Article 251 shall be concluded after the assent of the European Parliament has been obtained.

The Council and the European Parliament may, in an urgent situation, agree upon a time-limit for the assent.

4.   When concluding an agreement, the Council may, by way of derogation from paragraph 2, authorise the Commission to approve modifications on behalf of the Community where the agreement provides for them to be adopted by a simplified procedure or by a body set up by the agreement; it may attach specific conditions to such authorisation.

5.   When the Council envisages concluding an agreement which calls for amendments to this Treaty, the amendments must first be adopted in accordance with the procedure laid down in Article 48 of the Treaty on European Union.

6.   The Council, the Commission or a Member State may obtain the opinion of the Court of Justice as to whether an agreement envisaged is compatible with the provisions of this Treaty. Where the opinion of the Court of Justice is adverse, the agreement may enter into force only in accordance with Article 48 of the Treaty on European Union.

7.   Agreements concluded under the conditions set out in this Article shall be binding on the institutions of the Community and on Member States.

Article 301 (ex Article 228a) [Economic Sanctions Under the CFSP]

Where it is provided, in a common position or in a joint action adopted according to the provisions of the Treaty on European Union relating to the common foreign and security policy, for an action by the Community to interrupt or to reduce, in part or completely, economic relations with one or more third countries, the Council shall take the necessary urgent measures. The Council shall act by a qualified majority on a proposal from the Commission.

Article 302 (ex Article 229) [Relations with International Organizations]

It shall be for the Commission to ensure the maintenance of all appropriate relations with the organs of the United Nations and of its specialised agencies.

The Commission shall also maintain such relations as are appropriate with all international organisations.

Article 303 (ex Article 230) [Cooperation with the Council of Europe]

The Community shall establish all appropriate forms of cooperation with the Council of Europe.

Article 304 (ex Article 231) [Cooperation with the OECD]

The Community shall establish close cooperation with the Organisation for Economic Cooperation and Development, the details of which shall be determined by common accord.

Article 305 (ex Article 232) [Relationship to the Coal and Steel and Atomic Energy Treaties]

1. The provisions of this Treaty shall not affect the provisions of the Treaty establishing the European Coal and Steel Community, in particular as regards the rights and obligations of Member States, the powers of the institutions of that Community and the rules laid down by that Treaty for the functioning of the common market in coal and steel.
2. The provisions of this Treaty shall not derogate from those of the Treaty establishing the European Atomic Energy Community.

Article 306 (ex Article 233) [Regional Union of the BeNeLux-States]

The provisions of this Treaty shall not preclude the existence or completion of regional unions between Belgium and Luxembourg, or between Belgium, Luxembourg and the Netherlands, to the extent that the objectives of these regional unions are not attained by application of this Treaty.

Article 307 (ex Article 234) [Priority of Pre-Existing Treaties of the Member States]

The rights and obligations arising from agreements concluded before 1 January 1958 or, for acceding States, before the date of their accession, between one or more Member States on the one hand, and one or more third countries on the other, shall not be affected by the provisions of this Treaty.

To the extent that such agreements are not compatible with this Treaty, the Member State or States concerned shall take all appropriate steps to eliminate the incompatibilities established. Member States shall, where necessary, assist each other to this end and shall, where appropriate, adopt a common attitude.

In applying the agreements referred to in the first paragraph, Member States shall take into account the fact that the advantages accorded under this Treaty by each Member State form an integral part of the establishment of the Community and are thereby inseparably linked with the creation of common institutions, the conferring of powers upon them and the granting of the same advantages by all the other Member States.

Article 308 (ex Article 235) [Competence of the Council to Act in Unforeseen Cases]

If action by the Community should prove necessary to attain, in the course of the operation of the common market, one of the objectives of the Community and this Treaty has not provided the necessary powers, the Council shall, acting unanimously on a proposal from the Commission and after consulting the European Parliament, take the appropriate measures.

Article 309 (ex Article 236) [Voting in Case of a Serious and Persistent Breach of Community Principles]

1. Where a decision has been taken to suspend the voting rights of the representative of the government of a Member State in accordance with Article 7(2) of the Treaty on European Union, these voting rights shall also be suspended with regard to this Treaty.
2. Moreover, where the existence of a serious and persistent breach by a Member State of principles mentioned in Article 6(1) of the Treaty on European Union has been determined in accordance with Article 7(1) of that Treaty, the Council, acting by a qualified majority, may decide to suspend certain of the rights deriving from the application of this Treaty to the Member State in question. In doing so, the Council shall take into

account the possible consequences of such a suspension on the rights and obligations of natural and legal persons.

The obligations of the Member State in question under this Treaty shall in any case continue to be binding on that State.

3.   The Council, acting by a qualified majority, may decide subsequently to vary or revoke measures taken in accordance with paragraph 2 in response to changes in the situation which led to their being imposed.

4.   When taking decisions referred to in paragraphs 2 and 3, the Council shall act without taking into account the votes of the representative of the government of the Member State in question. By way of derogation from Article 205(2) a qualified majority shall be defined as the same proportion of the weighted votes of the members of the Council concerned as laid down in Article 205(2).

This paragraph shall also apply in the event of voting rights being suspended in accordance with paragraph 1. In such cases, a decision requiring unanimity shall be taken without the vote of the representative of the government of the Member State in question.

Article 310 (ex Article 238) [Association Agreements with Third Countries and International Organizations]
The Community may conclude with one or more States or international organisations agreements establishing an association involving reciprocal rights and obligations, common action and special procedure.

Article 311 (ex Article 239) [Protocols as Part of Primary Community Law]
The protocols annexed to this Treaty by common accord of the Member States shall form an integral part thereof.

Article 312 (ex Article 240) [Unlimited Duration]
This Treaty is concluded for an unlimited period.

FINAL PROVISIONS

Article 313 (ex Article 247) [Ratification and Entry into Force]
This Treaty shall be ratified by the High Contracting Parties in accordance with their respective constitutional requirements. The instruments of ratification shall be deposited with the Government of the Italian Republic.

This Treaty shall enter into force on the first day of the month following the deposit of the instrument of ratification by the last signatory State to take this step. If, however, such deposit is made less than 15 days before the beginning of the following month, this Treaty shall not enter into force until the first day of the second month after the date of such deposit.

Article 314 (ex Article 248) [Authentic Language Versions]
This Treaty, drawn up in a single original in the Dutch, French, German, and Italian languages, all four texts being equally authentic, shall be deposited in the archives of the Government of the Italian Republic, which shall transmit a certified copy to each of the Governments of the other signatory States.

Pursuant to the Accession Treaties, the Danish, English, Finnish, Greek, Irish, Portuguese, Spanish and Swedish versions of this Treaty shall also be authentic.

In witness whereof, the undersigned Plenipotentiaries have signed this Treaty.

Done at Rome this twenty-fifth day of March in the year [1957].

Protocols

Note: The references to Treaty articles, titles and sections contained in the protocols are adapted in accordance with the tables of equivalence set out in the original Annex to the Treaty of Amsterdam.

Protocols Annexed to the Treaty on European Union and the Treaty Establishing the European Community

Protocol No. 2 Integrating the Schengen Acquis Into the Framework of the European Union

THE HIGH CONTRACTING PARTIES,

NOTING that the Agreements on the gradual abolition of checks at common borders signed by some Member States of the European Union in Schengen on 14 June 1985 and on 19 June 1990, as well as related agreements and the rules adopted on the basis of these agreements, are aimed at enhancing European integration and, in particular, at enabling the European Union to develop more rapidly into an area of freedom, security and justice,
DESIRING to incorporate the abovementioned agreements and rules into the framework of the European Union,
CONFIRMING that the provisions of the Schengen *acquis* are applicable only if and as far as they are compatible with the European Union and Community law,
TAKING INTO ACCOUNT the special position of Denmark,
TAKING INTO ACCOUNT the fact that Ireland and the United Kingdom of Great Britain and Northern Ireland are not parties to and have not signed the abovementioned agreements; that provision should, however, be made to allow those Member States to accept some or all of the provisions thereof,
RECOGNISING that, as a consequence, it is necessary to make use of the provisions of the Treaty on European Union and of the Treaty establishing the European Community concerning closer cooperation between some Member States and that those provisions should only be used as a last resort,
TAKING INTO ACCOUNT the need to maintain a special relationship with the Republic of Iceland and the Kingdom of Norway, both States having confirmed their intention to become bound by the provisions mentioned above, on the basis of the Agreement signed in Luxembourg on 19 December 1996,
HAVE AGREED UPON the following provisions, which shall be annexed to the Treaty on European Union and to the Treaty establishing the European Community,

Article 1

The Kingdom of Belgium, the Kingdom of Denmark, the Federal Republic of Germany, the Hellenic Republic, the Kingdom of Spain, the French Republic, the Italian Republic, the Grand Duchy of Luxembourg, the Kingdom of the Netherlands, the Republic of Austria, the Portuguese Republic, the Republic of Finland and the Kingdom of Sweden, signatories to the Schengen agreements, are authorised to establish closer cooperation among themselves within the scope of those agreements and related provisions, as they are listed in the Annex to this Protocol, hereinafter referred to as the "Schengen *acquis*". This cooperation shall be conducted within the institutional and legal framework of the European Union and with respect for the relevant provisions of the Treaty on European Union and of the Treaty establishing the European Community.

Article 2

1. From the date of entry into force of the Treaty of Amsterdam, the Schengen *acquis*, including the decisions of the Executive Committee established by the Schengen agreements which have been adopted before this date, shall immediately apply to the thirteen Member States referred to in Article 1, without prejudice to the provisions of paragraph 2 of this Article. From the same date, the Council will substitute itself for the said Executive Committee.

The Council, acting by the unanimity of its Members referred to in Article 1, shall take any measure necessary for the implementation of this paragraph. The Council, acting unanimously, shall determine, in conformity with the relevant provisions of the Treaties, the legal basis for each of the provisions or decisions which constitute the Schengen *acquis*. With regard to such provisions and decisions and in accordance with that determination, the Court of Justice of the European Communities shall exercise the powers conferred upon it by the relevant applicable provisions of the Treaties. In any event, the Court of Justice shall have no jurisdiction on measures or decisions relating to the maintenance of law and order and the safeguarding of internal security.

As long as the measures referred to above have not been taken and without prejudice to Article 5(2), the provisions or decisions which constitute the Schengen *acquis* shall be regarded as acts based on Title VI of the Treaty on European Union.

2. The provisions of paragraph 1 shall apply to the Member States which have signed accession protocols to the Schengen agreements, from the dates decided by the Council, acting with the unanimity of its Members mentioned in Article 1, unless the conditions for the accession of any of those States to the Schengen *acquis* are met before the date of the entry into force of the Treaty of Amsterdam.

Article 3

Following the determination referred to in Article 2(1), second subparagraph, Denmark shall maintain the same rights and obligations in relation to the other signatories to the Schengen agreements, as before the said determination with regard to those parts of the Schengen *acquis* that are determined to have a legal basis in Title IIIa of the Treaty establishing the European Community.

With regard to those parts of the Schengen *acquis* that are determined to have legal base in Title VI of the Treaty on European Union, Denmark shall continue to have the same rights and obligations as the other signatories to the Schengen agreements.

Article 4

Ireland and the United Kingdom of Great Britain and Northern Ireland, which are not bound by the Schengen *acquis*, may at any time request to take part in some or all of the provisions of this *acquis*.

The Council shall decide on the request with the unanimity of its members referred to in Article 1 and of the representative of the Government of the State concerned.

Article 5

1.   Proposals and initiatives to build upon the Schengen *acquis* shall be subject to the relevant provisions of the Treaties.

In this context, where either Ireland or the United Kingdom or both have not notified the President of the Council in writing within a reasonable period that they wish to take part, the authorisation referred to in Article 5a of the Treaty establishing the European Community or Article K.12 of the Treaty on European Union shall be deemed to have been granted to the Members States referred to in Article 1 and to Ireland or the United Kingdom where either of them wishes to take part in the areas of cooperation in question.

2.   The relevant provisions of the Treaties referred to in the first subparagraph of paragraph 1 shall apply even if the Council has not adopted the measures referred to in Article 2(1), second subparagraph.

Article 6

The Republic of Iceland and the Kingdom of Norway shall be associated with the implementation of the Schengen *acquis* and its further development on the basis of the Agreement signed in Luxembourg on 19 December 1996. Appropriate procedures shall be agreed to that effect in an Agreement to be concluded with those States by the Council, acting by the unanimity of its Members mentioned in Article 1. Such Agreement shall include provisions on the contribution of Iceland and Norway to any financial consequences resulting from the implementation of this Protocol.

A separate Agreement shall be concluded with Iceland and Norway by the Council, acting unanimously, for the establishment of rights and obligations between Ireland and the United Kingdom of Great Britain and Northern Ireland on the one hand, and Iceland and Norway on the other, in domains of the Schengen *acquis* which apply to these States.

Article 7

The Council shall, acting by a qualified majority, adopt the detailed arrangements for the integration of the Schengen Secretariat into the General Secretariat of the Council.

Article 8

For the purposes of the negotiations for the admission of new Member States into the European Union, the Schengen *acquis* and further measures taken by the institutions within its scope shall be regarded as an *acquis* which must be accepted in full by all States candidates for admission.

ANNEX: SCHENGEN ACQUIS

1.   The Agreement, signed in Schengen on 14 June 1985, between the Governments of the States of the Benelux Economic Union, the Federal Republic of Germany and the French Republic on the gradual abolition of checks at their common borders.

2.   The Convention, signed in Schengen on 19 June 1990, between the Kingdom of Belgium, the Federal Republic of Germany, the French Republic, the Grand Duchy of Luxembourg and the Kingdom of the Netherlands, implementing the Agreement on the gradual abolition of checks at their common borders, signed in Schengen on 14 June 1985, with related Final Act and common declarations.

3.   The Accession Protocols and Agreements to the 1985 Agreement and the 1990 Implementation Convention with Italy (signed in Paris on 27 November 1990), Spain and Portugal (signed in Bonn on 25 June 1991), Greece (signed in Madrid on 6 November 1992), Austria

(signed in Brussels on 28 April 1995) and Denmark, Finland and Sweden (signed in Luxembourg on 19 December 1996), with related Final Acts and declarations.
4. Decisions and declarations adopted by the Executive Committee established by the 1990 Implementation Convention, as well as acts adopted for the implementation of the Convention by the organs upon which the Executive Committee has conferred decision making powers.

Protocol No. 3 on the Application of Certain Aspects of Article 14 of the Treaty Establishing the European Community to the United Kingdom and to Ireland

THE HIGH CONTRACTING PARTIES,

DESIRING to settle certain questions relating to the United Kingdom and Ireland,
HAVING REGARD to the existence for many years of special travel arrangements between the United Kingdom and Ireland,
HAVE AGREED UPON the following provisions, which shall be annexed to the Treaty establishing the European Community and to the Treaty on European Union,

Article 1
The United Kingdom shall be entitled, notwithstanding Article 14 of the Treaty establishing the European Community, any other provision of that Treaty or of the Treaty on European Union, any measure adopted under those Treaties, or any international agreement concluded by the Community or by the Community and its Member States with one or more third States, to exercise at its frontiers with other Member States such controls on persons seeking to enter the United Kingdom as it may consider necessary for the purpose:
(a) of verifying the right to enter the United Kingdom of citizens of States which are Contracting Parties to the Agreement on the European Economic Area and of their dependants exercising rights conferred by Community law, as well as citizens of other States on whom such rights have been conferred by an agreement by which the United Kingdom is bound; and
(b) of determining whether or not to grant other persons permission to enter the United Kingdom.
Nothing in Article 14 of the Treaty establishing the European Community or in any other provision of that Treaty or of the Treaty on European Union or in any measure adopted under them shall prejudice the right of the United Kingdom to adopt or exercise any such controls. References to the United Kingdom in this Article shall include territories for whose external relations the United Kingdom is responsible.

Article 2
The United Kingdom and Ireland may continue to make arrangements between themselves relating to the movement of persons between their territories ("the Common Travel Area"), while fully respecting the rights of persons referred to in Article 1, first paragraph, point (a) of this Protocol. Accordingly, as long as they maintain such arrangements, the provisions of Article 1 of this Protocol shall apply to Ireland under the same terms and conditions as for the United Kingdom. Nothing in Article 14 of the Treaty establishing the European Community, in any other provision of that Treaty or of the Treaty on European Union or in any measure adopted under them, shall affect any such arrangements.

Article 3

The other Member States shall be entitled to exercise at their frontiers or at any point of entry into their territory such controls on persons seeking to enter their territory from the United Kingdom or any territories whose external relations are under its responsibility for the same purposes stated in Article 1 of this Protocol, or from Ireland as long as the provisions of Article 1 of this Protocol apply to Ireland.

Nothing in Article 14 of the Treaty establishing the European Community or in any other provision of that Treaty or of the Treaty on European Union or in any measure adopted under them shall prejudice the right of the other Member States to adopt or exercise any such controls.

Protocol No. 4 on the Position of the United Kingdom and Ireland

THE HIGH CONTRACTING PARTIES,

DESIRING to settle certain questions relating to the United Kingdom and Ireland,
HAVING REGARD to the Protocol on the application of certain aspects of Article 14 of the Treaty establishing the European Community to the United Kingdom and to Ireland,
HAVE AGREED UPON the following provisions which shall be annexed to the Treaty establishing the European Community and to the Treaty on European Union,

Article 1

Subject to Article 3, the United Kingdom and Ireland shall not take part in the adoption by the Council of proposed measures pursuant to Title IIIa of the Treaty establishing the European Community. By way of derogation from Article 148(2) of the Treaty establishing the European Community, a qualified majority shall be defined as the same proportion of the weighted votes of the members of the Council concerned as laid down in the said Article 148(2). The unanimity of the members of the Council, with the exception of the representatives of the governments of the United Kingdom and Ireland, shall be necessary for decisions of the Council which must be adopted unanimously.

Article 2

In consequence of Article 1 and subject to Articles 3, 4 and 6, none of the provisions of Title IIIa of the Treaty establishing the European Community, no measure adopted pursuant to that Title, no provision of any international agreement concluded by the Community pursuant to that Title, and no decision of the Court of Justice interpreting any such provision or measure shall be binding upon or applicable in the United Kingdom or Ireland; and no such provision, measure or decision shall in any way affect the competences, rights and obligations of those States; and no such provision, measure or decision shall in any way affect the *acquis communautaire* nor form part of Community law as they apply to the United Kingdom or Ireland.

Article 3

1.   The United Kingdom or Ireland may notify the President of the Council in writing, within three months after a proposal or initiative has been presented to the Council pursuant to Title IIIa of the Treaty establishing the European Community, that it wishes to take part in the adoption and application of any such proposed measure, whereupon that State shall be entitled to do so. By way of derogation from Article 148(2) of the Treaty establishing the European Community, a qualified majority shall be defined as

the same proportion of the weighted votes of the members of the Council concerned as laid down in the said Article 148(2).

The unanimity of the members of the Council, with the exception of a member which has not made such a notification, shall be necessary for decisions of the Council which must be adopted unanimously. A measure adopted under this paragraph shall be binding upon all Member States which took part in its adoption.

2.   If after a reasonable period of time a measure referred to in paragraph 1 cannot be adopted with the United Kingdom or Ireland taking part, the Council may adopt such measure in accordance with Article 1 without the participation of the United Kingdom or Ireland. In that case Article 2 applies.

Article 4

The United Kingdom or Ireland may at any time after the adoption of a measure by the Council pursuant to Title IIIa of the Treaty establishing the European Community notify its intention to the Council and to the Commission that it wishes to accept that measure. In that case, the procedure provided for in Article 5a(3) of the Treaty establishing the European Community shall apply *mutatis mutandis*.

Article 5

A Member State which is not bound by a measure adopted pursuant to Title IIIa of the Treaty establishing the European Community shall bear no financial consequences of that measure other than administrative costs entailed for the institutions.

Article 6

Where, in cases referred to in this Protocol, the United Kingdom or Ireland is bound by a measure adopted by the Council pursuant to Title IIIa of the Treaty establishing the European Community, the relevant provisions of that Treaty, including Article 73p, shall apply to that State in relation to that measure.

Article 7

Articles 3 and 4 shall be without prejudice to the Protocol integrating the Schengen *acquis* into the framework of the European Union.

Article 8

Ireland may notify the President of the Council in writing that it no longer wishes to be covered by the terms of this Protocol. In that case, the normal treaty provisions will apply to Ireland.

Protocol No. 5 on the Position of Denmark

THE HIGH CONTRACTING PARTIES,

RECALLING the Decision of the Heads of State or Government, meeting within the European Council at Edinburgh on 12 December 1992, concerning certain problems raised by Denmark on the Treaty on European Union,

HAVING NOTED the position of Denmark with regard to Citizenship, Economic and Monetary Union, Defence Policy and Justice and Home Affairs as laid down in the Edinburgh Decision,

BEARING IN MIND Article 3 of the Protocol integrating the Schengen *acquis* into the framework of the European Union,

HAVE AGREED UPON the following provisions, which shall be annexed to the Treaty establishing the European Community and to the Treaty on European Union,

PART I

Article 1

Denmark shall not take part in the adoption by the Council of proposed measures pursuant to Title IIIa of the Treaty establishing the European Community. By way of derogation from Article 148(2) of the Treaty establishing the European Community, a qualified majority shall be defined as the same proportion of the weighted votes of the members of the Council concerned as laid down in the said Article 148(2). The unanimity of the members of the Council, with the exception of the representative of the government of Denmark, shall be necessary for the decisions of the Council which must be adopted unanimously.

Article 2

None of the provisions of Title IIIa of the Treaty establishing the European Community, no measure adopted pursuant to that Title, no provision of any international agreement concluded by the Community pursuant to that Title, and no decision of the Court of Justice interpreting any such provision or measure shall be binding upon or applicable in Denmark; and no such provision, measure or decision shall in any way affect the competences, rights and obligations of Denmark; and no such provision, measure or decision shall in any way affect the *acquis communautaire* nor form part of Community law as they apply to Denmark.

Article 3

Denmark shall bear no financial consequences of measures referred to in Article 1, other than administrative costs entailed for the institutions.

Article 4

Articles 1, 2 and 3 shall not apply to measures determining the third countries whose nationals must be in possession of a visa when crossing the external borders of the Member States, or measures relating to a uniform format for visas.

Article 5

1.   Denmark shall decide within a period of 6 months after the Council has decided on a proposal or initiative to build upon the Schengen *acquis* under the provisions of Title IIIa of the Treaty establishing the European Community, whether it will implement this decision in its national law. If it decides to do so, this decision will create an obligation under international law between Denmark and the other Member States referred to in Article 1 of the Protocol integrating the Schengen *acquis* into the framework of the European Union as well as Ireland or the United Kingdom if those Member States take part in the areas of cooperation in question.

2.   If Denmark decides not to implement a decision of the Council as referred to in paragraph 1, the Member States referred to in Article 1 of the Protocol integrating the Schengen *acquis* into the framework of the European Union will consider appropriate measures to be taken.

PART II

Article 6
With regard to measures adopted by the Council in the field of Articles J.3(1) and J.7 of the Treaty on European Union, Denmark does not participate in the elaboration and the implementation of decisions and actions of the Union which have defence implications, but will not prevent the development of closer cooperation between Member States in this area. Therefore Denmark shall not participate in their adoption. Denmark shall not be obliged to contribute to the financing of operational expenditure arising from such measures.

PART III

Article 7
At any time Denmark may, in accordance with its constitutional requirements, inform the other Member States that it no longer wishes to avail itself of all or part of this Protocol. In that event, Denmark will apply in full all relevant measures then in force taken within the framework of the European Union.

Protocol No. 7 on the Institutions with the Prospect of Enlargement of the European Union

THE HIGH CONTRACTING PARTIES,

HAVE AGREED UPON the following provisions, which shall be annexed to the Treaty on European Union and to the Treaties establishing the European Communities,

Article 1
At the date of entry into force of the first enlargement of the Union, notwithstanding Article 157(1) of the Treaty establishing the European Community, Article 9(1) of the Treaty establishing the European Coal and Steel Community and Article 126(1) of the Treaty establishing the European Atomic Energy Community, the Commission shall comprise one national of each of the Member States, provided that, by that date, the weighting of the votes in the Council has been modified, whether by re-weighting of the votes or by dual majority, in a manner acceptable to all Member States, taking into account all relevant elements, notably compensating those Member States which give up the possibility of nominating a second member of the Commission.

Article 2
At least one year before the membership of the European Union exceeds twenty, a conference of representatives of the governments of the Member States shall be convened in order to carry out a comprehensive review of the provisions of the Treaties on the composition and functioning of the institutions.

Protocol No. 8 on the Location of the Seats of the Institutions and of Certain Bodies and Departments of the European Communities and of Europol

THE REPRESENTATIVES OF THE GOVERNMENTS OF THE MEMBER STATES,

HAVING REGARD to Article 216 of the Treaty establishing the European Community, Article 77 of the Treaty establishing the European Coal and Steel Community and Article 189 of the Treaty establishing the European Atomic Energy Community,
HAVING REGARD to the Treaty on European Union,
RECALLING AND CONFIRMING the Decision of 8 April 1965, and without prejudice to the decisions concerning the seat of future institutions, bodies and departments,
HAVE AGREED UPON the following provisions, which shall be annexed to the Treaty on European Union and the Treaties establishing the European Communities,

Sole Article
(a) The European Parliament shall have its seat in Strasbourg where the 12 periods of monthly plenary sessions, including the budget session, shall be held. The periods of additional plenary sessions shall be held in Brussels. The committees of the European Parliament shall meet in Brussels. The General Secretariat of the European Parliament and its departments shall remain in Luxembourg.
(b) The Council shall have its seat in Brussels. During the months of April, June and October, the Council shall hold its meetings in Luxembourg.
(c) The Commission shall have its seat in Brussels. The departments listed in Articles 7, 8 and 9 of the Decision of 8 April 1965 shall be established in Luxembourg.
(d) The Court of Justice and the Court of First Instance shall have their seats in Luxembourg.
(e) The Court of Auditors shall have its seat in Luxembourg.
(f) The Economic and Social Committee shall have its seat in Brussels.
(g) The Committee of the Regions shall have its seat in Brussels.
(h) The European Investment Bank shall have its seat in Luxembourg.
(i) The European Monetary Institute and the European Central Bank shall have their seat in Frankfurt.
(j) The European Police Office (Europol) shall have its seat in The Hague.

Protocol No. 9 on the Role of National Parliaments in the European Union

THE HIGH CONTRACTING PARTIES,

RECALLING that scrutiny by individual national parliaments of their own government in relation to the activities of the Union is a matter for the particular constitutional organisation and practice of each Member State,
DESIRING, however, to encourage greater involvement of national parliaments in the activities of the European Union and to enhance their ability to express their views on matters which may be of particular interest to them,
HAVE AGREED UPON the following provisions, which shall be annexed to the Treaty on European Union and the Treaties establishing the European Communities,

I. INFORMATION FOR NATIONAL PARLIAMENTS OF MEMBER STATES

1. All Commission consultation documents (green and white papers and communications) shall be promptly forwarded to national parliaments of the Member States.
2. Commission proposals for legislation as defined by the Council in accordance with Article 151(3) of the Treaty establishing the European Community, shall be made available in good time so that the government of each Member State may ensure that its own national parliament receives them as appropriate.

3.   A six-week period shall elapse between a legislative proposal or a proposal for a measure to be adopted under Title VI of the Treaty on European Union being made available in all languages to the European Parliament and the Council by the Commission and the date when it is placed on a Council agenda for decision either for the adoption of an act or for adoption of a common position pursuant to Article 189b or 189c of the Treaty establishing the European Community, subject to exceptions on grounds of urgency, the reasons for which shall be stated in the act or common position.

II. THE CONFERENCE OF EUROPEAN AFFAIRS COMMITTEES

4.   The Conference of European Affairs Committees, hereinafter referred to as COSAC, established in Paris on 16-17 November 1989, may make any contribution it deems appropriate for the attention of the institutions of the European Union, in particular on the basis of draft legal texts which representatives of governments of the Member States may decide by common accord to forward to it, in view of the nature of their subject matter.
5.   COSAC may examine any legislative proposal or initiative in relation to the establishment of an area of freedom, security and justice which might have a direct bearing on the rights and freedoms of individuals. The European Parliament, the Council and the Commission shall be informed of any contribution made by COSAC under this point.
6.   COSAC may address to the European Parliament, the Council and the Commission any contribution which it deems appropriate on the legislative activities of the Union, notably in relation to the application of the principle of subsidiarity, the area of freedom, security and justice as well as questions regarding fundamental rights.
7.   Contributions made by COSAC shall in no way bind national parliaments or prejudge their position.

Protocol No. 18 on the Statute of the European System of Central Banks and of the European Central Bank

THE HIGH CONTRACTING PARTIES,

DESIRING to lay down the Statute of the European System of Central Banks and of the European Central Bank provided for in Article 4a of the Treaty establishing the European Community,
HAVE AGREED upon the following provisions, which shall be annexed to the Treaty establishing the European Community:

Chapter I Constitution of the ESCB

Article 1 The European System of Central Banks
1.1.   The European System of Central Banks (ESCB) and the European Central Bank (ECB) shall be established in accordance with Article 4a of this Treaty; they shall perform their tasks and carry on their activities in accordance with the provisions of this Treaty and of this Statute.
1.2.   In accordance with Article 106(1) of this Treaty, the ESCB shall be composed of the ECB and of the central banks of the Member States ("national central banks"). The Institut monetaire luxembourgeois will be the central bank of Luxembourg.

Chapter II Objectives and Tasks of the ESCB

Article 2 Objectives

In accordance with Article 105(1) of this Treaty, the primary objective of the ESCB shall be to maintain price stability. Without prejudice to the objective of price stability, it shall support the general economic policies in the Community with a view to contributing to the achievement of the objectives of the Community as laid down in Article 2 of this Treaty. The ESCB shall act in accordance with the principle of an open market economy with free competition, favouring an efficient allocation of resources, and in compliance with the principles set out in Article 3a of this Treaty.

Article 3 Tasks

3.1.   In accordance with Article 105(2) of this Treaty, the basic tasks to be carried out through the ESCB shall be:
—   to define and implement the monetary policy of the Community;
—   to conduct foreign-exchange operations consistent with the provisions of Article 109 of this Treaty;
—   to hold and manage the official foreign reserves of the Member States;
—   to promote the smooth operation of payment systems.
3.2.   In accordance with Article 105(3) of this Treaty, the third indent of Article 3.1 shall be without prejudice to the holding and management by the governments of Member States of foreign-exchange working balances.
3.3.   In accordance with Article 105(5) of this Treaty, the ESCB shall contribute to the smooth conduct of policies pursued by the competent authorities relating to the prudential supervision of credit institutions and the stability of the financial system.

Article 4 Advisory Functions

In accordance with Article 105(4) of this Treaty:
(a)   the ECB shall be consulted:
—   on any proposed Community act in its fields of competence;
—   by national authorities regarding any draft legislative provision in its fields of competence, but within the limits and under the conditions set out by the Council in accordance with the procedure laid down in Article 42;
(b)   the ECB may submit opinions to the appropriate Community institutions or bodies or to national authorities on matters in its fields of competence.

Article 5 Collection of Statistical Information

5.1.   In order to undertake the tasks of the ESCB, the ECB, assisted by the national central banks, shall collect the necessary statistical information either from the competent national authorities or directly from economic agents. For these purposes it shall cooperate with the Community institutions or bodies and with the competent authorities of the Member States or third countries and with international organizations.
5.2.   The national central banks shall carry out, to the extent possible, the tasks described in Article 5.1.
5.3.   The ECB shall contribute to the harmonization, where necessary, of the rules and practices governing the collection, compilation and distribution of statistics in the areas within its fields of competence.
5.4.   The Council, in accordance with the procedure laid down in Article 42, shall define the natural and legal persons subject to reporting requirements, the confidentiality regime and the appropriate provisions for enforcement.

Article 6 International Cooperation

6.1.   In the field of international cooperation involving the tasks entrusted to the ESCB, the ECB shall decide how the ESCB shall be represented.

6.2.   The ECB and, subject to its approval, the national central banks may participate in international monetary institutions.

6.3.   Articles 6.1 and 6.2 shall be without prejudice to Article 109(4) of this Treaty.

Chapter III Organization of The ESCB

Article 7 Independence

In accordance with Article 107 of this Treaty, when exercising the powers and carrying out the tasks and duties conferred upon them by this Treaty and this Statute, neither the ECB, nor a national central bank, nor any member of their decision-making bodies shall seek or take instructions from Community institutions or bodies, from any government of a Member State or from any other body. The Community institutions and bodies and the governments of the Member States undertake to respect this principle and not to seek to influence the members of the decision-making bodies of the ECB or of the national central banks in the performance of their tasks.

Article 8 General principle

The ESCB shall be governed by the decision-making bodies of the ECB.

Article 9 The European Central Bank

9.1.   The ECB which, in accordance with Article 106(2) of this Treaty, shall have legal personality, shall enjoy in each of the Member States the most extensive legal capacity accorded to legal persons under its law; it may, in particular, acquire or dispose of movable and immovable property and may be a party to legal proceedings.

9.2.   The ECB shall ensure that the tasks conferred upon the ESCB under Article 105(2), (3) and (5) of this Treaty are implemented either by its own activities pursuant to this Statute or through the national central banks pursuant to Articles 12.1 and 14.

9.3.   In accordance with Article 106(3) of this Treaty, the decision-making bodies of the ECB shall be the Governing Council and the Executive Board.

Article 10 The Governing Council

10.1. In accordance with Article 109a(1) of this Treaty, the Governing Council shall comprise the members of the Executive Board of the ECB and the Governors of the national central banks.

10.2. Subject to Article 10.3, only members of the Governing Council present in person shall have the right to vote. By way of derogation from this rule, the Rules of Procedure referred to in Article 12.3 may lay down that members of the Governing Council may cast their vote by means of teleconferencing. These rules shall also provide that a member of the Governing Council who is prevented from voting for a prolonged period may appoint an alternate as a member of the Governing Council.

Subject to Articles 10.3 and 11.3, each member of the Governing Council shall have one vote. Save as otherwise provided for in this Statute, the Governing Council shall act by a simple majority. In the event of a tie, the President shall have the casting vote.

In order for the Governing Council to vote, there shall be a quorum of two-thirds of the members. If the quorum is not met, the President may convene an extraordinary meeting at which decisions may be taken without regard to the quorum.

10.3. For any decisions to be taken under Articles 28, 29, 30, 32, 33 and 51, the votes in the Governing Council shall be weighted according to the national central banks' shares in the subscribed capital of the ECB. The weights of the votes of the members of the Executive Board shall be zero. A decision requiring a qualified majority shall be adopted if the votes cast in favour represent at least two-thirds of the subscribed capital of the ECB and represent at least half of the shareholders. If a Governor is unable to be present, he may nominate an alternate to cast his weighted vote.

10.4. The proceedings of the meetings shall be confidential. The Governing Council may decide to make the outcome of its deliberations public.

10.5. The Governing Council shall meet at least 10 times a year.

Article 11 The Executive Board

11.1. In accordance with Article 109a(2)(a) of this Treaty, the Executive Board shall comprise the President, the Vice-President and four other members.

The members shall perform their duties on a full-time basis. No member shall engage in any occupation, whether gainful or not, unless exemption is exceptionally granted by the Governing Council.

11.2. In accordance with Article 109a(2)(b) of this Treaty, the President, the Vice-President and the other Members of the Executive Board shall be appointed from among persons of recognized standing and professional experience in monetary or banking matters by common accord of the governments of the Member States at the level of the Heads of State or Government, on a recommendation from the Council after it has consulted the European Parliament and the Governing Council.

Their term of office shall be eight years and shall not be renewable.

Only nationals of Member States may be members of the Executive Board.

11.3. The terms and conditions of employment of the members of the Executive Board, in particular their salaries, pensions and other social security benefits shall be the subject of contracts with the ECB and shall be fixed by the Governing Council on a proposal from a Committee comprising three members appointed by the Governing Council and three members appointed by the Council. The members of the Executive Board shall not have the right to vote on matters referred to in this paragraph.

11.4. If a member of the Executive Board no longer fulfils the conditions required for the performance of his duties or if he has been guilty of serious misconduct, the Court of Justice may, on application by the Governing Council or the Executive Board, compulsorily retire him.

11.5. Each member of the Executive Board present in person shall have the right to vote and shall have, for that purpose, one vote. Save as otherwise provided, the Executive Board shall act by a simple majority of the votes cast. In the event of a tie, the President shall have the casting vote. The voting arrangements shall be specified in the Rules of Procedure referred to in Article 12.3.

11.6. The Executive Board shall be responsible for the current business of the ECB.

11.7. Any vacancy on the Executive Board shall be filled by the appointment of a new member in accordance with Article 11.2.

Article 12 Responsibilities of the Decision-making Bodies

12.1. The Governing Council shall adopt the guidelines and make the decisions necessary to ensure the performance of the tasks entrusted to the ESCB under this Treaty and this Statute. The Governing Council shall formulate the monetary policy of the Community including, as appropriate, decisions relating to intermediate monetary objectives, key interest rates and the supply of reserves in the ESCB, and shall establish the necessary guidelines for their implementation.

The Executive Board shall implement monetary policy in accordance with the guidelines and decisions laid down by the Governing Council. In doing so the Executive Board shall give the necessary instructions to national central banks. In addition the

Executive Board may have certain powers delegated to it where the Governing Council so decides.

To the extent deemed possible and appropriate and without prejudice to the provisions of this Article, the ECB shall have recourse to the national central banks to carry out operations which form part of the tasks of the ESCB.
12.2. The Executive Board shall have responsibility for the preparation of meetings of the Governing Council.
12.3. The Governing Council shall adopt Rules of Procedure which determine the internal organization of the ECB and its decision-making bodies.
12.4. The Governing Council shall exercise the advisory functions referred to in Article 4.
12.5. The Governing Council shall take the decisions referred to in Article 6.

Article 13 The President
13.1. The President or, in his absence, the Vice-President shall chair the Governing Council and the Executive Board of the ECB.
13.2. Without prejudice to Article 39, the President or his nominee shall represent the ECB externally.

Article 14 National Central Banks
14.1. In accordance with Article 108 of this Treaty, each Member State shall ensure, at the latest at the date of the establishment of the ESCB, that its national legislation, including the statutes of its national central bank, is compatible with this Treaty and this Statute.
14.2. The statutes of the national central banks shall, in particular, provide that the term of office of a Governor of a national central bank shall be no less than five years.

A Governor may be relieved from office only if he no longer fulfils the conditions required for the performance of his duties or if he has been guilty of serious misconduct. A decision to this effect may be referred to the Court of Justice by the Governor concerned or the Governing Council on grounds of infringement of this Treaty or of any rule of law relating to its application. Such proceedings shall be instituted within two months of the publication of the decision or of its notification to the plaintiff or, in the absence thereof, of the day on which it came to the knowledge of the latter, as the case may be.
14.3. The national central banks are an integral part of the ESCB and shall act in accordance with the guidelines and instructions of the ECB. The Governing Council shall take the necessary steps to ensure compliance with the guidelines and instructions of the ECB, and shall require that any necessary information be given to it.
14.4. National central banks may perform functions other than those specified in this Statute unless the Governing Council finds, by a majority of two thirds of the votes cast, that these interfere with the objectives and tasks of the ESCB. Such functions shall be performed on the responsibility and liability of national central banks and shall not be regarded as being part of the functions of the ESCB.

Article 15 Reporting Commitments
15.1. The ECB shall draw up and publish reports on the activities of the ESCB at least quarterly.
15.2. A consolidated financial statement of the ESCB shall be published each week.
15.3. In accordance with Article 109b(3) of this Treaty, the ECB shall address an annual report on the activities of the ESCB and on the monetary policy of both the previous and the current year to the European Parliament, the Council and the Commission, and also to the European Council.

15.4. The reports and statements referred to in this Article shall be made available to interested parties free of charge.

Article 16 Banknotes

In accordance with Article 105a(1) of this Treaty, the Governing Council shall have the exclusive right to authorize the issue of banknotes within the Community. The ECB and the national central banks may issue such notes. The banknotes issued by the ECB and the national central banks shall be the only such notes to have the status of legal tender within the Community.

The ECB shall respect as far as possible existing practices regarding the issue and design of banknotes.

Chapter IV Monetary Functions And Operations of The ESCB

Article 17 Accounts with the ECB and the National Central Banks

In order to conduct their operations, the ECB and the national central banks may open accounts for credit institutions, public entities and other market participants and accept assets, including book-entry securities, as collateral.

Article 18 Open Market and Credit Operations

18.1. In order to achieve the objectives of the ESCB and to carry out its tasks, the ECB and the national central banks may:

— operate in the financial markets by buying and selling outright (spot and forward) or under repurchase agreement and by lending or borrowing claims and marketable instruments, whether in Community or in non-Community currencies, as well as precious metals;

— conduct credit operations with credit institutions and other market participants, with lending being based on adequate collateral.

18.2. The ECB shall establish general principles for open market and credit operations carried out by itself or the national central banks, including for the announcement of conditions under which they stand ready to enter into such transactions.

Article 19 Minimum Reserves

19.1. Subject to Article 2, the ECB may require credit institutions established in Member States to hold minimum reserves on accounts with the ECB and national central banks in pursuance of monetary policy objectives. Regulations concerning the calculation and determination of the required minimum reserves may be established by the Governing Council. In cases of non-compliance the ECB shall be entitled to levy penalty interest and to impose other sanctions with comparable effect.

19.2. For the application of this Article, the Council shall, in accordance with the procedure laid down in Article 42, define the basis for minimum reserves and the maximum permissible ratios between those reserves and their basis, as well as the appropriate sanctions in cases of non-compliance.

Article 20 Other Instruments of Monetary Control

The Governing Council may, by a majority of two thirds of the votes cast, decide upon the use of such other operational methods of monetary control as it sees fit, respecting Article 2.

The Council shall, in accordance with the procedure laid down in Article 42, define the scope of such methods if they impose obligations on third parties.

Article 21 Operations with Public Entities

21.1. In accordance with Article 104 of this Treaty, overdrafts or any other type of credit facility with the ECB or with the national central banks in favour of Community institutions or bodies, central governments, regional, local or other public authorities, other bodies governed by public law, or public undertakings of Member States shall be prohibited, as shall the purchase directly from them by the ECB or national central banks of debt instruments.

21.2. The ECB and national central banks may act as fiscal agents for the entities referred to in Article 21.1.

21.3. The provisions of this Article shall not apply to publicly-owned credit institutions which, in the context of the supply of reserves by central banks, shall be given the same treatment by national central banks and the ECB as private credit institutions.

Article 22 Clearing and Payment Systems

The ECB and national central banks may provide facilities, and the ECB may make regulations, to ensure efficient and sound clearing and payment systems within the Community and with other countries.

Article 23 External operations

The ECB and national central banks may:
—   establish relations with central banks and financial institutions in other countries and, where appropriate, with international organizations;
—   acquire and sell spot and forward all types of foreign exchange assets and precious metals; the term "foreign exchange asset" shall include securities and all other assets in the currency of any country or units of account and in whatever form held;
—   hold and manage the assets referred to in this Article;
—   conduct all types of banking transactions in relations with third countries and international organizations, including borrowing and lending operations.

Article 24 Other Operations

In addition to operations arising from their tasks, the ECB and national central banks may enter into operations for their administrative purposes or for their staff.

Chapter V Prudential Supervision

Article 25 Prudential Supervision

25.1. The ECB may offer advice to and be consulted by the Council, the Commission and the competent authorities of the Member States on the scope and implementation of Community legislation relating to the prudential supervision of credit institutions and to the stability of the financial system.

25.2. In accordance with any decision of the Council under Article 105(6) of this Treaty, the ECB may perform specific tasks concerning policies relating to the prudential supervision of credit institutions and other financial institutions with the exception of insurance undertakings.

Chapter VI Financial Provisions of The ESCB

Article 26 Financial Accounts

26.1. The financial year of the ECB and national central banks shall begin on the first day of January and end on the last day of December.

26.2. The annual accounts of the ECB shall be drawn up by the Executive Board, in accordance with the principles established by the Governing Council. The accounts shall be approved by the Governing Council and shall thereafter be published.

26.3. For analytical and operational purposes, the Executive Board shall draw up a consolidated balance sheet of the ESCB, comprising those assets and liabilities of the national central banks that fall within the ESCB.

26.4. For the application of this Article, the Governing Council shall establish the necessary rules for standardizing the accounting and reporting of operations undertaken by the national central banks.

Article 27 Auditing

27.1. The accounts of the ECB and national central banks shall be audited by independent external auditors recommended by the Governing Council and approved by the Council. The auditors shall have full power to examine all books and accounts of the ECB and national central banks and obtain full information about their transactions.

27.2. The provisions of Article 188c of this Treaty shall only apply to an examination of the operational efficiency of the management of the ECB.

Article 28 Capital of the ECB

28.1. The capital of the ECB, which shall become operational upon its establishment, shall be ECU 5.000 million. The capital may be increased by such amounts as may be decided by the Governing Council acting by the qualified majority provided for in Article 10.3, within the limits and under the conditions set by the Council under the procedure laid down in Article 42.

28.2. The national central banks shall be the sole subscribers to and holders of the capital of the ECB. The subscription of capital shall be according to the key established in accordance with Article 29.

28.3. The Governing Council, acting by the qualified majority provided for in Article 10.3, shall determine the extent to which and the form in which the capital shall be paid up.

28.4. Subject to Article 28.5, the shares of the national central banks in the subscribed capital of the ECB may not be transferred, pledged or attached.

28.5. If the key referred to in Article 29 is adjusted, the national central banks shall transfer among themselves capital shares to the extent necessary to ensure that the distribution of capital shares corresponds to the adjusted key. The Governing Council shall determine the terms and conditions of such transfers.

Article 29 Key for Capital Subscription

29.1. When in accordance with the procedure referred to in Article 1091(1) of this Treaty the ESCB and the ECB have been established, the key for subscription of the ECB's capital shall be established. Each national central bank shall be assigned a weighting in this key which shall be equal to the sum of:

—   50% of the share of its respective Member State in the population of the Community in the penultimate year preceding the establishment of the ESCB;

—   50% of the share of its respective Member State in the gross domestic product at market prices of the Community as recorded in the last five years preceding the penultimate year before the establishment of the ESCB;

The percentages shall be rounded up to the nearest multiple of 0.05 percentage points.

29.2. The statistical data to be used for the application of this Article shall be provided by the Commission in accordance with the rules adopted by the Council under the procedure provided for in Article 42.

29.3. The weightings assigned to the national central banks shall be adjusted every five years after the establishment of the ESCB by analogy with the provisions laid down in Article 29.1. The adjusted key shall apply with effect from the first day of the following year.

29.4. The Governing Council shall take all other measures necessary for the application of this Article.

Article 30 Transfer of Foreign Reserve Assets to the ECB

30.1. Without prejudice to Article 28, the ECB shall be provided by the national central banks with foreign reserve assets, other than Member States' currencies, ECUs, IMF reserve positions and SDRs, up to an amount equivalent to ECU 50.000 million. The Governing Council shall decide upon the proportion to be called up by the ECB following its establishment and the amounts called up at later dates. The ECB shall have the full right to hold and manage the foreign reserves that are transferred to it and to use them for the purposes set out in this Statute.

30.2. The contributions of each national central bank shall be fixed in proportion to its share in the subscribed capital of the ECB.

30.3. Each national central bank shall be credited by the ECB with a claim equivalent to its contribution. The Governing Council shall determine the denomination and remuneration of such claims.

30.4. Further calls of foreign reserve assets beyond the limit set in Article 30.1 may be effected by the ECB, in accordance with Article 30.2, within the limits and under the conditions set by the Council in accordance with the procedure laid down in Article 42.

30.5. The ECB may hold and manage IMF reserve positions and SDRs and provide for the pooling of such assets.

30.6. The Governing Council shall take all other measures necessary for the application of this Article.

Article 31 Foreign Reserve Assets Held by National Central Banks

31.1. The national central banks shall be allowed to perform transactions in fulfilment of their obligations towards international organizations in accordance with Article 23.

31.2. All other operations in foreign reserve assets remaining with the national central banks after the transfers referred to in Article 30, and Member States' transactions with their foreign exchange working balances shall, above a certain limit to be established within the framework of Article 31.3, be subject to approval by the ECB in order to ensure consistency with the exchange rate and monetary policies of the Community.

31.3. The Governing Council shall issue guidelines with a view to facilitating such operations.

Article 32 Allocation of Monetary Income of National Central Banks

32.1. The income accruing to the national central banks in the performance of the ESCB's monetary policy function (hereinafter referred to as "monetary income") shall be allocated at the end of each financial year in accordance with the provisions of this Article.

32.2. Subject to Article 32.3, the amount of each national central bank's monetary income shall be equal to its annual income derived from its assets held against notes in circulation and deposit liabilities to credit institutions. These assets shall be earmarked by national central banks in accordance with guidelines to be established by the Governing Council.

32.3. If, after the start of the third stage, the balance sheet structures of the national central banks do not, in the judgment of the Governing Council, permit the application of Article 32.2, the Governing Council, acting by a qualified majority, may decide that, by way of derogation from Article 32.2, monetary income shall be measured according to an alternative method for a period of not more than five years.

32.4. The amount of each national central bank's monetary income shall be reduced by an amount equivalent to any interest paid by that central bank on its deposit liabilities to credit institutions in accordance with Article 19.

The Governing Council may decide that national central banks shall be indemnified against costs incurred in connection with the issue of banknotes or in exceptional circumstances for specific losses arising from monetary policy operations undertaken for the ESCB. Indemnification shall be in a form deemed appropriate in the judgment of the Governing Council; these amounts may be offset against the national central banks' monetary income.

32.5. The sum of the national central banks' monetary income shall be allocated to the national central banks in proportion to their paid-up shares in the capital of the ECB, subject to any decision taken by the Governing Council pursuant to Article 33.2.

32.6. The clearing and settlement of the balances arising from the allocation of monetary income shall be carried out by the ECB in accordance with guidelines established by the Governing Council.

32.7. The Governing Council shall take all other measures necessary for the application of this Article.

Article 33 Allocation of Net Profits and Losses of the ECB

33.1. The net profit of the ECB shall be transferred in the following order:
(a)   an amount to be determined by the Governing Council, which may not exceed 20% of the net profit, shall be transferred to the general reserve fund subject to a limit equal to 100% of the capital;
(b)   the remaining net profit shall be distributed to the shareholders of the ECB in proportion to their paid-up shares.

33.2. In the event of a loss incurred by the ECB, the shortfall may be offset against the general reserve fund of the ECB and, if necessary, following a decision by the Governing Council, against the monetary income of the relevant financial year in proportion and up to the amounts allocated to the national central banks in accordance with Article 32.5.

Chapter VII General Provisions

Article 34 Legal acts

34.1. In accordance with Article 108a of this Treaty, the ECB shall:
—   make regulations to the extent necessary to implement the tasks defined in Article 3.1, first indent, Articles 19.1, 22 or 25.2 and in cases which shall be laid down in the acts of the Council referred to in Article 42;
—   take decisions necessary for carrying out the tasks entrusted to the ESCB under this Treaty and this Statute;
—   make recommendations and deliver opinions.

34.2. A regulation shall have general application. It shall be binding in its entirety and directly applicable in all Member States.

Recommendations and opinions shall have no binding force.

A decision shall be binding in its entirety upon those to whom it is addressed.

Articles 190 to 192 of this Treaty shall apply to regulations and decisions adopted by the ECB.

The ECB may decide to publish its decisions, recommendations and opinions.

34.3. Within the limits and under the conditions adopted by the Council under the procedure laid down in Article 42, the ECB shall be entitled to impose fines or periodic penalty payments on undertakings for failure to comply with obligations under its regulations and decisions.

Article 35 Judicial Control and Related Matters

35.1. The acts or omissions of the ECB shall be open to review or interpretation by the Court of Justice in the cases and under the conditions laid down in this Treaty. The ECB may institute proceedings in the cases and under the conditions laid down in this Treaty.

35.2. Disputes between the ECB, on the one hand, and its creditors, debtors or any other person, on the other, shall be decided by the competent national courts, save where jurisdiction has been conferred upon the Court of Justice.

35.3. The ECB shall be subject to the liability regime provided for in Article 215 of this Treaty. The national central banks shall be liable according to their respective national laws.

35.4. The Court of Justice shall have jurisdiction to give judgment pursuant to any arbitration clause contained in a contract concluded by or on behalf of the ECB, whether that contract be governed by public or private law.

35.5. A decision of the ECB to bring an action before the Court of Justice shall be taken by the Governing Council.

35.6. The Court of Justice shall have jurisdiction in disputes concerning the fulfilment by a national central bank of obligations under this Statute. If the ECB considers that a national central bank has failed to fulfil an obligation under this Statute, it shall deliver a reasoned opinion on the matter after giving the national central bank concerned the opportunity to submit its observations. If the national central bank concerned does not comply with the opinion within the period laid down by the ECB, the latter may bring the matter before the Court of Justice.

Article 36 Staff

36.1. The Governing Council, on a proposal from the Executive Board, shall lay down the conditions of employment of the staff of the ECB.

36.2. The Court of Justice shall have jurisdiction in any dispute between the ECB and its servants within the limits and under the conditions laid down in the conditions of employment.

Article 37 Seat

Before the end of 1992, the decision as to where the seat of the ECB will be established shall be taken by common accord of the governments of the Member States at the level of Heads of State or Government.

Article 38 Professional Secrecy

38.1. Members of the governing bodies and the staff of the ECB and the national central banks shall be required, even after their duties have ceased, not to disclose information of the kind covered by the obligation of professional secrecy.

38.2. Persons having access to data covered by Community legislation imposing an obligation of secrecy shall be subject to such legislation.

Article 39 Signatories

The ECB shall be legally committed to third parties by the President or by two members of the Executive Board or by the signatures of two members of the staff of the ECB who have been duly authorized by the President to sign on behalf of the ECB.

Article 40 Privileges and Immunities

The ECB shall enjoy in the territories of the Member States such privileges and immunities as are necessary for the performance of its tasks, under the conditions laid down in the Protocol on the Privileges and Immunities of the European Communities annexed to the Treaty establishing a Single Council and a Single Commission of the European Communities.

Chapter VIII Amendment of The Statute And Complementary Legislation

Article 41 Simplified Amendment Procedure

41.1. In accordance with Article 106(5) of this Treaty, Articles 5.1, 5.2, 5.3, 17, 18, 19.1, 22, 23, 24, 26, 32.2, 32.3, 32.4, 32.6, 33.1(a) and 36 of this Statute may be amended by the Council, acting either by a qualified majority on a recommendation from the ECB and after consulting the Commission, or unanimously on a proposal from the Commission and after consulting the ECB. In either case the assent of the European Parliament shall be required.

41.2. A recommendation made by the ECB under this Article shall require a unanimous decision by the Governing Council.

Article 42 Complementary Legislation

In accordance with Article 106(6) of this Treaty, immediately after the decision on the date for the beginning of the third stage, the Council, acting by a qualified majority either on a proposal from the Commission and after consulting the European Parliament and the ECB or on a recommendation from the ECB and after consulting the European Parliament and the Commission, shall adopt the provisions referred to in Articles 4, 5.4, 19.2, 20, 28.1, 29.2, 30.4 and 34.3 of this Statute.

Chapter IX Transitional And Other Provisions For The ESCB

Article 43 General Provisions

43.1. A derogation as referred to in Article 109k(1) of this Treaty shall entail that the following Articles of this Statute shall not confer any rights or impose any obligations on the Member State concerned: 3, 6, 9.2, 12.1, 14.3, 16, 18, 19, 20, 22, 23, 26.2, 27, 30, 31, 32, 33, 34, 50 and 52.

43.2. The central banks of Member States with a derogation as specified in Article 109k(1) of this Treaty shall retain their powers in the field of monetary policy according to national law.

43.3. In accordance with Article 109k(4) of this Treaty, "Member States" shall be read as "Member States without a derogation" in the following Articles of this Statute: 3, 11.2, 19, 34.2 and 50.

43.4. "National central banks" shall be read as "central banks of Member States without a derogation" in the following Articles of this Statute: 9.2, 10.1, 10.3, 12.1, 16, 17, 18, 22, 23, 27, 30, 31, 32, 33.2 and 52.

43.5. "Shareholders" shall be read as "central banks of Member States without a derogation" in Articles 10.3 and 33.1.

43.6. "Subscribed capital of the ECB" shall be read as "capital of the ECB subscribed by the central banks of Member States without a derogation" in Articles 10.3 and 30.2.

Article 44 Transitional Tasks of the ECB

The ECB shall take over those tasks of the EMI which, because of the derogations of one or more Member States, still have to be performed in the third stage.

The ECB shall give advice in the preparations for the abrogation of the derogations specified in Article 109k of this Treaty.

Article 45 The General Council of the ECB

45.1. Without prejudice to Article 106(3) of this Treaty, the General Council shall be constituted as a third decision-making body of the ECB.

45.2. The General Council shall comprise the President and Vice-President of the ECB and the Governors of the national central banks. The other members of the Executive Board may participate, without having the right to vote, in meetings of the General Council.

45.3. The responsibilities of the General Council are listed in full in Article 47 of this Statute.

Article 46 Rules of Procedure of the General Council

46.1. The President or, in his absence, the Vice-President of the ECB shall chair the General Council of the ECB.

46.2. The President of the Council and a member of the Commission may participate, without having the right to vote, in meetings of the General Council.

46.3. The President shall prepare the meetings of the General Council.

46.4. By way of derogation from Article 12.3, the General Council shall adopt its Rules of Procedure.

46.5. The Secretariat of the General Council shall be provided by the ECB.

Article 47 Responsibilities of the General Council

47.1. The General Council shall:
— perform the tasks referred to in Article 44;
— contribute to the advisory functions referred to in Articles 4 and 25.1.

47.2. The General Council shall contribute to:
— the collection of statistical information as referred to in Article 5;
— the reporting activities of the ECB as referred to in Article 15;
— the establishment of the necessary rules for the application of Article 26 as referred to in Article 26.4.;
— the taking of all other measures necessary for the application of Article 29 as referred to in Article 29.4.;
— the laying down of the conditions of employment of the staff of the ECB as referred to in Article 36.

47.3. The General Council shall contribute to the necessary preparations for irrevocably fixing the exchange rates of the currencies of Member States with a derogation against the currencies, or the single currency, of the Member States without a derogation, as referred to in Article 109l(5) of this Treaty.

47.4. The General Council shall be informed by the President of the ECB of decisions of the Governing Council.

Article 48 Transitional Provisions for the Capital of the ECB

In accordance with Article 29.1 each national central bank shall be assigned a weighting in the key for subscription of the ECB's capital. By way of derogation from Article 28.3, central banks of Member States with a derogation shall not pay up their subscribed capital unless the General Council, acting by a majority representing at least two-thirds of the subscribed capital of the ECB and at least half of the shareholders, decides that a minimal percentage has to be paid up as a contribution to the operational costs of the ECB.

Article 49 Deferred Payment of Capital, Reserves and Provisions of the ECB
49.1. The central bank of a Member State whose derogation has been abrogated shall pay up its subscribed share of the capital of the ECB to the same extent as the central banks of other Member States without a derogation, and shall transfer to the ECB foreign reserve assets in accordance with Article 30.1. The sum to be transferred shall be determined by multiplying the ECU value at current exchange rates of the foreign reserve assets which have already been transferred to the ECB in accordance with Article 30.1, by the ratio between the number of shares subscribed by the national central bank concerned and the number of shares already paid up by the other national central banks.
49.2. In addition to the payment to be made in accordance with Article 49.1, the central bank concerned shall contribute to the reserves of the ECB, to those provisions equivalent to reserves, and to the amount still to be appropriated to the reserves and provisions corresponding to the balance of the profit and loss account as at 31 December of the year prior to the abrogation of the derogation. The sum to be contributed shall be determined by multiplying the amount of the reserves, as defined above and as stated in the approved balance sheet of the ECB, by the ratio between the number of shares subscribed by the central bank concerned and the number of shares already paid up by the other central banks.

Article 50 Initial Appointment of the Members of the Executive Board
When the Executive Board of the ECB is being established, the President, the Vice-President and the other members of the Executive Board shall be appointed by common accord of the governments of the Member States at the level of Heads of State or Government, on a recommendation from the Council and after consulting the European Parliament and the Council of the EMI. The President of the Executive Board shall be appointed for eight years. By way of derogation from Article 11.2, the Vice-President shall be appointed for four years and the other members of the Executive Board for terms of office of between five and eight years. No term of office shall be renewable. The number of members of the Executive Board may be smaller than provided for in Article 11.1, but in no circumstance shall it be less than four.

Article 51 Derogation from Article 32
51.1. If, after the start of the third stage, the Governing Council decides that the application of Article 32 results in significant changes in national central banks' relative income positions, the amount of income to be allocated pursuant to Article 32 shall be reduced by a uniform percentage which shall not exceed 60% in the first financial year after the start of the third stage and which shall decrease by at least 12 percentage points in each subsequent financial year.
51.2. Article 51.1 shall be applicable for not more than five financial years after the start of the third stage.

Article 52 Exchange of Banknotes in Community Currencies
Following the irrevocable fixing of exchange rates, the Governing Council shall take the necessary measures to ensure that banknotes denominated in currencies with irrevocably fixed exchange rates are exchanged by the national central banks at their respective par values.

Article 53 Applicability of the Transitional Provisions
If and as long as there are Member States with a derogation Articles 43 to 48 shall be applicable.

Protocol No. 20 on the Excessive Deficit Procedure

THE HIGH CONTRACTING PARTIES,

DESIRING to lay down the details of the excessive deficit procedure referred to in Article 104c of the Treaty establishing the European Community,
HAVE AGREED upon the following provisions, which shall be annexed to the Treaty establishing the European Community:

Article 1
The reference values referred to in Article 104c(2) of this Treaty are:
— 3% for the ratio of the planned or actual government deficit to gross domestic product at market prices;
— 60% for the ratio of government debt to gross domestic product at market prices.

Article 2
In Article 104c of this Treaty and in this Protocol:
— government means general government, that is central government, regional or local government and social security funds, to the exclusion of commercial operations, as defined in the European System of Integrated Economic Accounts;
— deficit means net borrowing as defined in the European System of Integrated Economic Accounts;
— investment means gross fixed capital formation as defined in the European System of Integrated Economic Accounts;
— debt means total gross debt at nominal value outstanding at the end of the year and consolidated between and within the sectors of general government as defined in the first indent.

Article 3
In order to ensure the effectiveness of the excessive deficit procedure, the governments of the Member States shall be responsible under this procedure for the deficits of general government as defined in the first indent of Article 2. The Member States shall ensure that national procedures in the budgetary area enable them to meet their obligations in this area deriving from this Treaty. The Member States shall report their planned and actual deficits and the levels of their debt promptly and regularly to the Commission.

Article 4
The statistical data to be used for the application of this Protocol shall be provided by the Commission.

Protocol No. 21 on the Convergence Criteria Referred to in Article 109j of the Treaty Establishing the European Community

THE HIGH CONTRACTING PARTIES,

DESIRING to lay down the details of the convergence criteria which shall guide the Community in taking decisions on the passage to the third stage of economic and monetary union, referred to in Article 109j(1) of this Treaty,
HAVE AGREED upon the following provisions, which shall be annexed to the Treaty establishing the European Community:

Article 1

The criterion on price stability referred to in the first indent of Article 109j(1) of this Treaty shall mean that a Member State has a price performance that is sustainable and an average rate of inflation, observed over a period of one year before the examination, that does not exceed by more than 1½ percentage points that of, at most, the three best performing Member States in terms of price stability. Inflation shall be measured by means of the consumer price index on a comparable basis, taking into account differences in national definitions.

Article 2

The criterion on the government budgetary position referred to in the second indent of Article 109j(1) of this Treaty shall mean that at the time of the examination the Member State is not the subject of a Council decision under Article 104c(6) of this Treaty that an excessive deficit exists.

Article 3

The criterion on participation in the exchange-rate mechanism of the European Monetary System referred to in the third indent of Article 109j(1) of this Treaty shall mean that a Member State has respected the normal fluctuation margins provided for by the exchange-rate mechanism of the European Monetary System without severe tensions for at least the last two years before the examination. In-particular, the Member State shall not have devalued its currency's bilateral central rate again any other Member State's currency on its own initiative for the same period.

Article 4

The criterion on the convergence of interest rates referred to in the fourth indent of Article 109j(1) of this Treaty shall mean that, observed over a period of one year before the examination, a Member State has had an average nominal long-term interest rate that does not exceed by more than two percentage points that of, at most, the three best performing Member States in terms of price stability. Interest rates shall be measured on the basis of long-term government bonds or comparable securities, taking into account differences in national definitions.

Article 5

The statistical data to be used for the application of this Protocol shall be provided by the Commission.

Article 6

The Council shall, acting unanimously on a proposal from the Commission and after consulting the European Parliament, the EMI or the ECB as the case may be, and the Committee referred to in Article 109c, adopt appropriate provisions to lay down the details of the convergence criteria referred to in Article 109j of this Treaty, which shall then replace this Protocol.

Protocol No. 24 on the Transition to the Third Stage of Economic and Monetary Union

THE HIGH CONTRACTING PARTIES,

Declare the irreversible character of the Community's movement to the third stage of economic and monetary union by signing the new Treaty provisions on economic and monetary union.

Therefore all Member States shall, whether they fulfil the necessary conditions for the adoption of a single currency or not, respect the will for the Community to enter swiftly into the third stage, and therefore no Member State shall prevent the entering into the third stage.

If by the end of 1997 the date of the beginning of the third stage has not been set, the Member States concerned, the Community institutions and other bodies involved shall expedite all preparatory work during 1998, in order to enable the Community to enter the third stage irrevocably on 1 January 1999 and to enable the ECB and the ESCB to start their full functioning from this date.

This Protocol shall be annexed to the Treaty establishing the European Community.

Protocol No. 25 on Certain Provisions Relating to the United Kingdom of Great Britain and Northern Ireland

THE HIGH CONTRACTING PARTIES,

RECOGNIZING that the United Kingdom shall not be obliged or committed to move to the third stage of economic and monetary union without a separate decision to do so by its government and Parliament,
NOTING the practice of the government of the United Kingdom to fund its borrowing requirement by the sale of debt to the private sector,
HAVE AGREED the following provisions, which shall be annexed to the Treaty establishing the European Community:

1.   The United Kingdom shall notify the Council whether it intends to move to the third stage before the Council makes its assessment under Article 109j(2) of this Treaty.

Unless the United Kingdom notifies the Council that it intends to move to the third stage, it shall be under no obligation to do so.

If no date is set for the beginning of the third stage under Article 109j(3) of this Treaty, the United Kingdom may notify its intention to move to the third stage before 1 January 1998.
2.   Paragraphs 3 to 9 shall have effect if the United Kingdom notifies the Council that it does not intend to move to the third stage.
3.   The United Kingdom shall not be included among the majority of Member States which fulfil the necessary conditions referred to in the second indent of Article 109j(2) and the first indent of Article 109j(3) of this Treaty.
4.   The United Kingdom shall retain its powers in the field of monetary policy according to national law.
5.   Articles 3a(2), 104c(1), (9) and (11), 105(1) to (5), 105a, 107, 108, 108a, 109, 109a(1) and (2)(b) and 109l(4) and (5) of this Treaty shall not apply to the United Kingdom. In these provisions references to the Community or the Member States shall not

include the United Kingdom and references to national central banks shall not include the Bank of England.

6. Articles 109e(4) and 109h and i of this Treaty shall continue to apply to the United Kingdom. Articles 109c(4) and 109m shall apply to the United Kingdom as if it had a derogation.

7. The voting rights of the United Kingdom shall be suspended in respect of acts of the Council referred to in the Articles listed in paragraph 5. For this purpose the weighted votes of the United Kingdom shall be excluded from any calculation of a qualified majority under Article 109k(5) of this Treaty.

The United Kingdom shall also have no right to participate in the appointment of the President, the Vice-President and the other members of the Executive Board of the ECB under Articles 109a(2)(b) and 109l(1) of this Treaty.

8. Articles 3, 4, 6, 7, 9.2, 10.1, 10.3, 11.2, 12.1, 14, 16, 18 to 20, 22, 23, 26, 27, 30 to 34, 50 and 52 of the Protocol on the Statute of the European System of Central Banks and of the European Central Bank ("the Statute") shall not apply to the United Kingdom.

In those Articles, references to the Community or the Member States shall not include the United Kingdom and references to national central banks or shareholders shall not include the Bank of England.

References in Articles 10.3 and 30.2 of the Statute to "subscribed capital of the ECB" shall not include capital subscribed by the Bank of England.

9. Article 109l(3) of this Treaty and Articles 44 to 48 of the Statute shall have effect, whether or not there is any Member State with a derogation, subject to the following amendments:

(a) References in Article 44 to the tasks of the ECB and the EMI shall include those tasks that still need to be performed in the third stage owing to any decision of the United Kingdom not to move to that stage.

(b) In addition to the tasks referred to in Article 47 the ECB shall also give advice in relation to and contribute to the preparation of any decision of the Council with regard to the United Kingdom taken in accordance with paragraphs 10(a) and 10(c).

(c) The Bank of England shall pay up its subscription to the capital of the ECB as a contribution to its operational costs on the same basis as national central banks of Member States with a derogation.

10. If the United Kingdom does not move to the third stage, it may change its notification at any time after the beginning of that stage. In that event:

(a) The United Kingdom shall have the right to move to the third stage provided only that it satisfies the necessary conditions. The Council, acting at the request of the United Kingdom and under the conditions and in accordance with the procedure laid down in Article 109k(2) of this Treaty, shall decide whether it fulfils the necessary conditions.

(b) The Bank of England shall pay up its subscribed capital, transfer to the ECB foreign reserve assets and contribute to its reserves on the same basis as the national central bank of a Member State whose derogation has been abrogated.

(c) The Council, acting under the conditions and in accordance with the procedure laid down in Article 109l(5) of this Treaty, shall take all other necessary decisions to enable the United Kingdom to move to the third stage.

If the United Kingdom moves to the third stage pursuant to the provisions of this Protocol, paragraphs 3 to 9 shall cease to have effect.

11. Notwithstanding Articles 104 and 109e(3) of this Treaty and Article 21.1 of the Statute, the government of the United Kingdom may maintain its "ways and means" facility with the Bank of England if and so long as the United Kingdom does not move to the third stage.

Protocol No. 28 on Economic and Social Cohesion

THE HIGH CONTRACTING PARTIES,

RECALLING that the Union has set itself the objective of promoting economic and social progress, inter alia, through the strengthening of economic and social cohesion,
RECALLING that Article 2 of the Treaty establishing the European Community includes the task of promoting economic and social cohesion and solidarity between Member States and that the strengthening of economic and social cohesion figures among the activities of the Community listed in Article 3,
RECALLING that the provisions of Part Three, Title XIV, on economic and social cohesion as a whole provide the legal basis for consolidating and further developing the Community's action in the field of economic and social cohesion, including the creation of a new fund,
RECALLING that the provisions of Part Three, Title XII on trans-European networks and Title XVI on environment envisage a cohesion fund to be set up before 31 December 1993,
STATING their belief that progress towards economic and monetary union will contribute to the economic growth of all Member States,
NOTING that the Community's structural Funds are being doubled in real terms between 1987 and 1993, implying large transfers, especially as a proportion of GDP of the less prosperous Member States,
NOTING that the European Investment Bank is lending large and increasing amounts for the benefit of the poorer regions,
NOTING the desire for greater flexibility in the arrangements for allocations from the structural funds,
NOTING the desire for modulation of the levels of Community participation in programmes and projects in certain countries,
NOTING the proposal to take greater account of the relative prosperity of Member States in the system of own resources,
REAFFIRM that the promotion of economic and social cohesion is vital to the full development and enduring success of the Community, and underline the importance of the inclusion of economic and social cohesion in Articles 2 and 3 of this Treaty,
REAFFIRM their conviction that the structural funds should continue to play a considerable part in the achievement of Community objectives in the field of cohesion,
REAFFIRM their conviction that the European Investment Bank should continue to devote the majority of its resources to the promotion of economic and social cohesion, and declare their willingness to review the capital needs of the European Investment Bank as soon as this is necessary for that purpose,
REAFFIRM the need for a thorough evaluation of the operation and effectiveness of the structural funds in 1992, and the need to review, on that occasion, the appropriate size of these funds in the light of the tasks of the Community in the area of economic and social cohesion,
AGREE that the cohesion fund to be set up before 31 December 1993 will provide Community financial contributions to projects in the fields of environment and trans-European networks in Member States with a per capita GNP of less than 90% of the Community average which have a programme leading to the fulfilment of the conditions of economic convergence as set out in Article 104c,
DECLARE their intention of allowing a greater margin of flexibility in allocating financing from the structural Funds to specific needs not covered under the present structural Funds regulations,

DECLARE their willingness to modulate the levels of Community participation in the context of programmes and projects of the structural funds, with a view to avoiding excessive increases in budgetary expenditure in the less prosperous Member States, RECOGNIZE the need to monitor regularly the progress made towards achieving economic and social cohesion and state their willingness to study all necessary measures in this respect,

DECLARE their intention of taking greater account of the contributive capacity of individual Member States in the system of own resources, and of examining means of correcting, for the less prosperous Member States, regressive elements existing in the present own resources system,

AGREE to annex this Protocol to the Treaty establishing the European Community.

Protocol No. 29 on Asylum for Nationals of Member States of the European Union

THE HIGH CONTRACTING PARTIES,

WHEREAS pursuant to the provisions of Article F(2) of the Treaty on European Union the Union shall respect fundamental rights as guaranteed by the European Convention for the Protection of Human Rights and Fundamental Freedoms signed in Rome on 4 November 1950;

WHEREAS the Court of Justice of the European Communities has jurisdiction to ensure that in the interpretation and application of Article F(2) of the Treaty on European Union the law is observed by the European Community;

WHEREAS pursuant to Article O of the Treaty on European Union any European State, when applying to become a Member of the Union, must respect the principles set out in Article F(1) of the Treaty on European Union;

BEARING IN MIND that Article 236 of the Treaty establishing the European Community establishes a mechanism for the suspension of certain rights in the event of a serious and persistent breach by a Member State of those principles;

RECALLING that each national of a Member State, as a citizen of the Union, enjoys a special status and protection which shall be guaranteed by the Member States in accordance with the provisions of Part Two of the Treaty establishing the European Community;

BEARING IN MIND that the Treaty establishing the European Community establishes an area without internal frontiers and grants every citizen of the Union the right to move and reside freely within the territory of the Member States;

RECALLING that the question of extradition of nationals of Member States of the Union is addressed in the European Convention on Extradition of 13 December 1957 and the Convention of 27 September 1996 drawn up on the basis of Article K.3 of the Treaty on European Union relating to extradition between the Member States of the European Union;

WISHING to prevent the institution of asylum being resorted to for purposes alien to those for which it is intended;

WHEREAS this Protocol respects the finality and the objectives of the Geneva Convention of 28 July 1951 relating to the status of refugees;

HAVE AGREED UPON the following provisions which shall be annexed to the Treaty establishing the European Community,

Sole Article

Given the level of protection of fundamental rights and freedoms by the Member States of the European Union, Member States shall be regarded as constituting safe countries of origin in respect of each other for all legal and practical purposes in relation to asylum matters.

Accordingly, any application for asylum made by a national of a Member State may be taken into consideration or declared admissible for processing by another Member State only in the following cases:

(a) if the Member State of which the applicant is a national proceeds after the entry into force of the Treaty of Amsterdam, availing itself of the provisions of Article 15 of the Convention for the Protection of Human Rights and Fundamental Freedoms, to take measures derogating in its territory from its obligations under that Convention;

(b) if the procedure referred to in Article F.1(1) of the Treaty on European Union has been initiated and until the Council takes a decision in respect thereof;

(c) if the Council, acting on the basis of Article F.1(1) of the Treaty on European Union, has determined, in respect of the Member State which the applicant is a national, the existence of a serious and persistent breach by that Member State of principles mentioned in Article F(1);

(d) if a Member State should so decide unilaterally in respect of the application of a national of another Member State; in that case the Council shall be immediately informed; the application shall be dealt with on the basis of the presumption that it is manifestly unfounded without affecting in any way, whatever the cases may be, the decision making power of the Member State.

Protocol No. 30 on the Application of the Principles of Subsidiarity and Proportionality

THE HIGH CONTRACTING PARTIES,

DETERMINED to establish the conditions for the application of the principles of subsidiarity and proportionality enshrined in Article 3b of the Treaty establishing the European Community with a view to defining more precisely the criteria for applying them and to ensure their strict observance and consistent implementation by all institutions;

WISHING to ensure that decisions are taken as closely as possible to the citizens of the Union;

TAKING ACCOUNT of the Interinstitutional Agreement of 25 October 1993 between the European Parliament, the Council and the Commission on procedures for implementing the principle of subsidiarity;

HAVE CONFIRMED that the conclusions of the Birmingham European Council on 16 October 1992 and the overall approach to the application of the subsidiarity principle agreed by the European Council meeting in Edinburgh on 11-12 December 1992 will continue to guide the action of the Union's institutions as well as the development of the application of the principle of subsidiarity, and, for this purpose,

HAVE AGREED UPON the following provisions which shall be annexed to the Treaty establishing the European Community:

1. In exercising the powers conferred on it, each institution shall ensure that the principle of subsidiarity is complied with. It shall also ensure compliance with the principle

of proportionality, according to which any action by the Community shall not go beyond what is necessary to achieve the objectives of the Treaty.

2.   The application of the principles of subsidiarity and proportionality shall respect the general provisions and the objectives of the Treaty, particularly as regards the maintaining in full of the *acquis communautaire* and the institutional balance; it shall not affect the principles developed by the Court of Justice regarding the relationship between national and Community law, and it should take into account Article F(4) of the Treaty on European Union, according to which "the Union shall provide itself with the means necessary to attain its objectives and carry through its policies".

3.   The principle of subsidiarity does not call into question the powers conferred on the European Community by the Treaty, as interpreted by the Court of Justice. The criteria referred to in the second paragraph of Article 3b of the Treaty shall relate to areas for which the Community does not have exclusive competence. The principle of subsidiarity provides a guide as to how those powers are to be exercised at the Community level.

Subsidiarity is a dynamic concept and should be applied in the light of the objectives set out in the Treaty. It allows Community action within the limits of its powers to be expanded where circumstances so require, and conversely, to be restricted or discontinued where it is no longer justified.

4.   For any proposed Community legislation, the reasons on which it is based shall be stated with a view to justifying its compliance with the principles of subsidiarity and proportionality; the reasons for concluding that a Community objective can be better achieved by the Community must be substantiated by qualitative or, wherever possible, quantitative indicators.

5.   For Community action to be justified, both aspects of the subsidiarity principle shall be met: the objectives of the proposed action cannot be sufficiently achieved by Member States' action in the framework of their national constitutional system and can therefore be better achieved by action on the part of the Community.

The following guidelines should be used in examining whether the abovementioned condition is fulfilled:

—   the issue under consideration has transnational aspects which cannot be satisfactorily regulated by action by Member States;

—   actions by Member States alone or lack of Community action would conflict with the requirements of the Treaty (such as the need to correct distortion of competition or avoid disguised restrictions on trade or strengthen economic and social cohesion) or would otherwise significantly damage Member States' interests;

—   action at Community level would produce clear benefits by reason of its scale or effects compared with action at the level of the Member States.

6.   The form of Community action shall be as simple as possible, consistent with satisfactory achievement of the objective of the measure and the need for effective enforcement. The Community shall legislate only to the extent necessary. Other things being equal, directives should be preferred to regulations and framework directives to detailed measures. Directives as provided for in Article 189 of the Treaty, while binding upon each Member State to which they are addressed as to the result to be achieved, shall leave to the national authorities the choice of form and methods.

7.   Regarding the nature and the extent of Community action, Community measures should leave as much scope for national decision as possible, consistent with securing the aim of the measure and observing the requirements of the Treaty. While respecting Community law, care should be taken to respect well established national arrangements and the organisation and working of Member States' legal systems. Where appropriate and subject to the need for proper enforcement, Community measures

should provide Member States with alternative ways to achieve the objectives of the measures.

8.　Where the application of the principle of subsidiarity leads to no action being taken by the Community, Member States are required in their action to comply with the general rules laid down in Article 5 of the Treaty, by taking all appropriate measures to ensure fulfilment of their obligations under the Treaty and by abstaining from any measure which could jeopardise the attainment of the objectives of the Treaty.

9.　Without prejudice to its right of initiative, the Commission should:

— except in cases of particular urgency or confidentiality, consult widely before proposing legislation and, wherever appropriate, publish consultation documents;

— justify the relevance of its proposals with regard to the principle of subsidiarity; whenever necessary, the explanatory memorandum accompanying a proposal will give details in this respect. The financing of Community action in whole or in part from the Community budget shall require an explanation;

— take duly into account the need for any burden, whether financial or administrative, falling upon the Community, national governments, local authorities, economic operators and citizens, to be minimised and proportionate to the objective to be achieved;

— submit an annual report to the European Council, the European Parliament and the Council on the application of Article 3b of the Treaty. This annual report shall also be sent to the Committee of the Regions and to the Economic and Social Committee.

10.　The European Council shall take account of the Commission report referred to in the fourth indent of point 9 within the report on the progress achieved by the Union which it is required to submit to the European Parliament in accordance with Article D of the Treaty on European Union.

11.　While fully observing the procedures applicable, the European Parliament and the Council shall, as an integral part of the overall examination of Commission proposals, consider their consistency with Article 3b of the Treaty. This concerns the original Commission proposal as well as amendments which the European Parliament and the Council envisage making to the proposal.

12.　In the course of the procedures referred to in Articles 189b and 189c of the Treaty, the European Parliament shall be informed of the Council's position on the application of Article 3b of the Treaty, by way of a statement of the reasons which led the Council to adopt its common position. The Council shall inform the European Parliament of the reasons on the basis of which all or part of a Commission proposal is deemed to be inconsistent with Article 3b of the Treaty.

13.　Compliance with the principle of subsidiarity shall be reviewed in accordance with the rules laid down by the Treaty.

TWO: THE INSTITUTIONS OF THE EUROPEAN UNION

European Parliament Rules of Procedure[1]

CONTENTS

---

1   Consolidated Version, OJ 1997 L 49, p. 1. Interpretations of the Rules (pursuant to Rule 162) are
     omitted.

Chapter I Members of The European Parliament

Rule 1 The European Parliament
1.   The European Parliament is the assembly elected pursuant to the Treaties, the Act of 20 September 1976 concerning the election of the representatives of the European Parliament by direct universal suffrage and national legislation deriving from the Treaties.
2.   Persons elected to the European Parliament shall be referred to as: [...] "Members of the European Parliament" [...].

Rule 2 The independent mandate
Members of the European Parliament shall exercise their mandate independently. They shall not be bound by any instructions and shall not receive a binding mandate.

Rule 3 Privileges and immunities
1.   Members shall enjoy privileges and immunities in accordance with the Protocol on the Privileges and Immunities of the European Communities, annexed to the Treaty of 8 April 1965 establishing a Single Council and a Single Commission of the European Communities.
2.   Passes to allow Members to circulate freely in the Member States shall be issued to them by the President of Parliament as soon as he has been notified of their election.

3. Members shall be entitled to inspect any files held by Parliament or a committee, other than personal files and accounts which only the Members concerned shall be allowed to inspect.

Rule 4 Attendance of Members at sittings and votes
1. An attendance register shall be laid open for signature by Members at each sitting.
2. The names of Members present, as shown in the attendance register, shall be recorded in the minutes of each sitting.
3. In the event of a roll-call vote the minutes shall record the names of Members who took part in the vote and how they voted.

Rule 5 Payment of expenses and allowances
The Bureau shall lay down rules governing the payment of expenses and allowances to Members.

Rule 6 Waiver of immunity
1. Any request addressed to the President by the appropriate authority of a Member State that the immunity of a Member be waived shall be announced in Parliament and referred to the committee responsible.
2. The committee shall consider such requests without delay and in the order in which they have been submitted.
3. The committee may ask the authority which has submitted the request to provide any information or explanation which the committee deems necessary for it to form an opinion on whether immunity should be waived. The Member concerned shall be heard at his request; he may bring any documents or other written evidence he deems relevant. He may be represented by another Member.
4. The committee's report shall contain a proposal for a decision which simply recommends the adoption or rejection of the request for the waiver of immunity. However, where the request seeks the waiver of immunity on several counts, each of these may be the subject of a separate proposal for a decision. The committee's report may, exceptionally, propose that the waiver of immunity shall apply solely to prosecution proceedings and that, until a final sentence is passed, the Member should be immune from any form of detention or remand or any other measure which prevents him from performing the duties proper to his mandate. Where the request for the waiver of immunity entails the possibility of obliging the Member to appear as a witness or expert witness thereby depriving him of his freedom, the committee shall:
— ascertain, before proposing that immunity be waived, that the Member will not be obliged to appear on a date or at a time which prevents him from performing, or makes it difficult for him to perform, his parliamentary duties, or that he will be able to provide a statement in writing or in any other form which does not make it difficult for him to fulfil his parliamentary obligations;
— seek clarification regarding the subject of the statement, in order to ensure that the Member is not obliged to testify concerning information obtained confidentially in the exercise of his mandate which he does not see fit to disclose.
5. The committee shall not, under any circumstances, pronounce on the guilt or otherwise of the Member nor on whether or not the opinions or acts attributed to him justify prosecution, even if, in considering the request, it acquires detailed knowledge of the facts of the case.
6. The report of the committee shall be placed at the head of the agenda of the first sitting following the day on which it was tabled. No amendment may be tabled to the proposal(s) for a decision. Discussion shall be confined to the reasons for or against

each proposal to waive or uphold immunity. The proposal(s) for a decision contained in the report shall be put to the vote at the first voting time following the debate.

7.   The President shall immediately communicate Parliament's decision to the appropriate authority of the Member State concerned, with a request, if immunity is waived, that he should be informed of any judicial rulings made as a consequence. When the President receives this information, he shall transmit it to Parliament in the way he considers most appropriate.

8.   Should a Member be arrested or prosecuted after having been found in the act of committing an offence, any other Member may request that the proceedings be suspended or that he be released. The President shall ensure that recourse is had to this right where the aim of the arrest or prosecution is to make the Member appear as a witness or expert witness against his will, without his immunity having been waived beforehand.

Rule 7 [omitted]

Rule 8 Term of office of Members

1.   A Member's term of office shall begin and end as laid down in the Act of 20 September 1976. It shall also end on death or resignation.

2.   Every Member shall remain in office until the opening of the first sitting of Parliament following the elections.

3.   A Member who resigns shall notify the President of his resignation in writing. This notification shall be made in an official record drawn up in the presence of the Secretary-General or his representative, signed by the latter and by the Member concerned and immediately submitted to the committee responsible, which shall enter it on the agenda of its first meeting following receipt of the document. If the committee responsible considers that the resignation is not in accordance with the spirit or the letter of the Act of 20 September 1976 it shall inform Parliament to this effect so that Parliament can decide whether or not to establish the vacancy. Otherwise, the vacancy shall be established automatically unless the resigning Member indicates a later date. There shall be no vote in Parliament on the subject.

4.   Incompatibilities resulting from national legislation shall be notified to Parliament, which shall take note thereof.

Where the competent authorities of the Member States or of the Union notify the President of appointments to an office incompatible with the office of Member of the European Parliament, the President shall inform Parliament, which shall establish that there is a vacancy.

5.   The following shall be considered as the date of the end of the term of office and the effective date of a vacancy:

—   in the event of resignation: the date on which the vacancy is established by Parliament, the date when the President receives the letter of resignation or a later (but not earlier) date specified in his letter by the resigning Member;

—   in the event of appointment to an office incompatible with the office of a Member of the European Parliament, either in respect of national electoral law, or in respect of Article 6 of the Act of 20 September 1976: the date notified by the competent authorities of the Member States or of the Union.

6.   When Parliament has established that a vacancy exists, it shall inform the Member State concerned thereof.

7.   Any dispute concerning the validity of the appointment of a Member whose credentials have already been verified shall be referred to the committee responsible, which shall report to Parliament without delay and no later than the beginning of the next part-session.

8.   Parliament shall reserve the right, where acceptance or termination of office appears to be based on material inaccuracy or vitiated consent, to declare the appointment under consideration to be invalid or refuse to establish the vacancy.

Rule 9 Code of conduct
1.   Parliament may lay down a code of conduct for its Members. The code shall be adopted pursuant to Rule 163 (2) and attached to these Rules of Procedure as an annex (2). The code shall not in any way prejudice or restrict a Member in the exercise of his office or of any political or other activity relating thereto.
2.   The Quaestors shall be responsible for issuing nominative passes valid for a maximum of one year to persons who wish to enter Parliament's premises frequently with a view to supplying information to Members within the framework of their parliamentary mandate in their own interests or those of third parties. In return, these persons shall be required to:
—   respect the code of conduct published as an annex to the Rules of Procedure (3);
—   sign a register kept by the Quaestors.
This register shall be made available to the public on request in all of Parliament's places of work and, in the form laid down by the Quaestors, in its information offices in the Member States. The provisions governing the application of this paragraph shall be laid down in an annex to the Rules of Procedure.

Chapter II Sessions of Parliament

Rule 10 Convening of Parliament
1.   The parliamentary term shall run concurrently with the term of office of Members provided for in the Act of 20 September 1976.
The session shall be the annual period prescribed by the Act and the Treaties. The part-session shall be the meeting of Parliament convened as a rule each month and subdivided into daily sittings.
2.   Parliament shall meet, without requiring to be convened, on the second Tuesday in March each year and shall itself determine the duration of adjournments of the session.
3.   Parliament shall, moreover, meet without requiring to be convened on the first Tuesday after expiry of an interval of one month from the end of the period referred to in Article 9 (1) of the Act of 20 September 1976.
4.   The Conference of Presidents, stating its reasons, may alter the duration of adjournments decided pursuant to paragraph 2 at least two weeks before the date previously fixed by Parliament for resuming the session; the date of resumption shall not, however, be postponed for more than two weeks.
5.   Exceptionally, after consulting the Conference of Presidents, the President shall convene Parliament at the request of a majority of its Members or at the request of the Commission or the Council. Exceptionally, with the approval of the Conference of Presidents, the President may convene Parliament at the request of one third of its Members.

Rule 11 Venue of sittings and meetings
1.   Parliament shall hold its sittings and its committee meetings at the place fixed as its seat under the provisions of the Treaties.
2.   Exceptionally, however, on a resolution adopted by a majority of its component Members, Parliament may decide to hold one or more sittings elsewhere than at its seat.

3.   Any committee may decide to ask that one or more meetings be held away from the said seat. Its request, with the reasons therefore, shall be made to the President, who shall place it before the Bureau. If the matter is urgent, the President may take the decision himself. Should the request be rejected by the Bureau or the President the reasons for the rejection shall be stated.

Chapter III Officers of Parliament

Rule 12 - 20 [omitted]

Chapter IV Parliament's Governing Bodies

Rule 21 - 28 [omitted]

Chapter V Political Groups

Rule 29 - 31 [omitted]

Chapter VI Relations With Other Institutions
Appointments

Rule 32 Nomination of the President of the Commission
1.   When the governments of the Member States have agreed on a nomination for President of the Commission, the President shall request the nominee to make a statement to Parliament. The statement shall be followed by a debate. The Council shall be invited to take part in the debate.
2.   Parliament shall approve or reject the nomination by a majority of the votes cast. The vote shall be taken by roll call.
3.   The President shall forward the result of the vote to the President of the European Council and to the governments of the Member States as Parliament's opinion.
4.   If the result of the vote in Parliament on the nomination for President of the Commission is negative, the President shall request the governments of the Member States to withdraw their nomination and submit a new nomination to Parliament.

Rule 33 Vote of approval of the Commission
1.   When the governments of the Member States have agreed on the other persons they intend to appoint as Members of the Commission, the President shall, after consulting the nominee for President of the Commission, request the nominees to appear before the appropriate committees according to their prospective fields of responsibility.
2.   The committee may invite the nominee to make a statement and answer questions. The committee shall report its conclusions to the President.
3.   The nominee for President shall present the programme of the nominated Commission at a sitting of Parliament which the whole Council shall be invited to attend. The statement shall be followed by a debate.
4.   In order to wind up the debate, any political group may table a motion for a resolution which shall contain a statement that:
(a) Parliament approves the nominated Commission, or
(b) Parliament rejects the nominated Commission, or
(c) in order to allow the reservations expressed by Parliament in the debate to be addressed, Parliament defers the vote until the next sitting.
5.   Parliament shall vote its approval of the Commission by a majority of the votes cast. The vote shall be taken by roll call.

6. If Parliament approves the nominated Commission, the President shall notify the governments of the Member States that the appointment of the Commission may now take place.

Rule 34 Motion of censure on the Commission

1. A motion of censure on the Commission may be submitted to the President by one tenth of the component Members of Parliament.
2. The motion shall be called "motion of censure" and supported by reasons. It shall be forwarded to the Commission.
3. The President shall announce to Members that a motion of censure has been tabled immediately he receives it.
4. The debate on the motion shall not take place until at least 24 hours after its receipt is announced to Members.
5. The vote on the motion shall be by roll call and shall not be taken until at least 48 hours after the beginning of the debate.
6. The debate and the vote shall take place, at the latest, during the part-session following the submission of the motion.
7. The motion of censure shall be adopted if it secures a two-thirds majority of the votes cast, representing a majority of the component Members of Parliament. The result of the vote shall be notified to the President of the Council and the President of the Commission.

Rule 35 Appointment of the Members of the Court of Auditors

1. Candidates nominated as Members of the Court of Auditors shall be invited to make a statement before the committee responsible and answer questions put by members.
2. The committee responsible shall make a recommendation to Parliament as to whether the nomination should be approved.
3. The vote shall take place within two months of the receipt of the nomination unless Parliament, at the request of the committee responsible, a political group or at least twenty-nine Members, decides otherwise.
4. If the opinion adopted by Parliament is negative, the President shall request the Council to withdraw its nomination and submit a new nomination to Parliament.

Rule 36 European Central Bank (European Monetary Institute)

1. The candidate nominated as President of the European Central Bank shall be invited to make a statement before the committee responsible and answer questions put by members.
2. The committee responsible shall make a recommendation to Parliament as to whether the nomination should be approved.
3. The vote shall take place within two months of the receipt of the nomination unless Parliament, at the request of the committee responsible, a political group or at least twenty-nine Members, decides otherwise.
4. If the opinion adopted by Parliament is negative, the President shall request the Council to withdraw its nomination and submit a new nomination to Parliament.
5. The same procedure shall apply for nominations for Vice-President and Executive Board Members of the European Central Bank and for President of the European Monetary Institute.

STATEMENTS

Rule 37 Statements by the Commission, Council and European Council
1.   Members of the Commission, Council and European Council may at any time ask
the President for permission to make a statement. The President shall decide when the
statement may be made. Such a statement may be followed by a debate.
2.   A committee, a political group, or at least twenty-nine Members may table a motion
for a resolution.
3   Motions for resolutions shall be put to the vote on the same day. The President
shall decide on any exceptions. Explanations of vote shall be admissible.
4.   A joint motion for a resolution shall replace the previous motions for resolutions
tabled by its signatories, but not those tabled by other committees, political groups or
Members.
5.   After a resolution has been adopted, no further motions may be put to the vote
except where the President, by way of exception, decides otherwise.
6.   If no debate is held, Members will be allowed a maximum of 30 minutes in which
to put brief and concise questions.

Rule 38 Statements by the Court of Auditors
1.   In the context of the discharge procedure or Parliament's activities in the sphere
of budgetary control, the President of the Court of Auditors may be invited to take the
floor in order to present the comments contained in the Annual Report, special reports
or opinions of the Court, or in order to explain the Court's work programme.
2.   Parliament may decide to hold a separate debate on any questions raised in such
statements with the participation of the Commission and Council.

Rule 39 Statements by the European Central Bank (European Monetary Institute)
1.   The President of the European Central Bank shall present the Annual Report of the
Bank to Parliament.
2.   Parliament may decide to hold a debate following this presentation.
3.   The President of the European Central Bank and other Executive Board Members
may be invited to attend a meeting of the committee responsible to make a statement
and answer questions. The President of the Bank shall attend such meetings twice a
year. He may be invited to attend additional meetings if circumstances justify it in the
opinion of the committee responsible confirmed by the Conference of Presidents.
4.   The same procedure shall apply to the President of the European Monetary Institute for the period of its existence.

QUESTIONS TO THE COUNCIL AND COMMISSION

Rule 40 Questions for oral answer
1.   Questions may be put to the Council or the Commission by a committee, a political
group or at least twenty-nine Members with a request that they be placed on the
agenda of Parliament. Such questions shall be submitted in writing to the President
who shall immediately refer them to the Conference of Presidents. The Conference of
Presidents shall decide whether and in what order questions should be placed on the
agenda.
2.   Questions to the Commission must be referred to that institution at least one week
before the sitting on whose agenda they are to appear and questions to the Council at
least three weeks before that date.
3.   Where the questions concern matters referred to in Articles J.7 and K.6 of the
Treaty on European Union, the time limit provided for in paragraph 2 of this Rule shall

not apply, and the Council must reply with sufficient promptness to keep Parliament properly informed.

4. One of the questioners may move the question for five minutes. One member of the institution concerned shall answer.

5. Rule 37 (2), (3) (4) and (5) shall apply *mutatis mutandis*.

Rule 41 Question Time

1. Question Time to the Council and Commission shall be held at each part-session at such times as may be decided by Parliament on a proposal from the Conference of Presidents. A specific period of time may be set aside for questions to the President and individual Members of the Commission.

2. No Member may put more than one question to the Council and the Commission at a given part-session.

3. Questions shall be submitted in writing to the President, who shall rule on their admissibility and on the order in which they are to be taken. The questioner shall be notified immediately of this decision.

4. The detailed procedure shall be governed by guidelines.

Rule 42 Questions for written answer

1. Questions for written answer may be put by any Member to the Council or the Commission.

2. Questions shall be submitted in writing to the President who shall forward them to the institution concerned.

3. Questions and answers shall be published in the Official Journal of the European Communities.

4. If a question cannot be answered within the time limit set it shall, at the request of the author, be placed on the agenda of the next meeting of the committee responsible. Rule 41 shall apply *mutatis mutandis*.

5. Questions which require an immediate answer but no detailed research (priority questions) shall be answered within three weeks. Each Member may table one priority question each month.

6. Other questions (non-priority questions) shall be answered within six weeks.

7. Members shall indicate which type of question they are submitting. The final decision shall be taken by the President.

REPORTS

Rule 43 Annual general report of the Commission

The annual general report by the Commission on the activities of the European Communities shall be referred to the committees, which may submit specific and fundamental questions to the plenary under the existing procedures.

Rule 44 Annual report of the Commission on the application of Community law

1. The annual report by the Commission on the application of Community law in the Member States shall be referred to the various committees concerned, each of which may deliver its opinion to the committee responsible for legal affairs which shall submit a report to the plenary.

2. The resolution adopted by Parliament and the report of the committee responsible shall be forwarded to the Council, the Commission and the governments and the parliaments of the Member States.

RESOLUTIONS AND RECOMMENDATIONS

Rule 45 Motions for resolutions

1.   Any Member may table a motion for a resolution on a matter falling within the sphere of activities of the European Union. The motion may not comprise more than 200 words.
2.   The committee responsible shall decide what procedure is to be adopted. It may combine the motion for a resolution with other motions for resolutions or reports. It may adopt an opinion, which may take the form of a letter. It may decide to draw up a report, in which case it shall require the approval of the Conference of Presidents.
3.   The authors of a motion for a resolution shall be informed of the decisions of the committee and the Conference of Presidents.
4.   The report shall contain the text of the motion for a resolution.
5.   Opinions in the form of a letter addressed to other institutions of the European Union shall be forwarded by the President.
6.   The author or authors of a motion for a resolution tabled pursuant to Rules 37 (2), 40 (5) or 47 (1) shall be entitled to withdraw it before the final vote.
7.   A motion for a resolution tabled pursuant to paragraph 1 may be withdrawn by its author, authors or first signatory before the committee responsible has decided, pursuant to paragraph 2, to draw up a report on it. Once the motion has been thus taken over by the committee, only the committee shall be empowered to withdraw it up until the opening of the final vote.
8.   A motion for a resolution withdrawn may be taken over and retabled immediately by a group, a committee or the same number of Members who are entitled to table it.

Rule 46 Recommendations to the Council

1.   At least twenty-nine Members or a political group may table a proposal for a recommendation to the Council concerning subjects under Titles V and VI of the Treaty on European Union.
2.   Such proposals shall be referred to the committee responsible for consideration. Where appropriate, the committee shall refer the matter to Parliament in accordance with the procedures laid down in these Rules.
3.   Where it presents a report, the committee responsible shall submit to Parliament a proposal for a recommendation to the Council, together with a brief explanatory statement and, where appropriate, the opinions of the committees consulted.
4.   In urgent cases the provisions of Rule 92 or Rule 94 shall apply.

Rule 47 Debates on topical and urgent subjects of major importance

1.   A political group or at least twenty-nine Members may ask the President in writing for a debate to be held on a topical and urgent subject of major importance (Rule 95 (3)). Such a request must be linked with a motion for a resolution. The President shall notify Parliament immediately of any such request.
2.   The Conference of Presidents shall draw up a list of subjects to be included on the agenda of the next debate on topical and urgent subjects of major importance on the basis of the requests referred to in paragraph 1 and in accordance with the provisions of Annex III. The total number of subjects included on the agenda shall not exceed five. The President shall notify Parliament of this list not later than at the resumption of the sitting on the afternoon of the same day. Up to the end of the sitting on the same day, a political group or at least twenty-nine Members may oppose this decision in writing, stating their reasons, and move that Parliament abandon a topic due to be debated and/or include an unscheduled topic in the debate without, however, exceeding the maximum number of topics laid down by this Rule. The President shall decide on the

admissibility of any objections raised. The vote on such objections shall take place without debate at the beginning of the next day's sitting.

3.   The total speaking time for the political groups and non-attached Members shall be allocated in accordance with the procedure laid down in Rule 106 (2) and (3) within the maximum time for debates of three hours per part-session. Any time remaining after taking account of the time required for the introduction of and vote on the motions for resolutions and the speaking time, if any, allocated to the Commission and Council, shall be broken down between the political groups and the non- attached Members.

4.   At the end of the debate there shall be an immediate vote. Rule 122 shall not apply.

5.   If two or more motions for resolutions are tabled on the same subject, the procedure set out in Rule 37 (4) shall apply.

6.   The President and political group chairmen may decide that a motion for a resolution shall be put to the vote without debate. Such a decision shall require the unanimous assent of all the political group chairmen.

Rule 48 Written declarations

1.   Any Member may submit a written declaration of not more than 200 words on a matter falling within the sphere of activities of the European Union. Written declarations shall be printed in the official languages, distributed and entered in a register.

2.   Any Member may add his signature to a declaration entered in the register.

3.   At the end of each part-session, the President shall announce how many signatures have been obtained by the declarations entered in the register.

4.   As soon as a declaration entered in the register has been signed by at least one half of the component Members of Parliament, the text of the declaration shall be forwarded to the institutions named by the author together with the names of the signatories. The President shall announce this at the next sitting and the text of the declaration and the names of the signatories shall be included in the minutes of that sitting as an annex. Once this announcement has been made, no more entries may be made in the register.

5.   A written declaration that has stood in the register for over two months and has not been signed by at least one half of the component Members of Parliament shall lapse.

Chapter VII Legislative Procedures
General Provisions

Rule 49 Annual legislative programme

1.   Parliament shall work together with the Commission and the Council to determine the legislative planning of the European Union.

2.   The Commission shall, in October, present its Annual Legislative Programme with an assessment of the previous year's Legislative Programme.

3.   The Annual Legislative Programme shall refer to:
(a) all proposals of a legislative nature,
(b) agreements with third countries.

The Programme shall also refer to any legislative proposals and documents requested by Parliament or the Council which the Commission has agreed to submit. Every act included in the Programme must indicate the legal basis and the timetable for adoption.

4.   Before the end of each year, Parliament shall adopt a resolution setting the political priorities for the Legislative Programme.

5.   In urgent and unforeseen circumstances, an institution may, on its own initiative and according to the procedures laid down in the Treaties, propose adding a legislative measure to those proposed in the Legislative Programme.

6.   The President shall forward the resolution adopted by Parliament to the other institutions which participate in the European Union's legislative procedure and to the parliaments of the Member States. The President shall ask the Council to express an opinion on the Commission's Annual Legislative Programme as well as Parliament's resolution.

7.   Where an institution is unable to comply with the timetable laid down it shall notify the other institution as to the reasons for the delay and propose a new timetable.

8.   Parliament shall review progress on the implementation of the Annual Legislative Programme every six months. The Programme may be revised at the beginning of the second half of the year.

Rule 50 Legislative initiative

1.   Parliament may request the Commission to submit to it any appropriate legislative proposal pursuant to Article 138b, second paragraph, of the EC Treaty by adopting a resolution on the basis of an own-initiative report from the committee responsible and authorized pursuant to Rule 148. The resolution shall be adopted by a majority of the component Members of Parliament. Parliament may at the same time fix a deadline for the submission of such a proposal.

2.   Before initiating the procedure under Rule 148, the committee responsible shall establish, in the following cases, that no such proposal is under preparation:
(a)   such a proposal is not included in the Annual Legislative Programme;
(b)   the preparations of such a proposal have not started or are unduly delayed;
(c)   the Commission has not responded positively to earlier requests either from the committee responsible or contained in resolutions adopted by Parliament with simple majority.

3.   Parliament's resolution shall indicate the appropriate legal basis and be accompanied by detailed recommendations as to the content of the required proposals, which shall respect the principle of subsidiarity and the fundamental rights of citizens.

4.   Where a proposal has financial implications, Parliament shall indicate how sufficient financial resources can be provided.

5.   The committee responsible shall monitor the progress of preparation of any legislative proposal drawn up following a particular request by Parliament.

6.   The provisions of this Rule shall apply *mutatis mutandis* in cases where the Treaties attribute the right of initiative to Parliament. The majority required shall be the majority indicated by the relevant article of the Treaty concerned.

Rule 51 Consideration of legislative documents

1.   Proposals from the Commission and other documents of a legislative nature shall be referred by the President to the committee responsible for consideration. Where a proposal is listed in the Annual Legislative Programme the committee responsible may decide to appoint a rapporteur to follow the preparatory phase of the proposal. Consultations by the Council or requests from the Commission for an opinion shall be forwarded by the President to the committee responsible for consideration of the proposal concerned. The provisions for the first reading as set out in Rules 53 to 63 shall apply to legislative proposals whether they require one, two or three readings.

2.   Common positions from the Council shall be referred for consideration to the committee responsible at the first reading. The provisions for the second reading as set out in Rules 64 to 73 shall apply to common positions.

3.   During the Conciliation procedure between Parliament and the Council following the second reading, no referral back to committee shall take place. The provisions for the third reading as set out in Rules 74 to 78 shall apply to the Conciliation procedure.

4.   Rules 52, 58 (1) and (3), 59, 60, 129, 143, 144 and 147 shall not apply during the second and third readings.

5.   In the event of a conflict between a provision of the Rules of Procedure relating to the second and third readings and any other provision of the Rules, the provision relating to the second and third readings shall take precedence.

Rule 52 Delegation of the power of decision to committees

1.   The Conference of Presidents may refer a consultation, a request for an opinion, an own-initiative report (Rule 148) or a report based on a motion for a resolution tabled pursuant to Rule 45 (1) to (5) to the appropriate committee for a decision.

2.   If, after referral to committee pursuant to paragraph 1, one third of the current members of the committee request that the power of decision be referred back to Parliament, the procedures for debate and amendment of committee reports in plenary shall apply.

3.   The meeting at which the committee takes its decision shall be open to the public.

4.   The deadline for tabling amendments shall be published in the Bulletin of the European Parliament.

5.   As soon as the committee has adopted its report, and subject to Rules 102 (1) and 103, the President shall place it on the agenda for the next part-session. The committee's resolution and amendments, if any, shall be deemed adopted and shall be recorded in the minutes unless, before the start of the second day of the part-session, one tenth of the component Members of Parliament from at least three political groups have tabled their opposition in writing. The President shall announce this opposition at the start of the second sitting of the part-session; in this case the committee's report shall be placed on the agenda for the same or the following part- session and shall be dealt with in accordance with the normal procedure. The President shall set a deadline for the tabling of amendments.

FIRST READING - COMMITTEE STAGE

Rule 53 Verification of legal basis

1.   For all Commission proposals and other documents of a legislative nature, the committee responsible shall first verify the validity and appropriateness of the chosen legal basis.

2.   If the committee responsible disputes the validity or the appropriateness of the legal basis, it shall request the opinion of the committee responsible for legal affairs.

3.   The committee responsible for legal affairs may also on its own initiative take up questions concerning the legal basis of proposals submitted by the Commission. In such cases it shall duly inform the committee responsible.

4.   If the committee responsible for legal affairs decides to dispute the validity or the appropriateness of the legal basis, it shall report its conclusions to Parliament.

5.   If amendments are tabled in Parliament to change the legal basis of a Commission proposal without the committee responsible having disputed the validity or appropriateness of the legal basis, the committee responsible for legal affairs must deliver an opinion on the amendments tabled before they are put to the vote.

Rule 54 Subsidiarity, fundamental rights, financial resources

1.   During the examination of a legislative proposal, Parliament shall pay particular attention to whether the proposal respects the principle of subsidiarity and the fundamental rights of citizens. Where a proposal has financial implications, Parliament shall establish whether sufficient financial resources are provided.

2.   If Parliament concludes that the principle of subsidiarity is not duly respected, or
that the fundamental rights of citizens are not sufficiently respected, or that the financial
resources provided are not sufficient, it shall request the Commission to make the
necessary modifications to its proposal.

Rule 55 Transparency in the legislative process
1.   Throughout the whole legislative procedure Parliament and its committees shall
request access to all documents relating to Commission proposals under the same
conditions as the Council and its working parties.
2.   During the examination of a Commission proposal, the committee responsible shall
request the Commission and the Council to keep it informed about the progress of this
proposal in the Council and its working parties and in particular to inform it of any
emerging compromises which will substantially amend the original Commission
proposal or of the intention of the Commission to withdraw its proposal.

Rule 56 Modification of a Commission proposal
1.   If the committee responsible, during its examination of a Commission proposal,
becomes aware that the Council intends to modify substantially this proposal, it shall
formally ask the Commission whether it intends to alter its proposal.
2.   If the Commission declares that it intends to alter its proposal, the committee
responsible shall postpone its examination of this proposal until it has been informed
about the new proposal or amendments by the Commission.
3.   During the examination of a Commission proposal in the committee responsible,
the Commission may also on its own initiative table amendments to its proposal directly
in the committee.
4.   If the Commission declares, following a request under paragraph 1, that it does not
intend to alter its proposal, the committee responsible shall proceed with its examination of the proposal. The declaration of the Commission shall be annexed to the
report and shall be considered by Parliament as binding on the Commission even after
the completion of the first reading.
5.   If, following a Commission declaration under paragraph 4, the Council, notwithstanding the position of the Commission, proceeds to a decision which substantially
modifies the original Commission proposal, the President of Parliament shall remind
the Council of its obligation to consult Parliament again.

Rule 57 Commission position on amendments
1.   Before the committee responsible proceeds to the final vote on a Commission
proposal, it shall request the Commission to state its position on all the amendments
to the proposal adopted by the committee.
2.   If the Commission is not in a position to make such a statement or declares that it
is not prepared to accept all the amendments adopted by the committee then the
committee may postpone the final vote.
3.   The position of the Commission shall be annexed to the report.

FIRST READING - PLENARY STAGE

Rule 58 Conclusion of first reading
1.   Without prejudice to Rules 52, 99 and 143 (1), Parliament shall discuss the
legislative proposal on the basis of the report drawn up by the committee responsible
pursuant to Rule 144.
2.   Parliament shall first vote on the amendments to the proposal with which the report
of the committee responsible is concerned, then on the proposal, amended or other-

wise, then on the amendments to the draft legislative resolution, then on the draft legislative resolution as a whole, which shall contain only a statement as to whether Parliament approves, rejects or proposes amendments to the Commission's proposal and any procedural requests. The consultation procedure is concluded if the draft legislative resolution is adopted.

3. The text of the proposal as approved by Parliament and the accompanying resolution shall be forwarded to the Council and Commission by the President as Parliament's opinion.

Rule 59 Rejection of a Commission proposal

1. If a Commission proposal fails to secure a majority of the votes cast, the President shall, before Parliament votes on the draft legislative resolution, request the Commission to withdraw the proposal.

2. If the Commission does so, the President shall hold the consultation procedure on the proposal to be superfluous and shall inform the Council accordingly.

3. If the Commission does not withdraw its proposal, Parliament shall refer the matter back to the committee responsible without voting on the draft legislative resolution. In this case, the committee responsible shall, orally or in writing, report back to Parliament within a period decided by Parliament which may not exceed two months.

4. If the committee responsible is unable to meet the deadline, it shall request referral back to committee pursuant to Rule 129 (1). If necessary, Parliament may set a new time limit pursuant to Rule 129 (4). If the committee's request is not accepted, Parliament shall move to the vote on the draft legislative resolution.

Rule 60 Adoption of amendments to a Commission proposal

1. Where the Commission proposal as a whole is approved, but on the basis of amendments which have also been adopted, the vote on the draft legislative resolution shall be postponed until the Commission has stated its position on each of Parliament's amendments. If the Commission is not in a position to make such a statement at the end of Parliament's vote on its proposal, it shall inform the President or the committee responsible as to when it will be in a position to do so; the proposal shall then be placed on the draft agenda of the first part-session thereafter.

2. Where the Commission announces that it does not intend to adopt all Parliament's amendments, the rapporteur of the committee responsible or, failing him, the chairman of that committee shall make a formal proposal to Parliament as to whether the vote on the draft legislative resolution should proceed. Before submitting this proposal, the rapporteur or chairman of the committee responsible may request the President to suspend consideration of the item. Should Parliament decide to postpone the vote, the matter shall be deemed to be referred back to the committee responsible for reconsideration. In this case, the committee responsible shall, orally or in writing, report back to Parliament within a period decided by Parliament which may not exceed two months. If the committee responsible is unable to meet the deadline, the procedure provided for in Rule 59 (4) shall be applied. Only amendments tabled by the committee responsible and seeking to reach a compromise with the Commission shall be admissible at this stage.

3. Application of paragraph 2 does not preclude a request for referral being tabled by other Members pursuant to Rule 129.

FIRST READING - FOLLOW-UP PROCEDURE

Rule 61 Follow-up to Parliament's opinion

1.   In the period following the adoption by Parliament of its opinion on a proposal by the Commission, the chairman and the rapporteur of the committee responsible shall monitor the progress of the proposal in the course of the procedure leading to its adoption by the Council to ensure that the undertakings made by the Commission to Parliament with respect to its amendments are properly observed.

2.   The Council or, if necessary, the Commission shall, during this period, and at least once every three months, furnish all necessary information to the committee responsible.

3.   The committee responsible shall, in particular, bring to Parliament's attention any potential or actual breach of undertakings made by the Commission to Parliament.

4.   At any stage of the follow-up procedure the committee responsible may, if it deems it necessary, table a motion for a resolution under this Rule inviting Parliament:
— to call upon the Commission to withdraw its proposal, or
— to call upon the Council to open a conciliation procedure with the Parliament, pursuant to Rule 63, or
— to call upon the Council to reconsult Parliament pursuant to Rule 62, or
— to decide to take such other action that it deems appropriate.

This motion shall be placed on the draft agenda of the part-session following the decision by the committee.

Rule 62 Renewed consultation

The President shall, at the request of the committee responsible, call on the Council to reconsult Parliament:
— where the Commission withdraws its initial proposal after Parliament has delivered its opinion in order to replace it with another text;
— where the Commission or the Council substantially amend or intend to amend the proposal on which Parliament originally delivered an opinion;
— where, through the passage of time or changes in circumstances, the nature of the problem with which the proposal is concerned substantially changes.

The President shall also request reconsultation in the circumstances defined in this Rule where Parliament so decides on a proposal from a political group or at least twenty-nine Members.

Rule 63 Conciliation procedure

1.   Where, in the case of certain important Community decisions, the Council intends to depart from the opinion of Parliament, a procedure for conciliation with the Council, with the active participation of the Commission, may be opened by Parliament when delivering its opinion.

2.   This procedure shall be initiated by Parliament, either at its own or at the Council's initiative.

3.   For the composition and procedure of the delegation to the conciliation committee Rule 75 (1) to (7) shall apply.

4.   The committee responsible shall report on the results of the conciliation. This report shall be debated and voted on by Parliament.

SECOND READING - COMMITTEE STAGE

Rule 64 Communication of the Council's common position

1.   Communication of the Council's common position pursuant to Articles 189b and 189c of the EC Treaty takes place when it is announced by the President in Parliament. On the day of the announcement, the President must have received the documents containing the common position itself, the reasons which led the Council to adopt its common position and the Commission's position, duly translated into the official languages of the European Union.
2.   A list of such communications shall be published in the minutes of the sitting together with the name of the committee responsible.

Rule 65 Time limits

1.   The President shall, on a request from the chairman or rapporteur of the committee responsible, ask the Council to agree to an extension, by a maximum of one month, of the three-month period following either the communication of the common position to Parliament or the presentation of the Commission's re-examined proposal.
2.   The President may, after consulting the chairman and the rapporteur of the committee responsible, on behalf of Parliament agree, on a request from the Council, to extend the period of three months following the communication of the common position to Parliament or the presentation of the Commission's re-examined proposal by a maximum of one month.

Rule 66 Referral to and procedure in the committee responsible

1.   On the day of its communication to Parliament pursuant to Rule 64 (1), the common position shall be deemed to have been referred automatically to the committee responsible and to the committees asked for their opinion at first reading.
2.   The common position shall be entered as the first item on the agenda of the first meeting of the committee responsible following the date of its communication.
3.   Unless otherwise decided, the rapporteur during second reading shall be the same as during first reading.
4.   The provisions for Parliament's second reading in Rules 69 (1), 71 (1) and 72 (2) and (4) shall apply to the proceedings in the committee responsible; only members or permanent substitutes of that committee may table proposals for rejection and amendments. The committee shall decide by a majority of the votes cast.
5.   The committee responsible may request a dialogue with the Council in order to reach a compromise.[1]
6.   The committee responsible shall submit a recommendation for second reading proposing the decision Parliament should take on the common position adopted by the Council. The recommendation shall include a short justification for the decision proposed.
7.   If the common position is approved without amendment, the recommendation may take the form of a letter.

---

1   See Rule 72 (2) (b).

SECOND READING - PLENARY STAGE

Rule 67 Conclusion of second reading

1.   The Council's common position and, where available, the recommendation for second reading of the committee responsible shall automatically be placed on the draft
agenda for the part-session whose Wednesday falls before and closest to the day of
expiry of the period of three months or, if extended in accordance with Rule 65, of four
months, unless the matter has been dealt with at an earlier part-session.

2.   The second reading shall be concluded when Parliament approves, rejects or
amends the common position within the time limits and in accordance with the conditions laid down by Articles 189b and 189c of the EC Treaty.

Rule 68 Approval without amendment of the Council's common position

Where no motion to reject the common position, and no amendments to the common
position, are adopted under Rules 71 and 72 within the time limits specified by Articles
189b and 189c of the EC Treaty, the President shall declare the common position
approved without a vote, unless Parliament has approved the common position by a
majority of the votes cast.

Rule 69 Intended rejection of the Council's common position

1.   For legislative proposals falling under Article 189b of the EC Treaty a committee,
a political group or at least twenty-nine Members may, in writing and before a deadline
set by the President, table a proposal for a declaration by Parliament of intended
rejection of the Council's common position. The proposal shall require for its approval
the votes of a majority of the component Members of Parliament. The proposal shall
be put to the vote before any amendments.

2.   If the proposal is approved, the President shall ask the Council whether it intends
to convene the Conciliation Committee. If the Council does not intend to convene the
Conciliation Committee, the President shall announce in Parliament that the procedure
is terminated and the proposed act shall be deemed not to have been adopted.

3.   For the composition and procedure of the delegation to the Conciliation Committee
Rule 75 shall apply.

Rule 70 Conciliation during second reading

1.   In the light of the conclusions of the Conciliation Committee convened pursuant to
Rule 69 (2), Parliament's delegation may recommend that Parliament confirm its rejection of the common position in a separate vote by a majority of its component Members. If Parliament confirms the rejection the President shall declare the legislative
procedure closed. If Parliament does not confirm the rejection with the required majority
then it shall proceed with the consideration of the common position and any amendments tabled to it.

2.   In the light of the conclusions of the Conciliation Committee, Parliament's delegation may recommend that consideration of the common position and any amendments
tabled to it be resumed or, in consultation with the committee responsible, propose new
amendments for consideration by Parliament in accordance with Rule 72. The delegation may recommend the application of Rule 115 (5) for the vote on the amendments.

Rule 71 Rejection of the Council's common position

1.   The committee responsible, a political group or at least twenty-nine Members may,
in writing and before a deadline set by the President, table a proposal to reject the common position of the Council. Such a proposal shall require for its adoption the votes of

a majority of the component Members of Parliament. A proposal to reject the common position shall be voted on before voting on any amendments.

2.   Notwithstanding a vote by Parliament against the initial proposal to reject the common position, Parliament may, on the recommendation of the rapporteur, consider a further proposal for rejection after voting on the amendments and hearing a statement from the Commission pursuant to Rule 72 (4).

3.   If the common position of the Council is rejected, the President shall request the Commission to withdraw its proposal.

4.   If the Commission does so, the President shall hold the cooperation procedure on the proposal to be superfluous and shall inform the Council accordingly.

Rule 72 Amendments to the Council's common position

1.   The committee responsible, a political group or at least twenty-nine Members may table amendments to the Council's common position for consideration in Parliament.

2.   An amendment to the common position shall be admissible only if it conforms to the provisions of Rules 124 and 125 and:

(a) it seeks to restore wholly or partly the position adopted by Parliament in its first reading; or

(b) it is a compromise amendment representing an agreement between the Council and Parliament; or

(c) it seeks to amend a part of the text of a common position which was not included in - or differs in content from - the proposal submitted in first reading and which does not amount to a substantial change within the meaning of Rule 62.

The President's discretion to declare an amendment admissible or inadmissible cannot be questioned.

3.   An amendment shall be adopted only if it secures the votes of a majority of the component Members of Parliament.

4.   If one or more of the amendments are adopted, the rapporteur of the committee responsible or, failing him, the chairman of that committee shall ask the Commission to state its position.

Rule 73 Consequences of the Commission failing to accept Parliament's amendments in its re-examined proposal

1.   For legislative proposals falling under Article 189c of the EC Treaty, the Conference of Presidents shall place the Commission's re-examined proposal on the draft agenda for the part-session following its adoption and the President shall request the Commission to inform Parliament of the reasons which led the Commission not to accept Parliament's amendments.

2.   Parliament may, by a majority of its component Members, request the Commission to withdraw its proposal.

THIRD READING - CONCILIATION

Rule 74 Convening of Conciliation Committee

Where the Council is unable to approve all Parliament's amendments to the common position, the President may, after consulting the chairmen of the political groups and the chairman and rapporteur of the committee responsible, agree to a time and place for a first meeting of the Conciliation Committee. The six-week deadline for the Conciliation Committee to agree a joint text shall run from the time at which the Committee first meets.

Rule 75 Delegation to Conciliation Committee

1.   Parliament's delegation to the Conciliation Committee shall consist of a number of members equal to the number of members of the Council delegation.

2.   The political composition of the delegation shall correspond to the composition of Parliament by political groups. The Conference of Presidents shall fix the exact number of Members from each political group.

3.   The members of the delegation shall be appointed by the political groups for each particular conciliation case, preferably from among the members of the committees concerned, except for three members who shall be appointed as permanent members of successive delegations for a period of twelve months. The three permanent members shall be appointed by the political groups from among the Vice-Presidents and shall represent at least two different political groups. The chairman and the rapporteur of the committee responsible in each particular case shall be members of the delegation.

4.   The political groups represented on the delegation may appoint substitutes who may only participate in the work of the Conciliation Committee if the full member is absent for the whole meeting.

5.   Political groups not represented on the delegation may each send one representative to any internal preparatory meeting of the delegation.

6.   The delegation shall be led by the President or by one of the three permanent members.

7.   The delegation shall decide by a majority of its members. Its deliberations shall be held in camera. The Conference of Presidents may lay down further procedural guidelines for the work of the delegation to the Conciliation Committee.

8.   The results of the conciliation including any proposed amendments or compromises shall be reported by the delegation to Parliament in due time to allow Parliament to complete any further procedural steps pursuant to the provisions of the EC Treaty.

Rule 76 Time limits

1.   The President shall, at the request of the delegation, ask the Council to agree to an extension, by a maximum of two weeks, of the six-week periods allowed for the work of the Conciliation Committee and for the approval of a joint text or the rejection of a Council text.

2.   The President may, after consultation with the delegation, agree on behalf of Parliament to a request from the Council for an extension, by a maximum of two weeks, of the six-week periods mentioned in paragraph 1.

THIRD READING - PLENARY STAGE

Rule 77 Joint text

1.   Where agreement on a joint text is reached within the Conciliation Committee, the matter shall automatically be placed on the agenda of the last part-session to fall within six or, if extended, eight weeks of the date of approval of the joint text by the Conciliation Committee unless the matter has been dealt with earlier.

2.   Parliament shall discuss the joint text on the basis of a report by its delegation to the Conciliation Committee.

3.   No amendments may be tabled to the joint text.

4.   The joint text as a whole shall be the subject of a single vote. The joint text shall be approved if it secures a majority of the votes cast.

Rule 78 Council text

1. Where no agreement is reached on a joint text within the Conciliation Committee, the President shall invite the Commission to withdraw its proposal, and invite the Council not to adopt under any circumstances a position pursuant to Article 189b (6) of the EC Treaty. Should the Council nonetheless confirm its common position, the President of the Council shall be invited to justify its decision before Parliament in plenary sitting. The matter shall automatically be placed on the agenda of the last part-session to fall within six or, if extended, eight weeks of the confirmation by the Council unless the matter has been dealt with at an earlier part-session.
2. Parliament shall discuss the Council text on the basis of a report from its delegation to the Conciliation Committee.
3. No amendments may be tabled to the Council text.
4. The Council text as a whole shall be the subject of a single vote. Parliament shall vote on a motion to reject the Council text. If this motion receives the votes of a majority of the component Members of Parliament, the President shall declare the proposed act not adopted.

Rule 79 Signature of adopted acts

For legislative acts adopted under the procedure in Article 189b of the EC Treaty, the President shall, after checking that all procedures have been properly completed, sign the act together with the President of the Council and arrange its publication in the Official Journal of the European Communities.

ASSENT PROCEDURE

Rule 80 Conclusion of assent procedure

1. Where Parliament is requested to give its assent to an international agreement or a legislative proposal, it shall consider the matter on the basis of a recommendation from the committee responsible to adopt or reject the document on which Parliament has been consulted. Parliament shall then take a decision on the document by means of a single vote, and no amendments may be tabled. The majority required for the adoption of the assent shall be the majority indicated in the relevant article of the EC Treaty.
2. For accession treaties and international agreements, Rules 89 and 90 shall apply respectively.
3. For legislative proposals the committee responsible may decide, in order to facilitate a positive outcome of the procedure, to present an interim report to Parliament with a motion for a resolution containing recommendations for modification or implementation of the proposal. If Parliament approves at least one recommendation with the same majority as required for the final assent, the President shall request the opening of a conciliation procedure with the Council. The committee responsible shall make its final recommendation for the assent of Parliament in the light of the outcome of the conciliation with the Council.

SUPERVISORY POWERS

Rule 81 Implementing provisions

When the Commission tables in Parliament an implementing measure which it has submitted to a management committee or a draft implementing measure which it has submitted to an advisory or regulatory committee, the President shall refer the document in question to the committee responsible for the proposal from which the implementing provisions derive.

Rule 82 Official codification of Community legislation
1.   When a Commission proposal for official codification of Community legislation is submitted to Parliament, it shall be referred to the committee responsible for legal matters. Provided that it is ascertained that the proposal does not entail any change of substance to existing Community legislation, the procedure laid down in Rule 143 (1) shall be followed.
2.   The chairman of the committee responsible or the rapporteur appointed by that committee may participate in the examination and revision of the proposal for codification. If necessary, the committee responsible may give its opinion beforehand.
3.   Notwithstanding the provisions of Rule 143 (3), the procedure without report may not be applied to a proposal for official codification where this procedure is opposed by a majority of the members of the committee responsible for legal matters or of the committee responsible.

Rule 83 Consequences of the Council failing to act following approval
of its common position
If, within three or, with the agreement of the Council, four months of the communication of the common position, Parliament has neither rejected nor amended the position, and the Council fails to adopt the proposed legislation in accordance with the common position, the President may, on behalf of Parliament and after consulting the committee responsible for legal affairs, bring an action against the Council in the Court of Justice under Article 175 of the EC Treaty.

Rule 84 Proceedings before the Court of Justice
1.   Parliament shall, within the time limits specified by the Treaties and the Statute of the Court of Justice for action by the institutions of the Union and by any natural or legal persons, examine Community legislation to ensure that its rights have been fully respected.
2.   The committee responsible shall report to Parliament, orally if necessary, where it suspects a breach of Parliament's rights.

Chapter VIII Budgetary Procedures

Rule 85 General Budget
Implementing procedures for examination of the General Budget of the European Union and supplementary budgets, in accordance with the budgetary provisions of the Treaties establishing the European Communities and the Treaty of 22 July 1975, shall be adopted by resolution of Parliament and annexed to these Rules.

Rule 86 Discharge to the Commission in respect of implementation of the budget
The provisions concerning the implementing procedures for the decision on the giving of a discharge to the Commission in respect of the implementation of the budget in accordance with the Treaty of 22 July 1975 and the Financial Regulation are attached to these Rules as an annex. This annex shall be adopted pursuant to Rule 163 (2).

Rule 87 Parliamentary control over implementation of the budget
1.   Parliament shall monitor the implementation of the current year's budget. It shall entrust this task to the committee responsible for budgetary control and the other committees concerned.
2.   Each year it shall, however, consider, before the first reading of the draft budget for the following financial year, the problems involved in the implementation of the cur-

rent budget, where appropriate on the basis of a motion for a resolution tabled by its committee responsible.

Chapter IX Treaties And International Agreements

Rule 88 ECSC Treaty amendments
1. Amendments proposed by the Commission and the Council under Article 95 of the ECSC Treaty shall be printed at the same time as the assenting opinion thereon delivered by the Court of Justice. These documents shall be distributed and referred to the appropriate committee. In its report the committee shall recommend either adoption or rejection of the proposed amendment as a whole.
2. No amendment thereto shall be admissible, and split voting shall not be permitted. For adoption the proposed amendment as a whole shall require a three-quarters majority of the votes cast, representing a two-thirds majority of the component Members of Parliament.
3. Any Member may table a motion for a resolution proposing to the Commission and Council amendments to the ECSC Treaty under Article 95 of that Treaty. Such motions shall be printed, distributed and referred to the appropriate committee. They shall be adopted only if they secure the votes of a majority of the component Members of Parliament.

Rule 89 Accession treaties
1. Any application by a European State to become a member of the European Union shall be referred to the appropriate committee for consideration.
2. Parliament may decide, on a proposal from the committee responsible, a political group or at least twenty-nine Members, to request the Commission and the Council to take part in a debate before negotiations with the applicant State commence.
3. Throughout the negotiations the Commission and the Council shall inform the committee responsible regularly and thoroughly of the progress in the negotiations, if necessary on a confidential basis.
4. At any stage of the negotiations Parliament may, on the basis of a report from the committee responsible, adopt recommendations and require these to be taken into account before the conclusion of a Treaty for the accession of an applicant State to the European Union. Such recommendations shall require the same majority as the final assent.
5. When the negotiations are completed, but before any agreement is signed, the draft agreement shall be submitted to Parliament for assent.
6. Parliament shall give its assent to an application by a European State to become a member of the European Union by a majority of its component Members on the basis of a report by the committee responsible.

Rule 90 International agreements
1. When it is intended to open negotiations on the conclusion, renewal or amendment of an international agreement, including agreements in specific areas such as monetary affairs or trade, the committee responsible shall ensure that Parliament is fully informed by the Commission about its recommendations for a negotiating mandate, if necessary on a confidential basis.
2. Parliament may, on a proposal from the committee responsible or a political group or at least twenty-nine Members, request the Council not to authorize the opening of negotiations until Parliament has stated its position on the proposed negotiating mandate on the basis of a report from the committee responsible.

3.   The committee responsible shall verify the chosen legal basis for international agreements pursuant to Rule 53.
4.   Throughout the negotiations the Commission and the Council shall inform the committee responsible regularly and thoroughly of the progress in the negotiations, if necessary on a confidential basis.
5.   At any stage of the negotiations Parliament may, on the basis of a report from the committee responsible, adopt recommendations and require that these be taken into account before the conclusion of the international agreement under consideration.
6.   When the negotiations are completed, but before any agreement is signed, the draft agreement shall be submitted to Parliament for opinion or for assent. For the assent procedure Rule 80 shall apply.
7.   Parliament shall give its opinion on, or its assent to, the conclusion, renewal or amendment of an international agreement or a financial protocol concluded by the European Community by a majority of the votes cast.
8.   If the opinion adopted by Parliament is negative, the President shall request the Council not to conclude the agreement in question.
9.   If Parliament, by a majority of the votes cast, withholds its assent to an international agreement, the President shall refer the agreement in question back to the Council for reconsideration.

Chapter X Common Foreign And Security Policy

Rule 91 Consultation of and provision of information to Parliament within the framework of the common foreign and security policy
1.   The committee responsible for the common foreign and security policy shall ensure that Parliament is consulted on such policies and that its opinions are duly taken into account, particularly in connection with the joint actions referred to in Article J.3 of the Treaty on European Union and the actions referred to in Article 228a of the EC Treaty.
2.   Where appropriate, the committee shall inform Parliament in accordance with these Rules.
3.   The Council and the Commission shall provide the committee responsible with full, regular and timely information on the development of the Union's common foreign and security policy.
4.   At the request of the Commission or the Council, a committee may decide to hold its proceedings in camera.

Rule 92 Recommendations within the framework of the common foreign and security policy
1.   The committee responsible for the common foreign and security policy may draw up recommendations to the Council in its areas of responsibility after obtaining authorization from the Conference of Presidents or on a proposal within the meaning of Rule 46. In urgent cases the authorization referred to in the first subparagraph may be granted by the President, who may likewise authorize an emergency meeting of the committee concerned.
2.   During the process for adopting these recommendations, which must be put to the vote in the form of a written text, Rule 102 shall not apply and oral amendments shall be admissible.
3.   Recommendations drawn up in this way shall be included on the agenda for the next part-session. Recommendations shall be deemed adopted unless, before the beginning of the part-session, a minimum of one tenth of the component Members of Parliament submit a written objection, in which case the committee's recommendations

shall be considered and each recommendation shall be put to the vote as a whole in plenary during the same part-session.

4.   The debates provided for under Article J.7 of the Treaty on European Union shall be held in accordance with the arrangements laid down in Rule 37 (2), (3) and (4).

Chapter XI Cooperation in The Fields of Justice And Home Affairs

Rule 93 Consultation of and provision of information to Parliament in the fields of justice and home affairs

1.   The committee responsible for matters relating to cooperation in the fields of justice and home affairs shall ensure that Parliament is fully informed and consulted on the activities covered by such cooperation and that its opinions are duly taken into consideration, particularly in connection with the joint positions, joint actions and conventions referred to in Article K.3 of the Treaty on European Union.

2.   Where appropriate, the committee shall inform Parliament in accordance with these Rules.

3.   The Council and Commission shall provide the committee responsible with full, regular and timely information on the development of cooperation in the fields of justice and home affairs.

4.   At the request of the Commission or the Council, a committee may decide to hold its proceedings in camera.

5.   The detailed rules for consultation and information, including procedures and frequency, will be included as an annex to these Rules.

Rule 94 Recommendations in the fields of justice and home affairs

1.   The committee responsible for matters relating to cooperation in the fields of justice and home affairs may draw up recommendations to the Council in its areas of responsibility after obtaining authorization from the Conference of Presidents or on a proposal within the meaning of Rule 46. In urgent cases the authorization referred to in the first subparagraph may be granted by the President of Parliament, who may likewise authorize an emergency meeting of the committee concerned. Recommendations drawn up in this way shall be included on the agenda for the next part-session.

2.   The debates provided for under Article K.6 of the Treaty on European Union shall be held in accordance with the arrangements laid down in Rule 37 (2), (3) and (4).

Chapter XII Order of Business of Parliament

Rule 95 - 100 [omitted]

Chapter XIII General Rules For The Conduct of Sittings

Rule 101 Access to the chamber

1.   No person may enter the chamber except Members of Parliament, Members of the Commission or Council, the Secretary-General of Parliament, members of the staff whose duties require their presence there, and experts or officials of the European Union.

2.   Only holders of an admission card duly issued by the President or Secretary-General of Parliament shall be admitted to the galleries.

3.   Members of the public admitted to the galleries shall remain seated and keep silent. Any person expressing approval or disapproval shall immediately be ejected by the ushers.

Rule 102 Languages

1. All documents of Parliament shall be drawn up in the official languages.
2. Speeches delivered in one of the official languages shall be simultaneously inter-preted into the other official languages and into any other language the Bureau may consider necessary.

Rule 103 - 111 [omitted]

Chapter XIV Quorum And Voting

Rule 112 Quorum

1. Parliament may deliberate, settle its agenda and approve the minutes of procee-dings, whatever the number of Members present.
2. A quorum shall exist when one third of the component Members of Parliament are present in the Chamber.
3. All votes shall be valid whatever the number of voters unless the President, on a request made before voting has begun by at least twenty-nine Members, establishes at the moment of voting that the quorum is not present. If the vote shows that the quorum is not present, the vote shall be placed on the agenda of the next sitting.
4. Members who have asked for the quorum to be established shall be counted as being present within the meaning of paragraph 2, even if they are no longer in the Chamber.
5. If fewer than twenty-nine Members are present, the President may rule that there is no quorum.

Rule 113 Voting procedure

1. The following voting procedure shall apply to reports:
(a) first, voting on any amendments to the text with which the report of the committee responsible is concerned,
(b) second, voting on the text as a whole, amended or otherwise,
(c) third, voting on the individual paragraphs of the motion for a resolution/draft legis-lative resolution, preceded in each case by voting on any amendments thereto,
(d) finally, voting on the motion for a resolution/draft legislative resolution as a whole (final vote).
Parliament shall not vote on the explanatory statement contained in the report.
2. The following procedure shall apply to second readings pursuant to the cooperation procedure:
(a) where no proposal to reject or amend the Council's common position has been tabled, the common position shall be deemed to have been approved in accor-dance with Rule 68;
(b) a proposal to reject the common position shall be voted upon before voting on any amendments (see Rule 71 (1));
(c) where several amendments to the common position have been tabled they shall be put to the vote in the order set out in Rule 115;
(d) where Parliament has proceeded to a vote to amend the common position, a further vote on the text as a whole may only be taken in accordance with Rule 71 (2).
3. Without prejudice to Rule 122, the only Member permitted to speak during the vote shall be the rapporteur, who shall have the opportunity of expressing briefly his committee's views on the amendments put to the vote.

Rule 113a Tied votes

1.   In the event of a tied vote under Rule 113 (1) (b) or (d), the text as a whole shall be referred back to committee. This shall also apply to votes under Rules 6 and 7 and to final votes under Rules 137 and 153, on the understanding that, for these two Rules, the matter is referred back to the Conference of Presidents.

2.   In the event of a tied vote on the Agenda as a whole (Rule 96) or the Minutes as a whole (Rule 133), or on a text put to a split vote under Rule 116, the text shall be deemed adopted.

3.   In all other cases where there is a tied vote, without prejudice to those Rules which require qualified majorities, the text or proposal shall be deemed rejected.

Rule 114 Principles governing voting

1.   Voting on a report shall take place on the basis of a recommendation from the committee responsible. The committee may delegate this task to its chairman and rapporteur.

2.   The committee may recommend that all or several amendments be put to the vote collectively, that they be accepted or rejected or declared void. It may also propose compromise amendments.

3.   Where the committee responsible recommends that amendments be put to the vote collectively, the collective vote on these amendments shall be taken first.

4.   Where the committee responsible proposes a compromise amendment it shall be given priority in voting.

5.   Amendments for which a roll call vote has been requested shall be put to the vote individually.

6.   A split vote shall not be admissible in the case of a collective vote or a vote on a compromise amendment.

Rule 115 Order of voting on amendments

1.   Amendments shall have priority over the text to which they relate and shall be put to the vote before that text.

2.   If two or more mutually exclusive amendments have been tabled to the same part of a text, the amendment that departs furthest from the original text shall have priority and shall be put to the vote first. If it is adopted the other amendments shall stand rejected. If it is rejected, the amendment next in priority shall be put to the vote and similarly for each of the remaining amendments. Where there is doubt as to priority, the President shall decide.

3.   The President may put the original text to the vote first, or put to the vote before the amendment that departs furthest from the original text an amendment that is closer to the original text. If either of these secures a majority, all other amendments tabled to the same text shall fall. Before applying this procedure, the President shall establish that it is not opposed by at least twenty-nine Members. If it is, he may not apply this procedure.

4.   Exceptionally, on a proposal from the President, amendments tabled after the close of the debate may be put to the vote if they are compromise amendments, or if there are technical problems. The President shall obtain the agreement of Parliament to putting such amendments to the vote. The following general criteria for admissibility may be applied:

— as a general rule, compromise amendments may not relate to parts of the text which have not been the subject of amendments prior to the conclusion of the debate;

— as a general rule, compromise amendments shall be tabled by political groups, the chairmen, rapporteurs or draftsmen of the committees concerned or the authors of other amendments;

— as a general rule, compromise amendments shall entail the withdrawal of other amendments to the same passage.

Only the President may propose that a compromise amendment be considered. In order for a compromise amendment to be put to the vote, the President must obtain the agreement of Parliament by asking whether there are any objections to such a vote being held. If an objection is raised, Parliament shall decide on the matter by a majority of the Members present.

5.   The President may put several amendments to the vote collectively when they are complementary, in particular when the committee responsible has tabled a set of amendments to the text with which its report is concerned. The President may seek the agreement of Parliament before doing so.

6.   The President may decide, following the adoption or rejection of a particular amendment, that several other amendments of similar content or with similar objectives be put to the vote collectively. The President may seek the agreement of Parliament before doing so.

Rule 116 Split voting

1.   Where the text to be put to the vote contains two or more provisions or references to two or more points or lends itself to division into two or more parts each with a distinct logical meaning and normative value, a split vote may be requested.

2.   The request may be made no later than one hour before the time at which voting begins, unless the President fixes a different deadline. The President shall decide on the request.

Rule 117 Right to vote

The right to vote is a personal right. Members shall cast their votes individually and in person.

Rule 118 Voting

1.   Normally Parliament shall vote by show of hands.

2.   If the President decides that the result is doubtful, a fresh vote shall be taken using the electronic voting system and, if the latter is not working, by sitting and standing.

3.   The result of the vote shall be recorded.

Rule 119 Voting by roll call

1.   In addition to the cases provided for under Rules 32 (2), 33 (5) and 34 (5), the vote shall be taken by roll call if so requested in writing by at least twenty-nine Members or a political group before voting has begun.

2.   The roll shall be called in alphabetical order, beginning with the name of a Member drawn by lot. The President shall be the last to be called to vote. Voting shall be by word of mouth and shall be expressed by "Yes", "No", or "I abstain". In calculating whether a motion has been adopted or rejected account shall be taken only of votes cast for and against. The President shall establish the result of the vote and announce it. Votes shall be recorded in the minutes of proceedings of the sitting by political group in the alphabetical order of Members' names.

Rule 120 Electronic voting

1.   The President may at any time decide that the voting operations indicated in Rules 118, 119 and 121 shall be carried out by means of an electronic voting system. Where

the electronic voting system cannot be used for technical reasons, voting shall take place pursuant to Rules 118, 119 (2) or 121. The technical instructions for the use of the electronic voting system shall be governed by instructions from the Bureau.
2.   Where an electronic vote is taken, only the numerical result of the vote shall be recorded. However, if a vote by roll call has been requested in accordance with Rule 119 (1), the votes shall be recorded in the minutes of proceedings of the sitting by political group in the alphabetical order of Members' names.
3.   The vote by roll call shall be taken in accordance with Rule 119 (2) if a majority of the Members present so request; the system indicated in paragraph 1 of this Rule may be used to determine whether a majority exists.

Rule 121 Voting by secret ballot
1.   In the case of appointments, voting shall be by secret ballot without prejudice to Rules 13 (1), 137 (1) and 142 (2) second subparagraph. Only ballot papers bearing the names of Members who have been nominated shall be taken into account in calculating the number of votes cast.
2.   Voting may also be by secret ballot if requested by at least one fifth of the component Members of Parliament. Such requests must be made before voting begins.
3.   A request for a secret ballot shall take priority over a request for a vote by roll call.
4.   Four Members chosen by lot shall count the votes cast in a secret ballot. In the case of votes pursuant to paragraph 1, candidates shall not act as tellers.

Rule 122 Explanations of vote
1.   Once the general debate has been concluded, any Member may give an oral explanation on the final vote for not longer than one minute or give a written explanation of no more than 200 words, which shall be included in the verbatim report of proceedings. Any political group may give an explanation of vote lasting not more than two minutes. No further requests to give explanations of vote shall be accepted once the first explanation of vote has begun.
2.   Explanations of vote shall not be admissible in cases of votes on procedural matters.
3.   When a Commission proposal or a report is on the agenda of Parliament pursuant to Rules 52 (5) or 99, Members may submit written explanations of vote pursuant to paragraph 1.

Rule 123 Disputes on voting
1.   The President shall declare votes open and closed.
2.   Once the President has declared a vote open, no-one except the President shall be allowed to speak until the vote is declared closed.
3.   Points of order concerning the validity of a vote may be raised after the President has declared it closed.
4.   After the result of a vote by show of hands has been announced, a Member may request that this result be cross-checked using the electronic voting system.
5.   The President shall decide whether the result announced is valid. His decision shall be final.

Rule 124 Tabling and moving amendments
1.   Any Member may table amendments for consideration in the committee responsible. Amendments for consideration in Parliament may be tabled by the committee responsible, a political group or at least twenty-nine Members. Amendments shall be tabled in writing and signed by their authors.

2.   Subject to the limitations laid down in Rule 125, an amendment may seek to change any part of a text, and may be directed to deleting, adding or substituting words or figures.

3.   The President shall set a deadline for the tabling of amendments.

4.   An amendment may be moved during the debate by its author or by any other Member appointed by the author to replace him.

5.   Where an amendment is withdrawn by its author, it shall fall unless immediately taken over by another Member.

6.   Amendments shall be put to the vote only after they have been printed and distributed in all the official languages, unless Parliament decides otherwise. Parliament may not decide otherwise if at least twelve Members object.

Rule 125 Admissibility of amendments

1.   No amendment shall be admissible if:

(a) it does not directly relate to the text which it seeks to amend;

(b) it seeks to delete or replace the whole of a text;

(c) where it seeks to delete part of a text, its purpose can be achieved by holding a split vote pursuant to Rule 116; this provision shall not however preclude the inclusion in a report on a consultation pursuant to Rule 51 of an amendment to delete a part of a Commission proposal;

(d) it seeks to amend more than one of the individual articles or paragraphs of the text to which it relates. This provision shall not apply to compromise amendments;

(e) it is established that the wording in at least one of the official languages of the text it is sought to amend does not call for amendment; in this case, the President shall seek out a suitable linguistic remedy together with those concerned.

2.   An amendment shall lapse if it is inconsistent with decisions previously taken on the text during the same vote.

3.   The President shall decide whether amendments are admissible.

Chapter XV Interruptive And Procedural Motions

Rule 126 - 132 [omitted]

Chapter XVI Public Record of Proceedings

Rule 133 Minutes

1.   The minutes of each sitting, containing the decisions of Parliament and the names of speakers, shall be distributed at least half an hour before the opening of the next sitting.

2.   At the beginning of each sitting the President shall place before Parliament, for its approval, the minutes of the previous sitting.

3.   If any objections are raised to the minutes Parliament shall, if necessary, decide whether the changes requested should be considered. No Member may speak on the minutes for more than one minute.

4.   The minutes shall be signed by the President and the Secretary-General and preserved in the records of Parliament. They shall be published within one month in the Official Journal of the European Communities.

Rule 134 Verbatim reports

1.   A verbatim report of the proceedings of each sitting shall be drawn up in the official languages.

2.   Speakers shall be required to return typescripts of their speeches to the Secretariat not later than the day following that on which they received them.
3.   The verbatim report shall be published as an annex to the Official Journal of the European Communities.

Chapter XVII Committees

Rule 135 Setting up of committees
1.   Parliament shall set up standing committees whose powers shall be defined in an annex to the Rules of Procedure. Their members shall be elected during the first part-session following the re-election of Parliament and again two and a half years thereafter.
2.   Parliament may at any time set up temporary committees, whose powers, composition and term of office shall be defined at the same time as the decision to set them up is taken; their term of office may not exceed twelve months, except where Parliament extends that term on its expiry.

Rule 136 Temporary committees of inquiry
1.   Parliament may, at the request of one quarter of its Members, set up a temporary committee of inquiry to investigate alleged contraventions of Community law or alleged maladministration in the application of Community law which would appear to be the act of an institution or body of the European Communities, of a public administrative body of a Member State, or of persons empowered by Community law to implement that law. The decision to set up a temporary committee of inquiry shall be published in the Official Journal of the European Communities within one month. In addition, Parliament shall take all the necessary steps to make this decision as widely known as possible.
2.   The *modus operandi* of a temporary committee of inquiry shall be governed by the provisions of these Rules of Procedure relating to committees, save as otherwise specifically provided for in this Rule and in the Decision of the European Parliament, the Council and the Commission of 19 April 1995 on the detailed provisions governing the exercise of the European Parliament's right of inquiry which is annexed to these Rules.[1]
3.   The request to set up a temporary committee of inquiry must specify precisely the subject of the inquiry and include a detailed statement of the grounds for it. Parliament, on a proposal by the Conference of Presidents, shall decide whether to set up a committee and, if it decides to do so, on its composition, in accordance with the provisions of Rule 137.
4.   A temporary committee of inquiry shall complete its work on the submission of a report within a maximum period of twelve months. Parliament may twice decide to extend this period by three months. Only full members or, in their absence, permanent substitutes may vote in a temporary committee of inquiry.
5.   A temporary committee of inquiry shall elect its chairman and two vice-chairmen and appoint one or more rapporteurs. The committee may also assign responsibilities, duties or specific tasks to its members who must subsequently report to the committee in detail thereon. In the interval between one meeting and another, the bureau of the committee shall, in cases of urgency or need, exercise the committee's powers, subject to ratification at the next meeting.

---

1   See Annex VIII.

6.   When a temporary committee of inquiry considers that one of its rights has been infringed, it shall propose that the President take appropriate measures.

7.   A temporary committee of inquiry may contact the institutions or persons referred to in Article 3 of the Decision referred to in paragraph 2 with a view to holding a hearing or obtaining documents. Travel and accommodation expenses of members and officials of Community institutions and bodies shall be borne by the latter. Travel and accommodation expenses of other persons who appear before a temporary committee of inquiry shall be reimbursed by the European Parliament in accordance with the rules governing hearings of experts. Any person called to give evidence before a temporary committee of inquiry may claim the rights they would enjoy if acting as a witness before a tribunal in their country of origin. They must be informed of these rights before they make a statement to the committee. With regard to the languages used, a temporary committee of inquiry shall apply the provisions of Rule 102 of the Rules of Procedure. However, the bureau of the committee:

—   may restrict interpretation to the official languages of those who are to take part in the deliberations, if it deems this necessary for reasons of confidentiality,

—   shall decide about translation of the documents received in such a way as to ensure that the committee can carry out its deliberations efficiently and rapidly and that the necessary secrecy and confidentiality are respected.

8.   The chairman of a temporary committee of inquiry shall, together with the bureau, ensure that the secrecy or confidentiality of the deliberations are respected and shall give members due notice to this effect. He shall also explicitly refer to the provisions of Article 2 (2) of the Decision referred to above. Annex VII to the Rules of Procedure shall apply.

9.   Secret or confidential documents which have been forwarded shall be examined using technical measures to ensure that only the members responsible for the case have personal access to them. The members in question shall give a solemn undertaking not to allow any other person access to secret or confidential information, in accordance with this Rule, and to use such information exclusively for the purposes of drawing up their report for the temporary committee of inquiry. Meetings shall be held on premises equipped in such a way as to make it impossible for any non- authorized persons to listen to the proceedings.

10. After completion of its work a temporary committee of inquiry shall submit to Parliament a report on the results of its work, containing minority opinions if appropriate. The report shall be published. At the request of the temporary committee of inquiry Parliament shall hold a debate on the report at the part-session following its submission. The committee may also submit to Parliament a draft recommendation addressed to institutions or bodies of the European Communities or the Member States.

11. The President shall instruct the committee responsible pursuant to Annex VI to the Rules of Procedure to monitor the action taken on the results of the work of the temporary committee of inquiry and, if appropriate, to report thereon. He shall take any further steps which are deemed appropriate to ensure that the conclusions of the inquiry are acted upon in practice. Only the proposal by the Conference of Presidents concerning the composition of a temporary committee of inquiry (paragraph 3) is open to amendments, in accordance with Rule 137 (2). The subject of the inquiry as defined by one quarter of Parliament's Members (paragraph 3) and the period laid down in paragraph 4 are not open to amendments.

Rule 137 - 152 [omitted]

Chapter XVIII Interparliamentary Delegations

Rule 153 - 155 [omitted]

Chapter XIX Petitions

Rule 156 Right of petition

1. Any citizen of the European Union, and any natural or legal person residing or having its registered office in a Member State, shall have the right to address, individually or in association with other citizens or persons, a petition to the European Parliament on a matter which comes within the European Union's fields of activity and which affects him, her or it directly.
2. Petitions to Parliament shall show the name, occupation, nationality and permanent address of each signatory.
3. Petitions must be written in one of the official languages of the European Union.
4. Petitions shall be entered in a register in the order in which they are received if they comply with the conditions laid down in paragraph 2; those that do not shall be filed, and the petitioner shall be informed of the reasons therefore.
5. Petitions entered in the register shall be forwarded by the President to the committee responsible, which shall first ascertain whether the petitions registered fall within the sphere of activities of the European Union.
6. Petitions declared inadmissible by the committee shall be filed; the petitioner shall be informed of the decision and the reasons therefore.
7. In such cases the committee may suggest to the petitioner that he contact the competent authority of the Member State concerned or of the European Union.
8. Where the committee deems it appropriate, it may refer the matter to the Ombudsman.
9. Petitions addressed to the European Parliament by natural or legal persons who are neither citizens of the European Union nor reside in a Member State nor have their registered office in a Member State shall be registered and filed separately. The President shall send a monthly record of such petitions received during the previous month, indicating their subject matter, to the committee responsible for considering petitions, which may request those which it wishes to consider.

Rule 157 Examination of petitions

1. The committee responsible may decide to draw up a report or otherwise express its opinion on petitions it has declared admissible. The committee may, particularly in the case of petitions which seek changes in existing law, request opinions from other committees pursuant to Rule 147.
2. When considering petitions, the committee may organize hearings or dispatch members to establish the facts of the situation in situ.
3. With a view to preparing its opinions, the committee may request the Commission to submit documents, to supply information and to grant it access to its facilities.
4. The committee shall, where necessary, submit motions for resolutions to Parliament on petitions which it has considered. The committee may also request that its opinions be forwarded by the President to the Commission or the Council.
5. The committee shall inform Parliament every six months of the outcome of its deliberations. The committee shall, in particular, inform Parliament of the measures taken by the Council or the Commission on petitions referred to them by Parliament.
6. The President shall inform petitioners of the decisions taken and the reasons therefore.

Rule 158 Notice of petitions

1. Notice shall be given in Parliament of the petitions entered in the register referred to in Rule 156 (4) and the main decisions on the procedure to be followed in relation to specific petitions. Such announcements shall be entered in the minutes of proceedings.

2. The texts of petitions entered in the register, together with the texts of the committee's opinions forwarded with them, shall be preserved in the records of Parliament, where they shall be available for inspection by Members.

Chapter XX Ombudsman

Rule 159 Appointment of the Ombudsman

1. At the start of each parliamentary term, immediately after his election or in the cases referred to in paragraph 8, the President shall call for nominations for the office of Ombudsman and set a time limit for submitting nominations. A notice calling for nominations shall be published in the Official Journal of the European Communities.

2. Nominations must have the support of a minimum of twenty-nine Members who are nationals of at least two Member States. Each Member may support only one nomination. Nominations shall include all the supporting documents needed to show conclusively that the nominee fulfils the conditions required by the Regulations on the Ombudsman.

3. Nominations shall be forwarded to the committee responsible, which may ask to hear the nominees. Such hearings shall be open to all Members.

4. A list of admissible nominations in alphabetical order shall then be submitted to the vote of Parliament.

5. The vote shall be held by secret ballot on the basis of a majority of the votes cast. If no candidate is elected after the first two ballots, only the two candidates obtaining the largest number of votes in the second ballot may continue to stand. In the event of any tie the eldest candidate shall prevail.

6. Before opening the vote, the President shall ensure that at least half of Parliament's component Members are present.

7. The person appointed shall immediately be called upon to take an oath before the Court of Justice.

8. The Ombudsman shall exercise his duties until his successor takes office, except in the case of his death or dismissal.

Rule 160 Dismissal of the Ombudsman

1. One tenth of Parliament's component Members may request the Ombudsman's dismissal if he no longer fulfils the conditions required for the performance of his duties or if he is guilty of serious misconduct.

2. The request shall be forwarded to the Ombudsman and to the committee responsible, which, if it decides by a majority of its members that the reasons are well-founded, shall submit a report to Parliament. If he so requests, the Ombudsman shall be heard before the report is put to the vote. Parliament shall, following a debate, take a decision by secret ballot.

3. Before opening the vote, the President shall ensure that half of Parliament's component Members are present.

4. If the vote is in favour of the Ombudsman's dismissal and he does not resign accordingly the President shall, at the latest by the part-session following that at which the vote was held, apply to the Court of Justice to have the Ombudsman dismissed with a request for a ruling to be given without delay. Resignation by the Ombudsman shall terminate the procedure.

Rule 161 Activities of the Ombudsman
1. The conditions governing referrals to the Ombudsman, together with the procedures and the rules governing the latter's powers, will be annexed to the Rules of Procedure. The Ombudsman may draw up a proposal to this end which shall be forwarded to the committee responsible for the Rules of Procedure, which shall report to Parliament.
2. The Ombudsman shall inform the committee responsible of his activities on a regular basis or when the committee requests him to do so.
3. The Ombudsman and the chairman of the committee responsible shall each safeguard the confidentiality of information made known to them in connection with the Ombudsman's activities. Such information shall be made available only to the judicial authorities and only where it is needed for criminal proceedings.

Chapter XXI Application And Amendment of The Rules of Procedure

Rule 162 Application of the Rules of Procedure
1. Should doubt arise over the application or interpretation of these Rules of Procedure, the President may, without prejudice to any previous decisions in this field, refer the matter to the committee responsible for examination. Where a point of order is raised under Rule 127, the President may also refer the matter to the committee responsible.
2. The committee shall decide whether it is necessary to propose an amendment to the Rules of Procedure. In this case it shall proceed in accordance with Rule 163.
3. Should the committee decide that an interpretation of the existing Rules is sufficient, it shall forward its interpretation to the President who shall inform Parliament.
4. Should a political group or at least twenty-nine Members contest the committee's interpretation, the matter shall be put to the vote in Parliament. Adoption of the text shall be by simple majority provided that at least one third of Parliament's Members are present. In the event of rejection, the matter shall be referred back to the committee.
5. Uncontested interpretations and interpretations adopted by Parliament shall be appended in italic print as explanatory notes to the appropriate Rule or Rules, together with decisions on the application of the Rules of Procedure.
6. These explanatory notes shall constitute precedents for the future application and interpretation of the Rules concerned.
7. The provisions on the application of the Rules of Procedure shall be reviewed regularly.
8. Where these Rules confer rights on a specific number of Members, that numbers shall be automatically adjusted to the nearest whole number representing the same percentage of Parliament's membership whenever the total size of Parliament is increased, notably following enlargements of the European Union.

Rule 163 Amendment of the Rules of Procedure
1. Any Member may propose amendments to these Rules. Such proposed amendments shall be translated, printed, distributed and referred to the committee responsible, which shall examine them and decide whether to submit them to Parliament.
2. Amendments to these Rules shall be adopted only if they secure the votes of a majority of the component Members of Parliament.
3. Unless otherwise specified when the vote is taken, amendments to these Rules shall enter into force on the first day of the part-session following their adoption.

Chapter XXII Secretariat of Parliament - Accounting

Rule 164 - 166 [omitted]

Chapter XXIII Miscellaneous Provisions

Rule 167 Unfinished business
At the end of the last part-session before elections, all Parliament's unfinished business shall be deemed to have lapsed, subject to the provisions of the second paragraph of this Rule. At the beginning of each parliamentary term the Conference of Presidents shall take a decision on reasoned requests from parliamentary committees and other institutions to resume or continue the consideration of such matters.

These provisions shall not apply to petitions and communications that do not require a decision.

ANNEX I - VII [OMITTED]

ANNEX VIII DETAILED PROVISIONS GOVERNING THE EXERCISE OF THE EUROPEAN PARLIAMENT'S RIGHT OF INQUIRY[1]

THE EUROPEAN PARLIAMENT, THE COUNCIL AND THE COMMISSION,

[...] HAVING REGARD to the Treaty establishing the European Community, and in particular Article 138c thereof, [...]
WHEREAS the detailed provisions governing the exercise of the European Parliament's right of inquiry should be determined with due regard for the provisions laid down by the Treaties establishing the European Communities;
WHEREAS temporary committees of inquiry must have the means necessary to perform their duties; whereas, to that end, it is essential that the Member States and the institutions and bodies of the European Communities take all steps to facilitate the performance of those duties;
WHEREAS the secrecy and confidentiality of the proceedings of temporary committees of inquiry must be protected;
WHEREAS, at the request of one of the three institutions concerned, the detailed provisions governing the exercise of the right of inquiry may be revised as from the end of the current term of the European Parliament in the light of experience,

HAVE BY COMMON ACCORD ADOPTED THIS DECISION:

Article 1
The detailed provisions governing the exercise of the European Parliament's right of inquiry shall be as laid down by this Decision, in accordance with Article 20b of the ECSC Treaty, Article 138c of the EC Treaty and Article 107b of the EAEC Treaty.

Article 2
1.   Subject to the conditions and limits laid down by the Treaties referred to in Article 1 and in the course of its duties, the European Parliament may, at the request of one quarter of its Members, set up a temporary committee of inquiry to investigate alleged contraventions or maladministration in the implementation of Community law which would appear to be the act of an institution or a body of the European Communities, of a public administrative body of a Member State or of persons empowered by Community law to implement that law. The European Parliament shall determine the composition and rules of procedure of temporary committees of inquiry. The decision to set up a temporary committee of inquiry, specifying in parti-

---

1   OJ 1995 L 113, p. 2.

cular its purpose and the time limit for submission of its report, shall be published in the Official Journal of the European Communities.

2. The temporary committee of inquiry shall carry out its duties in compliance with the powers conferred by the Treaties on the institutions and bodies of the European Communities. The members of the temporary committee of inquiry and any other persons who, by reason of their duties, have become acquainted with facts, information, knowledge, documents or objects in respect of which secrecy must be observed pursuant to provisions adopted by a Member State or by a Community institution shall be required, even after their duties have ceased, to keep them secret from any unauthorized person and from the public. Hearings and testimony shall take place in public. Proceedings shall take place in camera if requested by one quarter of the members of the committee of inquiry, or by the Community or national authorities, or where the temporary committee of inquiry is considering secret information. Witnesses and experts shall have the right to make a statement or provide testimony in camera.

3. A temporary committee of inquiry may not investigate matters at issue before a national or Community court of law until such time as the legal proceedings have been completed. Within a period of two months either of publication in accordance with paragraph 1 or of the Commission being informed of an allegation made before a temporary committee of inquiry of a contravention of Community law by a Member State, the Commission may notify the European Parliament that a matter to be examined by a temporary committee of inquiry is the subject of a Community pre-litigation procedure; in such cases the temporary committee of inquiry shall take all necessary steps to enable the Commission fully to exercise the powers conferred on it by the Treaties.

4. The temporary committee of inquiry shall cease to exist on the submission of its report within the time limit laid down when it was set up, or at the latest upon expiry of a period not exceeding twelve months from the date when it was set up, and In any event at the close of the parliamentary term. By means of a reasoned decision the European Parliament may twice extend the twelve-month period by three months. Such a decision shall be published in the Official Journal of the European Communities.

5. A temporary committee of inquiry may not be set up or re-established with regard to matters into which an inquiry has already been held by a temporary committee of inquiry until at least twelve months have elapsed since the submission of the report on that inquiry or the end of its assignment and unless any new facts have emerged.

Article 3

1. The temporary committee of inquiry shall carry out the inquiries necessary to verify alleged contraventions or maladministration in the implementation of Community law under the conditions laid down below.

2. The temporary committee of Inquiry may invite an institution or a body of the European Communities or the Government of a Member State to designate one of its members to take part in its proceedings.

3. On a reasoned request from the temporary committee of inquiry, the Member States concerned and the institutions or bodies of the European Communities shall designate the official or servant whom they authorize to appear before the temporary committee of inquiry, unless grounds of secrecy or public or national security dictate otherwise by virtue of national or Community legislation. The officials or servants in question shall speak on behalf of and as instructed by their Governments or institutions. They shall continue to be bound by the obligations arising from the rules to which they are subject.

4. The authorities of the Member States and the institutions or bodies of the European Communities shall provide a temporary committee of inquiry, where it so requests or on their own initiative, with the documents necessary for the performance of its duties, save where prevented from doing so by reasons of secrecy or public or national security arising out of national or Community legislation or rules.

5. Paragraphs 3 and 4 shall be without prejudice to any other provisions of the Member States which prohibit officials from appearing or documents from being forwarded. An obstacle arising from reasons of secrecy, public or national security or the provisions referred to in the first subparagraph shall be notified to the European Parliament by a representative authorized to commit the Government of the Member State concerned or the institution.

6.   Institutions or bodies of the European Communities shall not supply the temporary committee of inquiry with documents originating in a Member State without first informing the State concerned. They shall not communicate to the temporary committee of inquiry any documents to which paragraph 5 applies without first obtaining the consent of the Member State concerned.
7.   Paragraphs 3, 4 and 5 shall apply to natural or legal persons empowered by Community law to implement that law.
8.   Insofar as is necessary for the performance of its duties, the temporary committee of inquiry may request any other person to give evidence before it. The temporary committee of inquiry shall inform any person named in the course of an inquiry to whom this might prove prejudicial; it shall hear such a person if that person so requests.

Article 4
1.   The information obtained by the temporary committee of inquiry shall be used solely for the performance of its duties. It may not be made public if it contains material of a secret or confidential nature or names persons. The European Parliament shall adopt the administrative measures and procedural rules required to protect the secrecy and confidentiality of the proceedings of temporary committees of inquiry.
2.   The temporary committee of inquiry's report shall be submitted to the European Parliament, which may decide to make it public subject to the provisions of paragraph 1.
3.   The European Parliament may forward to the institutions or bodies of the European Communities or to the Member States any recommendations which it adopts on the basis of the temporary committee of inquiry's report. They shall draw therefrom the conclusions which they deem appropriate.

Article 5
Any communication addressed to the national authorities of the Member States for the purposes of applying this Decision shall be made through their Permanent Representations to the European Union.

Article 6
At the request of the European Parliament, the Council or the Commission, the above rules may be revised as from the end of the current term of the European Parliament in the light of experience.

Article 7
This Decision shall enter into force on the day of its publication in the Official Journal of the European Communities.

ANNEX IX PROVISIONS GOVERNING THE APPLICATION OF RULE 9 (2) LOBBYING IN PARLIAMENT

Article 1 Passes
1.   The pass shall consist of a plastic card, bearing a photograph of the holder, indicating the holder's surname and forenames and the name of the firm, organization or person for whom the holder works. Pass-holders shall at all times wear their pass visibly on all Parliament premises. Failure to do so may lead to its withdrawal. Passes shall be distinguished by their shape and colour from the passes issued to occasional visitors.
2.   Passes shall only be renewed if the holders have fulfilled the obligations referred to in Rule 9 (2). Any dispute by a Member as to the activity of a representative or lobby shall be referred to the Quaestors, who shall look into the matter and may decide whether to maintain or withdraw the pass concerned.
3.   Passes shall not, under any circumstances, entitle holders to attend meetings of Parliament or its bodies other than those declared open to the public and shall not, in this case, entitle the holder to derogations from access rules applicable to all other Union citizens.

Article 2 Assistants

1.   At the beginning of each parliamentary term the Quaestors shall determine the maximum number of assistants who may be registered by each Member. Upon taking up their duties, registered assistants shall make a written declaration of their professional activities and any other remunerated functions or activities.

2.   They shall have access to Parliament under the same conditions as staff of the Secretariat or the political groups.

3.   All other persons, including those working directly with Members, shall only have access to Parliament under the conditions laid down in Rule 9 (2).

Council Decision 99/385 of 3 May 1999 Adopting the Council's Rules of Procedure[1]

THE COUNCIL OF THE EUROPEAN UNION,

HAVING REGARD to the Treaty establishing the European Community, and in particular Article 207(3), first subparagraph, [...]

HAS DECIDED AS FOLLOWS:

Sole Article
The Rules of Procedure of the Council of 6 December 1993 (93/662), as amended on 6 February 1995 and 7 December 1998, shall be replaced by the following, which shall enter into force on 1 June 1999.

RULES OF PROCEDURE OF THE COUNCIL

Article 1 Notice and Venue of Meetings
1.   The Council shall meet when convened by its President on his own initiative or at the request of one of its members or of the Commission.
2.   The President shall make known the dates which he envisages for meetings of the Council during his period of office as President, seven months before the beginning thereof.
3.   The Council shall have its seat in Brussels. During the months of April, June and October, the Council shall hold its meetings in Luxembourg.
In exceptional circumstances and for duly substantiated reasons, the Council or the Permanent Representatives Committee (Coreper), acting unanimously, may decide that a Council meeting will be held elsewhere.

Article 2 Agenda
1.   The President shall draw up the provisional agenda for each meeting. The agenda shall be sent to the other members of the Council and to the Commission at least 14 days before the beginning of the meeting.
2.   The provisional agenda shall contain the items in respect of which a request for inclusion on the agenda, together with any documents relating thereto, has been received by the General Secretariat from a member of the Council or from the Commission at least 16 days before the beginning of that meeting.
The provisional agenda shall also indicate the items on which the Presidency, a member of the Council or the Commission may request a vote.
3.   Items relating to the adoption of an act or a common position on a legislative proposal or a proposal for a measure to be adopted under Title VI of the EU Treaty shall not be placed on the provisional agenda for a decision until the six-week period provided for in point 3 of the Protocol on the role of national parliaments in the European Union has elapsed.
The Council may unanimously derogate from the six-week period where the entry of an item is subject to the exception on grounds of urgency provided for in point 3 of that Protocol.

---

1   OJ 1999 L 147, p. 13, footnotes omitted.

4.   Only items in respect of which the documents have been sent to the members of the Council and to the Commission at the latest by the date on which the provisional agenda is sent may be placed on that agenda.

5.   The General Secretariat shall transmit to the members of the Council and to the Commission requests for the inclusion of items in the agenda, documents and indications concerning voting relating thereto in respect of which the time limits specified above were not respected.

6.   The agenda shall be adopted by the Council at the beginning of each meeting. The inclusion in the agenda of an item other than those appearing on the provisional agenda shall require unanimity in the Council. Items entered in this way may be put to the vote.

7.   The provisional agenda shall be divided into Part A and Part B. Items for which approval of the Council is possible without discussion shall be included in Part A, but this does not exclude the possibility of any member of the Council or of the Commission expressing an opinion at the time of the approval of these items and having statements included in the minutes.

8.   However, a "A" item shall be withdrawn from the agenda, unless the Council decides otherwise, if a position on an "A" item might lead to further discussion thereof or if a member of the Council or the Commission so requests.

9.   Any request for the inclusion of an "other business" item shall, in principle, be accompanied by an explanatory document.

Article 3 Representation of a Council Member Unable to Attend

Subject to the provisions of Article 9 on the delegation of voting rights, a member of the Council who is prevented from attending a meeting may arrange to be represented.

Article 4 Meetings and Public Debates

1.   Meetings of the Council shall not be public except in the cases referred to in paragraph 2.

2.   The Council shall hold policy debates on the six-monthly work programme submitted by the Presidency and, if appropriate, on the Commission's annual work programme. These debates shall be the subject of public transmission by audiovisual means.

The Council or Coreper may decide unanimously and on a case-by-case basis that other Council debates are to be the subject of public transmission by audiovisual means, in particular where they concern an important issue affecting the interests of the Union or an important new legislative proposal. To that end, it shall be for the Presidency, any member of the Council, or the Commission to propose issues or specific subjects for such a debate.

3.   The Commission shall be invited to take part in meetings of the Council. The same applies to the European Central Bank in cases where it exercises its right of initiative. The Council may, however, decide to deliberate without the presence of the Commission or of the European Central Bank.

4.   The members of the Council and of the Commission may be accompanied by officials who assist them. The number of such officials may be laid down by the Council.

The names and functions of such officials shall be notified in advance to the Secretary-General or the Deputy Secretary-General.

5.   Admission to meetings of the Council shall be subject to the production of a pass.

Article 5 Professional Secrecy and Production of Documents
in Legal Proceedings

1.   Without prejudice to Article 7 and other applicable provisions, the deliberations of the Council shall be covered by the obligation of professional secrecy, except insofar as the Council decides otherwise.

2.   The Council or Coreper may authorise the production for use in legal proceedings of a copy of or an extract from Council documents which have not been released to the public pursuant to these Rules or the Council's rules on public access to its documents.

Article 6 Cases Where the Council Acts in its Legislative Capacity

The Council acts in its legislative capacity within the meaning of the second subparagraph of Article 207(3)of the EC Treaty when it adopts rules which are legally binding in or for the Member States, by means of regulations, directives, framework decisions or decisions, on the basis of the relevant provisions of the Treaties, with the exception of discussions leading to the adoption of internal measures, administrative or budgetary acts, acts concerning inter-institutional or international relations or non-binding acts (such as conclusions, recommendations or resolutions).

Article 7 Making Deliberations Public

1.   Where the Council acts in its legislative capacity within the meaning of Article 6, the results of votes and explanations of votes by Council members, as well as the statements in the Council minutes and the items in those minutes relating to the adoption of legislative acts, shall be made public.

The results of votes and explanations of votes shall also be made public when the Council adopts a common position pursuant to Article 251 or 252 of the EC Treaty. The same rule shall apply for votes and explanations of votes by members of the Council or their representatives on the Conciliation Committee set up by Article 251 of the EC Treaty.

2.   The results of votes and explanations of votes shall also be made public when the Council establishes a convention on the basis of Title VI of the EU Treaty. The statements entered in the Council minutes and the items in those minutes relating to adoption of such conventions shall be made public by decision of the Council or Coreper, taken at the request of one of their members.

3.   The results of votes shall be made public:

(a) when the Council acts pursuant to Title V of the EU Treaty, by a unanimous Council or Coreper Decision taken at the request of one of their members;

(b) when the Council adopts a common position within the meaning of Title VI of the EU Treaty, by a unanimous Council or Coreper Decision taken at the request of one of their members;

(c) in other cases, by Council or Coreper Decision taken at the request of one of their members.

When the result of a vote in the Council is made public in accordance with sub-paragraphs (a), (b) and (c), the explanations of votes made when the vote was take shall also be made public at the request of the Council members concerned, with due regard for these Rules of Procedure, legal certainty and the interests of the Council.

Statements entered in the Council minutes and items in those minutes relating to the adoption of the acts referred to in subparagraphs (a), (b) and (c) shall be made public by Council or Coreper Decision taken at the request of one of their members.

4.   Votes shall not be made public in the case of discussions leading to indicative votes or the adoption of preparatory acts.

Article 8 Public Access to Council Documents
The detailed arrangements for public access to Council documents shall be adopted by the Council.

Article 9 Voting Arrangements and Quorum
1.   The Council shall vote on the initiative of its President.

The President shall, furthermore, be required to open a voting procedure on the initiative of a member of the Council or of the Commission, provided that a majority of the Council's members so decides.

2.   The members of the Council shall vote in the order of the Member States laid down in Article 203 of the EC Treaty and in the corresponding Articles of the other two Community Treaties, beginning with the member who, according to that order, follows the member holding the office of President.

3.   Where a vote is taken, any member of the Council may also act on behalf of not more than one other member.

4.   The presence of a majority of the members of the Council who are, under the Treaties, entitled to vote is required to enable the Council to vote.

Article 10 Written Procedure
1.   Acts of the Council on an urgent matter may be adopted by a written vote where the Council or Coreper unanimously decides to use that procedure. In special circumstances, the President may also propose the use of that procedure; in such a case, written votes may be used where all members of the Council agree to that procedure.

2.   Agreement by the Commission to the use of the written procedure shall be required where the written vote is on a matter which the Commission has brought before the Council.

3.   A summary of acts adopted by the written procedure shall be drawn up every month.

4.   On the initiative of the Presidency, the Council may also act for the purpose of implementing the common foreign and security policy by means of the simplified written procedure (COREU). In that case the proposal shall be deemed to be adopted at the end of the period laid down by the Presidency depending on the urgency of the matter, except where a member of the Council objects.

5.   On the initiative of the Presidency, the Council may also act for the purpose of deciding to consult other institutions or bodies by means of a streamlined written procedure wherever such consultation is required by Community law. In that case the decision to consult shall be deemed to be adopted at the end of the period laid down by the Presidency depending on the urgency of the matter, except where a member of the Council objects.

6.   The General Secretariat shall establish that the written procedures have been completed.

Article 11 Minutes
1.   Minutes of each meeting shall be drawn up and, when approved, shall be signed by the President-in-Office at the time of such approval and by the Secretary-General or the Deputy Secretary-General.

The minutes shall as a general rule indicate in respect of each item on the agenda:
— the documents submitted to the Council,
— the decisions taken or the conclusions reached by the Council,
— the statements made by the Council and those whose entry has been requested by a member of the Council or the Commission.

2.   The draft minutes shall be drawn up by the General Secretariat within fifteen days and submitted to the Council or to Coreper for approval.
3.   Prior to such approval any member of the Council, or the Commission, may request that more details be inserted in the minutes regarding any item on the agenda. These requests may be made in Coreper.

Article 12 Deliberations and Decisions on the Basis of Documents and Drafts Drawn up in the Languages Provided for by the Language Rules in Force

1.   Except as otherwise decided unanimously by the Council on grounds of urgency, the Council shall deliberate and take decisions only on the basis of documents and drafts drawn up in the languages specified in the rules in force governing languages.
2.   Any member of the Council may oppose discussion if the texts of any proposed amendments are not drawn up in such of the languages referred to in paragraph 1 as he or she may specify.

Article 13 Signing of Acts

The text of the acts adopted by the Council and that of the acts adopted jointly by the European Parliament and the Council shall be signed by the President-in-Office at the time of their adoption and by the Secretary-General or the Deputy Secretary-General. The Secretary-General and the Deputy Secretary-General may delegate their signatures to Directors-General of the General Secretariat.

Article 14 Absence of Entitlement to Vote

For the purposes of application of these Rules of Procedure, due account will be taken, in accordance with Annex I of cases in which, under the Treaties, one or more members of the Council are not entitled to vote.

Article 15 Publication of Acts in the Official Journal

1.   The following shall be published in the Official Journal by the Secretary-General or the Deputy Secretary-General:
(a) the acts referred to in Article 254(1) and (2) of the EC Treaty;
(b) the acts referred to in the first paragraph of Article 163 of the Euratom Treaty;
(c) the common positions adopted by the Council in accordance with the procedures referred to in Articles 251 and 252 of the EC Treaty, and the reasons underlying those common positions;
(d) the framework decisions and decisions referred to in Article 34(2) of the EU Treaty;
(e) the conventions established by the Council in accordance with Article 34(2) of the EU Treaty.
      Reference shall be made in the Official Journal to the entry into force of such conventions:
(f) the conventions signed between Member States on the basis of Article 293 of the EC Treaty.
      Reference shall be made in the Official Journal to the entry into force of such conventions:
(g) international agreements concluded by the Community or in accordance with Article 24 of the EU Treaty.
      Reference shall be made in the Official Journal to the entry into force of such agreements.
2.   Unless the Council or Coreper decides otherwise, the following shall be published in the Official Journal by the Secretary-General or the Deputy Secretary-General:

(a) initiatives presented to the Council by a Member State pursuant to Article 67(1) of the EC Treaty;
(b) initiatives presented to the Council by a Member State pursuant to Article 34(2) of the EU Treaty;
(c) the common positions referred to in Article 34(2) of the EU Treaty;
(d) directives other than those referred to in Article 254(1) and (2) of the EC Treaty, decisions other than those referred to in Article 254(1) of the EC Treaty and recommendations.

3. The Council or Coreper shall decide unanimously, on a case-by-case basis, whether there should be publication in the Official Journal by the Secretary-General or the Deputy Secretary-General of the common strategies, the joint actions and the common positions referred to in Article 12 of the EU Treaty.

4. The Council or Coreper shall decide, on a case-by-case basis and taking account of possible publication of the basic act, whether the following should be published in the Official Journal by the Secretary-General or the Deputy Secretary-General:
(a) the measures implementing the joint actions referred to in Article 12 of the EU Treaty;
(b) the joint actions, the common positions or any other decision adopted on the basis of a common strategy, as provided for in the first indent of Article 23(2) of the EU Treaty;
(c) any measures implementing the decisions referred to in Article 34(2) of the EU Treaty and any measures implementing conventions drawn up by the Council in accordance with Article 34(2) of the EU Treaty.

5. Where an agreement concluded between the Communities and one or more States or international organisations sets up a body vested with powers of decision, the Council shall decide, when such an agreement is concluded, whether decisions to be taken by that body should be published in the Official Journal.

Article 16 Notification of Acts

1. Directives other than those referred to in Article 254(1) and (2) of the EC Treaty and decisions other than those referred to in Article 254(1) of the EC Treaty shall be notified to their addressees by the Secretary-General, the Deputy Secretary-General or a Director-General acting on their behalf.

2. When they are not published in the Official Journal, the following acts shall be notified to their addressees by the Secretary-General, the Deputy Secretary-General or a Director-General acting on their behalf:
(a) recommendations;
(b) the common strategies, joint actions and common positions referred to in Article 12 of the EU Treaty;
(c) the common positions referred to in Article 34(2) of the EU Treaty;
(d) measures implementing the acts adopted on the basis of Articles 12 and 34 of the EU Treaty.

3. The Secretary-General, the Deputy Secretary-General or a Director-General acting on their behalf shall send to the Governments of the Member States and to the Commission authentic copies of Council Directives other than those referred to in Article 254(1) and (2) of the EC Treaty and Council Decisions and recommendations.

Article 17 Coreper, Committees and Working Parties

1. Coreper shall be responsible for preparing the work of the Council and for carrying out the tasks assigned to it by the Council. All items on the agenda for a Council meeting shall be examined in advance by Coreper unless the Council decides otherwise. Coreper shall endeavour to reach agreement at its level to be submitted to the

Council for adoption. It shall ensure adequate presentation of the dossiers to the Council. In the event of an emergency, the Council, acting unanimously, may decide to settle the matter without prior examination.

2.   Committees or working parties may be set up by, or with the approval of, Coreper with a view to carrying out certain preparatory work or studies defined in advance.

3.   Coreper shall be chaired, depending on the items on the agenda, by the Permanent Representative or the Deputy Permanent Representative of the Member State which holds the Presidency of the Council. Unless the Council decides otherwise, the various committees provided for in the Treaties shall also be chaired by a delegate of that Member State. The same shall apply to the committees and working parties referred to in paragraph 2, unless Coreper decides otherwise. For the preparation of meetings of Council compositions meeting once every six months and held during the first half of this period, the meetings of committees other than Coreper and those of working parties held during the preceding six months may be chaired by a delegate of the Member State whose turn it is to chair the said Council meetings.

4.   Coreper may adopt the following procedural decisions, provided that the items relating thereto have been included on its provisional agenda at least three working days before the meeting. Unanimity on the part of Coreper shall be required for any derogation from that period:

(a) decision to hold a Council meeting in a place other than Brussels or Luxembourg (second subparagraph of Article 1(3));

(b) decision that certain Council debates may be transmitted to the public (second subparagraph of Article 4(2));

(c) authorisation to produce a copy of or an extract from a Council document for use in legal proceedings (Article 5(2));

(d) decision to make the results of votes public in the cases laid down in Article 7(2) and (3);

(e) decision to use the written procedure (Article 10(1));

(f)   approval or amendment of Council minutes (Article 11(2) and (3));

(g) decision to publish a text or an act in the Official Journal (Article 15(2), (3) and (4));

(h) decision to consult an institution or body;

(i)   decision setting or extending a time-limit for consultation of an institution or body;

(j)   approval of the wording of a letter to be sent to an institution or body.

Article 18 Reports from Committees and Working Parties

Notwithstanding the other provisions of these Rules of Procedure, the Presidency shall organise the meetings of the various committees and working parties so that their reports are available before the Coreper meetings at which they are to be examined.

Article 19 Quality of Drafting

In order to assist the Council in its task of ensuring the drafting quality of the legislative acts which it adopts, the Legal Service shall be responsible for checking the drafting quality of proposals and draft acts at the appropriate stage, as well as for bringing drafting suggestions to the attention of the Council and its bodies, pursuant to the Interinstitutional Agreement of 22 December 1998.

Article 20 The General Secretariat

1.   The Council shall be assisted by a General Secretariat, under the responsibility of a Secretary-General, High Representative for the common foreign and security policy, who shall be assisted by a Deputy Secretary-General responsible for the running of the General Secretariat.

The Secretary-General and the Deputy Secretary-General shall be appointed by the Council acting unanimously.
2.   The Council shall decide on the organisation of the General Secretariat.
Under its authority the Secretary-General and the Deputy Secretary-General shall take all the measures necessary to ensure the smooth running of the General Secretariat.
3.   The Secretary-General or the Deputy Secretary-General shall submit to the Council the draft estimate of the expenditure of the Council in sufficient time to ensure that the time limits laid down by the financial provisions are met.
4.   In accordance with the provisions of the Financial Regulation referred to in Article 279 of the EC Treaty and in the corresponding articles of the other two Community Treaties, the Secretary-General or the Deputy Secretary-General shall administer the appropriations entered in Section II - Council - of the budget.

Article 21 Security
The rules on security shall be adopted by the Council.

Article 22 Duties as Depositary of Agreements and Conventions
In the event of the Secretary-General of the Council being designated as depositary of an agreement concluded in accordance with Article 24 of the EU Treaty or concluded by the Community and one or more States or international organisations, of a convention concluded between Member States or of a convention established pursuant to Article 34 of the EU Treaty, the acts of ratification, acceptance or approval of those agreements or conventions shall be deposited at the address of the Council.
In such instances the Secretary-General shall perform the duties of a depositary and shall also ensure that the dates of entry into force of such agreements or conventions are published in the Official Journal.

Article 23 Representation Before the European Parliament
Subject to special procedures, the Council may be represented by the Presidency or by any other of its members before the European Parliament or its committees. The Council may also be represented before those committees by its Secretary-General, its Deputy Secretary-General or by senior officials of the General Secretariat acting on instructions from the Presidency.
The Council may also present its views to the European Parliament by means of a written statement.

Article 24 Provisions Concerning the form of Acts
The provisions concerning the form of acts are set out in Annex II.

Article 25 Correspondence Addressed to the Council
Correspondence to the Council shall be sent to the President at the following address of the Council:
Council of the European Union
Rue de la Loi/Wetstraat, 175
B-1048 Brussels

ANNEXES [omitted]

Done at Brussels, 31 May 1999.
For the Council, The President, J. FISCHER

Commission Decision 93/492 of 17 February 1993 adopting the Rules of Procedure of the Commission[1]

THE COMMISSION OF THE EUROPEAN COMMUNITIES,

HAVING REGARD to the Treaty establishing a Single Council and a Single Commission of the European Communities, and in particular Article 16 thereof,

HAS ADOPTED THESE RULES OF PROCEDURE:

Chapter I The Commission

Article 1 [Collegiate Commission]
The Commission shall act collectively in accordance with these Rules.

Article 2 [Adoption of Decisions]
Commission decisions shall be adopted:
(a) at the Commission's meetings; or
(b) by written procedure, in accordance with Article 10; or
(c) by delegation, in accordance with Article 11.

Section I Meetings of the Commission
Article 3 [Meetings]
Meetings of the Commission shall be convened by the President. The Commission shall, as a general rule, meet at least once a week. It shall hold additional meetings whenever necessary.

Article 4 [Annual Programme]
Each year the Commission shall adopt an annual programme. The President shall adopt the agenda for each meeting in the light of this programme and a quarterly rolling programme which will normally include any items requiring a Commission decision. If a Member of the Commission requests the inclusion of an item that is not covered by the quarterly programme, it shall be placed on the agenda provided, save in exceptional circumstances, nine days' notice is given. The agenda and the necessary working documents shall be circulated to the Members of the Commission within the time limit and in the working languages prescribed by the Commission in accordance with Article 24. Any Member of the Commission may request or, in his absence, have a request made for an item to be withdrawn from the agenda, in which case the item shall be held over for a later meeting, but an item shall not be withdrawn if the effect would be to prevent the Commission from meeting a deadline where failure to meet it would have legal consequences. If any objection is raised to a further request for withdrawal of the same item, the Commission shall decide the matter. The Commission may decide by majority vote to discuss any question which is not on the agenda or for which the necessary working documents have been distributed late. It may decide by majority vote not to discuss any item on the agenda.

---

1   OJ 1993 L 230, p. 15, as amended by Commission Decision 95/148 of 8 March 1995.

Article 5 [Quorum]

The number of Members present required to constitute a quorum shall be equal to a majority of the number of Members specified in the Treaty.

Article 6 [Decision Making]

The Commission takes decisions on a proposal from one or more of its Members. A vote shall be taken if any Member so requests. The vote may be on a proposal as originally made or as amended by the Member or Members responsible or by the President. Commission decisions shall be adopted if a majority of the number of Members specified in the Treaty vote in favour. This provision shall apply to decisions of all kinds, subject to the first sentence of the fifth paragraph of Article 4.

Article 7 [Confidentiality]

Meetings of the Commission shall not be public. Discussions shall be confidential.

Article 8 [Admission to Meetings]

Save as otherwise decided by the Commission, the Secretary-General shall attend meetings. Attendance of other persons shall be determined in accordance with rules to give effect to these Rules of Procedure. In the absence of a Member of the Commission, his *chef de cabinet* may attend the meeting and, at the invitation of the President, state the views of the absent Member. The Commission may, by way of exception, decide to hear any other person.

Article 9 [Minutes]

Minutes shall be taken of all meetings of the Commission. The draft minutes shall be submitted to the Commission for approval at a subsequent meeting. The approved minutes shall be authenticated by the signatures of the President and the Secretary-General.

Section II Other decision-making procedures
Article 10 [Written Procedure]

The agreement of the Commission to a proposal by one or more of its Members may be obtained by means of a written procedure, provided the Directorates-General directly involved are in agreement and the proposal has been endorsed by the Legal Service.

For this purpose, the text of the proposal shall be circulated in writing to all Members of the Commission, in the languages prescribed by the Commission in accordance with Article 24, with a time limit within which Members must make known any reservations or amendments they wish to make.

Any Member of the Commission may, in the course of the written procedure, request that the proposal be discussed. In such case, the matter shall be placed on the agenda of the next meeting of the Commission.

A proposal on which no Member of the Commission has made a reservation and maintained it up to the time limit set for a written procedure shall be deemed to be agreed by the Commission. Proposals adopted shall be recorded in a day note which shall be noted in the minutes of the next meeting.

Article 11 [Delegation of Powers]

The Commission may, provided the principle of collective responsibility is fully respected, empower one or more of its Members to take, on its behalf and under its responsibility, clearly defined management or administrative measures, including instruments preparatory to a decision to be taken by the Commission collectively at a later time.

The Commission may also instruct one or more of its Members, with the agreement of the President, to adopt the definitive text of any instrument as defined in the first paragraph or of any proposal to be presented to other institutions the substance of which has already been determined in discussion.

Decisions adopted by delegation procedure shall be recorded in a day note which shall be noted in the minutes of the next meeting.

Powers conferred in this way may be subdelegated only as expressly provided in the enabling decision.

The provisions of the first to fourth paragraphs shall be without prejudice to the rules concerning delegation in respect of financial matters or the powers conferred on the appointing authority and the authority empowered to conclude contracts of employment.

Section III Preparation and implementation of Commission decisions
Article 12 [Commissioner's Areas of Responsibility]
The Commission may assign to its Members areas in which they will have special responsibility for preparing the Commission's business and for implementing its decisions. A Member of the Commission to whom an area of responsibility is so assigned shall give instructions to the relevant department or departments.

Article 13 [Working Groups]
The Commission may set up working groups of its Members; it shall appoint the chairman of any such group.

Article 14 [Cabinets of the Commissioners]
Members of the Commission may each appoint personal staff to assist them in their work and in preparing Commission decisions.

Article 15 [Secretary-General of the Commission]
The Secretary-General shall assist the President in preparing the proceedings and meetings of the Commission. He shall ensure that decision-making procedures are properly implemented and that effect is given to the decisions referred to in Article 2. He shall ensure the necessary coordination between departments in preparing the proceedings of the Commission and that the rules for submission of documents to the Commission are complied with. He shall take the necessary steps to ensure official notification and publication of Commission instruments in the Official Journal of the European Communities and that the documents of the Commission and its departments are transmitted to the other institutions of the European Communities. He shall be responsible for official relations with the other institutions of the European Communities, subject to any decision by the Commission to exercise any function itself or to assign it to its Members or departments. He shall monitor the proceedings of the other institutions of the European Communities and keep the Commission informed.

Article 16 [Authentic Instruments]
Instruments adopted by the Commission in the course of a meeting shall be attached, in the authentic language or languages, in such a way that they cannot be separated, to the minutes of the meeting at which they were adopted. They shall be authenticated by the signatures of the President and the Secretary-General on the first page of the minutes.

Instruments adopted by written procedure shall be attached, in the authentic language or languages, in such a way that they cannot be separated, to the day note referred to in Article 10. They shall be authenticated by the signature of the Secretary-General on the last page of the day note.

Instruments adopted by delegation procedure shall be attached, in the authentic language or languages, in such a way that they cannot be separated, to the day note referred to in Article 11. They shall be authenticated by the signature of the Secretary-General on the last page of the day note.

For the purposes of these Rules, "instruments" means any instrument as referred to in Article 14 of the ECSC Treaty, Article 189 of the EC Treaty or Article 161 of the Euratom Treaty.

For the purposes of these Rules, "authentic language or languages" means all the official languages of the Communities in the case of instruments of general application and, in other cases, the languages of those to whom they are addressed.

Chapter II Commission Departments

Article 17 [Directorates-General]
A number of departments forming a single administrative service shall assist the Commission in the performance of its official functions. The first paragraph is without prejudice to the provisions of Article 12.

Article 18 [Structure]
The administrative service of the Commission shall consist of Directorates-General and equivalent departments. Directorates-General and equivalent departments shall normally be divided into Directorates, and Directorates into Units.

Article 19 [Temporary Units]
The Commission may, in special cases, set up temporary structures to deal with particular matters and shall determine their responsibilities and method of operation.

Article 20 [Interdepartemental Co-operation]
Departments involved in the preparation or implementation of Commission decisions shall work together as closely as possible. Before submitting a document to the Commission, the department responsible shall, in sufficient time, consult other departments which are associated or concerned by virtue of their powers or responsibilities or the nature of the subject. The Legal Service shall be consulted on all drafts of or proposals for legal instruments and on all documents which may have legal implications. The Directorates-General responsible for the budgets, for personnel and for the administration shall be consulted on all documents which may have implications concerning the budget and finances or personnel and administration respectively. The Directorate-General responsible for financial control shall likewise be consulted, as need be. The department responsible shall endeavour to frame a proposal that has the agreement of the departments consulted. In the event of disagreement, it shall append to its proposal the different views expressed by these departments, subject to the provisions of Article 10.

Chapter III Deputizing

Article 21 [Replacement of the President]
If the President is prevented from exercising his functions, they shall be exercised by one of the Vice-Presidents or Members chosen in the order laid down by the Commission.

Article 22 [Replacement of the Secretary-General]
Where the Secretary-General is prevented from exercising his functions, they shall be exercised by the Deputy Secretary-General or, where this is not possible, by an official designated by the Commission.

Article 23 [Replacement of Other Staff]
Save as otherwise decided by the Commission, where any superior is prevented from exercising his functions, his place shall be taken by the longest-serving subordinate present, or (in the event of equal length of service) by the person who is the senior by age, in the highest category and grade. In the absence of the Head of one of the external delegations, the Director-General with responsibility for the delegation is empowered to appoint, with the agreement of the relevant Member of the Commission, a Chargé d'affaires who need not satisfy the conditions set out in the first paragraph.

FINAL PROVISIONS

Article 24 [Implementing Provisions]
The Commission shall determine, as necessary, rules to give effect to these Rules of Procedure.

Article 25 [Repeal of Former Rules]
The provisional Rules of Procedure of 6 July 1967 are hereby repealed.

Article 26 [Entry into Force]
These Rules of Procedure shall enter into force on 11 September 1993.

Article 27 [Publication]
These Rules of Procedure shall be published in the Official Journal of the European Communities.

Done at Brussels, 17 February 1993.
For the Commission, The President, Jacques DELORS

Council and Commission Decision 93/730 on a Code of Conduct Concerning Public Access to Council and Commission Documents[1]

THE COUNCIL AND THE COMMISSION,

HAVING REGARD to the declaration on the right of access to information annexed to the final act of the Treaty on European Union, which emphasizes that transparency of the decision-making process strengthens the democratic nature of the institutions and the public's confidence in the administration,
HAVING REGARD to the conclusions wherein the European Councils in Birmingham and Edinburgh agreed on a number of principles to promote a Community closer to its citizens,
HAVING REGARD to the conclusions of the European Council in Copenhagen, reaffirming the principle of giving citizens the greatest possible access to information and

---

1   So-called "Transparency Decision"; OJ 1993 L 340, p. 41.

calling on the Council and the Commission to adopt at an early date the necessary measures for putting this principle into practice,
CONSIDERING it desirable to establish by common agreement the principles which will govern access to Commission and Council documents, it being understood that it is for each of them to implement these principles by means of specific regulations,
WHEREAS the said principles are without prejudice to the relevant provisions on access to files directly concerning persons with a specific interest in them;
WHEREAS these principles will have to be implemented in full compliance with the provisions concerning classified information;
WHEREAS this code of conduct is an additional element in their information and communication policy,

HAVE AGREED AS FOLLOWS:

General principle
The public will have the widest possible access to documents held by the Commission and the Council. "Document" means any written text, whatever its medium, which contains existing data and is held by the Council or the Commission.

Processing of initial applications
An application for access to a document will have to be made in writing, in a sufficiently precise manner; it will have to contain information that will enable the document or documents concerned to be identified. Where necessary, the institution concerned will ask the applicant for further details.

Where the document held by an institution was written by a natural or legal person, a Member State, another Community institution or body or any other national or international body, the application must be sent direct to the author.

In consultation with the applicants, the institution concerned will find a fair solution to comply with repeat applications and/or those which relate to very large documents.

The applicant will have access to documents either by consulting them on the spot or by having a copy sent at his own expense; the fee will not exceed a reasonable sum. The institution concerned will be able to stipulate that a person to whom a document is released will not be allowed to reproduce or circulate the said document for commercial purposes through direct sale without its prior authorization.

Within one month the relevant departments of the institution concerned will inform the applicant either that his application has been approved or that they intend to advise the institution to reject it.

Processing of confirmatory applications
Where the relevant departments of the institution concerned intend to advise the institution to reject an application, they will inform the applicant thereof and tell him that he has one month to make a confirmatory application to the institution for that position to be reconsidered, failing which he will be deemed to have withdrawn his original application.

If a confirmatory application is submitted, and if the institution concerned decides to refuse to release the document, that decision, which must be made within a month of submission of the confirmatory application, will be notified in writing to the applicant as soon as possible. The grounds for the decision must be given, and the decision must indicate the means of redress that are available, i.e. judicial proceedings and complaints to the ombudsman under the conditions specified in, respectively, Articles 173 and 138e of the Treaty establishing the European Community.

Exceptions

The institutions will refuse access to any document whose disclosure could undermine:
— the protection of the public interest (public security, international relations, monetary stability, court proceedings, inspections and investigations),
— the protection of the individual and of privacy,
— the protection of commercial and industrial secrecy,
— the protection of the Community's financial interests,
— the protection of confidentiality as requested by the natural or legal persons that supplied the information or as required by the legislation of the Member State that supplied the information.

They may also refuse access in order to protect the institution's interest in the confidentiality of its proceedings.

Implementation

The Commission and the Council will severally take steps to implement these principles before 1 January 1994.

Review

The Council and the Commission agree that the code of conduct will, after two years of operation, be reviewed on the basis of reports drawn up by the Secretaries-General of the Council and the Commission.

THREE: LEGAL REMEDIES UNDER EU LAW

Protocol on the Statute of the Court of Justice of the European Community[1]

THE HIGH CONTRACTING PARTIES TO THE TREATY ESTABLISHING THE EUROPEAN COMMUNITY,

DESIRING to lay down the Statute of the Court provided for in Article 188 of this Treaty, [...]
HAVE AGREED upon the following provisions, which shall be annexed to the Treaty establishing the European Community.

Article 1 [Establishment of the Court]
The Court established by Article 4 of this Treaty shall be constituted and shall function in accordance with the provisions of this Treaty and of this Statute.

TITLE I
JUDGES AND ADVOCATES GENERAL

Article 2 [Oath of Office]
Before taking up his duties each Judge shall, in open court, take an oath to perform his duties impartially and conscientiously and to preserve the secrecy of the deliberations of the Court.

Article 3 [Immunity of Judges]
The Judges shall be immune from legal proceedings. After they have ceased to hold office, they shall continue to enjoy immunity in respect of acts performed by them in their official capacity including words spoken or written.
   The Court, sitting in plenary session, may waive the immunity.
   Where immunity has been waived and criminal proceedings are instituted against a Judge, he shall be tried, in any of the Member States, only by the Court competent to judge the members of the highest national judiciary.

Article 4 [Incompatibilities]
The Judges may not hold any political or administrative office.
   They may not engage in any occupation, whether gainful or not, unless exemption is exceptionally granted by the Council.
   When taking up their duties, they shall give a solemn undertaking that, both during and after their term of office, they will respect the obligations arising therefrom, in particular the duty to behave with integrity and discretion as regards the acceptance, after they have ceased to hold office, of certain appointments or benefits.
   Any doubt on this point shall be settled by decision of the Court.

Article 5 [Registration]
Apart from normal replacement, or death, the duties of a Judge shall end when he resigns.

---

1   As amended by subsequent acts of accession and by the decisions establishing the Court of First Instance.

Where a Judge resigns, his letter of resignation shall be addressed to the President of the Court for transmission to the President of the Council. Upon this notification a vacancy shall arise on the bench.

Save where Article 6 applies, a Judge shall continue to hold office until his successor takes up his duties.

Article 6 [Removal from Office]

A Judge may be deprived of his office or of his right to a pension or other benefits in its stead only if, in the unanimous opinion of the Judges and Advocates General of the Court, he no longer fulfils the requisite conditions or meets the obligations arising from his office. The Judge concerned shall not take part in any such deliberations.

The Registrar of the Court shall communicate the decision of the Court to the President of the European Parliament and to the President of the Commission and shall notify it to the President of the Council.

In the case of a decision depriving a Judge of his office, a vacancy shall arise on the bench upon this latter notification.

Article 7 [Appointment of Replacements]

A Judge who is to replace a member of the Court whose term of office has not expired shall be appointed for the remainder of his predecessor's term.

Article 8 [Advocates-General]

The provisions of Articles 2 to 7 shall apply to the Advocates-General.

TITLE II
ORGANIZATION

Article 9 [Registrar's Oath]

The Registrar shall take an oath before the Court to perform his duties impartially and conscientiously and to preserve the secrecy of the deliberations of the Court.

Article 10 [Replacement of Registrar]

The Court shall arrange for replacement of the Registrar on occasions when he is prevented from attending the Court.

Article 11 [Staff]

Officials and other servants shall be attached to the Court to enable it to function. They shall be responsible to the Registrar under the authority of the President.

Article 12 [Assistant Rapporteurs]

On a proposal from the Court, the Council may, acting unanimously, provide for the appointment of Assistant Rapporteurs and lay down the rules governing their service. The Assistant Rapporteurs may be required, under conditions laid down in the Rules of Procedure, to participate in preparatory inquiries in cases pending before the Court and to cooperate with the Judge who acts as Rapporteur.

The Assistant Rapporteurs shall be chosen from persons whose independence is beyond doubt and who possess the necessary legal qualifications; they shall be appointed by the Council. They shall take an oath before the Court to perform their duties impartially and conscientiously and to preserve the secrecy of the deliberations of the Court.

Article 13 [Residence in Luxembourg]
The Judges, the Advocates General and the Registrar shall be required to reside at the place where the Court has its seat.

Article 14 [Permanent Court]
The Court shall remain permanently in session. The duration of the judicial vacations shall be determined by the Court with due regard to the needs of its business.

Article 15 [Decisions]
Decisions of the Court shall be valid only when an uneven number of its members is sitting in the deliberations. Decisions of the full Court shall be valid if nine members are sitting. Decisions of the Chambers consisting of three or five Judges shall be valid only if three Judges are sitting. Decisions of the Chambers consisting of seven Judges shall be valid only if five Judges are sitting. In the event of one of the Judges of a Chamber being prevented from attending, a Judge of another Chamber may be called upon to sit in accordance with conditions laid down in the Rules of Procedure.

Article 16 [Disqualification]
No Judge or Advocate General may take part in the disposal of any case in which he has previously taken part as agent or adviser or has acted for one of the parties, or in which he has been called upon to pronounce as a member of a court or tribunal, of a commission of inquiry or in any other capacity.

If, for some special reason, any Judge or Advocate General considers that he should not take part in the judgment or examination of a particular case, he shall so inform the President. If, for some special reason, the President considers that any Judge or Advocate General should not sit or make submissions in a particular case, he shall notify him accordingly.

Any difficulty arising as to the application of this Article shall be settled by decision of the Court.

A party may not apply for a change in the composition of the Court or of one of its Chambers on the grounds of either the nationality of a Judge or the absence from the Court or from the Chamber of a Judge of the nationality of that party.

TITLE III
PROCEDURE

Article 17 [Appearance Before the Court]
The States and the institutions of the Community shall be represented before the Court by an agent appointed for each case; the agent may be assisted by an adviser or by a lawyer entitled to practise before a court of a Member State.

Other parties must be represented by a lawyer entitled to practise before a court of a Member State.

Such agents, advisers and lawyers shall, when they appear before the Court, enjoy the rights and immunities necessary to the independent exercise of their duties, under conditions laid down in the Rules of Procedure.

As regards such advisers and lawyers who appear before it, the Court shall have the powers normally accorded to courts of law, under conditions laid down in the Rules of Procedure.

University teachers being nationals of a Member State whose law accords them a right of audience shall have the same rights before the Court as are accorded by this Article to lawyers entitled to practise before a court of a Member State.

Article 18 [Procedure]

The procedure before the Court shall consist of two parts: written and oral.

The written procedure shall consist of the communication to the parties and to the institutions of the Community whose decisions are in dispute, of applications, statements of case, defences and observations, and of replies, if any, as well as of all papers and documents in support or of certified copies of them.

Communications shall be made by the Registrar in the order and within the time laid down in the Rules of Procedure.

The oral procedure shall consist of the reading of the report presented by a Judge acting as Rapporteur, the hearing by the Court of agents, advisers and lawyers entitled to practise before a court of a Member State and of the submissions of the Advocate General, as well as the hearing, if any, of witnesses and experts.

Article 19 [Application]

A case shall be brought before the Court by a written application addressed to the Registrar. The application shall contain the applicant's name and permanent address and the description of the signatory, the name of the party against whom the application is made, the subject matter of the dispute, the submissions and a brief statement of the grounds on which the application is based.

The application shall be accompanied, where appropriate, by the measure the annulment of which is sought or, in the circumstances referred to in Article 175 of this Treaty, by documentary evidence of the date on which an institution was, in accordance with that Article, requested to act. If the documents are not submitted with the application, the Registrar shall ask the party concerned to produce them within a reasonable period, but in that event the rights of the party shall not lapse even if such documents are produced after the time limit for bringing proceedings.

Article 20 [Preliminary References]

In the cases governed by Article 177 of this Treaty, the decision of the court or tribunal of a Member State which suspends its proceedings and refers a case to the Court shall be notified to the Court by the court or tribunal concerned. The decision shall then be notified by the Registrar of the Court to the parties, to the Member States and to the Commission, and also to the Council if the act the validity or interpretation of which is in dispute originates from the Council.

Within two months of this notification, the parties, the Member State, the Commission and, where appropriate, the Council, shall be entitled to submit statements of case or written observations to the Court.

Article 21 [Documentary Evidence]

The Court may require the parties to produce all documents and to supply all information which the Court considers desirable. Formal note shall be taken of any refusal.

The Court may also require the Member States and institutions not being parties to the case to supply all information which the Court considers necessary for the proceedings.

Article 22 [Expert Opinions]

The Court may at any time entrust any individual, body, authority, committee or other organization it chooses with the task of giving an expert opinion.

Article 23 [Witnesses]

Witnesses may be heard under conditions laid down in the Rules of Procedure.

Article 24 [Defaulting Witnesses]

With respect to defaulting witnesses the Court shall have the powers generally granted to courts and tribunals and may impose pecuniary penalties under conditions laid down in the Rules of Procedure.

Article 25 [Oath of Witnesses and Experts]

Witnesses and experts may be heard on oath taken in the form laid down in the Rules of Procedure or in the manner laid down by the law of the country of the witness or expert.

Article 26 [Hearing of Witnesses in Home Country]

The Court may order that a witness or expert be heard by the judicial authority of his place of permanent residence.

The order shall be sent for implementation to the competent judicial authority under conditions laid down in the Rules of Procedure. The documents drawn up in compliance with the letters rogatory shall be returned to the Court under the same conditions.

The Court shall defray the expenses, without prejudice to the right to charge them, where appropriate, to the parties.

Article 27 [Violation of an Oath]

A Member State shall treat any violation of an oath by a witness or expert in the same manner as if the offence had been committed before one of its courts with jurisdiction in civil proceedings. At the instance of the Court, the Member State concerned shall prosecute the offender before its competent court.

Article 28 [Public Hearing]

The hearing in court shall be public, unless the Court, of its own motion or on application by the parties, decides otherwise for serious reasons.

Article 29 [Examination of Experts, Witnesses and Parties]

During the hearings the Court may examine the experts, the witnesses and the parties themselves. The latter, however, may address the Court only through their representatives.

Articlo 30 [Minutes of Hearlngs]

Minutes shall be made of each hearing and signed by the President and the Registrar.

Article 31 [Case List]

The case list shall be established by the President.

Article 32 [Deliberations in Camera]

The deliberations of the Court shall be and shall remain secret.

Article 33 [Contents of Judgments]

Judgments shall state the reasons on which they are based. They shall contain the names of the Judges who took part in the deliberations.

Article 34 [Pronouncement of Judgments]

Judgments shall be signed by the President and the Registrar. They shall be read in open court.

Article 35 [Decision on Costs]
The Court shall adjudicate upon costs.

Article 36 [Intermediate Relief]
The President of the Court may, by way of summary procedure, which may, in so far as necessary, differ from some of the rules contained in this Statute and which shall be laid down in the Rules of Procedure, adjudicate upon applications to suspend execution, as provided for in Article 185 of this Treaty, or to prescribe interim measures in pursuance of Article 186, or to suspend enforcement in accordance with the last paragraph of Article 192.

Should the President be prevented from attending, his place shall be taken by another Judge under conditions laid down in the Rules of Procedure.

The ruling of the President or of the Judge replacing him shall be provisional and shall in no way prejudice the decision of the Court on the substance of the case.

Article 37 [Third Party Intervention]
Member States and institutions of the Community may intervene in cases before the Court.

The same right shall be open to any other person establishing an interest in the result of any case submitted to the Court, save in cases between Member States, between institutions of the Community or between Member States and institutions of the Community.

Submissions made in an application to intervene shall be limited to supporting the submissions of one of the parties.

Article 38 [Judgment by Default]
Where the defending party, after having been duly summoned, fails to file written submissions in defence, judgment shall be given against that party by default. An objection may be lodged against the judgment within one month of it being notified. The objection shall not have the effect of staying enforcement of the judgment by default unless the Court decides otherwise.

Article 39 [Contesting of Judgments]
Member States, institutions of the Community and any other natural or legal persons may, in cases and under conditions to be determined by the Rules of Procedure, institute third party proceedings to contest a judgment rendered without their being heard, where the judgment is prejudicial to their rights.

Article 40 [Interpretation of Judgments]
If the meaning or scope of a judgment is in doubt, the Court shall construe it on application by any party or any institution of the Community establishing an interest therein.

Article 41 [Revision of Judgments]
An application for revision of a judgment may be made to the Court only on discovery of a fact which is of such a nature as to be a decisive factor, and which, when the judgment was given, was unknown to the Court and to the party claiming the revision.

The revision shall be opened by a judgment of the Court expressly recording the existence of a new fact, recognizing that it is of such a character as to lay the case open to revision and declaring the application admissible on this ground.

No application for revision may be made after the lapse of 10 years from the date of the judgment.

Article 42 [Extension of Time Limits]
Periods of grace based on considerations of distance shall be determined by the Rules of Procedure.

No right shall be prejudiced in consequence of the expiry of a time limit if the party concerned proves the existence of unforeseeable circumstances or of force majeure.

Article 43 [Period of Limitation]
Proceedings against the Community in matters arising from non-contractual liability shall be barred after a period of five years from the occurrence of the event giving rise thereto. The period of limitation shall be interrupted if proceedings are instituted before the Court or if prior to such proceedings an application is made by the aggrieved party to the relevant institution of the Community. In the latter event the proceedings must be instituted within the period of two months provided for in Article 173; the provisions of the second paragraph of Article 175 shall apply where appropriate.

TITLE IV
THE COURT OF FIRST INSTANCE
OF THE EUROPEAN COMMUNITIES

Article 44 [Application of the Statute to the CFI]
Articles 2 to 8 and 13 to 16 of this Statute shall apply to the Court of First Instance and its members. The oath referred to in Article 2 shall be taken before the Court of Justice and the decisions referred to in Articles 3, 4 and 6 shall be adopted by that Court after hearing the Court of First Instance.

Article 45 [Staff of the CFI]
The Court of First Instance shall appoint its Registrar and lay down the rules governing his service. Articles 9, 10 and 13 of this Statute shall apply to the Registrar of the Court of First Instance mutatis mutandis.

The President of the Court of Justice and the President of the Court of First Instance shall determine, by common accord, the conditions under which officials and other servants attached to the Court of Justice shall render their services to the Court of First Instance to enable it to function. Certain officials or other servants shall be responsible to the Registrar of the Court of First Instance under the authority of the President of the Court of First Instance.

Article 46 [Procedure Before the CFI]
The procedure before the Court of First Instance shall be governed by Title III of this Statute, with the exception of Article 20.

Such further and more detailed provisions as may be necessary shall be laid down in the Rules of Procedure established in accordance with Article 168a(4) of this Treaty.

Notwithstanding the fourth paragraph of Article 18 of this Statute, the Advocate General may make his reasoned submissions in writing.

Article 47 [Cooperation Between ECJ and CFI]
Where an application or other procedural document addressed to the Court of First Instance is lodged by mistake with the Registrar of the Court of Justice, it shall be transmitted immediately by that Registrar to the Registrar of the Court of First Instance; likewise, where an application or other procedural document addressed to the Court of Justice is lodged by mistake with the Registrar of the Court of First Instance, it shall be transmitted immediately by that Registrar to the Registrar of the Court of Justice.

Where the Court of First Instance finds that it does not have jurisdiction to hear and determine an action in respect of which the Court of Justice has jurisdiction, it shall refer that action to the Court of Justice; likewise, where the Court of Justice finds that an action falls within the jurisdiction of the Court of First Instance, it shall refer that action to the Court of First Instance, whereupon that Court may not decline jurisdiction.

Where the Court of Justice and the Court of First Instance are seized of cases in which the same relief is sought, the same issue of interpretation is raised or the validity of the same act is called in question, the Court of First Instance may, after hearing the parties, stay the proceedings before it until such time as the Court of Justice shall have delivered judgment. Where applications are made for the same act to be declared void, the Court of First Instance may also decline jurisdiction in order that the Court of Justice may rule on such applications. In the cases referred to in this subparagraph, the Court of Justice may also decide to stay the proceedings before it; in that event, the proceedings before the Court of First Instance shall continue.

Article 48 [Notification of Judgments]
Final decisions of the Court of First Instance, decisions disposing of the substantive issues in part only or disposing of a procedural issue concerning a plea of lack of competence or inadmissibility, shall be notified by the Registrar of the Court of First Instance to all parties as well as all Member States and the Community institutions even if they did not intervene in the case before the Court of First Instance.

Article 49 [Appeals]
An appeal may be brought before the Court of Justice, within two months of the notification of the decision appealed against, against final decisions of the Court of First Instance and decisions of that Court disposing of the substantive issues in part only or disposing of a procedural issue concerning a plea of lack of competence or inadmissibility.

Such an appeal may be brought by any party which has been unsuccessful, in whole or in part, in its submissions. However, interveners other than the Member States and the Community institutions may bring such an appeal only where the decision of the Court of First Instance directly affects them.

With the exception of cases relating to disputes between the Community and its servants, an appeal may also be brought by Member States and Community institutions which did not intervene in the proceedings before the Court of First Instance. Such Member States and institutions shall be in the same position as Member States or institutions which intervened at first instance.

Article 50 [Procedural Appeals]
Any person whose application to intervene has been dismissed by the Court of First Instance may appeal to the Court of Justice within two weeks of the notification of the decision dismissing the application.

The parties to the proceedings may appeal to the Court of Justice against any decision of the Court of First Instance made pursuant to Articles 185 or 186 or the fourth paragraph of Article 192 of this Treaty within two months from their notification.

The appeal referred to in the first two paragraphs of this Article shall be heard and determined under the procedure referred to in Article 36 of this Statute.

Article 51 [Grounds for Appeals]
An appeal to the Court of Justice shall be limited to points of law. It shall lie on the grounds of lack of competence of the Court of First Instance, a breach of procedure

before it which adversely affects the interests of the appellant as well as the infringement of Community law by the Court of First Instance.

No appeal shall lie regarding only the amount of the costs or the party ordered to pay them.

Article 52 [Procedure of the ECJ upon Appeal]
Where an appeal is brought against a decision of the Court of First Instance, the procedure before the Court of Justice shall consist of a written part and an oral part. In accordance with conditions laid down in the Rules of Procedure the Court of Justice, having heard the Advocate General and the parties, may dispense with the oral procedure.

Article 53 [Suspension of Judgments of the CFI]
Without prejudice to Articles 185 and 186 of this Treaty, an appeal shall not have suspensory effect.

By way of derogation from Article 187 of this Treaty, decisions of the Court of First Instance declaring a regulation to be void shall take effect only as from the date of expiry of the period referred to in the first paragraph of Article 49 of this Statute or, if an appeal shall have been brought within that period, as from the date of dismissal of the appeal, without prejudice, however, to the right of a party to apply to the Court of Justice, pursuant to Articles 185 and 186 of this Treaty, for the suspension of the effects of the regulation which has been declared void or for the prescription of any other interim measure.

Article 54 [Successful Appeals]
If the appeal is well founded, the Court of Justice shall quash the decision of the Court of First Instance. It may itself give final judgment in the matter, where the state of the proceedings so permits, or refer the case back to the Court of First Instance for judgment.

Where a case is referred back to the Court of First Instance, that Court shall be bound by the decision of the Court of Justice on points of law.

When an appeal brought by a Member State or a Community institution, which did not intervene in the proceedings before the Court of First Instance, is well founded the Court of Justice may, if it considers this necessary, state which of the effects of the decision of the Court of First Instance which has been quashed shall be considered as definitive in respect of the parties to the litigation.

[FINAL PROVISIONS]
Article 55 [Rules of Procedure]
The Rules of Procedure of the Court provided for in Article 188 of this Treaty shall contain, apart from the provisions contemplated by this Statute, any other provisions necessary for applying and, where required, supplementing it.

Article 56 [Amendments of the Statute]
The Council may, acting unanimously, make such further adjustments to the provisions of this Statute as may be required by reason of measures taken by the Council in accordance with the last paragraph of Article 165 of this Treaty.

Article 57 [omitted]

IN WITNESS WHEREOF, the undersigned Plenipotentiaries have signed this Protocol. Done at Brussels this seventeenth day of April in the year [1957].

Rules of Procedure of the Court of Justice of the European Communities of 19 June 1991[1]

CONTENTS

---

1   OJ 1991 L 176, p. 7, as amended on 21 February 1995, OJ 1995 L 44, p. 61, and on 11 March 1997, OJ 1997 L 103, p. 1.

THE COURT OF JUSTICE,

HAVING REGARD to the powers conferred on the Court of Justice by the Treaty establishing the European Coal and Steel Community, the Treaty establishing the European Economic Community and the Treaty establishing the European Atomic Energy Community (Euratom),
Having regard to Article 55 of the Protocol on the Statute of the Court of Justice of the European Coal and Steel Community,
HAVING REGARD to the third paragraph of Article 188 of the Treaty establishing the European Economic Community,
HAVING REGARD to the third paragraph of Article 160 of the Treaty establishing the European Atomic Energy Community (Euratom),
WHEREAS it is necessary to revise the text of its Rules of Procedure in the various languages in order to ensure coherence and uniformity between those language versions;
WITH the unanimous approval of that revision, given by the Council on 29 April 1991;
AND WHEREAS, after the numerous amendments to its Rules of Procedure, it is necessary, in the interests of clarity and simplicity to establish a coherent authentic text,
WITH the unanimous approval of the Council, given on 7 June 1991,

REPLACES ITS RULES OF PROCEDURE BY THE FOLLOWING RULES:

INTERPRETATION

Article 1 [Definitions]
In these Rules:
- "EC Treaty" means the Treaty establishing the European Community,
- "EC Statute" means the Protocol on the Statute of the Court of Justice of the European Community,
- "ECSC Treaty" means the Treaty establishing the European Coal and Steel Community,
- "ECSC Statute" means the Protocol on the Statute of the Court of Justice of the European Coal and Steel Community,
- "Euratom Treaty" means the Treaty establishing the European Atomic Energy Community (Euratom),
- "Euratom Statute" means the Protocol on the Statute of the Court of Justice of the European Atomic Energy Community,
- "EEA Agreement" means the Agreement on the European Economic Area.

For the purposes of these Rules:
- "Institutions" means the institutions of the Communities and bodies which are established by the Treaties, or by an act adopted in implementation thereof, and which may be parties before the Court,
- "EFTA Surveillance Authority" means the surveillance authority referred to in the EEA Agreement.

TITLE I

ORGANIZATION OF THE COURT

Chapter 1 Judges and Advocates- General

Article 2 [Term of Office]

The term of office of a Judge shall begin on the date laid down in his instrument of appointment. In the absence of any provisions regarding the date, the term shall begin on the date of the instrument.

Article 3 [Oath]

1.   Before taking up his duties, a Judge shall at the first public sitting of the Court which he attends after his appointment take the following oath:
"I swear that I will perform my duties impartially and conscientiously; I swear that I will preserve the secrecy of the deliberations of the Court".
2.   Immediately after taking the oath, a Judge shall sign a declaration by which he solemnly undertakes that, both during and after his term of office, he will respect the obligations arising therefrom, and in particular the duty to behave with integrity and discretion as regards the acceptance, after he has ceased to hold office, of certain appointments and benefits.

Article 4 [Procedure for Removal of Judges]

When the Court is called upon to decide whether a Judge no longer fulfils the requisite conditions or no longer meets the obligations arising from his office, the President shall invite the Judge concerned to make representations to the Court, in closed session and in the absence of the Registrar.

Article 5 [Rules Applicable for Advocates-General]

Articles 2, 3 and 4 of these Rules shall apply in a corresponding manner to Advocates-General.

Article 6 [Ranking of Judges]

Judges and Advocates-General shall rank equally in precedence according to their seniority in office.
    Where there is equal seniority in office, precedence shall be determined by age.
    Retiring Judges and Advocates-General who are reappointed shall retain their former precedence.

Chapter 2 Presidency of The Court And Constitution of The Chambers

Article 7 [Election of the President]

1.   The Judges shall, immediately after the partial replacement provided for in Article 167 of the EC Treaty, Article 32b of the ECSC Treaty and Article 139 of the Euratom Treaty, elect one of their number as President of the Court for a term of three years.
2.   If the office of the President of the Court falls vacant before the normal date of expiry thereof, the Court shall elect a successor for the remainder of the term.

3.   The elections provided for in this Article shall be by secret ballot. If a Judge obtains an absolute majority he shall be elected. If no Judge obtains an absolute ma-jority, a second ballot shall be held and the Judge obtaining the most votes shall be elected. Where two or more Judges obtain an equal number of votes the oldest of them shall be deemed elected.

Article 8 [Functions of the President]
The President shall direct the judicial business and the administration of the Court; he shall preside at hearings and deliberations.

Article 9 [Chambers]
1.   The Court shall set up Chambers in accordance with the provisions of the second paragraph of Article 165 of the EC Treaty, the second paragraph of Article 32 of the ECSC Treaty and the second paragraph of Article 137 of the Euratom Treaty and shall decide which Judges shall be attached to them.
The composition of the Chambers shall be published in the Official Journal of the European Communities.
2.   As soon as an application initiating proceedings has been lodged, the President shall assign the case to one of the Chambers for any preparatory inquiries and shall designate a Judge from that Chamber to act as Rapporteur.
3.   The Court shall lay down criteria by which, as a rule, cases are to be assigned to Chambers.
4.   These Rules shall apply to proceedings before the Chambers.
In cases assigned to a Chamber the powers of the President of the Court shall be exercised by the President of the Chamber.

Article 10 [Appointment of Presidents of the Chambers and of the First Advocate-General]
1.   The Court shall appoint for a period of one year the Presidents of the Chambers and the First Advocate-General.
The provisions of Article 7 (2) and (3) shall apply.
Appointments made in pursuance of this paragraph shall be published in the Official Journal of the European Communities.
2.   The First Advocate-General shall assign each case to an Advocate-General as soon as the Judge-Rapporteur has been designated by the President. He shall take the necessary steps if an Advocate-General is absent or prevented from acting.

Article 11-23 [omitted]

Chapter 4 Assistant Rapporteurs

Article 24 [Possibility of Appointing Assistant Rapporteurs]
1.   Where the Court is of the opinion that the consideration of and preparatory inquiries in cases before it so require, it shall, pursuant to Article 2 of the EC Statute, Article 16 of the ECSC Statute and Article 2 of the Euratom Statute, propose the appointment of Assistant Rapporteurs.
2.   Assistant Rapporteurs shall in particular assist the President in connection with applications for the adoption of interim measures and assist the Judge-Rapporteurs in their work.
3.   In the performance of their duties the Assistant Rapporteurs shall be responsible to the President of the Court, the President of a Chamber or a Judge-Rapporteur, as the case may be.

4.   Before taking up his duties, an Assistant Rapporteur shall take before the Court the oath set out in Article 3 of these Rules.

Chapter 5 The Working of The Court

Article 25 [Sittings of the Court]
1.   The dates and times of the sittings of the Court shall be fixed by the President.
2.   The dates and times of the sittings of the Chambers shall be fixed by their respective Presidents.
3.   The Court and the Chambers may choose to hold one or more sittings in a place other than that in which the Court has its seat.

Article 26 [Participation in Deliberations]
1.   Where, by reason of a Judge being absent or prevented from attending, there is an even number of Judges, the most junior Judge within the meaning of Article 6 of these Rules shall abstain from taking part in the deliberations unless he is the Judge-Rapporteur. In that case the Judge immediately senior to him shall abstain from taking part in the deliberations.
2.   If, after the Court has been convened, it is found that the quorum referred to in Article 15 of the EC Statute, Article 18 of the ECSC Statute and Article 15 of the Euratom Statute has not been attained, the President shall adjourn the sitting until there is a quorum.
3.   If, in any Chamber, the quorum referred to in Article 15 of the EC Statute, Article 18 of the ECSC Statute and Article 15 of the Euratom Statute has not been attained, the President of that Chamber shall so inform the President of the Court, who shall designate another Judge to complete the Chamber.

Article 27 [Deliberations and Voting]
1.   The Court and Chambers shall deliberate in closed session.
2.   Only those Judges who were present at the oral proceedings and the Assistant Rapporteur, if any, entrusted with the consideration of the case may take part in the deliberations.
3.   Every Judge taking part in the deliberations shall state his opinion and the reasons for it.
4.   Any Judge may require that any questions be formulated in the language of his choice and communicated in writing to the Court or Chamber before being put to the vote.
5.   The conclusions reached by the majority of the Judges after final discussion shall determine the decision of the Court. Votes shall be cast in reverse order to the order of precedence laid down in Article 6 of these Rules.
6.   Differences of view on the substance, wording or order of questions, or on the interpretation of the voting shall be settled by decision of the Court or Chamber.
7.   Where the deliberations of the Court concern questions of its own administration, the Advocates-General shall take part and have a vote. The Registrar shall be present, unless the Court decides to the contrary.
8.   Where the court sits without the Registrar being present it shall, if necessary, instruct the most junior Judge within the meaning of Article 6 of these rules to draw up minutes. The minutes shall be signed by this Judge and by the President.

Article 28 [omitted]

Chapter 6 Languages

Article 29 [Language of a Case]

1.   The language of a case shall be Danish, Dutch, English, Finnish, French, German, Greek, Irish, Italian, Portuguese, Spanish or Swedish.

2.   The language of the case shall be chosen by the applicant, except that:

(a)   where the defendant is a Member State or a natural or legal person having the nationality of a Member State, the language of the case shall be the official language of that State; where that State has more than one official language, the applicant may choose between them;

(b)   at the joint request of the parties, the use of another of the languages mentioned in paragraph 1 for all or part of the proceedings may be authorized;

(c)   at the request of one of the parties, and after the opposite party and the Advocate-General have been heard, the use of another of the languages mentioned in paragraph 1 as the language of the case for all or part of the proceedings may be authorized by way of derogation from subparagraphs (a) and (b).

In cases to which Article 103 of these Rules applies, the language of the case shall be the language of the national court or tribunal which refers the matter to the Court. At the duly substantiated request of one of the parties to the main proceedings, and after the opposite party and the Advocate-General have been heard, the use of another of the languages mentioned in paragraph 1 may be authorized for the oral procedure.

Requests as above may be decided on by the President; the latter may and, where he wishes to accede to a request without the agreement of all the parties, must refer the request to the Court.

3.   The language of the case shall be used in the written and oral pleadings of the parties and in supporting documents, and also in the minutes and decisions of the Court.

Any supporting documents expressed in another language must be accompanied by a translation into the language of the case.

In the case of lengthy documents, translations may be confined to extracts. However, the Court or Chamber may, of its own motion or at the request of a party, at any time call for a complete or fuller translation.

Notwithstanding the foregoing provisions, a Member State shall be entitled to use its official language when intervening in a case before the Court or when taking part in any reference of a kind mentioned in Article 103. This provision shall apply both to written statements and to oral addresses. The Registrar shall cause any such statement or address to be translated into the language of the case.

The States, other than the Member States, which are parties to the EEA Agreement, and also the EFTA Surveillance Authority, may be authorized to use one of the languages mentioned in paragraph 1, other than the language of the case, when they intervene in a case before the Court or participate in preliminary ruling proceedings envisaged by Article 20 of the EC Statute. This provision shall apply both to written statements and oral addresses. The Registrar shall cause any such statement or address to be translated into the language of the case.

4.   Where a witness or expert states that he is unable adequately to express himself in one of the languages referred to in paragraph (1) of this Article, the Court or Chamber may authorize him to give his evidence in another language. The Registrar shall arrange for translation into the language of the case.

5.   The President of the Court and the Presidents of Chambers in conducting oral proceedings, the Judge Rapporteur both in his preliminary report and in his report for the hearing, Judges and Advocates-General in putting questions and Advocates-General in delivering their opinions may use one of the languages referred to in paragraph (1)

of this Article other than the language of the case. The Registrar shall arrange for translation into the language of the case.

Article 30 [Translations]
1.   The Registrar shall, at the request of any Judge, of the Advocate-General or of a party, arrange for anything said or written in the course of the proceedings before the Court or a Chamber to be translated into the languages he chooses from those referred to in Article 29 (1).
2.   Publications of the Court shall be issued in the languages referred to in Article 1 of Council Regulation No 1.

Article 31 [Authentic Texts]
The texts of documents drawn up in the language of the case or in any other language authorized by the Court pursuant to Article 29 of these rules shall be authentic.

Chapter 7 Rights And Obligations of Agents, Advisers And Lawyers

Article 32 [Privileges and Immunities of Agents, Advisors and Lawyers]
1.   Agents, advisers and lawyers appearing before the Court or before any judicial authority to which the Court has addressed letters rogatory, shall enjoy immunity in respect of words spoken or written by them concerning the case or the parties.
2.   Agents, advisers and lawyers shall enjoy the following further privileges and facilities:
(a) papers and documents relating to the proceedings shall be exempt from both search and seizure; in the event of a dispute the customs officials or police may seal those papers and documents; they shall then be immediately forwarded to the Court for inspection in the presence of the Registrar and of the person concerned;
(b) agents, advisers and lawyers shall be entitled to such allocation of foreign currency as may be necessary for the performance of their duties;
(c) agents, advisers and lawyers shall be entitled to travel in the course of duty without hindrance.

Article 33- 36 [omitted]

TITLE II
PROCEDURE
Chapter 1 Written Procedure

Article 37 [Submission of Written Pleadings]
1.   The original of every pleading must be signed by the party's agent or lawyer.
     The original, accompanied by all annexes referred to therein, shall be lodged together with five copies for the Court and a copy for every other party to the proceedings. Copies shall be certified by the party lodging them.
2.   Institutions shall in addition produce, within time-limits laid down by the Court, translations of all pleadings into the other languages provided for by Article 1 of Council Regulation No 1. The second subparagraph of paragraph (1) of this Article shall apply.
3.   All pleadings shall bear a date. In the reckoning of time-limits for taking steps in proceedings, only the date of lodgment at the Registry shall be taken into account.
4.   To every pleading there shall be annexed a file containing the documents relied on in support of it, together with a schedule listing them.
5.   Where in view of the length of a document only extracts from it are annexed to the pleading, the whole document or a full copy of it shall be lodged at the Registry.

Article 38 [Requirements of Form and Content for Written Pleadings]
1.   An application of the kind referred to in Article 19 of the EC Statute, Article 22 of the ECSC Statute and Article 19 of the Euratom Statute shall state:
(a) the name and address of the applicant;
(b) the designation of the party against whom the application is made;
(c) the subject-matter of the proceedings and a summary of the pleas in law on which the application is based;
(d) the form of order sought by the applicant;
(e) where appropriate, the nature of any evidence offered in support.
2.   For the purpose of the proceedings, the application shall state an address for service in the place where the Court has its seat and the name of the person who is authorized and has expressed willingness to accept service.

If the application does not comply with these requirements, all service on the party concerned for the purpose of the proceedings shall be effected, for so long as the defect has not been cured, by registered letter addressed to the agent or lawyer of that party. By way of derogation from Article 79, service shall then be deemed to be duly effected by the lodging of the registered letter at the post office of the place where the Court has its seat.
3.   The lawyer acting for a party must lodge at the Registry a certificate that he is authorized to practise before a court of a Member State or of another State which is a party to the EEA Agreement.
4.   The application shall be accompanied, where appropriate, by the documents specified in the second paragraph of Article 19 of the EC Statute, in the second paragraph of Article 22 of the ECSC Statute and in the second paragraph of Article 19 of the Euratom Statute.
5.   An application made by a legal person governed by private law shall be accompanied by:
(a) the instrument or instruments constituting or regulating that legal person or a recent extract from the register of companies, firms or associations or any other proof of its existence in law;
(b) proof that the authority granted to the applicant's lawyer has been properly conferred on him by someone authorized for the purpose.
6.   An application submitted under Articles 181 and 182 of the EC Treaty, Articles 42 and 89 of the ECSC Treaty and Articles 153 and 154 of the Euratom Treaty shall be accompanied by a copy of the arbitration clause contained in the contract governed by private or public law entered into by the Communities or on their behalf, or, as the case may be, by a copy of the special agreement concluded between the Member States concerned.
7.   If an application does not comply with the requirements set out in paragraphs (3) to (6) of this Article, the Registrar shall prescribe a reasonable period within which the applicant is to comply with them whether by putting the application itself in order or by producing any of the abovementioned documents. If the applicant fails to put the application in order or to produce the required documents within the time prescribed, the Court shall, after hearing the Advocate-General, decide whether the noncompliance with these conditions renders the application formally inadmissible.

Article 39 [Service on Defendant]
The application shall be served on the defendant. In a case where Article 38 (7) applies, service shall be effected as soon as the application has been put in order or the Court has declared it admissible notwithstanding the failure to observe the formal requirements set out in that Article.

Article 40 [Requirements of the Written Defence]

1.   Within one month after service on him of the application, the defendant shall lodge a defence, stating:
(a) the name and address of the defendant;
(b) the arguments of fact and law relied on;
(c) the form of order sought by the defendant;
(d) the nature of any evidence offered by him.
The provisions of Article 38 (2) to (5) of these Rules shall apply to the defence.
2. The time-limit laid down in paragraph (1) of this Article may be extended by the President on a reasoned application by the defendant.

Article 41 [Reply and Rejoinder]

1.   The application initiating the proceedings and the defence may be supplemented by a reply from the applicant and by a rejoinder from the defendant.
2.   The President shall fix the time-limits within which these pleadings are to be lodged.

Article 42 [Admissibility of New Pleas in the Reply or Rejoinder]

1.   In reply or rejoinder a party may offer further evidence. The party must, however, give reasons for the delay in offering it.
2.   No new plea in law may be introduced in the course of proceedings unless it is based on matters of law or of fact which come to light in the course of the procedure.
    If in the course of the procedure one of the parties puts forward a new plea in law which is so based, the President may, even after the expiry of the normal procedural time-limits, acting on a report of the Judge-Rapporteur and after hearing the Advocate-General, allow the other party time to answer on that plea.
    The decision on the admissibility of the plea shall be reserved for the final judgment.

Article 43 [Joining of Cases]

The President may, at any time, after hearing the parties and the Advocate-General, if the assignment referred to in Article 10 (2) has taken place, order that two or more cases concerning the same subject-matter shall, on account of the connection between them, be joined for the purposes of the written or oral procedure or of the final judgment. The cases may subsequently be disjoined. The President may refer these matters to the Court.

Article 44 [Preliminary Report by the Judge-Rapporteur]

1.   After the rejoinder provided for in Article 41 (1) of these Rules has been lodged, the President shall fix a date on which the Judge-Rapporteur is to present his preliminary report to the Court. The report shall contain recommendations as to whether a preparatory inquiry or any other preparatory step should be undertaken and whether the case should be referred to the Chamber to which it has been assigned under Article 9 (2).
    The Court shall decide, after hearing the Advocate-General, what action to take upon the recommendations of the Judge-Rapporteur.
    The same procedure shall apply:
(a) where no reply or no rejoinder has been lodged within the time-limit fixed in accordance with Article 41 (2) of these Rules;
(b) where the party concerned waives his right to lodge a reply or rejoinder.
2.   Where the Court orders a preparatory inquiry and does not undertake it itself, it shall assign the inquiry to the Chamber.

Where the Court decides to open the oral procedure without an inquiry, the President shall fix the opening date.

Article 44 (a) [Possibility to Dispense with Oral Hearing]
Without prejudice to any special provisions laid down in these Rules, and except in the specific cases in which, after the pleadings referred to in Article 40 (1) and, as the case may be, in Article 41 (1) have been lodged, the Court, acting on a report from the Judge-Rapporteur, after hearing the Advocate-General and with the express consent of the parties, decides otherwise, the procedure before the Court shall also include an oral part.

Chapter 2 Preparatory Inquiries

Section 1 - Measures of Inquiry
Article 45 [Available Measures of Inquiry]
1.   The Court, after hearing the Advocate-General, shall prescribe the measures of inquiry that it considers appropriate by means of an order setting out the facts to be proved. Before the Court decides on the measures of inquiry referred to in paragraph (2) (c), (d) and (e) the parties shall be heard.
The order shall be served on the parties.
2.   Without prejudice to Articles 21 and 22 of the EC Statute, Articles 24 and 25 of the ECSC Statute or Articles 22 and 23 of the Euratom Statute, the following measures of inquiry may be adopted:
(a) the personal appearance of the parties;
(b) a request for information and production of documents;
(c) oral testimony;
(d) the commissioning of an expert's report;
(e) an inspection of the place or thing in question.
3.   The measures of inquiry which the Court has ordered may be conducted by the Court itself, or be assigned to the Judge-Rapporteur.
The Advocate-General shall take part in the measures of inquiry.
4.   Evidence may be submitted in rebuttal and previous evidence may be amplified.

Article 46 [Inquiries by Chambers]
1.   A Chamber to which a preparatory inquiry has been assigned may exercise the powers vested in the Court by Articles 45 and 47 to 53 of these Rules; the powers vested in the President of the Court may be exercised by the President of the Chamber.
2.   Articles 56 and 57 of the Rules shall apply in a corresponding manner to proceedings before the Chamber.
3.   The parties shall be entitled to attend the measures of inquiry.

Section 2 - The summoning and examination of witnesses and experts
Article 47 [Summoning and Examination of Witnesses]
1.   The Court may, either of its own motion or an application by a party, and after hearing the Advocate-General, order that certain facts be proved by witnesses. The order of the Court shall set out the facts to be established.
The Court may summon a witness of its own motion or on application by a party or at the instance of the Advocate-General.
An application by a party for the examination of a witness shall state precisely about what facts and for what reasons the witness should be examined.
2.   The witness shall be summoned by an order of the Court containing the following information:

(a) the surname, forenames, description and address of the witness;
(b) an indication of the facts about which the witness is to be examined;
(c) where appropriate, particulars of the arrangements made by the Court for re-
    imbursement of expenses incurred by the witness, and of the penalties which may
    be imposed on defaulting witnesses.
The order shall be served on the parties and the witnesses.
3.   The Court may make the summoning of a witness for whose examination a party
has applied conditional upon the deposit with the cashier of the Court of a sum sufficient to cover the taxed costs thereof; the Court shall fix the amount of the payment.
     The cashier shall advance the funds necessary in connection with the examination
of any witness summoned by the Court of its own motion.
4.   After the identity of the witness has been established, the President shall inform
him that he will be required to vouch the truth of his evidence in the manner laid down
in these Rules.
     The witness shall give his evidence to the Court, the parties having been given
notice to attend. After the witness has given his main evidence the President may, at
the request of a party or of his own motion, put questions to him.
     The other Judges and the Advocate-General may do likewise.
     Subject to the control of the President, questions may be put to witnesses by the
representatives of the parties.
5.   After giving his evidence, the witness shall take the following oath:
"I swear that I have spoken the truth, the whole truth and nothing but the truth."
The Court may, after hearing the parties, exempt a witness from taking the oath.
6.   The Registrar shall draw up minutes in which the evidence of each witness is reproduced.
     The minutes shall be signed by the President or by the Judge-Rapporteur respon-
sible for conducting the examination of the witness, and by the Registrar. Before the
minutes are thus signed, witnesses must be given an opportunity to check the content
of the minutes and to sign them.
     The minutes shall constitute an official record.

Article 48 [Failure of Witnesses to Obey a Summons]
1.   Witnesses who have been duly summoned shall obey the summons and attend for
examination.
2.   If a witness who has been duly summoned fails to appear before the Court, the
Court may impose upon him a pecuniary penalty not exceeding ECU 5.000 and may
order that a further summons be served on the witness at his own expense.
     The same penalty may be imposed upon a witness who, without good reason, re-
fuses to give evidence or to take the oath or where appropriate to make a solemn affirmation equivalent thereto.
3.   If the witness proffers a valid excuse to the Court, the pecuniary penalty imposed
on him may be cancelled. The pecuniary penalty imposed may be reduced at the
request of the witness where he establishes that it is disproportionate to his income.
4.   Penalties imposed and other measures ordered under this Article shall be enforced
in accordance with Articles 187 and 192 of the EC Treaty, Article 44 and 92 of the
ECSC Treaty and Articles 159 and 164 of the Euratom Treaty.

Article 49 [Written Reports and Oral Examination of Experts]
1.   The Court may order that an expert's report be obtained. The order appointing
the expert shall define his task and set a time-limit within which he is to make his report.

2.   The expert shall receive a copy of the order, together with all the documents necessary for carrying out his task. He shall be under the supervision of the JudgeRapporteur, who may be present during his investigation and who shall be kept informed of his progress in carrying out his task.

The Court may request the parties or one of them to lodge security for the costs of the expert's report.

3.   At the request of the expert, the Court may order the examination of witnesses. Their examination shall be carried out in accordance with Article 47 of these Rules.

4.   The expert may give his opinion only on points which have been expressly referred to him.

5.   After the expert has made his report, the Court may order that he be examined, the parties having been given notice to attend.

Subject to the control of the President, questions may be put to the expert by the representatives of the parties.

6.   After making his report, the expert shall take the following oath before the Court: "I swear that I have conscientiously and impartially carried out my task."

The Court may, after hearing the parties, exempt the expert from taking the oath.

Article 50 [Objections to Witnesses or Experts]

1.   If one of the parties objects to a witness or to an expert on the ground that he is not a competent or proper person to act as witness or expert or for any other reason, or if a witness or expert refuses to give evidence, to take the oath or to make a solemn affirmation equivalent thereto, the matter shall be resolved by the Court.

2.   An objection to a witness or to an expert shall be raised within two weeks after service of the order summoning the witness or appointing the expert; the statement of objection must set out the grounds of objection and indicate the nature of any evidence offered.

Article 51 [Compensation for Witnesses and Experts]

1.   Witnesses and experts shall be entitled to reimbursement of their travel and subsistence expenses. The cashier of the Court may make a payment to them towards these expenses in advance.

2.   Witnesses shall be entitled to compensation for loss of earnings, and experts to fees for their services. The cashier of the Court shall pay witnesses and experts their compensation or fees after they have carried out their respective duties or tasks.

Article 52 [Letters Rogatory]

The Court may, on application by a party or of its own motion, issue letters rogatory for the examination of witnesses or experts, as provided for in the supplementary rules mentioned in Article 125 of these Rules.

Article 53 [Minutes of Hearings]

1.   The Registrar shall draw up minutes of every hearing. The minutes shall be signed by the President and by the Registrar and shall constitute an official record.

2.   The parties may inspect the minutes and any expert's report at the Registry and obtain copies at their own expense.

Section 3 - Closure of the Preparatory Inquiry
Article 54 [Closure of Written Stage and Opening of Oral procedure]

Unless the Court prescribes a period within which the parties may lodge written observations, the President shall fix the date for the opening of the oral procedure after the preparatory inquiry has been completed.

Where a period had been prescribed for the lodging of written observations, the President shall fix the date for the opening of the oral procedure after that period has expired.

Chapter 3 Oral Procedure

Article 55 [Order in Which Cases are Dealt With]
1.   Subject to the priority of decisions provided for in Article 85 of these Rules, the Court shall deal with the cases before it in the order in which the preparatory inquiries in them have been completed. Where the preparatory inquiries in several cases are completed simultaneously, the order in which they are to be dealt with shall be determined by the dates of entry in the register of the applications initiating them respectively.
2.   The President may in special circumstances order that a case be given priority over others.

The President may in special circumstances, after hearing the parties and the Advocate-General, either on his own initiative or at the request of one of the parties, defer a case to be dealt with at a later date. On a joint application by the parties the President may order that a case be deferred.

Article 56 [Opening of Hearings]
1.   The proceedings shall be opened and directed by the President, who shall be responsible for the proper conduct of the hearing.
2.   The oral proceedings in cases heard in camera shall not be published.

Article 57 [Questions in Hearings]
The President may in the course of the hearing put questions to the agents, advisers or lawyers of the parties.

The other Judges and the Advocate-General may do likewise.

Article 58 [Representation of Parties]
A party may address the Court only through his agent, adviser or lawyer.

Article 59 [Opinion of the Advocate-General and Closure of Oral Procedure]
1.   The Advocate-General shall deliver his opinion orally at the end of the oral procedure.
2.   After the Advocate-General has delivered his opinion, the President shall declare the oral procedure closed.

Article 60 [Additional Inquiries]
The Court may at any time, in accordance with Article 45 (1), after hearing the Advocate-General, order any measure of inquiry to be taken or that a previous inquiry be repeated or expanded. The Court may direct the Chamber or the Judge-Rapporteur to carry out the measures so ordered.

Article 61 [Reopening of the Oral Procedure]
The Court may after hearing the Advocate-General order the reopening of the oral procedure.

Article 62 [Minutes of the Hearing]
1.   The Registrar shall draw up minutes of every hearing. The minutes shall be signed by the President and by the Registrar and shall constitute an official record.

2.   The parties may inspect the minutes at the Registry and obtain copies at their own expense.

Chapter 4 Judgments

Article 63 [Contents of Judgments]

The judgment shall contain:
— a statement that it is the judgment of the Court,
— the date of its delivery,
— the names of the President and of the Judges taking part in it,
— the name of the Advocate-General,
— the name of the Registrar,
— the description of the parties,
— the names of the agents, advisers and lawyers of the parties,
— a statement of the forms of order sought by the parties,
— a statement that the Advocate-General has been heard,
— a summary of the facts,
— the grounds for the decision,
— the operative part of the judgment, including the decision as to costs.

Article 64 [Delivery of Judgments]

1.   The judgment shall be delivered in open court; the parties shall be given notice to attend to hear it.
2.   The original of the judgment, signed by the President, by the Judges who took part in the deliberations and by the Registrar, shall be sealed and deposited at the Registry; the parties shall be served with certified copies of the judgment.
3.   The Registrar shall record on the original of the judgment the date on which it was delivered.

Article 65 [Binding Effect of Judgments]

The judgment shall be binding from the date of its delivery.

Article 66 [Clarifications of Judgments]

1.   Without prejudice to the provisions relating to the interpretation of judgments the Court may, of its own motion or on application by a party made within two weeks after the delivery of a judgment, rectify clerical mistakes, errors in calculation and obvious slips in it.
2.   The parties, whom the Registrar shall duly notify, may lodge written observations within a period prescribed by the President.
3.   The Court shall take its decision in closed session after hearing the Advocate-General.
4.   The original of the rectification order shall be annexed to the original of the rectified judgment. A note of this order shall be made in the margin of the original of the rectified judgment.

Article 67 [Supplements to Judgments]

If the Court should omit to give a decision on a specific head of claim or on costs, any party may within a month after service of the judgment apply to the Court to supplement its judgment.

The application shall be served on the opposite party and the President shall prescribe a period within which that party may lodge written observations.

After these observations have been lodged, the Court shall, after hearing the Advocate-General, decide both on the admissibility and on the substance of the application.

Article 68 [Publication of Cases]

The Registrar shall arrange for the publication of reports of cases before the Court.

Chapter 5 Costs

Article 69 [Decisions as to Costs]

1. A decision as to costs shall be given in the final judgment or in the order which closes the proceedings.
2. The unsuccessful party shall be ordered to pay the costs if they have been applied for in the successful party's pleadings.

Where there are several unsuccessful parties the Court shall decide how the costs are to be shared.

3. Where each party succeeds on some and fails on other heads, or where the circumstances are exceptional, the Court may order that the costs be shared or that the parties bear their own costs.

The Court may order a party, even if successful, to pay costs which the Court considers that party to have unreasonably or vexatiously caused the opposite party to incur.

4. The Member States and institutions which intervene in the proceedings shall bear their own costs.

The States, other than the Member States, which are parties to the EEA Agreement, and also the EFTA Surveillance Authority, shall bear their own costs if they intervene in the proceedings.

The Court may order an intervener other than those mentioned in the preceding subparagraphs to bear his own costs.

5. A party who discontinues or withdraws from proceedings shall be ordered to pay the costs if they have been applied for in the other party's observations on the discontinuance pleadings. However, upon application by the party who discontinues or withdraws from proceedings, the costs shall be borne by the other party if this appears justified by the conduct of that party.

Where the parties have come to an agreement on costs, the decision as to costs shall be in accordance with that agreement.

If costs are not applied for, the parties shall bear their own costs.

6. Where a case does not proceed to judgment the costs shall be in the discretion of the Court.

Article 70 [Costs Borne by Institutions]

Without prejudice to the second subparagraph of Article 69 (3) of these Rules, in proceedings between the Communities and their servants the institutions shall bear their own costs.

Article 71 [National Scales for Refunds]

Costs necessarily incurred by a party in enforcing a judgment or order of the Court shall be refunded by the opposite party on the scale in force in the State where the enforcement takes place.

Article 72 [Costs of Proceedings]

Proceedings before the Court shall be free of charge, except that:

(a) where a party has caused the Court to incur avoidable costs the Court may, after hearing the Advocate-General, order that party to refund them;

(b) where copying or translation work is carried out at the request of a party, the cost shall, in so far as the Registrar considers it excessive, be paid for by that party on the scale of charges referred to in Article 16 (5) of these Rules.

Article 73 [Recoverable Costs]

Without prejudice to the preceding Article, the following shall be regarded as recoverable costs:

(a) sums payable to witnesses and experts under Article 51 of these Rules;

(b) expenses necessarily incurred by the parties for the purpose of the proceedings, in particular the travel and subsistence expenses and the remuneration of agents, advisers or lawyers.

Article 74 [Disputes Concerning Costs]

1. If there is a dispute concerning the costs to be recovered, the Chamber to which the case has been assigned shall, on application by the party concerned and after hearing the opposite party and the Advocate-General, make an order, from which no appeal shall lie.

2. The parties may, for the purposes of enforcement, apply for an authenticated copy of the order.

Article 75 [Payments]

1. Sums due from the cashier of the Court shall be paid in the currency of the country where the Court has its seat.

At the request of the person entitled to any sum, it shall be paid in the currency of the country where the expenses to be refunded were incurred or where the steps in respect of which payment is due were taken.

2. Other debtors shall make payment in the currency of their country of origin.

3. Conversions of currency shall be made at the official rates of exchange ruling on the day of payment in the country where the Court has its seat.

Chapter 6 Legal Aid

Article 76 [Applications for Legal Aid]

1. A party who is wholly or in part unable to meet the costs of the proceedings may at any time apply for legal aid.

The application shall be accompanied by evidence of the applicant's need of assistance, and in particular by a document from the competent authority certifying his lack of means.

2. If the application is made prior to proceedings which the applicant wishes to commence, it shall briefly state the subject of such proceedings. The application need not be made through a lawyer.

3. The President shall designate a Judge to act as Rapporteur. The Chamber to which the latter belongs shall, after considering the written observations of the opposite party and after hearing the Advocate-General, decide whether legal aid should be granted in full or in part, or whether it should be refused. The Chamber shall consider whether there is manifestly no cause of action.

The Chamber shall make an order without giving reasons, and no appeal shall lie therefrom.

4.   The Chamber may at any time, either of its own motion or on application, withdraw legal aid if the circumstances which led to its being granted alter during the proceedings.
5.   Where legal aid is granted, the cashier of the Court shall advance the funds necessary to meet the expenses.

In its decision as to costs the Court may order the payment to the cashier of the Court of the whole or any part of amounts advanced as legal aid.

The Registrar shall take steps to obtain the recovery of these sums from the party ordered to pay them.

Chapter 7 Discontinuance

Article 77 [Removal of Cases After Settlement]
If, before the Court has given its decision, the parties reach a settlement of their dispute and intimate to the Court the abandonment of their claims, the President shall order the case to be removed from the register and shall give a decision as to costs in accordance with Article 69 (5), having regard to any proposals made by the parties on the matter.

This provision shall not apply to proceedings under Articles 173 and 175 of the EC Treaty, Articles 33 and 35 of the ECSC Treaty or Articles 146 and 148 of the Euratom Treaty.

Article 78 [Removal of Cases on Request of the Applicant]
If the applicant informs the Court in writing that he wishes to discontinue the proceedings, the President shall order the case to be removed from the register and shall give a decision as to costs in accordance with Article 69 (5).

Chapter 8 Service

Article 79 [Service of Documents]
Where these Rules require that a document be served on a person, the Registrar shall ensure that service is effected at that person's address for service either by the dispatch of a copy of the document by registered post with a form for acknowledgement of receipt or by personal delivery of the copy against a receipt.

The Registrar shall prepare and certify the copies of documents to be served, save where the parties themselves supply the copies in accordance with Article 37 (1) of these Rules.

Chapter 9 Time Limits

Article 80 [Calculation of Time Limits]
1.   Any period of time prescribed by the EC, ECSC or Euratom Treaties, the Statutes of the Court or these Rules for the taking of any procedural step shall be reckoned as follows:
(a) where a period expressed in days, weeks, months or years is to be calculated from the moment at which an event occurs or an action takes place, the day during which that event occurs or that action takes place shall not be counted as falling within the period in question;
(b) a period expressed in weeks, months or in years shall end with the expiry of whichever day in the last week, month or year is the same day of the week, or falls on the same date, as the day during which the event or action from which the period is to be calculated occurred or took place. If, in a period expressed in months or in

years, the day on which it should expire does not occur in the last month, the period shall end with the expiry of the last day of that month;
(c) where a period is expressed in months and days, it shall first be reckoned in whole months, then in days;
(d) periods shall include official holidays, Sundays and Saturdays;
(e) periods shall not be suspended during the judicial vacations.
2.   If the period would otherwise end on a Saturday, Sunday or an official holiday, it shall be extended until the end of the first following working day.
      A list of official holidays drawn up by the Court shall be published in the Official Journal of the European Communities.

Article 81 [Time Limits Beginning with Publications in the Official Journal]
1.   Where the period of time allowed for initiating proceedings against a measure adopted by an institution runs from the publication of that measure, that period shall be calculated, for the purposes of Article 80 (1) (a), from the end of the 14th day after publication thereof in the Official Journal of the European Communities.
2.   The extensions, on account of distance, of prescribed time limits shall be provided for in a decision of the Court which shall be published in the Official Journal of the European Communities.

Article 82 [Extension of Time Limits]
Any time limit prescribed pursuant to these Rules may be extended by whoever prescribed it.
      The President and the Presidents of Chambers may delegate to the Registrar power of signature for the purpose of fixing time limits which, pursuant to these Rules, it falls to them to prescribe or of extending such time limits.

Chapter 10 Stay of Proceedings

Article 82a [Stay of Procedures]
1.   The proceedings may be stayed:
(a) in the circumstances specified in the third paragraph of Article 47 of the EC Statute, the third paragraph of Article 47 of the ECSC Statute and the third paragraph of Article 48 of the Euratom Statute, by order of the Court or of the Chamber to which the case has been assigned, made after hearing the Advocate-General;
(b) in all other cases, by decision of the President adopted after hearing the Advocate-General and, save in the case of references for a preliminary ruling as referred to in Article 103, the parties.
The proceedings may be resumed by order or decision, following the same procedure.
      The orders or decisions referred to in this paragraph shall be served on the parties.
2.   The stay of proceedings shall take effect on the date indicated in the order or decision of stay or, in the absence of such indication, on the date of that order or decision.
      While proceedings are stayed time shall cease to run for the purposes of prescribed time limits for all parties.
3.   Where the order or decision of stay does not fix the length of stay, it shall end on the date indicated in the order or decision of resumption or, in the absence of such indication, on the date of the order or decision of resumption.
      From the date of resumption time shall begin to run afresh for the purposes of the time limits.

TITLE III
SPECIAL FORMS OF PROCEDURE
Chapter 1 Suspension of Operation or Enforcement and Other Interim Measures

Article 83 [Applications for Interim Measures]

1. An application to suspend the operation of any measure adopted by an institution, made pursuant to Article 185 of the EC Treaty, the second paragraph of Article 39 of the ECSC Treaty or Article 157 of the Euratom Treaty, shall be admissible only if the applicant is challenging that measure in proceedings before the Court.

An application for the adoption of any other interim measure referred to in Article 186 of the EC Treaty, the third paragraph of Article 39 of the ECSC Treaty or Article 158 of the Euratom Treaty shall be admissible only if it is made by a party to a case before the Court and relates to that case.

2. An application of a kind referred to in paragraph (1) of this Article shall state the subject-matter of the proceedings, the circumstances giving rise to urgency and the pleas of fact and law establishing a prima facie case for the interim measures applied for.

3. The application shall be made by a separate document and in accordance with the provisions of Articles 37 and 38 of these Rules.

Article 84 [Procedure Concerning Interim Measures]

1. The application shall be served on the opposite party, and the President shall prescribe a short period within which that party may submit written or oral observations.

2. The President may order a preparatory inquiry.

The President may grant the application even before the observations of the opposite party have been submitted. This decision may be varied or cancelled even without any application being made by any party.

Article 85 [Decisions Concerning Interim Measures]

The President shall either decide on the application himself or refer it to the Court.

If the President is absent or prevented from attending, Article 11 of these Rules shall apply.

Where the application is referred to it, the Court shall postpone all other cases, and shall give a decision after hearing the Advocate-General. Article 84 shall apply.

Article 86 [Orders for Interim Measures]

1. The decision on the application shall take the form of a reasoned order, from which no appeal shall lie. The order shall be served on the parties forthwith.

2. The enforcement of the order may be made conditional on the lodging by the applicant of security, of an amount and nature to be fixed in the light of the circumstances.

3. Unless the order fixes the date on which the interim measure is to lapse, the measure shall lapse when final judgment is delivered.

4. The order shall have only an interim effect, and shall be without prejudice to the decision of the Court on the substance of the case.

Article 87 [Modification of Orders]

On application by a party, the order may at any time be varied or cancelled on account of a change in circumstances.

Article 88 [New Applications After Rejections]
Rejection of an application for an interim measure shall not bar the party who made it from making a further application on the basis of new facts.

Article 89 [Suspension of ECJ Decisions]
The provisions of this Chapter shall apply to applications to suspend the enforcement of a decision of the Court or of any measure adopted by another institution, submitted pursuant to Articles 187 and 192 of the EC Treaty, Articles 44 and 92 of the ECSC Treaty or Articles 159 and 164 of the Euratom Treaty.

The order granting the application shall fix, where appropriate, a date on which interim measure is to lapse.

Article 90 [Requirements for Applications for Interim Measures]
1.   An application of a kind referred to in the third and fourth paragraphs of Article 81 of the Euratom Treaty shall contain:
(a) the names and addresses of the persons or undertakings to be inspected;
(b) an indication of what is to be inspected and of the purpose of the inspection.
2.   The President shall give his decision in the form of an order. Article 86 of these Rules shall apply.

If the President is absent or prevented from attending, Article 11 of these Rules shall apply.

Chapter 2 Preliminary Issues

Article 91 [Applications for Preliminary Decisions]
1.   A party applying to the Court for a decision on a preliminary objection or other preliminary plea not going to the substance of the case shall make the application by a separate document.

The application must state the pleas of fact and law relied on and the form of order sought by the applicant; any supporting documents must be annexed to it.
2.   As soon as the application has been lodged, the President shall prescribe a period within which the opposite party may lodge a document containing a statement of the form of order sought by that party and its pleas in law.
3.   Unless the Court decides otherwise, the remainder of the proceedings shall be oral.
4.   The Court shall, after hearing the Advocate-General, decide on the application or reserve its decision for the final judgment.

If the Court refuses the application or reserves its decision, the President shall prescribe new time-limits for the further steps in the proceedings.

Article 92 [Manifestly Inadmissible Actions]
1.   Where it is clear that the Court has no jurisdiction to take cognizance of an action or where the action is manifestly inadmissible, the Court may, by reasoned order, after hearing the Advocate-General and without taking further steps in the proceedings, give a decision on the action.
2.   The Court may at any time of its own motion consider whether there exists any absolute bar to proceeding with a case or declare, after hearing the parties, that the action has become devoid of purpose and that there is no need to adjudicate on it; it shall give its decision in accordance with Article 91 (3) and (4) of these Rules.

Chapter 3 Intervention

Article 93 [Application to Intervene]

1. An application to intervene must be made within three months of the publication of the notice referred to in Article 16 (6) of these Rules. The application shall contain:
(a) the description of the case;
(b) the description of the parties;
(c) the name and address of the intervener;
(d) the intervener's address for service at the place where the Court has its seat;
(e) the form of order sought, by one or more of the parties, in support of which the intervener is applying for leave to intervene;
(f) a statement of the circumstances establishing the right to intervene, where the application is submitted pursuant to the second or third paragraph of Article 37 of the EC Statute, Article 34 of the ECSC Statute or the second paragraph of Article 38 of the Euratom Statute.

The intervener shall be represented in accordance with Article 17 of the EC Statute, Article 20 of the ECSC Statute and Article 17 of the Euratom Statute.

Articles 37 and 38 of these Rules shall apply.

2. The application shall be served on the parties.

The President shall give the parties an opportunity to submit their written or oral observations before deciding on the application.

The President shall decide on the application by order or shall refer the application to the Court.

3. If the President allows the intervention, the intervener shall receive a copy of every document served on the parties. The President may, however, on application by one of the parties, omit secret or confidential documents.

4. The intervener must accept the case as he finds it at the time of his intervention.

5. The President shall prescribe a period within which the intervener may submit a statement in intervention.

The statement in intervention shall contain:
(a) a statement of the form of order sought by the intervener in support of or opposing, in whole or in part, the form of order sought by one of the parties;
(b) the pleas in law and arguments relied on by the intervener;
(c) where appropriate, the nature of any evidence offered.

6. After the statement in intervention has been lodged, the President shall, where necessary, prescribe a time-limit within which the parties may reply to that statement.

Chapter 4 Judgments by Default And Applications to Set Them Aside

Article 94 [Judgment by Default]

1. If a defendant on whom an application initiating proceedings has been duly served fails to lodge a defence to the application in the proper form within the time prescribed, the applicant may apply for judgment by default.

The application shall be served on the defendant. The Court may decide to open the oral procedure on the application.

2. Before giving judgment by default the Court shall, after hearing the Advocate-General, consider whether the application initiating proceedings is admissible, whether the appropriate formalities have been complied with, and whether the application appears well founded. The Court may order a preparatory inquiry.

3. A judgment by default shall be enforceable. The Court may, however, grant a stay of execution until the Court has given its decision on any application under paragraph (4) to set aside the judgment, or it may make execution subject to the provision of

security of an amount and nature to be fixed in the light of the circumstances; this security shall be released if no such application is made or if the application fails.
4.   Application may be made to set aside a judgment by default.
      The application to set aside the judgment must be made within one month from the date of service of the judgment and must be lodged in the form prescribed by Articles 37 and 38 of these Rules.
5.   After the application has been served, the President shall prescribe a period within which the other party may submit his written observations.
      The proceedings shall be conducted in accordance with Articles 44 et seq. of these Rules.
6.   The Court shall decide by way of a judgment which may not be set aside. The original of this judgment shall be annexed to the original of the judgment by default. A note of the judgment on the application to set aside shall be made in the margin of the original of the judgment by default.

Chapter 5 Cases Assigned to Chambers

Article 95 [Assignment of Cases to Chambers]
1.   The Court may assign any case brought before it to a Chamber insofar as the difficulty or importance of the case or particular circumstances are not such as to require that the Court decide it in plenary session.
2.   The decision so to assign a case shall be taken by the Court at the end of the written procedure upon consideration of the preliminary report presented by the Judge-Rapporteur and after the Advocate-General has been heard.
      However, a case may not be so assigned if a Member State or an institution of the Communities, being a party to the proceedings, has requested that the case be decided in plenary session. In this subparagraph the expression "party to the proceedings" means any Member State or any institution which is a party to or an intervener in the proceedings or which has submitted written observations in any reference of a kind mentioned in Article 103 of these Rules.
      The request referred to in the preceding subparagraph may not be made in proceedings between the Communities and their servants.
3.   A Chamber may at any stage refer a case back to the Court.

Article 96 [repealed]

Chapter 6 Exceptional Review Procedures

Section 1 - Third-Party Proceedings
Article 97 [Contestation of a Judgment by a Third Party]
1.   Articles 37 and 38 of these Rules shall apply to an application initiating third-party proceedings. In addition such an application shall:
(a) specify the judgment contested;
(b) state how that judgment is prejudicial to the rights of the third party;
(c) indicate the reasons for which the third party was unable to take part in the original case.
      The application must be made against all the parties to the original case.
      Where the judgment has been published in the Official Journal of the European Communities, the application must be lodged within two months of the publication.
2.   The Court may, on application by the third party, order a stay of execution of the judgment. The provisions of Title III, Chapter I, of these Rules shall apply.
3.   The contested judgment shall be varied on the points on which the submissions of the third party are upheld.

The original of the judgment in the third-party proceedings shall be annexed to the original of the contested judgment. A note of the judgment in the third-party procee-dings shall be made in the margin of the original of the contested judgment.

Section 2 - Revision
Article 98 [Revision of Judgments]
An application for revision of a judgment shall be made within three months of the date on which the facts on which the application is based came to the applicant's know-ledge.

Article 99 [Applications for Revision]
1.   Articles 37 and 38 of these Rules shall apply to an application for revision. In addition such an application shall:
(a) specify the judgment contested;
(b) indicate the points on which the judgment is contested;
(c) set out the facts on which the application is based;
(d) indicate the nature of the evidence to show that there are facts justifying revision of the judgment, and that the time-limit laid down in Article 98 has been observed.
2.   The application must be made against all parties to the case in which the contested judgment was given.

Article 100 [Decisions Concerning Revisions]
1.   Without prejudice to its decision on the substance, the Court, in closed session, shall, after hearing the Advocate-General and having regard to the written observations of the parties, give in the form of a judgment its decision on the admissibility of the application.
2.   If the Court finds the application admissible, it shall proceed to consider the sub-stance of the application and shall give its decision in the form of a judgment in accor-dance with these Rules.
3.   The original of the revising judgment shall be annexed to the original of the judg-ment revised. A note of the revising judgment shall be made in the margin of the original of the judgment revised.

Chapter 7 Appeals Against Decisions of The Arbitration Committee

Article 101 [omitted]

Chapter 8 Interpretation of Judgments

Article 102 [Application for Interpretation]
1.   An application for interpretation of a judgment shall be made in accordance with Articles 37 and 38 of these Rules. In addition it shall specify:
(a) the judgment in question;
(b) the passages of which interpretation is sought.
The application must be made against all the parties to the case in which the judgment was given.
2.   The Court shall give its decision in the form of a judgment after having given the parties an opportunity to submit their observations and after hearing the Advocate-General.
The original of the interpreting judgment shall be annexed to the original of the judgment interpreted. A note of the interpreting judgment shall be made in the margin of the original of the judgment interpreted.

Chapter 9 Preliminary Rulings And Other References For Interpretation

Article 103 [References for Preliminary Rulings]

1.   In cases governed by Article 20 of the EC Statute and Article 21 of the Euratom Statute, the procedure shall be governed by the provisions of these Rules, subject to adaptations necessitated by the nature of the reference for a preliminary ruling.

2.   The provisions of paragraph (1) shall apply to the references for a preliminary ruling provided for in the Protocol concerning the interpretation by the Court of Justice of the Convention of 29 February 1968 on the mutual recognition of companies and legal persons and the Protocol concerning the interpretation by the Court of Justice of the Convention of 27 September 1968 on jurisdiction and the enforcement of judgments in civil and commercial matters, signed at Luxembourg on 3 June 1971, and to the references provided for by Article 4 of the latter Protocol.

The provisions of paragraph (1) shall apply also to references for interpretation provided for by other existing or future agreements.

3.   In cases provided for in Article 41 of the ECSC Treaty, the text of the decision to refer the matter shall be served on the parties in the case, the Member States, the Commission and the Council.

These parties, States and institutions may, within two months from the date of such service, lodge written statements of case or written observations.

The provisions of paragraph (1) shall apply.

Article 104 [Procedure for Preliminary Rulings]

1.   The decisions of national courts or tribunals referred to in Article 103 shall be communicated to the Member States in the original version, accompanied by a translation into the official language of the State to which they are addressed.

In the cases governed by Article 20 of the EC Statute, the decisions of national courts or tribunals shall be notified to the States, other than the Member States, which are parties to the EEA Agreement, and also to the EFTA Surveillance Authority, in the original version, accompanied by a translation into one of the languages mentioned in Article 29 (1), to be chosen by the addressee of the notification.

2.   As regards the representation and attendance of the parties to the main proceedings in the preliminary ruling procedure the Court shall take account of the rules of procedure of the national court or tribunal which made the reference.

3.   Where a question referred to the Court for a preliminary ruling is manifestly identical to a question on which the Court has already ruled, the Court may, after informing the court or tribunal which referred the question to it, hearing any observations submitted by the persons referred to in Article 20 of the EC Statute, Article 21 of the Euratom Statute and Article 103 (3) of these Rules and hearing the Advocate- General, give its decision by reasoned order in which reference is made to its previous judgment.

4.   Without prejudice to paragraph (3) of this Article, the procedure before the Court in the case of a reference for a preliminary ruling shall also include an oral part. However, after the statements of case or written observations referred to in Article 20 of the EC Statute, Article 21 of the Euratom Statute and Article 103 (3) of these Rules have been submitted, the Court, acting on a report from the Judge-Rapporteur, after informing the persons who under the aforementioned provisions are entitled to submit such statements or observations, may, after hearing the Advocate-General, decide otherwise, provided that none of those persons has asked to present oral argument.

5.   It shall be for the national court or tribunal to decide as to the costs of the reference.

In special circumstances the Court may grant, by way of legal aid, assistance for the purpose of facilitating the representation or attendance of a party.

Chapter 10 Special Procedures Under Articles 103 to 105 of The Euratom Treaty

Article 105 - 106 [omitted]

Chapter 11 Opinions

Article 107 [Opinions According to Art. 300 ECT (ex Art. 228)]
1.   A request by the Council for an opinion pursuant to Article 228 of the EC Treaty shall be served on the Commission and on the European Parliament. Such a request by the Commission shall be served on the Council, on the European Parliament and on the Member States. Such a request by a Member State shall be served on the Council, on the European Parliament and on the Member States. Such a request by a Member State shall be served on the Council, on the Commission, on the European Parliament and the other Member States.

The President shall prescribe a period within which the institutions and Member States which have been served with a request may submit their written observations.
2.   The Opinion may deal not only with the question whether the envisaged agreement is compatible which the provisions of the EC Treaty but also with the question whether the Community or any Community institution has the power to enter into that agreement.

Article 108 [Procedure for Opinions]
1.   As soon as the request for an Opinion has been lodged, the President shall designate a Judge to act as Rapporteur.
2.   The Court sitting in closed session shall, after hearing the Advocates-General, deliver a reasoned Opinion.
3.   The opinion, signed by the President, by the Judges who took part in the deliberations and by the Registrar, shall be served on the Council, the Commission, the European Parliament and the Member States.

Article 109 [omitted]

TITLE IV
APPEALS AGAINST DECISIONS OF THE COURT OF FIRST INSTANCE

Article 110 [Language of the Case]
Without prejudice to the arrangements laid down in Article 29 (2) (b) and (c) and the fourth subparagraph of Article 29 (3) of these Rules, in appeals against decisions of the Court of First Instance as referred to in Articles 49 and 50 of the EC Statute, Articles 49 and 50 of the ECSC Statute and Articles 50 and 51 of the Euratom Statute, the language of the case shall be the language of the decision of the Court of First Instance against which the appeal is brought.

Article 111 [Lodging an Appeal]
1.   An appeal shall be brought by lodging an application at the Registry of the Court of Justice or of the Court of First Instance.

2. The Registry of the Court of First Instance shall immediately transmit to the Registry of the Court of Justice the papers in the case at first instance and, where necessary, the appeal.

Article 112 [Requirements for an Appeal]
1. An appeal shall contain:
(a) the name and address of the appellant;
(b) the names of the other parties to the proceedings before the Court of First Instance;
(c) the pleas in law and legal arguments relied on;
(d) the form or order sought by the appellant.
Article 37 and Article 38 (2) and (3) of these Rules shall apply to appeals.
2. The decision of the Court of First Instance appealed against shall be attached to the appeal. The appeal shall state the date on which the decision appealed against was notified to the appellant.
3. If an appeal does not comply with Article 38 (3) or with paragraph (2) of this Article, Article 38 (7) of these Rules shall apply.

Article 113 [Subject-Matter of an Appeal]
1. An appeal may seek:
−   to set aside, in whole or in part, the decision of the Court of First Instance;
−   the same form of order, in whole or in part, as that sought at first instance and shall not seek a different form of order.
2. The subject-matter of the proceedings before the Court of First Instance may not be changed in the appeal.

Article 114 [Service on Other Parties]
Notice of the appeal shall be served on all the parties to the proceedings before the Court of First Instance. Article 39 of these Rules shall apply.

Article 115 [Response by Other Parties]
1. Any party to the proceedings before the Court of First Instance may lodge a response within two months after service on him of notice of the appeal. The time-limit for lodging a response shall not be extended.
2. A response shall contain:
(a) the name and address of the party lodging it;
(b) the date on which notice of the appeal was served on him;
(c) the pleas in law and legal arguments relied on;
(d) the form of order sought by the respondent.
Article 38 (2) and (3) of these Rules shall apply.

Article 116 [Subject-Matter of the Response]
1. A response may seek:
−   to dismiss, in whole or in part, the appeal or to set aside, in whole or in part, the decision of the Court of First Instance;
−   the same form of order, in whole or in part, as that sought at first instance and shall not seek a different form of order.
2. The subject-matter of the proceedings before the Court of First Instance may not be changed in the response.

Article 117 [Reply and Rejoinder]

1.   The appeal and the response may be supplemented by a reply and a rejoinder or any other pleading, where the President expressly, on application made within seven days of service of the response or of the reply, considers such further pleading necessary and expressly allows it in order to enable the party concerned to put forward its point of view or in order to provide a basis for the decision on the appeal.

2.   Where the response seeks to set aside, in whole or in part, the decision of the Court of First Instance on a plea in law which was not raised in the appeal, the appellant or any other party may submit a reply on that plea alone within two months of the service of the response in question.

Paragraph (1) shall apply to any further pleading following such a reply.

3.   Where the President allows the lodging of a reply and a rejoinder, or any other pleading, he shall prescribe the period within which they are to be submitted.

Article 118 [Procedure Concerning Appeals]

Subject to the following provisions, Articles 42 (2), 43, 44, 55 to 90, 93, 95 to 100 and 102 of these Rules shall apply to the procedure before the Court of Justice on appeal from a decision of the Court of First Instance.

Article 119 [Inadmissible or Unfounded Appeals]

Where the appeal is, in whole or in part, clearly inadmissible or clearly unfounded, the Court may at any time, acting on a report from the Judge-Rapporteur and after hearing the Advocate-General, by reasoned order dismiss the appeal in whole or in part.

Article 120 [Dispense with Oral Procedure]

After the submission of pleadings as provided for in Articles 115 (1) and, if any, Article 117 (1) and (2) of these Rules, the Court may, acting on a report from the Judge-Rapporteur and after hearing the Advocate-General and the parties, decide to dispense with the oral part of the procedure unless one of the parties objects on the ground that the written procedure did not enable him fully to defend his point of view.

Article 121 [Report by Judge-Rapporteur]

The report referred to in Article 44 (1) shall be presented to the Court after the pleadings provided for in Article 115 (1) and Article 117 (1) and (2) of these Rules have been lodged. The report shall contain, in addition to the recommendations provided for in Article 44 (1), a recommendation as to whether Article 120 of these Rules should be applied. Where no such pleadings are lodged, the same procedure shall apply after the expiry of the period prescribed for lodging them.

Article 122 [Decisions as to Costs]

Where the appeal is unfounded or where the appeal is well founded and the Court itself gives final judgment in the case, the Court shall make a decision as to costs.

In proceedings between the Communities and their servants:
−   Article 70 of these Rules shall apply only to appeals brought by institutions;
−   by way of derogation from Article 69 (2) of these Rules, the Court may, in appeals brought by officials or other servants of an institution, order the parties to share the costs where equity so requires.

If the appeal is withdrawn Article 69 (5) shall apply.

When an appeal brought by a Member State or an institution which did not intervene in the proceedings before the Court of First Instance is well founded, the Court of Justice may order that the parties share the costs or that the successful appellant pay the costs which the appeal has caused an unsuccessful party to incur.

Article 123 [Intervention in Appeal Proceedings]
An application to intervene made to the Court in appeal proceedings shall be lodged before the expiry of a period of one month running from the publication referred to in Article 16 (6).

TITLE V
PROCEDURES PROVIDED FOR BY THE EEA AGREEMENT

Article 123a - 127 [omitted]

Done at Luxembourg, 19 June 1991.

ANNEX I: DECISION ON OFFICIAL HOLIDAYS THE COURT OF JUSTICE OF THE EUROPEAN COMMUNITIES,

HAVING REGARD to Article 80 (2) of the Rules of Procedure, which requires the Court to draw up a list of official holidays;

DECIDES:
Article 1 [Official Holidays of the ECJ]
For the purposes of Article 80 (2) of the Rules of Procedure the following shall be official holidays:
New Year's Day;
Easter Monday;
1 May;
Ascension Day;
Whit Monday;
23 June;
24 June, where 23 June is a Sunday;
15 August;
1 November;
25 December;
26 December.
The official holidays referred to in the first paragraph hereof shall be those observed at the place where the Court of Justice has its seat.

Article 2-3 [omitted]

Done at Luxembourg, 19 June 1991.

ANNEX II: DECISION ON EXTENSION OF TIME LIMITS ON ACCOUNT OF DISTANCE THE COURT OF JUSTICE OF THE EUROPEAN COMMUNITIES,

HAVING REGARD to Article 81 (2) of the Rules of Procedure relating to the extension, on account of distance, of prescribed time limits;

DECIDES:
Article 1 [Extension of Time Limits]
In order to take account of distance, procedural time limits for all parties save those habitually resident in the Grand Duchy of Luxembourg shall be extended as follows:
– for the Kingdom of Belgium: two days,
– for the Federal Republic of Germany, the European territory of the French Republic and the European territory of the Kingdom of the Netherlands: six days,
– for the European territory of the Kingdom of Denmark, for the Kingdom of Spain, for Ireland, for the Hellenic Republic, for the Italian Republic, for the Republic of Austria, for the Portuguese Republic (with the exception of the Azores and Madeira), for the Republic of Finland, for the Kingdom of Sweden and for the United Kingdom: 10 days.

–   for other European countries and territories: two weeks,
–   for the autonomous regions of the Azores and Madeira of the Portuguese Republic: three
     weeks,
–   for other countries, departments and territories: one month.

Article 2 [omitted]

Rules of Procedure of the Court of First Instance of the European Communities of 2 May 1991[1]

TABLE OF CONTENTS

Interpretation (Article 1)

---

1   OJ 1991 L 136, p. 1, as amended on 15 September 1994, 17 February 1995, 6 July 1995, 12 March
     1997 and by the Amendments to the Rules of Procedure of the Court of First Instance of the
     European Communities to Enable it to Give Decisions in Cases When Constituted by a Single Judge
     of 17 May 1999.

THE COURT OF FIRST INSTANCE OF THE EUROPEAN COMMUNITIES,

HAVING REGARD [...] to Article 168a of the Treaty establishing the European Economic Community, [...]
HAVING REGARD to the Protocol on the Statute of the Court of Justice of the European Economic Community, signed in Brussels on 17 April 1957, [...]
HAVING REGARD to Council Decision 88/591 [...] establishing a Court of First Instance of the European Communities [...] and in particular Article 11 thereof,
HAVING REGARD to the agreement of the Court of Justice,
HAVING REGARD to the unanimous approval of the Council, given on 21 December 1990 and 29 April 1991,
WHEREAS the Court of First Instance is to establish its rules of procedure in agreement with the Court of Justice and with the unanimous approval of the Council and to adopt them immediately upon its constitution;
WHEREAS it is necessary to adopt the provisions laid down for the functioning of the Court of First Instance by the Treaties, by the Protocols on the Statutes of the Court of Justice and by the Council Decision of 24 October 1988 establishing a Court of First Instance of the European Communities and to adopt any other provisions necessary for applying and, where required, supplementing those instruments;
WHEREAS it is necessary to lay down for the Court of First Instance procedures adapted to the duties of such a court and to the task entrusted to the Court of First Instance of ensuring effective judicial protection of individual interests in cases requiring close examination of complex facts;
WHEREAS it is, moreover, desirable that the rules applicable to the procedure before the Court of First Instance should not differ more than is necessary from the rules applicable to the procedure before the Court of Justice under its Rules of Procedure adopted on 4 December 1974, as subsequently amended,

ADOPTS THE FOLLOWING

RULES OF PROCEDURE

INTERPRETATION
Article 1 [Definitions]
In these Rules:
— "EC Treaty" means the Treaty establishing the European Community,
— "EC Statute" means the Protocol on the Statute of the Court of Justice of the European Community,
— "ECSC Treaty" means the Treaty establishing the European Coal and Steel Community,
— "ECSC Statute" means the Protocol on the Statute of the Court of Justice of the European Coal and Steel Community,
— "Euratom Treaty" means the Treaty establishing the European Atomic Energy Community (Euratom),

— "Euratom Statute" means the Protocol on the Statute of the Court of Justice of the European Atomic Energy Community,
— "EEA Agreement" means the Agreement on the European Economic Area.
For the purpose of these Rules:
— "institutions" means the institutions of the Communities and bodies which are established by the Treaties, or by an act adopted in implementation thereof, and which may be parties before the Court of First Instance,
— "EFTA Surveillance Authority" means the surveillance authority referred to in the EEA Agreement.

TITLE I
ORGANIZATION OF THE COURT OF FIRST INSTANCE
Chapter 1 President and Members of the Court of First Instance

Article 2 [Judges and Advocates-General]
1.   Every Member of the Court of First Instance shall, as a rule, perform the function of Judge. Members of the Court of First Instance are hereinafter referred to as "Judges".
2.   Every Judge, with the exception of the President, may, in the circumstances specified in Articles 17 to 19, perform the function of Advocate-General in a particular case. References to the Advocate-General in these Rules shall apply only where a Judge has been designated as Advocate-General.

Article 3 [Beginning of Term]
The term of office of a Judge shall begin on the date laid down in his instrument of appointment. In the absence of any provision regarding the date, the term shall begin on the date of the instrument.

Article 4 [Oath of Office]
1.   Before taking up his duties, a Judge shall take the following oath before the Court of Justice of the European Communities: "I swear that I will perform my duties impartially and conscientiously; I swear that I will preserve the secrecy of the deliberations of the Court."
2.   Immediately after taking the oath, a Judge shall sign a declaration by which he solemnly undertakes that, both during and after his term of office, he will respect the obligations arising therefrom, and in particular the duty to behave with integrity and discretion as regards the acceptance, after he has ceased to hold office, of certain appointments and benefits.

Article 5 [Removal of a Judge]
When the Court of Justice is called upon to decide, after consulting the Court of First Instance, whether a Judge of the Court of First Instance no longer fulfils the requisite conditions or no longer meets the obligations arising from his office, the President of the Court of First Instance shall invite the Judge concerned to make representations to the Court of First Instance, in closed session and in the absence of the Registrar.
    The Court of First Instance shall state the reasons for its opinion.
    An opinion to the effect that a Judge of the Court of First Instance no longer fulfils the requisite conditions or no longer meets the obligations arising from his office must receive the votes of at least seven Judges of the Court of First Instance. In that event, particulars of the voting shall be communicated to the Court of Justice.
    Voting shall be by secret ballot; the Judge concerned shall not take part in the deliberations.

Article 6 [Ranking of Judges]

With the exception of the President of the Court of First Instance and of the Presidents of the Chambers, the Judges shall rank equally in precedence according to their seniority in office. Where there is equal seniority in office, precedence shall be determined by age.

Retiring Judges who are reappointed shall retain their former precedence.

Article 7 [Election of the President]

1. The Judges shall, immediately after the partial replacement provided for in Article 168a of the EC Treaty, Article 32d of the ECSC Treaty and Article 140a of the Euratom Treaty, elect one of their number as President of the Court of First Instance for a term of three years.

2. If the office of President of the Court of First Instance falls vacant before the normal date of expiry thereof, the Court of First Instance shall elect a successor for the remainder of the term.

3. The elections provided for in this Article shall be by secret ballot. If a Judge obtains an absolute majority he shall be elected. If no Judge obtains an absolute majority, a second ballot shall be held and the Judge obtaining the most votes shall be elected. Where two or more Judges obtain an equal number of votes the oldest of them shall be deemed elected.

Article 8 [Duties of the President]

The President of the Court of First Instance shall direct the judicial business and the administration of the Court of First Instance. He shall preside at plenary sittings and deliberations.

Article 9 [Replacement of the President]

When the President of the Court of First Instance is absent or prevented from attending or when the office of President is vacant, the functions of President shall be exercised by a President of a Chamber according to the order of precedence laid down in Article 6.

If the President of the Court and the Presidents of the Chambers are all prevented from attending at the same time, or their posts are vacant at the same time, the functions of President shall be exercised by one of the other Judges according to the order of precedence laid down in Article 6.

Chapter 2 Constitution of the Chambers and Designation of Judge-rapporteurs and Advocates-general

Article 10 [Creation of Chambers]

1. The Court of First Instance shall set up Chambers composed of three or five Judges and shall decide which Judges shall be attached to them.

2. The composition of the Chambers shall be published in the Official Journal of the European Communities.

Article 11 [Cases Heard in Plenary Court by a Chamber or by a Single Judge]

1. Cases before the Court of First Instance shall be heard by Chambers composed in accordance with Article 10.

Cases may be heard by the Court of First Instance sitting in plenary session under the conditions laid down in Articles 14, 51, 106, 118, 124, 127 and 129.

Cases may be heard by a single Judge where they are delegated to him under the conditions specified in Articles 14 and 51 or assigned to him pursuant to Article 124, Article 127(1) or Article 129(2).

2. In cases coming before a Chamber, the term "Court of First Instance" in these Rules shall designate that Chamber. In cases delegated or assigned to a single Judge the term "Court of First Instance" used in these Rules shall also designate that Judge.

Article 12 [Allocation of Cases to Chambers]
The Court of First Instance shall lay down criteria by which cases are to be allocated among the Chambers. The decision shall be published in the Official Journal of the European Communities.

Article 13 [Opening of Procedure]
1. As soon as the application initiating proceedings has been lodged, the President of the Court of First Instance shall assign the case to one of the Chambers.
2. The President of the Chamber shall propose to the President of the Court of First Instance, in respect of each case assigned to the Chamber, the designation of a Judge to act as Rapporteur; the President of the Court of First Instance shall decide on the proposal.

Article 14 [Decisions by Single Judge]
1. Whenever the legal difficulty or the importance of the case or special circumstances so justify, a case may be referred to the Court of First Instance sitting in plenary session or to a Chamber composed of a different number of Judges.
2. (1) The following cases, assigned to a Chamber composed of three Judges, may be heard and determined by the Judge-Rapporteur sitting as a single Judge where, having regard to the lack of difficulty of the questions of law or fact raised, to the limited importance of the case and to the absence of other special circumstances, they are suitable for being so heard and determined and have been delegated under the conditions laid down in Article 51:
    (a) cases brought pursuant to Article 179 of the EC Treaty or Article 152 of the EAEC Treaty;
    (b) cases brought pursuant to the fourth paragraph of Article 173, the third paragraph of Article 175 and Article 178 of the EC Treaty, to the second paragraph of Article 33, Article 35 and the first and second paragraphs of Article 40 of the ECSC Treaty and to the fourth paragraph of Article 146, the third paragraph of Article 148 and Article 151 of the EAEC Treaty that raise only questions already clarified by established case-law or that form part of a series of cases in which the same relief is sought and of which one has already been finally decided;
    (c) cases brought pursuant to Article 181 of the EC Treaty, Article 42 of the ECSC Treaty and Article 153 of the EAEC Treaty.
    (2) Delegation to a single Judge shall not be possible:
    (a) in cases which raise issues as to the legality of an act of general application;
    (b) in cases concerning the implementation of the rules:
    — on competition and on control of concentrations,
    — relating to aid granted by States,
    — relating to measures to protect trade,
    — relating to the common organisation of the agricultural markets, with the exception of cases that form part of a series of cases in which the same relief is sought and where one of those cases has already been finally decided;
    (c) in the cases referred to in Article 130(1).
    (3) The single Judge shall refer the case back to the Chamber if he finds that the conditions justifying delegation of the case are no longer satisfied.

3. The decisions to refer or to delegate a case which are provided for in paragraphs (1) and (2) shall be taken under the conditions laid down in Article 51.

Article 15 [Presidents of Chambers]

The Court of First Instance shall appoint for a period of one year the Presidents of the Chambers. The provisions of Article 7 (2) and (3) shall apply.

The appointments made in pursuance of this Article shall be published in the Official Journal of the European Communities.

Article 16 [Exercise of Presidential Powers]

In cases coming before a Chamber the powers of the President shall be exercised by the President of the Chamber.

In cases assigned or delegated to a single Judge the powers of the President, with the exception of those referred to in Articles 105 and 106, shall be exercised by that Judge.

Article 17 [Advocates-General in Plenary Court]

When the Court of First Instance sits in plenary session, it shall be assisted by an Advocate-General designated by the President of the Court of First Instance.

Article 18 [Advocates-General in Chambers]

A Chamber of the Court of First Instance may be assisted by an Advocate-General if it is considered that the legal difficulty or the factual complexity of the case so requires.

Article 19 [Decisions to Designate an Advocate-General]

The decision to designate an Advocate-General in a particular case shall be taken by the Court of First Instance sitting in plenary session at the request of the Chamber before which the case comes.

The President of the Court of First Instance shall designate the Judge called upon to perform the function of Advocate-General in that case.

Chapter 3 Registry

Section 1 - The Registrar
Article 20 [Appointment and Term]

1. The Court of First Instance shall appoint the Registrar.

Two weeks before the date fixed for making the appointment, the President of the Court of First Instance shall inform the Judges of the applications which have been submitted for the post.

2. An application shall be accompanied by full details of the candidate's age, nationality, university degrees, knowledge of any languages, present and past occupations and experience, if any, in judicial and international fields.

3. The appointment shall be made following the procedure laid down in Article 7 (3).

4. The Registrar shall be appointed for a term of six years. He may be reappointed.

5. Before he takes up his duties the Registrar shall take the oath before the Court of First Instance in accordance with Article 4.

6. The Registrar may be deprived of his office only if he no longer fulfils the requisite conditions or no longer meets the obligations arising from his office; the Court of First Instance shall take its decision after giving the Registrar an opportunity to make representations.

7. If the office of Registrar falls vacant before the usual date of expiry of the term thereof, the Court of First Instance shall appoint a new Registrar for a term of six years.

Article 21 [Assistant Registrars]

The Court of First Instance may, following the procedure laid down in respect of the Registrar, appoint one or more Assistant Registrars to assist the Registrar and to take his place in so far as the Instructions to the Registrar referred in Article 23 allow.

Article 22 [Replacement of the Registrar]

Where the Registrar is absent or prevented from attending and, if necessary, where the Assistant Registrar is absent or so prevented, or where their posts are vacant, the President of the Court of First Instance shall designate an official or servant to carry out the duties of Registrar.

Article 23 [Instructions to the Registrar]

Instructions to the Registrar shall be adopted by the Court of First Instance acting on a proposal from the President of the Court of First Instance.

Article 24 [The Registry]

1. There shall be kept in the Registry, under the control of the Registrar, a register initialled by the President of the Court of First Instance, in which all pleadings and supporting documents shall be entered in the order in which they are lodged.
2. When a document has been registered, the Registrar shall make a note to that effect on the original and, if a party so requests, on any copy submitted for the purpose.
3. Entries in the register and the notes provided for in the preceding paragraph shall be authentic.
4. Rules for keeping the register shall be prescribed by the Instructions to the Registrar referred to in Article 23.
5. Persons having an interest may consult the register at the Registry and may obtain copies or extracts on payment of a charge on a scale fixed by the Court of First Instance on a proposal from the Registrar.
    The parties to a case may on payment of the appropriate charge also obtain copies of pleadings and authenticated copies of orders and judgments.
6. Notice shall be given in the Official Journal of the European Communities of the date of registration of an application initiating proceedings, the names and addresses of the parties, the subject-matter of the proceedings, the form of order sought by the applicant and a summary of the pleas in law and of the main supporting arguments.
7. Where the Council or the Commission is not a party to a case, the Court of First Instance shall send to it copies of the application and of the defence, without the annexes thereto, to enable it to assess whether the inapplicability of one of its acts is being invoked under Article 184 of the EC Treaty, the third paragraph of Article 36 of the ECSC Treaty or Article 156 of the Euratom Treaty.

Article 25 [Duties of the Registrar]

1. The Registrar shall be responsible, under the authority of the President, for the acceptance, transmission and custody of documents and for effecting service as provided for by these Rules.
2. The Registrar shall assist the Court of First Instance, the Chambers, the President and the Judges in all their official functions.

Article 26 [Seals, Records and Publications]

The Registrar shall have custody of the seals. He shall be responsible for the records and be in charge of the publications of the Court of First Instance.

Article 27 [Attendance of Sittings]
Subject to Articles 5 and 33, the Registrar shall attend the sittings of the Court of First Instance and of the Chambers.

Section 2 - Other Departments
Article 28 [Other Staff]
The officials and other servants whose task is to assist directly the President, the Judges and the Registrar shall be appointed in accordance with the Staff Regulations. They shall be responsible to the Registrar, under the authority of the President of the Court of First Instance.

Article 29 [Oath of Office]
The officials and other servants referred to in Article 28 shall take the oath provided for in Article 20 (2) of the Rules of Procedure of the Court of Justice before the President of the Court of First Instance in the presence of the Registrar.

Article 30 [Financial Management]
The Registrar shall be responsible, under the authority of the President of the Court of First Instance, for the administration of the Court of First Instance, its financial management and its accounts; he shall be assisted in this by the departments of the Court of Justice.

Chapter 4 the Working of the Court of First Instance

Article 31 [Time and Place of Sittings]
1.   The dates and times of the sittings of the Court of First Instance shall be fixed by the President.
2.   The Court of First Instance may choose to hold one or more sittings in a place other than that in which the Court of First Instance has its seat.

Article 32 [Participation in Decisionmaking]
1.   Where, by reason of a Judge being absent or prevented from attending, there is an even number of Judges, the most junior Judge within the meaning of Article 6 shall abstain from taking part in the deliberations unless he is the Judge-Rapporteur. In this case, the Judge immediately senior to him shall abstain from taking part in the deliberations.
   Where, following the designation of an Advocate-General pursuant to Article 17, there is an even number of Judges in the Court of First Instance sitting in plenary session, the President of the Court shall designate, before the hearing and in accordance with a rota established in advance by the Court of First Instance and published in the Official Journal of the European Communities, the Judge who will not take part in the judgment of the case.
2.   If, after the Court of First Instance has been convened in plenary session, it is found that the quorum of nine Judges has not been attained, the President of the Court of First Instance shall adjourn the sitting until there is a quorum.
3.   If in any Chamber the quorum of three Judges has not been attained, the President of that Chamber shall so inform the President of the Court of First Instance who shall designate another Judge to complete the Chamber.
4.   If in any Chamber of three or five Judges the number of Judges assigned to that Chamber is higher than three or five respectively, the President of the Chamber shall decide which of the Judges will be called upon to take part in the judgment of the case.

5.   If the single Judge to whom the case has been delegated or assigned is absent or prevented from attending, the President of the Court of First Instance shall designate another Judge to replace that Judge.

Article 33 [Deliberations, Conclusions, Voting]
1.   The Court of First Instance shall deliberate in closed session.
2.   Only those Judges who were present at the oral proceedings may take part in the deliberations.
3.   Every Judge taking part in the deliberations shall state his opinion and the reasons for it.
4.   Any Judge may require that any question be formulated in the language of his choice and communicated in writing to the other Judges before being put to the vote.
5.   The conclusions reached by the majority of the Judges after final discussion shall determine the decision of the Court of First Instance. Votes shall be cast in reverse order to the order of precedence laid down in Article 6.
6.   Differences of view on the substance, wording or order of questions, or on the interpretation of a vote shall be settled by decision of the Court of First Instance.
7.   Where the deliberations of the Court of First Instance concern questions of its own administration, the Registrar shall be present, unless the Court of First Instance decides to the contrary.
8.   Where the Court of First Instance sits without the Registrar being present it shall, if necessary, instruct the most junior Judge within the meaning of Article 6 to draw up minutes. The minutes shall be signed by this Judge and by the President.

Article 34 [Court Vacations]
1.   Subject to any special decision of the Court of First Instance, its vacations shall be as follows:
— from 18 December to 10 January,
— from the Sunday before Easter to the second Sunday after Easter,
— from 15 July to 15 September.
During the vacations, the functions of President shall be exercised at the place where the Court of First Instance has its seat either by the President himself, keeping in touch with the Registrar, or by a President of Chamber or other Judge invited by the President to take his place.
2.   In a case of urgency, the President may convene the Judges during the vacations.
3.   The Court of First Instance shall observe the official holidays of the place where it has its seat.
4.   The Court of First Instance may, in proper circumstances, grant leave of absence to any Judge.

Chapter 5 Languages

Article 35 [Language of Cases]
1.   The language of a case shall be Danish, Dutch, English, Finnish, French, German, Greek, Irish, Italian, Portuguese, Spanish or Swedish.
2. The language of the case shall be chosen by the applicant, except that:
(a) at the joint request of the parties, the use of another of the languages mentioned in paragraph 1 for all or part of the proceedings may be authorized;
(b) at the request of one of the parties, and after the opposite party and the Advocate-General have been heard, the use of another of the languages mentioned in paragraph 1 as the language of the case for all or part of the proceedings may be authorized by way of derogation from subparagraph (a).

Requests as above may be decided on by the President; the latter may and, where he proposes to accede to a request without the agreement of all the parties, must refer the request to the Court of First Instance.

3.   The language of the case shall be used in the written and oral pleadings of the parties and in supporting documents, and also in the minutes and decisions of the Court of First Instance. Any supporting documents expressed in another language must be accompanied by a translation into the language of the case.

In the case of lengthy documents, translations may be confined to extracts. However, the Court of First Instance may, of its own motion or at the request of a party, at any time call for a complete or fuller translation.

Notwithstanding the foregoing provisions, a Member State shall be entitled to use its official language when intervening in a case before the Court of First Instance. This provision shall apply both to written statements and to oral addresses.

The Registrar shall cause any such statement or address to be translated into the language of the case.

The States, other than the Member States, which are parties to the EEA Agreement, and also the EFTA Surveillance Authority, may be authorized to use one of the languages mentioned in paragraph 1, other than the language of the case, when they intervene in a case before the Court of First Instance. This provision shall apply both to written statements and oral addresses. The Registrar shall cause any such statement or address to be translated into the language of the case.

4.   Where a witness or expert states that he is unable adequately to express himself in one of the languages referred to in paragraph (1) of this Article, the Court of First Instance may authorize him to give his evidence in another language. The Registrar shall arrange for translation into the language of the case.

5.   The President in conducting oral proceedings, the Judge-Rapporteur both in his preliminary report and in his report for the hearing, Judges and the Advocate-General in putting questions and the Advocate-General in delivering his opinion may use one of the languages referred to in paragraph (1) of this Article other than the language of the case. The Registrar shall arrange for translation into the language of the case.

Article 36 [Translations]

1.   The Registrar shall, at the request of any Judge, of the Advocate-General or of a party, arrange for anything said or written in the course of the proceedings before the Court of First Instance to be translated into the languages he chooses from those referred to in Article 35 (1).

2.   Publications of the Court of First Instance shall be issued in the language referred to in Article 1 of Council Regulation No 1.

Article 37 [Authentic Documents]

The texts of documents drawn up in the language of the case or in any other language authorized by the Court of First Instance pursuant to Article 35 shall be authentic.

Chapter 6 Rights and Obligations of Agents, Advisers and Lawyers

Article 38 [Privileges and Immunities of Counsel]

1.   Agents, advisers and lawyers, appearing before the Court of First Instance or before any judicial authority to which it has addressed letters rogatory, shall enjoy immunity in respect of words spoken or written by them concerning the case or the parties.

2.   Agents, advisers and lawyers shall enjoy the following further privileges and facilities:

(a) papers and documents relating to the proceedings shall be exempt from both
    search and seizure; in the event of a dispute the customs officials or police may
    seal those papers and documents; they shall then be immediately forwarded to the
    Court of First Instance for inspection in the presence of the Registrar and of the
    person concerned;
(b) agents, advisers and lawyers shall be entitled to such allocation of foreign currency
    as may be necessary for the performance of their duties;
(c) agents, advisers and lawyers shall be entitled to travel in the course of duty without
    hindrance.

Article 39 [Proof of Status]
In order to qualify for the privileges, immunities and facilities specified in Article 38,
persons entitled to them shall furnish proof of their status as follows:
(a) agents shall produce an official document issued by the party for whom they act
    and shall forward without delay a copy thereof to the Registrar.
(b) advisers and lawyers shall produce a certificate signed by the Registrar. The vali-
    dity of this certificate shall be limited to a specified period, which may be extended
    or curtailed according to the length of the proceedings.

Article 40 [Waiver of Immunity]
The privileges, immunities and facilities specified in Article 38 are granted exclusively
in the interests of the proper conduct of proceedings.
    The Court of First Instance may waive the immunity where it considers that the
proper conduct of proceedings will not be hindered thereby.

Article 41 [Exclusion of Counsel from Proceedings]
1. Any adviser or lawyer whose conduct towards the Court of First Instance, the President, a Judge or the Registrar is incompatible with the dignity of the Court of First Instance, or who uses his rights for purposes other than those for which they were granted, may at any time be excluded from the proceedings by an order of the Court of First
Instance; the person concerned shall be given an opportunity to defend himself.
    The order shall have immediate effect.
2. Where an adviser or lawyer is excluded from the proceedings, the proceedings
shall be suspended for a period fixed by the President in order to allow the party concerned to appoint another adviser or lawyer.
3. Decisions taken under this Article may be rescinded.

Article 42 [University Teachers as Counsel]
The provisions of this Chapter shall apply to university teachers who have a right of
audience before the Court of First Instance in accordance with Article 17 of the EC
Statute, Article 20 of the ECSC Statute and Article 17 of the Euratom Statute.

TITLE II
PROCEDURE
Chapter 1 Written Procedure

Article 43 [Written Pleadings]
1. The original of every pleading must be signed by the party's agent or lawyer.
    The original, accompanied by all annexes referred to therein, shall be lodged to-
gether with five copies for the Court of First Instance and a copy for every other party
to the proceedings. Copies shall be certified by the party lodging them.
2. Institutions shall in addition produce, within time-limits laid down by the Court of
First Instance, translations of all pleadings into the other languages provided for by

Article 1 of Council Regulation No 1. The second subparagraph of paragraph (1) of this Article shall apply.

3. All pleadings shall bear a date. In the reckoning of time-limits for taking steps in proceedings only the date of lodgment at the Registry shall be taken into account.

4. To every pleading there shall be annexed a file containing the documents relied on in support of it, together with a schedule listing them.

5. Where in view of the length of a document only extracts from it are annexed to the pleading, the whole document or a full copy of it shall be lodged at the Registry.

Article 44 [Contents of Written Pleadings]

1. An application of the kind referred to in Article 19 of the EC Statute, Article 22 of the ECSC Statute and Article 19 of the Euratom Statute shall state:
(a) the name and address of the applicant;
(b) the designation of the party against whom the application is made;
(c) the subject-matter of the proceedings and a summary of the pleas in law on which the application is based;
(d) the form of order sought by the applicant;
(e) where appropriate, the nature of any evidence offered in support.

2. For the purpose of the proceedings, the application shall state an address for service in the place where the Court of First Instance has its seat and the name of the person who is authorized and has expressed willingness to accept service. If the application does not comply with these requirements, all service on the party concerned for the purposes of the proceedings shall be effected, for so long as the defect has not been cured, by registered letter addressed to the agent or lawyer of that party. By way of derogation from Article 100, service shall then be deemed to have been duly effected by the lodging of the registered letter at the post office of the place where the Court of First Instance has its seat.

3. The lawyer acting for a party must lodge at the Registry a certificate that he is authorized to practise before a Court of a Member State or of another State which is a party to the EEA Agreement.

4. The application shall be accompanied, where appropriate, by the documents specified in the second paragraph of Article 19 of the EC Statute, in the second paragraph of Article 22 of the ECSC Statute and in the second paragraph of Article 19 of the Euratom Statute.

5. An application made by a legal person governed by private law shall be accompanied by:
(a) the instrument or instruments constituting and regulating that legal person or a recent extract from the register of companies, firms or associations or any other proof of its existence in law;
(b) proof that the authority granted to the applicant's lawyer has been properly conferred on him by someone authorized for the purpose.

5a. An application submitted under Article 181 of the EC Treaty, Article 42 of the ECSC Treaty or Article 153 of the Euratom Treaty pursuant to an arbitration clause contained in a contract governed by public or private law, entered into by the Community or on its behalf, shall be accompanied by a copy of the contract which contains that clause.

6. If an application does not comply with the requirements set out in paragraphs (3) to (5) of this Article, the Registrar shall prescribe a reasonable period within which the applicant is to comply with them whether by putting the application itself in order or by producing any of the abovementioned documents. If the applicant fails to put the application in order or to produce the required documents within the time prescribed, the Court of First Instance shall decide whether the non-compliance with these conditions renders the application formally inadmissible.

Article 45 [Service of Defendant]

The application shall be served on the defendant. In a case where Article 44 (6) applies, service shall be effected as soon as the application has been put in order or the Court of First Instance has declared it admissible notwithstanding the failure to observe the formal requirements set out in that Article.

Article 46 [Defence]

1. Within one month after service on him of the application, the defendant shall lodge a defence, stating:
(a) the name and address of the defendant;
(b) the arguments of fact and law relied on;
(c) the form of order sought by the defendant;
(d) the nature of any evidence offered by him.
The provisions of Article 44 (2) to (5) shall apply to the defence.
2. In proceedings between the Communities and their servants the defence shall be accompanied by the complaint within the meaning of Article 90 (2) of the Staff Regulations of Officials and by the decision rejecting the complaint together with the dates on which the complaint was submitted and the decision notified.
3. The time-limit laid down in paragraph (1) of this Article may be extended by the President on a reasoned application by the defendant.

Article 47 [Reply and Rejoinder]

1. The application initiating the proceedings and the defence may be supplemented by a reply from the applicant and by a rejoinder from the defendant.
2. The President shall fix the time-limits within which these pleadings are to be lodged.

Article 48 [Admitted Elements of Reply and Rejoinder]

1. In reply or rejoinder a party may offer further evidence. The party must, however, give reasons for the delay in offering it.
2. No new plea in law may be introduced in the course of proceedings unless it is based on matters of law or of fact which come to light in the course of the procedure.

If in the course of the procedure one of the parties puts forward a new plea in law which is so based, the President may, even after the expiry of the normal procedural time-limits, acting on a report of the Judge-Rapporteur and after hearing the Advocate-General, allow the other party time to answer on that plea.

Consideration of the admissibility of the plea shall be reserved for the final judgment.

Article 49 [Procedural Decisions]

At any stage of the proceedings the Court of First Instance may, after hearing the Advocate-General, prescribe any measure of organization of procedure or any measure of inquiry referred to in Articles 64 and 65 or order that a previous inquiry be repeated or expanded.

Article 50 [Joining and Disjoining Cases]

The President may, at any time, after hearing the parties and the Advocate-General, order that two or more cases concerning the same subject-matter shall, on account of the connexion between them, be joined for the purposes of the written or oral procedure or of the final judgment. The cases may subsequently be disjoined.

Article 51 [Delegation of cases]

1.   In the cases specified in Article 14(1), and at any stage in the proceedings, the Chamber hearing the case may, either on its own initiative or at the request of one of the parties, propose to the Court of First Instance sitting in plenary session that the case be referred to the Court of First Instance sitting in plenary session or to a Chamber composed of a different number of Judges. The Court of First Instance sitting in plenary session shall, after hearing the parties and the Advocate-General, decide whether or not to refer a case.

The case shall be maintained before or referred to a Chamber composed of five Judges where a Member State or an institution of the European Communities which is a party to the proceedings so requests.

2.   The decision to delegate a case to a single Judge in the situations set out in Article 14(2) shall be taken, after the parties have been heard, unanimously by the Chamber composed of three Judges before which the case is pending.

Where a Member State or an institution of the European Communities which is a party to the proceedings objects to the case being heard by a single Judge the case shall be maintained before or referred to the Chamber to which the Judge-Rapporteur belongs.

Article 52 [Report by the Judge-Rapporteur]

1.   Without prejudice to the application of Article 49, the President shall, after the rejoinder has been lodged, fix a date on which the Judge-Rapporteur is to present his preliminary report to the Court of First Instance. The report shall contain recommendations as to whether measures of organization of procedure or measures of inquiry should be undertaken and whether the case should be referred to the Court of First Instance sitting in plenary session or to a Chamber composed of a different number of Judges.

2.   The Court of First Instance shall decide, after hearing the Advocate-General, what action to take upon the recommendations of the Judge-Rapporteur.

The same procedure shall apply:

(a)   where no reply or no rejoinder has been lodged within the time-limit fixed in accordance with Article 47 (2);

(b)   where the party concerned waives his right to lodge a reply or rejoinder.

Article 53 [Opening of Oral Procedure]

Where the Court of First Instance decides to open the oral procedure without undertaking measures of organization of procedure or ordering a preparatory inquiry, the President of the Court of First Instance shall fix the opening date.

Article 54 [Opening of Oral Procedure After Measures of Inquiry]

Without prejudice to any measures of organization of procedure or measures of inquiry which may be arranged at the stage of the oral procedure, where, during the written procedure, measures of organization of procedure or measures of inquiry have been instituted and completed, the President shall fix the date for the opening of the oral procedure.

Chapter 2 Oral Procedure

Article 55 [Sequencing of Cases]

1.   Subject to the priority of decisions provided for in Article 106, the Court of First Instance shall deal with the cases before it in the order in which the preparatory inquiries in them have been completed. Where the preparatory inquiries in several cases are completed simultaneously, the order in which they are to be dealt with shall be de-

termined by the dates of entry in the register of the applications initiating them respectively.

2.   The President may in special circumstances order that a case be given priority over others.

The President may in special circumstances, after hearing the parties and the Advocate-General, either on his own initiative or at the request of one of the parties, defer a case to be dealt with at a later date. On a joint application by the parties the President may order that a case be deferred.

Article 56 [Duties of the President of the Hearings]
The proceedings shall be opened and directed by the President, who shall be responsible for the proper conduct of the hearing.

Article 57 [Hearings in Camera]
The oral proceedings in cases heard in camera shall not be published.

Article 58 [Examination of Counsel]
The President may in the course of the hearing put questions to the agents, advisers or lawyers of the parties. The other Judges and the Advocate-General may do likewise.

Article 59 [Requirement to be Represented by a Lawyer]
A party may address the Court of First Instance only through his agent, adviser or lawyer.

Article 60 [Closure of Oral Procedure]
Where an Advocate-General has not been designated in a case, the President shall declare the oral procedure closed at the end of the hearing.

Article 61 [Opinion of the Advocate-General]
1.   Where the Advocate-General delivers his opinion in writing, he shall lodge it at the Registry, which shall communicate it to the parties.
2.   After the delivery, orally or in writing, of the opinion of the Advocate-General the President shall declare the oral procedure closed.

Article 62 [Re-opening of Oral Proceedings]
The Court of First Instance may, after hearing the Advocate-General, order the re-opening of the oral procedure.

Article 63 [Minutes of the Hearings]
1.   The Registrar shall draw up minutes of every hearing. The minutes shall be signed by the President and by the Registrar and shall constitute an official record.
2.   The parties may inspect the minutes at the Registry and obtain copies at their own expense.

Chapter 3 Measures of Organization of Procedure and Measures of Inquiry

Section 1 - Measures of organization of procedure
Article 64 [Procedural Decisions]
1.   The purpose of measures of organization of procedure shall be to ensure that cases are prepared for hearing, procedures carried out and disputes resolved under the best possible conditions. They shall be prescribed by the Court of First Instance, after hearing the Advocate-General.
2.   Measures of organization of procedure shall, in particular, have as their purpose:

(a) to ensure efficient conduct of the written and oral procedure and to facilitate the taking of evidence;
(b) to determine the points on which the parties must present further argument or which call for measures of inquiry;
(c) to clarify the forms of order sought by the parties, their pleas in law and arguments and the points at issue between them;
(d) to facilitate the amicable settlement of proceedings.
3.   Measures of organization of procedure may, in particular, consist of:
(a) putting questions to the parties;
(b) inviting the parties to make written or oral submissions on certain aspects of the proceedings;
(c) asking the parties or third parties for information or particulars;
(d) asking for documents or any papers relating to the case to be produced;
(e) summoning the parties' agents or the parties in person to meetings.
4.   Each party may, at any stage of the procedure, propose the adoption or modification of measures of organization of procedure. In that case, the other parties shall be heard before those measures are prescribed.

Where the procedural circumstances so require, the Registrar shall inform the parties of the measures envisaged by the Court of First Instance and shall give them an opportunity to submit comments orally or in writing.
5.   If the Court of First Instance sitting in plenary session decides to prescribe measures of organization of procedure and does not undertake such measures itself, it shall entrust the task of so doing to the Chamber to which the case was originally assigned or to the Judge-Rapporteur.

If a Chamber prescribes measures of organization of procedure and does not undertake such measures itself, it shall entrust the task to the Judge-Rapporteur.

The Advocate-General shall take part in measures of organization of procedure.

Section 2 - Measures of inquiry
Article 65 [Evidence]
Without prejudice to Articles 21 and 22 of the EC Statute, Articles 24 and 25 of the ECSC Statute and Articles 22 and 23 of the Euratom Statute, the following measures of inquiry may be adopted:
(a) the personal appearance of the parties;
(b) a request for information and production of documents;
(c) oral testimony;
(d) the commissioning of an expert's report;
(e) an inspection of the place or thing in question.

Article 66 [Prescription of Measures of Inquiry]
1.   The Court of First Instance, after hearing the Advocate-General, shall prescribe the measures of inquiry that it considers appropriate by means of an order setting out the facts to be proved. Before the Court of First Instance decides on the measures of inquiry referred to in Article 65 (c), (d) and (e) the parties shall be heard.
The order shall be served on the parties.
2.   Evidence may be submitted in rebuttal and previous evidence may be amplified.

Article 67 [Conduct of Inquiry]
1.   Where the Court of First Instance sitting in plenary session orders a preparatory inquiry and does not undertake such an inquiry itself, it shall entrust the task of so doing to the Chamber to which the case was originally assigned or to the Judge-Rapporteur.

Where a Chamber orders a preparatory inquiry and does not undertake such an inquiry itself, it shall entrust the task of so doing to the Judge-Rapporteur.

The Advocate-General shall take part in the measures of inquiry.

2. The parties may be present at the measures of inquiry.

Section 3 - The summoning and examination of witnesses and experts
Article 68 [Examination of Witnesses]

1. The Court of First Instance may, either of its own motion or on application by a party, and after hearing the Advocate-General and the parties, order that certain facts be proved by witnesses. The order shall set out the facts to be established.

The Court of First Instance may summon a witness of its own motion or on application by a party or at the instance of the Advocate-General.

An application by a party for the examination of a witness shall state precisely about what facts and for what reasons the witness should be examined.

2. The witness shall be summoned by an order containing the following information:
(a) the surname, forenames, description and address of the witness;
(b) an indication of the facts about which the witness is to be examined;
(c) where appropriate, particulars of the arrangements made by the Court of First Instance for reimbursement of expenses incurred by the witness, and of the penalties which may be imposed on defaulting witnesses.

The order shall be served on the parties and the witnesses.

3. The Court of First Instance may make the summoning of a witness for whose examination a party has applied conditional upon the deposit with the cashier of the Court of First Instance of a sum sufficient to cover the taxed costs thereof; the Court of First Instance shall fix the amount of the payment.

The cashier of the Court of First Instance shall advance the funds necessary in connexion with the examination of any witness summoned by the Court of First Instance of its own motion.

4. After the identity of the witness has been established, the President shall inform him that he will be required to vouch the truth of his evidence in the manner laid down in paragraph (5) of this Article and in Article 71.

The witness shall give his evidence to the Court of First Instance, the parties having been given notice to attend. After the witness has given his main evidence the President may, at the request of a party or of his own motion, put questions to him.

The other Judges and the Advocate-General may do likewise.

Subject to the control of the President, questions may be put to witnesses by the representatives of the parties.

5. Subject to the provisions of Article 71, the witness shall, after giving his evidence, take the following oath: "I swear that I have spoken the truth, the whole truth and nothing but the truth."

The Court of First Instance may, after hearing the parties, exempt a witness from taking the oath.

6. The Registrar shall draw up minutes in which the evidence of each witness is reproduced. The minutes shall be signed by the President or by the Judge-Rapporteur responsible for conducting the examination of the witness, and by the Registrar. Before the minutes are thus signed, witnesses must be given an opportunity to check the content of the minutes and to sign them.

The minutes shall constitute an official record.

Article 69 [Penalties of Defaulting Witnesses]

1. Witnesses who have been duly summoned shall obey the summons and attend for examination.

2.   If a witness who has been duly summoned fails to appear before the Court of First Instance, the latter may impose upon him a pecuniary penalty not exceeding 5.000 ECU and may order that a further summons be served on the witness at his own expense.

The same penalty may be imposed upon a witness who, without good reason, refuses to give evidence or to take the oath or where appropriate to make a solemn affirmation equivalent thereto.

3.   If the witness proffers a valid excuse to the Court of First Instance, the pecuniary penalty imposed on him may be cancelled. The pecuniary penalty imposed may be reduced at the request of the witness where he establishes that it is disproportionate to his income.

4.   Penalties imposed and other measures ordered under this Article shall be enforced in accordance with Articles 187 and 192 of the EC Treaty, Articles 44 and 92 of the ECSC Treaty and Articles 159 and 164 of the Euratom Treaty.

Article 70 [Commissioning of Expert Reports]

1.   The Court of First Instance may order that an expert's report be obtained. The order appointing the expert shall define his task and set a time-limit within which he is to make his report.

2.   The expert shall receive a copy of the order, together with all the documents necessary for carrying out his task. He shall be under the supervision of the Judge-Rapporteur, who may be present during his investigation and who shall be kept informed of his progress in carrying out his task.

The Court of First Instance may request the parties or one of them to lodge security for the costs of the expert's report.

3.   At the request of the expert, the Court of First Instance may order the examination of witnesses. Their examination shall be carried out in accordance with Article 68.

4.   The expert may give his opinion only on points which have been expressly referred to him.

5.   After the expert has made his report, the Court of First Instance may order that he be examined, the parties having been given notice to attend.

Subject to the control of the President, questions may be put to the expert by the representatives of the parties.

6.   Subject to the provisions of Article 71, the expert shall, after making his report, take the following oath before the Court of First Instance: "I swear that I have conscientiously and impartially carried out my task."

The Court of First Instance may, after hearing the parties, exempt the expert from taking the oath.

Article 71 [Oath of Witnesses and Experts]

1.   The President shall instruct any person who is required to take an oath before the Court of First Instance, as witness or expert, to tell the truth or to carry out his task conscientiously and impartially, as the case may be, and shall warn him of the criminal liability provided for in his national law in the event of any breach of this duty.

2.   Witnesses and experts shall take the oath either in accordance with the first subparagraph of Article 68 (5) and the first subparagraph of Article 70 (6) or in the manner laid down by their national law.

3.   Where the national law provides the opportunity to make, in judicial proceedings, a solemn affirmation equivalent to an oath as well as or instead of taking an oath, the witnesses and experts may make such an affirmation under the conditions and in the form prescribed in their national law.

Where their national law provides neither for taking an oath nor for making a solemn affirmation, the procedure described in the first paragraph of this Article shall be followed.

Article 72 [Penalties for Injury]

1. The Court of First Instance may, after hearing the Advocate-General, decide to report to the competent authority referred to in Annex III to the Rules supplementing the Rules of Procedure of the Court of Justice of the Member State whose courts have penal jurisdiction in any case of perjury on the part of a witness or expert before the Court of First Instance, account being taken of the provisions of Article 71.
2. The Registrar shall be responsible for communicating the decision of the Court of First Instance. The decision shall set out the facts and circumstances on which the report is based.

Article 73 [Unsuitable Witnessses or Experts]

1. If one of the parties objects to a witness or to an expert on the ground that he is not a competent or proper person to act as witness or expert or for any other reason, or if a witness or expert refuses to give evidence, to take the oath or to make a solemn affirmation equivalent thereto, the matter shall be resolved by the Court of First Instance.
2. An objection to a witness or to an expert shall be raised within two weeks after service of the order summoning the witness or appointing the expert; the statement of objection must set out the grounds of objection and indicate the nature of any evidence offered.

Article 74 [Compensation of Witnesses and Experts]

1. Witnesses and experts shall be entitled to reimbursement of their travel and subsistence expenses. The cashier of the Court of First Instance may make a payment to them towards these expenses in advance.
2. Witnesses shall be entitled to compensation for loss of earnings, and experts to fees for their services. The cashier of the Court of First Instance shall pay witnesses and experts their compensation or fees after they have carried out their respective duties or tasks.

Article 75 [Letters Rogatory]

1. The Court of First Instance may, on application by a party or of its own motion, issue letters rogatory for the examination of witnesses or experts.
2. Letters rogatory shall be issued in the form of an order which shall contain the name, forenames, description and address of the witness or expert, set out the facts on which the witness or expert is to be examined, name the parties, their agents, lawyers or advisers, indicate their addresses for service and briefly describe the subject-matter of the proceedings.

Notice of the order shall be served on the parties by the Registrar.

3. The Registrar shall send the order to the competent authority named in Annex I to the Rules supplementing the Rules of Procedure of the Court of Justice of the Member State in whose territory the witness or expert is to be examined. Where necessary, the order shall be accompanied by a translation into the official language or languages of the Member State to which it is addressed.

The authority named pursuant to the first paragraph shall pass on the order to the judicial authority which is competent according to its national law.

The competent judicial authority shall give effect to the letters rogatory in accordance with its national law. After implementation the competent judicial authority shall transmit to the authority named pursuant to the first paragraph the order embodying the letters rogatory, any documents arising from the implementation and a detailed statement of costs. These documents shall be sent to the Registrar.

The Registrar shall be responsible for the translation of the documents into the language of the case.

4. The Court of First Instance shall defray the expenses occasioned by the letters rogatory without prejudice to the right to charge them, where appropriate, to the parties.

Article 76 [Minutes of Hearings]

1. The Registrar shall draw up minutes of every hearing. The minutes shall be signed by the President and by the Registrar and shall constitute an official record.
2. The parties may inspect the minutes and any expert's report at the Registry and obtain copies at their own expense.

Chapter 4 Stay of Proceedings and Declining of Jurisdiction by the Court of First Instance

Article 77 [Reasons for a Stay]

Without prejudice to Article 123 (4), Article 128 and Article 129 (4), proceedings may be stayed:
(a) in the circumstances specified in the third paragraph of Article 47 of the EC Statute, the third paragraph of Article 47 of the ECSC Statute and the third paragraph of Article 48 of the Euratom Statute;
(b) where an appeal is brought before the Court of Justice against a decision of the Court of First Instance disposing of the substantive issues in part only, disposing of a procedural issue concerning a plea of lack of competence or inadmissibility or dismissing an application to intervene;
(c) at the joint request of the parties.

Article 78 [Decisions to Stay]

The decision to stay the proceedings shall be made by order of the President after hearing the parties and the Advocate-General; the President may refer the matter to the Court of First Instance. A decision ordering that the proceedings be resumed shall be adopted in accordance with the same procedure. The orders referred to in this Article shall be served on the parties.

Article 79 [Effects of a Stay]

1. The stay of proceedings shall take effect on the date indicated in the order of stay or, in the absence of such an indication, on the date of that order.

While proceedings are stayed time shall, except for the purposes of the time-limit prescribed in Article 115 (1) for an application to intervene, cease to run for the purposes of prescribed time-limits for all parties.

2. Where the order of stay does not fix the length of the stay, it shall end on the date indicated in the order of resumption or, in the absence of such indication, on the date of the order of resumption.

From the date of resumption time shall begin to run afresh for the purposes of the time-limits.

Article 80 [Lack of Jurisdiction]

Decisions declining jurisdiction in the circumstances specified in the third paragraph of Article 47 of the EC Statute, the third paragraph of Article 47 of the ECSC Statute and the third paragraph of Article 48 of the Euratom Statute shall be made by the Court of First Instance by way of an order which shall be served on the parties.

Chapter 5 Judgments

Article 81 [Contents of Judgments]
The judgment shall contain:
— a statement that it is the judgment of the Court of First Instance,
— the date of its delivery,
— the names of the President and of the Judges taking part in it,
— the name of the Advocate-General, if designated,
— the name of the Registrar,
— the description of the parties,
— the names of the agents, advisers and lawyers of the parties,
— a statement of the forms of order sought by the parties,
— a statement, where appropriate, that the Advocate-General delivered his opinion,
— a summary of the facts,
— the grounds for the decision,
— the operative part of the judgment, including the decision as to costs.

Article 82 [Effects of Judgment]
1.   The judgment shall be delivered in open court; the parties shall be given notice to attend to hear it.
2.   The original of the judgment, signed by the President, by the Judges who took part in the deliberations and by the Registrar, shall be sealed and deposited at the Registry; the parties shall be served with certified copies of the judgment.
3.   The Registrar shall record on the original of the judgment the date on which it was delivered.

Article 83 [Rectification of Judgments]
Subject to the provisions of the second paragraph of Article 53 of the EC Statute, the second paragraph of Article 53 of the ECSC Statute and the second paragraph of Article 54 of the Euratom Statute, the judgment shall be binding from the date of its delivery.

Article 84 [Supplementing of Judgments]
1.   Without prejudice to the provisions relating to the interpretation of judgments, the Court of First Instance may, of its own motion or on application by a party made within two weeks after the delivery of a judgment, rectify clerical mistakes, errors in calculation and obvious slips in it.
2.   The parties, whom the Registrar shall duly notify, may lodge written observations within a period prescribed by the President.
3.   The Court of First Instance shall take its decision in closed session.
4.   The original of the rectification order shall be annexed to the original of the rectified judgment. A note of this order shall be made in the margin of the original of the rectified judgment.

Article 85 [Supplementing of Judgments]
If the Court of First Instance should omit to give a decision on costs, any party may within a month after service of the judgment apply to the Court of First Instance to supplement its judgment.

The application shall be served on the opposite party and the President shall prescribe a period within which that party may lodge written observations.

After these observations have been lodged, the Court of First Instance shall decide both on the admissibility and on the substance of the application.

Article 86 [Publication of Cases]
The Registrar shall arrange for the publication of cases before the Court of First Instance.

Chapter 6 Costs

Article 87 [Decision as to Costs]
1.   A decision as to costs shall be given in the final judgment or in the order which closes the proceedings.
2.   The unsuccessful party shall be ordered to pay the costs if they have been applied for in the successful party's pleadings.

Where there are several unsuccessful parties the Court of First Instance shall decide how the costs are to be shared.
3.   Where each party succeeds on some and fails on other heads, or where the circumstances are exceptional, the Court of First Instance may order that the costs be shared or that each party bear its own costs.

The Court of First Instance may order a party, even if successful, to pay costs which it considers that party to have unreasonably or vexatiously caused the opposite party to incur.
4.   The Member States and institutions which intervened in the proceedings shall bear their own costs.

The States, other than the Member States, which are parties to the EEA Agreement, and also the EFTA Surveillance Authority, shall bear their own costs if they intervene in the proceedings.

The Court of First Instance may order an intervener other than those mentioned in the preceding subparagraph to bear his own costs.
5.   A party who discontinues or withdraws from proceedings shall be ordered to pay the costs if they have been applied for in the observations of the other party on the discontinuance. However, upon application by the party who discontinues or withdraws from proceedings, the costs shall be borne by the other party if this appears justified by the conduct of that party.

Where the parties have come to an agreement on costs, the decision as to costs shall be in accordance with that agreement.

If costs are not applied for, the parties shall bear their own costs.
6.   Where a case does not proceed to judgment, the costs shall be in the discretion of the Court of First Instance.

Article 88 [Costs of Institutions]
Without prejudice to the second subparagraph of Article 87 (3), in proceedings between the Communities and their servants the institutions shall bear their own costs.

Article 89 [Costs of Enforcement]
Costs necessarily incurred by a party in enforcing a judgment or order of the Court of First Instance shall be refunded by the opposite party on the scale in force in the State where the enforcement takes place.

Article 90 [Court Fees]

Proceedings before the Court of First Instance shall be free of charge, except that:
(a) where a party has caused the Court of First Instance to incur avoidable costs, the Court of First Instance may order that party to refund them;
(b) where copying or translation work is carried out at the request of a party, the cost shall, in so far as the Registrar considers it excessive, be paid for by that party on the scale of charges referred to in Article 24 (5).

Article 91 [Recoverable Costs]

Without prejudice to the preceding Article, the following shall be regarded as recoverable costs:
(a) sums payable to witnesses and experts under Article 74;
(b) expenses necessarily incurred by the parties for the purpose of the proceedings, in particular the travel and subsistence expenses and the remuneration of agents, advisers or lawyers.

Article 92 [Dispute over Costs]

1.   If there is a dispute concerning the costs to be recovered, the Court of First Instance hearing the case shall, on application by the party concerned and after hearing the opposite party, make an order, from which no appeal shall lie.
2.   The parties may, for the purposes of enforcement, apply for an authenticated copy of the order.

Article 93 [Currency of Payment]

1.   Sums due from the cashier of the Court of First Instance shall be paid in the currency of the country where the Court of First Instance has its seat.
    At the request of the person entitled to any sum, it shall be paid in the currency of the country where the expenses to be refunded were incurred or where the steps in respect of which payment is due were taken.
2.   Other debtors shall make payment in the currency of their country of origin.
3.   Conversions of currency shall be made at the official rates of exchange ruling on the day of payment in the country where the Court of First Instance has its seat.

Chapter 7 Legal Aid

Article 94 [Application for Legal Aid]

1.   A party who is wholly or in part unable to meet the costs of the proceedings may at any time apply for legal aid. The application shall be accompanied by evidence of the applicant's need of assistance, and in particular by a document from the competent authority certifying his lack of means.
2.   If the application is made prior to proceedings which the applicant wishes to commence, it shall briefly state the subject of such proceedings.
    The application need not be made through a lawyer.
    The President shall, after considering the written observations of the opposite party, decide whether legal aid should be granted in full or in part, or whether it should be refused. He shall consider whether there is manifestly no cause of action.
    He may refer the matter to the Court of First Instance.
    The Decision shall be taken by way of an order without giving reasons, and no appeal shall lie therefrom.

Article 95 [Appointment of Counsel]

1.   The Court of First Instance, by any order by which it decides that a person is entitled to receive legal aid, shall order that a lawyer be appointed to act for him.

2.   If the person does not indicate his choice of lawyer, or if the Court of First Instance considers that his choice is unacceptable, the Registrar shall send a copy of the order and of the application for legal aid to the authority named in Annex II to the Rules supplementing the Rules of Procedure of the Court of Justice, being the competent authority of the State concerned.

3.   The Court of First Instance, in the light of the suggestions made by that authority, shall of its own motion appoint a lawyer to act for the person concerned.

4.   An order granting legal aid may specify an amount to be paid to the lawyer appointed to act for the person concerned or fix a limit which the lawyer's disbursements and fees may not, in principle, exceed.

Article 96 [Withdrawal of Legal Aid]

The Court of First Instance may at any time, either of its own motion or on application, withdraw legal aid if the circumstances which led to its being granted alter during the proceedings.

Article 97 [Legal Aid Granted]

1.   Where legal aid is granted, the cashier of the Court of First Instance shall advance the funds necessary to meet the expenses.

2.   The President, who may refer the matter to the Court of First Instance, shall adjudicate on the lawyer's disbursements and fees; he may, on application by the lawyer, order that he receive an advance.

3.   In its decision as to costs the Court of First Instance may order the payment to the cashier of the Court of First Instance of the whole or any part of amounts advanced as legal aid.

The Registrar shall take steps to obtain the recovery of these sums from the party ordered to pay them.

Chapter 8 Discontinuance

Article 98 [Removal of Pending Cases]

If, before the Court of First Instance has given its decision, the parties reach a settlement of their dispute and intimate to the Court of First Instance the abandonment of their claims, the President shall order the case to be removed from the register and shall give a decision as to costs in accordance with Article 87 (5) having regard to any proposals made by the parties on the matter.

This provision shall not apply to proceedings under Articles 173 and 175 of the EC Treaty, Articles 33 and 35 of the ECSC Treaty and Articles 146 and 148 of the Euratom Treaty.

Article 99 [Discontinuance]

If the applicant informs the Court of First Instance in writing that he wishes to discontinue the proceedings, the President shall order the case to be removed from the register and shall give a decision as to costs in accordance with Article 87 (5).

Chapter 9 Service

Article 100 [Service of Documents]

Where these Rules require that a document be served on a person, the Registrar shall ensure that service is effected at that person's address for service either by the dispatch of a copy of the document by registered post with a form for acknowledgement of receipt or by personal delivery of the copy against a receipt.

The Registrar shall prepare and certify the copies of documents to be served, save where the parties themselves supply the copies in accordance with Article 43 (1).

Chapter 10 Time-limits

Article 101 [Calculation of Time-Limits]

1. Any period of time prescribed by the EC, ECSC and Euratom Treaties, the Statutes of the Court of Justice or these Rules for the taking of any procedural step shall be reckoned as follows:
(a) Where a period expressed in days, weeks, months or years is to be calculated from the moment at which an event occurs or an action takes place, the day during which that event occurs or that action takes place shall not be counted as falling within the period in question;
(b) A period expressed in weeks, months or in years shall end with the expiry of whichever day in the last week, month or year is the same day of the week, or falls on the same date, as the day during which the event or action from which the period is to be calculated occurred or took place. If, in a period expressed in months or in years, the day on which it should expire does not occur in the last month, the period shall end with the expiry of the last day of that month;
(c) Where a period is expressed in months and days, it shall first be reckoned in whole months, then in days;
(d) Periods shall include official holidays, Sundays and Saturdays;
(e) Periods shall not be suspended during the judicial vacations.
2. If the period would otherwise end on a Saturday, Sunday or official holiday, it shall be extended until the end of the first following working day.

The list of official holidays drawn up by the Court of Justice and published in the Official Journal of the European Communities shall apply to the Court of First Instance.

Article 102 [Beginning of Time-Limits; Extentions on Account of Distance]

1. Where the period of time allowed for commencing proceedings against a measure adopted by an institution runs from the publication of that measure, that period shall be calculated, for the purposes of Article 101 (1), from the end of the 14th day after publication thereof in the Official Journal of the European Communities.
2. The extensions, on account of distance, of prescribed time-limits provided for in a decision of the Court of Justice and published in the Official Journal of the European Communities shall apply to the Court of First Instance.

Article 103 [Fixing and Extending Time-Limits in casu]

1. Any time-limit prescribed pursuant to these Rules may be extended by whoever prescribed it.
2. The President may delegate power of signature to the Registrar for the purpose of fixing time-limits which, pursuant to these Rules, it falls to the President to prescribe, or of extending such time-limits.

TITLE III
SPECIAL FORMS OF PROCEDURE
Chapter 1 Suspension of Operation or Enforcement and Other Interim Measures

Article 104 [Suspension of Measures of an Institution]
1. An application to suspend the operation of any measure adopted by an institution, made pursuant to Article 185 of the EC Treaty, the second paragraph of Article 39 of the ECSC Treaty and Article 157 of the Euratom Treaty, shall be admissible only if the applicant is challenging that measure in proceedings before the Court of First Instance.

An application for the adoption of any other interim measure referred to in Article 186 of the EC Treaty, the third paragraph of Article 39 of the ECSC Treaty and Article 158 of the Euratom Treaty shall be admissible only if it is made by a party to a case before the Court of First Instance and relates to that case.
2. An application of a kind referred to in paragraph (1) of this Article shall state the subject-matter of the proceedings, the circumstances giving rise to urgency and the pleas of fact and law establishing a prima facie case for the interim measures applied for.
3. The application shall be made by a separate document and in accordance with the provisions of Articles 43 and 44.

Article 105 [Procedure]
1. The application shall be served on the opposite party, and the President of the Court of First Instance shall prescribe a short period within which that party may submit written or oral observations.
2. The President of the Court of First Instance may order a preparatory inquiry.

The President of the Court of First Instance may grant the application even before the observations of the opposite party have been submitted. This decision may be varied or cancelled even without any application being made by any party.

Article 106 [Decision]
The President of the Court of First Instance shall either decide on the application himself or refer it to the Chamber to which the case has been assigned in the main proceedings or to the Court of First Instance sitting in plenary session if the case has been assigned to it.

If the President of the Court of First Instance is absent or prevented from attending, he shall be replaced by the President or the most senior Judge, within the meaning of Article 6, of the bench of the Court of First Instance to which the case has been assigned.

Where the application is referred to a bench of the Court of First Instance, that bench shall postpone all other cases and shall give a decision. Article 105 shall apply.

Article 107 [Form and Effect]
1. The decision on the application shall take the form of a reasoned order. The order shall be served on the parties forthwith.
2. The enforcement of the order may be made conditional on the lodging by the applicant of security, of an amount and nature to be fixed in the light of the circumstances.
3. Unless the order fixes the date on which the interim measure is to lapse, the measure shall lapse when final judgment is delivered.
4. The order shall have only an interim effect, and shall be without prejudice to the decision on the substance of the case by the Court of First Instance.

Article 108 [Change of Circumstances]
On application by a party, the order may at any time be varied or cancelled on account of a change in circumstances.

Article 109 [Rejection]
Rejection of an application for an interim measure shall not bar the party who made it from making a further application on the basis of new facts.

Article 110 [Suspension of CFI Decisions]
The provisions of this Chapter shall apply to applications to suspend the enforcement of a decision of the Court of First Instance or of any measure adopted by another institution, submitted pursuant to Articles 187 and 192 of the EC Treaty, Articles 44 and 92 of the ECSC Treaty and Articles 159 and 164 of the Euratom Treaty.

The order granting the application shall fix, where appropriate, a date on which the interim measure is to lapse.

Chapter 2 Preliminary Issues

Article 111 [Inadmissible Procedures]
Where it is clear that the Court of First Instance has no jurisdiction to take cognizance of an action or where the action is manifestly inadmissible or manifestly lacking any foundation in law, the Court of First Instance may, by reasoned order, after hearing the Advocate-General and without taking further steps in the proceedings, give a decision on the action.

Article 112 [Reference to the ECJ]
The decision to refer an action to the Court of Justice, pursuant to the second paragraph of Article 47 of the EC Statute, the second paragraph of Article 47 of the ECSC Statute and the second paragraph of Article 48 of the Euratom Statute, shall, in the case of manifest lack of competence, be made by reasoned order and without taking any further steps in the proceedings.

Article 113 [Removal of Ex-officio]
The Court of First Instance may at any time, of its own motion, consider whether there exists any absolute bar to proceeding with an action or declare, after hearing the parties, that the action has become devoid of purpose and that there is no need to adjudicate on it; it shall give its decision in accordance with Article 114 (3) and (4).

Article 114 [Application for a Decision on Admissibility]
1.   A party applying to the Court of First Instance for a decision on admissibility, on lack of competence or other preliminary plea not going to the substance of the case shall make the application by a separate document.

The application must contain the pleas of fact and law relied on and the form of order sought by the applicant; any supporting documents must be annexed to it.
2.   As soon as the application has been lodged, the President shall prescribe a period within which the opposite party may lodge a document containing a statement of the form of order sought by that party and its pleas in law.
3.   Unless the Court of First Instance otherwise decides, the remainder of the proceedings shall be oral.
4.   The Court of First Instance shall, after hearing the Advocate-General, decide on the application or reserve its decision for the final judgment. It shall refer the case to the Court of Justice if the case falls within the jurisdiction of that Court.

If the Court of First Instance refuses the application or reserves its decision, the President shall prescribe new time-limits for further steps in the proceedings.

Chapter 3 Intervention

Article 115 [Application for Intervention]

1. An application to intervene must be made within three months of the publication of the notice referred to in Article 24 (6).
2. The application shall contain:
(a) the description of the case;
(b) the description of the parties;
(c) the name and address of the intervener;
(d) the intervener's address for service at the place where the Court of First Instance has its seat;
(e) the form of order sought, by one or more of the parties, in support of which the intervener is applying for leave to intervene;
(f) a statement of the circumstances establishing the right to intervene, where the application is submitted pursuant to the second or third paragraph of Article 37 of the EC Statute, Article 34 of the ECSC Statute or the second paragraph of Article 38 of the Euratom Statute.
Articles 43 and 44 shall apply.
3. The intervener shall be represented in accordance with Article 17 of the EC Statute, the first and second paragraphs of Article 20 of the ECSC Statute and Article 17 of the Euratom Statute.

Article 116 [Procedure]

1. The application shall be served on the parties.
The President shall give the parties an opportunity to submit their written or oral observations before deciding on the application.
The President shall decide on the application by order or shall refer the decision to the Court of First Instance. The order must be reasoned if the application is dismissed.
2. If the President allows the intervention, the intervener shall receive a copy of every document served on the parties. The President may, however, on application by one of the parties, omit secret or confidential documents.
3. The intervener must accept the case as he finds it at the time of his intervention.
4. The President shall prescribe a period within which the intervener may submit a statement in intervention. The statement in intervention shall contain:
(a) a statement of the form of order sought by the intervener in support of or opposing, in whole or in part, the form of order sought by one of the parties;
(b) the pleas in law and arguments relied on by the intervener;
(c) where appropriate, the nature of any evidence offered.
5. After the statement in intervention has been lodged, the President shall, where necessary, prescribe a time-limit within which the parties may reply to that statement.

Chapter 4 Judgments of the Court of First Instance Delivered after its Decision Has Been Set Aside and the Case Referred Back to it

Article 117 [Re-Opening of Procedure]

Where the Court of Justice sets aside a judgment or an order of the Court of First Instance and refers the case back to that Court, the latter shall be seized of the case by the judgment so referring it.

Article 118 [Competent Judges]

1.   Where the Court of Justice sets aside a judgment or an order of a Chamber, the President of the Court of First Instance may assign the case to another Chamber composed of the same number of Judges.

2.   Where the Court of Justice sets aside a judgment delivered or an order made by the Court of First Instance sitting in plenary session, the case shall be assigned to that Court as so constituted.

2a. Where the Court of Justice sets aside a judgment delivered or an order made by a single Judge, the President of the Court of First Instance shall assign the case to a Chamber composed of three Judges of which that Judge is not a member.

3.   In the cases provided for in paragraphs (1), (2) and (2a) of this Article, Articles 13 (2), 14(1) and 51 shall apply.

Article 119 [Procedure]

1.   Where the written procedure before the Court of First Instance has been completed when the judgment referring the case back to it is delivered, the course of the procedure shall be as follows:

(a) Within two months from the service upon him of the judgment of the Court of Justice the applicant may lodge a statement of written observations.

(b) In the month following the communication to him of that statement, the defendant may lodge a statement of written observations. The time allowed to the defendant for lodging it may in no case be less than two months from the service upon him of the judgment of the Court of Justice.

(c) In the month following the simultaneous communication to the intervener of the observations of the applicant and the defendant, the intervener may lodge a statement of written observations. The time allowed to the intervener for lodging it may in no case be less than two months from the service upon him of the judgment of the Court of Justice.

2.   Where the written procedure before the Court of First Instance had not been completed when the judgment referring the case back to the Court of First Instance was delivered, it shall be resumed, at the stage which it had reached, by means of measures of organization of procedure adopted by the Court of First Instance.

3.   The Court of First Instance may, if the circumstances so justify, allow supplementary statements of written observations to be lodged.

Article 120 [Other Applicable Rules]

The procedure shall be conducted in accordance with the provisions of Title II of these Rules.

Article 121 [Costs]

The Court of First Instance shall decide on the costs relating to the proceedings instituted before it and to the proceedings on the appeal before the Court of Justice.

Chapter 5 Judgments by Default and Applications to Set Them Aside

Article 122 [Judgment by Default]

1.   If a defendant on whom an application initiating proceedings has been duly served fails to lodge a defence to the application in the proper form within the time prescribed, the applicant may apply to the Court of First Instance for judgment by default.

The application shall be served on the defendant. The Court of First Instance may decide to open the oral procedure on the application.

2.   Before giving judgment by default the Court of First Instance shall consider whether the application initiating proceedings is admissible, whether the appropriate formalities have been complied with, and whether the application appears well founded. It may order a preparatory inquiry.
3.   A judgment by default shall be enforceable. The Court of First Instance may, however, grant a stay of execution until it has given its decision on any application under paragraph (4) of this Article to set aside the judgment, or it may make execution subject to the provision of security of an amount and nature to be fixed in the light of the circumstances; this security shall be released if no such application is made or if the application fails.
4.   Application may be made to set aside a judgment by default.
     The application to set aside the judgment must be made within one month from the date of service of the judgment and must be lodged in the form prescribed by Articles 43 and 44.
5.   After the application has been served, the President shall prescribe a period within which the other party may submit his written observations.
     The proceedings shall be conducted in accordance with the provisions of Title II of these Rules.
6   The Court of First Instance shall decide by way of a judgment which may not be set aside. The original of this judgment shall be annexed to the original of the judgment by default. A note of the judgment on the application to set aside shall be made in the margin of the original of the judgment by default.

Chapter 6 Exceptional Review Procedures

Section 1 - Third-party proceedings
Article 123 [Application for Third-party Proceedings]
1.   Articles 43 and 44 shall apply to an application initiating third-party proceedings. In addition such an application shall:
(a) specify the judgment contested;
(b) state how that judgment is prejudicial to the rights of the third party;
(c) indicate the reasons for which the third party was unable to take part in the original case before the Court of First Instance.
The application must be made against all the parties to the original case.
     Where the judgment has been published in the Official Journal of the European Communities, the application must be lodged within two months of the publication.
2.   The Court of First Instance may, on application by the third party, order a stay of execution of the judgment. The provisions of Title III, Chapter 1, shall apply.
3.   The contested judgment shall be varied on the points on which the submissions of the third party are upheld. The original of the judgment in the third-party proceedings shall be annexed to the original of the contested judgment. A note of the judgment in the third-party proceedings shall be made in the margin of the original of the contested judgment.
4.   Where an appeal before the Court of Justice and an application initiating third-party proceedings before the Court of First Instance contest the same judgment of the Court of First Instance, the Court of First Instance may, after hearing the parties, stay the proceedings until the Court of Justice has delivered its judgment.

Article 124 [Competent Judges]
The application initiating third-party proceedings shall be assigned to the Chamber which delivered the judgment which is the subject of the application; if the Court of First Instance sitting in plenary session delivered the judgment, the application shall be

assigned to it. If the judgment has been delivered by a single Judge, the application initiating third-party proceedings shall be assigned to that Judge.

Section 2 - Revision
Article 125 [Time-Limit for Revisions]
Without prejudice to the period of ten years prescribed in the third paragraph of Article 41 of the EC Statute, the third paragraph of Article 38 of the ECSC Statute and the third paragraph of Article 42 of the Euratom Statute, an application for revision of a judgment shall be made within three months of the date on which the facts on which the application is based came to the applicant's knowledge.

Article 126 [Application for Revision]
1.   Articles 43 and 44 shall apply to an application for revision. In addition such an application shall:
(a) specify the judgment contested;
(b) indicate the points on which the application is based;
(c) set out the facts on which the application is based;
(d) indicate the nature of the evidence to show that there are facts justifying revision of the judgment, and that the time-limits laid down in Article 125 have been observed.
2.   The application must be made against all parties to the case in which the contested judgment was given.

Article 127 [Competent Judges]
1.   The application for revision shall be assigned to the Chamber which delivered the judgment which is the subject of the application; if the Court of First Instance sitting in plenary session delivered the judgment, the application shall be assigned to it. If the judgment has been delivered by a single Judge, the application for revision shall be assigned to that Judge.
2.   Without prejudice to its decision on the substance, the Court of First Instance shall, after hearing the Advocate-General, having regard to the written observations of the parties, give its decision on the admissibility of the application.
3.   If the Court of First Instance finds the application admissible, it shall proceed to consider the substance of the application and shall give its decision in the form of a judgment in accordance with these Rules.
4.   The original of the revising judgment shall be annexed to the original of the judgment revised. A note of the revising judgment shall be made in the margin of the original of the judgment revised.

Article 128 [Co-operation with the ECJ]
Where an appeal before the Court of Justice and an application for revision before the Court of First Instance concern the same judgment of the Court of First Instance, the Court of First Instance may, after hearing the parties, stay the proceedings until the Court of Justice has delivered its judgment.

Section 3 - Interpretation of Judgments
Article 129 [Application for Interpretation]
1.   An application for interpretation of a judgment shall be made in accordance with Articles 43 and 44. In addition it shall specify:
(a) the judgment in question;
(b) the passages of which interpretation is sought.

The application must be made against all the parties to the case in which the judgment was given.

2.   The application for interpretation shall be assigned to the Chamber which delivered the judgment which is the subject of the application; if the Court of First Instance sitting in plenary session delivered the judgment, the application shall be assigned to it. If the judgment has been delivered by a single Judge, the application for interpretation shall be assigned to that Judge.

3.   The Court of First Instance shall give its decision in the form of a judgment after having given the parties an opportunity to submit their observations and after hearing the Advocate-General.

The original of the interpreting judgment shall be annexed to the original of the judgment interpreted. A note of the interpreting judgment shall be made in the margin of the original of the judgment interpreted.

4.   Where an appeal before the Court of Justice and an application for interpretation before the Court of First Instance concern the same judgment of the Court of First Instance, the Court of First Instance may, after hearing the parties, stay the proceedings until the Court of Justice has delivered its judgment.

TITLE IV
PROCEEDINGS RELATING TO INTELLECTUAL PROPERTY RIGHTS

Article 130 [Jurisdiction of the CFI]

1.   Subject to the special provisions of this Title, the provisions of these Rules of Procedure shall apply to proceedings brought against the Office for Harmonization in the Internal Market (Trade Marks and Designs) and against the Community Plant Variety Office, (both hereinafter referred to as "the Office"), and concerning the application of the rules relating to an intellectual property regime.

2.   The provisions of this Title shall not apply to actions brought directly against the Office without prior proceedings before a Board of Appeal.

Article 131 [Language of an Application]

1.   The application shall be drafted in one of the languages described in Article 35 (1), according to the applicant's choice.

2.   The language in which the application is drafted shall become the language of the case if the applicant was the only party to the proceedings before the Board of Appeal or if another party to those proceedings does not object to this within a period laid down for that purpose by the Registrar after the application has been lodged.

If, within that period, the parties to the proceedings before the Board of Appeal inform the Registrar of their agreement on the choice, as the language of the case, of one of the languages referred to in Article 35 (1), that language shall become the language of the case before the Court of First Instance.

In the event of an objection to the choice of the language of the case made by the applicant within the period referred to above and in the absence of an agreement on the matter between the parties to the proceedings before the Board of Appeal, the language in which the application for registration in question was filed at the Office shall become the language of the case.

If, however, on a reasoned request by any party and after hearing the other parties, the President finds that the use of that language would not enable all parties to the proceedings before the Board of Appeal to follow the proceedings and defend their interests and that only the use of another language from among those mentioned in Article 35 (1) makes it possible to remedy that situation, he may designate that other language as the language of the case; the President may refer the matter to the Court of First Instance.

3.   In the pleadings and other documents addressed to the Court of First Instance and during the oral procedure, the applicant may use the language chosen by him in accordance with paragraph 1 and each of the other parties may use a language chosen by that party from those mentioned in Article 35 (1).

4.   If, by virtue of paragraph 2, a language other than that in which the application is drafted becomes the language of the case, the Registrar shall cause the application to be translated into the language of the case.

Each party shall be required, within a reasonable period to be prescribed for that purpose by the Registrar, to produce a translation into the language of the case of the pleadings or documents other than the application that are lodged by that party in a language other than the language of the case pursuant to paragraph 3. The party producing the translation, which shall be authentic within the meaning of Article 37, shall certify is accuracy. If the translation is not produced within the period prescribed, the pleading or the procedural document in question shall be removed from the file.

The Registrar shall cause everything said during the oral procedure to be translated into the language of the case and, at the request of any party, into the language used by that party in accordance with paragraph 3.

Article 132 [Contents of an Application]
1.   Without prejudice to Article 44, the application shall contain the names of all the parties to the proceedings before the Board of Appeal and the addresses which they had given for the purposes of the notifications to be effected in the course of those proceedings.

The contested decision of the Board of Appeal shall be appended to the application. The date on which the applicant was notified of that decision must be indicated.

2.   If the application does not comply with paragraph 1, Article 44 (6) shall apply.

Article 133 [Service on Defendant]
1.   The Registrar shall inform the Office and all the parties to the proceedings before the Board of Appeal of the lodging of the application. He shall arrange for service of the application after determining the language of the case in accordance with Article 131 (2).

2.   The application shall be served on the Office, as defendant, and on the parties to the proceedings before the Board of Appeal other than the applicant. Service shall be effected in the language of the case.

Service of the application on a party to the proceedings before the Board of Appeal shall be effected by registered post with a form of acknowledgment of receipt at the address given by the party concerned for the purposes of the notifications to be effected in the course of the proceedings before the Board of Appeal.

3.   Once the application has been served, the Office shall forward to the Court of First Instance the file relating to the proceedings before the Board of Appeal.

Article 134 [Intervention by Interested Parties]
1.   The parties to the proceedings before the Board of Appeal other than the applicant may participate, as interveners, in the proceedings before the Court of First Instance.

2.   The interveners referred to in paragraph 1 shall have the same procedural rights as the main parties.

They may support the form of order sought by a main party and they may apply for a form of order and put forward pleas in law independently of those applied for and put forward by the main parties.

3.   An intervener, as referred to in paragraph 1, may, in his response lodged in accordance with Article 135 (1), seek an order annulling or altering the decision of the Board of Appeal on a point not raised in the application and put forward pleas in law not raised in the application.

Such submissions seeking orders or putting forward pleas in law in the intervener's response shall cease to have effect should the applicant discontinue the proceedings.

4.   In derogation from Article 122, the default procedure shall not apply where an intervener, as referred to in paragraph 1 of this Article, has responded to the application in the manner and within the period prescribed.

Article 135 [Defence]

1.   The Office and the interveners referred to in Article 134 (1) may submit responses to the application within a period of two months from the service of the application.

Article 46 shall apply to the responses.

2.   The application and the responses may be supplemented by replies and rejoinders by the parties, including the interveners referred to in Article 134 (1), where the President, on a reasoned application made within two weeks of service of the responses or replies, considers such further pleading necessary and allows it in order to enable the party concerned to put forward its point of view.

The President shall prescribe the period within which such pleadings are to be submitted.

3.   Without prejudice to the foregoing, in the cases referred to in Article 134 (3), the other parties may, within a period of two months of service upon them of the response, submit a pleading confined to responding to the form of order sought and the pleas in law submitted for the first time in the response of a intervener. That period may be extended by the President on a reasoned application from the party concerned.

4.   The parties' pleadings may not change the subject-matter of the proceedings before the Board of Appeal.

Article 136 [Decision on Costs]

1.   Where an action against a decision of a Board of Appeal is successful, the Court of First Instance may order the Office to bear only its own costs.

2.   Costs necessarily incurred by the parties for the purposes of the proceedings before the Board of Appeal and costs incurred for the purposes of the production, prescribed by the second subparagraph of Article 131 (4), of translations of pleadings or other documents into the language of the case shall be regarded as recoverable costs.

In the event of inaccurate translations being produced, the second subparagraph of Article 87 (3) shall apply.

MISCELLANEOUS PROVISIONS

Article 137 [Publication and Entry into Force]

These Rules, which are authentic in the languages mentioned in Article 35 (1), shall be published in the Official Journal of the European Communities. They shall enter into force on the first day of the second month from the date of their publication.

Done at Luxembourg on 2 May 1991.
H. JUNG, Registrar; J. L. CRUZ VILAÇA, President

Advice for Lawyers and Agents Regarding the Written Procedure Before the Court of First Instance[1]

I. The purpose of the written procedure

The purpose of the written procedure before the Court of First Instance is to define the subject-matter of the action and to put before the Court all the claims of the parties by informing it of the relevant facts, forms of order sought, and the pleas and arguments of the parties so as to enable the Court to give judgment in the action.

II. The presentation and drafting of pleadings

1.   Pleadings should have a clear structure: each section should have a title and paragraphs should be numbered consecutively. In the case of lengthy pleadings, it is desirable to introduce each section with a brief summary of its contents and to include a table of contents in the pleading.

2.   Since the number of pleadings which each party may submit to the Court is limited (see Article 47 of the Rules of Procedure of the Court of First Instance) and new pleas may not be raised in the course of the proceedings except in certain limited circumstances (see Article 48 of the Rules of Procedure), it is advisable that a party should set out its entire case as fully as possible in its first pleading (the application or the defence).

3.   In view of the fact that the Judges will often study a set of pleadings by reading translations of them into another language, it is advisable to draft pleadings in a simple, straightforward and concise style which facilitates translation and to limit the number of pages to what is strictly necessary.

4.   When pleadings are drafted documents to which reference is made in them should be clearly identified and care should also be taken to ensure that all important documents are submitted. Documents should be identified by indicating, each time reference is made to them, the pleading to which the document concerned is annexed, with an indication of the annex number as it appears in the schedule of annexes attached to that pleading. It is desirable for each document to be identified in the same way throughout both the written and oral proceedings. Attaching to a pleading document already submitted to the Court as annexes to another pleading needlessly increases the volume of written evidence to be considered by the Court and may cause confusion.

5.   When addressing the arguments of another party it is advisable to refer to the relevant pages of the other party's pleading.

III. The structure of pleadings

1.   Originating applications must comply with Article 44 of the Rules of Procedure. Ideally, they should be structured as follows:

   1)   Indication of the parties
       See Article 44 (1) (a) and (b) and (2) of the Rules of Procedure.
   2)   Details of the type of dispute involved
       For example: "Application under Article 173 of the EC Treaty for the annulment of a decision of (the institution concerned) ..."
   3)   A summary of the relevant facts
       Supported by references to the documents and offers of evidence.
   4)   Any considerations relating to the admissibility of the action

---

1   Drawn up by the Registrar pursuant to Article 18 (2) of the Instructions to the Registrar of 3 March 1994, OJ 1994 C 120, p. 16.

5) A brief statement of all the pleas in law on which the action is based
6) A summary of the arguments put forward in support of each plea in law including, where appropriate, references to the relevant case-law of the Court of Justice and of the Court of First Instance.
7) Form of order sought
   Parties must set out the precise terms of the operative part of the order or judgment which they seek (for example: "1. annul the defendant's decision of ...; 2. order the defendant to pay the costs"). When drawing up the form of order sought, those acting for applicants should bear in mind what is laid down in Article 176 of the EC Treaty and that it is unnecessary to reiterate in the form of order sought pleas and arguments set out earlier in the application (for example, the following types of formulation should be avoided "... declare that the action is admissible and well-founded; declare that the contested decision does not state the reasons on which it is based and is contrary to the provisions of the Treaty and the principle of proportionality ..."). Reference should also be made to Article 87 of the Rules of Procedure as regards any order sought in the matter of costs.

2. In order to facilitate the drafting of the Official Journal notice provided for by Article 24 (6) of the Rules of Procedure and to ensure that the subject-matter of the case and the pleas in law and main arguments contained in the application are clearly identified, it is advisable to annex to the application a brief outline of the pleas in law and main arguments together with a table of contents.

IV. Production of annexes

1. Pleadings and procedural documents may be accompanied by documents annexed to them in order to substantiate or illustrate their contents. However, mere reference to an annex will be no substitute for including a summary of the facts, pleas and arguments in the body of the pleading or procedural document. Only annexes mentioned in the pleadings will be admissible.

2. A schedule of annexes must be submitted, as prescribed by Article 43 (4) of the Rules of Procedure and Article 6 (4) of the Instructions to the Registrar. Ideally, this schedule should set out the annex numbers, the date and nature of the documents annexed and the pages of the pleading on which reasons for the production of the respective annexes are given. In some cases, subnumbers will facilitate the identification of documents.

3. Lawyers and agents should ensure that the pleadings and evidence submitted are not made unnecessarily lengthy by the production of an excessive number of annexes and that the really important passages or information contained in annexes are still reproduced in the body of the pleadings.

European Parliament Decision 94/262 of 9 March 1994 on the Regulations and General Conditions Governing the Performance of the Ombudsman's Duties[1]

THE EUROPEAN PARLIAMENT,

HAVING REGARD to the Treaties establishing the European Communities, and in particular Article 138e (4) of the Treaty establishing the European Community, Article 20d (4) of the Treaty establishing the European Community, Article 107d (4) of the Treaty establishing the European Atomic Energy Community, [...]

(1) WHEREAS the regulations and general conditions governing the performance of the Ombudsman's duties should be laid down, [...];

(2) WHEREAS the conditions under which a complaint may be referred to the Ombudsman should be established as well as the relationship between the performance of the duties of Ombudsman and legal or administrative proceedings;

(3) WHEREAS the Ombudsman, who may also act on his own initiative, must have access to all the elements required for the performance of his duties; whereas to that end Community institutions and bodies are obliged to supply the Ombudsman, at his request, with any information which he requests of them, unless there are duly substantial grounds for secrecy, and without prejudice to the Ombudsman's obligation not to divulge such information; whereas the Member States' authorities are obliged to provide the Ombudsman with all necessary information save where such information is covered by laws or regulations on secrecy or by provisions preventing its being communicated; whereas if the Ombudsman finds that the assistance requested is not forthcoming, he shall inform the European Parliament, which shall make appropriate representations;

(4) WHEREAS it is necessary to lay down the procedures to be followed where the Ombudsman's enquiries reveal cases of maladministration; whereas provision should also be made for the submission of a comprehensive report by the Ombudsman to the European Parliament at the end of each annual session;

(5) WHEREAS the Ombudsman and his staff are obliged to treat in confidence any information which they have acquired in the course of their duties; whereas the Ombudsman is, however, obliged to inform the competent authorities of facts which he considers might relate to criminal law and which have come to this attention in the course of his enquiries;

(6) WHEREAS provision should be made for the possibility of cooperation between the Ombudsman and authorities of the same type in certain Member States, in compliance with the national laws applicable;

(7) WHEREAS it is for the European Parliament to appoint the Ombudsman at the beginning of its mandate and for the duration thereof, choosing him from among persons who are Union citizens and offer every requisite guarantee of independence and competence;

(8) WHEREAS conditions should be laid down for the cessation of the Ombudsman's duties;

(9) WHEREAS the Ombudsman must perform his duties with complete independence and give a solemn undertaking before the Court of Justice of the European Communities that he will do so when taking up his duties; whereas activities incompatible with the duties of Ombudsman should be laid down as should the remuneration, privileges and immunities of the Ombudsman;

---

1   OJ 1994 L 113, p. 15.

(10) WHEREAS provisions should be laid down regarding the officials and servants of the Ombudsman's secretariat which will assist him and the budget thereof; whereas the seat of the Ombudsman should be that of the European Parliament;
(11) WHEREAS it is for the Ombudsman to adopt the implementing provisions for this Decision; whereas furthermore certain transitional provisions should be laid down [...].

HAS DECIDED AS FOLLOWS:

Article 1 [Legal Basis]
1.   The regulations and general conditions governing the performance of the Ombudsman's duties shall be as laid down by this Decision in accordance with Article 138e (4) of the Treaty establishing the European Community, Article 20d (4) of the Treaty establishing the European Coal and Steel Community and Article 107d (4) of the Treaty establishing the European Atomic Energy Community.
2.   The Ombudsman shall perform his duties in accordance with the powers conferred on the Community institutions and bodies by the Treaties.
3.   The Ombudsman may not intervene in cases before courts or question the soundness of a court's ruling.

Article 2 [Tasks of the Ombudsperson]
1.   Within the framework of the aforementioned Treaties and the conditions laid down therein, the Ombudsman shall help to uncover maladministration in the activities of the Community institutions and bodies, with the exception of the Court of Justice and the Court of First Instance acting in their judicial role, and make recommendations with a view to putting an end to it. No action by any other authority or person may be the subject of a complaint to the Ombudsman.
2.   Any citizen of the Union or any natural or legal person residing or having its registered office in a Member State of the Union may, directly or through a Member of the European Parliament, refer a complaint to the Ombudsman in respect of an instance of maladministration in the activities of Community institutions or bodies, with the exception of the Court of Justice and the Court of First Instance acting in their judicial role. The Ombudsman shall inform the institution or body concerned as soon as a complaint is referred to him.
3.   The complaint must allow the person lodging the complaint and the object of the complaint to be identified; the person lodging the complaint may request that his complaint remain confidential.
4.   A complaint shall be made within two years of the date on which the facts on which it is based came to the attention of the person lodging the complaint and must be preceded by the appropriate administrate approaches to the institutions and bodies concerned.
5.   The Ombudsman may advise the person lodging the complaint to address it to another authority.
6.   Complaints submitted to the Ombudsman shall not affect time limits for appeals in administrative or judicial proceedings.
7.   When the Ombudsman, because of legal proceedings in progress or concluded concerning the facts which have been put forward, has to declare a complaint inadmissible or terminate consideration of it, the outcome of any enquiries he has carried out up to that point shall be filed without further action.
8.   No complaint may be made to the Ombudsman that concerns work relationships between the Community institutions and bodies and their officials and other servants unless all the possibilities for the submission of internal administrative requests and complaints, in particular the procedures referred to in Article 90 (1) and (2) of the Staff

Regulations, have been exhausted by the person concerned and the time limits for replies by the authority thus petitioned have expired.
9.   The Ombudsman shall as soon as possible inform the person lodging the complaint of the action he has taken on it.

Article 3 [Powers of Inquiry]

1.   The Ombudsman shall, on his own initiative or following a complaint, conduct all the enquiries which he considers justified to clarify any suspected maladministration in the activities of Community institutions and bodies. He shall inform the institution or body concerned of such action, which may submit any useful comment to him.
2.   The Community institutions and bodies shall be obliged to supply the Ombudsman with any information he has requested of them and give him access to the files concerned. They may refuse only on duly substantial grounds of secrecy.

They shall give access to documents originating in a Member State and classed as secret by law or regulation only where that Member State has given its prior agreement.

They shall give access to other documents originating in a Member State after having informed the Member State concerned. In both cases, in accordance with Article 4, the Ombudsman may not divulge the content of such documents.

Officials and other servants of Community institutions and bodies must testify at the request of the Ombudsman; they shall speak on behalf of and in accordance with instructions from their administrations and shall continue to be found by their duty of professional secrecy.
3.   The Member States' authorities shall be obliged to provide the Ombudsman, whenever he may so request, via the Permanent Representations of the Member States to the European Communities, with any information that may help to clarify instances of maladministration by Community institutions or bodies unless such information is covered by laws or regulations on secrecy or by provisions preventing its being communicated. Nonetheless, in the latter case, the Member State concerned may allow the Ombudsman to have this information provided that he undertakes not to divulge it.
4.   If the assistance which he requests is not forthcoming, the Ombudsman shall inform the European Parliament, which shall make appropriate representations.
5.   As far as possible, the Ombudsman shall seek a solution with the institution or body concerned to eliminate the instance of maladministration and satisfy the complaint.
6.   If the Ombudsman finds there has been maladministration, he shall inform the institution or body concerned, where appropriate making draft recommendations. The institution or body so informed shall send the Ombudsman a detailed opinion within three months.
7.   The Ombudsman shall then send a report to the European Parliament and to the institution or body concerned. He may make recommendations in his report. The person lodging the complaint shall be informed by the Ombudsman of the outcome of the inquiries, of the opinion expressed by the institution or body concerned and of any recommendations made by the Ombudsman.
8.   At the end of each annual session the Ombudsman shall submit to the European Parliament a report on the outcome of his inquiries.

Article 4 [Confidential Information]

1.   The Ombudsman and his staff, to whom Article 214 of the Treaty establishing the European Community, Article 47 (2) of the Treaty establishing the European Coal and Steel Community and Article 194 of the Treaty establishing the European Atomic Energy Community shall apply, shall be required not to divulge information or documents which they obtain in the course of their inquiries. They shall also be required to treat in confidence any information which could harm the person lodging the complaint or any other person involved, without prejudice to paragraph 2.

2.   If, in the course of inquiries, he learns of facts which he considers might relate to criminal law, the Ombudsman shall immediately notify the competent national authorities via the Permanent Representations of the Member States to the European Communities and, if appropriate, the Community institution with authority over the official or servant concerned, which may apply the second paragraph of Article 18 of the Protocol on the Privileges and Immunities of the European Communities. The Ombudsman may also inform the Community institution or body concerned of the facts calling into question the conduct of a member of their staff from a disciplinary point of view.

Article 5 [Cooperation with National Authorities]
Insofar as it may help to make his enquiries more efficient and better safeguard the rights and interests of persons who make complaints to him, the Ombudsman may cooperate with authorities of the same type in certain Member States provided he complies with the national law applicable. The Ombudsman may not by this means demand to see documents to which he would not have access under Article 3.

Article 6 [Appointment of the Ombudsperson]
1.   The Ombudsman shall be appointed by the European Parliament after each election to the European Parliament for the duration of the parliamentary term. He shall be eligible for reappointment.
2.   The Ombudsman shall be chosen from among persons who are Union citizens, have full civil and political rights, offer every guarantee of independence, and meet the conditions required for the exercise of the highest judicial office in their country or have the acknowledgement competence and experience to undertake the duties of Ombudsman.

Article 7 [End of Term; Succession]
1.   The Ombudsman shall cease to exercise his duties either at the end of this term of office or on his resignation or dismissal.
2.   Save in the event of his dismissal, the Ombudsman shall remain in office until his successor has been appointed.
3.   In the event of early cessation of duties, a successor shall be appointed within three months of the office's falling vacant for the remainder of the parliamentary term.

Article 8 [Dismissal]
An Ombudsman who no longer fulfils the conditions required for the performance of his duties or is guilty of serious misconduct may be dismissed by the Court of Justice of the European Communities at the request of the European Parliament.

Article 9 [Independence and Impartiality]
1.   The Ombudsman shall perform his duties with complete independence, in the general interest of the Communities and of the citizens of the Union. In the performance of his duties he shall neither seek nor accept instructions from any government or other body. He shall refrain from any act incompatible with the nature of his duties.
2.   When taking up his duties, the Ombudsman shall give a solemn undertaking before the Court of Justice of the European Communities that he will perform his duties with complete independence and impartiality and that during and after his term of office he will respect the obligations arising therefrom, in particular his duty to behave with integrity and discretion as regards the acceptance, after he has ceased to hold office, of certain appointments or benefits.

[Article 10 - 17 omitted]

FOUR: HUMAN RIGHTS AND CIVIL LIBERTIES

Convention for Protection of Human Rights and Fundamental Freedoms[1]

THE GOVERNMENTS SIGNATORY HERETO, BEING MEMBERS OF THE COUNCIL OF EUROPE,

CONSIDERING the Universal Declaration of Human Rights proclaimed by the General Assembly of the United Nations on 10th December 1948;
CONSIDERING that this Declaration aims at securing the universal and effective recognition and observance of the rights therein declared;
CONSIDERING that the aim of the Council of Europe is the achievement of greater unity between its members and that one of the methods by which that aim is to be pursued is the maintenance and further realisation of human rights and fundamental freedoms;
REAFFIRMING their profound belief in those fundamental freedoms which are the foundation of justice and peace in the world and are best maintained on the one hand by an effective political democracy and on the other by a common understanding and observance of the human rights upon which they depend;
BEING RESOLVED, as the governments of European countries which are like- minded and have a common heritage of political traditions, ideals, freedom and the rule of law, to take the first steps for the collective enforcement of certain of the rights stated in the Universal Declaration,

HAVE AGREED AS FOLLOWS:

Article 1 Obligation to respect human rights
The High Contracting Parties shall secure to everyone within their jurisdiction the rights and freedoms defined in Section I of this Convention.

Section I Rights and freedoms

Article 2 Right to life
1.   Everyone's right to life shall be protected by law. No one shall be deprived of his life intentionally save in the execution of a sentence of a court following his conviction of a crime for which this penalty is provided by law.
2.   Deprivation of life shall not be regarded as inflicted in contravention of this article when it results from the use of force which is no more than absolutely necessary:
a)   in defence of any person from unlawful violence;

---

1   Rome, 4 November 1950. The text of the Convention had been amended according to the provisions of Protocol No. 3 (ETS No. 45), which entered into force on 21 September 1970, of Protocol
No. 5 (ETS No. 55), which entered into force on 20 December 1971 and of Protocol No. 8 (ETS No.
118), which entered into force on 1 January 1990, and comprised also the text of Protocol No. 2
(ETS No. 44) which, in accordance with Article 5, paragraph 3 thereof, had been an integral part of
the Convention since its entry into force on 21 September 1970. All provisions which had been
amended or added by these Protocols are replaced by Protocol No. 11 (ETS No. 155), as from the
date of its entry into force on 1 November 1998. As from that date, Protocol No. 9 (ETS No. 140),
which entered into force on 1 October 1994, is repealed and Protocol No. 10 (ETS No. 146), which
has not entered into force, has lost its purpose.

b) in order to effect a lawful arrest or to prevent the escape of a person lawfully detained;
c) in action lawfully taken for the purpose of quelling a riot or insurrection.

Article 3 Prohibition of torture

No one shall be subjected to torture or to inhuman or degrading treatment or punishment.

Article 4 Prohibition of slavery and forced labour

1. No one shall be held in slavery or servitude.
2. No one shall be required to perform forced or compulsory labour.
3. For the purpose of this article the term "forced or compulsory labour" shall not include:
a) any work required to be done in the ordinary course of detention imposed according to the provisions of Article 5 of this Convention or during conditional release from such detention;
b) any service of a military character or, in case of conscientious objectors in countries where they are recognised, service exacted instead of compulsory military service;
c) any service exacted in case of an emergency or calamity threatening the life or well-being of the community;
d) any work or service which forms part of normal civic obligations.

Article 5 Right to liberty and security

1. Everyone has the right to liberty and security of person. No one shall be deprived of his liberty save in the following cases and in accordance with a procedure prescribed by law:
a) the lawful detention of a person after conviction by a competent court;
b) the lawful arrest or detention of a person for non-compliance with the lawful order of a court or in order to secure the fulfilment of any obligation prescribed by law;
c) the lawful arrest or detention of a person effected for the purpose of bringing him before the competent legal authority on reasonable suspicion of having committed an offence or when it is reasonably considered necessary to prevent his committing an offence or fleeing after having done so;
d) the detention of a minor by lawful order for the purpose of educational supervision or his lawful detention for the purpose of bringing him before the competent legal authority;
e) the lawful detention of persons for the prevention of the spreading of infectious diseases, of persons of unsound mind, alcoholics or drug addicts or vagrants;
f) the lawful arrest or detention of a person to prevent his effecting an unauthorised entry into the country or of a person against whom action is being taken with a view to deportation or extradition.
2. Everyone who is arrested shall be informed promptly, in a language which he understands, of the reasons for his arrest and of any charge against him.
3. Everyone arrested or detained in accordance with the provisions of paragraph 1.c of this article shall be brought promptly before a judge or other officer authorised by law to exercise judicial power and shall be entitled to trial within a reasonable time or to release pending trial. Release may be conditioned by guarantees to appear for trial.
4. Everyone who is deprived of his liberty by arrest or detention shall be entitled to take proceedings by which the lawfulness of his detention shall be decided speedily by a court and his release ordered if the detention is not lawful.

5.   Everyone who has been the victim of arrest or detention in contravention of the provisions of this article shall have an enforceable right to compensation.

Article 6 Right to a fair trial

1.   In the determination of his civil rights and obligations or of any criminal charge against him, everyone is entitled to a fair and public hearing within a reasonable time by an independent and impartial tribunal established by law. Judgment shall be pronounced publicly but the press and public may be excluded from all or part of the trial in the interests of morals, public order or national security in a democratic society, where the interests of juveniles or the protection of the private life of the parties so require, or to the extent strictly necessary in the opinion of the court in special circumstances where publicity would prejudice the interests of justice.

2.   Everyone charged with a criminal offence shall be presumed innocent until proved guilty according to law.

3.   Everyone charged with a criminal offence has the following minimum rights:
a)   to be informed promptly, in a language which he understands and in detail, of the nature and cause of the accusation against him;
b)   to have adequate time and facilities for the preparation of his defence;
c)   to defend himself in person or through legal assistance of his own choosing or, if he has not sufficient means to pay for legal assistance, to be given it free when the interests of justice so require;
d)   to examine or have examined witnesses against him and to obtain the attendance and examination of witnesses on his behalf under the same conditions as witnesses against him;
e)   to have the free assistance of an interpreter if he cannot understand or speak the language used in court.

Article 7 No punishment without law

1.   No one shall be held guilty of any criminal offence on account of any act or omission which did not constitute a criminal offence under national or international law at the time when it was committed. Nor shall a heavier penalty be imposed than the one that was applicable at the time the criminal offence was committed.

2.   This article shall not prejudice the trial and punishment of any person for any act or omission which, at the time when it was committed, was criminal according to the general principles of law recognised by civilised nations.

Article 8 Right to respect for private and family life

1.   Everyone has the right to respect for his private and family life, his home and his correspondence.

2.   There shall be no interference by a public authority with the exercise of this right except such as is in accordance with the law and is necessary in a democratic society in the interests of national security, public safety or the economic well-being of the country, for the prevention of disorder or crime, for the protection of health or morals, or for the protection of the rights and freedoms of others.

Article 9 Freedom of thought, conscience and religion

1.   Everyone has the right to freedom of thought, conscience and religion; this right includes freedom to change his religion or belief and freedom, either alone or in community with others and in public or private, to manifest his religion or belief, in worship, teaching, practice and observance.

2.   Freedom to manifest one's religion or beliefs shall be subject only to such limitations as are prescribed by law and are necessary in a democratic society in the in-

terests of public safety, for the protection of public order, health or morals, or for the protection of the rights and freedoms of others.

Article 10 Freedom of expression

1.   Everyone has the right to freedom of expression. This right shall include freedom to hold opinions and to receive and impart information and ideas without interference by public authority and regardless of frontiers. This article shall not prevent States from requiring the licensing of broadcasting, television or cinema enterprises.
2.   The exercise of these freedoms, since it carries with it duties and responsibilities, may be subject to such formalities, conditions, restrictions or penalties as are prescribed by law and are necessary in a democratic society, in the interests of national security, territorial integrity or public safety, for the prevention of disorder or crime, for the protection of health or morals, for the protection of the reputation or rights of others, for preventing the disclosure of information received in confidence, or for maintaining the authority and impartiality of the judiciary.

Article 11 Freedom of assembly and association

1.   Everyone has the right to freedom of peaceful assembly and to freedom of association with others, including the right to form and to join trade unions for the protection of his interests.
2   No restrictions shall be placed on the exercise of these rights other than such as are prescribed by law and are necessary in a democratic society in the interests of national security or public safety, for the prevention of disorder or crime, for the protection of health or morals or for the protection of the rights and freedoms of others. This article shall not prevent the imposition of lawful restrictions on the exercise of these rights by members of the armed forces, of the police or of the administration of the State.

Article 12 Right to marry

Men and women of marriageable age have the right to marry and to found a family, according to the national laws governing the exercise of this right.

Article 13 Right to an effective remedy

Everyone whose rights and freedoms as set forth in this Convention are violated shall have an effective remedy before a national authority notwithstanding that the violation has been committed by persons acting in an official capacity.

Article 14 Prohibition of discrimination

The enjoyment of the rights and freedoms set forth in this Convention shall be secured without discrimination on any ground such as sex, race, colour, language, religion, political or other opinion, national or social origin, association with a national minority, property, birth or other status.

Article 15 Derogation in time of emergency

1.   In time of war or other public emergency threatening the life of the nation any High Contracting Party may take measures derogating from its obligations under this Convention to the extent strictly required by the exigencies of the situation, provided that such measures are not inconsistent with its other obligations under international law.
2.   No derogation from Article 2, except in respect of deaths resulting from lawful acts of war, or from Articles 3, 4 (paragraph 1) and 7 shall be made under this provision.
3.   Any High Contracting Party availing itself of this right of derogation shall keep the Secretary General of the Council of Europe fully informed of the measures which it has taken and the reasons therefor. It shall also inform the Secretary General of the

Council of Europe when such measures have ceased to operate and the provisions of the Convention are again being fully executed.

Article 16 Restrictions on political activity of aliens
Nothing in Articles 10, 11 and 14 shall be regarded as preventing the High Contracting Parties from imposing restrictions on the political activity of aliens.

Article 17 Prohibition of abuse of rights
Nothing in this Convention may be interpreted as implying for any State, group or person any right to engage in any activity or perform any act aimed at the destruction of any of the rights and freedoms set forth herein or at their limitation to a greater extent than is provided for in the Convention.

Article 18 Limitation on use of restrictions on rights
The restrictions permitted under this Convention to the said rights and freedoms shall not be applied for any purpose other than those for which they have been prescribed.

Section II European Court of Human Rights

Article 19 Establishment of the Court
To ensure the observance of the engagements undertaken by the High Contracting Parties in the Convention and the Protocols thereto, there shall be set up a European Court of Human Rights, hereinafter referred to as "the Court". It shall function on a permanent basis.

Article 20 Number of judges
The Court shall consist of a number of judges equal to that of the High Contracting Parties.

Article 21 Criteria for office
1.   The judges shall be of high moral character and must either possess the qualifications required for appointment to high judicial office or be jurisconsults of recognised competence.
2.   The judges shall sit on the Court in their individual capacity.
3.   During their term of office the judges shall not engage in any activity which is incompatible with their independence, impartiality or with the demands of a full-time office; all questions arising from the application of this paragraph shall be decided by the Court.

Article 22 Election of judges
1.   The judges shall be elected by the Parliamentary Assembly with respect to each High Contracting Party by a majority of votes cast from a list of three candidates nominated by the High Contracting Party.
2.   The same procedure shall be followed to complete the Court in the event of the accession of new High Contracting Parties and in filling casual vacancies.

Article 23 Terms of office
1.   The judges shall be elected for a period of six years. They may be re-elected. However, the terms of office of one-half of the judges elected at the first election shall expire at the end of three years.

2. The judges whose terms of office are to expire at the end of the initial period of three years shall be chosen by lot by the Secretary General of the Council of Europe immediately after their election.

3. In order to ensure that, as far as possible, the terms of office of one-half of the judges are renewed every three years, the Parliamentary Assembly may decide, before proceeding to any subsequent election, that the term or terms of office of one or more judges to be elected shall be for a period other than six years but not more than nine and not less than three years.

4. In cases where more than one term of office is involved and where the Parliamentary Assembly applies the preceding paragraph, the allocation of the terms of office shall be effected by a drawing of lots by the Secretary General of the Council of Europe immediately after the election.

5. A judge elected to replace a judge whose term of office has not expired shall hold office for the remainder of his predecessor's term.

6. The terms of office of judges shall expire when they reach the age of 70.

7. The judges shall hold office until replaced. They shall, however, continue to deal with such cases as they already have under consideration.

Article 24 Dismissal

No judge may be dismissed from his office unless the other judges decide by a majority of two-thirds that he has ceased to fulfil the required conditions.

Article 25 Registry and legal secretaries

The Court shall have a registry, the functions and organisation of which shall be laid down in the rules of the Court. The Court shall be assisted by legal secretaries.

Article 26 Plenary Court

The plenary Court shall:

a) elect its President and one or two Vice-Presidents for a period of three years; they may be re-elected;
b) set up Chambers, constituted for a fixed period of time;
c) elect the Presidents of the Chambers of the Court; they may be re-elected;
d) adopt the rules of the Court, and
e) elect the Registrar and one or more Deputy Registrars.

Article 27 Committees, Chambers and Grand Chamber

1. To consider cases brought before it, the Court shall sit in committees of three judges, in Chambers of seven judges and in a Grand Chamber of seventeen judges. The Court's Chambers shall set up committees for a fixed period of time.

2. There shall sit as an ex officio member of the Chamber and the Grand Chamber the judge elected in respect of the State Party concerned or, if there is none or if he is unable to sit, a person of its choice who shall sit in the capacity of judge.

3. The Grand Chamber shall also include the President of the Court, the Vice-Presidents, the Presidents of the Chambers and other judges chosen in accordance with the rules of the Court. When a case is referred to the Grand Chamber under Article 43, no judge from the Chamber which rendered the judgment shall sit in the Grand Chamber, with the exception of the President of the Chamber and the judge who sat in respect of the State Party concerned.

Article 28 Declarations of inadmissibility by committees
A committee may, by a unanimous vote, declare inadmissible or strike out of its list of cases an application submitted under Article 34 where such a decision can be taken without further examination. The decision shall be final.

Article 29 Decisions by Chambers on admissibility and merits
1.   If no decision is taken under Article 28, a Chamber shall decide on the admissibility and merits of individual applications submitted under Article 34.
2.   A Chamber shall decide on the admissibility and merits of inter-State applications submitted under Article 33.
3.   The decision on admissibility shall be taken separately unless the Court, in exceptional cases, decides otherwise.

Article 30 Relinquishment of jurisdiction to the Grand Chamber
Where a case pending before a Chamber raises a serious question affecting the interpretation of the Convention or the protocols thereto, or where the resolution of a question before the Chamber might have a result inconsistent with a judgment previously delivered by the Court, the Chamber may, at any time before it has rendered its judgment, relinquish jurisdiction in favour of the Grand Chamber, unless one of the parties to the case objects.

Article 31 Powers of the Grand Chamber
The Grand Chamber shall:
a)   determine applications submitted either under Article 33 or Article 34 when a Chamber has relinquished jurisdiction under Article 30 or when the case has been referred to it under Article 43; and
b)   consider requests for advisory opinions submitted under Article 47.

Article 32 Jurisdiction of the Court
1.   The jurisdiction of the Court shall extend to all matters concerning the interpretation and application of the Convention and the protocols thereto which are referred to it as provided in Articles 33, 34 and 47.
2.   In the event of dispute as to whether the Court has jurisdiction, the Court shall decide.

Article 33 Inter-State cases
Any High Contracting Party may refer to the Court any alleged breach of the provisions of the Convention and the protocols thereto by another High Contracting Party.

Article 34 Individual applications
The Court may receive applications from any person, non-governmental organisation or group of individuals claiming to be the victim of a violation by one of the High Contracting Parties of the rights set forth in the Convention or the protocols thereto. The High Contracting Parties undertake not to hinder in any way the effective exercise of this right.

Article 35 Admissibility criteria
1.   The Court may only deal with the matter after all domestic remedies have been exhausted, according to the generally recognised rules of international law, and within a period of six months from the date on which the final decision was taken.
2.   The Court shall not deal with any application submitted under Article 34 that
a)   is anonymous; or

b) is substantially the same as a matter that has already been examined by the Court or has already been submitted to another procedure of international investigation or settlement and contains no relevant new information.
3. The Court shall declare inadmissible any individual application submitted under Article 34 which it considers incompatible with the provisions of the Convention or the protocols thereto, manifestly ill-founded, or an abuse of the right of application.
4. The Court shall reject any application which it considers inadmissible under this Article. It may do so at any stage of the proceedings.

Article 36 Third party intervention
1. In all cases before a Chamber of the Grand Chamber, a High Contracting Party one of whose nationals is an applicant shall have the right to submit written comments and to take part in hearings.
2. The President of the Court may, in the interest of the proper administration of justice, invite any High Contracting Party which is not a party to the proceedings or any person concerned who is not the applicant to submit written comments or take part in hearings.

Article 37 Striking out applications
1. The Court may at any stage of the proceedings decide to strike an application out of its list of cases where the circumstances lead to the conclusion that
a) the applicant does not intend to pursue his application; or
b) the matter has been resolved; or
c) for any other reason established by the Court, it is no longer justified to continue the examination of the application.
However, the Court shall continue the examination of the application if respect for human rights as defined in the Convention and the protocols thereto so requires.
2. The Court may decide to restore an application to its list of cases if it considers that the circumstances justify such a course.

Article 38 Examination of the case and friendly settlement proceedings
1. If the Court declares the application admissible, it shall
a) pursue the examination of the case, together with the representatives of the parties, and if need be, undertake an investigation, for the effective conduct of which the States concerned shall furnish all necessary facilities;
b) place itself at the disposal of the parties concerned with a view to securing a friendly settlement of the matter on the basis of respect for human rights as defined in the Convention and the protocols thereto.
2. Proceedings conducted under paragraph 1.b shall be confidential.

Article 39 Finding of a friendly settlement
If a friendly settlement is effected, the Court shall strike the case out of its list by means of a decision which shall be confined to a brief statement of the facts and of the solution reached.

Article 40 Public hearings and access to documents
1. Hearings shall be in public unless the Court in exceptional circumstances decides otherwise.
2. Documents deposited with the Registrar shall be accessible to the public unless the President of the Court decides otherwise.

Article 41 Just satisfaction

If the Court finds that there has been a violation of the Convention or the protocols thereto, and if the internal law of the High Contracting Party concerned allows only partial reparation to be made, the Court shall, if necessary, afford just satisfaction to the injured party.

Article 42 Judgments of Chambers

Judgments of Chambers shall become final in accordance with the provisions of Article 44, paragraph 2.

Article 43 Referral to the Grand Chamber

1.   Within a period of three months from the date of the judgment of the Chamber, any party to the case may, in exceptional cases, request that the case be referred to the Grand Chamber.
2.   A panel of five judges of the Grand Chamber shall accept the request if the case raises a serious question affecting the interpretation or application of the Convention or the protocols thereto, or a serious issue of general importance.
3.   If the panel accepts the request, the Grand Chamber shall decide the case by means of a judgment.

Article 44 Final judgments

1.   The judgment of the Grand Chamber shall be final.
2.   The judgment of a Chamber shall become final
a)   when the parties declare that they will not request that the case be referred to the Grand Chamber; or
b)   three months after the date of the judgment, if reference of the case to the Grand Chamber has not been requested; or
c)   when the panel of the Grand Chamber rejects the request to refer under Article 43.
3.   The final judgment shall be published.

Article 45 Reasons for judgments and decisions

1.   Reasons shall be given for judgments as well as for decisions declaring applications admissible or inadmissible.
2.   If a judgment does not represent, in whole or in part, the unanimous opinion of the judges, any judge shall be entitled to deliver a separate opinion.

Article 46 Binding force and execution of judgments

1.   The High Contracting Parties undertake to abide by the final judgment of the Court in any case to which they are parties.
2.   The final judgment of the Court shall be transmitted to the Committee of Ministers, which shall supervise its execution.

Article 47 Advisory opinions

1.   The Court may, at the request of the Committee of Ministers, give advisory opinions on legal questions concerning the interpretation of the Convention and the protocols thereto.
2.   Such opinions shall not deal with any question relating to the content or scope of the rights or freedoms defined in Section I of the Convention and the protocols thereto, or with any other question which the Court or the Committee of Ministers might have to consider in consequence of any such proceedings as could be instituted in accordance with the Convention.

3. Decisions of the Committee of Ministers to request an advisory opinion of the Court shall require a majority vote of the representatives entitled to sit on the Committee.

Article 48 Advisory jurisdiction of the Court
The Court shall decide whether a request for an advisory opinion submitted by the Committee of Ministers is within its competence as defined in Article 47.

Article 49 Reasons for advisory opinions
1. Reasons shall be given for advisory opinions of the Court.
2. If the advisory opinion does not represent, in whole or in part, the unanimous opinion of the judges, any judge shall be entitled to deliver a separate opinion.
3. Advisory opinions of the Court shall be communicated to the Committee of Ministers.

Article 50 Expenditure on the Court
The expenditure on the Court shall be borne by the Council of Europe.

Article 51 Privileges and immunities of judges
The judges shall be entitled, during the exercise of their functions, to the privileges and immunities provided for in Article 40 of the Statute of the Council of Europe and in the agreements made thereunder.

Section III Miscellaneous provisions

Article 52 Inquiries by the Secretary General
On receipt of a request from the Secretary General of the Council of Europe any High Contracting Party shall furnish an explanation of the manner in which its internal law ensures the effective implementation of any of the provisions of the Convention.

Article 53 Safeguard for existing human rights
Nothing in this Convention shall be construed as limiting or derogating from any of the human rights and fundamental freedoms which may be ensured under the laws of any High Contracting Party or under any other agreement to which it is a Party.

Article 54 Powers of the Committee of Ministers
Nothing in this Convention shall prejudice the powers conferred on the Committee of Ministers by the Statute of the Council of Europe.

Article 55 Exclusion of other means of dispute settlement
The High Contracting Parties agree that, except by special agreement, they will not avail themselves of treaties, conventions or declarations in force between them for the purpose of submitting, by way of petition, a dispute arising out of the interpretation or application of this Convention to a means of settlement other than those provided for in this Convention.

Article 56 Territorial application
1. Any State may at the time of its ratification or at any time thereafter declare by notification addressed to the Secretary General of the Council of Europe that the present Convention shall, subject to paragraph 4 of this Article, extend to all or any of the territories for whose international relations it is responsible.

2.   The Convention shall extend to the territory or territories named in the notification as from the thirtieth day after the receipt of this notification by the Secretary General of the Council of Europe.

3.   The provisions of this Convention shall be applied in such territories with due regard, however, to local requirements.

4.   Any State which has made a declaration in accordance with paragraph 1 of this article may at any time thereafter declare on behalf of one or more of the territories to which the declaration relates that it accepts the competence of the Court to receive applications from individuals, non-governmental organisations or groups of individuals as provided by Article 34 of the Convention.

Article 57 Reservations

1.   Any State may, when signing this Convention or when depositing its instrument of ratification, make a reservation in respect of any particular provision of the Convention to the extent that any law then in force in its territory is not in conformity with the provision. Reservations of a general character shall not be permitted under this article.

2.   Any reservation made under this article shall contain a brief statement of the law concerned.

Article 58 Denunciation

1.   A High Contracting Party may denounce the present Convention only after the expiry of five years from the date on which it became a party to it and after six months' notice contained in a notification addressed to the Secretary General of the Council of Europe, who shall inform the other High Contracting Parties.

2.   Such a denunciation shall not have the effect of releasing the High Contracting Party concerned from its obligations under this Convention in respect of any act which, being capable of constituting a violation of such obligations, may have been performed by it before the date at which the denunciation became effective.

3.   Any High Contracting Party which shall cease to be a member of the Council of Europe shall cease to be a Party to this Convention under the same conditions.

4.   The Convention may be denounced in accordance with the provisions of the preceding paragraphs in respect of any territory to which it has been declared to extend under the terms of Article 56.

Article 59 Signature and ratification

1.   This Convention shall be open to the signature of the members of the Council of Europe. It shall be ratified. Ratifications shall be deposited with the Secretary General of the Council of Europe.

2.   The present Convention shall come into force after the deposit of ten instruments of ratification.

3.   As regards any signatory ratifying subsequently, the Convention shall come into force at the date of the deposit of its instrument of ratification.

4.   The Secretary General of the Council of Europe shall notify all the members of the Council of Europe of the entry into force of the Convention, the names of the High Contracting Parties who have ratified it, and the deposit of all instruments of ratification which may be effected subsequently.

Done at Rome this 4th day of November 1950, in English and French, both texts being equally authentic, in a single copy which shall remain deposited in the archives of the Council of Europe. The Secretary General shall transmit certified copies to each of the signatories.

Protocols Annexed to the ECHR

Protocol to the Convention for the Protection of Human Rights and Fundamental Freedoms[1]

THE GOVERNMENTS SIGNATORY HERETO, BEING MEMBERS OF THE COUNCIL OF EUROPE,

BEING RESOLVED to take steps to ensure the collective enforcement of certain rights and freedoms other than those already included in Section I of the Convention for the Protection of Human Rights and Fundamental Freedoms signed at Rome on 4 November 1950 (hereinafter referred to as "the Convention"),

HAVE AGREED AS FOLLOWS:

Article 1 Protection of property
Every natural or legal person is entitled to the peaceful enjoyment of his possessions. No one shall be deprived of his possessions except in the public interest and subject to the conditions provided for by law and by the general principles of international law.

The preceding provisions shall not, however, in any way impair the right of a State to enforce such laws as it deems necessary to control the use of property in accordance with the general interest or to secure the payment of taxes or other contributions or penalties.

Article 2 Right to education
No person shall be denied the right to education. In the exercise of any functions which it assumes in relation to education and to teaching, the State shall respect the right of parents to ensure such education and teaching in conformity with their own religious and philosophical convictions.

Article 3 Right to free elections
The High Contracting Parties undertake to hold free elections at reasonable intervals by secret ballot, under conditions which will ensure the free expression of the opinion of the people in the choice of the legislature.

Article 4 Territorial application
Any High Contracting Party may at the time of signature or ratification or at any time thereafter communicate to the Secretary General of the Council of Europe a declaration stating the extent to which it undertakes that the provisions of the present Protocol shall apply to such of the territories for the international relations of which it is responsible as are named therein.

Any High Contracting Party which has communicated a declaration in virtue of the preceding paragraph may from time to time communicate a further declaration modifying the terms of any former declaration or terminating the application of the provisions of this Protocol in respect of any territory.

A declaration made in accordance with this article shall be deemed to have been made in accordance with paragraph 1 of Article 56 of the Convention.

---

1 Paris, 20 March 1952, as amended by Protocol No. 11.

Article 5 Relationship to the Convention
As between the High Contracting Parties the provisions of Articles 1, 2, 3 and 4 of this Protocol shall be regarded as additional articles to the Convention and all the provisions of the Convention shall apply accordingly.

Article 6 Signature and ratification
This Protocol shall be open for signature by the members of the Council of Europe, who are the signatories of the Convention; it shall be ratified at the same time as or after the ratification of the Convention. It shall enter into force after the deposit of ten instruments of ratification. As regards any signatory ratifying subsequently, the Protocol shall enter into force at the date of the deposit of its instrument of ratification.

The instruments of ratification shall be deposited with the Secretary General of the Council of Europe, who will notify all members of the names of those who have ratified.[...]

Protocol No. 4 to the Convention for the Protection of Human Rights and Fundamental Freedoms, Securing Certain Rights and Freedoms Other Than Those Already Included in the Convention and in the First Protocol Thereto[1]

THE GOVERNMENTS SIGNATORY HERETO, BEING MEMBERS OF THE COUNCIL OF EUROPE,

BEING RESOLVED to take steps to ensure the collective enforcement of certain rights and freedoms other than those already included in Section 1 of the Convention for the Protection of Human Rights and Fundamental Freedoms signed at Rome on 4th November 1950 (hereinafter referred to as the "Convention") and in Articles 1 to 3 of the First Protocol to the Convention, signed at Paris on 20th March 1952,

HAVE AGREED AS FOLLOWS:

Article 1 Prohibition of imprisonment for debt
No one shall be deprived of his liberty merely on the ground of inability to fulfil a contractual obligation.

Article 2 Freedom of movement
1)　Everyone lawfully within the territory of a State shall, within that territory, have the right to liberty of movement and freedom to choose his residence.
2)　Everyone shall be free to leave any country, including his own.
3)　No restrictions shall be placed on the exercise of these rights other than such as are in accordance with law and are necessary in a democratic society in the interests of national security or public safety, for the maintenance of ordre public, for the prevention of crime, for the protection of health or morals, or for the protection of the rights and freedoms of others.
4)　The rights set forth in paragraph 1 may also be subject, in particular areas, to restrictions imposed in accordance with law and justified by the public interest in a democratic society.

1　Strasbourg, 16. September 1963, as amended by Protocol No. 11.

Article 3 Prohibition of expulsion of nationals

1) No one shall be expelled, by means either of an individual or of a collective measure, from the territory of the State of which he is a national.

2) No one shall be deprived of the right to enter the territory of the state of which he is a national.

Article 4 Prohibition of collective expulsion of aliens

Collective expulsion of aliens is prohibited.

Article 5 Territorial application

1) Any High Contracting Party may, at the time of signature or ratification of this Protocol, or at any time thereafter, communicate to the Secretary General of the Council of Europe a declaration stating the extent to which it undertakes that the provisions of this Protocol shall apply to such of the territories for the international relations of which it is responsible as are named therein.

2) Any High Contracting Party which has communicated a declaration in virtue of the preceding paragraph may, from time to time, communicate a further declaration modifying the terms of any former declaration or terminating the application of the provisions of this Protocol in respect of any territory.

3) A declaration made in accordance with this article shall be deemed to have been made in accordance with paragraph 1 of Article 56 of the Convention.

4) The territory of any State to which this Protocol applies by virtue of ratification or acceptance by that State, and each territory to which this Protocol is applied by virtue of a declaration by that State under this article, shall be treated as separate territories for the purpose of the references in Articles 2 and 3 to the territory of a State.

5) Any State which has made a declaration in accordance with paragraph 1 or 2 of this Article may at any time thereafter declare on behalf of one or more of the territories to which the declaration relates that it accepts the competence of the Court to receive applications from individuals, non-governmental organisations or groups of individuals as provided in Article 34 of the Convention in respect of all or any of Articles 1 to 4 of this Protocol.

Article 6 Relationship to the Convention

As between the High Contracting Parties the provisions of Articles 1 to 5 of this Protocol shall be regarded as additional Articles to the Convention, and all the provisions of the Convention shall apply accordingly.

Article 7 Signature and ratification

1) This Protocol shall be open for signature by the members of the Council of Europe who are the signatories of the Convention; it shall be ratified at the same time as or after the ratification of the Convention. It shall enter into force after the deposit of five instruments of ratification. As regards any signatory ratifying subsequently, the Protocol shall enter into force at the date of the deposit of its instrument of ratification.

2) The instruments of ratification shall be deposited with the Secretary General of the Council of Europe, who will notify all members of the names of those who have ratified.

In witness whereof the undersigned, being duly authorised thereto, have signed this Protocol.[...]

Protocol No. 6 to the Convention for the Protection of Human Rights and Fundamental Freedoms Concerning the Abolition of the Death Penalty[1]

THE MEMBER STATES OF THE COUNCIL OF EUROPE, SIGNATORY TO THIS PROTOCOL TO THE CONVENTION FOR THE PROTECTION OF HUMAN RIGHTS AND FUNDAMENTAL FREEDOMS, SIGNED AT ROME ON 4 NOVEMBER 1950 (HEREINAFTER REFERRED TO AS "THE CONVENTION"),

CONSIDERING that the evolution that has occurred in several member States of the Council of Europe expresses a general tendency in favour of abolition of the death penalty;

HAVE AGREED AS FOLLOWS:

Article 1 Abolition of the death penalty
The death penalty shall be abolished. No-one shall be condemned to such penalty or executed.

Article 2 Death penalty in time of war
A State may make provision in its law for the death penalty in respect of acts committed in time of war or of imminent threat of war; such penalty shall be applied only in the instances laid down in the law and in accordance with its provisions. The State shall communicate to the Secretary General of the Council of Europe the relevant provisions of that law.

Article 3 Prohibition of derogations
No derogation from the provisions of this Protocol shall be made under Article 15 of the Convention.

Article 4 Prohibition of reservations
No reservation may be made under Article 57 of the Convention in respect of the provisions of this Protocol.

Article 5 Territorial application
1) Any State may at the time of signature or when depositing its instrument of ratification, acceptance or approval, specify the territory or territories to which this Protocol shall apply.
2) Any State may at any later date, by a declaration addressed to the Secretary General of the Council of Europe, extend the application of this Protocol to any other territory specified in the declaration. In respect of such territory the Protocol shall enter into force on the first day of the month following the date of receipt of such declaration by the Secretary General.
3) Any declaration made under the two preceding paragraphs may, in respect of any territory specified in such declaration, be withdrawn by a notification addressed to the Secretary General. The withdrawal shall become effective on the first day of the month following the date of receipt of such notification by the Secretary General.

---

1   Strasbourg, 28. April 1983, as amended by Protocol No. 11.

Article 6 Relationship to the Convention

As between the States Parties the provisions of Articles 1 to 5 of this Protocol shall be regarded as additional articles to the Convention and all the provisions of the Convention shall apply accordingly.

Article 7 Signature and ratification

The Protocol shall be open for signature by the member States of the Council of Europe, signatories to the Convention. It shall be subject to ratification, acceptance or approval. A member State of the Council of Europe may not ratify, accept or approve this Protocol unless it has, simultaneously or previously, ratified the Convention. Instruments of ratification, acceptance or approval shall be deposited with the Secretary General of the Council of Europe.

Article 8 Entry into force

1) This Protocol shall enter into force on the first day of the month following the date on which five member States of the Council of Europe have expressed their consent to be bound by the Protocol in accordance with the provisions of Article 7.
2) In respect of any member State which subsequently expresses its consent to be bound by it, the Protocol shall enter into force on the first day of the month following the date of the deposit of the instrument of ratification, acceptance or approval.

Article 9 Depositary functions

The Secretary General of the Council of Europe shall notify the member States of the Council of:
− any signature;
− the deposit of any instrument of ratification, acceptance or approval;
− any date of entry into force of this Protocol in accordance with Articles 5 and 8;
− any other act, notification or communication relating to this Protocol.

In witness whereof the undersigned, being duly authorised thereto, have signed this Protocol.[...]

Protocol No. 7 to the Convention for the Protection of Human Rights and Fundamental Freedoms[1]

THE MEMBER STATES OF THE COUNCIL OF EUROPE SIGNATORY HERETO,

BEING RESOLVED to take further steps to ensure the collective enforcement of certain rights and freedoms by means of the Convention for the Protection of Human Rights and Fundamental Freedoms signed at Rome on 4 November 1950 (hereinafter referred to as "the Convention"),

HAVE AGREED AS FOLLOWS :

---

1   Strasbourg, 22. November 1984, as amended by Protocol No. 11.

Article 1 Procedural safeguards relating to expulsion of aliens

1)   An alien lawfully resident in the territory of a State shall not be expelled therefrom except in pursuance of a decision reached in accordance with law and shall be allowed:
a)   to submit reasons against his expulsion,
b)   to have his case reviewed, and
c)   to be represented for these purposes before the competent authority or a person or persons designated by that authority.
2)   An alien may be expelled before the exercise of his rights under paragraph 1.a, b and c of this Article, when such expulsion is necessary in the interests of public order or is grounded on reasons of national security.

Article 2 Right of appeal in criminal matters

1)   Everyone convicted of a criminal offence by a tribunal shall have the right to have his conviction or sentence reviewed by a higher tribunal. The exercise of this right, including the grounds on which it may be exercised, shall be governed by law.
2)   This right may be subject to exceptions in regard to offences of a minor character, as prescribed by law, or in cases in which the person concerned was tried in the first instance by the highest tribunal or was convicted following an appeal against acquittal.

Article 3 Compensation for wrongful conviction

When a person has by a final decision been convicted of a criminal offence and when subsequently his conviction has been reversed, or he has been pardoned, on the ground that a new or newly discovered fact shows conclusively that there has been a miscarriage of justice, the person who has suffered punishment as a result of such conviction shall be compensated according to the law or the practice of the State concerned, unless it is proved that the non-disclosure of the unknown fact in time is wholly or partly attributable to him.

Article 4 Right not to be tried or punished twice

1)   No one shall be liable to be tried or punished again in criminal proceedings under the jurisdiction of the same State for an offence for which he has already been finally acquitted or convicted in accordance with the law and penal procedure of that State.
2)   The provisions of the preceding paragraph shall not prevent the reopening of the case in accordance with the law and penal procedure of the State concerned, if there is evidence of new or newly discovered facts, or if there has been a fundamental defect in the previous proceedings, which could affect the outcome of the case.
3)   No derogation from this Article shall be made under Article 15 of the Convention.

Article 5 Equality between spouses

Spouses shall enjoy equality of rights and responsibilities of a private law character between them, and in their relations with their children, as to marriage, during marriage and in the event of its dissolution. This Article shall not prevent States from taking such measures as are necessary in the interests of the children.

Article 6 Territorial application

1)   Any State may at the time of signature or when depositing its instrument of ratification, acceptance or approval, specify the territory or territories to which the Protocol shall apply and state the extent to which it undertakes that the provisions of this Protocol shall apply to such territory or territories.
2)   Any State may at any later date, by a declaration addressed to the Secretary General of the Council of Europe, extend the application of this Protocol to any other

territory specified in the declaration. In respect of such territory the Protocol shall enter into force on the first day of the month following the expiration of a period of two months after the date of receipt by the Secretary General of such declaration.

3) Any declaration made under the two preceding paragraphs may, in respect of any territory specified in such declaration, be withdrawn or modified by a notification addressed to the Secretary General. The withdrawal or modification shall become effective on the first day of the month following the expiration of a period of two months after the date of receipt of such notification by the Secretary General.

4) A declaration made in accordance with this Article shall be deemed to have been made in accordance with paragraph 1 of Article 56 of the Convention.

5) The territory of any State to which this Protocol applies by virtue of ratification, acceptance or approval by that State, and each territory to which this Protocol is applied by virtue of a declaration by that State under this Article, may be treated as separate territories for the purpose of the reference in Article 1 to the territory of a State.

6) Any State which has made a declaration in accordance with paragraph 1 or 2 of this Article may at any time thereafter declare on behalf of one or more of the territories to which the declaration relates that it accepts the competence of the Court to receive applications from individuals, non-governmental organisations or groups of individuals as provided in Article 34 of the Convention in respect of Articles 1 to 5 of this Protocol.

Article 7 Relationship to the Convention

As between the States Parties, the provisions of Article 1 to 6 of this Protocol shall be regarded as additional Articles to the Convention, and all the provisions of the Convention shall apply accordingly.

Article 8 Signature and ratification

This Protocol shall be open for signature by member States of the Council of Europe which have signed the Convention. It is subject to ratification, acceptance or approval. A member State of the Council of Europe may not ratify, accept or approve this Protocol without previously or simultaneously ratifying the Convention. Instruments of ratification, acceptance or approval shall be deposited with the Secretary General of the Council of Europe.

Article 9 Entry into force

1) This Protocol shall enter into force on the first day of the month following the expiration of a period of two months after the date on which seven member States of the Council of Europe have expressed their consent to be bound by the Protocol in accordance with the provisions of Article 8.

2) In respect of any member State which subsequently expresses its consent to be bound by it, the Protocol shall enter into force on the first day of the month following the expiration of a period of two months after the date of the deposit of the instrument of ratification, acceptance or approval.

Article 10 Depositary functions

The Secretary General of the Council of Europe shall notify all the member States of the Council of Europe of:

a) any signature;
b) the deposit of any instrument of ratification, acceptance or approval;
c) any date of entry into force of this Protocol in accordance with Articles 6 and 9;
d) any other act, notification or declaration relating to this Protocol.

In witness whereof the undersigned, being duly authorised thereto, have signed this Protocol.[...]

FIVE: ECONOMIC FREEDOMS IN THE INTERNAL MARKET

Free Movement of Goods

Commission Directive 70/50 of 22 December 1969 Based on the Provisions of Article 33 (7), on the Abolition of Measures Which Have an Equivalent Effect to Quantitative Restrictions on Imports and Are Not Covered by Other Provisions Adopted in Pursuance of the EEC Treaty[1]

THE COMMISSION OF THE EUROPEAN COMMUNITIES,

HAVING REGARD to the provisions of the Treaty establishing the European Economic Community, and in particular Article 33 (7) thereof;

(1) WHEREAS for the purpose of Article 30 *et seq.* "measures" means laws, regulations, administrative provisions, administrative practices, and all instruments issuing from a public authority, including recommendations;

(2) WHEREAS for the purposes of this Directive "administrative practices" means any standard and regularly followed procedure of a public authority; whereas "recommendations" means any instruments issuing from a public authority which, while not legally binding on the addressees thereof, cause them to pursue a certain conduct;

(3) WHEREAS the formalities to which imports are subject do not as a general rule have an effect equivalent to that of quantitative restrictions and, consequently, are not covered by this Directive;

(4) WHEREAS certain measures adopted by Member States other than those applicable equally to domestic and imported products, which were operative at the date of entry into force of the Treaty and are not covered by other provisions adopted in pursuance of the Treaty, either preclude importation or make it more difficult or costly than the disposal of domestic production;

(5) WHEREAS such measures must be considered to include those which make access of imported products to the domestic market, at any marketing stage, subject to a condition which is not laid down for domestic products or to a condition differing from that laid down for domestic products, and more difficult to satisfy, so that a burden is thus placed on imported products only;

(6) WHEREAS such measures must also be considered to include those which, at any marketing stage, grant to domestic products a preference, other than an aid, to which conditions may or may not be attached, and where such measures totally or partially preclude the disposal of imported products;

(7) WHEREAS such measures hinder imports which could otherwise take place, and thus have an effect equivalent to quantitative restrictions on imports;

(8) WHEREAS effects on the free movement of goods of measures which relate to the marketing of products and which apply equally to domestic and imported products are not as a general rule equivalent to those of quantitative restrictions, since such effects are normally inherent in the disparities between rules applied by Member States in this respect;

(9) WHEREAS, however, such measures may have a restrictive effect on the free movement of goods over and above that which is intrinsic to such rules;

(10) WHEREAS such is the case where imports are either precluded or made more difficult or costly than the disposal of domestic production and where such effect is not

---

1   OJ 1970 L 13, p. 29.

necessary for the attainment of an objective within the scope of the powers for the regulation of trade left to Member States by the Treaty; whereas such is in particular the case where the said objective can be attained just as effectively by other means which are less of a hindrance to trade; whereas such is also the case where the restrictive effect of these provisions on the free movement of goods is out of proportion to their purpose;

(11) WHEREAS these measures accordingly have an effect equivalent to that of quantitative restrictions on imports;

(12) WHEREAS the customs union cannot be achieved without the abolition of such measures having an equivalent effect to quantitative restrictions on imports;

(13) WHEREAS Member States must abolish all measures having equivalent effect by the end of the transitional period at the latest, even if no Commission Directive expressly requires them to do so;

(14) WHEREAS the provisions concerning the abolition of quantitative restrictions and measures having equivalent effect between Member States apply both to products originating in and exported by Member States and to products originating in third countries and put into free circulation in the other Member States;

(15) WHEREAS Article 33 (7) does not apply to measures of the kind referred to which fall under other provisions of the Treaty, and in particular those which fall under Articles 37 (1) and 44 of the Treaty or form an integral part of a national organisation of an agricultural market;

(16) WHEREAS Article 33 (7) does not apply to the charges and taxation referred to in Article 12 *et seq.* and Article 95 *et seq. or* to the aids mentioned in Article 9;

(17) WHEREAS the provisions of Article 33 (7) do not prevent the application, in particular, of Articles 36 and 223;

HAS ADOPTED THIS DIRECTIVE:

Article 1 [Abolition of Restrictions on the Free Movement of Goods]
The purpose of this Directive is to abolish the measures referred to in Articles 2 and 3, which were operative at the date of entry into force of the EEC Treaty.

Article 2 [Discriminatory Measures]
1.   This Directive covers measures, other than those applicable equally to domestic or imported products, which hinder imports which could otherwise take place, including measures which make importation more difficult or costly than the disposal of domestic production.

2.   In particular, it covers measures which make imports or the disposal, at any marketing stage, of imported products subject to a condition - other than a formality - which is required in respect of imported products only, or a condition differing from that required for domestic products and more difficult to satisfy. Equally, it covers, in particular, measures which favour domestic products or grant them a preference, other than an aid, to which conditions may or may not be attached.

3.   The measures referred to must be taken to include those measures which:

(a) lay down, for imported products only, minimum or maximum prices below or above which imports are prohibited, reduced or made subject to conditions liable to hinder importation;

(b) lay down less favourable prices for imported products than for domestic products;

(c) fix profit margins or any other price components for imported products only or fix these differently for domestic products and for imported products, to the detriment of the latter;

(d) preclude any increase in the price of the imported product corresponding to the supplementary costs and charges inherent in importation;
(e) fix the prices of products solely on the basis of the cost price or the quality of domestic products at such a level as to create a hindrance to importation;
(f) lower the value of an imported product, in particular by causing a reduction in its intrinsic value, or increase its costs;
(g) make access of imported products to the domestic market conditional upon having an agent or representative in the territory of the importing Member State;
(h) lay down conditions of payment in respect of imported products only, or subject imported products to conditions which are different from those laid down for domestic products and more difficult to satisfy;
(i) require, for imports only, the giving of guarantees or making of payments on account;
(j) subject imported products only to conditions, in respect, in particular of shape, size, weight, composition, presentation, identification or putting up, or subject imported products to conditions which are different from those for domestic products and more difficult to satisfy;
(k) hinder the purchase by private individuals of imported products only, or encourage, require or give preference to the purchase of domestic products only;
(l) totally or partially preclude the use of national facilities or equipment in respect of imported products only, or totally or partially confine the use of such facilities or equipment to domestic products only;
(m) prohibit or limit publicity in respect of imported products only, or totally or partially confine publicity to domestic products only;
(n) prohibit, limit or require stocking in respect of imported products only; totally or partially confine the use of stocking facilities to domestic products only, or make the stocking of imported products subject to conditions which are different from those required for domestic products and more difficult to satisfy;
(o) make importation subject to the granting of reciprocity by one or more Member States;
(p) prescribe that imported products are to conform, totally or partially, to rules other than those of the importing country;
(q) specific time limits for imported products which are insufficient or excessive in relation to the normal course of the various transactions to which these time limits apply;
(r) subject imported products to controls or, other than those inherent in the customs clearance procedure, to which domestic products are not subject or which are stricter in respect of imported products than they are in respect of domestic products, without this being necessary in order to ensure equivalent protection;
(s) confine names which are not indicative of origin or source to domestic products only.

Article 3 [Non-discriminatory Measures]
This Directive also covers measures governing the marketing of products which deal, in particular, with shape, size, weight, composition, presentation, identification or putting up and which are equally applicable to domestic and imported products, where the restrictive effect of such measures on the free movement of goods exceeds the effects intrinsic to trade rules.

This is the case, in particular, where:
— the restrictive effects on the free movement of goods are out of proportion to their purpose;

— the same objective can be attained by other means which are less of a hindrance to trade.

Article 4 [Obligations of Member States]
1. Member States shall take all necessary steps in respect of products which must be allowed to enjoy free movement pursuant to Articles 9 and 10 of the Treaty to abolish measures having an effect equivalent to quantitative restrictions on imports and covered by this Directive.
2. Member States shall inform the Commission of measures taken pursuant to this Directive.

Article 5 [Measures not Covered by this Directive]
1. This Directive does not apply to measures:
(a) which fall under Article 37 (1) of the EEC Treaty;
(b) which are referred to in Article 44 of the EEC Treaty or form an integral part of a national organisation of an agricultural market not yet replaced by a common organisation.
2. This Directive shall apply without prejudice to the application, in particular, of Articles 36 and 223 of the EEC Treaty.

Article 6 [omitted]

Done at Brussels, 22 December 1969.
For the Commission, The President, Jean REY

Council Regulation 2679/98 of 7 December 1998 on the Functioning of the Internal Market in Relation to the Free Movement of Goods Among the Member States[1]

THE COUNCIL OF THE EUROPEAN UNION,

HAVING REGARD to the Treaty establishing the European Community, and in particular Article 235 thereof, [...]
(1) WHEREAS, as provided for in Article 7a of the Treaty, the internal market comprises an area without internal frontiers in which, in particular, the free movement of goods is ensured in accordance with Articles 30 to 36 of the Treaty;
(2) WHEREAS breaches of this principle, such as occur when in a given Member State the free movement of goods is obstructed by actions of private individuals, may cause grave disruption to the proper functioning of the internal market and inflict serious losses on the individuals affected;
(3) WHEREAS, in order to ensure fulfilment of the obligations arising from the Treaty, and, in particular, to ensure the proper functioning of the internal market, Member States should, on the one hand, abstain from adopting measures or engaging in conduct liable to constitute an obstacle to trade and, on the other hand, take all necessary and proportionate measures with a view to facilitating the free movement of goods in their territory;

---

1   OJ 1998 L 337, p. 8.

(4) WHEREAS such measures must not affect the exercise of fundamental rights, including the right or freedom to strike;

(5) WHEREAS this Regulation does not prevent any actions which may be necessary in certain cases at Community level to respond to problems in the functioning of the internal market, taking into account, where appropriate, the application of this Regulation;

(6) WHEREAS Member States have exclusive competence as regards the maintenance of public order and the safeguarding of internal security as well as in determining whether, when and which measures are necessary and proportionate in order to facilitate the free movement of goods in their territory in a given situation;

(7) WHEREAS there should be adequate and rapid exchange of information between the Member States and the Commission on obstacles to the free movement of goods;

(8) WHEREAS a Member State on the territory of which obstacles to the free movement of goods occur should take all necessary and proportionate measures to restore as soon as possible the free movement of goods in their territory in order to avoid the risk that the disruption or loss in question will continue, increase or intensify and that there may be a breakdown in trade and in the contractual relations which underlie it; whereas such Member State should inform the Commission and, if requested, other Member States of the measures it has taken or intends to take in order to fulfil this objective;

(9) WHEREAS the Commission, in fulfilment of its duty under the Treaty, should notify the Member State concerned of its view that a breach has occurred and the Member State should respond to that notification;

(10) WHEREAS the Treaty provides for no powers, other than those in Article 235 thereof, for the adoption of this Regulation,

HAS ADOPTED THIS REGULATION:

Article 1 [Definitions]
For the purpose of this Regulation:

1.   the term "obstacle" shall mean an obstacle to the free movement of goods among Member States which is attributable to a Member State, whether it involves action or inaction on its part, which may constitute a breach of Articles 30 to 36 of the Treaty and which:

(a) leads to serious disruption of the free movement of goods by physically or otherwise preventing, delaying or diverting their import into, export from or transport across a Member State,

(b) causes serious loss to the individuals affected, and

(c) requires immediate action in order to prevent any continuation, increase or intensification of the disruption or loss in question;

2.   the term "inaction" shall cover the case when the competent authorities of a Member State, in the presence of an obstacle caused by actions taken by private individuals, fail to take all necessary and proportionate measures within their powers with a view to removing the obstacle and ensuring the free movement of goods in their territory.

Article 2 [Unaffected Rights]
This Regulation may not be interpreted as affecting in any way the exercise of fundamental rights as recognised in Member States, including the right or freedom to strike. These rights may also include the right or freedom to take other actions covered by the specific industrial relations systems in Member States.

Article 3 [Notification of Obstacles]
1.   When an obstacle occurs or when there is a threat thereof

(a) any Member State (whether or not it is the Member State concerned) which has relevant information shall immediately transmit it to the Commission, and

(b) the Commission shall immediately transmit to the Member States that information and any information from any other source which it may consider relevant.

2. The Member State concerned shall respond as soon as possible to requests for information from the Commission and from other Member States concerning the nature of the obstacle or threat and the action which it has taken or proposes to take.

Information exchange between Member States shall also be transmitted to the Commission.

Article 4 [Member State Duties]

1. When an obstacle occurs, and subject to Article 2, the Member State concerned shall

(a) take all necessary and proportionate measures so that the free movement of goods is assured in the territory of the Member State in accordance with the Treaty, and

(b) inform the Commission of the actions which its authorities have taken or intend to take.

2. The Commission shall immediately transmit the information received under paragraph 1(b) to the other Member States.

Article 5 [Commission Powers]

1. Where the Commission considers that an obstacle is occurring in a Member State, it shall notify the Member State concerned of the reasons that have led the Commission to such a conclusion and shall request the Member State to take all necessary and proportionate measures to remove the said obstacle within a period which it shall determine with reference to the urgency of the case.

2. In reaching its conclusion, the Commission shall have regard to Article 2.

3. The Commission may publish in the Official Journal of the European Communities the text of the notification which it has sent to the Member State concerned and shall immediately transmit the text to any party which requests it.

4. The Member State shall, within five working days of receipt of the text, either:

— inform the Commission of the steps which it has taken or intends to take to implement paragraph 1, or

— communicate a reasoned submission as to why there is no obstacle constituting a breach of Articles 30 to 36 of the Treaty.

5. In exceptional cases, the Commission may allow an extension of the deadline mentioned in paragraph 4 if the Member State submits a duly substantiated request and the grounds cited are deemed acceptable.

This Regulation shall be binding in its entirety and directly applicable in all Member States.

Done at Brussels, 7 December 1998.
For the Council, The President, J. FARNLEITNER

Directive 98/34 of the European Parliament and of the Council Laying down a Procedure for the Provision of Information in the Field of Technical Standards and Regulations and of Rules on Information Society Services[1]

THE EUROPEAN PARLIAMENT AND THE COUNCIL OF THE EUROPEAN UNION,

HAVING REGARD to the Treaty establishing the European Community, and in particular Articles 100a, 213 and 43 thereof, [...]
ACTING IN ACCORDANCE with the procedure laid down in Article 189b of the Treaty,
(1) WHEREAS Council Directive 83/189 of 28 March 1983 laying down a procedure for the provision of information in the field of technical standards and regulations has been variously and substantially amended; whereas for reasons of clarity and rationality the said Directive should be consolidated;
(2) WHEREAS the internal market comprises an area without internal frontiers in which the free movement of goods, persons, services and capital is ensured; whereas, therefore, the prohibition of quantitative restrictions on the movement of goods and of measures having an equivalent effect is one of the basic principles of the Community;
(3) WHEREAS in order to promote the smooth functioning of the internal market, as much transparency as possible should be ensured as regards national initiatives for the establishment of technical standards or regulations;
(4) WHEREAS barriers to trade resulting from technical regulations relating to products may be allowed only where they are necessary in order to meet essential requirements and have an objective in the public interest of which they constitute the main guarantee;
(5) WHEREAS it is essential for the Commission to have the necessary information at its disposal before the adoption of technical provisions; whereas, consequently, the Member States which are required to facilitate the achievement of its task pursuant to Article 5 of the Treaty must notify it of their projects in the field of technical regulations;
(6) WHEREAS all the Member States must also be informed of the technical regulations contemplated by any one Member State;
(7) WHEREAS the aim of the internal market is to create an environment that is conducive to the competitiveness of undertakings; whereas increased provision of information is one way of helping undertakings to make more of the advantages inherent in this market; whereas it is therefore necessary to enable economic operators to give their assessment of the impact of the national technical regulations proposed by other Member States, by providing for the regular publication of the titles of notified drafts and by means of the provisions relating to the confidentiality of such drafts;
(8) WHEREAS it is appropriate, in the interests of legal certainty, that Member States publicly announce that a national technical regulation has been adopted in accordance with the formalities laid down in this Directive;
(9) WHEREAS, as far as technical regulations for products are concerned, the measures designed to ensure the proper functioning or the continued development of the market include greater transparency of national intentions and a broadening of the criteria and conditions for assessing the potential effect of the proposed regulations on the market;

---

1   OJ 1998 L 204, p. 37, as amended by Directive 98/48 of the European Parliament and of the Council of 20 July 1998.

(10) WHEREAS it is therefore necessary to assess all the requirements laid down in respect of a product and to take account of developments in national practices for the regulation of products;

(11) WHEREAS requirements, other than technical specifications, referring to the life cycle of a product after it has been placed on the market are liable to affect the free movement of that product or to create obstacles to the proper functioning of the internal market;

(12) WHEREAS it is necessary to clarify the concept of a de facto technical regulation; whereas, in particular, the provisions by which the public authority refers to technical specifications or other requirements, or encourages the observance thereof, and the provisions referring to products with which the public authority is associated, in the public interest, have the effect of conferring on such requirements or specifications a more binding value than they would otherwise have by virtue of their private origin;

(13) WHEREAS the Commission and the Member States must also be allowed sufficient time in which to propose amendments to a contemplated measure, in order to remove or reduce any barriers which it might create to the free movement of goods;

(14) WHEREAS the Member State concerned must take account of these amendments when formulating the definitive text of the measure envisaged;

(15) WHEREAS it is inherent in the internal market that, in particular where the principle of mutual recognition cannot be implemented by the Member States, the Commission adopts or proposes the adoption of binding Community acts; whereas a specific temporary standstill period has been established in order to prevent the introduction of national measures from compromising the adoption of binding Community acts by the Council or the Commission in the same field;

(16) WHEREAS the Member State in question must, pursuant to the general obligations laid down in Article 5 of the Treaty, defer implementation of the contemplated measure for a period sufficient to allow either a joint examination of the proposed amendments or the preparation of a proposal for a binding act of the Council or the adoption of a binding act of the Commission; whereas the time limits laid down in the Agreement of the representatives of the Governments of the Member States meeting within the Council of 28 May 1969 providing for standstill and notification to the Commission, as amended by the Agreement of 5 March 1973, have proved inadequate in the cases concerned and should accordingly be extended;

(17) WHEREAS the procedure concerning the standstill arrangement and notification of the Commission contained in the abovementioned agreement of 28 May 1969 remains applicable to products subject to that procedure which are not covered by this Directive;

(18) WHEREAS, with a view to facilitating the adoption of Community measures by the Council, Member States should refrain from adopting technical regulations once the Council has adopted a common position on a Commission proposal concerning that sector;

(19) WHEREAS, in practice, national technical standards may have the same effects on the free movement of goods as technical regulations;

(20) WHEREAS it would therefore appear necessary to inform the Commission of draft standards under similar conditions to those which apply to technical regulations; whereas, pursuant to Article 213 of the Treaty, the Commission may, within the limits and under the conditions laid down by the Council in accordance with the provisions of the Treaty, collect any information and carry out any checks required for the performance of the tasks entrusted to it;

(21) WHEREAS it is also necessary for the Member States and the standards institutions to be informed of standards contemplated by standards institutions in the other Member States;

(22) WHEREAS systematic notification is actually necessary only in the case of new subjects for standardisation and in so far as the treatment of these subjects at national level may give rise to differences in national standards which are liable to disturb the functioning of the market as a result; whereas any subsequent notification or communication relating to the progress of national activities must depend on the interest in such activities expressed by those to whom this new subject has already been communicated;

(23) WHEREAS the Commission must nevertheless be able to request the communication of all or part of the national standardisation programmes so that it can review the development of standardisation activity in particular economic sectors;

(24) WHEREAS the European standardisation system must be organised by and for the parties concerned, on a basis of coherence, transparency, openness, consensus, independence of special interests, efficiency and decision-making based on national representation;

(25) WHEREAS the functioning of standardisation in the Community must be based on fundamental rights for the national standardisation bodies, such as the possibility of obtaining draft standards, being informed of the action taken in response to comments submitted, being associated with national standardisation activities or requesting the preparation of European standards in place of national standards; whereas it is for the Member States to take the appropriate measures in their power to ensure that their standardisation bodies observe these rights;

(26) WHEREAS the provisions concerning the standstill arrangements applicable to national standardisation bodies when a European standard is in preparation must be brought into line with the relevant provisions adopted by the standardisation bodies within the framework of the European standardisation bodies;

(27) WHEREAS it is necessary to set up a Standing Committee, the members of which will be appointed by the Member States with the task of helping the Commission to examine draft national standards and cooperating in its efforts to lessen any adverse effects thereof on the free movement of goods;

(28) WHEREAS the Standing Committee should be consulted on the draft standardisation requests referred to in this Directive;

(29) WHEREAS this Directive must not affect the obligations of the Member States concerning the deadlines for transposition of the Directives set out in Annex III, Part B,

HAVE ADOPTED THIS DIRECTIVE:

Article 1 [Definitions]
For the purposes of this Directive, the following meanings shall apply:
1. "product" any industrially manufactured product and any agricultural product, including fish products;
2. "service", any Information Society service, that is to say, any service normally provided for remuneration, at a distance, by electronic means and at the individual request of a recipient of services.

For the purposes of this definition:
— "at a distance" means that the service is provided without the parties being simultaneously present,
— "by electronic means" means that the service is sent initially and received at its destination by means of electronic equipment for the processing (including digital compression) and storage of data, and entirely transmitted, conveyed and received by wire, by radio, by optical means or by other electromagnetic means,
— "at the individual request of a recipient of services" means that the service is provided through the transmission of data on individual request.

An indicative list of services not covered by this definition is set out in Annex V. This Directive shall not apply to:
— radio broadcasting services,
— television broadcasting services covered by point (a) of Article 1 of Directive 89/552.[1]

3. "technical specification", a specification contained in a document which lays down the characteristics required of a product such as levels of quality, performance, safety or dimensions, including the requirements applicable to the product as regards the name under which the product is sold, terminology, symbols, testing and test methods, packaging, marking or labelling and conformity assessment procedures. The term "technical specification" also covers production methods and processes used in respect of agricultural products as referred to Article 38(1) of the Treaty, products intended for human and animal consumption, and medicinal products as defined in Article 1 of Directive 65/65[2], as well as production methods and processes relating to other products, where these have an effect on their characteristics;

4. "other requirements", a requirement, other than a technical specification, imposed on a product for the purpose of protecting, in particular, consumers or the environment, and which affects its life cycle after it has been placed on the market, such as conditions of use, recycling, reuse or disposal, where such conditions can significantly influence the composition or nature of the product or its marketing;

5. "rule on services", requirement of a general nature relating to the taking-up and pursuit of service activities within the meaning of point 2, in particular provisions concerning the service provider, the services and the recipient of services, excluding any rules which are not specifically aimed at the services defined in that point.

This Directive shall not apply to rules relating to matters which are covered by Community legislation in the field of telecommunications services, as defined by Directive 90/387.[3]

This Directive shall not apply to rules relating to matters which are covered by Community legislation in the field of financial services, as listed non-exhaustively in Annex VI to this Directive.

With the exception of Article 8(3), this Directive shall not apply to rules enacted by or for regulated markets within the meaning of Directive 93/22 or by or for other markets or bodies carrying out clearing or settlement functions for those markets.

For the purposes of this definition:
— a rule shall be considered to be specifically aimed at Information Society services where, having regard to its statement of reasons and its operative part, the specific aim and object of all or some of its individual provisions is to regulate such services in an explicit and targeted manner,
— a rule shall not be considered to be specifically aimed at Information Society services if it affects such services only in an implicit or incidental manner.

6. "standard", a technical specification approved by a recognised standardisation body for repeated or continuous application, with which compliance is not compulsory and which is one of the following:

---

1   OJ 1989 L 298, p. 23, [as amended].

2   Council Directive 65/65 of 26 January 1965 on the approximation of provisions laid down by law, regulation or administrative action relating to medicinal products, OJ 1965 No. 22, 9 February 1965, p. 369/65, [as amended].

3   OJ 1990 L 192, p. 1, [as amended].

— international standard: a standard adopted by an international standardisation organisation and made available to the public,
— European standard: a standard adopted by a European standardisation body and made available to the public,
— national standard: a standard adopted by a national standardisation body and made available to the public;

7. "standards programme", a work programme of a recognised standardisation body listing the subjects on which standardisation work is being carried out;

8. "draft standard", document containing the text of the technical specifications concerning a given subject, which is being considered for adoption in accordance with the national standards procedure, as that document stands after the preparatory work and as circulated for public comment or scrutiny;

9. "European standardisation body", a body referred to in Annex I;

10. "national standardisation body", a body referred to in Annex II;

11. "technical regulation", technical specifications and other requirements or rules on services, including the relevant administrative provisions, the observance of which is compulsory, de jure or de facto, in the case of marketing, provision of a service, establishment of a service operator or use in a Member State or a major part thereof, as well as laws, regulations or administrative provisions of Member States, except those provided for in Article 10, prohibiting the manufacture, importation, marketing or use of a product or prohibiting the provision or use of a service, or establishment as a service provider.

De facto technical regulations include:
— laws, regulations or administrative provisions of a Member State which refer either to technical specifications or to other requirements or to rules on services, or to professional codes or codes of practice which in turn refer to technical specifications or to other requirements or to rules on services, compliance with which confers a presumption of conformity with the obligations imposed by the aforementioned laws, regulations or administrative provisions,
— voluntary agreements to which a public authority is a contracting party and which provide, in the general interest, for compliance with technical specifications or other requirements or rules on services, excluding public procurement tender specifications,
— technical specifications or other requirements or rules on services which are linked to fiscal or financial measures affecting the consumption of products or services by encouraging compliance with such technical specifications or other requirements or rules on services; technical specifications or other requirements or rules on services linked to national social security systems are not included.

This comprises technical regulations imposed by the authorities designated by the Member States and appearing on a list to be drawn up by the Commission before 5 August 1999, in the framework of the Committee referred to in Article 5.

The same procedure shall be used for amending this list;

12. "draft technical regulation", the text of a technical specification or other requirement or of a rule on services, including administrative provisions, formulated with the aim of enacting it or of ultimately having it enacted as a technical regulation, the text being at a stage of preparation at which substantial amendments can still be made.

This Directive shall not apply to those measures Member States consider necessary under the Treaty for the protection of persons, in particular workers, when products are used, provided that such measures do not affect the products.

Article 2 [Systematic Information Regarding New or Amended Standards]

1.   The Commission and the standardisation bodies referred to in Annexes I and II shall be informed of the new subjects for which the national bodies referred to in Annex II have decided, by including them in their standards programme, to prepare or amend a standard, unless it is an identical or equivalent transposition of an international or European standard.

2.   The information referred to in paragraph 1 shall indicate, in particular, whether the standard concerned:
— will transpose an international standard without being the equivalent,
— will be a new national standard, or
— will amend a national standard.

After consulting the Committee referred to in Article 5, the Commission may draw up rules for the consolidated presentation of this information and a plan and criteria governing the presentation of this information in order to facilitate its evaluation.

3.   The Commission may ask for all or part of the standards programmes to be communicated to it. It shall make this information available to the Member States in a form which allows the different programmes to be assessed and compared.

4.   Where appropriate, the Commission shall amend Annex II on the basis of communications from the Member States.

5.   The Council shall decide, on the basis of a proposal from the Commission, on any amendment to Annex I.

Article 3 [Submission of Draft Standards]

The standardisation bodies referred to in Annexes I and II, and the Commission, shall be sent all draft standards on request; they shall be kept informed by the body concerned of the action taken on any comments they have made relating to drafts.

Article 4 [Duties of Member States]

1.   Member States shall take all necessary steps to ensure that their standardisation bodies:
— communicate information in accordance with Articles 2 and 3,
— publish the draft standards in such a way that comments may also be obtained from parties established in other Member States,
— grant the other bodies referred to in Annex II the right to be involved passively or actively (by sending an observer) in the planned activities,
— do not object to a subject for standardisation in their work programme being discussed at European level in accordance with the rules laid down by the European standardisation bodies and undertake no action which may prejudice a decision in this regard.

2.   Member States shall refrain in particular from any act of recognition, approval or use by reference to a national standard adopted in breach of Articles 2 and 3 and of paragraph 1 of this Article.

Article 5 [The Standing Committee]

A Standing Committee shall be set up consisting of representatives appointed by the Member States who may call on the assistance of experts or advisers; its chairman shall be a representative of the Commission. The Committee shall draw up its own rules of procedure.

Article 6 [Tasks of the Standing Committee]

1.   The Committee shall meet at least twice a year with the representatives of the standards institutions referred to in Annexes I and II.

The Committee shall meet in a specific composition to examine questions concerning Information Society services.

2. The Commission shall submit to the Committee a report on the implementation and application of the procedures set out in this Directive, and shall present proposals aimed at eliminating existing or foreseeable barriers to trade.

3. The Committee shall express its opinion on the communications and proposals referred to in paragraph 2 and may in this connection propose, in particular, that the Commission:

— request the European standards institutions to draw up a European standard within a given time limit,
— ensure where necessary, in order to avoid the risk of barriers to trade, that initially the Member States concerned decide amongst themselves on appropriate measures,
— take all appropriate measures,
— identify the areas where harmonisation appears necessary, and, should the case arise, undertake appropriate harmonisation in a given sector.

4. The Committee must be consulted by the Commission:
(a) before any amendment is made to the lists in Annexes I and II (Article 2(1));
(b) when drawing up the rules for the consolidated presentation of information and the plan and criteria for the presentation of standards programmes (Article 2(2));
(c) when deciding on the actual system whereby the exchange of information provided for in this Directive is to be effected and on any change to it;
(d) when reviewing the operation of the system set up by this Directive;
(e) on the requests to the standards institutions referred to in the first indent of paragraph 3.

5. The Committee may be consulted by the Commission on any preliminary draft technical regulation received by the latter.

6. Any question regarding the implementation of this Directive may be submitted to the Committee at the request of its chairman or of a Member State.

7. The proceedings of the Committee and the information to be submitted to it shall be confidential. However, the Committee and the national authorities may, provided that the necessary precautions are taken, consult, for an expert opinion, natural or legal persons, including persons in the private sector.

8. With respect to rules on services, the Commission and the Committee may consult natural or legal persons from industry or academia, and where possible representative bodies, capable of delivering an expert opinion on the social and societal aims and consequences of any draft rule on services, and take notice of their advice whenever requested to do so.

Article 7 [Standstill-Obligation During Preparation of European Standards]
1. Member States shall take all appropriate measures to ensure that, during the preparation of a European standard referred to in the first indent of Article 6(3) or after its approval, their standardisation bodies do not take any action which could prejudice the harmonisation intended and, in particular, that they do not publish in the field in question a new or revised national standard which is not completely in line with an existing European standard.

2. Paragraph 1 shall not apply to the work of standards institutions undertaken at the request of the public authorities to draw up technical specifications or a standard for specific products for the purpose of enacting a technical regulation for such products. Member States shall communicate all requests of the kind referred to in the preceding subparagraph to the Commission as draft technical regulations, in accordance with Article 8(1), and shall state the grounds for their enactment.

Article 8 [Submission of National Technical Regulations]
1.   Subject to Article 10, Member States shall immediately communicate to the Commission any draft technical regulation, except where it merely transposes the full text of an international or European standard, in which case information regarding the relevant standard shall suffice; they shall also let the Commission have a statement of the grounds which make the enactment of such a technical regulation necessary, where these have not already been made clear in the draft.

Where appropriate, and unless it has already been sent with a prior communication, Member States shall simultaneously communicate the text of the basic legislative or regulatory provisions principally and directly concerned, should knowledge of such text be necessary to assess the implications of the draft technical regulation.

Member States shall communicate the draft again under the above conditions if they make changes to the draft that have the effect of significantly altering its scope, shortening the timetable originally envisaged for implementation, adding specifications or requirements, or making the latter more restrictive.

Where, in particular, the draft seeks to limit the marketing or use of a chemical substance, preparation or product on grounds of public health or of the protection of consumers or the environment, Member States shall also forward either a summary or the references of all relevant data relating to the substance, preparation or product concerned and to known and available substitutes, where such information may be available, and communicate the anticipated effects of the measure on public health and the protection of the consumer and the environment, together with an analysis of the risk carried out as appropriate in accordance with the general principles for the risk evaluation of chemical substances as referred to in Article 10(4) of Regulation 793/93[1] in the case of an existing substance or in Article 3(2) of Directive 67/548[2], in the case of a new substance.

The Commission shall immediately notify the other Member States of the draft and all documents which have been forwarded to it; it may also refer this draft, for an opinion, to the Committee referred to in Article 5 and, where appropriate, to the committee responsible for the field in question.

With respect to the technical specifications or other requirements or rules on services referred to in the third indent of the second subparagraph of point 11 of Article 1, the comments or detailed opinions of the Commission or Member States may concern only aspects which may hinder trade or, in respect of rules on services, the free movement of services or the freedom of establishment of service operators and not the fiscal or financial aspects of the measure.
2.   The Commission and the Member States may make comments to the Member State which has forwarded a draft technical regulation; that Member State shall take such comments into account as far as possible in the subsequent preparation of the technical regulation.
3.   Member States shall communicate the definitive text of a technical regulation to the Commission without delay.
4.   Information supplied under this Article shall not be confidential except at the express request of the notifying Member State. Any such request shall be supported by

---

1   Council Regulation 793/93 of 23 March 1993 on the evaluation and control of the risks of existing substances, OJ 1993 L 84, p. 1.

2   Council Directive 67/548 of 27 June 1967 on the approximation of the laws, regulations and administrative provisions relating to the classification, packaging and labeling of dangerous substances, OJ 1967 L 196, [as amended].

reasons. In cases of this kind, if necessary precautions are taken, the Committee referred to in Article 5 and the national authorities may seek expert advice from physical or legal persons in the private sector.

5. When draft technical regulations form part of measures which are required to be communicated to the Commission at the draft stage under another Community act, Member States may make a communication within the meaning of paragraph 1 under that other act, provided that they formally indicate that the said communication also constitutes a communication for the purposes of this Directive. The absence of a reaction from the Commission under this Directive to a draft technical regulation shall not prejudice any decision which might be taken under other Community acts.

Article 9 [Obligation to Postpone the Adoption of National Technical Regulations]
1. Member States shall postpone the adoption of a draft technical regulation for three months from the date of receipt by the Commission of the communication referred to in Article 8(1).
2. Member States shall postpone:
— for four months the adoption of a draft technical regulation in the form of a voluntary agreement within the meaning of the second indent of the second subparagraph of point 11 of Article 1,
— without prejudice to paragraphs 3, 4 and 5, for six months the adoption of any other draft technical regulation (except for draft rules on services),
from the date of receipt by the Commission of the communication referred to in Article 8(1) if the Commission or another Member State delivers a detailed opinion, within three months of that date, to the effect that the measure envisaged may create obstacles to the free movement of goods within the internal market;
— without prejudice to paragraphs 4 and 5, for four months the adoption of any draft rule on services, from the date of receipt by the Commission of the communication referred to in Article 8(1) if the Commission or another Member State delivers a detailed opinion, within three months of that date, to the effect that the measure envisaged may create obstacles to the free movement of services or to the freedom of establishment of service operators within the internal market.
With regard to draft rules on services, detailed opinions from the Commission or Member States may not affect any cultural policy measures, in particular in the audiovisual sphere, which Member States might adopt in accordance with Community law, taking account of their linguistic diversity, their specific national and regional characteristics and their cultural heritage.

The Member State concerned shall report to the Commission on the action it proposes to take on such detailed opinions. The Commission shall comment on this reaction.

With respect to rules on services, the Member State concerned shall indicate, where appropriate, the reasons why the detailed opinions cannot be taken into account.
3. With the exclusion of draft rules relating to services, Member States shall postpone the adoption of a draft technical regulation for twelve months from the date of receipt by the Commission of the communication referred to in Article 8(1) if, within three months of that date, the Commission announces its intention of proposing or adopting a directive, regulation or decision on the matter in accordance with Article 189 of the Treaty.
4. Member States shall postpone the adoption of a draft technical regulation for 12 months from the date of receipt by the Commission of the communication referred to in Article 8(1) if, within the three months following that date, the Commission announces its finding that the draft technical regulation concerns a matter which is covered by

a proposal for a directive, regulation or decision presented to the Council in accordance with Article 189 of the Treaty.

5.   If the Council adopts a common position during the standstill period referred to in paragraphs 3 and 4, that period shall, subject to paragraph 6, be extended to 18 months.

6.   The obligations referred to in paragraphs 3, 4 and 5 shall lapse:
—   when the Commission informs the Member States that it no longer intends to propose or adopt a binding Community act,
—   when the Commission informs the Member States of the withdrawal of its draft or proposal,
—   when the Commission or the Council has adopted a binding Community act.

7.   Paragraphs 1 to 5 shall not apply in cases where:
—   for urgent reasons, occasioned by serious and unforeseeable circumstances relating to the protection of public health or safety, the protection of animals or the preservation of plants, and for rules on services, also for public policy, notably the protection of minors, a Member State is obliged to prepare technical regulations in a very short space of time in order to enact and introduce them immediately without any consultations being possible or
—   for urgent reasons occasioned by serious circumstances relating to the protection of the security and the integrity of the financial system, notably the protection of depositors, investors and insured persons, a Member State is obliged to enact and implement rules on financial services immediately.

In the communication referred to in Article 8, the Member State shall give reasons for the urgency of the measures taken. The Commission shall give its views on the communication as soon as possible. It shall take appropriate action in cases where improper use is made of this procedure. The European Parliament shall be kept informed by the Commission.

Article 10 [Exceptions to Articles 8 and 9]

1.   Articles 8 and 9 shall not apply to those laws, regulations and administrative provisions of the Member States or voluntary agreements by means of which Member States:
—   comply with binding Community acts which result in the adoption of technical specifications or rules on services,
—   fulfil the obligations arising out of international agreements which result in the adoption of common technical specifications or rules on services in the Community;
—   make use of safeguard clauses provided for in binding Community acts,
—   apply Article 8(1) of Directive 92/59,[1]
—   restrict themselves to implementing a judgment of the Court of Justice of the European Communities,
—   restrict themselves to amending a technical regulation within the meaning of point 11 of Article 1, in accordance with a Commission request, with a view to removing an obstacle to trade or, in the case of rules on services, to the free movement of services or the freedom of establishment of service operators.

2.   Article 9 shall not apply to the laws, regulations and administrative provisions of the Member States prohibiting manufacture insofar as they do not impede the free movement of products.

3.   Paragraphs 3 to 6 of Article 9 shall not apply to the voluntary agreements referred to in the second indent of the second subparagraph of point 11 of Article 1.

---

1   Council Directive 92/59 of 29 June 1992 on general product safety, see below, p. 587.

4.   Article 9 shall not apply to the technical specifications or other requirements or the rules on services referred to in the third indent of the second subparagraph of point 11 of Article 1.

Article 11 [Reports on the Functioning of this Directive]

The Commission shall report every two years to the European Parliament, the Council and the Economic and Social Committee on the results of the application of this Directive. Lists of standardisation work entrusted to the European standardisation organisations pursuant to this Directive, as well as statistics on the notifications received, shall be published on an annual basis in the Official Journal of the European Communities.

Article 12 [National References to this Directive]

When Member States adopt a technical regulation, it shall contain a reference to this Directive or shall be accompanied by such reference on the occasion of its official publication. The methods of making such reference shall be laid down by Member States.

Article 13 [Repeal of Preceding Legislation]

1.   The Directives and Decisions listed in Annex III, Part A are hereby repealed without prejudice to the obligations of the Member States concerning the deadlines for transposition of the said Directives, set out in Annex III, Part B.
2.   References to the repealed directives and decisions shall be construed as references to this Directive and shall be read in accordance with the correlation table set out in Annex IV.

Article 14 [Entry into Force]

This Directive shall enter into force on the 20th day following that of its publication in the Official Journal of the European Communities.

Article 15 [Addressees]

This Directive is addressed to the Member States.

Done at Luxembourg, 22 June 1998.
For the European Parliament, The President, J. M. GIL-ROBLES
For the Council, The President, J. CUNNINGHAM

ANNEX I: EUROPEAN STANDARDISATION BODIES
CEN: European Committee for Standardisation
Cenelec: European Committee for Electrotechnical Standardisation
ETSI: European Telecommunications Standards Institute

ANNEX II: NATIONAL STANDARDISATION BODIES [...]

ANNEX V: INDICATIVE LIST OF SERVICES NOT COVERED BY THE SECOND SUBPARAGRAPH OF POINT 2 OF ARTICLE 1
1.   Services not provided "at a distance"
Services provided in the physical presence of the provider and the recipient, even if they involve the use of electronic devices
(a) medical examinations or treatment at a doctor's surgery using electronic equipment where the patient is physically present;
(b) consultation of an electronic catalogue in a shop with the customer on site;
(c) plane ticket reservation at a travel agency in the physical presence of the customer by means of a network of computers;
(d) electronic games made available in a video-arcade where the customer is physically present.

2.   Services not provided "by electronic means"
—   Services having material content even though provided via electronic devices:
     (a)   automatic cash or ticket dispensing machines (banknotes, rail tickets);
     (b)   access to road networks, car parks, etc., charging for use, even if there are electronic
           devices at the entrance/exit controlling access and/or ensuring correct payment is
           made,
—   Off-line services: distribution of CD-ROMs or software on diskettes,
—   Services which are not provided via electronic processing/inventory systems:
     (a)   voice telephony services;
     (b)   telefax/telex services;
     (c)   services provided via voice telephony or fax;
     (d)   telephone/telefax consultation of a doctor;
     (e)   telephone/telefax consultation of a lawyer;
     (f)   telephone/telefax direct marketing.
3.   Services not supplied "at the individual request of a recipient of services"
Services provided by transmitting data without individual demand for simultaneous reception
by an unlimited number of individual receivers (point to multipoint transmission):
(a) television broadcasting services (including near-video on-demand services), covered by
     point (a) of Article 1 of Directive 89/552;
(b) radio broadcasting services;
(c) (televised) teletext.

ANNEX VI: INDICATIVE LIST OF THE FINANCIAL SERVICES COVERED BY THE THIRD
SUBPARAGRAPH OF POINT 5 OF ARTICLE 1
—   Investment services
—   Insurance and reinsurance operations
—   Banking services
—   Operations relating to pension funds
—   Services relating to dealings in futures or options
     Such services include in particular:
     (a)   investment services referred to in the Annex to Directive 93/22;[1] services of collective
           investment undertakings,
     (b)   services covered by the activities subject to mutual recognition referred to in the
           Annex to Directive 89/646,[2]
     (c)   operations covered by the insurance and reinsurance activities referred to in:
           —   Article 1 of Directive 73/239,[3]
           —   the Annex to Directive 79/267,[4]
           —   Directive 64/225,[5]
           —   Directives 92/49[6] and 92/96[7].

1   OJ 1993 L 141, p. 27.

2   OJ 1989 L 386, p. 1, [as amended].

3   OJ 1973 L 228, p. 3, [as amended].

4   OJ 1979 L 63, p. 1, [as amended].

5   OJ 1964 No. 56, p. 878/64, [as amended].

6   OJ 1992 L 228, p. 1.

7   OJ 1992 L 360, p. 1.

Council Regulation 2081/92 of 14 July 1992 on the Protection of Geographical Indications and Designations of Origin for Agricultural Products and Foodstuffs[1]

THE COUNCIL OF THE EUROPEAN COMMUNITIES,

HAVING REGARD to the Treaty establishing the European Economic Community, and in particular Article 43, [...]

(1) WHEREAS the production, manufacture and distribution of agricultural products and foodstuffs play an important role in the Community economy;

(2) WHEREAS, as part of the adjustment of the common agricultural policy the diversification of agricultural production should be encouraged so as to achieve a better balance between supply and demand on the markets; whereas the promotion of products having certain characteristics could be of considerable benefit to the rural economy, in particular to less-favoured or remote areas, by improving the incomes of farmers and by retaining the rural population in these areas;

(3) WHEREAS, moreover, it has been observed in recent years that consumers are tending to attach greater importance to the quality of foodstuffs rather than to quantity; whereas this quest for specific products generates a growing demand for agricultural products or foodstuffs with an identifiable geographical origin;

(4) WHEREAS in view of the wide variety of products marketed and of the abundance of information concerning them provided, consumers must, in order to be able to make the best choice, be given clear and succinct information regarding the origin of the product;

(5) WHEREAS the labelling of agricultural products and foodstuffs is subject to the general rules laid down in Council Directive 79/112 of 18 December 1978 on the approximation of the laws of the Member States relating to the labelling, presentation and advertising of foodstuffs;[2] whereas, in view of their specific nature, additional special provisions should be adopted for agricultural products and foodstuffs from a specified geographical area;

(6) WHEREAS the desire to protect agricultural products or foodstuffs which have an identifiable geographical origin has led certain Member States to introduce "registered designations of origin"; whereas these have proved successful with producers, who have secured higher incomes in return for a genuine effort to improve quality, and with consumers, who can purchase high quality products with guarantees as to the method of production and origin;

(7) WHEREAS, however, there is diversity in the national practices for implementing registered designations or origin and geographical indications; whereas a Community approach should be envisaged; whereas a framework of Community rules on protection will permit the development of geographical indications and designations of origin since, by providing a more uniform approach, such a framework will ensure fair competition between the producers of products bearing such indications and enhance the credibility of the products in the consumers' eyes;

(8) WHEREAS the planned rules should take account of existing Community legislation on wines and spirit drinks, which provide for a higher level of protection;

---

1 OJ 1992 L 208, p. 1, as amended by Council Regulation 535/97 of 17 March 1997, OJ 1997 L 83, p. 3, and Commission Regulation 1068/97 of 12 June 1997, OJ 1997 L 156, p. 10.

2 OJ 1979 L 33, p. 1. [as amended]

(9) WHEREAS the scope of this Regulation is limited to certain agricultural products and foodstuffs for which a link between product or foodstuff characteristics and geographical origin exists; whereas, however, this scope could be enlarged to encompass other products or foodstuffs;

(10) WHEREAS existing practices make it appropriate to define two different types of geographical description, namely protected geographical indications and protected designations of origin;

(11) WHEREAS an agricultural product or foodstuff bearing such an indication must meet certain conditions set out in a specification;

(12) WHEREAS to enjoy protection in every Member State geographical indications and designations of origin must be registered at Community level; whereas entry in a register should also provide information to those involved in trade and to consumers;

(13) WHEREAS the registration procedure should enable any person individually and directly concerned in a Member State to exercise his rights by notifying the Commission of his opposition;

(14) WHEREAS there should be procedures to permit amendment of the specification, after registration, in the light of technological progress or withdrawal from the register of the geographical indication or designation of origin of an agricultural product or foodstuff if that product or foodstuff ceases to conform to the specification on the basis of which the geographical indication or designation of origin was granted;

(15) WHEREAS provision should be made for trade with third countries offering equivalent guarantees for the issue and inspection of geographical indications or designations of origin granted on their territory;

(16) WHEREAS provision should be made for a procedure establishing close cooperation between the Member States and the Commission through a Regulatory Committee set up for that purpose,

HAS ADOPTED THIS REGULATION:

Article 1 [Scope of Application]
1.   This Regulation lays down rules on the protection of designations of origin and geographical indications of agricultural products intended for human consumption referred to in Annex II to the Treaty and of the foodstuffs referred to in Annex I to this Regulation and agricultural products listed in Annex II to this Regulation. However, this Regulation shall not apply to wine products or to spirit drinks. Annexes I and II may be amended in accordance with the procedure set out in Article 15.
2.   This Regulation shall apply without prejudice to other specific Community provisions.
3.   Council Directive 83/189 of 28 March 1983 laying down a procedure for the provision of information in the field of technical standards and regulations[1] shall not apply to the designations of origin and geographical indications covered by this Regulation.

Article 2 [Protected Designations of Origin and Protected Geographical Indications]
1.   Community protection of designations of origin and of geographical indications of agricultural products and foodstuffs shall be obtained in accordance with this Regulation.
2.   For the purposes of this Regulation:
(a) designation of origin: means the name of a region, a specific place or, in exceptional cases, a country, used to describe an agricultural product or a foodstuff:

---

1   This Directive has been replaced in the meantime by Dir 98/34, see above p. 311.

— originating in that region, specific place or country, and
— the quality or characteristics of which are essentially or exclusively due to a particular geographical environment with its inherent natural and human factors, and the production, processing and preparation of which take place in the defined geographical area;

(b) geographical indication: means the name of a region, a specific place or, in exceptional cases, a country, used to describe an agricultural product or a foodstuff:
— originating in that region, specific place or country, and
— which possesses a specific quality, reputation or other characteristics attributable to that geographical origin and the production and/or processing and/or preparation of which take place in the defined geographical area.

3. Certain traditional geographical or non-geographical names designating an agricultural product or a foodstuff originating in a region or a specific place, which fulfil the conditions referred to in the second indent of paragraph 2 (a) shall also be considered as designations of origin.

4. By way of derogation from Article 2 (a), certain geographical designations shall be treated as designations of origin where the raw materials of the products concerned come from a geographical area larger than or different from the processing area, provided that:
— the production area of the raw materials is limited,
— special conditions for the production of the raw materials exist, and
— there are inspection arrangements to ensure that those conditions are adhered to.

5. For the purposes of paragraph 4, only live animals, meat and milk may be considered as raw materials. Use of other raw materials may be authorized in accordance with the procedure laid down in Article 15.

6. In order to be eligible for the derogation provided for in paragraph 4, the designations in question may be or have already been recognized as designations of origin with national protection by the Member State concerned, or, if no such scheme exists, have a proven, traditional character and an exceptional reputation and renown.

7. In order to be eligible for the derogation provided for in paragraph 4, applications for registration must be lodged within two years of the entry into force of this Regulation.

Article 3 [Generic Names Not to Be Registered]

1. Names that have become generic may not be registered.

For the purposes of this Regulation, a "name that has become generic" means the name of an agricultural product or a foodstuff which, although it relates to the place or the region where this product or foodstuff was originally produced or marketed, has become the common name of an agricultural product or a foodstuff.

To establish whether or not a name has become generic, account shall be taken of all factors, in particular:
— the existing situation in the Member State in which the name originates and in areas of consumption,
— the existing situation in other Member States,
— the relevant national or Community laws.

Where, following the procedure laid down in Articles 6 and 7, an application of registration is rejected because a name has become generic, the Commission shall publish that decision in the Official Journal of the European Communities.

2. A name may not be registered as a designation of origin or a geographical indication where it conflicts with the name of a plant variety or an animal breed and as a result is likely to mislead the public as to the true origin of the product.

3.   Before the entry into force of this Regulation, the Council, acting by a qualified majority on a proposal from the Commission, shall draw up and publish in the Official Journal of the European Communities a non-exhaustive, indicative list of the names of agricultural products or foodstuffs which are within the scope of this Regulation and are regarded under the terms of paragraph 1 as being generic and thus not able to be registered under this Regulation.

Article 4 [Product Specifications]

1.   To be eligible to use a protected designation of origin (PDO) or a protected geographical indication (PGI) an agricultural product or foodstuff must comply with a specification.
2.   The product specification shall include at least:
(a) the name of the agricultural product or foodstuffs, including the designation of origin or the geographical indication;
(b) a description of the agricultural product or foodstuff including the raw materials, if appropriate, and principal physical, chemical, microbiological and/or organoleptic characteristics of the product or the foodstuff;
(c) the definition of the geographical area and, if appropriate, details indicating compliance with the requirements in Article 2 (4);
(d) evidence that the agricultural product or the foodstuff originates in the geographical area, within the meaning of Article 2 (2) (a) or (b), whichever is applicable;
(e) a description of the method of obtaining the agricultural product or foodstuff and, if appropriate, the authentic and unvarying local methods;
(f) the details bearing out the link with the geographical environment or the geographical origin within the meaning of Article 2 (2) (a) or (b), whichever is applicable;
(g) details of the inspection structures provided for in Article 10;
(h) the specific labelling details relating to the indication PDO or PGI, whichever is applicable, or the equivalent traditional national indications;
(i) any requirements laid down by Community and/or national provisions.

Article 5 [Applications for Registration]

1.   Only a group or, subject to certain conditions to be laid down in accordance with the procedure provided for in Article 15, a natural or legal person, shall be entitled to apply for registration.
   For the purposes of this Article, "Group" means any association, irrespective of its legal form or composition, of producers and/or processors working with the same agricultural product or foodstuff. Other interested parties may participate in the group.
2.   A group or a natural or legal person may apply for registration only in respect of agricultural products or foodstuffs which it produces or obtains within the meaning of Article 2 (2) (a) or (b).
3.   The application for registration shall include the product specification referred to in Article 4.
4.   The application shall be sent to the Member State in which the geographical area is located.
5.   The Member State shall check that the application is justified and shall forward the application, including the product specification referred to in Article 4 and other documents on which it has based its decision, to the Commission, if it considers that it satisfies the requirements of this Regulation.
   That Member State may, on a transitional basis only, grant on the national level a protection in the sense of the present Regulation to the name forwarded in the manner prescribed, and, where appropriate, an adjustment period, as from the date of such for-

warding; these may also be granted transitionally subject to the same conditions in connection with an application for the amendment of the product specification.

Such transitional national protection shall cease on the date on which a decision on registration under this Regulation is taken. When that decision is taken, a period of up to five years may be allowed for adjustment, on condition that the undertakings concerned have legally marketed the products in question, using the names concerned continuously, for at least five years prior to the date of the publication provided for in Article 6 (2).

The consequences of such national protection, where a name is not registered under this Regulation, shall be the sole responsibility of the Member State concerned.

The measures taken by Member States under the second subparagraph shall produce effects at national level only; they shall have no effect on intra-Community trade.

If the application concerns a name indicating a geographical area situated in another Member State also, that Member State shall be consulted before any decision is taken.

6.   Member States shall introduce the laws, regulations and administrative provisions necessary to comply with this Article.

Article 6 [Investigation Procedure]

1.   Within a period of six months the Commission shall verify, by means of a formal investigation, whether the registration application includes all the particulars provided for in Article 4. The Commission shall inform the Member State concerned of its findings.

2.   If, after taking account of paragraph 1, the Commission concludes that the name qualifies for protection, it shall publish in the Official Journal of the European Communities the name and address of the applicant, the name of the product, the main points of the application, the references to national provisions governing the preparation, production or manufacture of the product and, if necessary, the grounds for its conclusions.

3.   If no statement of objections is notified to the Commission in accordance with Article 7, the name shall be entered in a register kept by the Commission entitled "Register of protected designations of origin and protected geographical indications", which shall contain the names of the groups and the inspection bodies concerned.

4.   The Commission shall publish in the Official Journal of the European Communities:
— the names entered in the Register,
— amendments to the Register made in accordance with Article 9 and 11.

5.   If, in the light of the investigation provided for in paragraph 1, the Commission concludes that the name does not qualify for protection, it shall decide, in accordance with the procedure provided for in Article 15, not to proceed with the publication provided for in paragraph 2 of this Article.

Before publication as provided for in paragraphs 2 and 4 and registration as provided for in paragraph 3, the Commission may request the opinion of the Committee provided for in Article 15.

Article 7 [Objections to an Application or Registration]

1.   Within six months of the date of publication in the Official Journal of the European Communities referred to in Article 6 (2), any Member State may object to the registration.

2.   The competent authorities of the Member States shall ensure that all persons who can demonstrate a legitimate economic interest are authorized to consult the application. In addition and in accordance with the existing situation in the Member States, the Member States may provide access to other parties with a legitimate interest.

3.   Any legitimately concerned natural or legal person may object to the proposed registration by sending a duly substantiated statement to the competent authority of the Member State in which he resides or is established. The competent authority shall take the necessary measures to consider these comments or objection within the deadlines laid down.

4.   A statement of objection shall be admissible only if it:
— either shows non-compliance with the conditions referred to in Article 2,
— shows that the registration of the name proposed would jeopardize the existence of an entirely or partly identical name or of a mark or the existence of products which have been legally on the market for at least five years preceding the date of the publication provided for in Article 6 (2).
— or indicates the features which demonstrate that the name whose registration is applied for is generic in nature.

5.   Where an objection is admissible within the meaning of paragraph 4, the Commission shall ask the Member States concerned to seek agreement among themselves in accordance with their internal procedures within three months. If:

(a) agreement is reached, the Member States in question shall communicate to the Commission all the factors which made agreement possible together with the applicant's opinion and that of the objector. Where there has been no change to the information received under Article 5, the Commission shall proceed in accordance with Article 6 (4). If there has been a change, it shall again initiate the procedure laid down in Article 7;

(b) no agreement is reached, the Commission shall take a decision in accordance with the procedure laid down in Article 15, having regard to traditional fair practice and of the actual likelihood of confusion. Should it decide to proceed with registration, the Commission shall carry out publication in accordance with Article 6 (4).

Article 8 [Exclusivity of this Regulation]
The indications PDO, PGI or equivalent traditional national indications may appear only on agricultural products and foodstuffs that comply with this Regulation.

Article 9 [Amendments of Product Specifications]
The Member State concerned may request the amendment of a specification, in particular to take account of developments in scientific and technical knowledge or to redefine the geographical area. The Article 6 procedure shall apply *mutatis mutandis.*

The Commission may, however, decide, under the procedure laid down in Article 15, not to apply the Article 6 procedure in the case of a minor amendment.

Article 10 [Member States' Duty to Establish Inspection Structures]
1.   Member States shall ensure that not later than six months after the entry into force of this Regulation inspection structures are in place, the function of which shall be to ensure that agricultural products and foodstuffs bearing a protected name meet the requirements laid down in the specifications.

2.   An inspection structure may comprise one or more designated inspection authorities and/or private bodies approved for that purpose by the Member State. Member States shall send the Commission lists of the authorities and/or bodies approved and their respective powers. The Commission shall publish those particulars in the Official Journal of the European Communities.

3.   Designated inspection authorities and/or approved private bodies must offer adequate guarantees of objectivity and impartiality with regard to all producers or processors subject to their control and have permanently at their disposal the qualified

staff and resources necessary to carry out inspection of agricultural products and foodstuffs bearing a protected name.

If an inspection structure uses the services of another body for some inspections, that body must offer the same guarantees. In that event the designated inspection authorities and/or approved private bodies shall, however, continue to be responsible vis-á-vis the Member State for all inspections.

As from 1 January 1998, in order to be approved by the Member States for the purpose of this Regulation, private bodies must fulfil the requirements laid down in standard EN 45011 of 26 June 1989.

4.   If a designated inspection authority and/or private body in a Member State establishes that an agricultural product or a foodstuff bearing a protected name of origin in that Member State does not meet the criteria of the specification, they shall take the steps necessary to ensure that this Regulation is complied with. They shall inform the Member State of the measures taken in carrying out their inspections. The parties concerned must be notified of all decisions taken.

5.   A Member State must withdraw approval from an inspection body where the criteria referred to in paragraphs 2 and 3 are no longer fulfilled. It shall inform the Commission, which shall publish in the Official Journal of the European Communities a revised list of approved bodies.

6.   The Member States shall adopt the measures necessary to ensure that a producer who complies with this Regulation has access to the inspection system.

7.   The costs of inspections provided for under this Regulation shall be borne by the producers using the protected name.

Article 11 [Product Specifications Not Met by Lawful Users]

1.   Any Member State may submit that a condition laid down in the product specification of an agricultural product or foodstuff covered by a protected name has not been met.

2.   The Member State referred to in paragraph 1 shall make its submission to the Member State concerned. The Member State concerned shall examine the complaint and inform the other Member State of its findings and of any measures taken.

3.   In the event of repeated irregularities and the failure of the Member States concerned to come to an agreement, a duly substantiated application must be sent to the Commission.

4.   The Commission shall examine the application by consulting the Member States concerned. Where appropriate, having consulted the committee referred to in Article 15, the Commission shall take the necessary steps. These may include cancellation of the registration.

Article 12 [Third Country Products]

1.   Without prejudice to international agreements, this Regulation may apply to an agricultural product or foodstuff from a third country provided that:
—   the third country is able to give guarantees identical or equivalent to those referred to in Article 4,
—   the third country concerned has inspection arrangements equivalent to those laid down in Article 10,
—   the third country concerned is prepared to provide protection equivalent to that available in the Community to corresponding agricultural products for foodstuffs coming from the Community.

2.   If a protected name of a third country is identical to a Community protected name, registration shall be granted with due regard for local and traditional usage and the

practical risks of confusion. Use of such names shall be authorized only if the country of origin of the product is clearly and visibly indicated on the label.

Article 13 [Scope of Protection]

1. Registered names shall be protected against:
(a) any direct or indirect commercial use of a name registered in respect of products not covered by the registration in so far as those products are comparable to the products registered under that name or insofar as using the name exploits the reputation of the protected name;
(b) any misuse, imitation or evocation, even if the true origin of the product is indicated or if the protected name is translated or accompanied by an expression such as "style", "type", "method", "as produced in", "imitation" or similar;
(c) any other false or misleading indication as to the provenance, origin, nature or essential qualities of the product, on the inner or outer packaging, advertising material or documents relating to the product concerned, and the packing of the product in a container liable to convey a false impression as to its origin;
(d) any other practice liable to mislead the public as to the true origin of the product.
Where a registered name contains within it the name of an agricultural product or foodstuff which is considered generic, the use of that generic name on the appropriate agricultural product or foodstuff shall not be considered to be contrary to (a) or (b) in the first subparagraph.
2. By way of derogation from paragraph 1 (a) and (b), Member States may maintain national systems that permit the use of names registered under Article 17 for a period of not more than five years after the date of publication of registration, provided that:
— the products have been marketed legally using such names for at least five years before the date of publication of this Regulation,
— the undertakings have legally marketed the products concerned using those names continuously during the period referred to in the first indent,
— the labelling clearly indicates the true origin of the product.
However, this derogation may not lead to the marketing of products freely within the territory of a Member State where such names were prohibited.
3. Protected names may not become generic.
4. In the case of names, for which registration has been applied for under Article 5, provision may be made for a transitional period of up to five years under Article 7 (5) (b), solely where a statement of objection has been declared admissible on the grounds that registration of the proposed name would jeopardize the existence of an entirely or partly identical name or the existence of products which have been legally on the market for at least five years preceding the date of the publication provided for in Article 6 (2).

Such transitional period may be provided for only where undertakings have legally marketed the products concerned using the names in question continuously for at least five years preceding the date of the publication provided for in Article 6 (2).

Article 14 [Priority over Subsequent Applications for Trade Marks]

1. Where a designation of origin or geographical indication is registered in accordance with this Regulation, the application for registration of a trade mark corresponding to one of the situations referred to in Article 13 and relating to the same type of product shall be refused, provided that the application for registration of the trade mark was submitted after the date of the publication provided for in Article 6 (2).

Trade marks registered in breach of the first subparagraph shall be declared invalid.

This paragraph shall also apply where the application for registration of a trade mark was lodged before the date of publication of the application for registration provided for in Article 6 (2), provided that that publication occurred before the trade mark was registered.

2. With due regard for Community law, use of a trade mark corresponding to one of the situations referred to in Article 13 which was registered in good faith before the date on which application for registration of a designation of origin or geographical indication was lodged may continue notwithstanding the registration of a designation of origin or geographical indication, where there are no grounds for invalidity or revocation of the trade mark as provided respectively by Article 3 (1) (c) and (g) and Article 12 (2) (b) of First Council Directive 89/104 of 21 December 1988 to approximate the laws of the Member States relating to trade marks.[1]

3. A designation of origin or geographical indication shall not be registered where, in the light of a trade mark's reputation and renown and the length of time it has been used, registration is liable to mislead the consumer as to the true identity of the product.

Article 15 [Comitology]

The Commission shall be assisted by a committee composed of the representatives of the Member States and chaired by the representative of the Commission.

The representative of the Commission shall submit to the committee a draft of the measures to be taken. The committee shall deliver its opinion on the draft within a time limit which the chairman may lay down according to the urgency of the matter. The opinion shall be delivered by the majority laid down in Article 148 (2) of the Treaty in the case of decisions which the Council is required to adopt on a proposal from the Commission. The votes of the representatives of the Member States within the committee shall be weighted in the manner set out in that Article. The chairman shall not vote.

The Commission shall adopt the measures envisaged if they are in accordance with the opinion of the committee. If the measures envisaged are not in accordance with the opinion of the committee, or if no opinion is delivered, the Commission shall, without delay, submit to the Council a proposal relating to the measures to be taken. The Council shall act by a qualified majority.

If, on the expiry of a period of three months from the date of referral to the Council, the Council has not acted, the proposed measures shall be adopted by the Commission.

Article 16 [Detailed Rules of Application]

Detailed rules for applying this Regulation shall be adopted in accordance with the procedure laid down in Article 15.[2]

Article 17 [Registration of Nationally Protected Names]

1. Within six months of the entry into force of the Regulation, Member States shall inform the Commission which of their legally protected names or, in those Member States where there is no protection system, which of their names established by usage they wish to register pursuant to this Regulation.

---

1   OJ 1989 L 40, p. 1. Amended by Decision 92/10, OJ 1992 L 6, p. 35.

2   See Regulation 2037/93, below p. 332.

2.   In accordance with the procedure laid down in Article 15, the Commission shall register the names referred to in paragraph 1 which comply with Articles 2 and 4. Article 7 shall not apply. However, generic names shall not be added.
3.   Member States may maintain national protection of the names communicated in accordance with paragraph 1 until such time as a decision on registration has been taken.

Article 18 [Entry into Force]
This Regulation shall enter into force twelve months after the date of its publication in the Official Journal of the European Communities.
   This Regulation shall be binding in its entirety and directly applicable in all Member States.

Done at Brussels, 14 July 1992.
For the Council, The President, J. GUMMER

ANNEX I: Foodstuffs referred to in Article 1 (1)
— Beer,
— Natural mineral waters and spring waters,
— Beverages made from plant extracts,
— Bread, pastry, cakes, confectionery, biscuits and other baker's wares,
— Natural gums and resins.

ANNEX II: Agricultural products referred to in Article 1 (1) [omitted]

Commission Regulation 2037/93 of 27 July 1993 Laying Down Detailed Rules of Application of Council Regulation 2081/92 on the Protection of Geographical Indications and Designations of Origin for Agricultural Products and Foodstuffs[1]

THE COMMISSION OF THE EUROPEAN COMMUNITIES,

HAVING REGARD to the Treaty establishing the European Economic Community,
HAVING REGARD to Council Regulation 2081/92 of 14 July 1992 on the protection of geographical indications and designations of origin for agricultural products and food-stuffs,[2] and in particular Article 16 thereof,
(1) WHEREAS the conditions should be laid down in which a natural or legal person may apply exceptionally for registration;
(2) WHEREAS, in order to take account of the various legal situations in the Member States, a statement of objection within the meaning of Article 7 of Regulation 2081/92 presented by a group of individuals linked by a common interest may be admissible;
(3) WHEREAS, in order to ensure that Regulation 2081/92 is uniformly applied, precise deadlines should be set concerning objections, which would apply when the registration procedure is initiated;

---

1   OJ 1993 L 185, p. 5, as amended by Commission Regulation 1428/97 of 23 July 1997, OJ 1997 L 196, p. 39 and by Commission Regulation 1726/98 of 22 July 1998, OJ 1998, L 224, p.1.

2   See above, p. 323.

(4) WHEREAS, with a view to defining the cases referred to in Article 3 (1) of Regulation 2081/92 and the situations likely to mislead consumers in Member States within the meaning of Regulation 2081/92, the Commission may take appropriate action;
(5) WHEREAS these arrangements constitute a new Community system designed to protect designations of origin and geographical indications entailing distinctive new indications; whereas it is essential to explain their meaning to the public, without thereby removing the need for producers and/or processors to promote their respective products;
(6) WHEREAS the measures provided for in this Regulation are in accordance with the opinion of the Regulatory Committee on Geographical indications and Designations of Origin,

HAS ADOPTED THIS REGULATION:

Article 1 [Applications by Individuals]
1.   Applications for registration pursuant to Article 5 of Regulation 2081/92, may be submitted by a natural or legal person not complying with the definition laid down in the second subparagraph of paragraph 1 of that Article in exceptional, duly substantiated cases where the person concerned is the only producer in the geographical area defined at the time the application is submitted.
The application may be accepted only where:
(a) the said single person engages in authentic and unvarying local methods; and
(b) the geographical area defined possesses characteristics which differ appreciably from those of neighbouring areas and/or the characteristics of the product are different.
2.   In the case referred to in paragraph 1, the single natural or legal person who has submitted the application for registration shall be deemed to constitute a group within the meaning of Article 5 of Regulation 2081/92.

Article 2 [Applications by Groups Without Legal Personality]
Where national law treats a group of individuals without legal personality as a legal person, the said group of individuals shall be authorized to submit an application within the meaning of Article 1 of this Regulation, to consult the application within the meaning and subject to the conditions of Article 7 (2) of Regulation 2081/92 and to lodge an objection within the meaning and subject to the conditions of Article 7 (3) of that Regulation.

Article 3 [Calculation of Deadlines]
For the purposes of applying the deadline referred to in Article 7 (1) of Regulation 2081/92, account shall be taken of:
— either the date of dispatch of the statement of the objection by the Member State, the postmark being accepted as the date of dispatch, or
— the date of receipt where the statement of the objection by the Member State is delivered to the Commission directly or by telex or fax.

Article 4 [Commission Procedure]
The Commission may take all appropriate action in order to define the cases where a designation has become generic within the meaning of Article 3 (1) of Regulation 2081/92, as well as the situations likely to mislead consumers and in respect of which a decision has been taken in accordance with Article 15 of that Regulation.

Article 5 [Introduction of the Terms "Protected Designation of Origin" and "Protected Geographical Indication"]

For a period of five years after the date of entry into force of this Regulation, the Commission shall take the necessary steps to inform the public of the meaning of the indications "PDO", "PGI", "protected designation of origin" and "protected geographical indication" in the Community languages. Such steps shall not take the form of aid to producers and/or processors.

The five-year time limit provided for in the preceding paragraph is hereby extended by four years. The information measures implemented shall be evaluated.

Article 5a [Introduction of a Community Symbol]

1.   The names registered as protected designations of origin (PDOs) or protected geographical indications (PGIs) may be accompanied by a Community symbol to be determined in accordance with the procedure laid down in Article 15 of Regulation 2081/92.

2.   The Community symbol may appear only on products which comply with Regulation 2081/92.

3.   "PDO", "PGI", "protected designation of origin", "protected geographical indication" and the equivalent national traditional expressions may be used without the Community symbol.

Article 5b [Graphic Symbols]

The Community symbol referred to in Article 5a shall comprise the models in Annex I part A of this Regulation. The indications that can be used with the symbol are those listed in Annex I part B to this Regulation, as well as the equivalent traditional national terms.

To use the Community symbol and the indications, the technical reproduction rules laid down in the graphics manual in Annex II to this Regulation must be complied with.

Article 6 [Calculation of the Period Mentioned in Art. 7 (5)]

The period of three months referred to in Article 7 (5) of Regulation 2081/92 shall commence on the date of dispatch of the Commission's invitation to the Member States to reach agreement among themselves.

Article 6a [National Inspection Authorities]

A Member State may stipulate that the name of the inspection authority or body referred to in Article 10 of Regulation 2081/92 falling within its own inspection structure must appear on the label of the agricultural product or foodstuff.

Article 7 [Entry into Force]

This Regulation shall enter into force on 26 July 1993.

This Regulation shall be binding in its entirety and directly applicable in all Member States.

Done at Brussels, 27 July 1993.
For the Commission, René STEICHEN, Member of the Commission

ANNEX I [graphics omitted]

ANNEX II: GRAPHIC MANUAL
1.   INTRODUCTION
THE REASON FOR HAVING A LOGO?
The logo will allow producers of food products to increase awareness of their products among consumers in the European Union.

It is applied on products whose name has been registered in the context of a Community system to protect and enhance geographical designations, established by Regulation 2081/92.

In order to be registered under this Regulation, a designation must meet the criteria for a Protected Designation of Origin (PDO) or Protected Geographical Indication (PGI). Above all there must be a link between the product and the geographical area where it is produced. There categories, are differentiated only by the nature of the link, the protection afforded by the Regulation being identical for both.

The Community register links the geographical name to a particular set of specifications. Controls organised by Member States ensure the protection of the consumer by guaranteeing respect for the designation of origin and the specifications.

There is already a Community logo which guarantees the traditional specific character of certain products independently of their place of production; the new logo has been created on this model. Furthermore, the design is for the two classifications (PDO and PGI). This allows a synergy between the different graphic representations of the European systems and avoids a proliferation of symbols in the market place.

The presence of this logo is a genuine guarantee for all European consumers, making it clear that the special nature of this product lies in its geographical origin. Because of this, products will inspire more confidence.

As producers, the logo provides you with a marketing tool. You will be able to put the logo on the labels or packaging of your products, and also use it in your advertising.

This graphic manual is meant to act as a guide for you in reproducing the logo. Different possibilities for using it have been worked out, allowing you to make your choice depending on your requirements for printed material. [...]

Free Movement of Persons

Council Regulation 1612/68 of 15 October 1968 on Freedom of Movement for Workers Within the Community[1]

THE COUNCIL OF THE EUROPEAN COMMUNITIES,

HAVING REGARD to the Treaty establishing the European Economic Community, and in particular Article 49 thereof [...]

(1) WHEREAS freedom of movement for workers should be secured within the Community by the end of the transitional period at the latest;

(2) WHEREAS the attainment of this objective entails the abolition of any discrimination based on nationality between workers of the Member States as regards employment, remuneration and other conditions of work and employment, as well as the right of such workers to move freely within the Community in order to pursue activities as employed persons subject to any limitations justified on grounds of public policy, public security or public health;

(3) WHEREAS by reason in particular of the early establishment of the customs union and in order to ensure the simultaneous completion of the principal foundations of the Community, provisions should be adopted to enable the objectives laid down in Articles 48 And 49 of the Treaty in the field of freedom of movement to be achieved [...];

(4) WHEREAS freedom of movement constitutes a fundamental right of workers and their families;

(5) WHEREAS mobility of labour within the Community must be one of the means by which the worker is guaranteed the possibility of improving his living and working conditions and promoting his social advancement, while helping to satisfy the requirements of the economies of the Member States;

(6) WHEREAS the right of all workers in the Member States to pursue the activity of their choice within the Community should be affirmed;

(7) WHEREAS such right must be enjoyed without discrimination by permanent, seasonal and frontier workers and by those who pursue their activities for the purpose of providing services;

(8) WHEREAS the right of freedom of movement, in order that it may be exercised, by objective standards, in freedom and dignity, requires that equality of treatment shall be ensured in fact and in law in respect of all matters relating to the actual pursuit of activities as employed persons and to eligibility for housing, and also that obstacles to the mobility of workers shall be eliminated, in particular as regards the worker's right to be joined by his family and the conditions for the integration of that family into the host country;

(9) WHEREAS the principle of non-discrimination between Community workers entails that all nationals of Member States have the same priority as regards employment as is enjoyed by national workers;

(10) WHEREAS it is necessary to strengthen the machinery for vacancy clearance, in particular by developing direct co-operation between the central employment services and also between the regional services, as well as by increasing and co-ordinating the

---

1   OJ 1968 L 257, p. 2, as amended by Council Regulation 312/76 of 9 February 1976. Part II of the Regulation, which is omitted here, was also amended by Council Regulation 2434/92 of 27 July 1992, OJ 1992 L 245, p. 1.

exchange of information in order to ensure in a general way a clearer picture of the labour market;
(11) WHEREAS workers wishing to move should also be regularly informed of living and working conditions;
(12) WHEREAS, furthermore, measures should be provided for the case where a Member State undergoes or foresees disturbances on its labour market which may seriously threaten the standard of living and level of employment in a region or an industry;
(13) WHEREAS for this purpose the exchange of information, aimed at discouraging workers from moving to such a region or industry, constitutes the method to be applied in the first place but, where necessary, it should be possible to strengthen the results of such exchange of information by temporarily suspending the abovementioned machinery, any such Decision to be taken at Community level;
(14) WHEREAS close links exist between freedom of movement for workers, employ-ment and vocational training, particularly where the latter aims at putting workers in a position to take up offers of employment from other regions of the Community;
(15) WHEREAS such links make it necessary that the problems arising in this con-nection should no longer be studied in isolation but viewed as inter-dependent, account also being taken of the problems of employment at the regional level;
AND WHEREAS it is therefore necessary to direct the efforts of Member States toward co-ordinating their employment policies at Community level; [...]

HAS ADOPTED THIS REGULATION:

PART I
EMPLOYMENT AND WORKERS' FAMILIES
TITLE I
ELIGIBILITY FOR EMPLOYMENT

Article 1 [The Right to Take up Employment in Another Member State]
1. Any national of a Member State, shall, irrespective of his place of residence, have the right to take up an activity as an employed person, and to pursue such activity, within the territory of another Member State in accordance with the provisions laid down by law, Regulation or administrative action governing the employment of natio-nals of that state.
2. He shall, in particular, have the right to take up available employment in the territory of another Member State with the same priority as nationals of that state.

Article 2 [Applications and Offers for Employment]
Any national of a Member State and any employer pursuing an activity in the territory of a Member State may exchange their applications for and offers of employment, and may conclude and perform contracts of employment in accordance with the provisions in force laid down by law, Regulation or administrative action, without any discrimina-tion resulting therefrom.

Article 3 [Inapplicability of Restrictive National Measures]
Under this Regulation, provisions laid down by law, Regulation or administrative action or administrative practices of a Member State shall not apply:
— where they limit application for and offers of employment, or the right of foreign nationals to take up and pursue employment or subject these to conditions not applicable in respect of their own nationals, or

— where, though applicable irrespective of nationality, their exclusive or principal aim or effect is to keep nationals of other Member States away from the employment offered.

This provision shall not apply to conditions relating to linguistic knowledge required by reason of the nature of the post to be filled.

2.   There shall be included in particular among the provisions or practices of a Member State referred to in the first subparagraph of paragraph 1 those which:

(a) prescribe a special recruitment procedure for foreign nationals
(b) limit or restrict the advertising of vacancies in the press or through any other medium or subject it to conditions other than those applicable in respect of employers pursuing their activities in the territory of that Member State
(c) subject eligibility for employment to conditions of registration with employment offices or impede recruitment of individual workers, where persons who do not reside in the territory of that state are concerned.

Article 4 [Prohibition of National Quotas]

1.   Provisions laid down by law, Regulation or administrative action of the Member States which restrict by number or percentage the employment of foreign nationals in any undertaking, branch of activity or region, or at a national level, shall not apply to nationals of the other Member States.

2.   When in a Member State the granting of any benefit to undertakings is subject to a minimum percentage of national workers being employed, nationals of the other Member States shall be counted as national workers, subject to the provisions of the Council Directive of 15 October 1963.

Article 5 [The Right to Equal Assistance in the Search for Employment]

A national of a Member State who seeks employment in the territory of another Member State shall receive the same assistance there as that afforded by the employment offices in that state to their own nationals seeking employment.

Article 6 [Medical, Vocational and Other Criteria]

1.   The engagement and recruitment of a national of one Member State for a post in another Member State shall not depend on medical, vocational or other criteria which are discriminatory on grounds of nationality by comparison with those applied to nationals of the other Member State who wish to pursue the same activity.

2.   Nevertheless, a national who holds an offer in his name from an employer in a Member State other than that of which he is a national may have to undergo a vocational test, if the employer expressly requests this when making his offer of employment.

TITLE II
EMPLOYMENT AND EQUALITY OF TREATMENT

Article 7 [Scope of the Right to Equal Treatment]

1.   A worker who is a national of a Member State may not, in the territory of another Member State, be treated differently from national workers by reason of his nationality in respect of any conditions of employment and work, in particular as regards remuneration, dismissal, and should he become unemployed, reinstatement or reemployment

2.   He shall enjoy the same social and tax advantages as national workers.

3.   He shall also, by virtue of the same right and under the same conditions as national workers, have access to training in vocational schools and retraining centres.

4.   Any clause of a collective or individual agreement or of any other collective regulation concerning eligibility for employment, employment, remuneration and other conditions of work or dismissal shall be null and void in so far as it lays down or authorises discriminatory conditions in respect of workers who are nationals of the other Member States.

Article 8 [Access to Trade Unions and Offices Governed by Public Law]
A worker who is a national of a Member State and who is employed in the territory of another Member State shall enjoy equality of treatment as regards Membership of trade unions and the exercise of rights attaching thereto, including the right to vote and to be eligible for the administration or management posts of a trade union.

He may be excluded from taking part in the management of bodies governed by public law and from holding an office governed by public law. Furthermore, he shall have the right of eligibility for workers' representative bodies in the undertaking. The provisions of this article shall not affect laws or Regulations in certain Member States which grant more extensive rights to workers coming from the other Member States.

Article 9 [Housing Benefits]
1.   A worker who is a national of a Member State and who is employed in the territory of another Member State shall enjoy all the rights and benefits accorded to national workers in matters of housing, including ownership of the housing he needs.
2.   Such worker may, with the same right as nationals, put his name down on the housing lists in the region in which he is employed, where such lists exist

He shall enjoy the resultant benefits and priorities.

If his family has remained in the country whence he came, they shall be considered for this purpose as residing in the said region, where national workers benefit from a similar presumption.

TITLE III
WORKERS' FAMILIES

Article 10 [Definition of Family Members]
1.   The following shall, irrespective of their nationality, have the right to install themselves with a worker who is a national of one Member State and who is employed in the territory of another Member State:
(a)   his spouse and their descendants who are under the age of 21 years or are dependants
(b)   dependent relatives in the ascending line of the worker and his spouse.
2.   Member States shall facilitate the admission of any Member of the family not coming within the provisions of paragraph 1 if dependent on the worker referred to above or living under his roof in the country whence he comes.
3.   For the purposes of paragraphs 1 and 2, the worker must have available for his family housing considered as normal for national workers in the region where he is employed.

This provision, however must not give rise to discrimination between national workers and workers from the other Member States.

Article 11 [Right of Family Members to Take up Employment]
Where a national of a Member State is pursuing an activity as an employed or self-employed person in the territory of another Member State, his spouse and those of the children who are under the age of 21 years or dependent on him shall have the right

to take up any activity as an employed person throughout the territory of that same state, even if they are not nationals of any Member state.

Article 12 [Access of Children to the Educational System]
The children of a national of a Member State who is or has been employed in the territory of another Member State shall be admitted to that state's general educational, apprenticeship and vocational training courses under the same conditions as the nationals of that state, if such children are residing in its territory.

Member States shall encourage all efforts to enable such children to attend these courses under the best possible conditions.
[...]

Council Directive 68/360 of 15 October 1968 on the Abolition of Restrictions on Movement and Residence Within the Community for Workers of Member States and Their Families[1]

THE COUNCIL OF THE EUROPEAN COMMUNITIES,

HAVING REGARD to the Treaty establishing the European Economic Community, and in particular Article 49 thereof [...]
WHEREAS Council Regulation 1612/68[2] fixed the provisions governing freedom of movement for workers within the Community;
WHEREAS, consequently, measures should be adopted for the abolition of restrictions which still exist concerning movement and residence within the Community, which conform to the rights and privileges accorded by the said Regulation to nationals of any Member State who move in order to pursue activities as employed persons and to Members of their families;
WHEREAS the rules applicable to residence should, as far as possible, bring the position of workers from other Member States and Members of their families into line with that of nationals;
WHEREAS the co-ordination of special measures relating to the movement and residence of foreign nationals, justified on grounds of public policy, public security or public health, is the subject of the Council Directive of 25 February 1964[3], adopted in application of Article 56 (2) of the Treaty,

HAS ADOPTED THIS DIRECTIVE:

Article 1 [Elimination of Restrictions on the Freedom of Movement]
Member States shall, acting as provided in this Directive, abolish restrictions on the movement and residence of nationals of the said states and of Members of their families to whom Regulation 1612/68 applies.

---

1   OJ 1968 L 257, p. 13.

2   See above, p. 336.

3   See below, p. 346.

Article 2 [Right to Leave Home State]
1. Member States shall grant the nationals referred to in Article 1 the right to leave their territory in order to take up activities as employed persons and to pursue such activities in the territory of another Member State. Such right shall be exercised simply on production of a valid identity card or passport. Members of the family shall enjoy the same right as the national on whom they are dependent.
2. Member States shall, acting in accordance with their laws, issue to such nationals, or renew, an identity card or passport, which shall state in particular the holder's nationality.
3. The passport must be valid at least for all Member States and for countries through which the holder must pass when travelling between Member states. Where a passport is the only document on which the holder may lawfully leave the country, its period of validity shall be not less than five years.
4. Member States may not demand from the nationals referred to in Article 1 any exit visa or any equivalent document.

Article 3 [Right of Entry in the Host State]
1. Member States shall allow the persons referred to in Article 1 to enter their territory simply on production of a valid identity card or passport.
2. No entry visa or equivalent document may be demanded save from Members of the family who are not nationals of a Member State. Member States shall accord to such persons every facility for obtaining any necessary visas.

Article 4 [Right of Residence]
1. Member States shall grant the right of residence in their territory to the persons referred to in Article 1 who are able to produce the documents listed in paragraph 3.
2. As proof of the right of residence, a document entitled "residence permit for a national of a Member State of the EEC" shall be issued. This document must include a statement that it has been issued pursuant to Regulation 1612/68 and to the measures taken by the Member States for the implementation of the present Directive. The text of such statement is given in the Annex to this Directive.
3. For the issue of a residence permit for a national of a Member State of the EEC, Member States may require only the production of the following documents
— by the worker:
   (a) the document with which he entered their territory
   (b) a confirmation of engagement from the employer or a certificate of employment
— by the Members of the worker's family:
   (c) the document with which they entered the territory
   (d) a document issued by the competent authority of the state of origin or the state whence they came, proving their relationship
   (e) in the cases referred to in Article 10 (1) and (2) of Regulation 1612/68, a document issued by the competent authority of the state of origin or the state whence they came, testifying that they are dependent on the worker or that they live under his roof in such country.
4. A Member of the family who is not a national of a Member State shall be issued with a residence document which shall have the same validity as that issued to the worker on whom he is dependent.

Article 5 [Immediate Access to Employment]
Completion of the formalities for obtaining a residence permit shall not hinder the immediate beginning of employment under a contract concluded by the applicants.

Article 6 [Residence Permits]

1. The residence permit:
(a) must be valid throughout the territory of the Member State which issued it
(b) must be valid for at least five years from the date of issue and be automatically renewable.
2. Breaks in residence not exceeding six consecutive months and absence on military service shall not affect the validity of a residence permit.
3. Where a worker is employed for a period exceeding three months but not exceeding a year in the service of an employer in the host state or in the employ of a person providing services, the host Member State shall issue him a temporary residence permit, the validity of which may be limited to the expected period of the employment.

Subject to the provisions of Article 8 (1) (c), a temporary residence permit shall be issued also to a seasonal worker employed for a period of more than three months. The period of employment must be shown in the documents referred to in paragraph 4 (3) (b).

Article 7 [Renewal and Withdrawal of Residence Permits]

1. A valid residence permit may not be withdrawn from a worker solely on the grounds that he is no longer in employment, either because he is temporarily incapable of work as a result of illness or accident, or because he is involuntarily unemployed, this being duly confirmed by the competent employment office.
2. When the residence permit is renewed for the first time, the period of residence may be restricted, but not to less than twelve months, where the worker has been involuntarily unemployed in the Member State for more than twelve consecutive months.

Article 8 [Short Term and Seasonal Employment]

1. Member States shall, without issuing a residence permit, recognise the right of residence in their territory of:
(a) a worker pursuing an activity as an employed person, where the activity is not expected to last for more than three months. The document with which the person concerned entered the territory and a statement by the employer on the expected duration of the employment shall be sufficient to cover his stay
A statement by the employer shall not, however, be required in the case of workers coming within the provisions of the Council Directive of 25 February 1964 (5) on the attainment of freedom of establishment and freedom to provide services in respect of the activities of intermediaries in commerce, industry and small craft industries.
(b) a worker who, while having his residence in the territory of a Member state to which he returns as a rule, each day or at least once a week, is employed in the territory of another Member State. The competent authority of the state where he is employed may issue such worker with a special permit valid for five years and automatically renewable
(c) a seasonal worker who holds a contract of employment stamped by the competent authority of the Member State on whose territory he has come to pursue his activity.
2. In all cases referred to in paragraph 1, the competent authorities of the host Member State may require the worker to report his presence in the territory.

Article 9 [Procedures and Costs]

1. The residence documents granted to nationals of a Member State of the EEC referred to in this Directive shall be issued and renewed free of charge or on payment of an amount not exceeding the dues and taxes charged for the issue of identity cards to nationals.

2.   The visa referred to in Article 3 (2) and the stamp referred to in article 8 (1) (c) shall be free of charge.
3.   Member States shall take the necessary steps to simplify as much as possible the formalities and procedure for obtaining the documents mentioned in paragraph 1.

Article 10 [Derogations from the Fundamental Freedoms]
Member States shall not derogate from the provisions of this Directive save on grounds of public policy, public security or public health.

Article 11-14 [omitted]

Done at Luxembourg, 15 October 1968.

Council Directive 73/148 of 21 May 1973 on the Abolition of Restrictions on Movement and Residence Within the Community for Nationals of Member States with Regard to Establishment and the Provision of Services[1]

THE COUNCIL OF THE EUROPEAN COMMUNITIES,

HAVING REGARD to the Treaty establishing the European Economic Community, and in particular Article 54 (2) and Article 63 (2) thereof; [...]
(1) WHEREAS freedom of movement of persons as provided for in the Treaty and the general programmes for the abolition of restrictions on freedom of establishment and on freedom to provide services entails the abolition of restrictions on movement and residence within the Community for nationals of Member States wishing to establish themselves or to provide services within the territory of another Member State;
(2) WHEREAS freedom of establishment can be fully attained only if a right of permanent residence is granted to the persons who are to enjoy freedom of establishment;
(3) WHEREAS freedom to provide services entails that persons providing and receiving services should have the right of residence for the time during which the services are being provided;
(4) WHEREAS Council Directive of 25 February 1964 (4) on the abolition of restrictions on movement and residence within the Community for nationals of Member States with regard to establishment and the provision of services laid down the rules applicable in this area to activities as self-employed persons;
(5) WHEREAS Council Directive of 15 October 1968 (5) on the abolition of restrictions on movement and residence within the Community for workers of Member States and their families, which replaced the Directive of 25 March 1964 (6) bearing the same title, has in the meantime amended the rules applicable to employed persons;
(6) WHEREAS the provisions concerning movement and residence within the Community of self-employed persons and their families should likewise be improved;
(7) WHEREAS the coordination of special measures concerning the movement and residence of foreign nationals, justified on grounds of public policy, public security or public health, is already the subject of the Council Directive of 25 February 1964;[2]

---

1   OJ 1973 L 172, p. 14.

2   See below, p. 346.

HAS ADOPTED THIS DIRECTIVE:

Article 1 [Eliminations of Restrictions of the Freedom of Movement]

1.   The Member States shall, acting as provided in this Directive, abolish restrictions on the movements and residence of:

(a) nationals of a Member State who are established or who wish to establish them-selves in another Member State in order to pursue activities as self-employed persons, or who wish to provide services in that state;

(b) nationals of Member States wishing to go to another Member State as recipients of services;

(c) the spouse and the children under twenty-one years of age of such nationals, irrespective of their nationality;

(d) the relatives in the ascending and descending lines of such nationals and of the spouse of such nationals, which relatives are dependent on them, irrespective of their nationality.

2.   Member States shall favour the admission of any other member of the family of a national referred to in paragraph 1 (a) or (b) or of the spouse of that national, which member is dependent on that national or spouse of that national or who in the country of origin was living under the same roof.

Article 2 [Right to Leave Home State]

1.   Member States shall grant the persons referred to in Article 1 the right to leave their territory. Such right shall be exercised simply on production of a valid identity card or passport. Members of the family shall enjoy the same right as the national on whom they are dependent.

2.   Member States shall, acting in accordance with their laws, issue to their nationals, or renew, an identity card or passport, which shall state in particular the holder's natio-nality.

3.   The passport must be valid at least for all Member States and for countries through which the holder must pass when travelling between Member States. Where a pass-port is the only document on which the holder may lawfully leave the country, its period of validity shall be not less than five years.

4.   Member States may not demand from the persons referred to in Article 1 any exit visa or any equivalent requirement.

Article 3 [Right of Entry in the Host State]

1.   Member States shall grant to the persons referred to in Article 1 right to enter their territory merely on production of a valid identity card or passport.

2.   No entry visa or equivalent requirement may be demanded save in respect of members of the family who do have the nationality of a Member State. Member States shall afford to such persons every facility for obtaining any necessary visas.

Article 4 [Right of Residence]

1.   Each Member State shall grant the right of permanent residence to nationals of other Member States who establish themselves within its territory in order to pursue activities as self-employed persons, when the restrictions on these activities have been abolished pursuant to the Treaty.

As proof of the right of residence, a document entitled "residence permit for a natio-nal of a Member State of the European Communities" shall be issued. This document shall be valid for not less than five years from the date of issue and shall be automa-tically renewable.

Breaks in residence not exceeding six consecutive months and absence on military service shall not affect the validity of a residence permit.

A valid residence permit may not be withdrawn from a national referred to in Article 1 (1) (a) solely on the grounds that he is no longer in employment because he is temporarily incapable of work as a result of illness or accident.

Any national of a Member State who is not specified in the first subparagraph but who is authorized under the laws of another Member State to pursue an activity within its territory shall be granted a right of abode for a period not less than that of the authorization granted for the pursuit of the activity in question.

However, any national referred to in subparagraph 1 and to whom the provisions of the preceding subparagraph apply as a result of a change of employment shall retain his residence permit until the date on which it expires.

2. The right of residence for persons providing and receiving services shall be of equal duration with the period during which the services are provided.

Where such period exceeds three months, the Member State in the territory of which the services are performed shall issue a right of abode as proof of the right of residence.

Where the period does not exceed three months, the identity card of passport with which the person concerned entered the territory shall be sufficient to cover his stay. The Member State may, however, require the person concerned to report his presence in the territory.

3. A member of the family who is not a national of a Member State shall be issued with a residence document which shall have the same validity as that issued to the national on whom he is dependent.

Article 5 [Unlimited Territorial Coverage]
The right of residence shall be effective throughout the territory of the Member State concerned.

Article 6 [Applications for a Residence Permit]
An applicant for a residence permit or right of abode shall not be required by a Member State to produce anything other than the following, namely:
(a) the identity card or passport with which he or she entered its territory;
(b) proof that he or she comes within one of the classes of person referred to in Articles 1 and 4.

Article 7 [Procedures and Costs]
1. The residence documents granted to nationals of a Member State shall be issued and renewed free of charge or on payment of an amount not exceeding the dues and taxes charged for the issue of identity cards to nationals. These provisions shall also apply to documents and certificates required for the issue and renewal of such residence documents.
2. The visas referred to in Article 3 (2) shall be free of charge.
3. Member States shall take the necessary steps to simplify as much as possible the formalities and the procedure for obtaining the documents mentioned in paragraph 1.

Article 8 [Derogations from the Fundamental Freedoms]
Member States shall not derogate from the provisions of this Directive save on grounds of public policy, public security or public health.

Article 9 -11 [omitted]

Done at Brussels, 21 May 1973. For the Council, The President, E. Glinne

Council Directive 64/221 of 25 February 1964 on the Co-ordination of Special Measures Concerning the Movement and Residence of Foreign Nationals Which Are Justified on Grounds of Public Policy, Public Security or Public Health[1]

THE COUNCIL OF THE EUROPEAN ECONOMIC COMMUNITY,

HAVING REGARD to the Treaty establishing the European Economic Community, and in particular Article 56 (2) thereof; [...]

WHEREAS co-ordination of provisions laid down by law, Regulation or administrative action which provide for special treatment for foreign nationals on grounds of public policy, public security or public health should in the first place deal with the conditions for entry and residence of nationals of Member States moving within the Community either in order to pursue activities as employed or self-employed persons, or as recipients of services;

WHEREAS such co-ordination presupposes in particular an approximation of the procedures followed in each Member State when invoking grounds of public policy, public security or public health in matters connected with the movement or residence of foreign nationals;

WHEREAS, in each Member State, nationals of other Member States should have adequate legal remedies available to them in respect of the Decisions of the administration in such matters;

WHEREAS it would be of little practical use to compile a list of diseases and disabilities which might endanger public health, public policy or public security and it would be difficult to make such a list exhaustive;

WHEREAS it is sufficient to classify such diseases and disabilities in groups;

HAS ADOPTED THIS DIRECTIVE:

Article 1 [Coverage for Employed and Self-Employed Persons]
1.   The provisions of this Directive shall apply to any national of a Member state who resides in or travels to another Member State of the Community, either in order to pursue an activity as an employed or self-employed person, or as a recipient of services.
2.   These provisions shall apply also to the spouse and to members of the family who come within the provisions of the Regulations and Directives adopted in this field in pursuance of the Treaty.

Article 2 [Coverage for all Measures]
1.   This Directive relates to all measures concerning entry into their territory, issue or renewal of residence permits, or expulsion from their territory, taken by Member States on grounds of public policy, public security or public health.
2.   Such grounds shall not be invoked to service economic ends.

Article 3 [Individual and Concrete Measures]
1.   Measures taken on grounds of public policy or of public security shall be based exclusively on the personal conduct of the individual concerned.
2.   Previous criminal convictions shall not in themselves constitute grounds for the taking of such measures.

---

1   OJ 1964, No. 056, p. 850.

3.   Expiry of the identity card or passport used by the person concerned to enter the host country and to obtain a residence permit shall not justify expulsion from the territory.

4.   The state which issued the identity card or passport shall allow the holder of such document to re-enter its territory without any formality even if the document is no longer valid or the nationality of the holder is in dispute.

Article 4 [Diseases Justifying Restrictions]

1.   The only diseases or disabilities justifying refusal of entry into a territory or refusal to issue a first residence permit shall be those listed in the Annex to this Directive.

2.   Diseases or disabilities occurring after a first residence permit has been issued shall not justify refusal to renew the residence permit or expulsion from the territory.

3.   Member States shall not introduce new provisions or practices which are more restrictive than those in force at the date of notification of this Directive.

Article 5 [Decisions on First Residence Permits]

1.   A decision to grant or to refuse a first residence permit shall be taken as soon as possible and in any event not later than six months from the date of application for the permit.

The person concerned shall be allowed to remain temporarily in the territory pending a decision either to grant or to refuse a residence permit.

2.   The host country may, in cases where this is considered essential, request the Member State of origin of the applicant, and if need be other Member States, to provide information concerning any previous police record. Such enquiries shall not be made as a matter of routine. The Member State consulted shall give its reply within two months.

Article 6 [Notification of Reasons]

The person concerned shall be informed of the grounds of public policy, public security, or public health upon which the decision taken in his case is based, unless this is contrary to the interests of the security of the state involved.

Article 7 [Consequences of a Refusal]

The person concerned shall be officially notified of any decision to refuse the issue or renewal of a residence permit or to expel him from the territory. The period allowed for leaving the territory shall be stated in this notification. Save in cases of urgency, this period shall be not less than fifteen days if the person concerned has not yet been granted a residence permit and not less than one month in all other cases.

Article 8 [Legal Remedies]

The person concerned shall have the same legal remedies in respect of any decision concerning entry, or refusing the issue or renewal of a residence permit, or ordering expulsion from the territory, as are available to nationals of the State concerned in respect of acts of the administration.

Article 9 [Two Levels of Review]

1.   Where there is no right of appeal to a court of law, or where such appeal may be only in respect of the legal validity of the decision, or where the appeal cannot have suspensory effect, a decision refusing renewal of a residence permit or ordering the expulsion of the holder of a residence permit from the territory shall not be taken by the administrative authority, save in cases of urgency, until an opinion has been obtained from a competent authority of the host country before which the person concerned

enjoys such rights of defence and of assistance or representation as the domestic law of that country provides for.

This authority shall not be the same as that empowered to take the decision refusing renewal of the residence permit or ordering expulsion.

2.   Any decision refusing the issue of a first residence permit or ordering expulsion of the person concerned before the issue of the permit shall, where that person so requests, be referred for consideration to the authority whose prior opinion is required under paragraph 1. The person concerned shall then be entitled to submit his defence in person, except where this would be contrary to the interests of national security.

Article 10 [Implementation into National Law]

1.   Member States shall within six months of notification of this Directive put into force the measures necessary to comply with its provisions and shall forthwith inform the Commission thereof.

2.   Member States shall ensure that the texts of the main provisions of national law which they adopt in the field governed by this Directive are communicated to the Commission.

Article 11 [Addressees]

This Directive is addressed to the Member States.

Done at Brussels, 25 February 1964.
For the Council, The President, H. Fayat

ANNEX
A.   Diseases which might endanger public health:
1.   Diseases subject to quarantine listed in international health Regulation no 2 of the world health organisation of 25 May 1951
2.   Tuberculosis of the respiratory system in an active state or showing a tendency to develop
3.   Syphilis
4.   Other infectious diseases or contagious parasitic diseases if they are the subject of provisions for the protection of nationals of the host country.
B.   Diseases and disabilities which might threaten public policy or public security:
1.   Drug addiction
2.   Profound mental disturbance; manifest conditions of psychotic disturbance with agitation, delirium, hallucinations or confusion.

Commission Regulation 1251/70 of 29 June 1970 on the Right of Workers to Remain in the Territory of a Member State After Having Been Employed in that State[1]

THE COMMISSION OF THE EUROPEAN COMMUNITIES,

HAVING REGARD to the Treaty establishing the European Economic Community, and in particular Article 48 (3) (d) thereof, and Article 2 of the Protocol on the Grand Duchy of Luxembourg; [...]
(1) WHEREAS Council Regulation 1612/68[2] of 15 October 1968 and Council Directive 68/360 of 15 October 1968[3] enabled freedom of movement for workers to be secured at the end of a series of measures to be achieved progressively;
(2) WHEREAS the right of residence acquired by workers in active employment has as a corollary the right, granted by the Treaty to such workers, to remain in the territory of a Member State after having been employed in that state;
(3) WHEREAS it is important to lay down the conditions for the exercise of such right;
(4) WHEREAS the said Council Regulation and Council Directive contain the appropriate provisions concerning the right of workers to reside in the territory of a Member State for the purposes of employment;
(4) WHEREAS the right to remain, referred to in Article 48 (3) (d) of the Treaty, is interpreted therefore as the right of the worker to maintain his residence in the territory of a Member State when he ceases to be employed there;
(5) WHEREAS the mobility of labour in the Community requires that workers may be employed successively in several Member States without thereby being placed at a disadvantage;
(5) WHEREAS it is important, in the first place, to guarantee to the worker residing in the territory of a Member State the right to remain in that territory when he ceases to be employed in that state because he has reached retirement age or by reason of permanent incapacity to work;
(6) WHEREAS, however, it is equally important to ensure that right for the worker who, after a period of employment and residence in the territory of a Member state, works as an employed person in the territory of another Member State, while still retaining his residence in the territory of the first state;
(7) WHEREAS, to determine the conditions under which the right to remain arises, account should be taken of the reasons which have led to the termination of employment in the territory of the Member State concerned and, in particular, of the difference between retirement, the normal and foreseeable end of working life, and incapacity to work which leads to a premature and unforeseeable termination of activity;

---

1   OJ 1970 L 142, p. 24. Council Directive 72/194 of 18 May 1972, OJ 1972 L 121, p. 32, has extended the applicability of Directive 64/221 on the co-ordination of special measures concerning the movement and residence of foreign nationals which are justified on grounds of public policy, public security or public health (above, p. 346), to "nationals of Member States and members of their families who pursuant to Regulation 1251/70, exercise the right to remain in the territory of a Member State."

2   See above, p. 346.

3   See above, p. 340.

(8) WHEREAS special conditions must be laid down where termination of activity is the result of an accident at work or occupational disease, or where the worker's spouse is or was a national of the Member State concerned;

(9) WHEREAS the worker who has reached the end of his working life should have sufficient time in which to decide where he wishes to establish his final residence;

(10) WHEREAS the exercise by the worker of the right to remain entails that such right shall be extended to members of his family;

(11) WHEREAS in the case of the death of the worker during his working life, maintenance of the right of residence of the members of this family must also be recognised and be the subject of special conditions;

(12) WHEREAS persons to whom the right to remain applies must enjoy equality of treatment with national workers who have ceased their working lives;

HAS ADOPTED THIS REGULATION

Article 1 [Scope of Application]
The provisions of this Regulation shall apply to nationals of a Member State who have worked as employed persons in the territory of another Member State and to members of their families, as defined in Article 10 of Council Regulation 1612/68 on freedom of movement for workers within the Community.

Article 2 [Criteria for Employed Persons]
1.   The following shall have the right to remain permanently in the territory of a Member State:
(a) a worker who, at the time of termination of his activity, has reached the age laid down by the law of that Member State for entitlement to an old-age pension and who has been employed in that state for at least the last twelve months and has resided there continuously for more than three years;
(b) a worker who, having resided continuously in the territory of that state for more than two years, ceases to work there as an employed person as a result of permanent incapacity to work. If such incapacity is the result of an accident at work or an occupational disease entitling him to a pension for which an institution of that state is entirely or partially responsible, no condition shall be imposed as to length of residence;
(c) a worker who, after three years' continuous employment and residence in the territory of that state, works as an employed person in the territory of another Member State, while retaining his residence in the territory of the first state, to which he returns, as a rule, each day or at least once a week. Periods of employment completed in this way in the territory of the other Member State shall, for the purposes of entitlement to the rights referred to in subparagraphs (a) and (b), be considered as having been completed in the territory of the state of residence.
2.   The conditions as to length of residence and employment laid down in paragraph 1 (a) and the condition as to length of residence laid down in paragraph 1 (b) shall not apply if the worker's spouse is a national of the Member State concerned or has lost the nationality of that state by marriage to that worker.

Article 3 [Criteria for Members of Their Families]
1.   The members of a worker's family referred to in Article 1 of this Regulation who are residing which him in the territory of a Member State shall be entitled to remain there permanently if the worker has acquired the right to remain in the territory of that state in accordance with Article 2, and to do so even after his death.

2.   If, however, the worker dies during his working life and before having acquired the right to remain in the territory of the state concerned, members of his family shall be entitled to remain there permanently on condition that:
—   the worker, on the date of his decease, had resided continuously in the territory of that Member State for at least 2 years; or
—   his death resulted from an accident at work or an occupational disease; or
—   the surviving spouse is a national of the state of residence or lost the nationality of that state by marriage to that worker.

Article 4 [Calculation of Periods of Employment]
1.   Continuity of residence as provided for in Articles 2 (1) and 3 (2) may be attested by any means of proof in use in the country of residence. It shall not be affected by temporary absences not exceeding a total of three months per year, nor by longer absences due to compliance with the obligations of military service.
2.   Periods of involuntary unemployment, duly recorded by the competent employment office, and absences due to illness or accident shall be considered as periods of employment within the meaning of Article 2 (1).

Article 5 [Exercise of the Right to Remain in the Host State]
1.   The person entitled to the right to remain shall be allowed to exercise it within two years from the time of becoming entitled to such right pursuant to Article 2 (1) (a) and (b) and Article 3. During such period he may leave the territory of the Member State without adversely affecting such right.
2.   No formality shall be required on the part of the person concerned in respect of the exercise of the right to remain.

Article 6 [Procedures and Costs of Residence Permits]
1.   Persons coming under the provisions of this Regulation shall be entitled to a residence permit which:
(a) shall be issued and renewed free of charge or on payment of a sum not exceeding the dues and taxes payable by nationals for the issue or renewal identity documents;
(b) must be valid throughout the territory of the Member State issuing it;
(c) must be valid for at least five years and be renewable automatically.
2.   Periods of non-residence not exceeding six consecutive months shall not affect the validity of the residence permit.

Article 7 [Right to Equality of Treatment]
The right to equality of treatment, established by Council Regulation 1612/68, shall apply also to persons coming under the provisions of this Regulation.

Article 8 [More Favourable Member State Measures]
1.   This Regulation shall not affect any provisions laid down by law, regulation or administrative action of one Member State which would be more favourable to nationals of other Member States.
2.   Member States shall facilitate re-admission to their territories of workers who have left those territories after having resided there permanently for a long period and having been employed there and who wish to return there when they have reached retirement age or are permanently incapacitated for work.

Article 9 [omitted]

Done at Brussels, 29 June 1970. For the Commission, The President, Jean Rey

Council Directive 75/34 of 17 December 1974 Concerning the Right of Nationals of a Member State to Remain in the Territory of Another Member State After Having Pursued Therein an Activity in a Self-employed Capacity[1]

THE COUNCIL OF THE EUROPEAN COMMUNITIES,

HAVING REGARD to the Treaty establishing the European Economic Community, and in particular Article 235 thereof; [...]

(1) WHEREAS pursuant to Council Directive 73/148 of 21 May 1973 on the abolition of restrictions on movement and residence within the Community for nationals of Member States with regard to establishment and the provision of services,[2] each Member State grants the right of permanent residence to nationals of other Member States who establish themselves within its territory in order to pursue activities as self-employed persons, when the restrictions on these activities have been abolished pursuant to the Treaty;

(2) WHEREAS it is normal for a person to prolong a period of permanent residence in the territory of a Member State by remaining there after having pursued an activity there;

(3) WHEREAS the absence of a right so to remain in such circumstances is an obstacle to the attainment of freedom of establishment;

(4) WHEREAS, as regards employed persons, the conditions under which such a right may be exercised have already been laid down by Regulation 1251/70;[3]

(5) WHEREAS Article 48 (3) (d) of the Treaty recognizes the right of workers to remain in the territory of a Member State after having been employed in that state;

(6) WHEREAS Article 54 (2) does not expressly provide a similar right for self-employed persons;

(7) WHEREAS, nevertheless, the nature of establishment, together with attachments formed to the countries in which they have pursued their activities, means that such persons have a definite interest in enjoying the same right to remain as that granted to workers;

(8) WHEREAS in justification of this measure reference should be made to the Treaty provision enabling it to be taken;

(9) WHEREAS freedom of establishment within the Community requires that nationals of Member States may pursue self-employed activities in several Member States in succession without thereby being placed at a disadvantage;

(10) WHEREAS a national of a Member State residing in the territory of another Member State should be guaranteed the right to remain in that territory when he ceases to pursue an activity as a self-employed person in that state because he has reached retirement age or by reason of permanent incapacity to work;

(11) WHEREAS such a right should also be guaranteed to the national of a Member State who, after a period of activity in a self-employed capacity and residence in the territory of a second Member State, pursues an activity in the territory of a third Member State, while still retaining his residence in the territory of the second State;

---

1   OJ 1975 L 14, p. 10.

2   See above, p. 343.

3   See above, p. 349.

(12) WHEREAS, to determine the conditions under which the right to remain arises, account should be taken of the reasons which have led to the termination of activity in the territory of the Member State concerned and, in particular, of the difference between retirement, the normal and foreseeable end of working life, and permanent incapacity to work which leads to a premature and unforeseeable termination of activity;
(13) WHEREAS special conditions must be laid down where the spouse is or was a national of the Member State concerned, or where termination of activity is the result of an accident at work or occupational illness;
(14) WHEREAS a national of a Member State who has reached the end of his working life, after working in a self-employed capacity in the territory of another Member State, should have sufficient time in which to decide where he wishes to establish his final residence;
(15) WHEREAS the exercise of the right to remain by a national of a Member State working in a self-employed capacity entails extension of such right to the members of his family;
(16) WHEREAS in the case of the death of a national of a Member State working in a self-employed capacity during his working life the right of residence of the members of his family must also be recognized and be the subject of special conditions;
(17) WHEREAS persons to whom the right to remain applies must enjoy equality of treatment with nationals of the state concerned who have reached the end of their working lives;

HAS ADOPTED THIS DIRECTIVE:

Article 1 [Elimination of Restrictions on the Freedom of Movement]
Member States shall, under the conditions laid down in this Directive, abolish restrictions on the right to remain in their territory in favour of nationals of another Member State who have pursued activities as self-employed persons in their territory, and members of their families, as defined in Article 1 of Directive 73/148.

Article 2 [Criteria for Self-Employed Persons]
1.   Each Member State shall recognize the right to remain permanently in its territory of:
(a) any person who, at the time of termination of his activity, has reached the age laid down by the law of that state for entitlement to an old-age pension and who has pursued his activity in that state for at least the previous twelve months and has resided there continuously for more than three years.
       Where the law of that Member State does not grant the right to an old-age pension to certain categories of self-employed workers, the age requirement shall be considered as satisfied when the beneficiary reaches 65 years of age.
(b) any person who, having resided continuously in the territory of that state for more than two years, ceases to pursue his activity there as a result of permanent incapacity to work.
       If such incapacity is the result of an accident at work or an occupational illness entitling him to a pension which is payable in whole or in party by an institution of that state no condition shall be imposed as to length of residence.
(c) any person who, after three years' continuous activity and residence in the territory of that state, pursues his activity in the territory of another Member State, while retaining his residence in the territory of the first State, to which he returns, as a rule, each day or at least once a week.

Periods of activity so completed in the territory of the other Member State shall, for the purposes of entitlement to the rights referred to in (a) and (b), be considered as having been completed in the territory of the State of residence.

2.   The conditions as to length of residence and activity laid down in paragraph 1 (a) and the condition as to length of residence laid down in paragraph 1 (b) shall not apply if the spouse of the self-employed person is a national of the Member State concerned or has lost the nationality of that state by marriage to that person.

Article 3 [Criteria for Members of Their Families]

1.   Each Member State shall recognize the right of the members of the self-employed person's family referred to in Article 1 who are residing with him in the territory of that state to remain there permanently, if the person concerned has acquired the right to remain in the territory of that state in accordance with Article 2. This provision shall continue to apply even after the death of the person concerned.

2.   If, however, the self-employed person dies during his working life and before having acquired the right to remain in the territory of the state concerned, that state shall recognize the right of the members of his family to remain there permanently on condition that:
— the person concerned, on the date of his decease, had resided continuously in its territory for at least two years; or
— his death resulted from an accident at work or an occupational illness; or
— the surviving spouse is a national of that state or lost such nationality by marriage to the person concerned.

Article 4 [Calculation of Periods of Residence]

1.   Continuity of residence as provided for in Articles 2 (1) and 3 (2) may be attested by any means of proof in use in the country of residence. It may not be affected by temporary absences not exceeding a total of three months per year, nor by longer absences due to compliance with the obligations of military service.

2.   Periods of inactivity due to circumstances outside the control of the person concerned or of inactivity owing to illness or accident must be considered as periods of activity within the meaning of Article 2 (1).

Article 5 [Exercise of the Right to Remain in the Host State]

1.   Member States shall allow the person entitled to the right to remain to exercise such right within two years from the time of becoming entitled thereto pursuant to Article 2 (1) (a) and (b) and Article 3. During this period the beneficiary must be able to leave the territory of the Member State without adversely affecting such right.

2.   Member States shall not require the person concerned to comply with any particular formality in order to exercise the right to remain.

Article 6 [Procedures and Costs of Residence Permits]

1.   Member States shall recognize the right to remain in their territory to a residence permit, which must:
(a) be issued and renewed free of charge or on payment of a sum not exceeding the dues and taxes payable by nationals for the issue or renewal of identity cards;
(b) by valid throughout the territory of the Member State issuing it;
(c) be valid for five years and renewable automatically.

2.   Periods of non-residence not exceeding six consecutive months and longer absences due to compliance with the obligations of military service may not affect the validity of a residence permit.

Article 7 [Right to Equality of Treatment]
Member States shall apply to persons having the right to remain in their territory the right of equality of treatment recognized by the Council Directives on the abolition of restrictions on freedom of establishment pursuant to Title III of the general programme which provides for such abolition.

Article 8 [More Favourable Member State Measures]
1.   This Directive shall not affect any provisions laid down by law, regulation or administrative action of any Member State which would be more favourable to nationals of other Member States.
2.   Member States shall facilitate re-admission to their territories of self-employed persons who left those territories after having resided there permanently for a long period while pursuing an activity there and who whish to return when they have reached retirement age as defined in Article 2 (1) (a) or are permanently incapacitated for work.

Article 9 [Derogations from the Fundamental Freedoms]
Member States may not derogate from the provisions of this Directive save on grounds of public policy, public security or public health.

Article 10 [omitted]

Article 11 [Addressees]
This Directive is addressed to the Member States.

Done at Brussels, 17 December 1974.
For the Council, The President, M. Durafour

Council Directive 90/365 of 28 June 1990 on the Right of Residence for Employees and Self-employed Persons Who Have Ceased Their Occupational Activity[1]

THE COUNCIL OF THE EUROPEAN COMMUNITIES,

HAVING REGARD to the Treaty establishing the European Economic Community, and in particular Article 235 thereof, [...]
(1) WHEREAS Article 3 (c) of the Treaty provides that the activities of the Community shall include, as provided in the Treaty, the abolition, as between Member States, of obstacles to freedom of movement for persons;
(2) WHEREAS Article 8a of the Treaty provides that the internal market must be established by 31 December 1992; whereas the internal market comprises an area without internal frontiers in which the free movement of goods, persons, services and capital is ensured, in accordance with the provisions of the Treaty;
(3) WHEREAS Articles 48 and 52 of the Treaty provide for freedom of movement for workers and self-employed persons, which entails the right of residence in the Member States in which they pursue their occupational activity; whereas it is desirable that this right of residence also be granted to persons who have ceased their occupational

---

1   OJ 1990 L180, p. 28.

activity even if they have not exercised their right to freedom of movement during their working life;

(4) WHEREAS beneficiaries of the right of residence must not become an unreasonable burden on the public finances of the host Member State;

(5) WHEREAS under Article 10 of Regulation 1408/71, as amended [...], recipients of invalidity or old age cash benefits or pensions for accidents at work or occupational diseases are entitled to continue to receive these benefits and pensions even if they reside in the territory of a Member State other than that in which the institution responsible for payment is situated;

(6) WHEREAS this right can only be genuinely exercised if it is also granted to members of the family;

(7) WHEREAS the beneficiaries of this Directive should be covered by administrative arrangements similar to those laid down in particular by Directive 68/360[1] and Directive 64/221;[2]

(8) WHEREAS the Treaty does not provide, for the action concerned, powers other than those of Article 235,

HAS ADOPTED THIS DIRECTIVE:

Article 1 [Conditions for the Right of Residence]

1.   Member States shall grant the right of residence to nationals of Member States who have pursued an activity as an employee or self-employed person and to members of their families as defined in paragraph 2, provided that they are recipients of an invalidity or early retirement pension, or old age benefits, or of a pension in respect of an industrial accident or disease of an amount sufficient to avoid becoming a burden on the social security system of the host Member State during their period of residence and provided they are covered by sickness insurance in respect of all risks in the host Member State.

The resources of the applicant shall be deemed sufficient where they are higher than the level of resources below which the host Member State may grant social assistance to its nationals, taking into account the personal circumstances of persons admitted pursuant to paragraph 2.

Where the second subparagraph cannot be applied in a Member State, the resources of the applicant shall be deemed sufficient if they are higher than the level of the minimum social security pension paid by the host Member State.

2.   The following shall, irrespective of their nationality, have the right to install themselves in another Member State with the holder of the right of residence:

(a) his or her spouse and their descendants who are dependants;

(b) dependent relatives in the ascending line of the holder of the right of residence and his or her spouse.

Article 2 [Residence Permits]

1.   Exercise of the right of residence shall be evidenced by means of the issue of a document known as a "Residence permit for a national of a Member State of the EEC", whose validity may be limited to five years on a renewable basis. However, the Member States may, when they deem it to be necessary, require revalidation of the permit at the end of the first two years of residence. Where a member of the family does not

---

1   See above, p. 340.

2   See above, p. 346.

hold the nationality of a Member State, he or she shall be issued with a residence document of the same validity as that issued to the national on whom he or she depends.

For the purposes of issuing the residence permit or document, the Member State may require only that the applicant present a valid identity card or passport and provide proof that he or she meets the conditions laid down in Article 1.

2. Articles 2, 3, 6 (1) (a) and (2) and Article 9 of Directive 68/360 shall apply *mutatis mutandis* to the beneficiaries of this Directive.

The spouse and the dependent children of a national of a Member State entitled to the right of residence within the territory of a Member State shall be entitled to take up any employed or self-employed activity anywhere within the territory of that Member State, even if they are not nationals of a Member State.

Member States shall not derogate from the provisions of this Directive save on grounds of public policy, public security or public health. In that event, Directive 64/221 shall apply.

3. This Directive shall not affect existing law on the acquisition of second homes.

Article 3 [Duration of the Right of Residence]
The right of residence shall remain for as long as beneficiaries of that right fulfil the conditions laid down in Article 1.

Article 4 [Monitoring]
The Commission shall, not more than three years after the date of implementation of this Directive, and at three-yearly intervals thereafter, draw up a report on the application of this Directive and submit it to the European Parliament and the Council.

Article 5 [Implementation into National Law]
Member States shall bring into force the laws, regulations and administrative provisions necessary to comply with this Directive not later than 30 June 1992. They shall forthwith inform the Commission thereof.

Article 6 [Addressees]
This Directive is addressed to the Member States.

Done at Luxembourg, 28 June 1990.
For the Council, The President, M. GEOGHEGAN-QUINN

Council Directive 93/96 of 29 October 1993 on the Right of Residence for Students[1]

THE COUNCIL OF THE EUROPEAN COMMUNITIES,

HAVING REGARD to the Treaty establishing the European Economic Community, and in particular the second paragraph of Article 7 thereof, [...]
(1) WHEREAS Article 3 (c) of the Treaty provides that the activities of the Community shall include, as provided in the Treaty, the abolition, as between Member States, of obstacles to freedom of movement for persons;
(2) WHEREAS Article 8a of the Treaty provides that the internal market must be established by 31 December 1992; whereas the internal market comprises an area without internal frontiers in which the free movement of goods, persons, services and capital is ensured in accordance with the provisions of the Treaty;
(3) WHEREAS, as the Court of Justice has held, Articles 128 and 7 of the Treaty prohibit any discrimination between nationals of the Member States as regards access to vocational training in the Community; whereas access by a national of one Member State to vocational training in another Member State implies, for that national, a right of residence in that other Member State;
(4) WHEREAS, accordingly, in order to guarantee access to vocational training, the conditions likely to facilitate the effective exercise of that right of residence should be laid down;
(5) WHEREAS the right of residence for students forms part of a set of related measures designed to promote vocational training;
(6) WHEREAS beneficiaries of the right of residence must not become an unreasonable burden on the public finances of the host Member State;
(7) WHEREAS, in the present state of Community law, as established by the case law of the Court of Justice, assistance granted to students, does not fall within the scope of the Treaty within the meaning of Article 7 thereof;
(8) WHEREAS the right of residence can only be genuinely exercised if it is also granted to the spouse and their dependent children;
(9) WHEREAS the beneficiaries of this Directive should be covered by administrative arrangements similar to those laid down in particular in Council Directive 68/360 of 15 October 1968 on the abolition of restrictions on movement and residence within the Community for workers of Member States and their families and Council Directive 64/221 of 25 February 1964 on the coordination of special measures concerning the movement and residence of foreign nationals which are justified on grounds of public policy, public security or public health;
(10) WHEREAS this Directive does not apply to students who enjoy the right of residence by virtue of the fact that they are or have been effectively engaged in economic activities or are members of the family of a migrant worker;
(11) WHEREAS, by its judgment of 7 July 1992 in Case C-295/90, the Court of Justice annulled Council Directive 90/366 of 28 June 1990 on the right of residence for students, while maintaining the effects of the annulled Directive until the entry into force of a directive adopted on the appropriate legal basis;
(12) WHEREAS the effects of Directive 90/366 should be maintained during the period up to 31 December 1993, the date by which Member States are to have adopted the laws, regulations and administrative provisions necessary to comply with this Directive,

---

1   OJ 1993 L 317, p. 59.

HAS ADOPTED THIS DIRECTIVE:

Article 1 [Conditions for the Right of Residence]

In order to lay down conditions to facilitate the exercise of the right of residence and with a view to guaranteeing access to vocational training in a non-discriminatory manner for a national of a Member State who has been accepted to attend a vocational training course in another Member State, the Member States shall recognize the right of residence for any student who is a national of a Member State and who does not enjoy that right under other provisions of Community law, and for the student's spouse and their dependent children, where the student assures the relevant national authority, by means of a declaration or by such alternative means as the student may choose that are at least equivalent, that he has sufficient resources to avoid becoming a burden on the social assistance system of the host Member State during their period of residence, provided that the student is enrolled in a recognized educational establishment for the principal purpose of following a vocational training course there and that he is covered by sickness insurance in respect of all risks in the host Member State.

Article 2 [Residence Permits]

1. The right of residence shall be restricted to the duration of the course of studies in question.

The right of residence shall be evidenced by means of the issue of a document known as a "residence permit for a national of a Member State of the Community", the validity of which may be limited to the duration of the course of studies or to one year where the course lasts longer; in the latter event it shall be renewable annually.

Where a member of the family does not hold the nationality of a Member State, he or she shall be issued with a residence document of the same validity as that issued to the national on whom he or she depends.

For the purpose of issuing the residence permit or document, the Member State may require only that the applicant present a valid identity card or passport and provide proof that he or she meets the conditions laid down in Article 1.

2. Articles 2, 3 and 9 of Directive 68/360 shall apply mutatis mutandis to the beneficiaries of this Directive.

The spouse and the dependent children of a national of a Member State entitled to the right of residence within the territory of a Member State shall be entitled to take up any employed or self-employed activity anywhere within the territory of that Member State, even if they are not nationals of a Member State.

Member States shall not derogate from the provisions of this Directive save on grounds of public policy, public security or public health; in that event, Articles 2 to 9 of Directive 64/221 shall apply.

Article 3 [No Claim to Financial Support]

This Directive shall not establish any entitlement to the payment of maintenance grants by the host Member State on the part of students benefiting from the right of residence.

Article 4 [Duration of the Right of Residence]

The right of residence shall remain for as long as beneficiaries of that right fulfil the conditions laid down in Article 1.

Article 5 [Monitoring]

The Commission shall, not more than three years after the date of implementation of this Directive, and at three-yearly intervals thereafter, draw up a report on the application of this Directive and submit it to the European Parliament and the Council.

The Commission shall pay particular attention to any difficulties to which the implementation of Article 1 might give rise in the Member States; it shall, if appropriate, submit proposals to the Council with the aim of remedying such difficulties.

Article 6 [Implementation into National Law]
Member States shall bring into force the laws, regulations and administrative provisions necessary to comply with this Directive not later than 31 December 1993. They shall forthwith inform the Commission thereof.

For the period preceding that date, the effects of Directive 90/366 shall be maintained.

When Member States adopt those measures, they shall contain a reference to this Directive or shall be accompanied by such a reference on the occasion of their official publication. The methods of making such references shall be laid down by the Member States.

Article 7 [Addressees]
This Directive is addressed to the Member States.

Done at Brussels, 29 October 1993.
For the Council, The President, R. URBAIN

Council Directive 90/364 of 28 June 1990 on the Right of Residence[1]

THE COUNCIL OF THE EUROPEAN COMMUNITIES,

HAVING REGARD to the Treaty establishing the European Economic Community, and in particular Article 235 thereof, [...]
(1) WHEREAS Article 3 (c) of the Treaty provides that the activities of the Community shall include, as provided in the Treaty, the abolition, as between Member States, of obstacles to freedom of movement for persons;
(2) WHEREAS Article 8a of the Treaty provides that the internal market must be established by 31 December 1992; whereas the internal market comprises an area without internal frontiers in which the free movement of goods, persons, services and capital is ensured in accordance with the provisions of the Treaty;
(3) WHEREAS national provisions on the right of nationals of the Member States to reside in a Member State other than their own must be harmonized to ensure such freedom of movement;
(4) WHEREAS beneficiaries of the right of residence must not become an unreasonable burden on the public finances of the host Member State;
(5) WHEREAS this right can only be genuinely exercised if it is also granted to members of the family;
(6) WHEREAS the beneficiaries of this Directive should be covered by administrative arrangements similar to those laid down in particular in Directive 68/360[2] and Directive 64/221;[3]

---

1   OJ 1990 L 180, p. 26.

2   See above, p. 340.

3   See above, p. 346.

(7) WHEREAS the Treaty does not provide, for the action concerned, powers other than those of Article 235,

HAS ADOPTED THIS DIRECTIVE:

Article 1 [Conditions for the Right of Residence]

1. Member States shall grant the right of residence to nationals of Member States who do not enjoy this right under other provisions of Community law and to members of their families as defined in paragraph 2, provided that they themselves and the members of their families are covered by sickness insurance in respect of all risks in the host Member State and have sufficient resources to avoid becoming a burden on the social assistance system of the host Member State during their period of residence.

The resources referred to in the first subparagraph shall be deemed sufficient where they are higher than the level of resources below which the host Member State may grant social assistance to its nationals, taking into account the personal circumstances of the applicant and, where appropriate, the personal circumstances of persons admitted pursuant to paragraph 2.

Where the second subparagraph cannot be applied in a Member State, the resources of the applicant shall be deemed sufficient if they are higher than the level of the minimum social security pension paid by the host Member State.

2. The following shall, irrespective of their nationality, have the right to install themselves in another Member State with the holder of the right of residence:

(a) his or her spouse and their descendants who are dependants;

(b) dependent relatives in the ascending line of the holder of the right of residence and his or her spouse.

Article 2 [Residence Permits]

1. Exercise of the right of residence shall be evidenced by means of the issue of a document known as a "Residence permit for a national of a Member State of the EEC", the validity of which may be limited to five years on a renewable basis. However, the Member States may, when they deem it to be necessary, require revalidation of the permit at the end of the first two years of residence. Where a member of the family does not hold the nationality of a Member State, he or she shall be issued with a residence document of the same validity as that issued to the national on whom he or she depends.

For the purpose of issuing the residence permit or document, the Member State may require only that the applicant present a valid identity card or passport and provide proof that he or she meets the conditions laid down in Article 1.

2. Articles 2, 3, 6 (1) (a) and (2) and Article 9 of Directive 68/360 shall apply mutatis mutandis to the beneficiaries of this Directive.

The spouse and the dependent children of a national of a Member State entitled to the right of residence within the territory of a Member State shall be entitled to take up any employed or self-employed activity anywhere within the territory of that Member State, even if they are not nationals of a Member State.

Member States shall not derogate from the provisions of this Directive save on grounds of public policy, public security or public health. In that event, Directive 64/221 shall apply.

3. This Directive shall not affect existing law on the acquisition of second homes.

Article 3 [Duration of the Right of Residence]

The right of residence shall remain for as long as beneficiaries of that right fulfil the conditions laid down in Article 1.

Article 4 [Monitoring]
The Commission shall, not more than three years after the date of implementation of this Directive, and at three-yearly intervals thereafter, draw up a report on the application of this Directive and submit it to the European Parliament and the Council.

Article 5 [Implementation into National Law]
Member States shall bring into force the laws, regulations and administrative provisions necessary to comply with this Directive not later than 30 June 1992. They shall forthwith inform the Commission thereof.

Article 6 [Addressees]
This Directive is addressed to the Member States.

Done at Luxembourg, 28 June 1990.

Council Directive 89/48 of 21 December 1988 on a General System for the Recognition of Higher-education Diplomas Awarded on Completion of Professional Education and Training of at Least Three Years' Duration[1]

THE COUNCIL OF THE EUROPEAN COMMUNITIES,

HAVING REGARD to the Treaty establishing the European Economic Community, and in particular Articles 49, 57 (1) and 66 thereof, [...]
(1) WHEREAS, pursuant to Article 3 (c) of the Treaty the abolition, as between Member States, of obstacles to freedom of movement for persons and services constitutes one of the objectives of the Community;
(2) WHEREAS, for nationals of the Member States, this means in particular the possibility of pursuing a profession, whether in a self-employed or employed capacity, in a Member State other than that in which they acquired their professional qualifications;
(3) WHEREAS the provisions so far adopted by the Council, and pursuant to which Member States recognize mutually and for professional purposes higher-education diplomas issued within their territory, concern only a few professions;
(4) WHEREAS the level and duration of the education and training governing access to those professions have been regulated in a similar fashion in all the Member States or have been the subject of the minimal harmonization needed to establish sectoral systems for the mutual recognition of diplomas;
(5) WHEREAS, in order to provide a rapid response to the expectations of nationals of Community countries who hold higher-education diplomas awarded on completion of professional education and training issued in a Member State other than that in which they wish to pursue their profession, another method of recognition of such diplomas should also be put in place such as to enable those concerned to pursue all those professional activities which in a host Member State are dependent on the completion of post-secondary education and training, provided they hold such a diploma preparing

---

1   OJ 1989 L 19, p. 16. For shorter and other types of training see also Council Directive 92/51 of 18 June 1992 on a second general system for the recognition of professional education and training to supplement Directive 89/48, OJ 1992 L 209, p. 25.

them for those activities awarded on completion of a course of studies lasting at least three years and issued in another Member State;

(6) WHEREAS this objective can be achieved by the introduction of a general system for the recognition of higher-education diplomas awarded on completion of professional education and training of at least three years' duration;

(7) WHEREAS, for those professions for the pursuit of which the Community has not laid down the necessary minimum level of qualification, Member States reserve the option of fixing such a level with a view to guaranteeing the quality of services provided in their territory;

(8) WHEREAS, however, they may not, without infringing their obligations laid down in Article 5 of the Treaty, require a national of a Member State to obtain those qualifications which in general they determine only by reference to diplomas issued under their own national education systems, where the person concerned has already acquired all or part of those qualifications in another Member State;

(9) WHEREAS, as a result, any host Member State in which a profession is regulated is required to take account of qualifications acquired in another Member State and to determine whether those qualifications correspond to the qualifications which the Member State concerned requires;

(10) WHEREAS collaboration between the Member States is appropriate in order to facilitate their compliance with those obligations;

(11) WHEREAS, therefore, the means of organizing such collaboration should be established;

(12) WHEREAS the term "regulated professional activity" should be defined so as to take account of differing national sociological situations;

(13) WHEREAS the term should cover not only professional activities access to which is subject, in a Member State, to the possession of a diploma, but also professional activities, access to which is unrestricted when they are practised under a professional title reserved for the holders of certain qualifications;

(14) WHEREAS the professional associations and organizations which confer such titles on their members and are recognized by the public authorities cannot invoke their private status to avoid application of the system provided for by this Directive;

(15) WHEREAS it is also necessary to determine the characteristics of the professional experience or adaptation period which the host Member State may require of the person concerned in addition to the higher-education diploma, where the person's qualifications do not correspond to those laid down by national provisions;

(16) WHEREAS an aptitude test may also be introduced in place of the adaptation period; whereas the effect of both will be to improve the existing situation with regard to the mutual recognition of diplomas between Member States and therefore to facilitate the free movement of persons within the Community;

(17) WHEREAS their function is to assess the ability of the migrant, who is a person who has already received his professional training in another Member State, to adapt to this new professional environment;

(18) WHEREAS, from the migrant's point of view, an aptitude test will have the advantage of reducing the length of the practice period;

(19) WHEREAS, in principle, the choice between the adaptation period and the aptitude test should be made by the migrant; whereas, however, the nature of certain professions is such that Member States must be allowed to prescribe, under certain conditions, either the adaptation period or the test;

(20) WHEREAS, in particular, the differences between the legal systems of the Member States, whilst they may vary in extent from one Member State to another, warrant special provisions since, as a rule, the education or training attested by the diploma, certificate or other evidence of formal qualifications in a field of law in the Member State

of origin does not cover the legal knowledge required in the host Member State with respect to the corresponding legal field;

(21) WHEREAS, moreover, the general system for the recognition of higher-education diplomas is intended neither to amend the rules, including those relating to professional ethics, applicable to any person pursuing a profession in the territory of a Member State nor to exclude migrants from the application of those rules;

(22) WHEREAS that system is confined to laying down appropriate arrangements to ensure that migrants comply with the professional rules of the host Member State;

(23) WHEREAS Articles 49, 57 (1) and 66 of the Treaty empower the Community to adopt provisions necessary for the introduction and operation of such a system;

(24) WHEREAS the general system for the recognition of higher-education diplomas is entirely without prejudice to the application of Article 48 (4) and Article 55 of the Treaty;

(25) WHEREAS such a system, by strengthening the right of a Community national to use his professional skills in any Member State, supplements and reinforces his right to acquire such skills wherever he wishes;

(26) WHEREAS this system should be evaluated, after being in force for a certain time, to determine how efficiently it operates and in particular how it can be improved or its field of application extended,

HAS ADOPTED THIS DIRECTIVE:

Article 1 [Definitions]
For the purposes of this Directive the following definitions shall apply:
(a) diploma: any diploma, certificate or other evidence of formal qualifications or any set of such diplomas, certificates or other evidence:
— which has been awarded by a competent authority in a Member State, designated in accordance with its own laws, regulations or administrative provisions;
— which shows that the holder has successfully completed a post-secondary course of at least three years' duration, or of an equivalent duration part- time, at a university or establishment of higher education or another establishment of similar level and, where appropriate, that he has successfully completed the professional training required in addition to the post-secondary course, and
— which shows that the holder has the professional qualifications required for the taking up or pursuit of a regulated profession in that Member State, provided that the education and training attested by the diploma, certificate or other evidence of formal qualifications were received mainly in the Community, or the holder thereof has three years' professional experience certified by the Member State which recognized a third-country diploma, certificate or other evidence of formal qualifications.

The following shall be treated in the same way as a diploma, within the meaning of the first subparagraph: any diploma, certificate or other evidence of formal qualifications or any set of such diplomas, certificates or other evidence awarded by a competent authority in a Member State if it is awarded on the successful completion of education and training received in the Community and recognized by a competent authority in that Member State as being of an equivalent level and if it confers the same rights in respect of the taking up and pursuit of a regulated profession in that Member State;

(b) host Member State: any Member State in which a national of a Member State applies to pursue a profession subject to regulation in that Member State, other than the State in which he obtained his diploma or first pursued the profession in question;

(c) a regulated profession: the regulated professional activity or range of activities which constitute this profession in a Member State;

(d) regulated professional activity: a professional activity, in so far as the taking up or pursuit of such activity or one of its modes of pursuit in a Member State is subject, directly or indirectly by virtue of laws, regulations or administrative provisions, to the possession of a diploma. The following in particular shall constitute a mode of pursuit of a regulated professional activity:

— pursuit of an activity under a professional title, in so far as the use of such a title is reserved to the holders of a diploma governed by laws, regulations or administrative provisions,

— pursuit of a professional activity relating to health, in so far as remuneration and/or reimbursement for such an activity is subject by virtue of national social security arrangements to the possession of a diploma.

Where the first subparagraph does not apply, a professional activity shall be deemed to be a regulated professional activity if it is pursued by the members of an association or organization the purpose of which is, in particular, to promote and maintain a high standard in the professional field concerned and which, to achieve that purpose, is recognized in a special form by a Member State and:

— awards a diploma to its members,

— ensures that its members respect the rules of professional conduct which it prescribes, and

— confers on them the right to use a title or designatory letters, or to benefit from a status corresponding to that diploma.

A non-exhaustive list of associations or organizations which, when this Directive is adopted, satisfy the conditions of the second subparagraph is contained in the Annex. Whenever a Member State grants the recognition referred to in the second subparagraph to an association or organization, it shall inform the Commission thereof, which shall publish this information in the Official Journal of the European Communities.

(e) professional experience: the actual and lawful pursuit of the profession concerned in a Member State;

(f) adaptation period: the pursuit of a regulated profession in the host Member State under the responsibility of a qualified member of that profession, such period of supervised practice possibly being accompanied by further training. This period of supervised practice shall be the subject of an assessment. The detailed rules governing the adaptation period and its assessment as well as the status of a migrant person under supervision shall be laid down by the competent authority in the host Member States;

(g) aptitude test: a test limited to the professional knowledge of the applicant, made by the competent authorities of the host Member State with the aim of assessing the ability of the applicant to pursue a regulated profession in that Member State.

In order to permit this test to be carried out, the competent authorities shall draw up a list of subjects which, on the basis of a comparison of the education and training required in the Member State and that received by the applicant, are not covered by the diploma or other evidence of formal qualifications possessed by the applicant.

The aptitude test must take account of the fact that the applicant is a qualified professional in the Member State of origin or the Member State from which he comes. It shall cover subjects to be selected from those on the list, knowledge of which is essential in order to be able to exercise the profession in the host Member

State. The test may also include knowledge of the professional rules applicable to the activities in question in the host Member State. The detailed application of the aptitude test shall be determined by the competent authorities of that State with due regard to the rules of Community law.

The status, in the host Member State, of the applicant who wishes to prepare himself for the aptitude test in that State shall be determined by the competent authorities in that State.

Article 2 [Scope]

This Directive shall apply to any national of a Member State wishing to pursue a regulated profession in a host Member State in a self-employed capacity or as an employed person.

This Directive shall not apply to professions which are the subject of a separate Directive establishing arrangements for the mutual recognition of diplomas by Member States.

Article 3 [Conditions for Mutual Recognition]

Where, in a host Member State, the taking up or pursuit of a regulated profession is subject to possession of a diploma, the competent authority may not, on the grounds of inadequate qualifications, refuse to authorize a national of a Member State to take up or pursue that profession on the same conditions as apply to its own nationals:

(a) if the applicant holds the diploma required in another Member State for the taking up or pursuit of the profession in question in its territory, such diploma having been awarded in a Member State; or

(b) if the applicant has pursued the profession in question full-time for two years during the previous ten years in another Member State which does not regulate that profession, within the meaning of Article 1 (c) and the first subparagraph of Article 1 (d), and possesses evidence of one or more formal qualifications:

— which have been awarded by a competent authority in a Member State, designated in accordance with the laws, regulations or administrative provisions of such State,

— which show that the holder has successfully completed a post-secondary course of at least three years' duration, or of an equivalent duration part-time, at a university or establishment of higher education or another establishment of similar level of a Member State and, where appropriate, that he has successfully completed the professional training required in addition to the post-secondary course and which have prepared the holder for the pursuit of his profession.

The following shall be treated in the same way as the evidence of formal qualifications referred to in the first subparagraph: any formal qualifications or any set of such formal qualifications awarded by a competent authority in a Member State if it is awarded on the successful completion of training received in the Community and is recognized by that Member State as being of an equivalent level, provided that the other Member States and the Commission have been notified of this recognition.

Article 4 [Additional Requirements Imposed by Host Member State]

1. Notwithstanding Article 3, the host Member State may also require the applicant:

(a) to provide evidence of professional experience, where the duration of the education and training adduced in support of his application, as laid down in Article 3 (a) and (b), is at least one year less than that required in the host Member State. In this event, the period of professional experience required:

— may not exceed twice the shortfall in duration of education and training where the shortfall relates to post-secondary studies and/or to a period of probationary practice carried out under the control of a supervising professional person and ending with an examination,

— may not exceed the shortfall where the shortfall relates to professional practice acquired with the assistance of a qualified member of the profession.

In the case of diplomas within the meaning of the last subparagraph of Article 1 (a), the duration of education and training recognized as being of an equivalent level shall be determined as for the education and training defined in the first subparagraph of Article 1 (a).

When applying these provisions, account must be taken of the professional experience referred to in Article 3 (b).

At all events, the professional experience required may not exceed four years;

(b) to complete an adaptation period not exceeding three years or take an aptitude test:

— where the matters covered by the education and training he has received as laid down in Article 3 (a) and (b), differ substantially from those covered by the diploma required in the host Member State, or

— where, in the case referred to in Article 3 (a), the profession regulated in the host Member State comprises one or more regulated professional activities which are not in the profession regulated in the Member State from which the applicant originates or comes and that difference corresponds to specific education and training required in the host Member State and covers matters which differ substantially from those covered by the diploma adduced by the applicant, or

— where, in the case referred to in Article 3 (b), the profession regulated in the host Member State comprises one or more regulated professional activities which are not in the profession pursued by the applicant in the Member State from which he originates or comes, and that difference corresponds to specific education and training required in the host Member State and covers matters which differ substantially from those covered by the evidence of formal qualifications adduced by the applicant.

Should the host Member State make use of this possibility, it must give the applicant the right to choose between an adaptation period and an aptitude test. By way of derogation from this principle, for professions whose practice requires precise knowledge of national law and in respect of which the provision of advice and/or assistance concerning national law is an essential and constant aspect of the professional activity, the host Member State may stipulate either an adaptation period or an aptitude test. Where the host Member State intends to introduce derogations for other professions as regards an applicant's right to choose, the procedure laid down in Article 10 shall apply.

2. However, the host Member State may not apply the provisions of paragraph 1 (a) and (b) cumulatively.

Article 5 [Supplementary Training in Host Member States]

Without prejudice to Articles 3 and 4, a host Member State may allow the applicant, with a view to improving his possibilities of adapting to the professional environment in that State, to undergo there, on the basis of equivalence, that part of his professional education and training represented by professional practice, acquired with the assistance of a qualified member of the profession, which he has not undergone in his Member State of origin or the Member State from which he has come.

Article 6 [Requirement of Proof of Good Repute]
1.   Where the competent authority of a host Member State requires of persons wishing to take up a regulated profession proof that they are of good character or repute or that they have not been declared bankrupt, or suspends or prohibits the pursuit of that profession in the event of serious professional misconduct or a criminal offence, that State shall accept as sufficient evidence, in respect of nationals of Member States wishing to pursue that profession in its territory, the production of documents issued by competent authorities in the Member State of origin or the Member State from which the foreign national comes showing that those requirements are met.

Where the competent authorities of the Member State of origin or of the Member State from which the foreign national comes do not issue the documents referred to in the first subparagraph, such documents shall be replaced by a declaration on oath - or, in States where there is no provision for declaration on oath, by a solemn declaration - made by the person concerned before a competent judicial or administrative authority or, where appropriate, a notary or qualified professional body of the Member State of origin or the Member State from which the person comes; such authority or notary shall issue a certificate attesting the authenticity of the declaration on oath or solemn declaration.
2.   Where the competent authority of a host Member State requires of nationals of that Member State wishing to take up or pursue a regulated profession a certificate of physical or mental health, that authority shall accept as sufficient evidence in this respect the production of the document required in the Member State of origin or the Member State from which the foreign national comes.

Where the Member State of origin or the Member State from which the foreign national comes does not impose any requirements of this nature on those wishing to take up or pursue the profession in question, the host Member State shall accept from such nationals a certificate issued by a competent authority in that State corresponding to the certificates issued in the host Member State.
3.   The competent authorities of host Member States may require that the documents and certificates referred to in paragraphs 1 and 2 are presented no more than three months after their date of issue.
4.   Where the competent authority of a host Member State requires nationals of that Member State wishing to take up or pursue a regulated profession to take an oath or make a solemn declaration and where the form of such oath or declaration cannot be used by nationals of other Member States, that authority shall ensure that an appropriate and equivalent form of oath or declaration is offered to the person concerned.

Article 7 [Professional Titles]
1.   The competent authorities of host Member States shall recognize the right of nationals of Member States who fulfil the conditions for the taking up and pursuit of a regulated profession in their territory to use the professional title of the host Member State corresponding to that profession.
2.   The competent authorities of host Member States shall recognize the right of nationals of Member States who fulfil the conditions for the taking up and pursuit of a regulated profession in their territory to use their lawful academic title and, where appropriate, the abbreviation thereof deriving from their Member State of origin or the Member State from which they come, in the language of that State. Host Member State may require this title to be followed by the name and location of the establishment or examining board which awarded it.
3.   Where a profession is regulated in the host Member State by an association or organization referred to in Article 1 (d), nationals of Member States shall only be en-

titled to use the professional title or designatory letters conferred by that organization or association on proof of membership.

Where the association or organization makes membership subject to certain qualification requirements, it may apply these to nationals of other Member States who are in possession of a diploma within the meaning of Article 1 (a) or a formal qualification within the meaning of Article 3 (b) only in accordance with this Directive, in particular Articles 3 and 4.

Article 8 [Examination of Applications]

1. The host Member State shall accept as proof that the conditions laid down in Articles 3 and 4 are satisfied the certificates and documents issued by the competent authorities in the Member States, which the person concerned shall submit in support of his application to pursue the profession concerned.

2. The procedure for examining an application to pursue a regulated profession shall be completed as soon as possible and the outcome communicated in a reasoned decision of the competent authority in the host Member State not later than four months after presentation of all the documents relating to the person concerned. A remedy shall be available against this decision, or the absence thereof, before a court or tribunal in accordance with the provisions of national law.

Article 9 [Competent Authorities]

1. Member States shall designate, within the period provided for in Article 12, the competent authorities empowered to receive the applications and take the decisions referred to in this Directive. They shall communicate this information to the other Member States and to the Commission.

2. Each Member State shall designate a person responsible for coordinating the activities of the authorities referred to in paragraph 1 and shall inform the other Member States and the Commission to that effect. His role shall be to promote uniform application of this Directive to all the professions concerned. A coordinating group shall be set up under the aegis of the Commission, composed of the coordinators appointed by each Member State or their deputies and chaired by a representative of the Commission.

The task of this group shall be:
— to facilitate the implementation of this Directive,
— to collect all useful information for its application in the Member States.
The group may be consulted by the Commission on any changes to the existing system that may contemplated.

3. Member States shall take measures to provide the necessary information on the recognition of diplomas within the framework of this Directive. They may be assisted in this task by the information centre on the academic recognition of diplomas and periods of study established by the Member States within the framework of the Resolution of the Council and the Ministers of Education meeting within the Council of 9 February 1976, and, where appropriate, the relevant professional associations or organizations. The Commission shall take the necessary initiatives to ensure the development and coordination of the communication of the necessary information.

Article 10 [Exception to Choice Between Adaption Period and Aptitude Test]

1. If, pursuant to the third sentence of the second subparagraph of Article 4 (1) (b), a Member State proposes not to grant applicants the right to choose between an adaptation period and an aptitude test in respect of a profession within the meaning of this Directive, it shall immediately communicate to the Commission the corresponding

draft provision. It shall at the same time notify the Commission of the grounds which make the enactment of such a provision necessary.

The Commission shall immediately notify the other Member States of any draft it has received; it may also consult the coordinating group referred to in Article 9 (2) of the draft.

2. Without prejudice to the possibility for the Commission and the other Member States of making comments on the draft, the Member State may adopt the provision only if the Commission has not taken a decision to the contrary within three months.

3. At the request of a Member State or the Commission, Member States shall communicate to them, without delay, the definitive text of a provision arising from the application of this Article.

Article 11 [Member State Reports]

Following the expiry of the period provided for in Article 12, Member States shall communicate to the Commission, every two years, a report on the application of the system introduced.

In addition to general remarks, this report shall contain a statistical summary of the decisions taken and a description of the main problems arising from application of the Directive.

Article 12 [Implementation into National Law]

Member States shall take the measures necessary to comply with this Directive within two years of its notification[1]. They shall forthwith inform the Commission thereof.

Member States shall communicate to the Commission the texts of the main provisions of national law which they adopt in the field governed by this Directive.

Article 13 [Monitoring]

Five years at the latest following the date specified in Article 12, the Commission shall report to the European Parliament and the Council on the state of application of the general system for the recognition of higher-education diplomas awarded on completion of professional education and training of at least three years' duration.

After conducting all necessary consultations, the Commission shall, on this occasion, present its conclusions as to any changes that need to be made to the system as it stands. At the same time the Commission shall, where appropriate, submit proposals for improvements in the present system in the interest of further facilitating the freedom of movement, right of establishment and freedom to provide services of the persons covered by this Directive.

Article 14 [Addressees]

This Directive is addressed to the Member States.

Done at Brussels, 21 December 1988.

ANNEX
List of professional associations or organizations which satisfy the conditions of the second subparagraph of Article 1 (d) [...]

---

1   The Directive was notified to the Member States on 4 January 1989.

The Freedom to Provide Services and the Freedom of Establishment

Council Directive 77/249 of 22 March 1977 to Facilitate the Effective Exercise by Lawyers of Freedom to Provide Services[1]

THE COUNCIL OF THE EUROPEAN COMMUNITIES,

HAVING REGARD to the Treaty establishing the European Economic Community, and in particular Articles 57 and 66 thereof, [...]
WHEREAS, pursuant to the Treaty, any restriction on the provision of services which is based on nationality or on conditions of residence has been prohibited since the end of the transitional period
WHEREAS this Directive deals only with measures to facilitate the effective pursuit of the activities of lawyers by way of provision of services
WHEREAS more detailed measures will be necessary to facilitate the effective exercise of the right of establishment
WHEREAS if lawyers are to exercise effectively the freedom to provide services host Member States must recognize as lawyers those persons practising the profession in the various Member States
WHEREAS, since this Directive solely concerns provision of services and does not contain provisions on the mutual recognition of diplomas, a person to whom the Directive applies must adopt the professional title used in the Member state in which he is established, hereinafter referred to as "the Member state from which he comes",

HAS ADOPTED THIS DIRECTIVE:

Article 1 [Scope]
1.   This Directive shall apply, within the limits and under the conditions laid down herein, to the activities of lawyers pursued by way of provision of services.
    Notwithstanding anything contained in this Directive, Member States may reserve to prescribed categories of lawyers the preparation of formal documents for obtaining title to administer estates of deceased persons, and the drafting of formal documents creating or transferring interests in land.
2. "lawyer" means any person entitled to pursue his professional activities under one of the following designations:

Belgium:	Avocat - advocaat
Denmark:	Advokat
Germany:	Rechtsanwalt
Greece:	Δικηγόρος
France:	Avocat
Ireland:	Barrister, Solicitor
Italy:	Avvocato
Luxembourg:	Avocat-avoué
Netherlands:	Advocaat
Portugal:	Advogado
Spain:	Abogado
United Kingdom:	Advocate, Barrister, Solicitor
Austria:	Rechtsanwalt

---

1   OJ 1977 L 78, p. 17, as amended by the various treaties of accession.

Finland: Asianajaja/Advokat
Sweden: Advokat

Article 2 [Mutual Recognition]
Each Member State shall recognize as a lawyer for the purpose of pursuing the activities specified in Article 1 (1) any person listed in paragraph 2 of that article.

Article 3 [Professional Titles of Home State]
A person referred to in Article 1 shall adopt the professional title used in the Member State from which he comes, expressed in the language or one of the languages, of that state, with an indication of the professional organization by which he is authorized to practise or the court of law before which he is entitled to practise pursuant to the laws of that state.

Article 4 [National Treatment in Host State]
1.   Activities relating to the representation of a client in legal proceedings or before public authorities shall be pursued in each host Member State under the conditions laid down for lawyers established in that state, with the exception of any conditions requiring residence, or registration with a professional organization, in that state.
2.   A lawyer pursuing these activities shall observe the rules of professional conduct of the host Member State, without prejudice to his obligations in the Member State from which he comes.
3.   When these activities are pursued in the United Kingdom, "rules of professional conduct of the host Member State" means the rules of professional conduct appli-cable to solicitors, where such activities are not reserved for barristers and advocates. Otherwise the rules of professional conduct applicable to the latter shall apply. However, barristers from Ireland shall always be subject to the rules of professional conduct applicable in the United Kingdom to barristers and advocates.
     When these activities are pursued in Ireland "rules of professional conduct of the host Member State" means, in so far as they govern the oral presentation of a case in court, the rules of professional conduct applicable to barristers. In all other cases the rules of professional conduct applicable to solicitors shall apply. However, barristers and advocates from the united Kingdom shall always be subject to the rules of professional conduct applicable in Ireland to barristers.
4.   A lawyer pursuing activities other than those referred to in paragraph 1 shall remain subject to the conditions and rules of professional conduct of the Member State from which he comes without prejudice to respect for the rules, whatever their source, which govern the profession in the host Member state, especially those concerning the incompatibility of the exercise of the activities of a lawyer with the exercise of other activities in that state, professional secrecy, relations with other lawyers, the prohibition on the same lawyer acting for parties with mutually conflicting interests, and publicity. The latter rules are applicable only if they are capable of being observed by a lawyer who is not established in the host Member State and to the extent to which their observance is objectively justified to ensure, in that state, the proper exercise of a lawyer's activities, the standing of the profession and respect for the rules concerning incompatibility.

Article 5 [Representation of Clients in Legal Proceedings in Host State]
For the pursuit of activities relating to the representation of a client in legal proceedings, a Member State may require lawyers to whom Article 1 applies:
—   to be introduced, in accordance with local rules or customs, to the presiding judge and, where appropriate, to the President of the relevant bar in the host Member State

— to work in conjunction with a lawyer who practises before the judicial authority in question and who would, where necessary, be answerable to that authority, or with an "avoué" or "procuratore" practising before it.

Article 6 [Corporate Counsel]

Any Member State may exclude lawyers who are in the salaried employment of a public or private undertaking from pursuing activities relating to the representation of that undertaking in legal proceedings in so far as lawyers established in that state are not permitted to pursue those activities.

Article 7 [Proof of Qualifications]

1.   The competent authority of the host Member State may request the person providing the services to establish his qualifications as a lawyer.

2.   In the event of non-compliance with the obligations referred to in article 4 and in force in the host Member State, the competent authority of the latter shall determine in accordance with its own rules and procedures the consequences of such non-compliance, and to this end may obtain any appropriate professional information concerning the person providing services.

It shall notify the competent authority of the Member State from which the person comes of any Decision taken. Such exchanges shall not affect the confidential nature of the information supplied.

Article 8 [Implementation into National Law]

1.   Member States shall bring into force the measures necessary to comply with this Directive within two years of its notification and shall forthwith inform the Commission thereof.

2.   Member States shall communicate to the Commission the texts of the main provisions of national law which they adopt in the field covered by this Directive.

Article 9 [Addressees]

This Directive is addressed to the Member States.

Done at Brussels, 22 March 1977.
For the Council, The President, Judith Hart

Directive 98/5 of the European Parliament and of the Council of 16 February 1998 to Facilitate Practice of the Profession of Lawyer on a Permanent Basis in a Member State Other than that in Which the Qualification was Obtained[1]

THE EUROPEAN PARLIAMENT AND THE COUNCIL OF THE EUROPEAN UNION,

HAVING REGARD to the Treaty establishing the European Community, and in particular Article 49, Article 57(1) and the first and third sentences of Article 57(2) thereof,
[...]
(1) WHEREAS, pursuant to Article 7a of the Treaty, the internal market is to comprise an area without internal frontiers; whereas, pursuant to Article 3(c) of the Treaty, the

---

1   OJ 1998 L 77, p. 36.

abolition, as between Member States, of obstacles to freedom of movement for persons and services constitutes one of the objectives of the Community; whereas, for nationals of the Member States, this means among other things the possibility of practising a profession, whether in a self-employed or a salaried capacity, in a Member State other than that in which they obtained their professional qualifications;

(2) WHEREAS, pursuant to Council Directive 89/48 of 21 December 1988 on a general system for the recognition of higher-education diplomas awarded on completion of professional education and training of at least three years' duration[1], a lawyer who is fully qualified in one Member State may already ask to have his diploma recognised with a view to establishing himself in another Member State in order to practise the profession of lawyer there under the professional title used in that State;

(3) WHEREAS the objective of Directive 89/48 is to ensure that a lawyer is integrated into the profession in the host Member State, and the Directive seeks neither to modify the rules regulating the profession in that State nor to remove such a lawyer from the ambit of those rules;

(4) WHEREAS while some lawyers may become quickly integrated into the profession in the host Member State, inter alia by passing an aptitude test as provided for in Directive 89/48, other fully qualified lawyers should be able to achieve such integration after a certain period of professional practice in the host Member State under their home-country professional titles or else continue to practise under their home-country professional titles;

(5) WHEREAS at the end of that period the lawyer should be able to integrate into the profession in the host Member States after verification that the possesses professional experience in that Member State;

(6) WHEREAS action along these lines is justified at Community level not only because, compared with the general system for the recognition of diplomas, it provides lawyers with an easier means whereby they can integrate into the profession in a host Member State, but also because, by enabling lawyers to practise under their home-country professional titles on a permanent basis in a host Member State, it meets the needs of consumers of legal services who, owing to the increasing trade flows resulting, in particular, from the internal market, seek advice when carrying out cross-border transactions in which international law, Community law and domestic laws often overlap;

(7) WHEREAS action is also justified at Community level because only a few Member States already permit in their territory the pursuit of activities of lawyers, otherwise than by way of provision of services, by lawyers from other Member States practising under their home-country professional titles; whereas, however, in the Member States where this possibility exists, the practical details concerning, for example, the area of activity and the obligation to register with the competent authorities differ considerably;

(8) WHEREAS such a diversity of situations leads to inequalities and distortions in competition between lawyers from the Member States and constitutes an obstacle to freedom of movement;

(9) WHEREAS only a directive laying down the conditions governing practice of the profession, otherwise than by way of provision of services, by lawyers practising under their home-country professional titles is capable of resolving these difficulties and of affording the same opportunities to lawyers and consumers of legal services in all Member States;

(10) WHEREAS, in keeping with its objective, this Directive does not lay down any rules concerning purely domestic situations, and where it does affect national rules re-

---

1   See above, p. 362.

gulating the legal profession it does so no more than is necessary to achieve its purpose effectively;

(11) WHEREAS it is without prejudice in particular to national legislation governing access to and practice of the profession of lawyer under the professional title used in the host Member State;

(12) WHEREAS lawyers covered by the Directive should be required to register with the competent authority in the host Member State in order that that authority may ensure that they comply with the rules of professional conduct in force in that State;

(13) WHEREAS the effect of such registration as regards the jurisdictions in which, and the levels and types of court before which, lawyers may practise is determined by the law applicable to lawyers in the host Member State;

(14) WHEREAS lawyers who are not integrated into the profession in the host Member State should practise in that State under their home-country professional titles so as to ensure that consumers are properly informed and to distinguish between such lawyers and lawyers from the host Member State practising under the professional title used there;

(15) WHEREAS lawyers covered by this Directive should be permitted to give legal advice in particular on the law of their home Member States, on Community law, on international law and on the law of the host Member State;

(16) WHEREAS this is already allowed as regards the provision of services under Council Directive 77/249 of 22 March 1977 to facilitate the effective exercise by lawyers of freedom to provide services[1];

(17) WHEREAS, however, provision should be made, as in Directive 77/249, for the option of excluding from the activities of lawyers practising under their home-country professional titles in the United Kingdom and Ireland the preparation of certain formal documents in the conveyancing and probate spheres;

(18) WHEREAS this Directive in no way affects the provisions under which, in every Member State, certain activities are reserved for professions other than the legal profession;

(19) WHEREAS the provision in Directive 77/249 concerning the possibility of the host Member State to require a lawyer practising under his home-country professional title to work in conjunction with a local lawyer when representing or defending a client in legal proceedings should also be incorporated in this Directive;

(20) WHEREAS that requirement must be interpreted in the light of the case law of the Court of Justice of the European Communities, in particular its judgment of 25 February 1988 in Case 427/85, Commission v. Germany;[2]

(21) WHEREAS to ensure the smooth operation of the justice system Member States should be allowed, by means of specific rules, to reserve access to their highest courts to specialist lawyers, without hindering the integration of Member States' lawyers fulfilling the necessary requirements;

(22) WHEREAS a lawyer registered under his home-country professional title in the host Member State must remain registered with the competent authority in his home Member State if he is to retain his status of lawyer and be covered by this Directive;

(23) WHEREAS for that reason close collaboration between the competent authorities is indispensable, in particular in connection with any disciplinary proceedings;

---

1   See above, p. 371.

2   [1988] ECR 1123.

(24) WHEREAS lawyers covered by this Directive, whether salaried or self-employed in their home Member States, may practise as salaried lawyers in the host Member State, where that Member State offers that possibility to its own lawyers;

(25) WHEREAS the purpose pursued by this Directive in enabling lawyers to practise in another Member State under their home-country professional titles is also to make it easier for them to obtain the professional title of that host Member State;

(26) WHEREAS under Articles 48 and 52 of the Treaty as interpreted by the Court of Justice the host Member State must take into consideration any professional experience gained in its territory;

(27) WHEREAS after effectively and regularly pursuing in the host Member State an activity in the law of that State including Community law for a period of three years, a lawyer may reasonably be assumed to have gained the aptitude necessary to become fully integrated into the legal profession there;

(28) WHEREAS at the end of that period the lawyer who can, subject to verification, furnish evidence of his professional competence in the host Member State should be able to obtain the professional title of that Member State;

(29) WHEREAS if the period of effective and regular professional activity of at least three years includes a shorter period of practice in the law of the host Member State, the authority shall also take into consideration any other knowledge of that State's law, which it may verify during an interview;

(30) WHEREAS if evidence of fulfilment of these conditions is not provided, the decision taken by the competent authority of the host State not to grant the State's professional title under the facilitation arrangements linked to those conditions must be substantiated and subject to appeal under national law;

(31) WHEREAS, for economic and professional reasons, the growing tendency for lawyers in the Community to practise jointly, including in the form of associations, has become a reality;

(32) WHEREAS the fact that lawyers belong to a grouping in their home Member State should not be used as a pretext to prevent or deter them from establishing themselves in the host Member State;

(33) WHEREAS Member States should be allowed, however, to take appropriate measures with the legitimate aim of safeguarding the profession's independence; (34) WHEREAS certain guarantees should be provided in those Member States which permit joint practice,

HAVE ADOPTED THIS DIRECTIVE:

Article 1 Object, scope and definitions

1. The purpose of this Directive is to facilitate practice of the profession of lawyer on a permanent basis in a self-employed or salaried capacity in a Member State other than that in which the professional qualification was obtained.

2. For the purposes of this Directive:

(a) "lawyer" means any person who is a national of a Member State and who is authorised to pursue his professional activities under one of the following professional titles:

Austria:	Rechtsanwalt
Belgium:	Avocat - advocaat
Denmark:	Advokat
Finland:	Asianajaja/Advokat
France:	Avocat
Germany:	Rechtsanwalt
Greece:	Δικηγόρος

Ireland:	Barrister, Solicitor
Italy:	Avvocato
Luxembourg:	Avocat-avoué
Netherlands:	Advocaat
Portugal:	Advogado
Spain:	Abogado
Sweden:	Advokat
United Kingdom:	Advocate, Barrister, Solicitor

(b) "home Member State" means the Member State in which a lawyer acquired the right to use one of the professional titles referred to in (a) before practising the profession of lawyer in another Member State;

(c) "host Member State" means the Member State in which a lawyer practises pursuant to this Directive;

(d) "home-country professional title" means the professional title used in the Member State in which a lawyer acquired the right to use that title before practising the profession of lawyer in the host Member State;

(e) "grouping" means any entity, with or without legal personality, formed under the law of a Member State, within which lawyers pursue their professional activities jointly under a joint name;

(f) "relevant professional title" or "relevant profession" means the professional title or profession governed by the competent authority with whom a lawyer has registered under Article 3, and "competent authority" means that authority.

3. This Directive shall apply both to lawyers practising in a self-employed capacity and to lawyers practising in a salarial capacity in the home Member State and, subject to Article 8, in the host Member State.

4. Practice of the profession of lawyer within the meaning of this Directive shall not include the provision of services, which is covered by Directive 77/249.

Article 2 Right to practise under the home-country professional title

Any lawyer shall be entitled to pursue on a permanent basis, in any other Member State under his home-country professional title, the activities specified in Article 5. Integration into the profession of lawyer in the host Member State shall be subject to Article 10.

Article 3 Registration with the competent authority

1. A lawyer who wishes to practise in a Member State other than that in which he obtained his professional qualification shall register with the competent authority in that State.

2. The competent authority in the host Member State shall register the lawyer upon presentation of a certificate attesting to his registration with the competent authority in the home Member State. It may require that, when presented by the competent authority of the home Member State, the certificate be not more than three months old. It shall inform the competent authority in the home Member State of the registration.

3. For the purpose of applying paragraph 1:

— in the United Kingdom and Ireland, lawyers practising under a professional title other than those used in the United Kingdom or Ireland shall register either with the authority responsible for the profession of barrister or advocate or with the authority responsible for the profession of solicitor,

— in the United Kingdom, the authority responsible for a barrister from Ireland shall be that responsible for the profession of barrister or advocate, and the authority responsible for a solicitor from Ireland shall be that responsible for the profession of solicitor,

— in Ireland, the authority responsible for a barrister or an advocate from the United Kingdom shall be that responsible for the profession of barrister, and the authority responsible for a solicitor from the United Kingdom shall be that responsible for the profession of solicitor.

4.   Where the relevant competent authority in a host Member State publishes the names of lawyers registered with it, it shall also publish the names of lawyers registered pursuant to this Directive.

Article 4 Practice under the home-country professional title

1.   A lawyer practising in a host Member State under his home-country professional title shall do so under that title, which must be expressed in the official language or one of the official languages of his home Member State, in an intelligible manner and in such a way as to avoid confusion with the professional title of the host Member State.

2.   For the purpose of applying paragraph 1, a host Member State may require a lawyer practising under his home-country professional title to indicate the professional body of which he is a member in his home Member State or the judicial authority before which he is entitled to practise pursuant to the laws of his home Member State. A host Member State may also require a lawyer practising under his home-country professional title to include a reference to his registration with the competent authority in that State.

Article 5 Area of activity

1.   Subject to paragraphs 2 and 3, a lawyer practising under his home-country professional title carries on the same professional activities as a lawyer practising under the relevant professional title used in the host Member State and may, inter alia, give advice on the law of his home Member State, on Community law, on international law and on the law of the host Member State. He shall in any event comply with the rules of procedure applicable in the national courts.

2.   Member States which authorise in their territory a prescribed category of lawyers to prepare deeds for obtaining title to administer estates of deceased persons and for creating or transferring interests in land which, in other Member States, are reserved for professions other than that of lawyer may exclude from such activities lawyers practising under a home-country professional title conferred in one of the latter Member States.

3.   For the pursuit of activities relating to the representation or defence of a client in legal proceedings and insofar as the law of the host Member State reserves such activities to lawyers practising under the professional title of that State, the latter may require lawyers practising under their home-country professional titles to work in conjunction with a lawyer who practises before the judicial authority in question and who would, where necessary, be answerable to that authority or with an "avoué" practising before it. Nevertheless, in order to ensure the smooth operation of the justice system, Member States may lay down specific rules for access to supreme courts, such as the use of specialist lawyers.

Article 6 Rules of professional conduct applicable

1.   Irrespective of the rules of professional conduct to which he is subject in his home Member State, a lawyer practising under his home-country professional title shall be subject to the same rules of professional conduct as lawyers practising under the relevant professional title of the host Member State in respect of all the activities he pursues in its territory.

2.   Lawyers practising under their home-country professional titles shall be granted appropriate representation in the professional associations of the host Member State.

Such representation shall involve at least the right to vote in elections to those associations' governing bodies.

3. The host Member State may require a lawyer practising under his home-country professional title either to take out professional indemnity insurance or to become a member of a professional guarantee fund in accordance with the rules which that State lays down for professional activities pursued in its territory. Nevertheless, a lawyer practising under his home-country professional title shall be exempted from that requirement if he can prove that he is covered by insurance taken out or a guarantee provided in accordance with the rules of his home Member State, insofar as such insurance or guarantee is equivalent in terms of the conditions and extent of cover. Where the equivalence is only partial, the competent authority in the host Member State may require that additional insurance or an additional guarantee be contracted to cover the elements which are not already covered by the insurance or guarantee contracted in accordance with the rules of the home Member State.

Article 7 Disciplinary proceedings

1. In the event of failure by a lawyer practising under his home-country professional title to fulfil the obligations in force in the host Member State, the rules of procedure, penalties and remedies provided for in the host Member State shall apply.

2. Before initiating disciplinary proceedings against a lawyer practising under his home-country professional title, the competent authority in the host Member State shall inform the competent authority in the home Member State as soon as possible, furnishing it with all the relevant details.

The first subparagraph shall apply mutatis mutandis where disciplinary proceedings are initiated by the competent authority of the home Member State, which shall inform the competent authority of the host Member State(s) accordingly.

3. Without prejudice to the decision-making power of the competent authority in the host Member State, that authority shall cooperate throughout the disciplinary proceedings with the competent authority in the home Member State. In particular, the host Member State shall take the measures necessary to ensure that the competent authority in the home Member State can make submissions to the bodies responsible for hearing any appeal.

4. The competent authority in the home Member State shall decide what action to take, under its own procedural and substantive rules, in the light of a decision of the competent authority in the host Member State concerning a lawyer practising under his home-country professional title.

5. Although it is not a prerequisite for the decision of the competent authority in the host Member State, the temporary or permanent withdrawal by the competent authority in the home Member State of the authorisation to practise the profession shall automatically lead to the lawyer concerned being temporarily or permanently prohibited from practising under his home-country professional title in the host Member State.

Article 8 Salaried practice

A lawyer registered in a host Member State under his home-country professional title may practise as a salaried lawyer in the employ of another lawyer, an association or firm of lawyers, or a public or private enterprise to the extent that the host Member State so permits for lawyers registered under the professional title used in that State.

Article 9 Statement of reasons and remedies

Decisions not to effect the registration referred to in Article 3 or to cancel such registration and decisions imposing disciplinary measures shall state the reasons on which they are based.

A remedy shall be available against such decisions before a court or tribunal in accordance with the provisions of domestic law.

Article 10 Like treatment as a lawyer of the host Member State

1.　A lawyer practising under his home-country professional title who has effectively and regularly pursued for a period of at least three years an activity in the host Member State in the law of that State including Community law shall, with a view to gaining admission to the profession of lawyer in the host Member State, be exempted from the conditions set out in Article 4(1)(b) of Directive 89/48, "Effective and regular pursuit" means actual exercise of the activity without any interruption other than that resulting from the events of everyday life.

It shall be for the lawyer concerned to furnish the competent authority in the host Member State with proof of such effective regular pursuit for a period of at least three years of an activity in the law of the host Member State.

To that end:

(a) the lawyer shall provide the competent authority in the host Member State with any relevant information and documentation, notably on the number of matters he has dealt with and their nature;

(b) the competent authority of the host Member State may verify the effective and regular nature of the activity pursued and may, if need be, request the lawyer to provide, orally or in writing, clarification of or further details on the information and documentation mentioned in point (a).

Reasons shall be given for a decision by the competent authority in the host Member State not to grant an exemption where proof is not provided that the requirements laid down in the first subparagraph have been fulfilled, and the decision shall be subject to appeal under domestic law.

2.　A lawyer practising under his home-country professional title in a host Member State may, at any time, apply to have his diploma recognised in accordance with Directive 89/48 with a view to gaining admission to the profession of lawyer in the host Member State and practising it under the professional title corresponding to the profession in that Member State.

3.　A lawyer practising under his home-country professional title who has effectively and regularly pursued a professional activity in the host Member State for a period of at least three years but for a lesser period in the law of that Member State may obtain from the competent authority of that State admission to the profession of lawyer in the host Member State and the right to practise it under the professional title corresponding to the profession in that Member State, without having to meet the conditions referred to in Article 4(1)(b) of Directive 89/48, under the conditions and in accordance with the procedures set out below:

(a) The competent authority of the host Member State shall take into account the effective and regular professional activity pursued during the abovementioned period and any knowledge and professional experience of the law of the host Member State, and any attendance at lectures or seminars on the law of the host Member State, including the rules regulating professional practice and conduct.

(b) The lawyer shall provide the competent authority of the host Member State with any relevant information and documentation, in particular on the matters he has dealt with. Assessment of the lawyer's effective and regular activity in the host Member State and assessment of his capacity to continue the activity he has pursued there shall be carried out by means of an interview with the competent authority of the host Member State in order to verify the regular and effective nature of the activity pursued.

Reasons shall be given for a decision by the competent authority in the host Member State not to grant authorisation where proof is not provided that the requirements laid down in the first subparagraph have been fulfilled, and the decision shall be subject to appeal under domestic law.

4.   The competent authority of the host Member State may, by reasoned decision subject to appeal under domestic law, refuse to allow the lawyer the benefit of the provisions of this Article if it considers that this would be against public policy, in a particular because of disciplinary proceedings, complaints or incidents of any kind.

5.   The representatives of the competent authority entrusted with consideration of the application shall preserve the confidentiality of any information received.

6.   A lawyer who gains admission to the profession of lawyer in the host Member State in accordance with paragraphs 1, 2 and 3 shall be entitled to use his home-country professional title, expressed in the official language or one of the official languages of his home Member State, alongside the professional title corresponding to the profession of lawyer in the host Member State.

Article 11 Joint practice

Where joint practise is authorised in respect of lawyers carrying on their activities under the relevant professional title in the host Member State, the following provisions shall apply in respect of lawyers wishing to carry on activities under that title or registering with the competent authority:

(1)   One or more lawyers who belong to the same grouping in their home Member State and who practise under their home-country professional title in a host Member State may pursue their professional activities in a branch or agency of their grouping in the host Member State. However, where the fundamental rules governing that grouping in the home Member State are incompatible with the fundamental rules laid down by law, regulation or administrative action in the host Member State, the latter rules shall prevail insofar as compliance therewith is justified by the public interest in protecting clients and third parties.

(2)   Each Member State shall afford two or more lawyers from the same grouping or the same home Member State who practise in its territory under their home-country professional titles access to a form of joint practice. If the host Member State gives its lawyers a choice between several forms of joint practice, those same forms shall also be made available to the aforementioned lawyers. The manner in which such lawyers practise jointly in the host

Member State shall be governed by the laws, regulations and administrative provisions of that State.

(3)   The host Member State shall take the measures necessary to permit joint practice also between:

(a)   several lawyers from different Member States practising under their home-country professional titles;

(b)   one or more lawyers covered by point (a) and one or more lawyers from the host Member State.

The manner in which such lawyers practice jointly in the host Member State shall be governed by the laws, regulations and administrative provisions of that State.

(4) A lawyer who wishes to practise under his home-country professional title shall inform the competent authority in the host Member State of the fact that he is a member of a grouping in his home Member State and furnish any relevant information on that grouping.

(5) Notwithstanding points 1 to 4, a host Member State, insofar as it prohibits lawyers practising under its own relevant professional title from practising the profession of

lawyer within a grouping in which some persons are not members of the profession, may refuse to allow a lawyer registered under his home-country professional title to practice in its territory in his capacity as a member of his grouping. The grouping is deemed to include persons who are not members of the profession if
— the capital of the grouping is held entirely or partly, or
— the name under which it practises is used, or
— the decision-making power in that grouping is exercised, de facto or de jure, by persons who do not have the status of lawyer within the meaning of Article 1(2).
Where the fundamental rules governing a grouping of lawyers in the home Member State are incompatible with the rules in force in the host Member State or with the provisions of the first subparagraph, the host Member State may oppose the opening of a branch or agency within its territory without the restrictions laid down in point (1).

Article 12 Name of the grouping
Whatever the manner in which lawyers practise under their home-country professional titles in the host Member State, they may employ the name of any grouping to which they belong in their home Member State.

The host Member State may require that, in addition to the name referred to in the first subparagraph, mention be made of the legal form of the grouping in the home Member State and/or of the names of any members of the grouping practising in the host Member State.

Article 13 Cooperation between the competent authorities in the home and host Member States and confidentiality
In order to facilitate the application of this Directive and to prevent its provisions from being misapplied for the sole purpose of circumventing the rules applicable in the host Member State, the competent authority in the host Member State and the competent authority in the home Member State shall collaborate closely and afford each other mutual assistance. They shall preserve the confidentiality of the information they exchange.

Article 14 Designation of the competent authorities
Member States shall designate the competent authorities empowered to receive the applications and to take the decisions referred to in this Directive by 14 March 2000. They shall communicate this information to the other Member States and to the Commission.

Article 15 Report by the Commission
Ten years at the latest from the entry into force of this Directive, the Commission shall report to the European Parliament and to the Council on progress in the implementation of the Directive.

After having held all the necessary consultations, it shall on that occasion present its conclusions and any amendments which could be made to the existing system.

Article 16 Implementation
1.   Member States shall bring into force the laws, regulations and administrative provisions necessary to comply with this Directive by 14 March 2000. They shall forthwith inform the Commission thereof.

When Member States adopt these measures, they shall contain a reference to this Directive or shall be accompanied by such reference on the occasion of their official publication. The methods of making such reference shall be adopted by Member States.

2. Member States shall communicate to the Commission the texts of the main provisions of domestic law which they adopt in the field covered by this Directive.

Article 17 [Entry into Force]

This Directive shall enter into force on the date of its publication in the Official Journal of the European Communities.

Article 18 Addressees

This Directive is addressed to the Member States.

Done at Brussels, 16 February 1998.
For the European Parliament, The President, J. M. GIL-ROBLES
For the Council, The President, J. CUNNINGHAM

SIX: EUROPEAN UNION COMPETITION POLICY

Cartels and Abuses of Dominant Positions

Council Regulation No 17: First Regulation Implementing Articles 85 and 86 of the Treaty[1]

THE COUNCIL OF THE EUROPEAN ECONOMIC COMMUNITY,

HAVING REGARD to the Treaty establishing the European Economic Community, and in particular Article 87 thereof [...]

(1) WHEREAS, in order to establish a system ensuring that competition shall not be distorted in the common market, it is necessary to provide for balanced application of Articles 85 and 86 in a uniform manner in the Member States;

(2) WHEREAS in establishing the rules for applying Article 85 (3) account must be taken of the need to ensure effective supervision and to simplify administration to the greatest possible extent;

(3) WHEREAS it is accordingly necessary to make it obligatory, as a general principle, for undertakings which seek application of Article 85 (3) to notify to the Commission their agreements, Decisions and concerted practices;

(4) WHEREAS, on the one hand, such agreements, decisions and concerted practices are probably very numerous and cannot therefore all be examined at the same time and, on the other hand, some of them have special features which may make them less prejudicial to the development of the common market;

(5) WHEREAS there is consequently a need to make more flexible arrangements for the time being in respect of certain categories of agreement, decision and concerted practice without prejudging their validity under Article 85;

(6) WHEREAS it may be in the interest of undertakings to know whether any agreements, decisions or practices to which they are party, or propose to become party, may lead to action on the part of the Commission pursuant to Article 85 (1) or Article 86;

(7) WHEREAS, in order to secure uniform application of Articles 85 and 86 in the common market, rules must be made under which the Commission, acting in close and constant liaison with the competent authorities of the Member States, may take the requisite measures for applying those articles;

(8) WHEREAS for this purpose the Commission must have the co-operation of the competent authorities of the Member States and be empowered, throughout the common market, to require such information to be supplied and to undertake such investigations as are necessary to bring to light any agreement, decision or concerted practice prohibited by Article 85 (1) or any abuse of a dominant position prohibited by Article 86;

(9) WHEREAS, in order to carry out its duty of ensuring that the provisions of the Treaty are applied, the Commission must be empowered to address to undertakings or associations of undertakings Recommendations and Decisions for the purpose of bringing to an end infringements of Articles 85 and 86;

---

1   OJ 1962 No. 013, p. 204, as amended by Council Regulation 59 of 3 July 1962, Council Regulation 118/63 of 5 November 1963 and Council Regulation 2822/71 of 20 December 1971.

(10) WHEREAS compliance with Articles 85 and 86 and the fulfilment of obligations imposed on undertakings and associations of undertakings under this Regulation must be enforceable by means of fines and periodic penalty payments;
(11) WHEREAS undertakings concerned must be accorded the right to be heard by the Commission, third parties whose interests may be affected by a Decision must be given the opportunity of submitting their comments beforehand, and it must be ensured that wide publicity is given to Decisions taken;
(12) WHEREAS all Decisions taken by the Commission under this Regulation are subject to review by the Court of Justice under the conditions specified in the Treaty;
(13) WHEREAS it is moreover desirable to confer upon the Court of Justice, pursuant to Article 172, unlimited jurisdiction in respect of Decisions under which the Commission imposes fines or periodic penalty payments;
(14) WHEREAS this Regulation may enter into force without prejudice to any other provisions that may hereafter be adopted pursuant to Article 87:

HAS ADOPTED THIS REGULATION:

Article 1 Basic provision
Without prejudice to Articles 6, 7 and 23 of this Regulation, agreements, decisions and concerted practices of the kind described in Article 85 (1) of the Treaty and the abuse of a dominant position in the market, within the meaning of Article 86 of the Treaty, shall be prohibited, no prior Decision to that effect being required.

Article 2 Negative clearance
Upon application by the undertakings or associations of undertakings concerned, the Commission may certify that, on the basis of the facts in its possession, there are no grounds under Article 85 (1) or Article 86 of the Treaty for action on its part in respect of an agreement, decision or practice.

Article 3 Termination of infringements
1.   Where the Commission, upon application or upon its own initiative, finds that there is infringement of Article 85 or Article 86 of the Treaty, it may by Decision require the undertakings or associations of undertakings concerned to bring such infringement to an end.
2.   Those entitled to make application are:
(a) Member States;
(b) natural or legal persons who claim a legitimate interest.
3.   Without prejudice to the other provisions of this Regulation, the Commission may, before taking a Decision under paragraph 1, address to the undertakings or associations of undertakings concerned Recommendations for termination of the infringement.

Article 4 Notification of new agreements, decisions and practices
1.   Agreements, decisions and concerted practices of the kind described in Article 85 (1) of the Treaty which come into existence after the entry into force of this Regulation and in respect of which the parties seek application of Article 85 (3) must be notified to the Commission. Until they have been notified, no Decision in application of Article 85 (3) may be taken.
2.   Paragraph 1 shall not apply to agreements, decisions or concerted practices where:
(1) the only parties thereto are undertakings from one Member State and the agreements, decisions or practices do not relate either to imports or to exports between Member States;

(2) not more than two undertakings are party thereto, and the agreements only:
  (a) restrict the freedom of one party to the contract in determining the prices or conditions of business upon which the goods which he has obtained from the other party to the contract may be resold; or
  (b) impose restrictions on the exercise of the rights of the assignee or user of industrial property rights - in particular patents, utility models, designs or trade marks - or of the person entitled under a contract to the assignment, or grant, of the right to use a method of manufacture or knowledge relating to the use and to the application of industrial processes;
(3) they have as their sole object:
  (a) the development or uniform application of standards or types; or
  (b) joint research and development;
  (c) specialisation in the manufacture of products, including agreements necessary for achieving this,
      — where the products which are the subject of specialisation do not, in a substantial part of the common market, represent more than 15% of the volume of business done in identical products or those considered by consumers to be similar by reason of their characteristics, price and use, and
      — where the total annual turnover of the participating undertakings does not exceed 200 million units of account.
These agreements, decisions and practices may be notified to the Commission.

Article 5 Notification of existing agreements, decisions and practices

1. Agreements, decisions and concerted practices of the kind described in Article 85 (1) of the Treaty which are in existence at the date of entry into force of this Regulation and in respect of which the parties seek application of Article 85 (3) shall be notified to the Commission before 1 August 1962. However, notwithstanding the foregoing provisions, any agreements, decisions and concerted practices to which not more than two undertakings are party shall be notified before 1 February 1963.
2. Paragraph 1 shall not apply to agreements, decisions or concerted practices falling within Article 4 (2).
These may be notified to the Commission.

Article 6 Decisions pursuant to Article 85 (3)

1. Whenever the Commission takes a Decision pursuant to Article 85 (3) of the Treaty, it shall specify therein the date from which the Decision shall take effect. Such date shall not be earlier than the date of notification.
2. The second sentence of paragraph 1 shall not apply to agreements, decisions or concerted practices falling within Article 4 (2) and Article 5 (2), nor to those falling within Article 5 (1) which have been notified within the time limit specified in Article 5 (1).

Article 7 Special provisions for existing agreements, decisions and practices

1. Where agreements, decisions and concerted practices in existence at the date of entry into force of this Regulation and notified before 1 August 1962 do not satisfy the requirements of Article 85 (3) of the Treaty and the undertakings or associations of undertakings concerned cease to give effect to them or modify them in such manner that they no longer fall within the prohibition contained in Article 85 (1) or that they satisfy the requirements of Article 85 (3), the prohibition contained in Article 85 (1) shall apply only for a period fixed by the Commission. A Decision by the Commission pursuant to the foregoing sentence shall not apply as against undertakings and associations of undertakings which did not expressly consent to the notification.

2.   Paragraph 1 shall apply to agreements, decisions and concerted practices falling within Article 4 (2) which are in existence at the date of entry into force of this Regulation if they are notified before 1 January 1967.

Article 8 Duration and revocation of Decisions under Article 85 (3)

1.   A Decision in application of Article 85 (3) of the Treaty shall be issued for a specified period and conditions and obligations may be attached thereto.
2.   A Decision may on application be renewed if the requirements of Article 85 (3) of the Treaty continue to be satisfied.
3.   The Commission may revoke or amend its Decision or prohibit specified acts by the parties:
(a) where there has been a change in any of the facts which were basic to the making of the Decision;
(b) where the parties commit a breach of any obligation attached to the Decision;
(c) where the Decision is based on incorrect information or was induced by deceit;
(d) where the parties abuse the exemption from the provisions of Article 85 (1) of the Treaty granted to them by the Decision.
In cases to which subparagraphs (b), (c) or (d) apply, the Decision may be revoked with retroactive effect.

Article 9 Powers

1.   Subject to review of its Decision by the Court of Justice, the Commission shall have sole power to declare Article 85 (1) inapplicable pursuant to Article 85 (3) of the Treaty.
2.   The Commission shall have power to apply Article 85 (1) and Article 86 of the Treaty.
      This power may be exercised notwithstanding that the time limits specified in Article 5 (1) and in Article 7 (2) relating to notification have not expired.
3.   As long as the Commission has not initiated any procedure under Articles 2, 3 or 6, The authorities of the Member States shall remain competent to apply Article 85 (1) and Article 86 in accordance with Article 88 of the Treaty.
      They shall remain competent in this respect notwithstanding that the time limits specified in Article 5 (1) and in Article 7 (2) relating to notification have not expired.

Article 10 Liaison with the authorities of the Member States

1.   The Commission shall forthwith transmit to the competent authorities of the Member States a copy of the applications and notifications together with copies of the most important documents lodged with the Commission for the purpose of establishing the existence of infringements of Articles 85 or 86 of the Treaty or of obtaining negative clearance or a Decision in application of Article 85 (3).
2.   The Commission shall carry out the procedure set out in paragraph 1 in close and constant liaison with the competent authorities of the Member States.
      Such authorities shall have the right to express their views upon that procedure.
3.   An advisory committee on restrictive practices and monopolies shall be consulted prior to the taking of any Decision following upon a procedure under paragraph 1, and of any Decision concerning the renewal, amendment or revocation of a Decision pursuant to Article 85 (3) of the Treaty.
4.   The advisory committee shall be composed of officials competent in the matter of restrictive practices and monopolies. Each Member State shall appoint an official to represent it who, if prevented from attending, may be replaced by another official.
5.   The consultation shall take place at a joint meeting convened by the Commission. Such meeting shall be held not earlier than fourteen days after dispatch of the notice convening it. The notice shall, in respect of each case to be examined, be accompa-

nied by a summary of the case together with an indication of the most important documents, and a preliminary Draft Decision.
6.   The advisory committee may deliver an opinion notwithstanding that some of its
Members or their alternates are not present. A report of the outcome of the consultative
proceedings shall be annexed to the Draft Decision. It shall not be made public.

Article 11 Requests for information

1.   In carrying out the duties assigned to it by Article 89 and by provisions adopted under Article 87 of the Treaty, the Commission may obtain all necessary information from
the governments and competent authorities of the Member States and from undertakings and associations of undertakings.
2.   When sending a request for information to an undertaking or association of undertakings, the Commission shall at the same time forward a copy of the request to the
competent authority of the Member State in whose territory the seat of the undertaking
or association of undertakings is situated.
3.   In its request the Commission shall state the legal basis and the purpose of the
request and also the penalties provided for in Article 15 (1) (b) for supplying incorrect
information.
4.   The owners of the undertakings or their representatives and, in the case of legal
persons, companies or firms, or of associations having no legal personality, the persons authorised to represent them by law or by their constitution shall supply the information requested.
5.   Where an undertaking or association of undertakings does not supply the information requested within the time limit fixed by the Commission, or supplies incomplete information, the Commission shall by Decision require the information to be supplied.
The Decision shall specify what information is required, fix an appropriate time limit
within which it is to be supplied and indicate the penalties provided for in Article 15 (1)
(b) and Article 16 (1) (c) and the right to have the Decision reviewed by the Court of
Justice.
6.   The Commission shall at the same time forward a copy of its Decision to the competent authority of the Member State in whose territory the seat of the under-taking or
association of undertakings is situated.

Article 12 Inquiry into sectors of the economy

1.   If in any sector of the economy the trend of trade between Member States, price
movements, inflexibility of prices or other circumstances suggest that in the economic
sector concerned competition is being restricted or distorted within the common market, the Commission may decide to conduct a general inquiry into that economic sector
and in the course thereof may request undertakings in the sector concerned to supply
the information necessary for giving effect to the principles formulated in Articles 85
and 86 of the Treaty and for carrying out the duties entrusted to the Commission.
2.   The Commission may in particular request every undertaking or association of undertakings in the economic sector concerned to communicate to it all agreements, Decisions and concerted practices which are exempt from notification by virtue of Article
4 (2) and Article 5 (2).
3.   When making inquiries pursuant to paragraph 2, the Commission shall also request
undertakings or groups of undertakings whose size suggests that they occupy a dominant position within the common market or a substantial part thereof to supply to the
Commission such particulars of the structure of the undertakings and of their behaviour
as are requisite to an appraisal of their position in the light of Article 86 of the Treaty.
4.   Article 10 (3) to (6) and Articles 11, 13 and 14 shall apply correspondingly.

Article 13 Investigations by the authorities of the Member States

1. At the request of the Commission, the competent authorities of the Member States shall undertake the investigations which the Commission considers to be necessary under Article 14 (1), or which it has ordered by Decision pursuant to Article 14 (3). The officials of the competent authorities of the Member states responsible for conducting these investigations shall exercise their powers upon production of an authorisation in writing issued by the competent authority of the Member State in whose territory the investigation is to be made. Such authorisation shall specify the subject matter and purpose of the investigation.
2. If so requested by the Commission or by the competent authority of the Member State in whose territory the investigation is to be made, the officials of the Commission may assist the officials of such authorities in carrying out their duties.

Article 14 Investigating powers of the Commission

1. In carrying out the duties assigned to it by Article 89 and by provisions adopted under Article 87 of the Treaty, the Commission may undertake all necessary investigations into undertakings and associations of undertakings. to this end the officials authorised by the Commission are empowered:
(a) to examine the books and other business records;
(b) to take copies of or extracts from the books and business records;
(c) to ask for oral explanations on the spot;
(d) to enter any premises, land and means of transport of undertakings.
2. The officials of the Commission authorised for the purpose of these investigations shall exercise their powers upon production of an authorisation in writing specifying the subject matter and purpose of the investigation and the penalties provided for in Article 15 (1) (c) in cases where production of the required books or other business records is incomplete. In good time before the investigation, the Commission shall inform the competent authority of the Member State in whose territory the same is to be made of the investigation and of the identity of the authorised officials.
3. Undertakings and associations of undertakings shall submit to investigations ordered by Decision of the Commission. The Decision shall specify the subject matter and purpose of the investigation, appoint the date on which it is to begin and indicate the penalties provided for in Article 15 (1) (c) and Article 16 (1) (d) and the right to have the Decision reviewed by the Court of Justice.
4. The Commission shall take Decisions referred to in paragraph 3 after consultation with the competent authority of the Member State in whose territory the investigation is to be made.
5. Officials of the competent authority of the Member State in whose territory the investigation is to be made may, at the request of such authority or of the Commission, assist the officials of the Commission in carrying out their duties.
6. Where an undertaking opposes an investigation ordered pursuant to this Article, the Member State concerned shall afford the necessary assistance to the officials authorised by the Commission to enable them to make their investigation. Member States shall, after consultation with the Commission, take the necessary measures to this end before 1 October 1962.

Article 15 Fines

1. The Commission may by Decision impose on undertakings or associations of undertakings fines of from 100 to 5.000 units of account where, intentionally or negligently
(a) they supply incorrect or misleading information in an application pursuant to Article 2 or in a notification pursuant to Articles 4 or 5; or

(b) they supply incorrect information in response to a request made pursuant to Article 11 (3) or (5) or to Article 12, or do not supply information within the time limit fixed by a Decision taken under Article 11 (5); or

(c) they produce the required books or other business records in incomplete form during investigations under Article 13 or 14, or refuse to submit to an investigation ordered by Decision issued in implementation of Article 14 (3).

2.   The Commission may by Decision impose on undertakings or associations of undertakings fines of from 1.000 to 1.000.000 units of account, or a sum in excess thereof but not exceeding 10% of the turnover in the preceding business year of each of the undertakings participating in the infringement where, either intentionally or negligently:

(a) they infringe Article 85 (1) or Article 86 of the Treaty; or

(b) they commit a breach of any obligation imposed pursuant to Article 8 (1).

In fixing the amount of the fine, regard shall be had both to the gravity and to the duration of the infringement.

3.   Article 10 (3) to (6) shall apply.

4.   Decisions taken pursuant to paragraphs 1 and 2 shall not be of a criminal law nature.

5.   The fines provided for in paragraph 2 (a) shall not be imposed in respect of acts taking place:

(a) after notification to the Commission and before its Decision in application of Article 85 (3) of the Treaty, provided they fall within the limits of the activity described in the notification;

(b) before notification and in the course of agreements, decisions or concerted practices in existence at the date of entry into force of this Regulation, provided that notification was effected within the time limits specified in Article 5 (1) and Article 7 (2).

6.   Paragraph 5 shall not have effect where the Commission has informed the undertakings concerned that after preliminary examination it is of opinion that Article 85 (1) of the Treaty applies and that application of Article 85 (3) is not justified.

Article 16 Periodic penalty payments

1.   The Commission may by Decision impose on undertakings or associations of undertakings periodic penalty payments of from 50 to 1.000 units of account per day, calculated from the date appointed by the Decision, in order to compel them:

(a) to put an end to an infringement of Article 85 or 86 of the Treaty, in accordance with a Decision taken pursuant to Article 3 of this Regulation;

(b) to refrain from any act prohibited under Article 8 (3);

(c) to supply complete and correct information which it has requested by Decision taken pursuant to Article 11 (5);

(d) to submit to an investigation which it has ordered by Decision taken pursuant to Article 14 (3).

2.   Where the undertakings or associations of undertakings have satisfied the obligation which it was the purpose of the periodic penalty payment to enforce, the Commission may fix the total amount of the periodic penalty payment at a lower figure than that which would arise under the original Decision.

3.   Article 10 (3) to (6) shall apply.

Article 17 Review by the Court of Justice

The Court of Justice shall have unlimited jurisdiction within the meaning of Article 172 of the Treaty to review Decisions whereby the Commission has fixed a fine or periodic penalty payment.

It may cancel, reduce or increase the fine or periodic penalty payment imposed.

Article 18 Unit of account

For the purposes of applying Articles 15 to 17 the unit of account shall be that adopted in drawing up the budget of the Community in accordance with Articles 207 and 209 of the Treaty.

Article 19 Hearing of the parties and of third persons

1.   Before taking Decisions as provided for in Articles 2, 3, 6, 7, 8, 15 and 16, the Commission shall give the undertakings or associations of undertakings concerned the opportunity of being heard on the matters to which the Commission has taken objection.

2.   If the Commission or the competent authorities of the Member States consider it necessary, they may also hear other natural or legal persons. applications to be heard on the part of such persons shall, where they show a sufficient interest, be granted.

3.   Where the Commission intends to give negative clearance pursuant to Article 2 or take a Decision in application of Article 85 (3) of the Treaty, it shall publish a summary of the relevant application or notification and invite all interested third parties to submit their observations within a time limit which it shall fix being not less than one month. Publication shall have regard to the legitimate interest of undertakings in the protection of their business secrets.

Article 20 Professional secrecy

1.   Information acquired as a result of the application of Articles 11, 12, 13 and 14 shall be used only for the purpose of the relevant request or investigation.

2.   Without prejudice to the provisions of Articles 19 and 21, the Commission and the competent authorities of the Member States, their officials and other servants shall not disclose information acquired by them as a result of the application of this Regulation and of the kind covered by the obligation of professional secrecy.

3.   The provisions of paragraphs 1 and 2 shall not prevent publication of general information or surveys which do not contain information relating to particular undertakings or associations of undertakings.

Article 21 Publication of Decisions

1.   The Commission shall publish the Decisions which it takes pursuant to Articles 2, 3, 6, 7 and 8.

2.   The publication shall state the names of the parties and the main content of the Decision.

   It shall have regard to the legitimate interest of undertakings in the protection of their business secrets.

Article 22 Special provisions

1.   The Commission shall submit to the Council proposals for making certain categories of agreement, decision and concerted practice falling within Article 4 (2) or Article 5 (2) compulsorily notifiable under Article 4 or 5.

2.   Within one year from the date of entry into force of this Regulation, the Council shall examine, on a proposal from the Commission, what special provisions might be made for exempting from the provisions of this Regulation agreements, decisions and concerted practices falling within Article 4 (2) or Article 5 (2).

Article 23 Transitional provisions applicable to Decisions of authorities of the Member States

1.   Agreements, decisions and concerted practices of the kind described in Article 85 (1) of the Treaty to which, before the entry into force of this Regulation, the competent

authority of a Member State has declared Article 85 (1) to be inapplicable pursuant to Article 85 (3) shall not be subject to compulsory notification under Article 5. The Decision of the competent authority of the Member State shall be deemed to be a Decision within the meaning of Article 6.

It shall cease to be valid upon expiration of the period fixed by such authority but in any event not more than three years after the entry into force of this Regulation. Article 8 (3) shall apply.

2.   Applications for renewal of Decisions of the kind described in paragraph 1 shall be decided upon by the Commission in accordance with Article 8 (2).

Article 24 Implementing provisions

The Commission shall have power to adopt implementing provisions concerning the form, content and other details of applications pursuant to Articles 2 and 3 and of notifications pursuant to Articles 4 and 5, and concerning hearings pursuant to Article 19 (1) and (2).

This Regulation shall be binding in its entirety and directly applicable in all Member States.

Done at Brussels, 6 February 1962.
For the Council, The President, M. Couve de Murville

Commission Regulation 3385/94 of 21 December 1994 on the Form, Content and Other Details of Applications and Notifications Provided for in Council Regulation No 17[1]

THE COMMISSION OF THE EUROPEAN COMMUNITIES,

HAVING REGARD to the Treaty establishing the European Community, [...]
HAVING REGARD to Council Regulation No 17 of 6 February 1962, First Regulation implementing Articles 85 and 86 of the Treaty,[2] as [...] amended [...], and in particular Article 24 thereof,
(1) WHEREAS Commission Regulation No 27 of 3 May 1962, First Regulation implementing Council Regulation No 17, [...] no longer meets the requirements of efficient administrative procedure; whereas it should therefore be replaced by a new regulation;
(2) WHEREAS, on the one hand, applications for negative clearance under Article 2 and notifications under Articles 4, 5 and 25 of Regulation No 17 have important legal consequences, which are favourable to the parties to an agreement, a decision or a practice, while, on the other hand, incorrect or misleading information in such applications or notifications may lead to the imposition of fines and may also entail civil law disadvantages for the parties; whereas it is therefore necessary in the interests of legal certainty to define precisely the persons entitled to submit applications and notifications, the subject matter and content of the information which such applications and notifications must contain, and the time when they become effective;

---

1   OJ 1994 L 377, p. 28. See also Commission Regulation 2842/98 of 22 December 1998 on the hearing of parties in certain proceedings under Articles 85 and 86 of the EC Treaty, OJ 1998 L 354, p. 18.

2   See above, p. 392.

(3) WHEREAS each of the parties should have the right to submit the application or the notification to the Commission; whereas, furthermore, a party exercising the right should inform the other parties in order to enable them to protect their interests; whereas applications and notifications relating to agreements, decisions or practices of associations of undertakings should be submitted only by such association;

(4) WHEREAS it is for the applicants and the notifying parties to make full and honest disclosure to the Commission of the facts and circumstances which are relevant for coming to a decision on the agreements, decisions or practices concerned;

(5) WHEREAS, in order to simplify and expedite their examination, it is desirable to prescribe that a form be used for applications for negative clearance relating to Article 85 (1) and for notifications relating to Article 85 (3); whereas the use of this form should also be possible in the case of applications for negative clearance relating to Article 86;

(6) WHEREAS the Commission, in appropriate cases, will give the parties, if they so request, an opportunity before the application or the notification to discuss the intended agreement, decision or practice informally and in strict confidence; whereas, in addition, it will, after the application or notification, maintain close contact with the parties to the extent necessary to discuss with them any practical or legal problems which it discovers on a first examination of the case and if possible to remove such problems by mutual agreement; [...]

HAS ADOPTED THIS REGULATION:

Article 1 Persons entitled to submit applications and notifications

1.   The following may submit an application under Article 2 of Regulation No 17 relating to Article 85 (1) of the Treaty or a notification under Articles 4, 5 and 25 of Regulation No 17:

(a) any undertaking and any association of undertakings being a party to agreements or to concerted practices; and

(b) any association of undertakings adopting decisions or engaging in practices; which may fall within the scope of Article 85 (1).

Where the application or notification is submitted by some, but not all, of the parties, referred to in point (a) of the first subparagraph, they shall give notice to the other parties.

2.   Any undertaking which may hold, alone or with other undertakings, a dominant position within the common market or in a substantial part of it, may submit an application under Article 2 of Regulation No 17 relating to Article 86 of the Treaty.

3.   Where the application or notification is signed by representatives of persons, undertakings or associations of undertakings, such representatives shall produce written proof that they are authorized to act.

4.   Where a joint application or notification is made, a joint representative should be appointed who is authorized to transmit and receive documents on behalf of all the applicants or notifying parties.

Article 2 Submission of applications and notifications

1.   Applications under Article 2 of Regulation No 17 relating to Article 85 (1) of the Treaty and notifications under Articles 4, 5 and 25 of Regulation No 17 shall be submitted in the manner prescribed by Form A/B as shown in the Annex to this Regulation. Form A/B may also be used for applications under Article 2 of Regulation No 17 relating to Article 86 of the Treaty. Joint applications and joint notifications shall be submitted on a single form.

2.   Seventeen copies of each application and notification and three copies of the Annexes thereto shall be submitted to the Commission at the address indicated in Form A/B.

3.   The documents annexed to the application or notification shall be either originals or copies of the originals; in the latter case the applicant or notifying party shall confirm that they are true copies of the originals and complete.

4.   Applications and notifications shall be in one of the official languages of the Community. This language shall also be the language of the proceeding for the applicant or notifying party. Documents shall be submitted in their original language. Where the original language is not one of the official languages, a translation into the language of the proceeding shall be attached.

5.   [...]

Article 3 Content of applications and notifications

1.   Applications and notifications shall contain the information, including documents, required by Form A/B. The information must be correct and complete.

2.   Applications under Article 2 of Regulation No 17 relating to Article 86 of the Treaty shall contain a full statement of the facts, specifying, in particular, the practice concerned and the position of the undertaking or undertakings within the common market or a substantial part thereof in regard to the products or services to which the practice relates.

3.   The Commission may dispense with the obligation to provide any particular information, including documents, required by Form A/B where the Commission considers that such information is not necessary for the examination of the case.

4.   The Commission shall, without delay, acknowledge in writing to the applicant or notifying party receipt of the application or notification, and of any reply to a letter sent by the Commission pursuant to Article 4 (2).

Article 4 Effective date of submission of applications and notifications

1.   Without prejudice to paragraphs 2 to 5, applications and notifications shall become effective on the date on which they are received by the Commission. Where, however, the application or notification is sent by registered post, it shall become effective on the date shown on the postmark of the place of posting.

2.   Where the Commission finds that the information, including documents, contained in the application or notification is incomplete in a material respect, it shall, without delay, inform the applicant or notifying party in writing of this fact and shall fix an appropriate time limit for the completion of the information. In such cases, the application or notification shall become effective on the date on which the complete information is received by the Commission.

3.   Material changes in the facts contained in the application or notification which the applicant or notifying party knows or ought to know must be communicated to the Commission voluntarily and without delay.

4.   Incorrect or misleading information shall be considered to be incomplete information.

5.   Where, at the expiry of a period of one month following the date on which the application or notification has been received, the Commission has not provided the applicant or notifying party with the information referred to in paragraph 2, the application or notification shall be deemed to have become effective on the date of its receipt by the Commission.

Article 5 Repeal

Regulation No 27 is repealed.

Article 6 Entry into force
This Regulation shall enter into force on 1 March 1995.
This Regulation shall be binding in its entirety and directly applicable in all Member States.

Done at Brussels, 21 December 1994.
For the Commission: Karel VAN MIERT

Form A/B for Applications for Negative Clearance of Agreements or Practices Which May Fall Under Article 85 (1) or Article 86

INTRODUCTION

Form A/B, as its Annex, is an integral part of the Commission Regulation 3385/94 of 21 December 1994 on the form, content and other details of applications and notifications provided for in Council Regulation No 17 (hereinafter referred to as "the Regulation"). It allows undertakings and associations of undertakings to apply to the Commission for negative clearance agreements or practices which may fall within the prohibitions of Article 85 (1) and Article 86 of the EC Treaty, or within Articles 53 (1) and 54 of the EEA Agreement or to notify such agreement and apply to have it exempted from the prohibition set out in Article 85 (1) by virtue of the provisions of Article 85 (3) of the EC Treaty or from the prohibition of Article 53 (1) by virtue of the provisions of Article 53 (3) of the EEA Agreement.
To facilitate the use of the Form A/B the following pages set out:
— in which situations it is necessary to make an application or a notification (Point A),
— to which authority (the Commission or the EFTA Surveillance Authority) the application or notification should be made (Point B),
— for which purposes the application or notification can be used (Point C),
— what information must be given in the application or notification (Points D, E and F),
— who can make an application or notification (Point G),
— how to make an application or notification (Point H),
— how the business secrets of the undertakings can be protected (Point I),
— how certain technical terms used in the operational part of the Form A/B should be interpreted (Point J), and
— the subsequent procedure after the application or notification has been made (Point K).

A. In which situations is it necessary to make an application or a notification?
I. Purpose of the competition rules of the EC Treaty and the EEA Agreement
1. Purpose of the EC Competition Rules
The purpose of the competition rules is to prevent the distortion of competition in the common market by restrictive practices or the abuse of dominant positions. They apply to any enterprise trading directly or indirectly in the common market, wherever established.

Article 85 (1) of the EC Treaty (the text of Articles 85 and 86 is reproduced in Annex I to this form) prohibits restrictive agreements, decisions or concerted practices (arrangements) which may affect trade between Member States, and Article 85 (2) declares agreements and decisions containing such restrictions void (although the Court of Justice has held that if restrictive terms of agreements are severable, only those terms are void); Article 85 (3), however, provides for exemption of arrangements with beneficial effects, if its conditions are met. Article 86 prohibits the abuse of a dominant position which may affect trade between Member States. The original procedures for implementing these Articles, which provide for "negative clearance" and exemption pursuant to Article 85 (3), were laid down in Regulation No 17.

2.   Purpose of the EEA competition rules [...]

II.   The scope of the competition rules of the EC Treaty and the EEA Agreement

The applicability of Articles 85 and 86 of the EC Treaty and Articles 53 and 54 of the EEA Agreement depends on the circumstances of each individual case. It presupposes that the arrangement or behaviour satisfies all the conditions set out in the relevant provisions. This question must consequently be examined before any application for negative clearance or any notification is made.

1)   Negative clearance

The negative clearance procedure allows undertakings to ascertain whether the Commission considers that their arrangement or their behaviour is or is not prohibited by Article 85 (1), or Article 86 of the EC Treaty or by Article 53 (1) or Article 54 of the EEA Agreement. This procedure is governed by Article 2 of Regulation No 17. The negative clearance takes the form of a decision by which the Commission certifies that, on the basis of the facts in its possession, there are no grounds pursuant to Article 85 (1) or Article 86 of the EC Treaty or under Article 53 (1) or Article 54 of the EEA Agreement for action on its part in respect of the arrangement or behaviour.

There is, however, no point in making an application when the arrangements or the behaviour are manifestly not prohibited by the abovementioned provisions. Nor is the Commission obliged to give negative clearance. Article 2 of Regulation No 17 states that "... the Commission may certify...". The Commission issues negative clearance decisions only where an important problem of interpretation has to be solved. In the other cases it reacts to the application by sending a comfort letter.

The Commission has published several notices relating the interpretation of Article 85 (1) of the EC Treaty. They define certain categories of agreements which, by their nature or because of their minor importance, are not caught by the prohibition.[1]

2)   Exemption

The procedure for exemption pursuant to Article 85 (3) of the EC Treaty and Article 53 (3) of the EEA Agreement allows companies to enter into arrangements which, in fact, offer economic advantages but which, without exemption, would be prohibited by Article 85 (1) of the EC Treaty or by Article 53 (1) of the EEA Agreement. This procedure is governed by Articles 4, 6 and 8 and, for the new Member States, also by Articles 5, 7 and 25 of Regulation No 17. The exemption takes the form of a decision by the Commission declaring Article 85 (1) of the EC Treaty or Article 53 (1) of the EEA Agreement to be inapplicable to the arrangements described in the decision. Article 8 requires the Commission to specify the period of validity of any such decision, allows the Commission to attach conditions and obligations and provides for decisions to be amended or revoked or specified acts by the parties to be prohibited in certain circumstances, notably if the decisions were based on incorrect information or if there is any material change in the facts.

The Commission has adopted a number of regulations granting exemptions to categories of agreements.[2] Some of these regulations provide that some agreements may benefit from exemption only if they are notified to the Commission pursuant to Article 4 or 5 of Regulation No 17 with a view to obtaining exemption, and the benefit of the opposition procedure is claimed in the notification.

---

1   See Annex II.

2   See Annex II.

A decision granting exemption may have retroactive effect, but, with certain exceptions, cannot be made effective earlier than the date of notification (Article 6 of Regulation No 17). Should the Commission find that notified arrangements are indeed prohibited and cannot be exempted and, therefore, take a decision condemning them, the participants are nevertheless protected, between the date of the notification and the date of the decision, against fines for any infringement described in the notification (Article 3 and Article 15 (5) and (6) of Regulation No 17).

Normally the Commission issues exemption decisions only in cases of particular legal, economic or political importance. In the other cases it terminates the procedure by sending a comfort letter.

B. To which authority should application or notification be made?

The applications and notifications must be made to the authority which has competence for the matter. The Commission is responsible for the application of the competition rules of the EC Treaty. However there is shared competence in relation to the application of the competition rules of the EEA agreement.

The competence of the Commission and of the EFTA Surveillance Authority to apply the EEA competition rules follows from Article 56 of the EEA Agreement. Applications and notifications relating to agreements, decisions or concerted practices liable to affect trade between Member States should be addressed to the Commission unless their effects on trade between Member States or on competition within the Community are not appreciable within the meaning of the Commission notice of 1986 on agreements of minor importance. Furthermore, all restrictive agreements, decisions or concerted practices affecting trade between one Member State and one or more EFTA States fall within the competence of the Commission, provided that the undertakings concerned achieve more than 67% of their combined EEA-wide turnover within the Community. However, if the effects of such agreements, decisions or concerted practices on trade between Member States or on competition within the Community are not appreciable, the notification should, where necessary, be addressed to the EFTA Surveillance Authority. All other agreements, decisions and concerted practices falling under Article 53 of the EEA Agreement should be notified to the EFTA Surveillance Authority (the address of which is given in Annex III).

Applications for negative clearance regarding Article 54 of the EEA Agreement should be lodged with the Commission if the dominant position exists only in the Community, or with the EFTA Surveillance Authority, if the dominant position exists only in the whole of the territory of the EFTA States, or a substantial part of it. Only where the dominant position exists within both territories should the rules outlined above with respect to Article 53 be applied.

The Commission will apply, as a basis for appraisal, the competition rules of the EC Treaty. Where the case falls under the EEA Agreement and is attributed to the Commission pursuant to Article 56 of that Agreement, it will simultaneously apply the EEA rules.

C. The purpose of this form

Form A/B lists the questions that must be answered and the information and documents that must be provided when applying for the following:
— a negative clearance with regard to Article 85 (1) of the EC Treaty and/or Article 53 (1) of the EEA Agreement, pursuant to Article 2 of Regulation No 17, with respect to agreements between undertakings, decisions by associations of undertakings and concerted practices,

— an exemption pursuant to Article 85 (3) of the EC Treaty and/or Article 53 (3) of the EEA Agreement with respect to agreements between undertakings, decisions by associations of undertakings and concerted practices,
— the benefit of the opposition procedure contained in certain Commission regulations granting exemption by category.

This form allows undertakings applying for negative clearance to notify, at the same time, in order to obtain an exemption in the event that the Commission reaches the conclusion that no negative clearance can be granted.

Applications for negative clearance and notifications relating to Article 85 of the EC Treaty shall be submitted in the manner prescribed by form A/B (see Article 2 (1), first sentence of the Regulation).

This form can also be used by undertakings that wish to apply for a negative clearance from Article 86 of the EC Treaty or Article 53 of the EEA Agreement, pursuant to Article 2 of Regulation No 17. Applicants requesting negative clearance from Article 86 are not required to use form A/B. They are nonetheless strongly recommended to give all the information requested below to ensure that their application gives a full statement of the facts (see Article 2 (1), second sentence of the Regulation).

The applications or notifications made on the form A/B issued by the EFTA side are equally valid. However, if the agreements, decisions or practices concerned fall solely within Articles 85 or 86 of the EC Treaty, i. e. have no EEA relevance whatsoever, it is advisable to use the present form established by the Commission.

D. Which chapters of the form should be completed?

The operational part of this form is sub-divided into four chapters. Undertakings wishing to make an application for a negative clearance or a notification must complete Chapters I, II and IV. An exception to this rule is provided for in the case where the application or notification concerns an agreement concerning the creation of a cooperative joint venture of a structural character if the parties wish to benefit from an accelerated procedure. In this situation Chapters I, III and IV should be completed.

In 1992, the Commission announced that it had adopted new internal administrative rules that provided that certain applications and notifications - those of cooperative joint ventures which are structural in nature - would be dealt with within fixed deadlines. In such cases the services of the Commission will, within two months of receipt of the complete notification of the agreement, inform the parties in writing of the results of the initial analysis of the case and, as appropriate, the nature and probable length of the administrative procedure they intend to engage.

The contents of this letter may vary according to the characteristics of the case under investigation:
— in cases not posing any problems, the Commission will send a comfort letter confirming the compatibility of the agreement with Article 85 (1) or (3),
— if a comfort letter cannot be sent because of the need to settle the case by formal decision, the Commission will inform the undertakings concerned of its intention to adopt a decision either granting or rejecting exemption,
— if the Commission has serious doubts as to the compatibility of the agreement with the competition rules, it will send a letter to the parties giving notice of an in-depth examination which may, depending on the case, result in a decision either prohibiting, exempting subject to conditions and obligations, or simply exempting the agreement in question.

This new accelerated procedure, applicable since 1 January 1993, is based entirely on the principle of self-discipline. The deadline of two months from the complete notification - intended for the initial examination of the case - does not constitute a statutory term and is therefore in no way legally binding. However, the Commission will do its best to abide by it. The Commission reserves the right, moreover, to extend this accelerated procedure to other forms of cooperation between undertakings.

A cooperative joint venture of a structural nature is one that involves an important change in the structure and organization of the business assets of the parties to the agreement. This may occur because the joint venture takes over or extends existing activities of the parent companies or because it undertakes new activities on their behalf. Such operations are characterized by the commitment of significant financial, material and/or non-tangible assets such as intellectual property rights and know how. Structural joint ventures are therefore normally intended to operate on a medium- or long-term basis.

This concept includes certain "partial function" joint ventures which take over one or several specific functions within the parents' business activity without access to the market, in particular research and development and/or production. It also covers those "full function" joint ventures which give rise to coordination of the competitive behaviour of independent undertakings, in particular between the parties to the joint venture or between them and the joint venture.[1]

In order to respect the internal deadline, it is important that the Commission has available on notification all the relevant information reasonably available to the notifying parties that is necessary for it to assess the impact of the operation in question on competition. Form A/B therefore contains a special section (Chapter III) that must be completed only by persons notifying cooperative joint ventures of a structural character that wish to benefit from the accelerated procedure.

Persons notifying joint ventures of a structural character that wish to claim the benefit of the aforementioned accelerated procedure should therefore complete Chapters I, III and IV of this form. Chapter III contains a series of detailed questions necessary for the Commission to assess the relevant market(s) and the position of the parties to the joint venture on that (those) market(s).

Where the parties do not wish to claim the benefit of an accelerated procedure for their joint ventures of a structural character they should complete Chapters I, II and IV of this form. Chapter II contains a far more limited range of questions on the relevant market(s) and the position of the parties to the operation in question on that (those) market(s), but sufficient to enable the Commission to commence its examination and investigation.

E. The need for complete information

The receipt of a valid notification by the Commission has two main consequences. First, it affords immunity from fines from the date that the valid notification is received by the Commission with respect to applications made in order to obtain exemption (see Article 15 (5) of Regulation No 17). Second, until a valid notification is received, the Commission cannot grant an exemption pursuant to Article 85 (3) of the EC Treaty and/or Article 53 (3) of the EEA Agreement, and any exemption that is granted can be effective only from the date of receipt of a valid notification.[2] Thus, whilst there is no legal obligation to notify as such, unless and until an arrangement that falls within the scope of Article 85 (1) and/or Article 53 (1) has not been notified and is, therefore, not

---

1   See the Commission Notice on p. 498.

2   Subject to the qualification provided for in Article 4 (2) of Regulation No 17.

capable of being exempted, it may be declared void by a national court pursuant to Article 85 (2) and/or Article 53 (2).[1]

Where an undertaking is claiming the benefit of a group exemption by recourse to an opposition procedure, the period within which the Commission must oppose the exemption by category only applies from the date that a valid notification is received. This is also true of the two months' period imposed on the Commission services for an initial analysis of applications for negative clearance and notifications relating to cooperative joint ventures of a structural character which benefit from the accelerated procedure.

A valid application or notification for this purpose means one that is not incomplete (see Article 3 (1) of the Regulation). This is subject to two qualifications. First, if the information or documents required by this form are not reasonably available to you in part or in whole, the Commission will accept that a notification is complete and thus valid notwithstanding the failure to provide such information, providing that you give reasons for the unavailability of the information, and provide your best estimates for missing data together with the sources for the estimates. Indications as to where any of the requested information or documents that are unavailable to you could be obtained by the Commission must also be provided. Second, the Commission only requires the submission of information relevant and necessary to its inquiry into the notified operation. In some cases not all the information required by this form will be necessary for this purpose. The Commission may therefore dispense with the obligation to provide certain information required by this form (see Article 3 (3) of the Regulation). This provision enables, where appropriate, each application or notification to be tailored to each case so that only the information strictly necessary for the Commission's examination is provided. This avoids unnecessary administrative burdens being imposed on undertakings, in particular on small and medium-sized ones. Where the information or documents required by this form are not provided for this reason, the application or notification should indicate the reasons why the information is considered to be unnecessary to the Commission's investigation.

Where the Commission finds that the information contained in the application or notification is incomplete in a material respect, it will, within one month from receipt, inform the applicant or the notifying party in writing of this fact and the nature of the missing information. In such cases, the application or notification shall become effective on the date on which the complete information is received by the Commission. If the Commission has not informed the applicant or the notifying party within the one month period that the application or notification is incomplete in a material respect, the application or notification will be deemed to be complete and valid (see Article 4 of the Regulation).

It is also important that undertakings inform the Commission of important changes in the factual situation including those of which they become aware after the application or notification has been submitted. The Commission must, therefore, be informed immediately of any changes to an agreement, decision or practice which is the subject of an application or notification (see Article 4 (3) of the Regulation). Failure to inform the Commission of such relevant changes could result in any negative clearance decision being without effect or in the withdrawal of any exemption decision[2] adopted by the Commission on the basis of the notification.

---

1   For further details of the consequences of non-notification see the Commission notice on cooperation between national Courts and the Commission, OJ 1993 C 39, p. 6.

2   See point (a) of Article 8 (3) of Regulation No 17.

F. The need for accurate information

In addition to the requirement that the application or notification be complete, it is important that you ensure that the information provided is accurate (see Article 3 (1) of the Regulation). Article 15 (1) (a) of Regulation No 17 states that the Commission may, by decision, impose on undertakings or associations of undertakings fines of up to ECU 5.000 where, intentionally or negligently, they supply incorrect or misleading information in an application for negative clearance or notification. Such information is, moreover, considered to be incomplete (see Article 4 (4) of the Regulation), so that the parties cannot benefit from the advantages of the opposition procedure or accelerated procedure (see above, Point E).

G. Who can lodge an application or a notification?

Any of the undertakings party to an agreement, decision or practice of the kind described in Articles 85 or 86 of the EC Treaty and Articles 53 or 54 of the EEA Agreement may submit an application for negative clearance, in relation to Article 85 and Article 53, or a notification requesting an exemption. An association of undertakings may submit an application or a notification in relation to decisions taken or practices pursued into in the operation of the association.

In relation to agreements and concerted practices between undertakings it is common practice for all the parties involved to submit a joint application or notification. Although the Commission strongly recommends this approach, because it is helpful to have the views of all the parties directly concerned at the same time, it is not obligatory. Any of the parties to an agreement may submit an application or notification in their individual capacities, but in such circumstances the notifying party should inform all the other parties to the agreement, decision or practice of that fact (see Article 1 (3) of the Regulation). They may also provide them with a copy of the completed form, where relevant once confidential information and business secrets have been deleted (see below, operational part, question 1.2).

Where a joint application or notification is submitted, it has also become common practice to appoint a joint representative to act on behalf of all the undertakings involved, both in making the application or notification, and in dealing with any subsequent contacts with the Commission (see Article 1 (4) of the Regulation). Again, whilst this is helpful, it is not obligatory, and all the undertakings jointly submitting an application or a notification may sign it in their individual capacities.

H. How to submit an application or notification

Applications and notifications may be submitted in any of the official languages of the European Community or of an EFTA State (see Article 2 (4) and (5) of the Regulation). In order to ensure rapid proceedings, it is, however, recommended to use, in case of an application or notification to the EFTA Surveillance Authority one of the official languages of an EFTA State or the working language of the EFTA Surveillance Authority, which is English, or, in case of an application or notification to the Commission, one of the official languages of the Community or the working language of the EFTA Surveillance Authority. This language will thereafter be the language of the proceeding for the applicant or notifying party.

Form A/B is not a form to be filled in. Undertakings should simply provide the information requested by this form, using its sections and paragraph numbers, signing a declaration as stated in Section 19 below, and annexing the required supporting documentation.

Supporting documents shall be submitted in their original language; where this is not an official language of the Community they must be translated into the language of the proceeding. The supporting documents may be originals or copies of the originals (see Article 2 (4) of the Regulation).

All information requested in this form shall, unless otherwise stated, relate to the calendar year preceding that of the application or notification. Where information is not reasonably available on this basis (for example if accounting periods are used that are not based on the calendar year, or the previous year's figures are not yet available) the most recently available information should be provided and reasons given why figures on the basis of the calendar year preceding that of the application or notification cannot be provided.

Financial data may be provided in the currency in which the official audited accounts of the undertaking(s) concerned are prepared or in Ecus. In the latter case the exchange rate used for the conversion must be stated.

Seventeen copies of each application or notification, but only three copies of all supporting documents must be provided (see Article 2 (2) of the Regulation).

The application or notification is to be sent to:

> Commission of the European Communities,
> Directorate-General for Competition (DG IV),
> The Registrar,
> 200, Rue de la Loi,
> B-1049 Brussels.

or be delivered by hand during Commission working days and official working hours at the following address:

> Commission of the European Communities,
> Directorate-General for Competition (DG IV),
> The Registrar,
> 158, Avenue de Cortenberg,
> B-1040 Brussels.

I.   Confidentiality

Article 214 of the EC Treaty, Article 20 of Regulation No 17, Article 9 of Protocol 23 to the EEA Agreement, Article 122 of the EEA Agreement and Articles 20 and 21 of Chapter II of Protocol 4 to the Agreement between the EFTA States on the establishment of a Surveillance Authority and of a Court of Justice require the Commission, the Member States, the EEA Surveillance Authority and EFTA States not to disclose information of the kind covered by the obligation of professional secrecy. On the other hand, Regulation No 17 requires the Commission to publish a summary of the application or notification, should it intend to take a favourable decision. In this publication, the Commission "... shall have regard to the legitimate interest of undertakings in the protection of their business secrets" (Article 19 (3) of Regulation No 17; see also Article 21 (2) in relation to the publication of decisions). In this connection, if an undertaking believes that its interests would be harmed if any of the information it is asked to supply were to be published or otherwise divulged to other undertakings, it should put all such information in a separate annex with each page clearly marked "Business Secrets". It should also give reasons why any information identified as confidential or secret should not be divulged or published. (See below, Section 5 of the operational part that requests a non-confidential summary of the notification).

J.   Subsequent Procedure

The application or notification is registered in the Registry of the Directorate-General for Competition (DG IV). The date of receipt by the Commission (or the date of posting if sent by registered post) is the effective date of the submission (see Article 4 (1) of the

Regulation). However, special rules apply to incomplete applications and notifications (see above under Point E).

The Commission will acknowledge receipt of all applications and notifications in writing, indicating the case number attributed to the file. This number must be used in all future correspondence regarding the notification. The receipt of acknowledgement does not prejudge the question whether the application or notification is valid.

Further information may be sought from the parties or from third parties (Articles 11 to 14 of Regulation No 17) and suggestions might be made as to amendments to the arrangements that might make them acceptable. Equally, a short preliminary notice may be published in the C series of the Official Journal of the European Communities, stating the names of the interested undertakings, the groups to which they belong, the economic sectors involved and the nature of the arrangements, and inviting third party comments (see below, operational part, Section 5).

Where a notification is made together for the purpose of the application of the opposition procedure, the Commission may oppose the grant of the benefit of the group exemption with respect to the notified agreement. If the Commission opposes the claim, and unless it subsequently withdraws its opposition, that notification will then be treated as an application for an individual exemption.

If, after examination, the Commission intends to grant the application for negative clearance or exemption, it is obliged (by Article 19 (3) of Regulation No 17) to publish a summary and invite comments from third parties. Subsequently, a preliminary draft decision has to be submitted to and discussed with the Advisory Committee on Restrictive Practices and Dominant Positions composed of officials of the competent authorities of the Member States in the matter of restrictive practices and monopolies (Article 10 of Regulation No 17) and attended, where the case falls within the EEA Agreement, by representatives of the EFTA Surveillance Authority and the EFTA States which will already have received a copy of the application or notification. Only then, and providing nothing has happened to change the Commission's intention, can it adopt the envisaged decision.

Files are often closed without any formal decision being taken, for example, because it is found that the arrangements are already covered by a block exemption, or because they do not call for any action by the Commission, at least in circumstances at that time. In such cases comfort letters are sent. Although not a Commission decision, a comfort letter indicates how the Commission's departments view the case on the facts currently in their possession which means that the Commission could where necessary - for example, if it were to be asserted that a contract was void under Article 85 (2) of the EC Treaty and/or Article 53 (2) of the EEA Agreement - take an appropriate decision to clarify the legal situation.

K. Definitions used in the operational part of this form

— Agreement: The word "agreement" is used to refer to all categories of arrangements, i. e. agreements between undertakings, decisions by associations of undertakings and concerted practices.
— Year: All references to the word "year" in this form shall be read as meaning calendar year, unless otherwise stated.
— Group: A group relationship exists for the purpose of this form where one undertaking:
— owns more than half the capital or business assets of another undertaking, or
— has the power to exercise more than half the voting rights in another undertaking, or
— has the power to appoint more than half the members of the supervisory board, board of directors or bodies legally representing the undertaking, or

— has the right to manage the affairs of another undertaking.
An undertaking which is jointly controlled by several other undertakings (joint venture) forms part of the group of each of these undertakings.
— Relevant product market: questions 6.1 and 11.1 of this form require the undertaking or individual submitting the notification to define the relevant product and/or service market(s) that are likely to be affected by the agreement in question.[1] That definition(s) is then used as the basis for a number of other questions contained in this form. The definition(s) thus submitted by the notifying parties are referred to in this form as the relevant product market(s). These words can refer to a market made up either of products or of services.
— Relevant geographic market: questions 6.2 and 11.2 of this form require the undertaking or individual submitting the notification to define the relevant geographic market(s) that are likely to be affected by the agreement in question. That definition(s) is then used as the basis for a number of other questions contained in this form. The definition(s) thus submitted by the notifying parties are referred to in this form as the relevant geographic market(s).
— Relevant product and geographic market: by virtue of the combination of their replies to questions 6 and 11 the parties provide their definition of the relevant market(s) affected by the notified agreement(s). That (those) definition(s) is (are) then used as the basis for a number of other questions contained in this form. The definition(s) thus submitted by the notifying parties is referred to in this form as the relevant geographic and product market(s).
— Notification: this form can be used to make an application for negative clearance and/or a notification requesting an exemption. The word "notification" is used to refer to either an application or a notification.
— Parties and notifying party: the word "party" is used to refer to all the undertakings which are party to the agreement being notified. As a notification may be submitted by only one of the undertakings which are party to an agreement, "notifying party" is used to refer only to the undertaking or undertakings actually submitting the notification.

OPERATIONAL PART

Please make sure that the first page of your application or notification contains the words "application for negative clearance/notification in accordance with form A/B".

Chapter I
Sections concerning the parties, their groups and the agreement
(to be completed for all notifications)
Section 1 Identity of the undertakings or persons submitting the notification
1.1. Please list the undertakings on behalf of which the notification is being submitted and indicate their legal denomination or commercial name, shortened or commonly used as appropriate (if it differs from the legal denomination).
1.2. If the notification is being submitted on behalf of only one or some of the undertakings party to the agreement being notified, please confirm that the remaining undertakings have been informed of that fact and indicate whether they have received a copy

---

1   See the Commission Notice on p. 501.

of the notification, with relevant confidential information and business secrets deleted.[1] (In such circumstances a copy of the edited copy of the notification which has been provided to such other undertakings should be annexed to this notification.)

1.3. If a joint notification is being submitted, has a joint representative[2] been appointed[3]?

If yes, please give the details requested in 1.3.1 to 1.3.3 below.

If no, please give details of any representatives who have been authorized to act for each or either of the parties to the agreement indicating who they represent.

    1.3.1. Name of representative.

    1.3.2. Address of representative.

    1.3.3. Telephone and fax number of representative.

1.4. In cases where one or more representatives have been appointed, an authority to act on behalf of the undertaking(s) submitting the notification must accompany the notification.

Section 2 Information on the parties to the agreement and the groups to which they belong

2.1. State the name and address of the parties to the agreement being notified, and the country of their incorporation.

2.2. State the nature of the business of each of the parties to the agreement being notified.

2.3. For each of the parties to the agreement, give the name of a person that can be contacted, together with his or her name, address, telephone number, fax number and position held in the undertaking.

2.4. Identify the corporate groups to which the parties to the agreement being notified belong. State the sectors in which these groups are active, and the world-wide turnover of each group.

Section 3 Procedural matters

3.1. Please state whether you have made any formal submission to any other competition authorities in relation to the agreement in question. If yes, state which authorities, the individual or department in question, and the nature of the contact. In addition to this, mention any earlier proceedings or informal contacts, of which you are aware, with the Commission and/or the EFTA Surveillance Authority and any earlier proceedings with any national authorities or courts in the Community or in EFTA concerning these or any related agreements.

---

1   The Commission is aware that in exceptional cases it may not be practicable to inform non-notifying parties to the notified agreement of the fact that it has been notified, or to provide them a copy of the notification. This may be the case, for example, where a standard agreement is being notified that is concluded with a large number of undertakings. Where this is the case you should state the reasons why it has not been practicable to follow the standard procedure set out in this question.

2   Note: For the purposes of this question a representative means an individual or undertaking formally appointed to make the notification or application on behalf of the party or parties submitting the notification. This should be distinguished from the situation where the notification is signed by an officer of the company or companies in question. In the latter situation no representative is appointed.

3   Note: It is not mandatory to appoint representatives for the purpose of completing and/or submitting this notification. This question only requires the identification of representatives where the notifying parties have chosen to appoint them.

3.2. Please summarize any reasons for any claim that the case involves an issue of exceptional urgency.

3.3. The Commission has stated that where notifications do not have particular political, economic or legal significance for the Community they will normally be dealt with by means of comfort letter.[1] Would you be satisfied with a comfort letter? If you consider that it would be inappropriate to deal with the notified agreement in this manner, please explain the reasons for this view.

3.4. State whether you intend to produce further supporting facts or arguments not yet available and, if so, on which points.[2]

Section 4 Full details of the arrangements

4.1. Please summarize the nature, content and objectives pursued by the agreement being notified.

4.2. Detail any provisions contained in the agreements which may restrict the parties in their freedom to take independent commercial decisions, for example regarding:
— buying or selling prices, discounts or other trading conditions,
— the quantities of goods to be manufactured or distributed or services to be offered,
— technical development or investment,
— the choice of markets or sources of supply,
— purchases from or sales to third parties,
— whether to apply similar terms for the supply of equivalent goods or services,
— whether to offer different services separately or together.
If you are claiming the benefit of the opposition procedure, identify in this list the restrictions that exceed those automatically exempted by the relevant regulation.

4.3. State between which Member States of the Community and/or EFTA States trade may be affected by the arrangements. Please give reasons for your reply to this question, giving data on trade flows where relevant. Furthermore please state whether trade between the Community or the EEA territory and any third countries is affected, again giving reasons for your reply.

Section 5 Non-confidential Summary

Shortly following receipt of a notification, the Commission may publish a short notice inviting third party comments on the agreement in question.[3] As the objective pursued by the Commission in publishing an informal preliminary notice is to receive third party comments as soon as possible after the notification has been received, such a notice is usually published without first providing it to the notifying parties for their comments. This section requests the information to be used in an informal preliminary notice in the event that the Commission decides to issue one. It is important, therefore, that your

---

1   See paragraph 14 of the notice on cooperation between national courts and the Commission in applying Articles 85 and 86 of the EC Treaty (OJ 1993 C 39, p. 6).

2   Note: In so far as the notifying parties provide the information required by this form that was reasonably available to them at the time of notification, the fact that the parties intend to provide further supporting facts or documentation in due course does not prevent the notification being valid at the time of notification and, in the case of structural joint ventures where the accelerated procedure is being claimed, the two month deadline commencing.

3   Such a notice should be distinguished from a formal notice published pursuant to Article 19 (3) of Regulation No 17. An Article 19 (3) notice is relatively detailed, and gives an indication of the Commission's current approach in the case in question. Section 5 only seeks information that will be used in a short preliminary notice, and not a notice published pursuant to Article 19 (3).

replies to these questions do not contain any business secrets or other confidential information.

1.   State the names of the parties to the agreement notified and the groups of undertakings to which they belong.

2.   Give a short summary of the nature and objectives of the agreement. As a guideline this summary should not exceed 100 words.

3.   Identify the product sectors affected by the agreement in question.

Chapter II
Section concerning the relevant market

(to be completed for all notifications except those relating to structural joint ventures for which accelerated treatment is claimed)

Section 6 The relevant market

A relevant product market comprises all those products and/or services which are regarded as interchangeable or substitutable by the consumer, by reason of the products' characteristics, their prices and their intended use.

The following factors are normally considered to be relevant to the determination of the relevant product market and should be taken into account in this analysis:[1]

— the degree of physical similarity between the products/services in question,
— any differences in the end use to which the goods are put,
— differences in price between two products,
— the cost of switching between two potentially competing products,
— established or entrenched consumer preferences for one type or category of product over another,
— industry-wide product classifications (e. g. classifications maintained by trade associations).

The relevant geographic market comprises the area in which the undertakings concerned are involved in the supply of products or services, in which the conditions of competition are sufficiently homogeneous and which can be distinguished from neighbouring areas because, in particular, conditions of competition are appreciably different in those areas.

Factors relevant to the assessment of the relevant geographic market include[2] the nature and characteristics of the products or services concerned, the existence of entry barriers or consumer preferences, appreciable differences of the undertakings' market share or substantial price differences between neighbouring areas, and transport costs.

6.1. In the light of the above please explain the definition of the relevant product market or markets that in your opinion should form the basis of the Commission's analysis of the notification.

In your answer, please give reasons for assumptions or findings, and explain how the factors outlined above have been taken into account. In particular, please state the specific products or services directly or indirectly affected by the agreement being notified and identify the categories of goods viewed as substitutable in your market definition.

In the questions figuring below, this (or these) definition(s) will be referred to as "the relevant product market(s)".

---

1   This list is not, however, exhaustive, and notifying parties may refer to other factors. [In this context, see also the Commission Notice on p. 501.]

2   This list is not, however, exhaustive, and notifying parties may refer to other factors.

6.2. Please explain the definition of the relevant geographic market or markets that in your opinion should form the basis of the Commission's analysis of the notification. In your answer, please give reasons for assumptions or findings, and explain how the factors outlined above have been taken into account. In particular, please identify the countries in which the parties are active in the relevant product market(s), and in the event that you consider the relevant geographic market to be wider than the individual Member States of the Community or EFTA on which the parties to the agreement are active, give the reasons for this.

In the questions below, this (or these) definition(s) will be referred to as "the relevant geographic market(s)".

Section 7 Group members operating on the same markets as the parties
7.1. For each of the parties to the agreement being notified, provide a list of all undertakings belonging to the same group which are:
    7.1.1. active in the relevant product market(s);
    7.1.2. active in markets neighbouring the relevant product market(s) (i.e. active in products and/or services that represent imperfect and partial substitutes for those included in your definition of the relevant product market(s)).

Such undertakings must be identified even if they sell the product or service in question in other geographic areas than those in which the parties to the notified agreement operate. Please list the name, place of incorporation, exact product manufactured and the geographic scope of operation of each group member.

Section 8 The position of the parties on the affected relevant product markets
Information requested in this section must be provided for the groups of the parties as a whole. It is not sufficient to provide such information only in relation to the individual undertakings directly concerned by the agreement.
8.1. In relation to each relevant product market(s) identified in your reply to question 6.1 please provide the following information:
    8.1.1. the market shares of the parties on the relevant geographic market during the previous three years;
    8.1.2. where different, the market shares of the parties in (a) the EEA territory as a whole, (b) the Community, (c) the territory of the EFTA States and (d) each EC Member State and EFTA State during the previous three years.[1] For this section, where market shares are less than 20%, please state simply which of the following bands are relevant: 0 to 5%, 5 to 10%, 10 to 15%, 15 to 20%.

For the purpose of answering these questions, market share may be calculated either on the basis of value or volume. Justification for the figures provided must be given. Thus, for each answer, total market value/volume must be stated, together with the sales/turnover of each of the parties in question. The source or sources of the information should also be given (e.g. official statistics, estimates, etc.), and where possible, copies should be provided of documents from which information has been taken.

---

1   Where the relevant geographic market has been defined as world wide, these figures must be given regarding the EEA, the Community, the territory of the EFTA States, and each EC Member State. Where the relevant geographic market has been defined as the Community, these figures must be given for the EEA, the territory of the EFTA States, and each EC Member State. Where the market has been defined as national, these figures must be given for the EEA, the Community and the territory of the EFTA States.

Section 9 The position of competitors and customers on the relevant product market(s)

Information requested in this section must be provided for the group of the parties as a whole and not in relation to the individual companies directly concerned by the agreement notified.

For the (all) relevant product and geographic market(s) in which the parties have a combined market share exceeding 15%, the following questions must be answered.

9.1. Please identify the five main competitors of the parties. Please identify the company and give your best estimate as to their market share in the relevant geographic market(s). Please also provide address, telephone and fax number, and, where possible, the name of a contact person at each company identified.

9.2. Please identify the five main customers of each of the parties. State company name, address, telephone and fax numbers, together with the name of a contact person.

Section 10 Market entry and potential competition in product and geographic terms

For the (all) relevant product and geographic market(s) in which the parties have a combined market share exceeding 15%, the following questions must be answered.

10.1. Describe the various factors influencing entry in product terms into the relevant product market(s) that exist in the present case (i.e. what barriers exist to prevent undertakings that do not presently manufacture goods within the relevant product market(s) entering this market(s)). In so doing take account of the following where appropriate:

— to what extent is entry to the markets influenced by the requirement of government authorization or standard setting in any form? Are there any legal or regulatory controls on entry to these markets?

— to what extent is entry to the markets influenced by the availability of raw materials?

— to what extent is entry to the markets influenced by the length of contracts between an undertaking and its suppliers and/or customers?

— describe the importance of research and development and in particular the importance of licensing patents, know-how and other rights in these markets.

10.2. Describe the various factors influencing entry in geographic terms into the relevant geographic market(s) that exist in the present case (i.e. what barriers exist to prevent undertakings already producing and/or marketing products within the relevant product market(s) but in areas outside the relevant geographic market(s) extending the scope of their sales into the relevant geographic market(s)?). Please give reasons for your answer, explaining, where relevant, the importance of the following factors:

— trade barriers imposed by law, such as tariffs, quotas etc.,

— local specification or technical requirements,

— procurement policies,

— the existence of adequate and available local distribution and retailing facilities,

— transport costs,

— entrenched consumer preferences for local brands or products,

— language.

10.3. Have any new undertakings entered the relevant product market(s) in geographic areas where the parties sell during the last three years? Please provide this information with respect to both new entrants in product terms and new entrants in geographic terms. If such entry has occurred, please identify the undertaking(s) concerned (name, address, telephone and fax numbers, and, where possible, contact person), and provide your best estimate of their market share in the relevant product and geographic market(s).

Chapter III
Section concerning the relevant market only for structural joint ventures for which accelerated treatment is claimed
Section 11 The relevant market

A relevant product market comprises all those products and/or services which are regarded as interchangeable or substitutable by the consumer, by reason of the products' characteristics, their prices and their intended use.

The following factors are normally considered to be relevant[1] to the determination of the relevant product market and should be taken into account in this analysis:
—   the degree of physical similarity between the products/services in question,
—   any differences in the end use to which the goods are put,
—   differences in price between two products,
—   the cost of switching between two potentially competing products,
—   established or entrenched consumer preferences for one type or category of product over another,
—   different or similar industry-wide product classifications (e.g. classifications maintained by trade associations).

The relevant geographic market comprises the area in which the undertakings concerned are involved in the supply of products or services, in which the conditions of competition are sufficiently homogeneous and which can be distinguished from neighbouring areas because, in particular, conditions of competition are appreciably different in those areas.

Factors relevant to the assessment of the relevant geographic market include[2] the nature and characteristics of the products or services concerned, the existence of entry barriers or consumer preferences, appreciable differences of the undertakings' market share or substantial price differences between neighbouring areas, and transport costs.

Part 11.1: The notifying parties' analysis of the relevant market
11.1.1. In the light of the above, please explain the definition of the relevant product market or markets that in the opinion of the parties should form the basis of the Commission's analysis of the notification.

In your answer, please give reasons for assumptions or findings, and explain how the factors outlined above have been taken into account.

In the questions figuring below, this (or these) definition(s) will be referred to as "the relevant product market(s)".
11.1.2. Please explain the definition of the relevant geographic market or markets that in the opinion of the parties should form the basis of the Commission's analysis of the notification.

In your answer, please give reasons for assumptions or findings, and explain how the factors outlined above have been taken into account.

Part 11.2: Questions on the relevant product and geographic market(s)
Answers to the following questions will enable the Commission to verify whether the product and geographic market definitions put forward by you in Section 11.1 are compatible with definitions figuring above.

---

1   This list is not, however, exhaustive, and notifying parties may refer to other factors.

2   This list is not, however, exhaustive, and notifying parties may refer to other factors.

Product market definition

11.2.1. List the specific products or services directly or indirectly affected by the agreement being notified.

11.2.2. List the categories of products and/or services that are, in the opinion of the notifying parties, close economic substitutes for those identified in the reply to question 11.2.1. Where more than one product or service has been identified in the reply to question 11.2.1, a list for each product must be provided for this question.

The products identified in this list should be ordered in their degree of substitutability, first listing the most perfect substitute for the products of the parties, finishing with the least perfect substitute.[1]

Please explain how the factors relevant to the definition of the relevant product market have been taken into account in drawing up this list and in placing the products/services in their correct order.

Geographic market definition

11.2.3. List all the countries in which the parties are active in the relevant product market(s). Where they are active in all countries within any given groups of countries or trading area (e. g. the whole Community or EFTA, the EEA countries, world-wide) it is sufficient to indicate the area in question.

11.2.4. Explain the manner in which the parties produce and sell the goods and/or services in each of these various countries or areas. For example, do they manufacture

---

1 Close economic substitute; most perfect substitute; least perfect substitute these definitions are only relevant to those filling out Chapter III of the form, i.e. those notifying structural joint ventures requesting the accelerated procedure).

For any given product (for the purposes of this definition "product" is used to refer to products or services) a chain of substitutes exists. This chain is made up of all conceivable substitutes for the product in question, i.e. all those products that will, to a greater or lesser extent, fulfil the needs of the consumer in question. The substitutes will range from very close (or perfect) ones (products to which consumers would turn immediately in the event of, for example, even a very small price increase for the product in question) to very distant (or imperfect) substitutes (products to which customers would only turn to in the event of a very large price rise for the product in question). When defining the relevant market, and calculating market shares, the Commission only takes into account close economic substitutes of the products in question. Close economic substitutes are ones to which customers would turn to in response to a small but significant price increase for the product in question (say 5%). This enables the Commission to assess the market power of the notifying companies in the context of a relevant market made up of all those products that consumers of the products in question could readily and easily turn to.

However, this does not mean that the Commission fails to take into account the constraints on the competitive behavior of the parties in question resulting from the existence of imperfect substitutes (those to which a consumer could not turn to in response to a small but significant price increase (say 5%) for the products in question). These effects are taken into account once the market has been defined, and the market shares determined.

It is therefore important for the Commission to have information regarding both close economic substitutes for the products in question, as well as less perfect substitutes.

For example, assume two companies active in the luxury watch sector conclude a research and development agreement. They both manufacture watches costing ECU 1.800 to 2.000. Close economic substitutes are likely to be watches of other manufactures in the same or similar price category, and these will be taken into account when defining the relevant product market. Cheaper watches, and in particular disposable plastic watches, will be imperfect substitutes, because it is unlikely that a potential purchaser of a ECU 2.000 watch will turn to one costing ECU 20 if the expensive one increased its price by 5%.

locally, do they sell through local distribution facilities, or do they distribute through exclusive, or non-exclusive, importers and distributors?

11.2.5. Are there significant trade flows in the goods/services that make up the relevant product market(s) (i) between the EC Member States (please specify which and estimate the percentage of total sales made up by imports in each Member State in which the parties are active), (ii) between all or part of the EC Member States and all or part of the EFTA States (again, please specify and estimate the percentage of total sales made up by imports), (iii) between the EFTA States (please specify which and estimate the percentage of total sales made up by imports in each such State in which the parties are active), and (iv) between all or part of the EEA territory and other countries? (again, please specify and estimate the percentage of total sales made up by imports.)

11.2.6. Which producer undertakings based outside the Community or the EEA territory sell within the EEA territory in countries in which the parties are active in the affected products? How do these undertakings market their products? Does this differ between different EC Member States and/or EFTA States?

Section 12 Group members operating on the same markets as the parties to the notified agreement

12.1. For each of the parties to the agreement being notified, provide a list of all undertakings belonging to the same group which are:

12.1.1. active in the relevant product market(s);

12.1.2. active in markets neighbouring the relevant product market(s) (i.e. active in products/services that represent imperfect and partial substitutes[1] for those included in your definition of the relevant product market(s);

12.1.3. active in markets upstream and/or downstream from those included in the relevant product market(s).

Such undertakings must be identified even if they sell the product or service in question in other geographic areas than those in which the parties to the notified agreement operate. Please list the name, place of incorporation, exact product manufactured and the geographic scope of operation of each group member.

Section 13 The position of the parties on the relevant product market(s)

Information requested in this section must be provided for the group of the parties as a whole and not in relation to the individual companies directly concerned by the agreement notified.

13.1. In relation to each relevant product market(s), as defined in your reply to question 11.1.2, please provide the following information:

13.1.1. the market shares of the parties on the relevant geographic market during the previous three years;

13.1.2. where different, the market shares of the parties in (a) the EEA territory as a whole, (b) the Community, (c) the territory of the EFTA States and (d) each EC Member State and EFTA State during the previous three years.[2] For this section, where

---

1   The following are considered to be partial substitutes: products and services which may replace each other solely in certain geographic areas, solely during part of the year or solely for certain uses.

2   Where the relevant geographic market has been defined as world wide, these figures must be given regarding the EEA, the Community, the territory of the EFTA States, and each EC Member State and EFTA State. Where the relevant geographic market has been defined as the Community, these figures must be given for the EEA, the territory of the EFTA States, and each EC Member State and EFTA State. Where the market has been defined as national, these figures must be given for the

market shares are less than 20%, please state simply which of the following bands are relevant: 0 to 5%, 5 to 10%, 10 to 15%, 15 to 20% in terms of value or volume.

For the purpose of answering these questions, market share may be calculated either on the basis of value or volume. Justification for the figures provided must be given. Thus, for each answer, total market value/volume must be stated, together with the sales/turnover of each the parties in question. The source or sources of the information should also be given, and where possible, copies should be provided of documents from which information has been taken.

13.2. If the market shares in question 13.1 were to be calculated on a basis other than that used by the parties, would the resultant market shares differ by more than 5% in any market (i.e. if the parties have calculated market shares on the basis of volume, what would be the relevant figure if it was calculated on the basis of value?) If the figure were to differ by more than 5% please provide the information requested in question 13.1 on the basis of both value and volume.

13.3. Give your best estimate of the current rate of capacity utilization of the parties and in the industry in general in the relevant product and geographic market(s).

Section 14 The position of competitors and customers on the relevant product market(s)

Information requested in this section must be provided for the group of the parties as a whole and not in relation to the individual companies directly concerned by the agreement notified.

For the (all) relevant product market(s) in which the parties have a combined market share exceeding 10% in the EEA as a whole, the Community, the EFTA territory or in any EC Member State or EFTA Member State, the following questions must be answered.

14.1. Please identify the competitors of the parties on the relevant product market(s) that have a market share exceeding 10% in any EC Member State, EFTA State, in the territory of the EFTA States, in the EEA, or world-wide. Please identify the company and give your best estimate as to their market share in these geographic areas. Please also provide the address, telephone and fax numbers, and, where possible, the name of a contact person at each company identified.

14.2. Please describe the nature of demand on the relevant product market(s). For example, are there few or many purchasers, are there different categories of purchasers, are government agencies or departments important purchasers?

14.3. Please identify the five largest customers of each of the parties for each relevant product market(s). State company name, address, telephone and fax numbers, together with the name of a contact person.

Section 15 Market entry and potential competition

For the (all) relevant product market(s) in which the parties have a combined market share exceeding 10% in the EEA as a whole, the Community, the EFTA territory or in any EC Member State or EFTA State, the following questions must be answered.

15.1. Describe the various factors influencing entry into the relevant product market(s) that exist in the present case. In so doing take account of the following where appropriate:

—   to what extent is entry to the markets influenced by the requirement of government authorization or standard setting in any form? Are there any legal or regulatory controls on entry to these markets?

EEA, the Community and the territory of the EFTA States.

— to what extent is entry to the markets influenced by the availability of raw materials?

— to what extent is entry to the markets influenced by the length of contracts between an undertaking and its suppliers and/or customers?

— what is the importance of research and development and in particular the importance of licensing patents, know-how and other rights in these markets.

15.2. Have any new undertakings entered the relevant product market(s) in geographic areas where the parties sell during the last three years? If so, please identify the undertaking(s) concerned (name, address, telephone and fax numbers, and, where possible, contact person), and provide your best estimate of their market share in each EC Member State and EFTA State that they are active and in the Community, the territory of the EFTA States and the EEA territory as a whole.

15.3. Give your best estimate of the minimum viable scale for the entry into the relevant product market(s) in terms of appropriate market share necessary to operate profitably.

15.4. Are there significant barriers to entry preventing companies active on the relevant product market(s):

15.4.1. in one EC Member State or EFTA State selling in other areas of the EEA territory;

15.4.2. outside the EEA territory selling into all or parts of the EEA territory.

Please give reasons for your answers, explaining, where relevant, the importance of the following factors:

— trade barriers imposed by law, such as tariffs, quotas etc.,

— local specification or technical requirements,

— procurement policies,

— the existence of adequate and available local distribution and retailing facilities,

— transport costs,

— entrenched consumer preferences for local brands or products,

— language.

Chapter IV Final sections
To be completed for all notifications
Section 16 Reasons for the application for negative clearance

If you are applying for negative clearance state:

16.1. why, i.e. state which provision or effects of the agreement or behaviour might, in your view, raise questions of compatibility with the Community's and/or the EEA rules of competition. The object of this subheading is to give the Commission the clearest possible idea of the doubts you have about your agreement or behaviour that you wish to have resolved by a negative clearance.

Then, under the following three references, give a statement of the relevant facts and reasons as to why you consider Article 85 (1) or 86 of the EC Treaty and/or Article 53 (1) or 54 of the EEA Agreement to be inapplicable, i.e.:

16.2. why the agreements or behaviour do not have the object or effect of preventing, restricting or distorting competition within the common market or within the territory of the EFTA States to any appreciable extent, or why your undertaking does not have or its behaviour does not abuse a dominant position; and/or

16.3. why the agreements or behaviour do not have the object or effect of preventing, restricting or distorting competition within the EEA territory to any appreciable extent, or why your undertaking does not have or its behaviour does not abuse a dominant position; and/or

16.4. why the agreements or behaviour are not such as may affect trade between Member States or between the Community and one or more EFTA States, or between EFTA States to any appreciable extent.

Section 17 Reasons for the application for exemption

If you are notifying the agreement, even if only as a precaution, in order to obtain an exemption under Article 85 (3) of the EC Treaty and/or Article 53 (3) of the EEA Agreement, explain how:

17.1. the agreement contributes to improving production or distribution, and/or promoting technical or economic progress. In particular, please explain the reasons why these benefits are expected to result from the collaboration; for example, do the parties to the agreement possess complementary technologies or distribution systems that will produce important synergies? (if, so, please state which). Also please state whether any documents or studies were drawn up by the notifying parties when assessing the feasibility of the operation and the benefits likely to result therefrom, and whether any such documents or studies provided estimates of the savings or efficiencies likely to result. Please provide copies of any such documents or studies;

17.2. a proper share of the benefits arising from such improvement or progress accrues to consumers;

17.3. all restrictive provisions of the agreement are indispensable to the attainment of the aims set out under 17.1 (if you are claiming the benefit of the opposition procedure, it is particularly important that you should identify and justify restrictions that exceed those automatically exempted by the relevant Regulations). In this respect please explain how the benefits resulting from the agreement identified in your reply to question 17.1 could not be achieved, or could not be achieved so quickly or efficiently or only at higher cost or with less certainty of success (i) without the conclusion of the agreement as a whole and (ii) without those particular clauses and provisions of the agreement identified in your reply to question 4.2;

17.4. the agreement does not eliminate competition in respect of a substantial part of the goods or services concerned.

Section 18 Supporting documentation

The completed notification must be drawn up and submitted in one original. It shall contain the last versions of all agreements which are the subject of the notification and be accompanied by the following:

(a) sixteen copies of the notification itself;

(b) three copies of the annual reports and accounts of all the parties to the notified agreement, decision or practice for the last three years;

(c) three copies of the most recent in-house or external long-term market studies or planning documents for the purpose of assessing or analysing the affected markets) with respect to competitive conditions, competitors (actual and potential), and market conditions. Each document should indicate the name and position of the author;

(d) three copies of reports and analyses which have been prepared by or for any officer(s) or director(s) for the purposes of evaluating or analysing the notified agreement.

Section 19 Declaration

The notification must conclude with the following declaration which is to be signed by or on behalf of all the applicants or notifying parties.[1]

"The undersigned declare that the information given in this notification is correct to the best of their knowledge and belief, that complete copies of all documents requested by form A/B have been supplied to the extent that they are in the possession of the group

---

1 Applications and notifications which have not been signed are invalid.

of undertakings to which the applicant(s) or notifying party(ies) belong(s) and are accessible to the latter, that all estimates are identified as such and are their best estimates of the underlying facts and that all the opinions expressed are sincere.

They are aware of the provisions of Article 15 (1) (a) of Regulation No 17.
Place and date:
Signatures:"
Please add the name(s) of the person(s) signing the application or notification and their function(s).

ANNEX I: TEXT OF ARTICLES 85 AND 86 OF THE EC TREATY, ARTICLES 53, 54 AND 56 OF THE EEA AGREEMENT, AND OF ARTICLES 2, 3 AND 4 OF PROTOCOL 22 TO THAT AGREEMENT [...]

ANNEX II: LIST OF RELEVANT ACTS (as of 1 March 1995)
(If you think it possible that your arrangements do not need to be notified by virtue of any of these regulations or notices it may be worth your while to obtain a copy.)
IMPLEMENTING REGULATIONS
Council Regulation of 6 February 1992: First Regulation implementing Articles 85 and 86 of the Treaty
Commission Regulation 3385/94 on the form, content and other details of applications and notifications provided for in Council Regulation No 17.
REGULATIONS GRANTING BLOCK EXEMPTION IN RESPECT OF A WIDE RANGE OF AGREEMENTS
Commission Regulation 1983/83 on the application of Article 85 (3) of the Treaty to categories of exclusive distribution agreements [see below, p. 423]
Commission Regulation 1984/83 on the application of Article 85 (3) of the Treaty to categories of exclusive purchasing agreements [see below, p. 428]
Commission Regulation 2349/84 on the application of Article 85 (3) of the Treaty to certain categories of patent licensing agreements
Commission Regulation 123/85 on the application of Article 85 (3) of the Treaty to certain categories of motor vehicle distributing and servicing agreements
Commission Regulation 417/85 on the application of Article 85 (3) of the Treaty to categories of specialization agreements
Commission Regulation 418/85 on the application of Article 85 (3) of the Treaty to categories of research and development cooperation agreements
Commission Regulation 4087/88 on the application of Article 85 (3) of the Treaty to categories of franchise agreements
Commission Regulation 556/89 on the application of Article 85 (3) of the Treaty to certain categories of know-how licensing agreements
Commission Regulation 3932/92 on the application of Article 85 (3) of the Treaty to certain categories of agreements, decisions and concerted practices in the insurance sector
NOTICES OF A GENERAL NATURE
Commission notice on exclusive dealing contracts with commercial agents. This states that the Commission does not consider most such agreements to fall under the prohibition of Article 85 (1).
Commission notice concerning agreements, decisions and concerted practices in the field of cooperation between enterprises. This defines the sorts of cooperation on market studies, accounting, R & D, joint use of production, storage or transport, ad hoc consortia, selling or after-sales service, advertising or quality labelling that the Commission considers not to fall under the prohibition of Article 85 (1).
Commission notice concerning its assessment of certain subcontracting agreements in relation to Article 85 (1) of the Treaty
Commission notice on agreements, decisions and concerted practices of minor importance which do not fall under Article 85 (1) of the Treaty - in the main, those where the parties have less than 5% of the market between them, and a combined annual turnover of less than ECU 300 million.

Commission guidelines on the application of EEC competition rules in the telecommunications sector. These guidelines aim at clarifying the application of Community competition rules to the market participants in the telecommunications sector.
Commission notice on cooperation between national courts and the Commission in applying Articles 85 and 86. This notice sets out the principles on the basis of which such cooperation takes place.
Commission notice concerning the assessment of cooperative joint ventures pursuant to Article 85 of the EC Treaty. This notice sets out the principles on the assessment of joint ventures.

ANNEX III [...]

Notice on Agreements of Minor Importance Which Do not Fall Within the Meaning of Article 85 (1) of the Treaty Establishing the European Community[1]

I. [Purpose and Scope of Application]

1.   The Commission considers it important to facilitate cooperation between undertakings where such cooperation is economically desirable without presenting difficulties from the point of view of competition policy. To this end, it published the notice concerning agreements, decisions and concerted practices in the field of co-operation between enterprises[2] listing a number of agreements that by their nature cannot be regarded as being in restraint of competition. Furthermore, in the notice concerning its assessment of certain subcontracting agreements[3] the Commission considered that that type of contract, which offers all undertakings opportunities for development, does not automatically fall within the scope of Article 85 (1). The notice concerning the assessment of cooperative joint ventures pursuant to Article 85 of the EC Treaty[4] describes in detail the conditions under which the agreements in question do not fall under the prohibition of restrictive agreements. By issuing this notice which replaces the Commission notice of 3 September 1986, the Commission is taking a further step towards defining the scope of Article 85 (1), in order to facilitate cooperation between undertakings.
2.   Article 85 (1) prohibits agreements which may affect trade between Member States and which have as their object or effect the prevention, restriction or distortion of competition within the common market. The Court of Justice of the European Communities has clarified that this provision is not applicable where the impact of the agreement on intra-Community trade or on competition is not appreciable. Agreements which are not capable of significantly affecting trade between Member States are not caught by Article 85. They should therefore be examined on the basis, and within the framework, of national legislation alone. This is also the case for agreements whose actual or potential effect remains limited to the territory of only one Member State or of one or more third countries. Likewise, agreements which do not have as their object or their effect an appreciable restriction of competition are not caught by the prohibition contained in Article 85 (1).

---

1   OJ 1997 C 372, p. 13.

2   OJ 1968 C 75, p. 3, as corrected in OJ 1968 C 84, p. 14.

3   OJ 1979 C 1, p. 2.

4   OJ 1993 C 43, p. 2.

3.   In this notice the Commission, by setting quantitative criteria and by explaining their application, has given a sufficiently concrete meaning to the term "appreciable" for undertakings to be able to judge for themselves whether their agreements do not fall within the prohibition pursuant to Article 85 (1) by virtue of their minor importance. The quantitative definition of appreciability, however, serves only as a guideline: in individual cases even agreements between undertakings which exceed the threshold set out below may still have only a negligible effect on trade between Member States or on competition within the common market and are therefore not caught by Article 85 (1). This notices does not contain an exhaustive description of restrictions which fall outside Article 85 (1). It is generally recognized that even agreements which are not of minor importance can escape the prohibition on agreements on account of their exclusively favourable impact on competition.

4.   The benchmarks provided by the Commission in this notice should eliminate the need to have the legal status of agreements covered by it established through individual Commission decisions; notification for this purpose will no longer be necessary for such agreements. However, if it is doubtful whether, in an individual case, an agreement is likely to affect trade between Member States or to restrict competition to any significant extent, undertakings are free to apply for negative clearance or to notify the agreement pursuant to Council Regulations No 17, [...].

5.   In cases covered by this notice, and subject to points 11 and 20, the Commission will not institute any proceedings either on application or on its own initiative. Where undertakings have failed to notify an agreement falling within the scope of Article 85 (1) because they assumed in good faith that the agreement was covered by this notice, the Commission will not consider imposing fines.

6.   This notice is likewise applicable to decisions by associations of undertakings and to concerted practices.

7.   This notice is without prejudice to the competence of national courts to apply Article 85. However, it constitutes a factor which those courts may take into account when deciding a pending case. It is also without prejudice to any interpretation of Article 85 which may be given by the Court of Justice or the Court of First Instance of the European Communities.

8.   This notice is without prejudice to the application of national competition laws.

II. [Exemption for Agreements of Minor Importance]

9.   The Commission holds the view that agreements between undertakings engaged in the production or distribution of goods or in the provision of services do not fall under the prohibition in Article 85 (1) if the aggregate market shares held by all of the participating undertakings do not exceed, on any of the relevant markets:

(a) the 5 % threshold, where the agreement is made between undertakings operating at the same level of production or of marketing ("horizontal" agreement);

(b) the 10 % threshold, where the agreement is made between undertakings operating at different economic levels ("vertical" agreement).

In the case of a mixed horizontal/vertical agreement or where it is difficult to classify the agreement as either horizontal or vertical, the 5% threshold is applicable.

10. The Commission also holds the view that the said agreements do not fall under the prohibition of Article 85 (1) if the market shares given at point 9 are exceeded by no more than one 10th during two successive financial years.

11. With regard to:

(a) horizontal agreements which have as their object
    — to fix prices or to limit production or sales, or
    — to share markets or sources of supply,

(b) vertical agreements which have as their object

— to fix resale prices, or
— to confer territorial protection on the participating undertakings or third undertakings, the applicability of Article 85 (1) cannot be ruled out even where the
aggregate market shares held by all of the participating undertakings remain
below the thresholds mentioned in points 9 and 10.

The Commission considers, however, that in the first instance it is for the authorities
and courts of the Member States to take action on any agreements envisaged above
in (a) and (b). Accordingly, it will only intervene in such cases when it considers that the
interest of the Community so demands, and in particular if the agreements impair the
proper functioning of the internal market.

12. For the purposes of this notice, "participating undertakings" are:
(a) undertakings being parties to the agreement;
(b) undertakings in which a party to the agreement, directly or indirectly,
— owns more than half of the capital or business assets, or
— has the power to exercise more than half of the voting rights, or
— has the power to appoint more than half of the members of the supervisory
board, board of management or bodies legally representing the undertakings,
or
— has to the right to manage the undertaking's business;
(c) undertakings which directly or indirectly have over a party to the agreement the
rights or powers listed in (b);
(d) undertakings over which an undertaking referred to in (c) has, directly or indirectly,
the rights or powers listed in (b).

Undertakings over which several undertakings as referred to in (a) to (d) jointly have,
directly or indirectly, the rights or powers set out in (b) shall also be considered to be
participating undertakings.

13. In order to calculate the market share, it is necessary to determine the relevant
market; for this, the relevant product market and the relevant geographic market must
be defined.

14. The relevant product market comprises any products or services which are regarded as interchangeable or substitutable by the consumer, by reason of their characteristics, prices and intended use.

15. The relevant geographic market comprises the area in which the participating undertakings are involved in the supply of relevant products or services, in which the conditions of competition are sufficiently homogeneous, and which can be distinguished
from neighbouring geographic areas because, in particular, conditions of competition
are appreciably different in those areas.

16. When applying points 14 and 15, reference should be had to the notice (on the definition of the relevant market under Community competition law.[1]

17. In the case of doubt about the delimitation of the relevant geographic market, undertakings may take the view that their agreement has no appreciable effect on intra-
Community trade or on competition when the market share thresholds indicated in
points 9 and 10 are not exceeded in any Member State. This view, however, does not
preclude the application of national competition law to the agreements in question.

18. Chapter II of this notice shall not apply where in a relevant market competition is
restricted by the cumulative effects of parallel networks of similar agreements established by several manufacturers or dealers.

---

1   OJ 1997 C 372, p. 5.

III. [Exemption for Agreements Between Small and Medium Sized Undertakings]
19. Agreements between small and medium-sized undertakings, as defined in the Annex to Commission recommendation 96/280[1] are rarely capable of significantly affecting trade between Member States and competition within the common market. Consequently, as a general rule, they are not caught by the prohibition in Article 85 (1). In cases where such agreements exceptionally meet the conditions for the application of that provision, they will not be of sufficient Community interest to justify any intervention. This is why the Commission will not institute any proceedings, either on request or on its own initiative, to apply the provisions of Article 85 (1) to such agreements, even if the thresholds set out in points 9 and 10 above are exceeded.
20. The Commission nevertheless reserves the right to intervene in such agreements:
(a) where they significantly impede competition in a substantial part of the relevant market,
(b) where, in the relevant market, competition is restricted by the cumulative effect of parallel networks of similar agreements made between several producers or dealers.

---

1   OJ 1996 L 107, p. 4.

Block Exemption Regulations

Regulation No 19/65 of 2 March 1965 of the Council on Application of Article 85 (3) of the Treaty to Certain Categories of Agreements and Concerted Practices[1]

THE COUNCIL OF THE EUROPEAN ECONOMIC COMMUNITY,

HAVING REGARD to the Treaty establishing the European Economic Community, and in particular Article 87 thereof; [...]
(1) WHEREAS Article 85 (1) of the Treaty may in accordance with Article 85 (3) be declared inapplicable to certain categories of agreements, decisions and concerted practices which fulfil the conditions contained in Article 85 (3);
(2) WHEREAS the provisions for implementation of Article 85 (3) must be adopted by way of regulation pursuant to Article 87;
(3) WHEREAS in view of the large number of notifications submitted in pursuance of Regulation No 17[2] it is desirable that in order to facilitate the task of the Commission it should be enabled to declare by way of regulation that the provisions of Article 85 (1) do not apply to certain categories of agreements and concerted practices;
(4) WHEREAS it should be laid down under what conditions the Commission, in close and constant liaison with the competent authorities of the Member States, may exercise such powers after sufficient experience has been gained in the light of individual decisions and it becomes possible to define categories of agreements and concerted practices in respect of which the conditions of Article 85 (3) may be considered as being fulfilled;
(5) WHEREAS the Commission has indicated by the action it has taken, in particular by Regulation No 153, that there can be no easing of the procedures prescribed by Regulation No 17 in respect of certain types of agreements and concerted practices that are particularly liable to distort competition in the common market;
(6) WHEREAS under Article 6 of Regulation No 17 the Commission may provide that a decision taken pursuant to Article 85 (3) of the Treaty shall apply with retroactive effect; whereas it is desirable that the Commission be also empowered to adopt, by regulation, provisions to the like effect;
(7) WHEREAS under Article 7 of Regulation No 17 agreements, decisions and concerted practices may, by decision of the Commission, be exempted from prohibition in particular if they are modified in such manner that they satisfy the requirements of Article 85 (3); whereas it is desirable that the Commission be enabled to grant like exemption by regulation to such agreements and concerted practices if they are modified in such manner as to fall within a category defined in an exempting regulation;
(8) WHEREAS, since there can be no exemption if the conditions set out in Article 85 (3) are not satisfied, the Commission must have power to lay down by decision the conditions that must be satisfied by an agreement or concerted practice which owing to special circumstances has certain effects incompatible with Article 85 (3);

HAS ADOPTED THIS REGULATION:

---

1   OJ 1965 No. 036, p. 533.
2   See above, p. 384.

Article 1 [Legal Basis for Block Exemption Regulations]

1. Without prejudice to the application of Council Regulation No 17 and in accordance with Article 85 (3) of the Treaty the Commission may by regulation declare that Article 85 (1) shall not apply to categories of agreements to which only two undertakings are party and:
(a) —   whereby one party agrees with the other to supply only to that other certain goods for resale within a defined area of the common market; or
—   whereby one party agrees with the other to purchase only from that other certain goods for resale; or
—   whereby the two undertakings have entered into obligations, as in the two preceding subparagraphs, with each other in respect of exclusive supply and purchase for resale;
(b) which include restrictions imposed in relation to the acquisition or use of industrial property rights - in particular of patents, utility models, designs or trade marks - or to the rights arising out of contracts for assignment of, or the right to use, a method of manufacture or knowledge relating to the use or to the application of industrial processes.
2. The regulation shall define the categories of agreements to which it applies and shall specify in particular:
(a) the restrictions or clauses which must not be contained in the agreements;
(b) the clauses which must be contained in the agreements, or the other conditions which must be satisfied.
3. Paragraphs 1 and 2 shall apply by analogy to categories of concerted practices to which only two undertakings are party.

Article 2 [Duration of Exemptions]

1. A regulation pursuant to Article 1 shall be made for a specified period.
2. It may be repealed or amended where circumstances have changed with respect to any factor which was basic to its being made; in such case, a period shall be fixed for modification of the agreements and concerted practices to which the earlier regulation applies.

Article 3 [Retroactivity of Exemptions]

A regulation pursuant to Article 1 may stipulate that it shall apply with retroactive effect to agreements and concerted practices to which, at the date of entry into force of that regulation, a decision issued with retroactive effect in pursuance of Article 6 of Regulation No 17 would have applied.

Article 4 [Pre-existing Agreements]

1. A regulation pursuant to Article 1 may stipulate that the prohibition contained in Article 85 (1) of the Treaty shall not apply, for such period as shall be fixed by that regulation, to agreements and concerted practices already in existence on 13 March 1962 which do not satisfy the conditions of Article 85 (3), where:
—   within three months from the entry into force of the Regulation, they are so modified as to satisfy the said conditions in accordance with the provisions of the regulation; and
—   the modifications are brought to the notice of the Commission within the time limit fixed by the regulation.
2. Paragraph 1 shall apply to agreements and concerted practices which had to be notified before 1 February 1963, in accordance with Article 5 of Regulation No 17, only where they have been so notified before that date.

3. The benefit of the provisions laid down pursuant to paragraph 1 may not be claimed in actions pending at the date of entry into force of a regulation adopted pursuant to Article 1; neither may it be relied on as grounds for claims for damages against third parties.

Article 5 [Consultation Procedure]

Before adopting a regulation, the Commission shall publish a draft thereof and invite all persons concerned to submit their comments within such time limit, being not less than one month, as the Commission shall fix.

Article 6 [Advisory Committee on Restrictive Practices]

1. The Commission shall consult the Advisory Committee on Restrictive Practices and Monopolies:
(a) before publishing a draft regulation;
(b) before adopting a regulation.
2. Article 10 (5) and (6) of Regulation No 17, relating to consultation with the Advisory Committee, shall apply by analogy, it being understood that joint meetings with the Commission shall take place not earlier than one month after dispatch of the notice convening them.

Article 7 [Withdrawal of Exemptions]

Where the Commission, either on its own initiative or at the request of a Member State or of natural or legal persons claiming a legitimate interest, finds that in any particular case agreements or concerted practices to which a regulation adopted pursuant to Article 1 of this Regulation applies have nevertheless certain effects which are incompatible with the conditions laid down in Article 85 (3) of the Treaty, it may withdraw the benefit of application of that regulation and issue a decision in accordance with Articles 6 and 8 of Regulation No 17, without any notification under Article 4 (1) of Regulation No 17 being required.

Article 8 [Entry into Force]

The Commission shall, before 1 January 1970, submit to the Council a proposal for a Regulation for such amendment of this Regulation as may prove necessary in the light of experience.

This Regulation shall be binding in its entirety and directly applicable in all Member States.

Done at Brussels, 2 March 1965.
For the Council, The President, M. COUVE DE MURVILLE

Commission Regulation 1983/83 of 22 June 1983 on the Application of Article 85 (3) of the Treaty to Categories of Exclusive Distribution Agreements[1]

THE COMMISSION OF THE EUROPEAN COMMUNITIES,

HAVING REGARD to the Treaty establishing the European Economic Community, [...]

---

1   OJ 1983 L 173, p. 1, as amended by Commission Regulation 1582/97 of 30 July 1997.

(1) WHEREAS Regulation No 19/65 empowers the Commission to apply Article 85 (3) of the Treaty by Regulation to certain categories of bilateral exclusive distribution agreements and analogous concerted practices falling within Article 85 (1);

(2) WHEREAS experience to date makes it possible to define a category of agreements and concerted practices which can be regarded as normally satisfying the conditions laid down in Article 85 (3);

(3) WHEREAS exclusive distribution agreements of the category defined in Article 1 of this Regulation may fall within the prohibition contained in Article 85 (1) of the Treaty; whereas this will apply only in exceptional cases to exclusive agreements of this kind to which only undertakings from one Member State are party and which concern the resale of goods within that Member State; whereas however, to the extent that such agreements may affect trade between Member States and also satisfy all the requirements set out in this Regulation there is no reason to withhold from them the benefit of the exemption by category;

(4) WHEREAS it is not necessary expressly to exclude from the defined category those agreements which do not fulfil the conditions of Article 85 (1) of the Treaty;

(5) WHEREAS exclusive distribution agreements lead in general to an improvement in distribution because the undertaking is able to concentrate its sales activities, does not need to maintain numerous business relations with a larger number of dealers and is able, by dealing with only one dealer, to overcome more easily distribution difficulties in international trade resulting from linguistic, legal and other differences;

(6) WHEREAS exclusive distribution agreements facilitate the promotion of sales of a product and lead to intensive marketing and to continuity of supplies while at the same time rationalizing distribution; whereas they stimulate competition between the products of different manufacturers; whereas the appointment of an exclusive distributor who will take over sales promotion, customer services and carrying of stocks is often the most effective way, and sometimes indeed the only way, for the manufacturer to enter a market and compete with other manufacturers already present; whereas this is particularly so in the case of small and medium-sized undertakings; whereas it must be left to the contracting parties to decide whether and to what extent they consider it desirable to incorporate in the Agreements terms providing for the promotion of sales;

(7) WHEREAS, as a rule, such exclusive distribution agreements also allow consumers a fair share of the resulting benefit as they gain directly from the improvement in distribution, and their economic and supply position is improved as they can obtain products manufactured in particular in other countries more quickly and more easily;

(8) WHEREAS this Regulation must define the obligations restricting competition which may be included in exclusive distribution agreements; whereas the other restrictions on competition allowed under this Regulation in addition to the exclusive supply obligation produce a clear division of functions between the parties and compel the exclusive distributor to concentrate his sales efforts on the contract goods and the contract territory; whereas they are, where they are agreed only for the duration of the agreement, generally necessary in order to attain the improvement in the distribution of goods sought through exclusive distribution; whereas it may be left to the contracting parties to decide which of these obligations they include in their agreements; whereas further restrictive obligations and in particular those which limit the exclusive distributor's choice of customers or his freedom to determine his prices and conditions of sale cannot be exempted under this Regulation;

(9) WHEREAS the exemption by category should be reserved for agreements for which it can be assumed with sufficient certainty that they satisfy the conditions of Article 85 (3) of the Treaty;

(10) WHEREAS it is not possible, in the absence of a case-by-case examination, to consider that adequate improvements in distribution occur where a manufacturer en-

trusts the distribution of his goods to another manufacturer with whom he is in competition; whereas such agreements should, therefore, be excluded from the exemption by category; whereas certain derogations from this rule in favour of small and medium-sized undertakings can be allowed;

(11) WHEREAS consumers will be assured of a fair share of the benefits resulting from exclusive distribution only if parallel imports remain possible; whereas agreements relating to goods which the user can obtain only from the exclusive distributor should therefore be excluded from the exemption by category; whereas the parties cannot be allowed to abuse industrial property rights or other rights in order to create absolute territorial protection; whereas this does not prejudice the relationship between competition law and industrial property rights, since the sole object here is to determine the conditions for exemption by category;

(12) WHEREAS, since competition at the distribution stage is ensured by the possibility of parallel imports, the exclusive distribution agreements covered by this Regulation will not normally afford any possibility of eliminating competition in respect of a substantial part of the products in question; whereas this is also true of agreements that allot to the exclusive distributor a contract territory covering the whole of the common market.

(13) WHEREAS, in particular cases in which agreements or concerted practices satisfying the requirements of this Regulation nevertheless have effects incompatible with Article 85 (3) of the Treaty, the Commission may withdraw the benefit of the exemption by category from the undertakings party to them;

(14) WHEREAS agreements and concerted practices which satisfy the conditions set out in this Regulation need not be notified; whereas an undertaking may nonetheless in a particular case where real doubt exists, request the Commission to declare whether its agreements comply with this Regulation;

(15) WHEREAS this Regulation does not affect the applicability of Commission Regulation 3604/82 of 23 December 1982 on the application of article 85 (3) of the Treaty to categories of specialization agreements[1]; whereas it does not exclude the application of Article 86 of the Treaty,

HAS ADOPTED THIS REGULATION:

Article 1 [The Block Exemption]
Pursuant to Article 85 (3) of the Treaty and subject to the provisions of this Regulation, it is hereby declared that Article 85 (1) of the Treaty shall not apply to agreements to which only two undertakings are party and whereby one party agrees with the other to supply certain goods for resale within the whole or a defined area of the common market only to that other.

Article 2 [White List]
1. Apart from the obligation referred to in Article 1 no restriction on competition shall be imposed on the supplier other than the obligation not to supply the contract goods to users in the contract territory.

2. No restriction on competition shall be imposed on the exclusive distributor other than:

(a) the obligation not to manufacture or distribute goods which compete with the contract goods;

(b) the obligation to obtain the contract goods for resale only from the other party;

---

1   OJ 1982 L 376, p. 33.

(c) the obligation to refrain, outside the contract territory and in relation to the contract goods, from seeking customers, from establishing any branch and from maintaining any distribution depot.

3.   Article 1 shall apply notwithstanding that the exclusive distributor undertakes all or any of the following obligations:

(a) to purchase complete ranges of goods or minimum quantities;

(b) to sell the contract goods under trade marks, or packed and presented as specified by the other party;

(c) to take measures for promotion of sales, in particular:
— To advertise,
— To maintain a sales network or stock of goods,
— To provide customer and guarantee services,
— To employ staff having specialized or technical training.

Article 3 [Black List]

Article 1 shall not apply where:

(a) manufacturers of identical goods or of goods which are considered by users as equivalent in view of their characteristics, price and intended use enter into reciprocal exclusive distribution agreements between themselves in respect of such goods;

(b) manufacturers of identical goods or of goods which are considered by users as equivalent in view of their characteristics, price and intended use enter into a non-reciprocal exclusive distribution agreement between themselves in respect of such goods unless at least one of them has a total annual turnover of no more than 100 million ECU;

(c) users can obtain the contract goods in the contract territory only from the exclusive distributor and have no alternative source of supply outside the contract territory;

(d) one or both of the parties makes it difficult for intermediaries or users to obtain the contract goods from other dealers inside the common market or, in so far as no alternative source of supply is available there, from outside the common market, in particular where one or both of them:
1)   Exercises industrial property rights so as to prevent dealers or users from obtaining outside, or from selling in, the contract territory properly marked or otherwise properly marketed contract goods;
2)   Exercises other rights or takes other measures so as to prevent dealers or users from obtaining outside, or from selling in, the contract territory contract goods.

Article 4 [Connected Undertakings]

1.   Article 3 (a) and (b) shall also apply where the goods there referred to are manufactured by an undertaking connected with a party to the Agreement.

2.   Connected undertakings are:

(a) undertakings in which a party to the Agreement, directly or indirectly:
— Owns more than half the capital or business assets, or
— Has the power to exercise more than half the voting rights, or
— Has the power to appoint more than half the Members of the supervisory board, board of directors or bodies legally representing the undertaking, or
— Has the right to manage the affairs;

(b) undertakings which directly or indirectly have in or over a party to the agreement the rights or powers listed in (a)

(c) undertakings in which an undertaking referred to in (b) directly or indirectly has the rights or powers listed in (a).

3.   Undertakings in which the parties to the Agreement or undertakings connected with them jointly have the rights or powers set out in paragraph 2 (a) shall be considered to be connected with each of the parties to the agreement.

Article 5 [Calculation of Turnover]

1.   For the purpose of Article 3 (b), the ECU is the unit of account used for drawing up the budget of the Community pursuant to Articles 207 and 209 of the Treaty.
2.   Article 1 shall remain applicable where during any period of two consecutive financial years the total turnover referred to in Article 3 (B) is exceeded by no more than 10%.
3.   For the purpose of calculating total turnover within the meaning of Article 3 (b), the turnovers achieved during the last financial year by the party to the Agreement and connected undertakings in respect of all goods and services, excluding all taxes and other duties, shall be added together. For this purpose no account shall be taken of dealings between the party to the Agreement and its connected undertakings or between its connected undertakings.

Article 6 [Withdrawal of the Benefits in Particular Cases]

The Commission may withdraw the benefit of this Regulation, pursuant to Article 7 of Regulation No 19/65, when it finds in a particular case that an agreement which is exempted by this Regulation nevertheless has certain effects which are incompatible with the conditions set out in Article 85 (3) of the Treaty, and in particular where:
(a) the contract goods are not subject, in the contract territory, to effective competition from identical goods or goods considered by users as equivalent in view of their characteristics, price and intended use;
(b) access by other suppliers to the different stages of distribution within the contract territory is made difficult to a significant extent;
(c) for reasons other than those referred to in Article 3 (c) and (d) it is not possible for intermediaries or users to obtain supplies of the contract goods from dealers outside the contract territory on the terms there customary;
(d) the exclusive distributor:
  1) Without any objectively justified reason refuses to supply in the contract territory categories of purchasers who cannot obtain contract goods elsewhere on suitable terms or applies to them differing prices or conditions of sale;
  2) Sells the contract goods at excessively high prices.

Article 7 [omitted]

Article 8 [No Application to Beer Supply Agreements and Service Station Agreements]

This Regulation shall not apply to agreements entered into for the resale of drinks in premises used for the sale and consumption of drinks or for the resale of petroleum products in service stations.

Article 9 [Application to Concerted Practices]

This Regulation shall apply *mutatis mutandis* to concerted practices of the type defined in Article 1.

Article 10 [Entry into Force and Expiry]

This Regulation shall enter into force on 1 July 1983.
    It shall expire on 31 December 1999.

This Regulation shall be binding in its entirety and directly applicable in all Member States.

Done at Brussels, 22 June 1983.
For the Commission, Frans Andriessen, Member of the Commission

Commission Regulation 1984/83 of 22 June 1983 on the Application of Article 85 (3) of the Treaty to Categories of Exclusive Purchasing Agreements[1]

THE COMMISSION OF THE EUROPEAN COMMUNITIES,

HAVING REGARD to the Treaty establishing the European Economic Community, [...]
(1) WHEREAS Regulation No 19/65 empowers the Commission to apply Article 85 (3) of the Treaty by Regulation to certain categories of bilateral exclusive purchasing agreements entered into for the purpose of the resale of goods and corresponding concerted practices falling within Article 85 (1);
(2) WHEREAS experience to date makes it possible to define three categories of agreements and concerted practices which can be regarded as normally satisfying the conditions laid down in Article 85 (3); whereas the first category comprises exclusive purchasing agreements of short and medium duration in all sectors of the economy; whereas the other two categories comprise long-term exclusive purchasing agreements entered into for the resale of drinks (beer supply agreements) and of petroleum products in service stations (service station agreements);
(3) WHEREAS exclusive purchasing agreements of the categories defined in this Regulation may fall within the prohibition contained in Article 85 (1) of the Treaty; whereas this will often be the case with agreements concluded between undertakings from different Member States; whereas an exclusive purchasing agreement to which undertakings from only one Member State are party and which concerns the resale of goods within that Member State may also be caught by the prohibition; whereas this is in particular the case where it is one of a number of similar agreements which together may affect trade between Member States;
(4) WHEREAS it is not necessary expressly to exclude from the defined categories those agreements which do not fulfil the conditions of Article 85 (1) of the Treaty;
(5) WHEREAS the exclusive purchasing agreements defined in this Regulation lead in general to an improvement in distribution; whereas they enable the supplier to plan the sales of his goods with greater precision and for a longer period and ensure that the reseller's requirements will be met on a regular basis for the duration of the agreement; whereas this allows the parties to limit the risk to them of variations in market conditions and to lower distribution costs;
(6) WHEREAS such agreements also facilitate the promotion of the sales of a product and lead to intensive marketing because the supplier, in consideration for the exclusive purchasing obligation, is as a rule under an obligation to contribute to the improvement of the structure of the distribution network, the quality of the promotional effort or the sales success; whereas, at the same time, they stimulate competition between the products of different manufacturers; whereas the appointment of several resellers, who are bound to purchase exclusively from the manufacturer and who take over sales pro-

---

1   OJ 1983 L 173, p. 5, as amended by Commission Regulation 1582/97 of 30 July 1997.

motion, customer services and carrying of stock, is often the most effective way, and sometimes the only way, for the manufacturer to penetrate a market and compete with other manufacturers already present; whereas this is particularly so in the case of small and medium-sized undertakings; whereas it must be left to the contracting parties to decide whether and to what extent they consider it desirable to incorporate in their agreements terms concerning the promotion of sales;

(7) WHEREAS, as a rule, exclusive purchasing agreements between suppliers and resellers also allow consumers a fair share of the resulting benefit as they gain the advantages of regular supply and are able to obtain the contract goods more quickly and more easily;

(8) WHEREAS this Regulation must define the obligations restricting competition which may be included in an exclusive purchasing agreement; whereas the other restrictions of competition allowed under this Regulation in addition to the exclusive purchasing obligation lead to a clear division of functions between the parties and compel the reseller to concentrate his sales efforts on the contract goods; whereas they are, where they are agreed only for the duration of the agreement, generally necessary in order to attain the improvement in the distribution of goods sought through exclusive purchasing; whereas further restrictive obligations and in particular those which limit the reseller's choice of customers or his freedom to determine his prices and conditions of sale cannot be exempted under this Regulation;

(9) WHEREAS the exemption by categories should be reserved for agreements for which it can be assumed with sufficient certainty that they satisfy the conditions of Article 85 (3) of the Treaty;

(10) WHEREAS it is not possible, in the absence of a case-by-case examination, to consider that adequate improvements in distribution occur where a manufacturer imposes an exclusive purchasing obligation with respect to his goods on a manufacturer with whom he is in competition; whereas such agreements should, therefore, be excluded from the exemption by categories; whereas certain derogations from this rule in favour of small and medium-sized undertakings can be allowed;

(11) WHEREAS certain conditions must be attached to the exemption by categories so that access by other undertakings to the different stages of distribution can be ensured; whereas, to this end, limits must be set to the scope and to the duration of the exclusive purchasing obligation; whereas it appears appropriate as a general rule to grant the benefit of a general exemption from the prohibition on restrictive agreements only to exclusive purchasing agreements which are concluded for a specified product or range of products and for not more than five years;

(12) WHEREAS, in the case of beer supply agreements and service-station agreements, different rules should be laid down which take account of the particularities of the markets in question

(13) WHEREAS these agreements are generally distinguished by the fact that, on the one hand, the supplier confers on the reseller special commercial or financial advantages by contributing to his financing, granting him or obtaining for him a loan on favourable terms, equipping him with a site or premises for conducting his business, providing him with equipment or fittings, or undertaking other investments for his benefit and that, on the other hand, the reseller enters into a long-term exclusive purchasing obligation which in most cases is accompanied by a ban on dealing in competing products;

(14) WHEREAS beer supply and service-station agreements, like the other exclusive purchasing agreements dealt with in this Regulation, normally produce an appreciable improvement in distribution in which consumers are allowed a fair share of the resulting benefit;

(15) WHEREAS the commercial and financial advantages conferred by the supplier on the reseller make it significantly easier to establish, modernize, maintain and operate

premises used for the sale and consumption of drinks and service stations; whereas the exclusive purchasing obligation and the ban on dealing in competing products imposed on the reseller incite the reseller to devote all the resources at his disposal to the sale of the contract goods; whereas such agreements lead to durable cooperation between the parties allowing them to improve or maintain the quality of the contract goods and of the services to the customer and sales efforts of the reseller; whereas they allow long-term planning of sales and consequently a cost effective organization of production and distribution; whereas the pressure of competition between products of different makes obliges the undertakings involved to determine the number and character of premises used for the sale and consumption of drinks and service stations, in accordance with the wishes of customers;

(16) WHEREAS consumers benefit from the improvements described, in particular because they are ensured supplies of goods of satisfactory quality at fair prices and conditions while being able to choose between the products of different manufacturers;

(17) WHEREAS the advantages produced by beer supply agreements and service-station agreements cannot otherwise be secured to the same extent and with the same degree of certainty; whereas the exclusive purchasing obligation on the reseller and the non-competition clause imposed on him are essential components of such agreements and thus usually indispensable for the attainment of these advantages; whereas, however, this is true only as long as the reseller's obligation to purchase from the supplier is confined in the case of premises used for the sale and consumption of drinks to beers and other drinks of the types offered by the supplier, and in the case of service stations to petroleum-based fuel for motor vehicles and other petroleum-based fuels; whereas the exclusive purchasing obligation for lubricants and related petroleum-based products can be accepted only on condition that the supplier provides for the reseller or finances the procurement of specific equipment for the carrying out of lubrication work; whereas this obligation should only relate to products intended for use within the service station;

(18) WHEREAS, in order to maintain the reseller's commercial freedom and to ensure access to the retail level of distribution on the part of other suppliers, not only the scope but also the duration of the exclusive purchasing obligation must be limited; whereas it appears appropriate to allow drinks suppliers a choice between a medium-term exclusive purchasing agreement covering a range of drinks and a long-term exclusive purchasing agreement for beer; whereas it is necessary to provide special rules for those premises used for the sale and consumption of drinks which the supplier lets to the reseller; whereas, in this case, the reseller must have the right to obtain from other undertakings, under the conditions specified in this Regulation, other drinks, except beer, supplied under the Agreement or of the same type but bearing a different trademark; whereas a uniform maximum duration should be provided for service-station agreements, with the exception of tenancy agreements between the supplier and the reseller, which takes account of the long-term character of the relationship between the parties;

(19) WHEREAS to the extent that Member States provide, by law or administrative measures, for the same upper limit of duration for the exclusive purchasing obligation upon the reseller in service-station agreements as laid down in this Regulation but provide for a permissible duration which varies in proportion to the consideration provided by the supplier or generally provide for a shorter duration than that permitted by this Regulation, such laws or measures are not contrary to the objectives of this Regulation which, in this respect, merely sets an upper limit to the duration of service-station agreements; whereas the application and enforcement of such national laws or measures must therefore be regarded as compatible with the provisions of this Regulation;

(20) WHEREAS the limitations and conditions provided for in this Regulation are such as to guarantee effective competition on the markets in question; whereas, therefore, the Agreements to which the exemption by category applies do not normally enable the participating undertakings to eliminate competition for a substantial part of the products in question;
(21) WHEREAS, in particular cases in which agreements or concerted practices satisfying the conditions of this Regulation nevertheless have effects incompatible with Article 85 (3) of the Treaty, the Commission may withdraw the benefit of the exemption by category from the undertakings party thereto;
(22) WHEREAS agreements and concerted practices which satisfy the conditions set out in this Regulation need not be notified; whereas an undertaking may nonetheless, in a particular case where real doubt exists, request the Commission to declare whether its agreements comply with this Regulation;
(23) WHEREAS this Regulation does not affect the applicability of Commission Regulation 3604/82 of 23 December 1982 on the application of article 85 (3) of the Treaty to categories of specialization agreements;[1] whereas it does not exclude the application of Article 86 of the Treaty,

HAS ADOPTED THIS REGULATION:

TITLE I
GENERAL PROVISIONS

Article 1 [The Block Exemption]
Pursuant to Article 85 (3) of the Treaty, and subject to the conditions set out in Articles 2 to 5 of this Regulation, it is hereby declared that Article 85 (1) of the Treaty shall not apply to agreements to which only two undertakings are party and whereby one party, the reseller, agrees with the other, the supplier, to purchase certain goods specified in the Agreement for resale only from the supplier or from a connected undertaking or from another undertaking which the supplier has entrusted with the sale of his goods.

Article 2 [White List]
1.   No other restriction of competition shall be imposed on the supplier than the obligation not to distribute the contract goods or goods which compete with the contract goods in the reseller's principal sales area and at the reseller's level of distribution.
2.   Apart from the obligation described in Article 1, no other restriction of competition shall be imposed on the reseller than the obligation not to manufacture or distribute goods which compete with the contract goods.
3.   Article 1 shall apply notwithstanding that the reseller undertakes any or all of the following obligations
(a) to purchase complete ranges of goods;
(b) to purchase minimum quantities of goods which are subject to the exclusive purchasing obligation;
(c) to sell the contract goods under trademarks, or packed and presented as specified by the supplier;
(d) to take measures for the promotion of sales, in particular:
— To advertise,
— To maintain a sales network or stock of goods,
— To provide customer and guarantee services,

---

1   OJ 1982 L 376, p. 33.

— To employ staff having specialized or technical training.

Article 3 [Black List]

Article 1 shall not apply where:

(a) manufacturers of identical goods or of goods which are considered by users as equivalent in view of their characteristics, price and intended use enter into reciprocal exclusive purchasing agreements between themselves in respect of such goods;

(b) manufacturers of identical goods or of goods which are considered by users as equivalent in view of their characteristics, price and intended use enter into a non-reciprocal exclusive purchasing agreement between themselves in respect of such goods, unless at least one of them has a total annual turnover of no more than 100 million ECU;

(c) the exclusive purchasing obligation is agreed for more than one type of goods where these are neither by their nature nor according to commercial usage connected to each other;

(d) the Agreement is concluded for an indefinite duration or for a period of more than five years.

Article 4 [Connected Undertakings]

1. Article 3 (a) and (b) shall also apply where the goods there referred to are manufactured by an undertaking connected with a party to the Agreement.

2. Connected undertakings are:

(a) undertakings in which a party to the Agreement, directly or indirectly:
   — Owns more than half the capital or business assets, or
   — Has the power to exercise more than half the voting rights, or
   — Has the power to appoint more than half the Members of the supervisory board, board of directors or bodies legally representing the undertaking, or
   — Has the right to manage the affairs;

(b) undertakings which directly or indirectly have in or over a party to the agreement the rights or powers listed in (a);

(c) undertakings in which an undertaking referred to in (b) directly or indirectly has the rights or powers listed in (a).

3. Undertaking in which the parties to the Agreement or undertakings connected with them jointly have the rights or powers set out in paragraph 2 (a) shall be considered to be connected with each of the parties to the agreement.

Article 5 [Calculation of Turnover]

1. For the purpose of Article 3 (b), the ECU is the unit of account used for drawing up the budget of the Community pursuant to Articles 207 and 209 of the Treaty.

2. Article 1 shall remain applicable where during any period of two consecutive financial years the total turnover referred to in Article 3 (b) is exceeded by no more than 10%.

3. For the purpose of calculating total turnover within the meaning of Article 3 (b), the turnovers achieved during the last financial year by the party to the Agreement and connected undertakings in respect of all goods and services, excluding all taxes and other duties, shall be added together.

For this purpose no account shall be taken of dealings between the party to the Agreement and its connected undertakings or between its connected undertakings.

TITLE II
SPECIAL PROVISIONS FOR BEER SUPPLY AGREEMENTS

Article 6 [The Block Exemption]
1.   Pursuant to Article 85 (3) of the Treaty, and subject to Articles 7 to 9 of this Regulation, it is hereby declared that Article 85 (1) of the Treaty shall not apply to agreements to which only two undertakings are party and whereby one party, the reseller, agrees with the other, the supplier, in consideration for the according of special commercial or financial advantages, to purchase only from the supplier, an undertaking connected with the supplier or another undertaking entrusted by the supplier with the distribution of his goods, certain beers, or certain beers and certain other drinks, specified in the Agreement for resale in premises used for the sale and consumption of drinks and designated in the Agreement.
2.   The Declaration in paragraph 1 shall also apply where exclusive purchasing obligations of the kind described in paragraph 1 are imposed on the reseller in favour of the supplier by another undertaking which is itself not a supplier.

Article 7 [White List]
1.   Apart from the obligation referred to in Article 6, no restriction on competition shall be imposed on the reseller other than:
(a) the obligation not to sell beers and other drinks which are supplied by other undertakings and which are of the same type as the beers or other drinks supplied under the Agreement in the premises designated in the Agreement;
(b) the obligation, in the event that the reseller sells in the premises designated in the Agreement beers which are supplied by other undertakings and which are of a different type from the beers supplied under the Agreement, to sell such beers only in bottles, cans or other small packages, unless the sale of such beers in draught form is customary or is necessary to satisfy a sufficient demand from consumers;
(c) the obligation to advertise goods supplied by other undertakings within or outside the premises designated in the Agreement only in proportion to the share of these goods in the total turnover realized in the premises.
2.   Beers or other drinks are of different types where they are clearly distinguishable by their composition, appearance or taste.

Article 8 [Black List]
1.   Article 6 shall not apply where:
(a) the supplier or a connected undertaking imposes on the reseller exclusive purchasing obligations for goods other than drinks or for services;
(b) the supplier restricts the freedom of the reseller to obtain from an undertaking of his choice either services or goods for which neither an exclusive purchasing obligation nor a ban on dealing in competing products may be imposed;
(c) the Agreement is concluded for an indefinite duration or for a period of more than five years and the exclusive purchasing obligation relates to specified beers and other drinks;
(d) the Agreement is concluded for an indefinite duration or for a period of more than 10 years and the exclusive purchasing obligation relates only to specified beers;
(e) the supplier obliges the reseller to impose the exclusive purchasing obligation on his successor for a longer period than the reseller would himself remain tied to the supplier.
2.   Where the Agreement relates to premises which the supplier lets to the reseller or allows the reseller to occupy on some other basis in lax or in fact, the following provisions shall also apply:

(a) notwithstanding paragraphs (1) (c) and (d), the exclusive purchasing obligations and bans on dealing in competing products specified in this title may be imposed on the reseller for the whole period for which the reseller in fact operates the premises;

(b) the Agreement must provide for the reseller to have the right to obtain:
— Drinks, except beer, supplied under the Agreement from other undertakings where these undertakings offer them on more favourable conditions which the supplier does not meet,
— Drinks, except beer, which are of the same type as those supplied under the agreement but which bear different trade marks, from other undertakings where the supplier does not offer them.

Article 9
Articles 2 (1) and (3), 3 (a) and (b), 4 and 5 shall apply *mutatis mutandis*.

TITLE III
SPECIAL PROVISIONS FOR SERVICE-STATION AGREEMENTS

Article 10 *[The Block Exemption]*
Pursuant to Article 85 (3) of the Treaty and subject to Articles 11 to 13 of this Regulation, it is hereby declared that Article 85 (1) of the Treaty shall not apply to agreements to which only two undertakings are party and whereby one party, the reseller, agrees with the other, the supplier, in consideration for the according of special commercial or financial advantages, to purchase only from the supplier, an undertaking connected with the supplier or another undertaking entrusted by the supplier with the distribution of his goods, certain petroleum-based motor-vehicle fuels or certain petroleum-based motor-vehicle and other fuels specified in the Agreement for resale in a service station designated in the Agreement.

Article 11 *[White List]*
Apart from the obligation referred to in Article 10, no restriction on competition shall be imposed on the reseller other than:
(a) the obligation not to sell motor-vehicle fuel and other fuels which are supplied by other undertakings in the service station designated in the agreement;
(b) the obligation not to use lubricants or related petroleum-based products which are supplied by other undertakings within the service station designated in the Agreement where the supplier or a connected undertaking has made available to the reseller, or financed, a lubrication bay or other motor-vehicle lubrication equipment;
(c) the obligation to advertise goods supplied by other undertakings within or outside the service station designated in the Agreement only in proportion to the share of these goods in the total turnover realized in the service station;
(d) the obligation to have equipment owned by the supplier or a connected undertaking or financed by the supplier or a connected undertaking serviced by the supplier or an undertaking designated by him.

Article 12 *[Black List]*
1. Article 10 shall not apply where:
(a) the supplier or a connected undertaking imposes on the reseller exclusive purchasing obligations for goods other than motor-vehicle and other fuels or for services, except in the case of the obligations referred to in Article 11 (b) and (d);
(b) the supplier restricts the freedom of the reseller to obtain from an undertaking of his choice goods or services for which under the provisions of this title neither an

exclusive purchasing obligation nor a ban on dealing in competing products may be imposed;
(c) the Agreement is concluded for an indefinite duration or for a period of more than 10 years;
(d) the supplier obliges the reseller to impose the exclusive purchasing obligation on his successor for a longer period than the reseller would himself remain tied to the supplier.
2.   Where the Agreement relates to a service station which the supplier lets to the reseller, or allows the reseller to occupy on some other basis, in law or in fact, exclusive purchasing obligations or bans on dealing in competing products specified in this title may, notwithstanding paragraph 1 (c), be imposed on the reseller for the whole period for which the reseller in fact operates the premises.

Article 13
Articles 2 (1) and (3), 3 (a) and (b), 4 and 5 of this Regulation shall apply *mutatis mutandis*.

TITLE IV
MISCELLANEOUS PROVISIONS

Article 14 [Withdrawal of the Benefits in Particular Cases]
The Commission may withdraw the benefit of this Regulation, pursuant to Article 7 of Regulation No 19/65, when it finds in a particular case that an agreement which is exempted by this Regulation nevertheless has certain effects which are incompatible with the conditions set out in Article 85 (3) of the Treaty, and in particular where:
(a) the contract goods are not subject, in a substantial part of the common market, to effective competition from identical goods or goods considered by users as equivalent in view of their characteristics, price and intended use;
(b) access by of other suppliers to the different stages of distribution in a substantial part of the common market is made difficult to a significant extent;
(c) the supplier without any objectively justified reason:
  1) Refuses to supply categories of resellers who cannot obtain the contract goods elsewhere on suitable terms or applies to them differing prices or conditions of sale;
  2) Applies less favourable prices or conditions of sale to resellers bound by an exclusive purchasing obligation as compared with other resellers at the same level of distribution.

Article 15 [omitted]

Article 16 [Exclusive Distribution]
This Regulation shall not apply to agreements by which the supplier undertakes with the reseller to supply only to the reseller certain goods for resale, in the whole or in a defined part of the Community, and the reseller undertakes with the supplier to purchase these goods only from the supplier.

Article 17 [Combined Agreements]
This Regulation shall not apply where the parties or connected undertakings, for the purpose of resale in one and the same premises used for the sale and consumption of drinks or service station, enter into agreements both of the kind referred to in title I and of a kind referred to in title II or III.

Article 18 [Application to Concerted Practices]
This Regulation shall apply *mutatis mutandis* to the categories of concerted practices defined in Articles 1, 6 and 10.

Article 19 [Entry into Force and Expiry]
This Regulation shall enter into force on 1 July 1983.
It shall expire on 31 December 1997.
     This Regulation shall be binding in its entirety and directly applicable in all Member States.

Done at Brussels, 22 June 1983.
For the Commission, Frans Andriessen, Member of the Commission

Commission Regulation 240/96 of 31 January 1996 on the Application of Article 85 (3) of the Treaty to Certain Categories of Technology Transfer Agreements[1]

THE COMMISSION OF THE EUROPEAN COMMUNITIES,

HAVING REGARD to the Treaty establishing the European Community,
HAVING REGARD to Council Regulation 19/65 of 2 March 1965 on the application of Article 85 (3) of the Treaty to certain categories of agreements and concerted practices, [...]
WHEREAS:
(1) Regulation 19/65 empowers the Commission to apply Article 85 (3) of the Treaty by regulation to certain categories of agreements and concerted practices falling within the scope of Article 85 (1) which include restrictions imposed in relation to the acquisition or use of industrial property rights - in particular of patents, utility models, designs or trademarks - or to the rights arising out of contracts for assignment of, or the right to use, a method of manufacture of knowledge relating to use or to the application of industrial processes.
(2) The Commission has made use of this power by adopting Regulation 2349/84 of 23 July 1984 on the application of Article 85 (3) of the Treaty to certain categories of patent licensing agreements,[2] as [...] amended [...], and Regulation 556/89 of 30 November 1988 on the application of Article 85 (3) of the Treaty to certain categories of know-how licensing agreements,[3] as [...] amended [...].
(3) These two block exemptions ought to be combined into a single regulation covering technology transfer agreements, and the rules governing patent licensing agreements and agreements for the licensing of know-how ought to be harmonized and simplified as far as possible, in order to encourage the dissemination of technical knowledge in the Community and to promote the manufacture of technically more sophisticated products. In those circumstances Regulation 556/89 should be repealed.

---

1   OJ 1996 L 31, p. 2.

2   OJ 1984 L 219, p. 15.

3   OJ 1989 L 61, p. 1.

(4) This Regulation should apply to the licensing of Member States' own patents, Community patents[1] and European patents[2] ("pure" patent licensing agreements). It should also apply to agreements for the licensing of non-patented technical information such as descriptions of manufacturing processes, recipes, formulae, designs or drawings, commonly termed "know-how" ("pure" know-how licensing agreements), and to combined patent and know-how licensing agreements ("mixed" agreements), which are playing an increasingly important role in the transfer of technology. For the purposes of this Regulation, a number of terms are defined in Article 10.

(5) Patent or know-how licensing agreements are agreements whereby one undertaking which holds a patent or know-how ("the licensor") permits another undertaking ("the licensee") to exploit the patent thereby licensed, or communicates the know-how to it, in particular for purposes of manufacture, use or putting on the market. In the light of experience acquired so far, it is possible to define a category of licensing agreements covering all or part of the common market which are capable of falling within the scope of Article 85 (1) but which can normally be regarded as satisfying the conditions laid down in Article 85 (3), where patents are necessary for the achievement of the objects of the licensed technology by a mixed agreement or where know-how - whether it is ancillary to patents or independent of them - is secret, substantial and identified in any appropriate form. These criteria are intended only to ensure that the licensing of the know-how or the grant of the patent licence justifies a block exemption of obligations restricting competition. This is without prejudice to the right of the parties to include in the contract provisions regarding other obligations, such as the obligation to pay royalties, even if the block exemption no longer applies.

(6) It is appropriate to extend the scope of this Regulation to pure or mixed agreements containing the licensing of intellectual property rights other than patents (in particular, trademarks, design rights and copyright, especially software protection), when such additional licensing contributes to the achievement of the objects of the licensed technology and contains only ancillary provisions.

(7) Where such pure or mixed licensing agreements contain not only obligations relating to territories within the common market but also obligations relating to non-member countries, the presence of the latter does not prevent this Regulation from applying to the obligations relating to territories within the common market. Where licensing agreements for non-member countries or for territories which extend beyond the frontiers of the Community have effects within the common market which may fall within the scope of Article 85 (1), such agreements should be covered by this Regulation to the same extent as would agreements for territories within the common market.

(8) The objective being to facilitate the dissemination of technology and the improvement of manufacturing processes, this Regulation should apply only where the licensee himself manufactures the licensed products or has them manufactured for his account, or where the licensed product is a service, provides the service himself or has the service provided for his account, irrespective of whether or not the licensee is also entitled to use confidential information provided by the licensor for the promotion and sale of the licensed product. The scope of this Regulation should therefore exclude agreements solely for the purpose of sale. Also to be excluded from the scope of this Regulation are agreements relating to marketing know-how communicated in the context of franchising arrangements and certain licensing agreements entered into in connection with arrangements such as joint ventures or patent pools and other arrangements in

---

1   OJ 1994 L 377, p. 28.

2   Ibid.

which a licence is granted in exchange for other licences not related to improvements to or new applications of the licensed technology. Such agreements pose different problems which cannot at present be dealt with in a single regulation (Article 5).

(9) Given the similarity between sale and exclusive licensing, and the danger that the requirements of this Regulation might be evaded by presenting as assignments what are in fact exclusive licenses restrictive of competition, this Regulation should apply to agreements concerning the assignment and acquisition of patents or know-how where the risk associated with exploitation remains with the assignor. It should also apply to licensing agreements in which the licensor is not the holder of the patent or know-how but is authorized by the holder to grant the licence (as in the case of sub-licences) and to licensing agreements in which the parties' rights or obligations are assumed by connected undertakings (Article 6).

(10) Exclusive licensing agreements, i.e. agreements in which the licensor undertakes not to exploit the licensed technology in the licensed territory himself or to grant further licences there, may not be in themselves incompatible with Article 85 (1) where they are concerned with the introduction and protection of a new technology in the licensed territory, by reason of the scale of the research which has been undertaken, of the increase in the level of competition, in particular inter-brand competition, and of the competitiveness of the undertakings concerned resulting from the dissemination of innovation within the Community. In so far as agreements of this kind fall, in other circumstances, within the scope of Article 85 (1), it is appropriate to include them in Article 1 in order that they may also benefit from the exemption.

(11) The exemption of export bans on the licensor and on the licensees does not prejudice any developments in the case law of the Court of Justice in relation to such agreements, notably with respect to Articles 30 to 36 and Article 85 (1). This is also the case, in particular, regarding the prohibition on the licensee from selling the licensed product in territories granted to other licensees (passive competition).

(12) The obligations listed in Article 1 generally contribute to improving the production of goods and to promoting technical progress. They make the holders of patents or know-how more willing to grant licences and licensees more inclined to undertake the investment required to manufacture, use and put on the market a new product or to use a new process. Such obligations may be permitted under this Regulation in respect of territories where the licensed product is protected by patents as long as these remain in force.

(13) Since the point at which the know-how ceases to be secret can be difficult to determine, it is appropriate, in respect of territories where the licensed technology comprises know-how only, to limit such obligations to a fixed number of years. Moreover, in order to provide sufficient periods of protection, it is appropriate to take as the starting-point for such periods the date on which the product is first put on the market in the Community by a licensee.

(14) Exemption under Article 85 (3) of longer periods of territorial protection for know-how agreements, in particular in order to protect expensive and risky investment or where the parties were not competitors at the date of the grant of the licence, can be granted only by individual decision. On the other hand, parties are free to extend the term of their agreements in order to exploit any subsequent improvement and to provide for the payment of additional royalties. However, in such cases, further periods of territorial protection may be allowed only starting from the date of licensing of the secret improvements in the Community, and by individual decision. Where the research for improvements results in innovations which are distinct from the licensed technology the parties may conclude a new agreement benefiting from an exemption under this Regulation.

(15) Provision should also be made for exemption of an obligation on the licensee not to put the product on the market in the territories of other licensees, the permitted period for such an obligation (this obligation would ban not just active competition but passive competition too) should, however, be limited to a few years from the date on which the licensed product is first put on the market in the Community by a licensee, irrespective of whether the licensed technology comprises know-how, patents or both in the territories concerned.

(16) The exemption of territorial protection should apply for the whole duration of the periods thus permitted, as long as the patents remain in force or the know-how remains secret and substantial. The parties to a mixed patent and know-how licensing agreement must be able to take advantage in a particular territory of the period of protection conferred by a patent or by the know-how, whichever is the longer.

(17) The obligations listed in Article 1 also generally fulfil the other conditions for the application of Article 85 (3). Consumers will, as a rule, be allowed a fair share of the benefit resulting from the improvement in the supply of goods on the market. To safeguard this effect, however, it is right to exclude from the application of Article 1 cases where the parties agree to refuse to meet demand from users or resellers within their respective territories who would resell for export, or to take other steps to impede parallel imports. The obligations referred to above thus only impose restrictions which are indispensable to the attainment of their objectives.

(18) It is desirable to list in this Regulation a number of obligations that are commonly found in licensing agreements but are normally not restrictive of competition, and to provide that in the event that because of the particular economic or legal circumstances they should fall within Article 85 (1), they too will be covered by the exemption. This list, in Article 2, is not exhaustive.

(19) This Regulation must also specify what restrictions or provisions may not be included in licensing agreements if these are to benefit from the block exemption. The restrictions listed in Article 3 may fall under the prohibition of Article 85 (1), but in their case there can be no general presumption that, although they relate to the transfer of technology, they will lead to the positive effects required by Article 85 (3), as would be necessary for the granting of a block exemption. Such restrictions can be declared exempt only by an individual decision, taking account of the market position of the undertakings concerned and the degree of concentration on the relevant market.

(20) The obligations on the licensee to cease using the licensed technology after the termination of the agreement (Article 2 (1) (3)) and to make improvements available to the licensor (Article 2 (1) (4)) do not generally restrict competition. The post-term use ban may be regarded as a normal feature of licensing, as otherwise the licensor would be forced to transfer his know-how or patents in perpetuity. Undertakings by the licensee to grant back to the licensor a licence for improvements to the licensed know-how and/or patents are generally not restrictive of competition if the licensee is entitled by the contract to share in future experience and inventions made by the licensor. On the other hand, a restrictive effect on competition arises where the agreement obliges the licensee to assign to the licensor rights to improvements of the originally licensed technology that he himself has brought about (Article 3 (6)).

(21) The list of clauses which do not prevent exemption also includes an obligation on the licensee to keep paying royalties until the end of the agreement independently of whether or not the licensed know-how has entered into the public domain through the action of third parties or of the licensee himself (Article 2 (1) (7)). Moreover, the parties must be free, in order to facilitate payment, to spread the royalty payments for the use of the licensed technology over a period extending beyond the duration of the licensed patents, in particular by setting lower royalty rates. As a rule, parties do not need to be protected against the foreseeable financial consequences of an agreement freely en-

tered into, and they should therefore be free to choose the appropriate means of financing the technology transfer and sharing between them the risks of such use. However, the setting of rates of royalty so as to achieve one of the restrictions listed in Article 3 renders the agreement ineligible for the block exemption.

(22) An obligation on the licensee to restrict his exploitation of the licensed technology to one or more technical fields of application ("fields of use") or to one or more product markets is not caught by Article 85 (1) either, since the licensor is entitled to transfer the technology only for a limited purpose (Article 2 (1) (8)).

(23) Clauses whereby the parties allocate customers within the same technological field of use or the same product market, either by an actual prohibition on supplying certain classes of customer or through an obligation with an equivalent effect, would also render the agreement ineligible for the block exemption where the parties are competitors for the contract products (Article 3 (4)). Such restrictions between undertakings which are not competitors remain subject to the opposition procedure. Article 3 does not apply to cases where the patent or know-how licence is granted in order to provide a single customer with a second source of supply. In such a case, a prohibition on the second licensee from supplying persons other than the customer concerned is an essential condition for the grant of a second licence, since the purpose of the transaction is not to create an independent supplier in the market. The same applies to limitations on the quantities the licensee may supply to the customer concerned (Article 2 (1) (13)).

(24) Besides the clauses already mentioned, the list of restrictions which render the block exemption inapplicable also includes restrictions regarding the selling prices of the licensed product or the quantities to be manufactured or sold, since they seriously limit the extent to which the licensee can exploit the licensed technology and since quantity restrictions particularly may have the same effect as export bans (Article 3 (1) and (5)). This does not apply where a licence is granted for use of the technology in specific production facilities and where both a specific technology is communicated for the setting-up, operation and maintenance of these facilities and the licensee is allowed to increase the capacity of the facilities or to set up further facilities for its own use on normal commercial terms. On the other hand, the licensee may lawfully be prevented from using the transferred technology to set up facilities for third parties, since the purpose of the agreement is not to permit the licensee to give other producers access to the licensor's technology while it remains secret or protected by patent (Article 2 (1) (12)).

(25) Agreements which are not automatically covered by the exemption because they contain provisions that are not expressly exempted by this Regulation and not expressly excluded from exemption, including those listed in Article 4 (2), may, in certain circumstances, nonetheless be presumed to be eligible for application of the block exemption. It will be possible for the Commission rapidly to establish whether this is the case on the basis of the information undertakings are obliged to provide under Commission Regulation 3385/94.[1] The Commission may waive the requirement to supply specific information required in form A/B but which it does not deem necessary. The Commission will generally be content with communication of the text of the agreement and with an estimate, based on directly available data, of the market structure and of the licensee's market share. Such agreements should therefore be deemed to be covered by the exemption provided for in this Regulation where they are notified to the Commission and the Commission does not oppose the application of the exemption within a specified period of time.

---

1   See above, p. 392.

(26) Where agreements exempted under this Regulation nevertheless have effects incompatible with Article 85 (3), the Commission may withdraw the block exemption, in particular where the licensed products are not faced with real competition in the licensed territory (Article 7). This could also be the case where the licensee has a strong position on the market. In assessing the competition the Commission will pay special attention to cases where the licensee has more than 40% of the whole market for the licensed products and of all the products or services which customers consider interchangeable or substitutable on account of their characteristics, prices and intended use.

(27) Agreements which come within the terms of Articles 1 and 2 and which have neither the object nor the effect of restricting competition in any other way need no longer be notified. Nevertheless, undertakings will still have the right to apply in individual cases for negative clearance or for exemption under Article 85 (3) in accordance with Council Regulation No 17 (2), as last amended by the Act of Accession of Austria, Finland and Sweden. They can in particular notify agreements obliging the licensor not to grant other licences in the territory, where the licensee's market share exceeds or is likely to exceed 40%,

HAS ADOPTED THIS REGULATION:

Article 1 [The Block Exemption]

1. Pursuant to Article 85 (3) of the Treaty and subject to the conditions set out below, it is hereby declared that Article 85 (1) of the Treaty shall not apply to pure patent licensing or know-how licensing agreements and to mixed patent and know-how licensing agreements, including those agreements containing ancillary provisions relating to intellectual property rights other than patents, to which only two undertakings are party and which include one or more of the following obligations:

(1) an obligation on the licensor not to license other undertakings to exploit the licensed technology in the licensed territory;

(2) an obligation on the licensor not to exploit the licensed technology in the licensed territory himself;

(3) an obligation on the licensee not to exploit the licensed technology in the territory of the licensor within the common market;

(4) an obligation on the licensee not to manufacture or use the licensed product, or use the licensed process, in territories within the common market which are licensed to other licensees;

(5) an obligation on the licensee not to pursue an active policy of putting the licensed product on the market in the territories within the common market which are licensed to other licensees, and in particular not to engage in advertising specifically aimed at those territories or to establish any branch or maintain a distribution depot there;

(6) an obligation on the licensee not to put the licensed product on the market in the territories licensed to other licensees within the common market in response to unsolicited orders;

(7) an obligation on the licensee to use only the licensor's trademark or get up to distinguish the licensed product during the term of the agreement, provided that the licensee is not prevented from identifying himself as the manufacturer of the licensed products;

(8) an obligation on the licensee to limit his production of the licensed product to the quantities he requires in manufacturing his own products and to sell the licensed product only as an integral part of or a replacement part for his own products or

otherwise in connection with the sale of his own products, provided that such quantities are freely determined by the licensee.

2.   Where the agreement is a pure patent licensing agreement, the exemption of the obligations referred to in paragraph 1 is granted only to the extent that and for as long as the licensed product is protected by parallel patents, in the territories respectively of the licensee (points (1), (2), (7) and (8)), the licensor (point (3)) and other licensees (points (4) and (5). The exemption of the obligation referred to in point (6) of paragraph 1 is granted for a period not exceeding five years from the date when the licensed product is first put on the market within the common market by one of the licensees, to the extent that and for as long as, in these territories, this product is protected by parallel patents.

3.   Where the agreement is a pure know-how licensing agreement, the period for which the exemption of the obligations referred to in points (1) to (5) of paragraph 1 is granted may not exceed ten years from the date when the licensed product is first put on the market within the common market by one of the licensees.

The exemption of the obligation referred to in point (6) of paragraph 1 is granted for a period not exceeding five years from the date when the licensed product is first put on the market within the common market by one of the licensees.

The obligations referred to in points (7) and (8) of paragraph 1 are exempted during the lifetime of the agreement for as long as the know-how remains secret and substantial.

However, the exemption in paragraph 1 shall apply only where the parties have identified in any appropriate form the initial know-how and any subsequent improvements to it which become available to one party and are communicated to the other party pursuant to the terms of the agreement and to the purpose thereof, and only for as long as the know-how remains secret and substantial.

4.   Where the agreement is a mixed patent and know-how licensing agreement, the exemption of the obligations referred to in points (1) to (5) of paragraph 1 shall apply in Member States in which the licensed technology is protected by necessary patents for as long as the licensed product is protected in those Member States by such patents if the duration of such protection exceeds the periods specified in paragraph 3.

The duration of the exemption provided in point (6) of paragraph 1 may not exceed the five-year period provided for in paragraphs 2 and 3.

However, such agreements qualify for the exemption referred to in paragraph 1 only for as long as the patents remain in force or to the extent that the know-how is identified and for as long as it remains secret and substantial whichever period is the longer.

5.   The exemption provided for in paragraph 1 shall also apply where in a particular agreement the parties undertake obligations of the types referred to in that paragraph but with a more limited scope than is permitted by that paragraph.

Article 2 [White List]

1.   Article 1 shall apply notwithstanding the presence in particular of any of the following clauses, which are generally not restrictive of competition:

(1)   an obligation on the licensee not to divulge the know-how communicated by the licensor; the licensee may be held to this obligation after the agreement has expired;

(2)   an obligation on the licensee not to grant sublicences or assign the licence;

(3)   an obligation on the licensee not to exploit the licensed know-how or patents after termination of the agreement in so far and as long as the know-how is still secret or the patents are still in force;

(4) an obligation on the licensee to grant to the licensor a licence in respect of his own improvements to or his new applications of the licensed technology, provided:
— that, in the case of severable improvements, such a licence is not exclusive, so that the licensee is free to use his own improvements or to license them to third parties, in so far as that does not involve disclosure of the know-how communicated by the licensor that is still secret,
— and that the licensor undertakes to grant an exclusive or non-exclusive licence of his own improvements to the licensee;

(5) an obligation on the licensee to observe minimum quality specifications, including technical specifications, for the licensed product or to procure goods or services from the licensor or from an undertaking designated by the licensor, in so far as these quality specifications, products or services are necessary for:
(a) a technically proper exploitation of the licensed technology; or
(b) ensuring that the product of the licensee conforms to the minimum quality specifications that are applicable to the licensor and other licensees; and to allow the licensor to carry out related checks;

(6) obligations:
(a) to inform the licensor of misappropriation of the know-how or of infringements of the licensed patents; or
(b) to take or to assist the licensor in taking legal action against such misappropriation or infringements;

(7) an obligation on the licensee to continue paying the royalties:
(a) until the end of the agreement in the amounts, for the periods and according to the methods freely determined by the parties, in the event of the know-how becoming publicly known other than by action of the licensor, without prejudice to the payment of any additional damages in the event of the know-how becoming publicly known by the action of the licensee in breach of the agreement;
(b) over a period going beyond the duration of the licensed patents, in order to facilitate payment;

(8) an obligation on the licensee to restrict his exploitation of the licensed technology to one or more technical fields of application covered by the licensed technology or to one or more product markets;

(9) an obligation on the licensee to pay a minimum royalty or to produce a minimum quantity of the licensed product or to carry out a minimum number of operations exploiting the licensed technology;

(10) an obligation on the licensor to grant the licensee any more favourable terms that the licensor may grant to another undertaking after the agreement is entered into;

(11) an obligation on the licensee to mark the licensed product with an indication of the licensor's name or of the licensed patent;

(12) an obligation on the licensee not to use the licensor's technology to construct facilities for third parties; this is without prejudice to the right of the licensee to increase the capacity of his facilities or to set up additional facilities for his own use on normal commercial terms, including the payment of additional royalties;

(13) an obligation on the licensee to supply only a limited quantity of the licensed product to a particular customer, where the licence was granted so that the customer might have a second source of supply inside the licensed territory; this provision shall also apply where the customer is the licensee, and the licence which was granted in order to provide a second source of supply provides that the customer is himself to manufacture the licensed products or to have them manufactured by a subcontractor;

(14) a reservation by the licensor of the right to exercise the rights conferred by a patent to oppose the exploitation of the technology by the licensee outside the licensed territory;
(15) a reservation by the licensor of the right to terminate the agreement if the licensee contests the secret or substantial nature of the licensed know-how or challenges the validity of licensed patents within the common market belonging to the licensor or undertakings connected with him;
(16) a reservation by the licensor of the right to terminate the licence agreement of a patent if the licensee raises the claim that such a patent is not necessary;
(17) an obligation on the licensee to use his best endeavours to manufacture and market the licensed product;
(18) a reservation by the licensor of the right to terminate the exclusivity granted to the licensee and to stop licensing improvements to him when the licensee enters into competition within the common market with the licensor, with undertakings connected with the licensor or with other undertakings in respect of research and development, production, use or distribution of competing products, and to require the licensee to prove that the licensed know-how is not being used for the production of products and the provision of services other than those licensed.
2.   In the event that, because of particular circumstances, the clauses referred to in paragraph 1 fall within the scope of Article 85 (1), they shall also be exempted even if they are not accompanied by any of the obligations exempted by Article 1.
3.   The exemption in paragraph 2 shall also apply where an agreement contains clauses of the types referred to in paragraph 1 but with a more limited scope than is permitted by that paragraph.

Article 3 [Black List]
Article 1 and Article 2 (2) shall not apply where:
(1) one party is restricted in the determination of prices, components of prices or discounts for the licensed products;
(2) one party is restricted from competing within the common market with the other party, with undertakings connected with the other party or with other undertakings in respect of research and development, production, use or distribution of competing products without prejudice to the provisions of Article 2 (1) (17) and (18);
(3) one or both of the parties are required without any objectively justified reason:
    (a) to refuse to meet orders from users or resellers in their respective territories who would market products in other territories within the common market;
    (b) to make it difficult for users or resellers to obtain the products from other resellers within the common market, and in particular to exercise intellectual property rights or take measures so as to prevent users or resellers from obtaining outside, or from putting on the market in the licensed territory products which have been lawfully put on the market within the common market by the licensor or with his consent; or do so as a result of a concerted practice between them;
(4) the parties were already competing manufacturers before the grant of the licence and one of them is restricted, within the same technical field of use or within the same product market, as to the customers he may serve, in particular by being prohibited from supplying certain classes of user, employing certain forms of distribution or, with the aim of sharing customers, using certain types of packaging for the products, save as provided in Article 1 (1) (7) and Article 2 (1) (13);
(5) the quantity of the licensed products one party may manufacture or sell or the number of operations exploiting the licensed technology he may carry out are subject to limitations, save as provided in Article (1) (8) and Article 2 (1) (13);

(6) the licensee is obliged to assign in whole or in part to the licensor rights to improvements to or new applications of the licensed technology;

(7) the licensor is required, albeit in separate agreements or through automatic prolongation of the initial duration of the agreement by the inclusion of any new improvements, for a period exceeding that referred to in Article 1 (2) and (3) not to license other undertakings to exploit the licensed technology in the licensed territory, or a party is required for a period exceeding that referred to in Article 1 (2) and (3) or Article 1 (4) not to exploit the licensed technology in the territory of the other party or of other licensees.

Article 4 [Grey List]

1. The exemption provided for in Articles 1 and 2 shall also apply to agreements containing obligations restrictive of competition which are not covered by those Articles and do not fall within the scope of Article 3, on condition that the agreements in question are notified to the Commission in accordance with the provisions of Articles 1, 2 and 3 of Regulation 3385/94 and that the Commission does not oppose such exemption within a period of four months.

2. Paragraph 1 shall apply, in particular, where:

(a) the licensee is obliged at the time the agreement is entered into to accept quality specifications or further licences or to procure goods or services which are not necessary for a technically satisfactory exploitation of the licensed technology or for ensuring that the production of the licensee conforms to the quality standards that are respected by the licensor and other licensees;

(b) the licensee is prohibited from contesting the secrecy or the substantiality of the licensed know-how or from challenging the validity of patents licensed within the common market belonging to the licensor or undertakings connected with him.

3. The period of four months referred to in paragraph 1 shall run from the date on which the notification takes effect in accordance with Article 4 of Regulation 3385/94.

4. The benefit of paragraphs 1 and 2 may be claimed for agreements notified before the entry into force of this Regulation by submitting a communication to the Commission referring expressly to this Article and to the notification. Paragraph 3 shall apply *mutatis mutandis*.

5. The Commission may oppose the exemption within a period of four months. It shall oppose exemption if it receives a request to do so from a Member State within two months of the transmission to the Member State of the notification referred to in paragraph 1 or of the communication referred to in paragraph 4. This request must be justified on the basis of considerations relating to the competition rules of the Treaty.

6. The Commission may withdraw the opposition to the exemption at any time. However, where the opposition was raised at the request of a Member State and this request is maintained, it may be withdrawn only after consultation of the Advisory Committee on Restrictive Practices and Dominant Positions.

7. If the opposition is withdrawn because the undertakings concerned have shown that the conditions of Article 85 (3) are satisfied, the exemption shall apply from the date of notification.

8. If the opposition is withdrawn because the undertakings concerned have amended the agreement so that the conditions of Article 85 (3) are satisfied, the exemption shall apply from the date on which the amendments take effect.

9. If the Commission opposes exemption and the opposition is not withdrawn, the effects of the notification shall be governed by the provisions of Regulation No 17.

Article 5 [Agreements not Covered by the Block Exemption]

1. This Regulation shall not apply to:

(1) agreements between members of a patent or know-how pool which relate to the pooled technologies;

(2) licensing agreements between competing undertakings which hold interests in a joint venture, or between one of them and the joint venture, if the licensing agreements relate to the activities of the joint venture;

(3) agreements under which one party grants the other a patent and/or know-how licence and in exchange the other party, albeit in separate agreements or through connected undertakings, grants the first party a patent, trademark or know-how licence or exclusive sales rights, where the parties are competitors in relation to the products covered by those agreements;

(4) licensing agreements containing provisions relating to intellectual property rights other than patents which are not ancillary;

(5) agreements entered into solely for the purpose of sale.

2. This Regulation shall nevertheless apply:

(1) to agreements to which paragraph 1 (2) applies, under which a parent undertaking grants the joint venture a patent or know-how licence, provided that the licensed products and the other goods and services of the participating undertakings which are considered by users to be interchangeable or substitutable in view of their characteristics, price and intended use represent:

— in case of a licence limited to production, not more than 20%, and

— in case of a licence covering production and distribution, not more than 10% of the market for the licensed products and all interchangeable or substitutable goods and services;

(2) to agreements to which paragraph 1 (1) applies and to reciprocal licences within the meaning of paragraph 1 (3), provided the parties are not subject to any territorial restriction within the common market with regard to the manufacture, use or putting on the market of the licensed products or to the use of the licensed or pooled technologies.

3. This Regulation shall continue to apply where, for two consecutive financial years, the market shares in paragraph 2 (1) are not exceeded by more than one-tenth; where that limit is exceeded, this Regulation shall continue to apply for a period of six months from the end of the year in which the limit was exceeded.

Article 6 [Related Forms of Agreement]

This Regulation shall also apply to:

(1) agreements where the licensor is not the holder of the know-how or the patentee, but is authorized by the holder or the patentee to grant a licence;

(2) assignments of know-how, patents or both where the risk associated with exploitation remains with the assignor, in particular where the sum payable in consideration of the assignment is dependent on the turnover obtained by the assignee in respect of products made using the know-how or the patents, the quantity of such products manufactured or the number of operations carried out employing the know-how or the patents;

(3) licensing agreements in which the rights or obligations of the licensor or the licensee are assumed by undertakings connected with them.

Article 7 [Withdrawal of the Benefits in Particular Cases]

The Commission may withdraw the benefit of this Regulation, pursuant to Article 7 of Regulation 19/65, where it finds in a particular case that an agreement exempted by this Regulation nevertheless has certain effects which are incompatible with the conditions laid down in Article 85 (3) of the Treaty, and in particular where:

(1) the effect of the agreement is to prevent the licensed products from being exposed to effective competition in the licensed territory from identical goods or services or from goods or services considered by users as interchangeable or substitutable in view of their characteristics, price and intended use, which may in particular occur where the licensee's market share exceeds 40%;

(2) without prejudice to Article 1 (1) (6), the licensee refuses, without any objectively justified reason, to meet unsolicited orders from users or resellers in the territory of other licensees;

(3) the parties:
(a) without any objectively justified reason, refuse to meet orders from users or resellers in their respective territories who would market the products in other territories within the common market; or
(b) make it difficult for users or resellers to obtain the products from other resellers within the common market, and in particular where they exercise intellectual property rights or take measures so as to prevent resellers or users from obtaining outside, or from putting on the market in the licensed territory products which have been lawfully put on the market within the common market by the licensor or with his consent;

(4) the parties were competing manufacturers at the date of the grant of the licence and obligations on the licensee to produce a minimum quantity or to use his best endeavours as referred to in Article 2 (1), (9) and (17) respectively have the effect of preventing the licensee from using competing technologies.

Article 8 [Scope of "Patents"]

1. For purposes of this Regulation:
(a) patent applications;
(b) utility models;
(c) applications for registration of utility models;
(d) topographies of semiconductor products;
(e) *certificats d'utilité* and *certificats d'addition* under French law;
(f) applications for *certificats d'utilité* and *certificats d'addition* under French law;
(g) supplementary protection certificates for medicinal products or other products for which such supplementary protection certificates may be obtained;
(h) plant breeder's certificates,
shall be deemed to be patents.

2. This Regulation shall also apply to agreements relating to the exploitation of an invention if an application within the meaning of paragraph 1 is made in respect of the invention for a licensed territory after the date when the agreements were entered into but within the time-limits set by the national law or the international convention to be applied.

3. This Regulation shall furthermore apply to pure patent or know-how licensing agreements or to mixed agreements whose initial duration is automatically prolonged by the inclusion of any new improvements, whether patented or not, communicated by the licensor, provided that the licensee has the right to refuse such improvements or each party has the right to terminate the agreement at the expiry of the initial term of an agreement and at least every three years thereafter.

Article 9 [Confidentiality]

1. Information acquired pursuant to Article 4 shall be used only for the purposes of this Regulation.

2.   The Commission and the authorities of the Member States, their officials and other servants shall not disclose information acquired by them pursuant to this Regulation of the kind covered by the obligation of professional secrecy.
3.   The provisions of paragraphs 1 and 2 shall not prevent publication of general information or surveys which do not contain information relating to particular undertakings or associations of undertakings.

Article 10 [Definitions]

For purposes of this Regulation:
(1) "know-how" means a body of technical information that is secret, substantial and identified in any appropriate form;
(2) "secret" means that the know-how package as a body or in the precise configuration and assembly of its components is not generally known or easily accessible, so that part of its value consists in the lead which the licensee gains when it is communicated to him; it is not limited to the narrow sense that each individual component of the know-how should be totally unknown or unobtainable outside the licensor's business;
(3) "substantial" means that the know-how includes information which must be useful, i.e. can reasonably be expected at the date of conclusion of the agreement to be capable of improving the competitive position of the licensee, for example by helping him to enter a new market or giving him an advantage in competition with other manufacturers or providers of services who do not have access to the licensed secret know-how or other comparable secret know-how;
(4) "identified" means that the know-how is described or recorded in such a manner as to make it possible to verify that it satisfies the criteria of secrecy and substantiality and to ensure that the licensee is not unduly restricted in his exploitation of his own technology, to be identified the know-how can either be set out in the licence agreement or in a separate document or recorded in any other appropriate form at the latest when the know-how is transferred or shortly thereafter, provided that the separate document or other record can be made available if the need arises;
(5) "necessary patents" are patents where a licence under the patent is necessary for the putting into effect of the licensed technology in so far as, in the absence of such a licence, the realization of the licensed technology would not be possible or would by possible only to a lesser extent or in more difficult or costly conditions. Such patents must therefore be of technical, legal or economic interest to the licensee;
(6) "licensing agreement" means pure patent licensing agreements and pure know-how licensing agreements as well as mixed patent and know-how licensing agreements;
(7) "licensed technology" means the initial manufacturing know-how or the necessary product and process patents, or both, existing at the time the first licensing agreement is concluded, and improvements subsequently made to the know-how or patents, irrespective of whether and to what extent they are exploited by the parties or by other licensees;
(8) "the licensed products" are goods or services the production or provision of which requires the use of the licensed technology;
(9) "the licensee's market share" means the proportion which the licensed products and other goods or services provided by the licensee, which are considered by users to be interchangeable or substitutable for the licensed products in view of their characteristics, price and intended use, represent the entire market for the licensed products and all other interchangeable or substitutable goods and services in the common market or a substantial part of it;

(10) "exploitation" refers to any use of the licensed technology in particular in the production, active or passive sales in a territory even if not coupled with manufacture in that territory, or leasing of the licensed products;
(11) "the licensed territory" is the territory covering all or at least part of the common market where the licensee is entitled to exploit the licensed technology;
(12) "territory of the licensor" means territories in which the licensor has not granted any licences for patents and/or know-how covered by the licensing agreement;
(13) "parallel patents" means patents which, in spite of the divergences which remain in the absence of any unification of national rules concerning industrial property, protect the same invention in various Member States;
(14) "connected undertakings" means:
(a) undertakings in which a party to the agreement, directly or indirectly:
— owns more than half the capital or business assets, or
— has the power to exercise more than half the voting rights, or
— has the power to appoint more than half the members of the supervisory board, board of directors or bodies legally representing the undertaking, or
— has the right to manage the affairs of the undertaking;
(b) undertakings which, directly or indirectly, have in or over a party to the agreement the rights or powers listed in (a);
(c) undertakings in which an undertaking referred to in (b), directly or indirectly, has the rights or powers listed in (a);
(d) undertakings in which the parties to the agreement or undertakings connected with them jointly have the rights or powers listed in (a): such jointly controlled undertakings are considered to be connected with each of the parties to the agreement;
(15) "ancillary provisions" are provisions relating to the exploitation of intellectual property rights other than patents, which contain no obligations restrictive of competition other than those also attached to the licensed know-how or patents and exempted under this Regulation;
(16) "obligation" means both contractual obligation and a concerted practice;
(17) "competing manufacturers" or manufacturers of "competing products" means manufacturers who sell products which, in view of their characteristics, price and intended use, are considered by users to be interchangeable or substitutable for the licensed products.

Article 11 [Repeals]
1. Regulation 556/89 is hereby repealed with effect from 1 April 1996.
2. Regulation 2349/84 shall continue to apply until 31 March 1996.
3. The prohibition in Article 85 (1) of the Treaty shall not apply to agreements in force on 31 March 1996 which fulfil the exemption requirements laid down by Regulation 2349/84 or 556/89.

Article 12 [Monitoring]
1. The Commission shall undertake regular assessments of the application of this Regulation, and in particular of the opposition procedure provided for in Article 4.
2. The Commission shall draw up a report on the operation of this Regulation before the end of the fourth year following its entry into force and shall, on that basis, assess whether any adaptation of the Regulation is desirable.

Article 13 [Entry into Force and Expiry]
This Regulation shall enter into force on 1 April 1996.
It shall apply until 31 March 2006.
Article 11 (2) of this Regulation shall, however, enter into force on 1 January 1996.

This Regulation shall be binding in its entirety and directly applicable in all Member States.

Done at Brussels, 31 January 1996.
For the Commission, Karel VAN MIERT, Member of the Commission

Merger Control

Council Regulation 4064/89 of 21 December 1989 on the Control of Concentrations Between Undertakings[1]

THE COUNCIL OF THE EUROPEAN COMMUNITIES,

HAVING REGARD to the Treaty establishing the European Economic Community, and in particular Articles 87 and 235 thereof, [...]

(1) WHEREAS, for the achievement of the aims of the Treaty establishing the European Economic Community, Article 3 (f) gives the Community the objective of instituting "a system ensuring that competition in the common market is not distorted";

(2) WHEREAS this system is essential for the achievement of the internal market by 1992 and its further development;

(3) WHEREAS the dismantling of internal frontiers is resulting and will continue to result in major corporate re-organizations in the Community, particularly in the form of concentrations;

(4) WHEREAS such a development must be welcomed as being in line with the requirements of dynamic competition and capable of increasing the competitiveness of European industry, improving the conditions of growth and raising the standard of living in the Community;

(5) WHEREAS, however, it must be ensured that the process of re-organization does not result in lasting damage to competition; whereas Community law must therefore include provisions governing those concentrations which may significantly impede effective competition in the common market or in a substantial part of it;

(6) WHEREAS Articles 85 and 86, while applicable, according to the case-law of the Court of Justice, to certain concentrations, are not, however, sufficient to cover all operations which may prove to be incompatible with the system of undistorted competition envisaged in the Treaty;

(7) WHEREAS a new legal instrument should therefore be created in the form of a Regulation to permit effective monitoring of all concentrations from the point of view of their effect on the structure of competition in the Community and to be the only instrument applicable to such concentrations;

(8) WHEREAS this Regulation should therefore be based not only on 87 but, principally, on Article 235 of the Treaty, under which the Community may give itself the additional powers of action necessary for the attainment of its objectives, and also with regard to concentrations on the markets for agricultural products listed in Annex II to the Treaty;

(9) WHEREAS the provisions to be adopted in this Regulation should apply to significant structural changes the impact of which on the market goes beyond the national borders of any one Member State;

(10) WHEREAS the scope of application of this Regulation should therefore be defined according to the geographical area of activity of the undertakings concerned and be limited by quantitative thresholds in order to cover those concentrations which have a Community dimension; whereas, at the end of an initial phase of the implementation of this Regulation, these thresholds should be reviewed in the light of the experience gained;

---

1   OJ 1990 L 257, p. 13, as amended by Council Regulation 1310/97 of 30 June 1997.

(11) WHEREAS a concentration with a Community dimension exists where the aggregate turnover of the undertakings concerned exceeds given levels worldwide and throughout the Community and where at least two of the undertakings concerned have their sole or main fields of activities in different Member States or where, although the undertakings in question act mainly in one and the same Member State, at least one of them has substantial operations in at least one other Member State; whereas that is also the case where the concentrations are effected by undertakings which do not have their principal fields of activities in the Community but which have substantial operations there;

(12) WHEREAS the arrangements to be introduced for the control of concentrations should, without prejudice to Article 90 (2) of the Treaty, respect the principle of non-discrimination between the public and the private sectors; whereas, in the public sector, calculation of the turnover of an undertaking concerned in a concentration needs, therefore, to take account of undertakings making up an economic unit with an independent power of decision, irrespective of the way in which their capital is held or of the rules of administrative supervision applicable to them;

(13) WHEREAS it is necessary to establish whether concentrations with a Community dimension are compatible or not with the common market from the point of view of the need to preserve and develop effective competition in the common market; whereas, in so doing, the Commission must place its appraisal within the general framework of the achievement of the fundamental objectives referred to in Article 2 of the Treaty, including that of strengthening the Community's economic and social cohesion, referred to in Article 130a;

(14) WHEREAS this Regulation should establish the principle that a concentration with a Community dimension which creates or strengthens a position as result of which effective competition in the common market or in a substantial part of it is significantly impeded is to be declared incompatible with the common market;

(15) WHEREAS concentrations which, by reason of the limited market share of the undertakings concerned, are not liable to impede effective competition may be presumed to be compatible with the common market; whereas, without prejudice to Articles 85 and 86 of the Treaty, an indication to this effect exists, in particular, where the market share of the undertakings concerned does not exceed 25% either in the common market or in a substantial part of it;

(15) WHEREAS the Commission should have the task of taking all decisions necessary to establish whether or not concentrations of a Community dimension are compatible with the common market, as well as decisions designed to restore effective competition;

(16) WHEREAS to ensure effective control undertakings should be obliged to give prior notification of concentrations with a Community dimension and provision should be made for the suspension of concentrations for a limited period, and for the possibility of extending or waiving a suspension where necessary; whereas in the interests of legal certainty the validity of transactions must nevertheless be protected as much as necessary;

(17) WHEREAS a period within which the Commission must initiate a proceeding in respect of a notified concentration and a period within which it must give a final decision on the compatibility or incompatibility with the common market of a notified concentration should be laid down;

(18) WHEREAS the undertakings concerned must be accorded the right to be heard by the Commission as soon as a proceeding has been initiated; whereas the members of management and supervisory organs and recognized workers' representatives in the undertakings concerned, together with third parties showing a legitimate interest, must also be given the opportunity to be heard;

(19) WHEREAS the Commission should act in close and constant liaison with the competent authorities of the Member States from which it obtains comments and information;

(20) WHEREAS, for the purposes of this Regulation, and in accordance with the case-law of the Court of Justice, the Commission must be afforded the assistance of the Member States and must also be empowered to require information to be given and to carry out the necessary investigations in order to appraise concentrations;

(21) WHEREAS compliance with this Regulation must be enforceable by means of fines and periodic penalty payments; whereas the Court of Justice should be given unlimited jurisdiction in that regard pursuant to Article 172 of the Treaty;

(22) WHEREAS it is appropriate to define the concept of concentration in such a manner as to cover only operations bringing about a durable change in the structure of the undertakings concerned; whereas it is therefore necessary to exclude from the scope of this Regulation those operations which have as their object or effect the coordination of the competitive behaviour of independent undertakings, since such operations fall to be examined under the appropriate provisions of Regulations implementing Article 85 or Article 86 of the Treaty; whereas it is appropriate to make this distinction specifically in the case of the creation of joint ventures;

(23) WHEREAS there is no coordination of competitive behaviour within the meaning of this Regulation where two or more undertakings agree to acquire jointly control of one or more other undertakings with the object and effect of sharing amongst themselves such undertakings or their assets;

(24) WHEREAS the application of this Regulation is not excluded where the undertakings concerned accept restrictions directly related and necessary to the implementation of the concentration;

(25) WHEREAS the Commission should be given exclusive competence to apply this Regulation, subject to review by the Court of Justice;

(26) WHEREAS the Member States may not apply their national legislation on competition to concentrations with a Community dimension, unless the Regulation makes provision therefor; whereas the relevant powers of national authorities should be limited to cases where, failing intervention by the Commission, effective competition is likely to be significantly impeded within the territory of a Member State and where the competition interests of that Member State cannot be sufficiently protected otherwise than by this Regulation; whereas the Member States concerned must act promptly in such cases; whereas this Regulation cannot, because of the diversity of national law, fix a single deadline for the adoption of remedies;

(27) WHEREAS, furthermore, the exclusive application of this Regulation to concentrations with a Community dimension is without prejudice to Article 223 of the Treaty, and does not prevent the Member States' taking appropriate measures to protect legitimate interests other than those pursued by this Regulation, provided that such measures are compatible with the general principles and other provisions of Community law;

(28) WHEREAS concentrations not referred to in this Regulation come, in principle, within the jurisdiction of the Member States; whereas, however, the Commission should have the power to act, at the request of a Member State concerned, in cases where effective competition would be significantly impeded within that Member State's territory;

(29) WHEREAS the conditions in which concentrations involving Community undertakings are carried out in non-member countries should be observed, and provision should be made for the possibility of the Council's giving the Commission an appropriate mandate for negotiation with a view to obtaining non-discriminatory treatment for Community undertakings;

(30) WHEREAS this Regulation in no way detracts from the collective rights of workers as recognized in the undertakings concerned,

HAS ADOPTED THIS REGULATION:

Article 1 Scope

1.   Without prejudice to Article 22, this Regulation shall apply to all concentrations with a Community dimension as defined in paragraphs 2 and 3.

2.   For the purposes of this Regulation, a concentration has a Community dimension where;

(a) the aggregate worldwide turnover of all the undertakings concerned is more than ECU 5.000 million, and

(b) the aggregate Community-wide turnover of each of at least two of the undertakings concerned is more than ECU 250 million, unless each of the undertakings concerned achieves more than two-thirds of its aggregate Community-wide turnover within one and the same Member State.

3.   For the purposes of this Regulation, a concentration that does not meet the thresholds laid down in paragraph 2 has a Community dimension where:

(a) the combined aggregate worldwide turnover of all the undertakings concerned is more than ECU 2.500 million;

(b) in each of at least three Member States, the combined aggregate turnover of all the undertakings concerned is more than ECU 100 million;

(c) in each of at least three Member States included for the purpose of point (b), the aggregate turnover of each of at least two of the undertakings concerned is more than ECU 25 million; and

(d) the aggregate Community-wide turnover of each of at least two of the undertakings concerned is more than ECU 100 million;

unless each of the undertakings concerned achieves more than two-thirds of its aggregate Community-wide turnover within one and the same Member State.

4.   Before 1 July 2000 the Commission shall report to the Council on the operation of the thresholds and criteria set out in paragraphs 2 and 3.

5.   Following the report referred to in paragraph 4 and on a proposal from the Commission, the Council, acting by a qualified majority, may revise the thresholds and criteria mentioned in paragraph 3.

Article 2 Appraisal of concentrations

1.   Concentrations within the scope of this Regulation shall be appraised in accordance with the following provisions with a view to establishing whether or not they are compatible with the common market.

In making this appraisal, the Commission shall take into account:

(a) the need to preserve and develop effective competition within the common market in view of, among other things, the structure of all the markets concerned and the actual or potential competition from undertakings located either within or without the Community;

(b) the market position of the undertakings concerned and their economic and financial power, the opportunities available to suppliers and users, their access to supplies or markets, any legal or other barriers to entry, supply and demand trends for the relevant goods and services, the interests of the intermediate and ultimate consumers, and the development of technical and economic progress provided that it is to consumers' advantage and does not form an obstacle to competition.

2.   A concentration which does not create or strengthen a dominant position as a result of which effective competition would be significantly impeded in the common market or in a substantial part of it shall be declared compatible with the common market.
3.   A concentration which creates or strengthens a dominant position as a result of which effective competition would be significantly impeded in the common market or in a substantial part of it shall be declared incompatible with the common market.
4.   To the extent that the creation of a joint venture constituting a concentration pursuant to Article 3 has as its object or effect the coordination of the competitive behaviour of undertakings that remain independent, such coordination shall be appraised in accordance with the criteria of Article 85 (1) and (3) of the Treaty, with a view to establishing whether or not the operation is compatible with the common market.
     In making this appraisal, the Commission shall take into account in particular:
—   whether two or more parent companies retain to a significant extent activities in the same market as the joint venture or in a market which is downstream or upstream from that of the joint venture or in a neighbouring market closely related to this market,
—   whether the coordination which is the direct consequence of the creation of the joint venture affords the undertakings concerned the possibility of eliminating competition in respect of a substantial part of the products or services in question.

Article 3 Definition of concentration
1.   A concentration shall be deemed to arise where:
(a) two or more previously independent undertakings merge, or
(b) one or more persons already controlling at least one undertaking, or
(c) one or more undertakings acquire, whether by purchase of securities or assets, by contract or by any other means, direct or indirect control of the whole or parts of one or more other undertakings.
2.   The creation of a joint venture performing on a lasting basis all the functions of an autonomous economic entity shall constitute a concentration within the meaning of paragraph 1 (b).
3.   For the purposes of this Regulation, control shall be constituted by rights, contracts or any other means which, either separately or jointly and having regard to the considerations of fact or law involved, confer the possibility of exercising decisive influence on an undertaking, in particular by:
(a) ownership or the right to use all or part of the assets of an undertaking;
(b) rights or contracts which confer decisive influence on the composition, voting or decisions of the organs of an undertaking.
4.   Control is acquired by persons or undertakings which:
(a) are holders of the rights or entitled to rights under the contracts concerned, or
(b) while not being holders of such rights or entitled to rights under such contracts, have the power to exercise the rights deriving therefrom.
5.   A concentration shall not be deemed to arise where:
(a) credit institutions or other financial institutions or insurance companies, the normal activities of which include transactions and dealing in securities for their own account or for the account of others, hold on a temporary basis securities which they have acquired in an undertaking with a view to reselling them, provided that they do not exercise voting rights in respect of those securities with a view to determining the competitive behaviour of that undertaking or provided that they exercise such voting rights only with a view to preparing the sale of all or part of that undertaking or of its assets or the sale of those securities and that any such sale takes place within one year of the date of acquisition; that period may be extended by the

Commission on request where such institutions or companies justify the fact that the sale was not reasonably possible within the period set;

(b) control is acquired by an office holder according to the law of a Member State relating to liquidation, winding up, insolvency, cessation of payments, compositions or analogous proceedings;

(c) the operations referred to in paragraph 1 (b) are carried out by the financial holding companies referred to in Article 5 (3) of the Fourth Council Directive 78/660 of 25 July 1978 on the annual accounts of certain types of companies, [as amended], provided however that the voting rights in respect of the holding are exercised, in particular in relation to the appointment of members of the management and supervisory bodies of the undertakings in which they have holdings, only to maintain the full value of those investments and not to determine directly or indirectly the competitive conduct of those undertakings.

Article 4 Prior notification of concentrations

1. Concentrations with a Community dimension as referred to by this Regulation shall be notified to the Commission not more than one week after the conclusion of the agreement, or the announcement of the public bid, or the acquisition of a controlling interest. That week shall begin when the first of those events occurs.

2. A concentration which consists of a merger within the meaning of Article 3 (1) (a) or in the acquisition of joint control within the meaning of Article 3 (1) (b) shall be notified jointly by the parties to the merger or by those acquiring joint control as the case may be.

In all other cases, the notification shall be effected by the person or undertaking acquiring control of the whole or parts of one or more undertakings.

3. Where the Commission finds that a notified concentration falls within the scope of this Regulation, it shall publish the fact of the notification, at the same time indicating the names of the parties, the nature of the concentration and the economic sectors involved. The Commission shall take account of the legitimate interest of undertakings in the protection of their business secrets.

Article 5 Calculation of turnover

1. Aggregate turnover within the meaning of Article 1 (2) shall comprise the amounts derived by the undertakings concerned in the preceding financial year from the sale of products and the provision of services falling within the undertakings' ordinary activities after deduction of sales rebates and of value added tax and other taxes directly related to turnover. The aggregate turnover of an undertaking concerned shall not include the sale of products or the provision of services between any of the undertakings referred to in paragraph 4.

Turnover, in the Community or in a Member State, shall comprise products sold and services provided to undertakings or consumers, in the Community or in that Member State as the case may be.

2. By way of derogation from paragraph 1, where the concentration consists in the acquisition of parts, whether or not constituted as legal entities, of one or more undertakings, only the turnover relating to the parts which are the subject of the transaction shall be taken into account with regard to the seller or sellers.

However, two or more transactions within the meaning of the first subparagraph which take place within a two-year period between the same persons or undertakings shall be treated as one and the same concentration arising on the date of the last transaction.

3. In place of turnover the following shall be used:

(a) for credit institutions and other financial institutions, as regards Article 1 (2) and (3), the sum of the following income items as defined in Council Directive 86/635 of 8 December 1986 on the annual accounts and consolidated accounts of banks and other financial institutions[1], after deduction of value added tax and other taxes directly related to those items, where appropriate:
  (i) interest income and similar income;
  (ii) income from securities:
  — income from shares and other variable yield securities,
  — income from participating interests,
  — income from shares in affiliated undertakings;
  (iii) commissions receivable;
  (iv) net profit on financial operations;
  (v) other operating income.
  The turnover of a credit or financial institution in the Community or in a Member State shall comprise the income items, as defined above, which are received by the branch or division of that institution established in the Community or in the Member State in question, as the case may be;
(b) for insurance undertakings, the value of gross premiums written which shall comprise all amounts received and receivable in respect of insurance contracts issued by or on behalf of the insurance undertakings, including also outgoing reinsurance premiums, and after deduction of taxes and parafiscal contributions or levies charged by reference to the amounts of individual premiums or the total volume of premiums; as regards Article 1 (2) (b) and (3) (b), (c) and (d) and the final part of Article 1 (2) and (3), gross premiums received from Community residents and from residents of one Member State respectively shall be taken into account.

4. Without prejudice to paragraph 2, the aggregate turnover of an undertaking concerned within the meaning of Article 1 (2) and (3) shall be calculated by adding together the respective turnovers of the following:
(a) the undertaking concerned;
(b) those undertakings in which the undertaking concerned, directly or indirectly;
  — owns more than half the capital or business assets, or
  — has the power to exercise more than half the voting rights, or
  — has the power to appoint more than half the members of the supervisory board, the administrative board or bodies legally representing the undertakings, or
  — has the right to manage the undertakings' affairs;
(c) those undertakings which have in an undertaking concerned the rights or powers listed in (b);
(d) those undertakings in which an undertaking as referred to in (c) has the rights or powers listed in (b);
(e) those undertakings in which two or more undertakings as referred to in (a) to (d) jointly have the rights or powers listed in (b).

5. Where undertakings concerned by the concentration jointly have the rights or powers listed in paragraph 4 (b), in calculating the aggregate turnover of the undertakings concerned for the purposes of Article 1 (2) and (3):
(a) no account shall be taken of the turnover resulting from the sale of products or the provision of services between the joint undertaking and each of the undertakings concerned or any other undertaking connected with any one of them, as set out in paragraph 4 (b) to (e);

---

1 OJ 1986 L 372, p. 1.

(b) account shall be taken of the turnover resulting from the sale of products and the provision of services between the joint undertaking and any third undertakings. This turnover shall be apportioned equally amongst the undertakings concerned.

Article 6 Examination of the notification and initiation of proceedings
1. The Commission shall examine the notification as soon as it is received.
(a) Where it concludes that the concentration notified does not fall within the scope of this Regulation, it shall record that finding by means of a decision.
(b) Where it finds that the concentration notified, although falling within the scope of this Regulation, does not raise serious doubts as to its compatibility with the common market, it shall decide not to oppose it and shall declare that it is compatible with the common market.
      The decision declaring the concentration compatible shall also cover restrictions directly related and necessary to the implementation of the concentration.
(c) Without prejudice to paragraph 1 (a), where the Commission finds that the concentration notified falls within the scope of this Regulation and raises serious doubts as to its compatibility with the common market, it shall decide to initiate proceedings.
1a. Where the Commission finds that, following modification by the undertakings concerned, a notified concentration no longer raises serious doubts within the meaning of paragraph 1 (c), it may decide to declare the concentration compatible with the common market pursuant to paragraph 1 (b).
      The Commission may attach to its decision under paragraph 1 (b) conditions and obligations intended to ensure that the undertakings concerned comply with the commitments they have entered into vis-à-vis the Commission with a view to rendering the concentration compatible with the common market.
1b. The Commission may revoke the decision it has taken pursuant to paragraph 1 (a) or (b) where:
(a) the decision is based on incorrect information for which one of the undertakings is responsible or where it has been obtained by deceit, or
(b) the undertakings concerned commit a breach of an obligation attached to the decision.
1c. In the cases referred to in paragraph 1 (b), the Commission may take a decision under paragraph 1, without being bound by the deadlines referred to in Article 10 (1).
2.   The Commission shall notify its decision to the undertakings concerned and the competent authorities of the Member States without delay.

Article 7 Suspension of concentrations
1.   A concentration as defined in Article 1 shall not be put into effect either before its notification or until it as been declared compatible with the common market pursuant to a decision under Article 6 (1) (b) or Article 8 (2) or on the basis of a presumption according to Article 10 (6).
2.   deleted
3.   Paragraph 1 shall not impede the implementation of a public bid which has been notified to the Commission in accordance with Article 4 (1) by the date of its announcement, provided that the acquirer does not exercise the voting rights attached to the securities in question or does so only to maintain the full value of those investments and on the basis of a derogation granted by the Commission pursuant to paragraph 4.
4.   The Commission may, on request, grant a derogation from the obligations imposed in paragraphs 1 or 3. The request to grant a derogation must be reasoned. In deciding on the request, the Commission shall take into account inter alia the effects of the suspension on one or more undertakings concerned by a concentration or on a third party

and the threat to competition posed by the concentration. That derogation may be made subject to conditions and obligations in order to ensure conditions of effective competition. A derogation may be applied for and granted at any time, even before notification or after the transaction.

5.   The validity of any transaction carried out in contravention of paragraph 1 shall be dependent on a decision pursuant to Article 6 (1) (b) or Article 8 (2) or (3) or on a presumption pursuant to Article 10 (6).

This Article shall, however, have no effect on the validity of transactions in securities including those convertible into other securities admitted to trading on a market which is regulated and supervised by authorities recognized by public bodies, operates regularly and is accessible directly or indirectly to the public, unless the buyer and seller knew or ought to have known that the transaction was carried out in contravention of paragraph 1.

Article 8 Powers of decision of the Commission

1.   Without prejudice to Article 9, each proceeding initiated pursuant to Article 6 (1) (c) shall be closed by means of a decision as provided for in paragraphs 2 to 5.

2.   Where the Commission finds that, following modification by the undertakings concerned if necessary, a notified concentration fulfils the criterion laid down in Article 2 (2) and, in the cases referred to in Article 2 (4), the criteria laid down in Article 85 (3) of the Treaty, it shall issue a decision declaring the concentration compatible with the common market.

It may attach to its decision conditions and obligations intended to ensure that the undertakings concerned comply with the commitments they have entered into vis-à-vis the Commission with a view to rendering the concentration compatible with the common market. The decision declaring the concentration compatible with the common market shall also cover restrictions directly related and necessary to the implementation of the concentration.

3.   Where the Commission finds that a concentration fulfils the criterion defined in Article 2 (3) or, in the cases referred to in Article 2 (4), does not fulfil the criteria laid down in Article 85 (3) of the Treaty, it shall issue a decision declaring that the concentration is incompatible with the common market.

4.   Where a concentration has already been implemented, the Commission may, in a decision pursuant to paragraph 3 or by a separate decision, require the undertakings or assets brought together to be separated or the cessation of joint control or any other action that may be appropriate in order to restore conditions of effective competition.

5.   The Commission may revoke the decision it has taken pursuant to paragraph 2 where:

(a) the declaration of compatibility is based on incorrect information for which one of the undertakings concerned is responsible or where it has been obtained by deceit, or

(b) the undertakings concerned commit a breach of an obligation attached to the decision.

6.   In the case referred to in paragraph 5, the Commission may take a decision pursuant to paragraph 3, without being bound by the deadline referred to in Article 10 (3).

Article 9 Referral to the competent authorities of the Member States

1.   The Commission may, by means of a decision notified without delay to the undertakings concerned and the competent authorities of the other Member States, refer a notified concentration to the competent authorities of the Member State concerned in the following circumstances.

2.   Within three weeks of the date of receipt of the copy of the notification a Member State may inform the Commission, which shall inform the undertakings concerned, that:
(a) a concentration threatens to create or to strengthen a dominant position as a result of which effective competition will be significantly impeded on a market within that Member State, which presents all the characteristics of a distinct market, or
(b) a concentration affects competition on a market within that Member State, which presents all the characteristics of a distinct market and which does not constitute a substantial part of the common market.
3.   If the Commission considers that, having regard to the market for the products or services in question and the geographical reference market within the meaning of paragraph 7, there is such a distinct market and that such a threat exists either:
(a) it shall itself deal with the case in order to maintain or restore effective competition on the market concerned, or
(b) it shall refer the whole or part of the case to the competent authorities of the Member State concerned with a view to the application of that State's national competition law.
If, however, the Commission considers that such a distinct market or threat does not exist it shall adopt a decision to that effect which it shall address to the Member State concerned.
    In cases where a Member State informs the Commission that a concentration affects competition in a distinct market within its territory that does not form a substantial part of the common market, the Commission shall refer the whole or part of the case relating to the distinct market concerned, if it considers that such a distinct market is affected.
4.   A decision to refer or not to refer pursuant to paragraph 3 shall be taken where:
(a) as a general rule within the six-week period provided for in Article 10 (1), second subparagraph, where the Commission has not initiated proceedings pursuant to Article 6 (1) (b), or
(b) within three months at most of the notification of the concentration concerned where the Commission has initiated proceedings under Article 6 (1) (c), without taking the preparatory steps in order to adopt the necessary measures pursuant to Article 8 (2), second subparagraph, (3) or (4) to maintain or restore effective competition on the market concerned.
5.   If within the three months referred to in paragraph 4 (b) the Commission, despite a reminder from the Member State concerned, has taken no decision on referral in accordance with paragraph 3 or taken the preparatory steps referred to in paragraph 4 (b), it shall be deemed to have taken a decision to refer the case to the Member State concerned in accordance with paragraph 3 (b).
6.   The publication of any report or the announcement of the findings of the examination of the concentration by the competent authority of the Member State concerned shall be effected not more than four months after the Commission's referral.
7.   The geographical reference market shall consist of the area in which the undertakings concerned are involved in the supply of products or services, in which the conditions of competition are sufficiently homogeneous and which can be distinguished from neighbouring areas because, in particular, conditions of competition are appreciably different in those areas. This assessment should take account in particular of the nature and characteristics of the products or services concerned, of the existence of entry barriers or of consumer preferences, of appreciable differences of the undertakings' market shares between neighbouring areas or of substantial price differences.

8. In applying the provisions of this Article, the Member State concerned may take only the measures strictly necessary to safeguard or restore effective competition on the market concerned.

9. In accordance with the relevant provisions of the Treaty, any Member State may appeal to the Court of Justice, and in particular request the application of Article 186, for the purpose of applying its national competition law.

10. This Article may be re-examined at the same time as the thresholds referred to in Article 1.

Article 10 Time limits for initiating proceedings and for decisions

1. The decisions referred to in Article 6 (1) must be taken within one month at most. That period shall begin on the day following the receipt of a notification or, if the information to be supplied with the notification is incomplete, on the day following the receipt of the complete information.

That period shall be increased to six weeks if the Commission receives a request from a Member State in accordance with Article 9 (2) or where, after notification of a concentration, the undertakings concerned submit commitments pursuant to Article 6 (1a), which are intended by the parties to form the basis for a decision pursuant to Article 6 (1) (b).

2. Decisions taken pursuant to Article 8 (2) concerning notified concentrations must be taken as soon as it appears that the serious doubts referred to in Article 6 (1) (c) have been removed, particularly as a result of modifications made by the undertakings concerned, and at the latest by the deadline laid down in paragraph 3.

3. Without prejudice to Article 8 (6), decisions taken pursuant to Article 8 (3) concerning notified concentrations must be taken within not more than four months of the date on which the proceeding is initiated.

4. The period set by paragraphs 1 and 3 shall exceptionally be suspended where, owing to circumstances for which one of the undertakings involved in the concentration is responsible, the Commission has had to request information by decision pursuant to Article 11 or to order an investigation by decision pursuant to Article 13.

5. Where the Court of Justice gives a judgment which annuls the whole or part of a Commission decision taken under this Regulation, the periods laid down in this Regulation shall start again from the date of the judgment.

6. Where the Commission has not taken a decision in accordance with Article 6 (1) (b) or (c) or Article 8 (2) or (3) within the deadlines set in paragraphs 1 and 3 respectively, the concentration shall be deemed declared compatible with the common market, without prejudice to Article 9.

Article 11 Requests for information

1. In carrying out the duties assigned to it by this Regulation, the Commission may obtain all necessary information from the Governments and competent authorities of the Member States, from the persons referred to in Article 3 (1) (b), and from undertakings and associations of undertakings.

2. When sending a request for information to a person, an undertaking or an association of undertakings, the Commission shall at the same time send a copy of the request to the competent authority of the Member State within the territory of which the residence of the person or the seat of the undertaking or association of undertakings is situated.

3. In its request the Commission shall state the legal basis and the purpose of the request and also the penalties provided for in Article 14 (1) (b) for supplying incorrect information.

4.   The information requested shall be provided, in the case of undertakings, by their owners or their representatives and, in the case of legal persons, companies or firms, or of associations having no legal personality, by the persons authorized to represent them by law or by their statutes.

5.   Where a person, an undertaking or an association of undertakings does not provide the information requested within the period fixed by the Commission or provides incomplete information, the Commission shall by decision require the information to be provided. The decision shall specify what information is required, fix an appropriate period within which it is to be supplied and state the penalties provided for in Articles 14 (1) (b) and 15 (1) (a) and the right to have the decision reviewed by the Court of Justice.

6.   The Commission shall at the same time send a copy of its decision to the competent authority of the Member State within the territory of which the residence of the person or the seat of the undertaking or association of undertakings is situated.

Article 12 Investigations by the authorities of the Member States

1.   At the request of the Commission, the competent authorities of the Member States shall undertake the investigations which the Commission considers to be necessary pursuant to Article 13 (1), or which it has ordered by decision pursuant to Article 13 (3). The officials of the competent authorities of the Member States responsible for conducting those investigations shall exercise their powers upon production of an authorization in writing issued by the competent authority of the Member State within the territory of which the investigation is to be carried out. Such authorization shall specify the subject matter and purpose of the investigation.

2.   If so requested by the Commission or by the competent authority of the Member State within the territory of which the investigation is to be carried out, officials of the Commission may assist the officials of that authority in carrying out their duties.

Article 13 Investigative powers of the Commission

1.   In carrying out the duties assigned to it by this Regulation, the Commission may undertake all necessary investigations into undertakings and associations of undertakings.

To that end the officials authorized by the Commission shall be empowered:
(a) to examine the books and other business records;
(b) to take or demand copies of or extracts from the books and business records;
(c) to ask for oral explanations on the spot;
(d) to enter any premises, land and means of transport of undertakings.

2.   The officials of the Commission authorized to carry out the investigations shall exercise their powers on production of an authorization in writing specifying the subject matter and purpose of the investigation and the penalties provided for in Article 14 (1) (c) in cases where production of the required books or other business records is incomplete. In good time before the investigation, the Commission shall inform, in writing, the competent authority of the Member State within the territory of which the investigation is to be carried out of the investigation and of the identities of the authorized officials.

3.   Undertakings and associations of undertakings shall submit to investigations ordered by decision of the Commission. The decision shall specify the subject matter and purpose of the investigation, appoint the date on which it shall begin and state the penalties provided for in Articles 14 (1) (c) and 15 (1) (b) and the right to have the decision reviewed by the Court of Justice.

4.   The Commission shall in good time and in writing inform the competent authority of the Member State within the territory of which the investigation is to be carried out

of its intention of taking a decision pursuant to paragraph 3. It shall hear the competent authority before taking its decision.

5. Officials of the competent authority of the Member State within the territory of which the investigation is to be carried out may, at the request of that authority or of the Commission, assist the officials of the Commission in carrying out their duties.

6. Where an undertaking or association of undertakings opposes an investigation ordered pursuant to this Article, the Member State concerned shall afford the necessary assistance to the officials authorized by the Commission to enable them to carry out their investigation. To this end the Member States shall, after consulting the Commission, take the necessary measures within one year of the entry into force of this Regulation.

Article 14 Fines

1. The Commission may by decision impose on the persons referred to in Article 3 (1) (b), undertakings or associations of undertakings fines of from ECU 1.000 to 50.000 where intentionally or negligently:
(a) they omit to notify a concentration in accordance with Article 4;
(b) they supply incorrect or misleading information in a notification pursuant to Article 4;
(c) they supply incorrect information in response to a request made pursuant to Article 11 or fail to supply information within the period fixed by a decision taken pursuant to Article 11;
(d) they produce the required books or other business records in incomplete form during investigations pursuant to Article 12 or 13, or refuse to submit to an investigation ordered by decision taken pursuant to Article 13.

2. The Commission may by decision impose fines not exceeding 10% of the aggregate turnover of the undertakings concerned within the meaning of Article 5 on the persons or undertakings concerned where, either intentionally or negligently, they;
(a) fail to comply with an obligation imposed by decision pursuant to Article 7 (4) or 8 (2), second subparagraph;
(b) put into effect a concentration in breach of Article 7 (1) or disregard a decision taken pursuant to Article 7 (2);
(c) put into effect a concentration declared incompatible with the common market by decision pursuant to Article 8 (3) or do not take the measures ordered by decision pursuant to Article 8 (4).

3. In setting the amount of a fine, regard shall be had to the nature and gravity of the infringement.

4. Decisions taken pursuant to paragraphs 1 and 2 shall not be of a criminal law nature.

Article 15 Periodic penalty payments

1. The Commission may by decision impose on the persons referred to in Article 3 (1) (b), undertakings or associations of undertakings concerned periodic penalty payments of up to ECU 25.000 for each day of the delay calculated from the date set in the decision, in order to compel them:
(a) to supply complete and correct information which it has requested by decision pursuant to Article 11;
(b) to submit to an investigation which it has ordered by decision pursuant to Article 13.

2. The Commission may by decision impose on the persons referred to in Article 3 (1) (b) or on undertakings periodic penalty payments of up to ECU 100.000 for each day of the delay calculated from the date set in the decision, in order to compel them:

(a) to comply with an obligation imposed by decision pursuant to Article 7 (4) or 8 (2), second subparagraph, or

(b) to apply the measures ordered by decision pursuant to Article 8 (4).

3.   Where the persons referred to in Article 3 (1) (b), undertakings or associations of undertakings have satisfied the obligation which it was the purpose of the periodic penalty payment to enforce, the Commission may set the total amount of the periodic penalty payments at a lower figure than that which would arise under the original decision.

Article 16 Review by the Court of Justice

The Court of Justice shall have unlimited jurisdiction within the meaning of Article 172 of the Treaty to review decisions whereby the Commission has fixed a fine or periodic penalty payments; it may cancel, reduce or increase the fine or periodic penalty payment imposed.

Article 17 Professional secrecy

1.   Information acquired as a result of the application of Articles 11, 12, 13 and 18 shall be used only for the purposes of the relevant request, investigation or hearing.

2.   Without prejudice to Articles 4 (3), 18 and 20, the Commission and the competent authorities of the Member States, their officials other servants shall not disclose information they have acquired through the application of this Regulation of the kind covered by the obligation of professional secrecy.

3.   Paragraphs 1 and 2 shall not prevent publication of general information or of surveys which do not contain information relating to particular undertakings or associations of undertakings.

Article 18 Hearing of the parties and of third persons

1.   Before taking any decision provided for in Article 7 (4), 8 (2), second subparagraph, and (3) to (5), 14 and 15, the Commission shall give the persons, undertakings and associations of undertakings concerned the opportunity, at every stage of the procedure up to the consultation of the Advisory Committee, of making known their views on the objections against them.

2.   By way of derogation from paragraph 1, a decision to grant a derogation from suspension as referred to in Article 7 (4) may be taken provisionally, without the persons, undertakings or associations of undertakings concerned being given the opportunity to make known their views beforehand, provided that the Commission gives them that opportunity as soon as possible after having taken its decision.

3.   The Commission shall base its decision only on objections on which the parties have been able to submit their observations. The rights of the defence shall be fully respected in the proceedings. Access to the file shall be open at least to the parties directly involved, subject to the legitimate interest of undertakings in the protection of their business secrets.

4.   Insofar as the Commission and the competent authorities of the Member States deem it necessary, they may also hear other natural or legal persons. Natural or legal persons showing a legitimate interest and especially members of the administrative or management organs of the undertakings concerned or recognized workers' representatives of those undertakings shall be entitled, upon application, to be heard.

Article 19 Liaison with the authorities of the Member States

1.   The Commission shall transmit to the competent authorities of the Member States copies of notifications within three working days and, as soon as possible, copies of the most important documents lodged with or issued by the Commission pursuant to this

Regulation. Such documents shall include commitments which are intended by the parties to form the basis for a decision pursuant to Articles 6 (1) (b) or 8 (2).

2.   The Commission shall carry out the procedures set out in this Regulation in close and constant liaison with the competent authorities of the Member States, which may express their views upon those procedures. For the purposes of Article 9 it shall obtain information from the competent authority of the Member State as referred to in paragraph 2 of that Article and give it the opportunity to make known its views at every stage of the procedure up to the adoption of a decision pursuant to paragraph 3 of that Article; to that end it shall give it access to the file.

3.   An Advisory Committee on concentrations shall be consulted before any decision is taken pursuant to Articles 8 (2) to (5), 14 or 15, or any provisions are adopted pursuant to Article 23.

4.   The Advisory Committee shall consist of representatives of the authorities of the Member States. Each Member State shall appoint one or two representatives; if unable to attend, they may be replaced by other representatives. At least one of the representatives of a Member State shall be competent in matters of restrictive practices and dominant positions.

5.   Consultation shall take place at a joint meeting convened at the invitation of and chaired by the Commission. A summary of the facts, together with the most important documents and a preliminary draft of the decision to be taken for each case considered, shall be sent with the invitation. The meeting shall take place not less than 14 days after the invitation has been sent. The Commission may in exceptional cases shorten that period as appropriate in order to avoid serious harm to one or more of the undertakings concerned by a concentration.

6.   The Advisory Committee shall deliver an opinion on the Commission's draft decision, if necessary by taking a vote. The Advisory Committee may deliver an opinion even if some members are absent and unrepresented. The opinion shall be delivered in writing and appended to the draft decision. The Commission shall take the utmost account of the opinion delivered by the Committee. It shall inform the Committee of the manner in which its opinion has been taken into account.

7.   The Advisory Committee may recommend publication of the opinion. The Commission may carry out such publication. The decision to publish shall take due account of the legitimate interest of undertakings in the protection of their business secrets and of the interest of the undertakings concerned in such publication taking place.

Article 20 Publication of decisions

1.   The Commission shall publish the decisions which it takes pursuant to Article 8 (2), where conditions and obligations are attached to them, and to Article 8 (2) to (5) in the Official Journal of the European Communities.

2.   The publication shall state the names of the parties and the main content of the decision; it shall have regard to the legitimate interest of undertakings in the protection of their business secrets.

Article 21 Jurisdiction

1.   Subject to review by the Court of Justice, the Commission shall have sole competence to take the decisions provided for in this Regulation.

2.   No Member State shall apply its national legislation on competition to any concentration that has a Community dimension.

The first subparagraph shall be without prejudice to any Member State's power to carry out any inquiries necessary for the application of Article 9 (2) or after referral, pursuant to Article 9 (3), first subparagraph, indent (b), or (5), to take the measures strictly necessary for the application of Article 9 (8).

3.   Notwithstanding paragraphs 1 and 2, Member States may take appropriate measures to protect legitimate interests other than those taken into consideration by this Regulation and compatible with the general principles and other provisions of Community law. Public security, plurality of the media and prudential rules shall be regarded as legitimate interests within the meaning of the first subparagraph.

Any other public interest must be communicated to the Commission by the Member State concerned and shall be recognized by the Commission after an assessment of its compatibility with the general principles and other provisions of Community law before the measures referred to above may be taken. The Commission shall inform the Member State concerned of its decision within one month of that communication.

Article 22 Application of the Regulation

1.   This Regulation alone shall apply to concentrations as defined in Article 3, and Regulations No 17[1], 1017/68, 4056/86 and 3975/87 shall not apply, except in relation to joint ventures that do not have a Community dimension and which have their object or effect the coordination of the competitive behaviour of undertakings that remain independent.

2.   deleted

3.   If the Commission finds, at the request of a Member State or at the joint request of two or more Member States, that a concentration as defined in Article 3 that has no Community dimension within the meaning of Article 1 creates or strengthens a dominant position as a result of which effective competition would be significantly impeded within the territory of the Member State or States making the joint request, it may, insofar as that concentration affects trade between Member States, adopt the decisions provided for in Article 8 (2), second subparagraph, (3) and (4).

4.   Articles 2 (1) (a) and (b), 5, 6, 8 and 10 to 20 shall apply to a request made pursuant to paragraph 3. Article 7 shall apply to the extent that the concentration has not been put into effect on the date on which the Commission informs the parties that a request has been made.

The period within which proceedings may be initiated pursuant to Article 10 (1) shall begin on the day following that of the receipt of the request from the Member State or States concerned. The request must be made within one month at most of the date on which the concentration was made known to the Member State or to all Member States making a joint request or effected. This period shall begin on the date of the first of those events.

5.   Pursuant to paragraph 3 the Commission shall take only the measures strictly necessary to maintain or restore effective competition within the territory of the Member State or States at the request of which it intervenes.

Article 23 Implementing provisions

The Commission shall have the power to adopt implementing provisions concerning the form, content and other details of notifications pursuant to Article 4, time limits pursuant to Articles 7, 9, 10 and 22, and hearings pursuant to Article 18.

The Commission shall have the power to lay down the procedure and time limits for the submission of commitments pursuant to Articles 6 (1a) and 8 (2).

---

1   See above, p. 384.

Article 24 Relations with non-member countries

1.   The Member States shall inform the Commission of any general difficulties encountered by their undertakings with concentrations as defined in Article 3 in a non- member country.

2.   Initially not more than one year after the entry into force of this Regulation and thereafter periodically the Commission shall draw up a report examining the treatment accorded to Community undertakings, in the terms referred to in paragraphs 3 and 4, as regards concentrations in non-member countries. The Commission shall submit those reports to the Council, together with any recommendations.

3.   Whenever it appears to the Commission, either on the basis of the reports referred to in paragraph 2 or on the basis of other information, that a non-member country does not grant Community undertakings treatment comparable to that granted by the Community to undertakings from that non-member country, the Commission may submit proposals to the Council for the appropriate mandate for negotiation with a view to obtaining comparable treatment for Community undertakings.

4.   Measures taken pursuant to this Article shall comply with the obligations of the Community or of the Member States, without prejudice to Article 234 of the Treaty, under international agreements, whether bilateral or multilateral.

Article 25 Entry into force

1.   This Regulation shall enter into force on 21 September 1990.

2.   This Regulation shall not apply to any concentration which was the subject of an agreement or announcement or where control was acquired within the meaning of Article 4 (1) before the date of this Regulation's entry into force and it shall not in any circumstances apply to any concentration in respect of which proceedings were initiated before that date by a Member State's authority with responsibility for competition.

This Regulation shall be binding in its entirety and directly applicable in all Member States.
Done at Brussels, 21 December 1989.

Commission Regulation 447/98 of 1 March 1998 on the Notifications, Time Limits and Hearings Provided for in Council Regulation 4064/89 on the Control of Concentrations Between Undertakings[1]

THE COMMISSION OF THE EUROPEAN COMMUNITIES,

HAVING REGARD to the Treaty establishing the European Community, [...]
HAVING REGARD to Council Regulation 4064/89 of 21 December 1989 on the control of concentrations between undertakings,[2] [...]
(1) WHEREAS Regulation 4064/89 and in particular Article 23 thereof has been amended by Regulation 1310/97;
(2) WHEREAS Commission Regulation 3384/94, implementing Regulation 4064/89, must be modified in order to take account of those amendments; whereas experience in the application of Regulation 3384/94 has revealed the need to improve certain pro-

---

1   OJ 1998 L 61, p. 1.

2   See above, p. 451.

cedural aspects thereof; whereas for the sake of clarity it should therefore be replaced by a new regulation;

(3) WHEREAS the Commission has adopted Decision 94/810 of 12 December 1994 on the terms of reference of hearing officers in competition procedures before the Commission;[1]

(4) WHEREAS Regulation 4064/89 is based on the principle of compulsory notification of concentrations before they are put into effect; whereas, on the one hand, a notification has important legal consequences which are favourable to the parties to the concentration plan, while, on the other hand, failure to comply with the obligation to notify renders the parties liable to a fine and may also entail civil law disadvantages for them; whereas it is therefore necessary in the interests of legal certainty to define precisely the subject matter and content of the information to be provided in the notification;

(5) WHEREAS it is for the notifying parties to make full and honest disclosure to the Commission of the facts and circumstances which are relevant for taking a decision on the notified concentration;

(6) WHEREAS in order to simplify and expedite examination of the notification, it is desirable to prescribe that a form be used;

(7) WHEREAS since notification sets in motion legal time limits pursuant to Regulation 4064/89, the conditions governing such time-limits and the time when they become effective must also be determined;

(8) WHEREAS rules must be laid down in the interests of legal certainty for calculating the time limits provided for in Regulation 4064/89; whereas in particular, the beginning and end of the period and the circumstances suspending the running of the period must be determined, with due regard to the requirements resulting from the exceptionally short legal time-limits referred to above; whereas in the absence of specific provisions the determination of rules applicable to periods, dates and time-limits should be based on the principles of Council Regulation 1182/71;[2]

(9) WHEREAS the provisions relating to the Commission's procedure must be framed in such a way as to safeguard fully the right to be heard and the rights of defence; whereas for these purposes the Commission should distinguish between the parties who notify the concentration, other parties involved in the concentration plan, third parties and parties regarding whom the Commission intends to take a decision imposing a fine or periodic penalty payments;

(10) WHEREAS the Commission should give the notifying parties and other parties involved, if they so request, an opportunity before notification to discuss the intended concentration informally and in strict confidence; whereas in addition it should, after notification, maintain close contact with those parties to the extent necessary to discuss with them any practical or legal problems which it discovers on a first examination of the case and if possible to remove such problems by mutual agreement;

(11) WHEREAS in accordance with the principle of the rights of defence, the notifying parties must be given the opportunity to submit their comments on all the objections which the Commission proposes to take into account in its decisions; whereas the other parties involved should also be informed of the Commission's objections and granted the opportunity to express their views;

(12) WHEREAS third parties having sufficient interest must also be given the opportunity of expressing their views where they make a written application;

---

1   OJ 1994 L 330, p. 67.

2   OJ 1971 L 124, p. 1.

(13) WHEREAS the various persons entitled to submit comments should do so in writing, both in their own interest and in the interest of good administration, without prejudice to their right to request a formal oral hearing where appropriate to supplement the written procedure; whereas in urgent cases, however, the Commission must be able to proceed immediately to formal oral hearings of the notifying parties, other parties involved or third parties;

(14) WHEREAS it is necessary to define the rights of persons who are to be heard, to what extent they should be granted access to the Commission's file and on what conditions they may be represented or assisted;

(15) WHEREAS the Commission must respect the legitimate interest of undertakings in the protection of their business secrets and other confidential information;

(16) WHEREAS, in order to enable the Commission to carry out a proper assessment of commitments that have the purpose of rendering the concentration compatible with the common market, and to ensure due consultation with other parties involved, third parties and the authorities of the Member States as provided for in Regulation 4064/89, in particular Article 18(1) and (4) thereof, the procedure and time-limits for submitting such commitments as provided for in Article 6(2) and Article 8(2) of Regulation 4064/89 must be laid down;

(17) WHEREAS it is also necessary to define the rules for fixing and calculating the time limits for reply fixed by the Commission;

(18) WHEREAS the Advisory Committee on Concentrations must deliver its opinion on the basis of a preliminary draft decision; whereas it must therefore be consulted on a case after the inquiry into that case has been completed; whereas such consultation does not, however, prevent the Commission from reopening an inquiry if need be,

HAS ADOPTED THIS REGULATION:

Chapter I Notifications

Article 1 Persons entitled to submit notifications
1. Notifications shall be submitted by the persons or undertakings referred to in Article 4(2) of Regulation 4064/89.
2. Where notifications are signed by representatives of persons or of undertakings, such representatives shall produce written proof that they are authorised to act.
3. Joint notifications should be submitted by a joint representative who is authorised to transmit and to receive documents on behalf of all notifying parties.

Article 2 Submission of notifications
1. Notifications shall be submitted in the manner prescribed by form CO as shown in the Annex. Joint notifications shall be submitted on a single form.
2. One original and 23 copies of the form CO and the supporting documents shall be submitted to the Commission at the address indicated in form CO.
3. The supporting documents shall be either originals or copies of the originals; in the latter case the notifying parties shall confirm that they are true and complete.
4. Notifications shall be in one of the official languages of the Community. This language shall also be the language of the proceeding for the notifying parties. Supporting documents shall be submitted in their original language. Where the original language is not one of the official languages of the Community, a translation into the language of the proceeding shall be attached.
5. Where notifications are made pursuant to Article 57 of the EEA Agreement, [...]

Article 3 Information and documents to be provided

1.   Notifications shall contain the information, including documents, requested by form CO. The information must be correct and complete.

2.   The Commission may dispense with the obligation to provide any particular information, including documents, requested by form CO where the Commission considers that such information is not necessary for the examination of the case.

3.   The Commission shall without delay acknowledge in writing to the notifying parties or their representatives receipt of the notification and of any reply to a letter sent by the Commission pursuant to Article 4(2) and (4).

Article 4 Effective date of notification

1.   Subject to paragraphs 2, 3 and 4, notifications shall become effective on the date on which they are received by the Commission.

2.   Where the information, including documents, contained in the notification is incomplete in a material respect, the Commission shall inform the notifying parties or their representatives in writing without delay and shall set an appropriate time-limit for the completion of the information. In such cases, the notification shall become effective on the date on which the complete information is received by the Commission.

3.   Material changes in the facts contained in the notification which the notifying parties know or ought to have known must be communicated to the Commission without delay. In such cases, when these material changes could have a significant effect on the appraisal of the concentration, the notification may be considered by the Commission as becoming effective on the date on which the information on the material changes is received by the Commission; the Commission shall inform the notifying parties or their representatives of this in writing and without delay.

4.   Incorrect or misleading information shall be considered to be incomplete information.

5.   When the Commission publishes the fact of the notification pursuant to Article 4(3) of Regulation 4064/89, it shall specify the date upon which the notification has been received. Where, further to the application of paragraphs 2, 3 and 4, the effective date of notification is later than the date specified in this publication, the Commission shall issue a further publication in which it will state the later date.

Article 5 Conversion of notifications

1.   Where the Commission finds that the operation notified does not constitute a concentration within the meaning of Article 3 of Regulation 4064/89, it shall inform the notifying parties or their representatives in writing. In such a case, the Commission shall, if requested by the notifying parties, as appropriate and subject to paragraph 2 of this Article, treat the notification as an application within the meaning of Article 2 or a notification within the meaning of Article 4 of Regulation No 17, as an application within the meaning of Article 12 or a notification within the meaning of Article 14 of Regulation 1017/68, as an application within the meaning of Article 12 of Regulation 4056/86 or as an application within the meaning of Article 3(2) or of Article 5 of Regulation 3975/87.

2.   In cases referred to in paragraph 1, second sentence, the Commission may require that the information given in the notification be supplemented within an appropriate time-limit fixed by it in so far as this is necessary for assessing the operation on the basis of the Regulations referred to in that sentence. The application or notification shall be deemed to fulfil the requirements of such Regulations from the date of the original notification where the additional information is received by the Commission within the time-limit fixed.

Chapter II Time-limits

Article 6 Beginning of periods

1.   The period referred to in Article 9(2) of Regulation 4064/89 shall start at the beginning of the working day following the date of the receipt of the copy of the notification by the Member State.

2.   The period referred to in Article 9(4)(b) of Regulation 4064/89 shall start at the beginning of the working day following the effective date of the notification, within the meaning of Article 4 of this Regulation.

3.   The period referred to in Article 9(6) of Regulation 4064/89 shall start at the beginning of the working day following the date of the Commission's referral.

4.   The periods referred to in Article 10(1) of Regulation 4064/89 shall start at the beginning of the working day following the effective date of the notification, within the meaning of Article 4 of this Regulation.

5.   The period referred to in Article 10(3) of Regulation 4064/89 shall start at the beginning of the working day following the day on which proceedings were initiated.

6.   The period referred to in Article 22(4), second subparagraph, second sentence, of Regulation 4064/89 shall start at the beginning of the working day following the date of the first of the events referred to.

Article 7 End of periods

1.   The period referred to in Article 9(2) of Regulation 4064/89 shall end with the expiry of the day which in the third week following that in which the period began is the same day of the week as the day from which the period runs.

2.   The period referred to in Article 9(4)(b) of Regulation 4064/89 shall end with the expiry of the day which in the third month following that in which the period began falls on the same date as the day from which the period runs. Where such a day does not occur in that month, the period shall end with the expiry of the last day of that month.

3.   The period referred to in Article 9(6) of Regulation 4064/89 shall end with the expiry of the day which in the fourth month following that in which the period began falls on the same date as the day from which the period runs. Where such a day does not occur in that month, the period shall end with the expiry of the last day of that month.

4.   The period referred to in Article 10(1), first subparagraph, of Regulation 4064/89 shall end with the expiry of the day which in the month following that in which the period began falls on the same date as the day from which the period runs. Where such a day does not occur in that month, the period shall end with the expiry of the last day of that month.

5.   The period referred to in Article 10(1), second subparagraph, of Regulation 4064/89 shall end with the expiry of the day which in the sixth week following that in which the period began is the same day of the week as the day from which the period runs.

6.   The period referred to in Article 10(3) of Regulation 4064/89 shall end with the expiry of the day which in the fourth month following that in which the period began falls on the same date as the day from which the period runs. Where such a day does not occur in that month, the period shall end with the expiry of the last day of that month.

7.   The period referred to in Article 22(4), second subparagraph, second sentence, of Regulation 4064/89 shall end with the expiry of the day which in the month following that in which the period began falls on the same date as the day from which the period runs. Where such a day does not occur in that month, the period shall end with the expiry of the last day of that month.

8.   Where the last day of the period is not a working day, the period shall end with the expiry of the following working day.

Article 8 Recovery of holidays

Once the end of the period has been determined in accordance with Article 7, if public holidays or other holidays of the Commission referred to in Article 23 fall within the periods referred to in Articles 9, 10 and 22 of Regulation 4064/89, a corresponding number of working days shall be added to those periods.

Article 9 Suspension of time limit

1.   The periods referred to in Article 10(1) and (3) of Regulation 4064/89 shall be suspended where the Commission, pursuant to Article 11(5) and Article 13(3) of that Regulation, has to take a decision because:

(a) information which the Commission has requested pursuant to Article 11(1) of Regulation 4064/89 from one of the notifying parties or another involved party, as defined in Article 11 of this Regulation, is not provided or not provided in full within the time limit fixed by the Commission;

(b) information which the Commission has requested pursuant to Article 11(1) of Regulation 4064/89 from a third party, as defined in Article 11 of this Regulation, is not provided or not provided in full within the time limit fixed by the Commission owing to circumstances for which one of the notifying parties or another involved party, as defined in Article 11 of this Regulation, is responsible;

(c) one of the notifying parties or another involved party, as defined in Article 11 of this Regulation, has refused to submit to an investigation deemed necessary by the Commission on the basis of Article 13(1) of Regulation 4064/89 or to cooperate in the carrying out of such an investigation in accordance with that provision;

(d) the notifying parties have failed to inform the Commission of material changes in the facts contained in the notification.

2.   The periods referred to in Article 10(1) and (3) of Regulation 4064/89 shall be suspended:

(a) in the cases referred to in paragraph 1(a) and (b), for the period between the end of the time limit fixed in the request for information and the receipt of the complete and correct information required by decision;

(b) in the cases referred to in paragraph 1(c), for the period between the unsuccessful attempt to carry out the investigation and the completion of the investigation ordered by decision;

(c) in the cases referred to in paragraph 1(d), for the period between the occurrence of the change in the facts referred to therein and the receipt of the complete and correct information requested by decision or the completion of the investigation ordered by decision.

3.   The suspension of the time limit shall begin on the day following that on which the event causing the suspension occurred. It shall end with the expiry of the day on which the reason for suspension is removed. Where such a day is not a working day, the suspension of the time-limit shall end with the expiry of the following working day.

Article 10 Compliance with the time-limits

1.   The time limits referred to in Article 9(4) and (5), and Article 10(1) and (3) of Regulation 4064/89 shall be met where the Commission has taken the relevant decision before the end of the period.

2.   The time limit referred to in Article 9(2) of Regulation 4064/89 shall be met where a Member State informs the Commission before the end of the period in writing.

3.   The time limit referred to in Article 9(6) of Regulation 4064/89 shall be met where the competent authority of the Member State concerned publishes any report or announces the findings of the examination of the concentration before the end of the period.

4.   The time limit referred to in Article 22(4), second subparagraph, second sentence, of Regulation 4064/89 shall be met where the request made by the Member State or the Member States is received by the Commission before the end of the period.

Chapter III Hearing of the Parties and of Third Parties

Article 11 Parties to be heard

For the purposes of the rights to be heard pursuant to Article 18 of Regulation 4064/89, the following parties are distinguished:
(a) notifying parties, that is, persons or undertakings submitting a notification pursuant to Article 4(2) of Regulation 4064/89;
(b) other involved parties, that is, parties to the concentration plan other than the notifying parties, such as the seller and the undertaking which is the target of the concentration;
(c) third parties, that is, natural or legal persons showing a sufficient interest, including customers, suppliers and competitors, and especially members of the administration or management organs of the undertakings concerned or recognised workers' representatives of those undertakings;
(d) parties regarding whom the Commission intends to take a decision pursuant to Article 14 or 15 of Regulation 4064/89.

Article 12 Decisions on the suspension of concentrations

1.   Where the Commission intends to take a decision pursuant to Article 7(4) of Regulation 4064/89 which adversely affects one or more of the parties, it shall, pursuant to Article 18(1) of that Regulation, inform the notifying parties and other involved parties in writing of its objections and shall fix a time limit within which they may make known their views.
2.   Where the Commission, pursuant to Article 18(2) of Regulation 4064/89, has taken a decision referred to in paragraph 1 of this Article provisionally without having given the notifying parties and other involved parties the opportunity to make known their views, it shall without delay send them the text of the provisional decision and shall fix a time limit within which they may make known their views. Once the notifying parties and other involved parties have made known their views, the Commission shall take a final decision annulling, amending or confirming the provisional decision. Where they have not made known their views within the time limit fixed, the Commission's provisional decision shall become final with the expiry of that period.
3.   The notifying parties and other involved parties shall make known their views in writing or orally within the time limit fixed. They may confirm their oral statements in writing.

Article 13 Decisions on the substance of the case

1.   Where the Commission intends to take a decision pursuant to Article 8(2), second subparagraph, or Article 8(3), (4) or (5) of Regulation 4064/89, it shall, before consulting the Advisory Committee on Concentrations, hear the parties pursuant to Article 18(1) and (3) of that Regulation.
2.   The Commission shall address its objections in writing to the notifying parties. The Commission shall, when giving notice of objections, set a time limit within which the notifying parties may inform the Commission of their views in writing. The Commission shall inform other involved parties in writing of these objections. The Commission shall also set a time limit within which those other involved parties may inform the Commission of their views in writing.

3.   After having addressed its objections to the notifying parties, the Commission shall, upon request, give them access to the file for the purpose of enabling them to exercise their rights of defence. The Commission shall, upon request, also give the other involved parties who have been informed of the objections access to the file in so far as this is necessary for the purposes of preparing their observations.

4.   The parties to whom the Commission's objections have been addressed or who have been informed of those objections shall, within the time limit fixed, make known in writing their views on the objections. In their written comments, they may set out all matters relevant to the case and may attach any relevant documents in proof of the facts set out. They may also propose that the Commission hear persons who may corroborate those facts. They shall submit one original and 29 copies of their response to the Commission at the address indicated in form CO.

5.   Where the Commission intends to take a decision pursuant to Article 14 or 15 of Regulation 4064/89 it shall, before consulting the Advisory Committee on Concentrations, hear pursuant to Article 18(1) and (3) of that Regulation the parties regarding whom the Commission intends to take such a decision. The procedure provided for in paragraph 2, first and second subparagraphs, paragraph 3, first subparagraph, and paragraph 4 is applicable, *mutatis mutandis*.

Article 14 Oral hearings

1.   The Commission shall afford the notifying parties who have so requested in their written comments the opportunity to put forward their arguments orally in a formal hearing if such parties show a sufficient interest. It may also in other cases afford such parties the opportunity of expressing their views orally.

2.   The Commission shall afford other involved parties who have so requested in their written comments the opportunity to express their views orally in a formal hearing if they show a sufficient interest. It may also in other cases afford such parties the opportunity of expressing their views orally.

3.   The Commission shall afford parties on whom it proposes to impose a fine or periodic penalty payment who have so requested in their written comments the opportunity to put forward their arguments orally in a formal hearing. It may also in other cases afford such parties the opportunity of expressing their views orally.

4.   The Commission shall invite the persons to be heard to attend on such date as it shall appoint.

5.   The Commission shall invite the competent authorities of the Member States, to take part in the hearing.

Article 15 Conduct of formal oral hearings

1.   Hearings shall be conducted by the Hearing Officer.

2.   Persons invited to attend shall either appear in person or be represented by legal representatives or by representatives authorised by their constitution as appropriate. Undertakings and associations of undertakings may be represented by a duly authorised agent appointed from among their permanent staff.

3.   Persons heard by the Commission may be assisted by their legal adviser or other qualified persons admitted by the Hearing Officer.

4.   Hearings shall not be public. Each person shall be heard separately or in the presence of other persons invited to attend. In the latter case, regard shall be had to the legitimate interest of the undertakings in the protection of their business secrets and other confidential information.

5.   The statements made by each person heard shall be recorded.

Article 16 Hearing of third parties

1. If third parties apply in writing to be heard pursuant to Article 18(4), second sentence, of Regulation 4064/89, the Commission shall inform them in writing of the nature and subject matter of the procedure and shall fix a time limit within which they may make known their views.
2. The third parties referred to in paragraph 1 shall make known their views in writing within the time limit fixed. The Commission may, where appropriate, afford the parties who have so requested in their written comments the opportunity to participate in a formal hearing. It may also in other cases afford such parties the opportunity of expressing their views orally.
3. The Commission may likewise afford to any other third parties the opportunity of expressing their views.

Article 17 Confidential information

1. Information, including documents, shall not be communicated or made accessible in so far as it contains business secrets of any person or undertaking, including the notifying parties, other involved parties or of third parties, or other confidential information the disclosure of which is not considered necessary by the Commission for the purpose of the procedure, or where internal documents of the authorities are concerned.
2. Any party which makes known its views under the provisions of this Chapter shall clearly identify any material which it considers to be confidential, giving reasons, and provide a separate non-confidential version within the time limit fixed by the Commission.

Chapter IV Commitments Rendering the Concentration Compatible

Article 18 Time limits for commitments

1. Commitments proposed to the Commission by the undertakings concerned pursuant to Article 6(2) of Regulation 4064/89 which are intended by the parties to form the basis for a decision pursuant to Article 6(1)(b) of that Regulation shall be submitted to the Commission within not more than three weeks from the date of receipt of the notification.
2. Commitments proposed to the Commission by the undertakings concerned pursuant to Article 8(2) of Regulation 4064/89 which are intended by the parties to form the basis for a decision pursuant to that Article shall be submitted to the Commission within not more than three months from the date on which proceedings were initiated. The Commission may in exceptional circumstances extend this period.
3. Articles 6 to 9 shall apply *mutatis mutandis* to paragraphs 1 and 2 of this Article.

Article 19 Procedure for commitments

1. One original and 29 copies of commitments proposed to the Commission by the undertakings concerned pursuant to Article 6(2) or Article 8(2) of Regulation 4064/89 shall be submitted to the Commission at the address indicated in form CO.
2. Any party proposing commitments to the Commission pursuant to Articles 6(2) or Article 8(2) of Regulation 4064/89 shall clearly identify any material which it considers to be confidential, giving reasons, and provide a separate non-confidential version within the time limit fixed by the Commission.

Chapter V Miscellaneous Provisions

Article 20 Transmission of documents

1.   Transmission of documents and invitations from the Commission to the addressees may be effected in any of the following ways:
(a) delivery by hand against receipt;
(b) registered letter with acknowledgement of receipt;
(c) fax with a request for acknowledgement of receipt;
(d) telex;
(e) electronic mail with a request for acknowledgement of receipt.
2.   Unless otherwise provided in this Regulation, paragraph 1 also applies to the transmission of documents from the notifying parties, from other involved parties or from
third parties to the Commission.
3.   Where a document is sent by telex, by fax or by electronic mail, it shall be presumed that it has been received by the addressee on the day on which it was sent.

Article 21 Setting of time limits

In fixing the time limits provided for pursuant to Article 4(2), Article 5(2), Article12(1)
and (2), Article 13(2) and Article 16(1), the Commission shall have regard to the time
required for preparation of statements and to the urgency of the case. It shall also take
account of working days as well as public holidays in the country of receipt of the Commission's communication. These time limits shall be set in terms of a precise calendar
date.

Article 22 Receipt of documents by the Commission

1.   In accordance with the provisions of Article 4(1) of this Regulation, notifications
must be delivered to the Commission at the address indicated in form CO or have
been dispatched by registered letter to the address indicated in form CO before the expiry of the period referred to in Article 4(1) of Regulation 4064/89. Additional information
requested to complete notifications pursuant to Article 4(2) and (4) or to supplement
notifications pursuant to Article 5(2) must reach the Commission at the aforesaid
address or have been dispatched by registered letter before the expiry of the time limit
fixed in each case. Written comments on Commission communications pursuant to Article 12(1) and (2), Article 13(2) and Article 16(1) must have reached the Commission
at the aforesaid address before the expiry of the time limit fixed in each case.
2.   Time limits referred to in subparagraphs two and three of paragraph 1 shall be determined in accordance with Article 21.
3.   Should the last day of a time limit fall on a day which is not a working day or which
is a public holiday in the country of dispatch, the time limit shall expire on the following
working day.

Article 23 Definition of working days

The expression "working days" in this Regulation means all days other than Saturdays,
Sundays, public holidays and other holidays as determined by the Commission and
published in the Official Journal of the European Communities before the beginning of
each year.

Article 24 Repeal

Regulation 3384/94 is repealed.

Article 25 Entry into force

This Regulation shall enter into force on 21 March 1998.

This Regulation shall be binding in its entirety and directly applicable in all Member States.

Done at Brussels, 1 March 1998.
For the Commission, Karel VAN MIERT, Member of the Commission

Form CO Relating to the Notification of a Concentration Pursuant to Regulation 4064/89

INTRODUCTION

A. The purpose of this form
This form specifies the information that must be provided by an undertaking or undertakings when notifying the Commission of a concentration with a Community dimension. A "concentration" is defined in Article 3 of Regulation 4064/89 (hereinafter referred to as "the Merger Regulation") and "Community dimension" in Article 1 thereof. Your attention is drawn to the Merger Regulation and to Regulation 447/98 (hereinafter referred to as "the Implementing Regulation") and to the corresponding provisions of the Agreement on the European Economic Area (hereinafter referred to as "the EEA Agreement"). Experience has shown that pre-notification meetings are extremely valuable to both the notifying parties and the Commission in determining the precise amount of information required in a notification and, in the large majority of cases, will result in a significant reduction of the information required. Accordingly, notifying parties are encouraged to consult the Commission regarding the possibility of dispensing with the obligation to provide certain information (see Section B(g) on the possibility of dispensation).

B. The need for a correct and complete notification
All information required by this form must be correct and complete. The information required must be supplied in the appropriate section of this form. Annexes to this form shall only be used to supplement the information supplied in the form itself. In particular you should note that:
(a) In accordance with Article 10(1) of the Merger Regulation and Article 4(2) and (4) of the Implementing Regulation, the time limits of the Merger Regulation linked to the notification will not begin to run until all the information that has to be supplied with the notification has been received by the Commission. This requirement is to ensure that the Commission is able to assess the notified concentration within the strict time-limits provided by the Merger Regulation.
(b) The notifying parties should check carefully, in the course of preparing their notification, that contact names and numbers, and in particular fax numbers, provided to the Commission are accurate, relevant and up-to-date.
(c) Incorrect or misleading information in the notification will be considered to be incomplete information (Article 4(4) of the Implementing Regulation).
(d) If a notification is incomplete, the Commission will inform the notifying parties or their representatives of this in writing and without delay. The notification will only become effective on the date on which the complete and accurate information is received by the Commission (Article 10(1) of the Merger Regulation, Article 4(2) and (4) of the Implementing Regulation).
(e) Article 14(1)(b) of the Merger Regulation provides that incorrect or misleading information, where supplied intentionally or negligently, can make the notifying party or parties liable to fines of up to ECU 50.000. In addition, pursuant to Article 6(3)(a)

and Article 8(5)(a) of the Merger Regulation the Commission may also revoke its decision on the compatibility of a notified concentration where it is based on incorrect information for which one of the undertakings is responsible.

(f) You may request that the Commission accept that the notification is complete notwithstanding the failure to provide information required by this form, if such information is not reasonably available to you in part or in whole (for example, because of the unavailability of information on a target company during a contested bid). The Commission will consider such a request, provided that you give reasons for the unavailability of that information, and provide your best estimates for missing data together with the sources for the estimates. Where possible, indications as to where any of the requested information that is unavailable to you could be obtained by the Commission should also be provided.

(g) You may request that the Commission accept that the notification is complete notwithstanding the failure to provide information required by this form, if you consider that any particular information requested by this form, in the full or short form version, may not be necessary for the Commission's examination of the case. The Commission will consider such a request, provided that you give reasons why that information is not relevant and necessary to its inquiry into the notified operation. You may explain this during your pre-notification contacts with the Commission and/or in your notification and ask the Commission to dispense with the obligation to provide that information, pursuant to Article 3(2) of the Implementing Regulation.

C. Notification in short form

(a) In cases where a joint venture has no, or *de minimis*, actual or foreseen activities within the EEA territory, the Commission intends to allow notification of the operation by means of short form. Such cases occur where joint control is acquired by two or more undertakings, and where:

(i) the turnover[1] of the joint venture and/or the turnover of the contributed activities,[2] is less than ECU 100 million in the EEA territory; and

(ii) the total value of assets[3] transferred to the joint venture is less than ECU 100 million in the EEA territory.[4]

---

1   The turnover of the joint venture should be determined according to the most recent audited accounts of the parent companies, or the joint venture itself, depending upon the availability of separate accounts for the resources combined in the joint venture.

2   The expression "and/or" refers to the variety of situations covered by the short form; for example:
    —   in the case of the joint acquisition of a target company, the turnover to be taken into account is the turnover of this target (the joint venture),
    —   in the case of the creation of a joint venture to which the parent companies contribute their activities, the turnover to be taken into account is that of the contributed activities,
    —   in the case of entry of a new controlling party into an existing joint venture, the turnover of the joint venture and the turnover of the activities contributed by the new parent company (if any) must be taken into account.

3   The total value of assets of the joint venture should be determined according to the last regularly prepared and approved balance sheet of each parent company. The term "assets" includes: (1) all tangible and intangible assets that will be transferred to the joint venture (examples of tangible assets include production plants, wholesale or retail outlets, and inventory of goods), and (2) any amount of credit or any obligations of the joint venture which any parent company of the joint venture has agreed to extend or guarantee.

4   Where the assets transferred generate turnover, then neither the value of the assets nor that of the turnover may exceed ECU 100 million.

(b) If you consider that the operation to be notified meets these qualifications, you may explain this in your notification and ask the Commission to dispense with the obligation to provide the full-form notification, pursuant to Article 3(2) of the Implementing Regulation, and to allow you to notify by means of short form.

(c) Short-form notification allows the notifying parties to limit the information provided in the notification to the following sections and questions:
— Section 1,
— Section 2, except questions 2.1 (a, b and d), 2.3.4, and 2.3.5,
— Section 3, only questions 3.1 and 3.2 (a),
— Section 5, only questions 5.1 and 5.3,
— Section 6,
— Section 10,
— Section 11 (optional for the convenience of the parties), and
— Section 12,
— the five largest independent customers, the five largest independent suppliers, and the five largest competitors in the markets in which the joint venture will be active. Provide the name, address, telephone number, fax number and appropriate contact person of each such customer, supplier and competitor.

(d) In addition, with respect to the affected markets of the joint venture as defined in Section 6, indicate for the EEA territory, for the Community as a whole, for each Member State and EFTA State, and where different, in the opinion of the notifying parties, for the relevant geographic market, the sales in value and volume, as well as the market shares, for the year preceding the operation.

(e) The Commission may require full, or where appropriate partial, notification under the form CO where:
— the notified operation does not meet the short-form thresholds, or
— this appears to be necessary for an adequate investigation with respect to possible competition problems.

In such cases, the notification may be considered incomplete in a material respect pursuant to Article 4(2) of the Implementing Regulation. The Commission will inform the notifying parties or their representatives of this in writing and without delay and will fix a deadline for the submission of a full or, where appropriate, partial notification. The notification will only become effective on the date on which all information required is received.

D. Who must notify

In the case of a merger within the meaning of Article 3(1)(a) of the Merger Regulation or the acquisition of joint control in an undertaking within the meaning of Article 3(1)(b) of the Merger Regulation, the notification shall be completed jointly by the parties to the merger or by those acquiring joint control as the case may be. In case of the acquisition of a controlling interest in one undertaking by another, the acquirer must complete the notification.

In the case of a public bid to acquire an undertaking, the bidder must complete the notification. Each party completing the notification is responsible for the accuracy of the information which it provides.

E. How to notify

The notification must be completed in one of the official languages of the European Community. This language will thereafter be the language of the proceedings for all notifying parties. [...] The information requested by this form is to be set out using the sections and paragraph numbers of the form, signing a declaration as provided in Section 12, and annexing supporting documentation. Supporting documents are to be submitted in their original language; where this is not an official language of the Community, they must be translated into the language of the proceeding (Article 2(4) of the Implementing Regulation). Supporting documents may be originals or copies of the originals. In the latter case, the notifying party must confirm that they are true and complete. One original and 23 copies of the form CO and all supporting documents must be provided.

The notification must be delivered to the Commission on working days as defined by Article 23 of the Implementing Regulation. In order to enable it to be registered on the same day, it must be delivered before 17.00 on Mondays to Thursdays and before 16.00 on Fridays, at the following address:

Commission of the European Communities
Directorate-General for Competition (DG IV)
Merger Task Force
150 avenue de Cortenberg/Kortenberglaan 150
B-1049 Brussels.

F. Confidentiality
Article 214 of the Treaty and Article 17(2) of the Merger Regulation as well as the corresponding provisions of the EEA Agreement require the Commission, the Member States, the EFTA Surveillance Authority and the EFTA States, their officials and other servants not to disclose information they have acquired through the application of the Regulation of the kind covered by the obligation of professional secrecy. The same principle must also apply to protect confidentiality between notifying parties.

If you believe that your interests would be harmed if any of the information you are asked to supply were to be published or otherwise divulged to other parties, submit this information separately with each page clearly marked "Business Secrets". You should also give reasons why this information should not be divulged or published.

In the case of mergers or joint acquisitions, or in other cases where the notification is completed by more than one of the parties, business secrets may be submitted under separate cover, and referred to in the notification as an annex. All such annexes must be included in the submission in order for a notification to be considered complete.

G. Definitions and instructions for purposes of this form
— Notifying party or parties: in cases where a notification is submitted by only one of the undertakings party to an operation, "notifying parties" is used to refer only to the undertaking actually submitting the notification.
— Party(parties) to the concentration: these terms relate to both the acquiring and acquired parties, or to the merging parties, including all undertakings in which a controlling interest is being acquired or which is the subject of a public bid.

Except where otherwise specified, the terms "notifying party(parties)" and "party(parties) to the concentration" include all the undertakings which belong to the same groups as those "parties".
— Affected markets: Section 6 of this form requires the notifying parties to define the relevant product markets, and further to identify which of those relevant markets are likely to be affected by the notified operation. This definition of affected market is used as the basis for requiring information for a number of other questions contained in this form. The definitions thus submitted by the notifying parties are referred to in this form as the affected market(s). This term can refer to a relevant market made up either of products or of services.
— Year: all references to the word "year" in this form should be read as meaning calendar year, unless otherwise stated. All information requested in this form must,

unless otherwise specified, relate to the year preceding that of the notification. The financial data requested in Sections 2.3 to 2.5 must be provided in ecus at the average conversion rates prevailing for the years or other periods in question. All references contained in this form are to the relevant Articles and paragraphs of Council Regulation 4064/89, unless otherwise stated.

Section 1 Background Information

1.1. Information on notifying party (or parties)
Give details of:
1.1.1. name and address of undertaking;
1.1.2. nature of the undertaking's business;
1.1.3. name, address, telephone number, fax number and/or telex of, and position held by, the appropriate contact person.
1.2. Information on other parties[1] to the concentration
For each party to the concentration (except the notifying party or parties) give details of:
1.2.1. name and address of undertaking;
1.2.2. nature of undertaking's business;
1.2.3. name, address, telephone number, fax number and/or telex of, and position held by the appropriate contact person.
1.3. Address for service
Give an address (in Brussels if available) to which all communications may be made and documents delivered.
1.4. Appointment of representatives
Where notifications are signed by representatives of undertakings, such representatives must produce written proof that they are authorised to act. If a joint notification is being submitted, has a joint representative been appointed? If yes, please give the details requested in Sections 1.4.1 to 1.4.4. If no, please give details of information of any representatives who have been authorised to act for each of the parties to the concentration, indicating whom they represent:
1.4.1. name of representative;
1.4.2. address of representative;
1.4.3. name of person to be contacted (and address, if different from 1.4.2);
1.4.4. telephone number, fax number and/or telex.

Section 2 Details of the Concentration

2.1. Describe the nature of the concentration being notified. In doing so state:
(a) whether the proposed concentration is a full legal merger, an acquisition of sole or joint control, a full-function joint venture within the meaning of Article 3(2) of the Merger Regulation or a contract or other means of conferring direct or indirect control within the meaning of Article 3(3) of the Merger Regulation;
(b) whether the whole or parts of parties are subject to the concentration;
(c) a brief explanation of the economic and financial structure of the concentration;
(d) whether any public offer for the securities of one party by another party has the support of the former's supervisory boards of management or other bodies legally representing that party;
(e) the proposed or expected date of any major events designed to bring about the completion of the concentration;

---

1 This includes the target company in the case of a contested bid, in which case the details should be completed as far as is possible.

(f) the proposed structure of ownership and control after the completion of the con-
     centration;
(g) any financial or other support received from whatever source (including public
     authorities) by any of the parties and the nature and amount of this support.
2.2. List the economic sectors involved in the concentration
2.3. For each of the undertakings concerned by the concentration[1] provide the following
data[2] for the last financial year:
2.3.1. worldwide turnover;
2.3.2. Community-wide turnover;
2.3.3. EFTA- wide turnover;
2.3.4. turnover in each Member State;
2.3.5. turnover in each EFTA State;
2.3.6. the Member State, if any, in which more than two thirds of Community-wide turnover is achieved;[3]
2.3.7. the EFTA State, if any, in which more than two thirds of EFTA-wide turnover is
achieved.
2.4. For the purposes of Article 1(3) of the Merger Regulation, if the operation does not
meet the thresholds set out in Article 1(2), provide the following data for the last financial year:
2.4.1. the Member States, if any, in which the combined aggregate turnover of all the
undertakings concerned is more than ECU 100 million;
2.4.2. the Member States, if any, in which the aggregate turnover of each of at least
two of the undertakings concerned is more than ECU 25 million.
2.5. Provide the following information with respect to the last financial year:
2.5.1. does the combined turnover of the undertakings concerned in the territory of the
EFTA States equal 25% or more of their total turnover in the EEA territory?
2.5.2. does each of at least two undertakings concerned have a turnover exceeding
ECU 250 million in the territory of the EFTA States?

Section 3 Ownership and Control[4]

For each of the parties to the concentration provide a list of all undertakings belonging
to the same group. This list must include:
3.1. all undertakings or persons controlling these parties, directly or indirectly;
3.2. all undertakings active on any affected market[5] that are controlled, directly or indirectly:
(a) by these parties;
(b) by any other undertaking identified in 3.1. For each entry listed above, the nature
     and means of control should be specified. The information sought in this section

---

1 See Commission notice on the concept of undertakings concerned.

2 See, generally, the Commission notice on calculation of turnover. Turnover of the acquiring party
   or parties to the concentration should include the aggregated turnover of all undertakings within the
   meaning of Article 5(4). Turnover of the acquired party or parties should include the turnover relating
   to the parts subject to the transaction within the meaning of Article 5(2). Special provisions are
   contained in Articles 5(3), (4) and 5(5) for credit, insurance, other financial institutions and joint
   undertakings.

3 See Guidance Note III for the calculation of turnover in one Member State with respect to
   Community-wide turnover.

4 See Article 3(3), (4) and (5) and Article 5(4).

5 See Section 6 for the definition of affected markets.

may be illustrated by the use of organisation charts or diagrams to show the structure of ownership and control of the undertakings.

Section 4 Personal and Financial Links and Previous Acquisitions

With respect to the parties to the concentration and each undertaking or person identified in response to Section 3, provide:

4.1. a list of all other undertakings which are active on affected markets (affected markets are defined in Section 6 in which the undertakings, or persons, of the group hold individually or collectively 10% or more of the voting rights, issued share capital or other securities; in each case identify the holder and state the percentage held;

4.2. a list for each undertaking of the members of their boards of management who are also members of the boards of management or of the supervisory boards of any other undertaking which is active on affected markets; and (where applicable) for each undertaking a list of the members of their supervisory boards who are also members of the boards of management of any other undertaking which is active on affected markets; in each case identify the name of the other undertaking and the positions held;

4.3. details of acquisitions made during the last three years by the groups identified above (Section 3) of undertakings active in affected markets as defined in Section 6. Information provided here may be illustrated by the use of organisation charts or diagrams to give a better understanding.

Section 5 Supporting Documentation

Notifying parties must provide the following:

5.1. copies of the final or most recent versions of all documents bringing about the concentration, whether by agreement between the parties to the concentration, acquisition of a controlling interest or a public bid;

5.2. in a public bid, a copy of the offer document; if it is unavailable at the time of notification, it should be submitted as soon as possible and not later than when it is posted to shareholders;

5.3. copies of the most recent annual reports and accounts of all the parties to the concentration;

5.4. where at least one affected market is identified: copies of analyses, reports, studies and surveys submitted to or prepared for any member(s) of the board of directors, the supervisory board, or the shareholders' meeting, for the purpose of assessing or analysing the concentration with respect to competitive conditions, competitors (actual and potential), and market conditions.

Section 6 Market Definitions

The relevant product and geographic markets determine the scope within which the market power of the new entity resulting from the concentration must be assessed.[1] The notifying party or parties must provide the data requested having regard to the following definitions:

I. Relevant product markets

A relevant product market comprises all those products and/or services which are regarded as interchangeable or substitutable by the consumer, by reason of the products' characteristics, their prices and their intended use. A relevant product market may in some cases be composed of a number of individual products and/or services

---

1   See Commission notice on the definition of the relevant market for the purposes of Community competition law, [below at p. 501].

which present largely identical physical or technical characteristics and are inter-changeable. Factors relevant to the assessment of the relevant product market include the analysis of why the products or services in these markets are included and why others are excluded by using the above definition, and having regard to, for example, substitutability, conditions of competition, prices, cross-price elasticity of demand or other factors relevant for the definition of the product markets.

II. Relevant geographic markets

The relevant geographic market comprises the area in which the undertakings concerned are involved in the supply and demand of relevant products or services, in which the conditions of competition are sufficiently homogeneous and which can be distinguished from neighbouring geographic areas because, in particular, conditions of competition are appreciably different in those areas. Factors relevant to the assessment of the relevant geographic market include the nature and characteristics of the products or services concerned, the existence of entry barriers, consumer preferences, appreciable differences in the undertakings' market shares between neighbouring geographic areas or substantial price differences.

III. Affected markets

For purposes of information required in this form, affected markets consist of relevant product markets where, in the EEA territory, in the Community, in the territory of the EFTA States, in any Member State or in any EFTA State:
(a) two or more of the parties to the concentration are engaged in business activities in the same product market and where the concentration will lead to a combined market share of 15% or more. These are horizontal relationships;
(b) one or more of the parties to the concentration are engaged in business activities in a product market, which is upstream or downstream of a product market in which any other party to the concentration is engaged, and any of their individual or combined market shares is 25% or more, regardless of whether there is or is not any existing supplier/customer relationship between the parties to the concentration. These are vertical relationships.
On the basis of the above definitions and market share thresholds, provide the following information:
6.1. Identify each affected market within the meaning of Section III, at:
(a) the EEA, Community or EFTA level;
(b) the individual Member States or EFTA States level.

IV. Markets related to affected markets within the meaning of Section III

6.2. Describe the relevant product and geographic markets concerned by the notified operation, which are closely related to the affected market(s) (in upstream, downstream and horizontal neighbouring markets), where any of the parties to the concentration are active and which are not themselves affected markets within the meaning of Section III.

V. Non-affected markets

6.3. In case there are no affected markets in the meaning of Section 6.1, describe the product and geographic scope of the markets on which the notified operation would have an impact.

Section 7 Information on Affected Markets

For each affected relevant product market, for each of the last three financial years:[1]

(a) for the EEA territory,

(b) for the Community as a whole,

(c) for the territory of the EFTA States as a whole,

(d) individually for each Member State and EFTA State where the parties to the concentration do business,

(e) and, where in the opinion of the notifying parties, the relevant geographic market is different, provide the following:

7.1. an estimate of the total size of the market in terms of sales value (in ecus) and volume (units).[2] Indicate the basis and sources for the calculations and provide documents where available to confirm these calculations;

7.2. the sales in value and volume, as well as an estimate of the market shares, of each of the parties to the concentration;

7.3. an estimate of the market share in value (and where appropriate volume) of all competitors (including importers) having at least 10% of the geographic market under consideration. Provide documents where available to confirm the calculation of these market shares and provide the name, address, telephone number, fax number and appropriate contact person, of these competitors;

7.4. an estimate of the total value and volume and source of imports from outside the EEA territory and identify:

(a) the proportion of such imports that are derived from the groups to which the parties to the concentration belong,

(b) an estimate of the extent to which any quotas, tariffs or non-tariff barriers to trade, affect these imports, and

(c) an estimate of the extent to which transportation and other costs affect these imports,

7.5. the extent to which trade among States within the EEA territory is affected by:

(a) transportation and other costs, and

(b) other non-tariff barriers to trade;

7.6. the manner in which the parties to the concentration produce and sell the products and/or services; for example, whether they manufacture locally, or sell through local distribution facilities;

7.7. a comparison of price levels in each Member State and EFTA State by each party to the concentration and a similar comparison of price levels between the Community, the EFTA States and other areas where these products are produced (e.g. eastern Europe, the United States of America, Japan, or other relevant areas);

7.8. the nature and extent of vertical integration of each of the parties to the concentration compared with their largest competitors.

---

1 Without prejudice to Article 3(2) of the Implementing Regulation, the information required under 7.1 and 7.2 below must be provided with regard to all the territories under (a), (b), (c), (d) and (e).

2 The value and volume of a market should reflect output less exports plus imports for the geographic areas under consideration.

Section 8 General conditions in affected markets

8.1. Identify the five largest independent[1] suppliers to the parties and their individual shares of purchases from each of these suppliers (of raw materials or goods used for purposes of producing the relevant products). Provide the name, address, telephone number, fax number and appropriate contact person, of these suppliers.

Structure of supply in affected markets

8.2. Explain the distribution channels and service networks that exist on the affected markets. In so doing, take account of the following where appropriate:
(a) the distribution systems prevailing on the market and their importance. To what extent is distribution performed by third parties and/or undertakings belonging to the same group as the parties identified in Section 3?
(b) the service networks (for example, maintenance and repair) prevailing and their importance in these markets. To what extent are such services performed by third parties and/or undertakings belonging to the same group as the parties identified in Section 3?

8.3. Where appropriate, provide an estimate of the total Community-wide and EFTA-wide capacity for the last three years. Over this period what proportion of this capacity is accounted for by each of the parties to the concentration, and what have been their respective rates of capacity utilisation.

8.4. If you consider any other supply-side considerations to be relevant, they should be specified.

Structure of demand in affected markets

8.5. Identify the five largest independent customers of the parties in each affected market and their individual share of total sales for such products accounted for by each of those customers. Provide the name, address, telephone number, fax number and appropriate contact person, of each of these customers.

8.6. Explain the structure of demand in terms of:
(a) the phases of the markets in terms of, for example, take-off, expansion, maturity and decline, and a forecast of the growth rate of demand;
(b) the importance of customer preferences, in terms of brand loyalty, product differentiation and the provision of a full range of products;
(c) the degree of concentration or dispersion of customers;
(d) segmentation of customers into different groups with a description of the "typical customer" of each group;
(e) the importance of exclusive distribution contracts and other types of long-term contracts;
(f) the extent to which public authorities, government agencies, State enterprises or similar bodies are important participants as a source of demand.

Market entry

8.7. Over the last five years, has there been any significant entry into any affected markets? If the answer is "yes", where possible provide their name, address, telephone number, fax number and appropriate contact person, and an estimate of their current market shares.

---

1   That is suppliers which are not subsidiaries, agents or undertakings forming part of the group of the party in question. In addition to those five independent suppliers the notifying parties can, if they consider it necessary for a proper assessment of the case, identify the intra-group suppliers. The same will apply in 8.5 in relation with customers.

8.8. In the opinion of the notifying parties are there undertakings (including those at present operating only in extra-Community or extra-EEA markets) that are likely to enter the market? If the answer is "yes", please explain why and identify such entrants by name, address, telephone number, fax number and appropriate contact person, and an estimate of the time within which such entry is likely to occur.

8.9. Describe the various factors influencing entry into affected markets that exist in the present case, examining entry from both a geographical and product viewpoint. In so doing, take account of the following where appropriate:

(a) the total costs of entry R&D, establishing distribution systems, promotion, advertising, servicing, etc.) on a scale equivalent to a significant viable competitor, indicating the market share of such a competitor;

(b) any legal or regulatory barriers to entry, such as government authorisation or standard setting in any form;

(c) any restrictions created by the existence of patents, know-how and other intellectual property rights in these markets and any restrictions created by licensing such rights;

(d) the extent to which each of the parties to the concentration are licensees or licensors of patents, know-how and other rights in the relevant markets;

(e) the importance of economies of scale for the production of products in the affected markets;

(f) access to sources of supply, such as availability of raw materials.

Research and development

8.10. Give an account of the importance of research and development in the ability of a firm operating on the relevant market(s) to compete in the long term. Explain the nature of the research and development in affected markets carried out by the parties to the concentration.

In so doing, take account of the following, where appropriate:

(a) trends and intensities of research and development[1] in these markets and for the parties to the concentration;

(b) the course of technological development for these markets over an appropriate time period (including developments in products and/or services, production processes, distribution systems, etc.);

(c) the major innovations that have been made in these markets and the undertakings responsible for these innovations;

(d) the cycle of innovation in these markets and where the parties are in this cycle of innovation.

Cooperative agreements

8.11. To what extent do cooperative agreements (horizontal or vertical) exist in the affected markets?

8.12. Give details of the most important cooperative agreements engaged in by the parties to the concentration in the affected markets, such as research and development, licensing, joint production, specialisation, distribution, long term supply and exchange of information agreements.

Trade associations

8.13. With respect to the trade associations in the affected markets:

---

1   Research and development intensity is defined as research development expenditure as a proportion of turnover.

(a) identify those in which the parties to the concentration are members;
(b) identify the most important trade associations to which the customers and suppliers of the parties to the concentration belong. Provide the name, address, telephone number, fax number and appropriate contact person of all trade associations listed above.

Section 9 General Market Information

Market data on conglomerate aspects
Where any of the parties to the concentration hold individually a market share of 25% or more for any product market in which there is no horizontal or vertical relationship as described above, provide the following information:

9.1. a description of each product market and explain why the products and/or services in these markets are included (and why others are excluded) by reason of their characteristics, prices and their intended use;

9.2. an estimate of the value of the market and the market shares of each of the groups to which the parties belong for each product market identified in 9.1 for the last financial year:
(a) for the EEA territory as a whole;
(b) for the Community as a whole;
(c) for the territory of the EFTA States as a whole;
(d) individually for each Member State and EFTA State where the groups to which the parties belong do business;
(e) and, where different, for the relevant geographic market.

Overview of the markets
9.3. Describe the worldwide context of the proposed concentration, indicating the position of each of the parties to the concentration outside of the EEA territory in terms of size and competitive strength.

9.4. Describe how the proposed concentration is likely to affect the interests of intermediate and ultimate consumers and the development of technical and economic progress.

Section 10 Cooperative Effects of a Joint Venture

10. For the purpose of Article 2(4) of the Merger Regulation please answer the following questions:
(a) Do two or more parents retain to a significant extent activities in the same market as the joint venture or in a market which is downstream or upstream from that of the joint venture or in a neighbouring market closely related to this market?[1] If the answer is affirmative, please indicate for each of the markets referred to here:
— the turnover of each parent company in the preceding financial year,
— the economic significance of the activities of the joint venture in relation to this turnover,
— the market share of each parent.
If the answer is negative, please justify your answer.
(b) If the answer to (a) is affirmative and in your view the creation of the joint venture does not lead to coordination between independent undertakings that restricts competition within the meaning of Article 85(1) of the EC Treaty, give your reasons.
(c) Without prejudice to the answers to (a) and (b) and in order to ensure that a complete assessment of the case can be made by the Commission, please explain

---

1   For market definitions refer to Section 6.

how the criteria of Article 85(3) apply. Under Article 85(3), the provisions of Article 85(1) may be declared inapplicable if the operation:
(i)   contributes to improving the production or distribution of goods, or to promoting technical or economic progress;
(ii) allows consumers a fair share of the resulting benefit;
(iii) does not impose on the undertakings concerned restrictions which are not indispensable to the attainment of these objectives; and
(iv) does not afford such undertakings the possibility of eliminating competition in respect of a substantial part of the products in question.

For guidance, please refer to form A/B, and in particular Sections 16 and 17 thereof, annexed to Commission Regulation 3385/94.[1]

Section 11 General Matters
Ancillary restraints
11.1. If the parties to the concentration, and/or other involved parties (including the seller and minority shareholders), enter into ancillary restrictions directly related and necessary to the implementation of the concentration, these restrictions may be assessed in conjunction with the concentration itself (see Article 6(1)(b) and Article 8(2) of the Merger Regulation, recital 25 to the Merger Regulation, recital 7 to Regulation 1310/97 and the Commission notice on restrictions ancillary to concentrations).[2]
(a) Identify each ancillary restriction in the agreements provided with the notification for which you request an assessment in conjunction with the concentration; and
(b) explain why these are directly related and necessary to the implementation of the concentration.

Conversion of notification
11.2. In the event that the Commission finds that the operation notified does not constitute a concentration within the meaning of Article 3 of the Merger Regulation, do you request that it be treated as an application for negative clearance from, or a notification to obtain an exemption from Article 85 of the EC Treaty?

Section 12 Declaration
Article 1(2) of the Implementing Regulation states that where notifications are signed by representatives of undertakings, such representatives must produce written proof that they are authorised to act. Such written authorisation must accompany the notification. The notification must conclude with the following declaration which is to be signed by or on behalf of all the notifying parties:

The undersigned declare that, to the best of their knowledge and belief, the information given in this notification is true, correct, and complete, that complete copies of documents required by form CO, have been supplied, and that all estimates are identified as such and are their best estimates of the underlying facts and that all the opinions expressed are sincere. They are aware of the provisions of Article 14(1)(b) of the Merger Regulation.
Place and date:
Signatures:
Name/s:
On behalf of:

---

1   See above, p. 392 and p. 395.

2   OJ 1997 L 180, p. 1.

GUIDANCE NOTE I: Calculation of turnover for insurance undertakings [...]
GUIDANCE NOTE II: Calculation of turnover for joint undertakings [...]
GUIDANCE NOTE III: Application of the two-thirds rule (Article 1) [...]

Commission Notice on the Concept of Concentration Under Council Regulation 4064/89 on the Control of Concentrations Between Undertakings[1]

I. Introduction

1.   The purpose of this Notice is to provide guidance as to how the Commission interprets the term "concentration" used in Article 3 of Council Regulation 4064/89 as [amended][2] (hereinafter referred to as "the Merger Regulation"). This formal guidance on the interpretation of Article 3 should enable firms to establish more quickly, in advance of any contact with the Commission, whether and to what extent their operations may be covered by Community merger control. This Notice replaces the Notice on the notion of a concentration.

This Notice deals with paragraphs (1), (3), (4) and (5) of Article 3. The interpretation of Article 3 in relation to joint ventures, dealt with in particular under Article 3(2), is set out in the Commission's Notice on the concept of full-function joint ventures.

2.   The guidance set out in this Notice reflects the Commission's experience in applying the Merger Regulation since it entered into force on 21 December 1990. The principles contained here will be applied and further developed by the Commission in individual cases.

3.   According to recital 23 to Regulation 4064/89, the concept of concentration is defined as covering only operations which bring about a lasting change in the structure of the undertakings concerned. Article 3(1) provides that such a structural change is brought about either by a merger between two previously independent undertakings or by the acquisition of control over the whole or part of another undertaking.

4. The determination of the existence of a concentration under the Merger Regulation is based upon qualitative rather than quantitative criteria, focussing on the concept of control. These criteria include considerations of both law and fact. It follows, therefore, that a concentration may occur on a legal or a *de facto* basis.

5.   Article 3(1) of the Merger Regulation defines two categories of concentration:
—   those arising from a merger between previously independent undertakings (point (a));
—   those arising from an acquisition of control (point (b)).
These are treated respectively in Sections II and III below.

II. Mergers between previously independent undertakings

6.   A merger within the meaning of Article 3(1)(a) of the Merger Regulation occurs when two or more independent undertakings amalgamate into a new undertaking and cease to exist as separate legal entities. A merger may also occur when an undertaking is absorbed by another, the latter retaining its legal identity while the former ceases to exist as a legal entity.

---

1   Footnotes with references to ECJ case-law are omitted.

2   See above, p. 451.

7. A merger within the meaning of Article 3(1)(a) may also occur where, in the absence of a legal merger, the combining of the activities of previously independent undertakings results in the creation of a single economic unit.

This may arise in particular where two or more undertakings, while retaining their individual legal personalities, establish contractually a common economic management.

If this leads to a *de facto* amalgamation of the undertakings concerned into a genuine common economic unit, the operation is considered to be a merger. A prerequisite for the determination of a common economic unit is the existence of a permanent, single economic management. Other relevant factors may include internal profit and loss compensation as between the various undertakings within the group, and their joint liability externally.

The *de facto* amalgamation may be reinforced by cross-shareholdings between the undertakings forming the economic unit.

III. Acquisition of control

8. Article 3(1)(b) provides that a concentration occurs in the case of an acquisition of control. Such control may be acquired by one undertaking acting alone or by two or more undertakings acting jointly.

Control may also be acquired by a person in circumstances where that person already controls (whether solely or jointly) at least one other undertaking or, alternatively, by a combination of persons (which controls another undertaking) and/or undertakings. The term "person" in this context extends to public bodies and private entities, as well as individuals.

As defined, a concentration within the meaning of the Merger Regulation is limited to changes in control. Internal restructuring within a group of companies, therefore, cannot constitute a concentration.

An exceptional situation exists where both the acquiring and acquired undertakings are public companies owned by the same State (or by the same public body). In this case, whether the operation is to be regarded as an internal restructuring depends in turn on the question whether both undertakings were formerly part of the same economic unit within the meaning of recital 12 to Regulation 4064/89. Where the undertakings were formerly part of different economic units having an independent power of decision, the operation will be deemed to constitute a concentration and not an internal restructuring.

Such independent power of decision does not normally exist, however, where the undertakings are within the same holding company.

9. Whether an operation gives rise to an acquisition of control depends on a number of legal and/or factual elements. The acquisition of property rights and shareholders' agreements are important, but are not the only elements involved: purely economic relationships may also play a decisive role. Therefore, in exceptional circumstances, a situation of economic dependence may lead to control on a *de facto* basis where, for example, very important long-term supply agreements or credits provided by suppliers or customers, coupled with structural links, confer decisive influence.

There may also be acquisition of control even if it is not the declared intention of the parties. Moreover, the Merger Regulation clearly defines control as having "the possibility of exercising decisive influence" rather than the actual exercise of such influence.

10. Control is nevertheless normally acquired by persons or undertakings which are the holders of the rights or are entitled to rights conferring control (Article 3(4)(a)). There may be exceptional situations where the formal holder of a controlling interest differs from the person or undertaking having in fact the real power to exercise the

rights resulting from this interest. This may be the case, for example, where an undertaking uses another person or undertaking for the acquisition of a controlling interest and exercises the rights through this person or undertaking, even though the latter is formally the holder of the rights. In such a situation, control is acquired by the undertaking which in reality is behind the operation and in fact enjoys the power to control the target undertaking (Article 3(4)(b)). The evidence needed to establish this type of indirect control may include factors such as the source of financing or family links.

11. The object of control can be one or more undertakings which constitute legal entities, or the assets of such entities, or only some of these assets.

The assets in question, which could be brands or licences, must constitute a business to which a market turnover can be clearly attributed.

12. The acquisition of control may be in the form of sole or joint control. In both cases, control is defined as the possibility of exercising decisive influence on an undertaking on the basis of rights, contracts or any other means (Article 3(3)).

III.1 Sole control

13. Sole control is normally acquired on a legal basis where an undertaking acquires a majority of the voting rights of a company. It is not in itself significant that the acquired shareholding is 50% of the share capital plus one share or that it is 100% of the share capital. In the absence of other elements, an acquisition which does not include a majority of the voting rights does not normally confer control even if it involves the acquisition of a majority of the share capital.

14. Sole control may also be acquired in the case of a "qualified minority". This can be established on a legal and/or *de facto* basis.

On a legal basis it can occur where specific rights are attached to the minority shareholding.

These may be preferential shares leading to a majority of the voting rights or other rights enabling the minority shareholder to determine the strategic commercial behaviour of the target company, such as the power to appoint more than half of the members of the supervisory board or the administrative board.

A minority shareholder may also be deemed to have sole control on a *de facto* basis. This is the case, for example, where the shareholder is highly likely to achieve a majority at the shareholders' meeting, given that the remaining shares are widely dispersed.

In such a situation it is unlikely that all the smaller shareholders will be present or represented at the shareholders' meeting. The determination of whether or not sole control exists in a particular case is based on the evidence resulting from the presence of shareholders in previous years. Where, on the basis of the number of shareholders attending the shareholders' meeting, a minority shareholder has a stable majority of the votes at this meeting, then the large minority shareholder is taken to have sole control.

Sole control can also be exercised by a minority shareholder who has the right to manage the activities of the company and to determine its business policy.

15. An option to purchase or convert shares cannot in itself confer sole control unless the option will be exercised in the near future according to legally binding agreements.

However, the likely exercise of such an option can be taken into account as an additional element which, together with other elements, may lead to the conclusion that there is sole control.

16. A change from joint to sole control of an undertaking is deemed to be a concentration within the meaning of the Merger Regulation because decisive influence exercised alone is substantially different from decisive influence exercised jointly. For the same reason, an operation involving the acquisition of joint control of one part of an

undertaking and sole control of another part is in principle regarded as two separate concentrations under the Merger Regulation.

17. The concept of control under the Merger Regulation may be different from that applied in specific areas of legislation concerning, for example, prudential rules, taxation, air transport or the media. In addition, national legislation within a Member State may provide specific rules on the structure of bodies representing the organization of decision-making within an undertaking, in particular, in relation to the rights of representatives of employees. While such legislation may confer some power of control upon persons other than the shareholders, the concept of control under the Merger Regulation is related only to the means of influence normally enjoyed by the owners of an undertaking. Finally, the prerogatives exercised by a State acting as a public authority rather than as a shareholder, in so far as they are limited to the protection of the public interest, do not constitute control within the meaning of the Merger Regulation to the extent that they have neither the aim nor the effect of enabling the State to exercise a decisive influence over the activity of the undertaking.

III.2 Joint control

18. As in the case of sole control, the acquisition of joint control (which includes changes from sole control to joint control) can also be established on a legal or de facto basis. There is joint control if the shareholders (the parent companies) must reach agreement on major decisions concerning the controlled undertaking (the joint venture).

19. Joint control exists where two or more undertakings or persons have the possibility of exercising decisive influence over another undertaking. Decisive influence in this sense normally means the power to block actions which determine the strategic commercial behaviour of an undertaking. Unlike sole control, which confers the power upon a specific shareholder to determine the strategic decisions in an undertaking, joint control is characterized by the possibility of a deadlock situation resulting from the power of two or more parent companies to reject proposed strategic decisions. It follows, therefore, that these shareholders must reach a common understanding in determining the commercial policy of the joint venture.

III.2.1 Equality in voting rights or appointment to decision-making bodies

20. The clearest form of joint control exists where there are only two parent companies which share equally the voting rights in the joint venture. In this case, it is not necessary for a formal agreement to exist between them. However, where there is a formal agreement, it must be consistent with the principle of equality between the parent companies, by laying down, for example, that each is entitled to the same number of representatives in the management bodies and that none of the members has a casting vote.

Equality may also be achieved where both parent companies have the right to appoint an equal number of members to the decision-making bodies of the joint venture.

III.2.2 Veto rights

21. Joint control may exist even where there is no equality between the two parent companies in votes or in representation in decision-making bodies or where there are more than two parent companies. This is the case where minority shareholders have additional rights which allow them to veto decisions which are essential for the strategic commercial behaviour of the joint venture.

These veto rights may be set out in the statute of the joint venture or conferred by agreement between its parent companies. The veto rights themselves may operate by means of a specific quorum required for decisions taken at the shareholders' meeting or by the board of directors to the extent that the parent companies are represented on this board. It is also possible that strategic decisions are subject to approval by a body, e.g. supervisory board, where the minority shareholders are represented and form part of the quorum needed for such decisions.

22. These veto rights must be related to strategic decisions on the business policy of the joint venture. They must go beyond the veto rights normally accorded to minority shareholders in order to protect their financial interests as investors in the joint venture. This normal protection of the rights of minority shareholders is related to decisions on the essence of the joint venture, such as changes in the statute, an increase or decrease in the capital or liquidation. A veto right, for example, which prevents the sale or winding-up of the joint venture does not confer joint control on the minority shareholder concerned.

23. In contrast, veto rights which confer joint control typically include decisions and issues such as the budget, the business plan, major investments or the appointment of senior management. The acquisition of joint control, however, does not require that the acquirer has the power to exercise decisive influence on the day-to-day running of an undertaking. The crucial element is that the veto rights are sufficient to enable the parent companies to exercise such influence in relation to the strategic business behaviour of the joint venture. Moreover, it is not necessary to establish that an acquirer of joint control of the joint venture will actually make use of its decisive influence. The possibility of exercising such influence and, hence, the mere existence of the veto rights, is sufficient.

24. In order to acquire joint control, it is not necessary for a minority shareholder to have all the veto rights mentioned above. It may be sufficient that only some, or even one such right, exists. Whether or not this is the case depends upon the precise content of the veto right itself and also the importance of this right in the context of the specific business of the joint venture.

Appointment of management and determination of budget

25. Normally the most important veto rights are those concerning decisions on the appointment of the management and the budget. The power to co-determine the structure of the management confers upon the holder the power to exercise decisive influence on the commercial policy of an undertaking. The same is true with respect to decisions on the budget since the budget determines the precise framework of the activities of the joint venture and, in particular, the investments it may make.

Business plan

26. The business plan normally provides details of the aims of a company together with the measures to be taken in order to achieve those aims. A veto right over this type of business plan may be sufficient to confer joint control even in the absence of any other veto right. In contrast, where the business plan contains merely general declarations concerning the business aims of the joint venture, the existence of a veto right will be only one element in the general assessment of joint control but will not, on its own, be sufficient to confer joint control.

Investments

27. In the case of a veto right on investments, the importance of this right depends, first, on the level of investments which are subject to the approval of the parent companies and, secondly, on the extent to which investments constitute an essential feature of the market in which the joint venture is active. In relation to the first criterion, where the level of investments necessitating approval of the parent companies is extremely high, this veto right may be closer to the normal protection of the interests of a minority

shareholder than to a right conferring a power of co-determination over the commercial policy of the joint venture. With regard to the second, the investment policy of an undertaking is normally an important element in assessing whether or not there is joint control. However, there may be some markets where investment does not play a significant role in the market behaviour of an undertaking.

Market-specific rights

28. Apart from the typical veto rights mentioned above, there exist a number of other veto rights related to specific decisions which are important in the context of the particular market of the joint venture. One example is the decision on the technology to be used by the joint venture where technology is a key feature of the joint venture's activities. Another example relates to markets characterized by product differentiation and a significant degree of innovation. In such markets, a veto right over decisions relating to new product lines to be developed by the joint venture may also be an important element in establishing the existence of joint control.

Overall context

29. In assessing the relative importance of veto rights, where there are a number of them, these rights should not be evaluated in isolation. On the contrary, the determination of whether or not joint control exists is based upon an assessment of these rights as a whole. However, a veto right which does not relate either to commercial policy and strategy or to the budget or business plan cannot be regarded as giving joint control to its owner.

III.2.3 Joint exercise of voting rights

30. Even in the absence of specific veto rights, two or more undertakings acquiring minority shareholdings in another undertaking may obtain joint control. This may be the case where the minority shareholdings together provide the means for controlling the target undertaking. This means that the minority shareholders, together, will have a majority of the voting rights; and they will act together in exercising these voting rights. This can result from a legally binding agreement to this effect, or it may be established on a *de facto* basis.

31. The legal means to ensure the joint exercise of voting rights can be in the form of a holding company to which the minority shareholders transfer their rights, or an agreement by which they undertake to act in the same way (pooling agreement).

32. Very exceptionally, collective action can occur on a de facto basis where strong common interests exist between the minority shareholders to the effect that they would not act against each other in exercising their rights in relation to the joint venture.

33. In the case of acquisitions of minority shareholdings, the prior existence of links between the minority shareholders or the acquisition of the shareholdings by means of concerted action will be factors indicating such a common interest.

34. In the case where a new joint venture is established, as opposed to the acquisition of minority shareholdings in a pre-existing company, there is a higher probability that the parent companies are carrying out a deliberate common policy. This is true, in particular, where each parent company provides a contribution to the joint venture which is vital for its operation (e.g. specific technologies, local know-how or supply agreements). In these circumstances, the parent companies may be able to operate the joint venture with full cooperation only with each other's agreement on the most important strategic decisions even if there is no express provision for any veto rights. The greater the number of parent companies involved in such a joint venture, however, the more remote is the likelihood of this situation occurring.

35. In the absence of strong common interests such as those outlined above, the possibility of changing coalitions between minority shareholders will normally exclude the assumption of joint control. Where there is no stable majority in the decision-making procedure and the majority can on each occasion be any of the various combinations possible amongst the minority shareholders, it cannot be assumed that the minority shareholders will jointly control the undertaking. In this context, it is not sufficient that there are agreements between two or more parties having an equal shareholding in the capital of an undertaking which establish identical rights and powers between the parties. For example, in the case of an undertaking where three shareholders each own one-third of the share capital and each elect one-third of the members of the Board of Directors, the shareholders do not have joint control since decisions are re-quired to be taken on the basis of a simple majority.

The same considerations also apply in more complex structures, for example, where the capital of an undertaking is equally divided between three shareholders and where the Board of Directors is composed of twelve members, each of the share-holders A, B and C electing two, another two being elected by A, B and C jointly, whilst the remaining four are chosen by the other eight members jointly. In this case also there is no joint control, and hence no control at all within the meaning of the Merger Regulation.

III.2.4 Other considerations related to joint control
36. Joint control is not incompatible with the fact that one of the parent companies enjoys specific knowledge of and experience in the business of the joint venture. In such a case, the other parent company can play a modest or even non-existent role in the daily management of the joint venture where its presence is motivated by con-siderations of a financial, long-term-strategy, brand image or general policy nature.

Nevertheless, it must always retain the real possibility of contesting the decisions taken by the other parent company, without which there would be sole control.
37. For joint control to exist, there should not be a casting vote for one parent company only.

However, there can be joint control when this casting vote can be exercised only after a series of stages of arbitration and attempts at reconciliation or in a very limited field.

III.2.5 Joint control for a limited period
38. Where an operation leads to joint control for a starting-up period but, according to legally binding agreements, this joint control will be converted to sole control by one of the shareholders, the whole operation will normally be considered to be an acquisition of sole control.

III.3 Control by a single shareholder on the basis of veto rights
39. An exceptional situation exists where only one shareholder is able to veto strategic decisions in an undertaking, but this shareholder does not have the power, on his own, to impose such decisions. This situation occurs either where one shareholder holds 50% in an undertaking whilst the remaining 50% is held by two or more minority share-holders, or where there is a quorum required for strategic decisions which in fact con-fers a veto right upon only one minority shareholder.

In these circumstances, a single shareholder possesses the same level of in-fluence as that normally enjoyed by several jointly-controlling shareholders, i.e. the power to block the adoption of strategic decisions. However, this shareholder does not enjoy the powers which are normally conferred on an undertaking with sole control, i.e. the power to impose strategic decisions. Since this shareholder can produce a deadlock situation comparable to that in normal cases of joint control, he acquires decisive influence and therefore control within the meaning of the Merger Regulation.

III.4 Changes in the structure of control

40. A concentration may also occur where an operation leads to a change in the structure of control. This includes the change from joint control to sole control as well as an increase in the number of shareholders exercising joint control. The principles for determining the existence of a concentration in these circumstances are set out in detail in the Notice on the concept of undertakings concerned.

IV. Exceptions

41. Article 3(5) sets out three exceptional situations where the acquisition of a controlling interest does not constitute a concentration under the Merger Regulation.

42. First, the acquisition of securities by companies whose normal activities include transactions and dealing in securities for their own account or for the account of others is not deemed to constitute a concentration if such an acquisition is made in the framework of these businesses and if the securities are held on only a temporary basis (Article 3(5)(a)). In order to fall within this exception, the following requirements must be fulfilled:

— the acquiring undertaking must be a credit or other financial institution or insurance company the normal activities of which are described above;
— the securities must be acquired with a view to their resale;
— the acquiring undertaking must not exercise the voting rights with a view to determining the strategic commercial behaviour of the target company or must exercise these rights only with a view to preparing the total or partial disposal of the undertaking, its assets or securities;
— the acquiring undertaking must dispose of its controlling interest within one year of the date of the acquisition, that is, it must reduce its shareholding within this one-year period at least to a level which no longer confers control. This period, however, may be extended by the Commission where the acquiring undertaking can show that the disposal was not reasonably possible within the one-year period.

43. Secondly, there is no change of control, and hence no concentration within the meaning of the Merger Regulation, where control is acquired by an office-holder according to the law of a Member State relating to liquidation, winding-up, insolvency, cessation of payments, compositions or analogous proceedings (Article 3(5)(b));

44. Thirdly, a concentration does not arise where a financial holding company within the meaning of the Fourth Council Directive 78/660 acquires control, provided that this company exercises its voting rights only to maintain the full value of its investment and does not otherwise determine directly or indirectly the strategic commercial conduct of the controlled undertaking.

45. In the context of the exceptions under Article 3(5), the question may arise whether a rescue operation constitutes a concentration under the Merger Regulation. A rescue operation typically involves the conversion of existing debt into a new company, through which a syndicate of banks may acquire joint control of the company concerned. Where such an operation meets the criteria for joint control, as outlined above, it will normally be considered to be a concentration. Although the primary intention of the banks is to restructure the financing of the undertaking concerned for its subsequent resale, the exception set out in Article 3(5)(a) is normally not applicable to such an operation. This is because the restructuring programme normally requires the controlling banks to determine the strategic commercial behaviour of the rescued undertaking.

Furthermore, it is not normally a realistic proposition to transform a rescued company into a commercially viable entity and to resell it within the permitted one-year period. Moreover, the length of time needed to achieve this aim may be so uncertain that it would be difficult to grant an extension of the disposal period.

V. Final

46. The Commission's interpretation of Article 3 as set out in this Notice is without prejudice to the interpretation which may be given by the Court of Justice or the Court of First Instance of the European Communities.

Commission Notice on the Concept of Full-function Joint Ventures Under Council Regulation 4064/89 on the Control of Concentrations Between Undertakings[1]

I. Introduction

1.   The purpose of this notice is to provide guidance as to how the Commission interprets Article 3 of Council Regulation 4064/89 as [amended] (hereinafter referred to as the Merger Regulation)[2] in relation to joint ventures.

2.   This Notice replaces the Notice on the distinction between concentrative and cooperative joint ventures. Changes made in this Notice reflect the amendments made to the Merger Regulation as well as the experience gained by the Commission in applying the Merger Regulation since its entry into force on 21 September 1990. The principles set out in this Notice will be followed and further developed by the Commission's practice in individual cases.

3.   Under the Community competition rules, joint ventures are undertakings which are jointly controlled by two or more other undertakings. In practice joint ventures encompass a broad range of operations, from merger-like operations to cooperation for particular functions such as R&D, production or distribution.

4.   Joint ventures fall within the scope of the Merger Regulation if they meet the requirements of a concentration set out in Article 3 thereof.

5.   According to recital 23 to Council Regulation 4064/89 it is appropriate to define the concept of concentration in such a manner as to cover only operations bringing about a lasting change in the structure of the undertakings concerned.

6.   The structural changes brought about by concentrations frequently reflect a dynamic process of restructuring in the markets concerned. They are permitted under the Merger Regulation unless they result in serious damage to the structure of competition by creating or strengthening a dominant position.

7.   The Merger Regulation deals with the concept of full-function joint ventures in Article 3(2) as follows: "The creation of a joint venture performing on a lasting basis all the functions of an autonomous economic entity shall constitute a concentration within the meaning of paragraph 1(b)."

II. Joint Ventures Under Article 3 of the Merger Regulation

8.   In order to be a concentration within the meaning of Article 3 of the Merger Regulation, an operation must fulfil the following requirements:

---

1   Footnotes with references to ECJ case-law are omitted.

2   See above, p. 451.

1) Joint control

9.   A joint venture may fall within the scope of the Merger Regulation where there is an acquisition of joint control by two or more undertakings, that is, its parent companies (Article 3(1)(b)). The concept of control is set out in Article 3(3). This provides that control is based on the possibility of exercising decisive influence over an undertaking, which is determined by both legal and factual considerations.

10.   The principles for determining joint control are set out in detail in the Commission's Notice on the concept of concentration.

2) Structural change of the undertakings

11.   Article 3(2) provides that the joint venture must perform, on a lasting basis, all the functions of an autonomous economic entity. Joint ventures which satisfy this requirement bring about a lasting change in the structure of the undertakings concerned. They are referred to in this Notice as "full-function" joint ventures.

12.   Essentially this means that a joint venture must operate on a market, performing the functions normally carried out by undertakings operating on the same market. In order to do so the joint venture must have a management dedicated to its day-to-day operations and access to sufficient resources including finance, staff, and assets (tangible and intangible) in order to conduct on a lasting basis its business activities within the area provided for in the joint-venture agreement.

13.   A joint venture is not full-function if it only takes over one specific function within the parent companies' business activities without access to the market. This is the case, for example, for joint ventures limited to R&D or production. Such joint ventures are auxiliary to their parent companies' business activities. This is also the case where a joint venture is essentially limited to the distribution or sales of its parent companies' products and, therefore, acts principally as a sales agency. However, the fact that a joint venture makes use of the distribution network or outlet of one or more of its parent companies normally will not disqualify it as "full-function" as long as the parent companies are acting only as agents of the joint venture.

14.   The strong presence of the parent companies in upstream or downstream markets is a factor to be taken into consideration in assessing the full-function character of a joint venture where this presence leads to substantial sales or purchases between the parent companies and the joint venture. The fact that the joint venture relies almost entirely on sales to its parent companies or purchases from them only for an initial start-up period does not normally affect the full-function character of the joint venture. Such a start-up period may be necessary in order to establish the joint venture on a market. It will normally not exceed a period of three years, depending on the specific conditions of the market in question.

Where sales from the joint venture to the parent companies are intended to be made on a lasting basis, the essential question is whether, regardless of these sales, the joint venture is geared to play an active role on the market. In this respect the relative proportion of these sales compared with the total production of the joint venture is an important factor.

Another factor is whether sales to the parent companies are made on the basis of normal commercial conditions.

In relation to purchases made by the joint venture from its parent companies, the full-function character of the joint venture is questionable in particular where little value is added to the products or services concerned at the level of the joint venture itself. In such a situation, the joint venture may be closer to a joint sales agency. However, in contrast to this situation where a joint venture is active in a trade market and performs the normal functions of a trading company in such a market, it normally will not be an auxiliary sales agency but a full-function joint venture. A trade market is characterised by the existence of companies which specialise in the selling and distribution of products without being vertically integrated in addition to those which are integrated, and where different sources of supply are available for the products in question. In addition, many trade markets may require operators to invest in specific facilities such as outlets, stockholding, warehouses, depots, transport fleets and sales personnel. In order to constitute a full-function joint venture in a trade market, an undertaking must have the necessary facilities and be likely to obtain a substantial proportion of its supplies not only from its parent companies but also from other competing sources.

15. Furthermore, the joint venture must be intended to operate on a lasting basis. The fact that the parent companies commit to the joint venture the resources described above normally demonstrates that this is the case. In addition, agreements setting up a joint venture often provide for certain contingencies, for example, the failure of the joint venture or fundamental disagreement as between the parent companies.

This may be achieved by the incorporation of provisions for the eventual dissolution of the joint venture itself or the possibility for one or more parent companies to withdraw from the joint venture. This kind of provision does not prevent the joint venture from being considered as operating on a lasting basis. The same is normally true where the agreement specifies a period for the duration of the joint venture where this period is sufficiently long in order to bring about a lasting change in the structure of the undertakings concerned, or where the agreement provides for the possible continuation of the joint venture beyond this period. By contrast, the joint venture will not be considered to operate on a lasting basis where it is established for a short finite duration. This would be the case, for example, where a joint venture is established in order to construct a specific project such as a power plant, but it will not be involved in the operation of the plant once its construction has been completed.

III. Final

16. The creation of a full-function joint venture constitutes a concentration within the meaning of Article 3 of the Merger Regulation. Restrictions accepted by the parent companies of the joint venture that are directly related and necessary for the implementation of the concentration ("ancillary restrictions"), will be assessed together with the concentration itself.

Further, the creation of a full-function joint venture may as a direct consequence lead to the coordination of the competitive behaviour of undertakings that remain independent. In such cases Article 2(4) of the Merger Regulation provides that those cooperative effects will be assessed within the same procedure as the concentration. This assessment will be made in accordance with the criteria of Article 85(1) and (3) of the Treaty with a view to establishing whether or not the operation is compatible with the common market.

The applicability of Article 85 of the Treaty to other restrictions of competition, that are neither ancillary to the concentration, nor a direct consequence of the creation of the joint venture, will normally have to be examined by means of Regulation No 17.

17. The Commission's interpretation of Article 3 of the Merger Regulation with respect to joint ventures is without prejudice to the interpretation which may be given by the Court of Justice or the Court of First Instance of the European Communities.

Commission Notice on the Definition of the Relevant Market for the Purposes of Community Competition Law[1]

I. Introduction

The purpose of this notice is to provide guidance as to how the Commission applies the concept of relevant product and geographic market in its ongoing enforcement of Community competition law, in particular the application of Regulations 17/62 and 4064/89, their equivalents in other sectoral applications such as transport, coal and steel, and agriculture, [...].

Market definition is a tool to identify and define the boundaries of competition between firms. It allows to establish the framework within which competition policy is applied by the Commission. The main purpose of market definition is to identify in a systematic way the competitive constraints that the undertakings involved[2] face. The objective of defining a market in both its product and geographic dimension is to identify those actual competitors of the undertakings involved that are capable of constraining their behaviour and of preventing them from behaving independently of an effective competitive pressure. It is from this perspective, that the market definition makes it possible, inter alia, to calculate market shares that would convey meaningful information regarding market power for the purposes of assessing dominance or for the purposes of applying Article 85.

It follows from the above, that the concept of relevant market is different from other concepts of market often used in other contexts. For instance, companies often use the term market to refer to the area where it sells its products or to refer broadly to the industry or sector where it belongs.

The definition of the relevant market in both its product and geographic dimensions often has a decisive influence on the assessment of a competition case. By rendering public the procedures the Commission follows when considering market definition and by indicating the criteria and evidence on which it relies to reach a decision, the Commission expects to increase the transparency of its policy and decision making in the area of competition policy.

Increased transparency will also result in companies and their advisors being able to better anticipate the possibility that the Commission would raise competition concerns in an individual case. Companies could, therefore, take such a possibility into account in their own internal decision making when contemplating for instance, acquisitions, the creation of joint ventures or the establishment of certain agreements. It is also intended that companies are in a better position to understand what sort of information the Commission considers relevant for the purposes of market definition.

The Commission's interpretation of the notion of relevant market is without prejudice to the interpretation which may be given by the Court of Justice or the Court of First Instance of the European Communities.

II. Definition of Relevant Market

Definition of relevant product and relevant geographic market.

The regulations based on Articles 85 and 86 of the Treaty, in particular in section 6 of Form A/B with respect to Regulation 17, as well as in section 6 of Form CO with

---

1   OJ 1997 C 372.

2   For the purposes of this notice, the undertakings involved will be in the case of a concentration the parties to the concentration; in investigations under Article 86 of the Treaty, the undertaking being investigated or the complainants; for investigations under Article 85, the parties to the agreement.

respect to regulation 4064/89 on the control of concentrations of a Community dimension have laid down the following definitions. Relevant product markets are defined as follows:

"A relevant product market comprises all those products and/or services which are regarded as interchangeable or substitutable by the consumer, by reason of the products' characteristics, their prices and their intended use."

Relevant geographic markets are defined as follows:

"The relevant geographic market comprises the area in which the undertakings concerned are involved in the supply and demand of products or services, in which the conditions of competition are sufficiently homogeneous and which can be distinguished from neighbouring areas because the conditions of competition are appreciably different in those areas".

The relevant market within which to assess a given competition issue is therefore established by the combination of the product and geographic markets. The Commission interprets the definitions at paragraphs 7 and 8 (which reflect the jurisprudence of the Court of Justice and the Court of First Instance as well as its own decisional practice) according to the orientations defined in this Notice.

Concept of relevant market and objectives of Community competition policy.

The concept of relevant market is closely related to the objectives pursued under Community competition policy. For example under the Community's merger control, the objective in controlling structural changes in the supply of a product/service is to prevent the creation or reinforcement of a dominant position as a result of which effective competition would be significantly impeded in a substantial part of the common market. Under the Community's competition policy, a dominant position is such that a firm or group of firms would be in a position to behave to an appreciable extent independently of its competitors, customers and ultimately of its consumers.[1] Such a position would usually arise when a firm or group of firms would account for a large share of the supply in any given market, provided that other factors analysed in the assessment (such as entry barriers, capacity of reaction of customers, etc.) point in the same direction.

The same approach is followed by the Commission in its application of Article 86 of the Treaty to firms that enjoy a single or collective dominant position. Under Regulation 17 the Commission has the power to investigate and bring to an end abuses of such a dominant position, which must also be defined by reference to the relevant market. Markets may also need to be defined in the application of Article 85 of the Treaty, in particular, in determining whether an appreciable restriction of competition exists or in establishing if the condition under Article 85 (3) b) for an exemption from the application of Article 85(1) is met.

The criteria to define the relevant market are applied generally for the analysis of certain behaviours in the market and for the analysis of structural changes in the supply of products. This methodology, though, might lead to different results depending on the nature of the competition issue being examined. For instance, the scope of the geographic market might be different when analysing a concentration, where the analysis is essentially prospective, than when analysing past behaviour. The different time horizon considered in each case might lead to the result that different geographic markets are defined for the same products depending on whether the Commission is

---

1   Definition given by the Court of Justice in Case 85/76, Hoffmann La Roche, judgment of 13 February 1979, and confirmed in subsequent judgments.

examining a change in the structure of supply, such as a concentration or a cooperative joint venture, or issues relating to certain past behaviour.

Basic principles for market definition.
Competitive constraints

Firms are subject to three main sources of competitive constraints: demand substitutability, supply substitutability and potential competition. From an economic point of view, for the definition of the relevant market, demand substitution constitutes the most immediate and effective disciplinary force on the suppliers of a given product, in particular in relation to their pricing decisions. A firm or a group of firms cannot have a significant impact on the prevailing conditions of sale, such as prices, if its customers are in a position to switch easily to available substitute products or to suppliers located elsewhere. Basically, the exercise of market definition consists in identifying the effective alternative sources of supply for the customers of the undertakings involved, both in terms of products/services and geographic location of suppliers.

The competitive constraints arising from supply side substitutability other than those described in para 20-23 and from potential competition are in general less immediate and in any case require an analysis of additional factors. As a result such constraints are taken into account at the assessment stage of competition analysis.

Demand substitution

The assessment of demand substitution entails a determination of the range of products which are viewed as substitutes by the consumer. One way of making this determination can be viewed, as a thought experiment, postulating a hypothetical small, non-transitory change in relative prices and evaluating the likely reactions of customers to that increase. The exercise of market definition focuses on prices for operational and practical purposes, and more precisely on demand substitution arising from small, permanent changes in relative prices. This concept can provide clear indications as to the evidence that is relevant to define markets.

Conceptually, this approach implies that starting from the type of products that the undertakings involved sell and the area in which they sell them, additional products and areas will be included into or excluded from the market definition depending on whether competition from these other products and areas affect or restrain sufficiently the pricing of the parties' products in the short term.

The question to be answered is whether the parties' customers would switch to readily available substitutes or to suppliers located elsewhere in response to an hypothetical small (in the range 5%-10%), permanent relative price increase in the products and areas being considered. If substitution would be enough to make the price increase unprofitable because of the resulting loss of sales, additional substitutes and areas are included in the relevant market. This would be done until the set of products and geographic areas is such that small, permanent increases in relative prices would be profitable. The equivalent analysis is applicable in cases concerning the concentration of buying power, where the starting point would then be the supplier and the price test allows to identify the alternative distribution channels or outlets for the supplier's products. In the application of these principles, careful account should be taken of certain particular situations as described under paragraphs 56 and 58.

A practical example of this test can be provided by its application to a merger of, for instance, soft drink bottlers. An issue to examine in such a case would be to decide whether different flavours of soft drinks belong to the same market. In practice, the question to address would be if consumers of flavour A would switch to other flavours when confronted with a permanent price increase of 5% to 10% for flavour A. If a sufficient number of consumers would switch to, say, flavour B, to such an extent that the price increase for flavour A would not be profitable due to the resulting loss of sales, then the market would comprise at least flavours A and B. The process would have to be extended in addition to other available flavours until a set of products is identified for which a price rise would not induce a sufficient substitution in demand.

Generally, and in particular for the analysis of merger cases, the price to take into account will be the prevailing market price. This might not be the case where the prevailing price has been determined in the absence of sufficient competition. In particular for investigation of abuses of dominant positions, the fact that the prevailing price might already have been substantially increased will be taken into account.

Supply substitution

Supply-side substitutability may also be taken into account when defining markets in those situations in which its effects are equivalent to those of demand substitution in terms of effectiveness and immediacy. This requires that suppliers be able to switch production to the relevant products and market them in the short term[1] without incurring significant additional costs or risks in response to small and permanent changes in relative prices. When these conditions are met, the additional production that is put on the market will have a disciplinary effect on the competitive behaviour of the companies involved. Such an impact in terms of effectiveness and immediacy is equivalent to the demand substitution effect.

These situations typically arise when companies market a wide range of qualities or grades of one product; even if for a given final customer or group of consumers, the different qualities are not substitutable, the different qualities will be grouped into one product market provided that most of the suppliers are able to offer and sell the various qualities under the conditions of immediacy and absence of significant increase in costs described above. In such cases, the relevant product market will encompass all products that are substitutable in demand and supply, and the current sales of those products will be summed to calculate the total value or volume of the market. The same reasoning may lead to group different geographic areas.

A practical example of the approach to supply side substitutability when defining product markets is to be found in the case of paper. Paper is usually supplied in a range of different qualities, from standard writing paper to high quality papers to be used for instance to publish art books. From a demand point of view, different qualities of paper cannot be used for a specific use, i.e. an art book or a high quality publication cannot be based on lower quality papers. However, paper plants are prepared to manufacture the different qualities, and production can be adjusted with negligible costs and in a short time frame. In the absence of particular difficulties in distribution, paper manufacturers are able therefore to compete for orders of the various qualities, in particular if orders are passed with a sufficient lead time to allow to modify production plans. Under such circumstances, the Commission would not define a separate market for each quality of paper and respective usage. The various qualities of paper are included in the relevant market, and their sales added up to estimate total market value and volume.

When supply side substitutability would imply the need to adjust significantly existing tangible and intangible assets, additional investments, strategic decisions or time delays, it will not be considered at the stage of market definition. Examples where supply side substitution did not lead the Commission to enlarge the market are offered in the area of consumer products, in particular for branded beverages. Although

---

1   I.e. the period which does not imply a significant adjustment of existing tangible and intangible assets.

bottling plants may in principle bottle different beverages, there are costs and lead times involved (in terms of advertising, product testing and distribution) before the products can actually be sold. In these cases, the effects of supply side substitutability and other forms of potential competition would then be examined at a later stage.

Potential competition

The third source of competitive constraint, potential competition, is not taken into account when defining markets, since the conditions under which potential competition will actually represent an effective competitive constraint depend on the analysis of specific factors and circumstances related to the conditions of entry. If required, this analysis is only carried out at a subsequent stage, in general once the position of the companies involved in the relevant market has already been ascertained, and such position is indicative of concerns from a competition point of view.

III. Evidence relied upon to define relevant markets [...]

IV. Calculation of market shares.

The definition of the relevant market in both its product and geographic dimensions allows to identify the suppliers and the customers/consumers active on that market. On that basis, a total market size and market shares for each supplier can be calculated on the basis of their sales of the relevant products on the relevant area. In practice, the total market size and market shares are often available from market sources, i.e. companies' estimates, studies commissioned to industry consultants and/or trade associations. When this is not the case, or also when available estimates are not reliable, the Commission will usually ask each supplier in the relevant market to provide its own sales in order to calculate total market size and market shares.

If sales are usually the reference to calculate market shares, there are nevertheless other indications that, depending on the specific products or industry in question, can offer useful information such as, in particular, capacity, the number of players in bidding markets, units of fleet as in aerospace, or the reserves held in the case of sectors such as mining.

As a rule of thumb, both volume sales and value sales provide useful information. In cases of differentiated products, sales in value and their associated market share will usually be considered to better reflect the relative position and strength of each supplier.

V. Additional considerations.

There are certain areas where the application of the principles above has to be undertaken with care. This is the case when considering primary and secondary markets, in particular, when the behaviour of undertakings at a point in time has to be analysed under Article 86. The method to define markets in these cases is the same, i.e. to assess the responses of customers based on their purchasing decisions to relative price changes, but taking into account as well constraints on substitution imposed by conditions in the connected markets. A narrow definition of market for secondary products, for instance, spare parts, may result when compatibility with the primary product is important. Problems of finding compatible secondary products together with the existence of high prices and a long life time of the primary products may render relative price increases of secondary products profitable. A different market definition may result if significant substitution between secondary products is possible or if the characteristics of the primary products make quick and direct consumer responses to relative price increases of the secondary products feasible.

In certain cases, the existence of chains of substitution might lead to the definition of a relevant market where products or areas at the extreme of the market are not directly substitutable. An example might be provided by the geographic dimension of a product with significant transport costs. In such cases, deliveries from a given plant are limited to a certain area around each plant by the impact of transport costs. In principle, such area could constitute the relevant geographic market. However, if the distribution of plants is such that there are considerable overlaps between the areas around different plants, it is possible that the pricing of those products will be constrained by a chain substitution effect, and lead to define a broader geographic market. The same reasoning may apply if product B is a demand substitute for products A and C. Even if products A and C are not direct demand substitutes they might be found to be in the same relevant product market since their respective pricing might be constrained by substitution to B.

From a practical perspective, the concept of chains of substitution has to be corroborated by actual evidence, for instance related to price interdependence at the extremes of the chains of substitution, in order to lead to an extension of the relevant market in an individual case. Price levels at the extremes of the chains would have to be as well of the same magnitude.

SEVEN: EXTERNAL TRADE LAW OF THE EUROPEAN UNION

Council Regulation 384/96 of 22 December 1995 on Protection Against Dumped Imports From Countries Not Members of the European Community[1]

THE COUNCIL OF THE EUROPEAN UNION,

HAVING REGARD to the Treaty establishing the European Community, and in particular Article 113 thereof,
HAVING REGARD to the Regulations establishing the common organization of agricultural markets and the Regulations adopted pursuant to Article 235 of the Treaty applicable to goods manufactured from agricultural products, and in particular the provisions of those Regulations which allow for derogation from the general principle that protective measures at frontiers may be replaced solely by the measures provided for in those Regulations, [...]
(1) WHEREAS, by Regulation 2423/88, the Council adopted common rules for protection against dumped or subsidized imports from countries which are not members of the European Community;
(2) WHEREAS those rules were adopted in accordance with existing international obligations, in particular those arising from Article VI of the General Agreement on Tariffs and Trade (hereinafter referred to as "GATT"), from the Agreement on Implementation of Article VI of the GATT (1979 Anti-Dumping Code) and from the Agreement on Interpretation and Application of Articles VI, XVI and XXIII of the GATT (Code on Subsidies and Countervailing Duties);
(3) WHEREAS the multilateral trade negotiations concluded in 1994 have led to new Agreements on the implementation of Article VI of GATT and it is therefore appropriate to amend the Community rules in the light of these new Agreements; whereas is it also desirable, in the light of the different nature of the new rules for dumping and subsidies respectively, to have a separate body of Community rules in each of those two areas; whereas, consequently, the new rules on protection against subsidies and countervailing duties are contained in a separate Regulation;
(4) WHEREAS, in applying the rules it is essential, in order to maintain the balance of rights and obligations which the GATT Agreement establishes, that the Community take account of how they are interpreted by the Community's major trading partners;
(5) WHEREAS the new agreement on dumping, namely, the Agreement on Implementation of Article VI of the General Agreement on Tariffs and Trade 1994 (hereinafter referred to as "the 1994 Anti-Dumping Agreement"), contains new and detailed rules, relating in particular to the calculation of dumping, procedures for initiating and pursuing an investigation, including the establishment and treatment of the facts, the imposition of provisional measures, the imposition and collection of anti-dumping duties, the duration and review of anti-dumping measures and the public disclosure of information relating to anti-dumping investigations; whereas, in view of the extent of the changes and to ensure a proper and transparent application of the new rules, the language of the new agreements should be brought into Community legislation as far as possible;
(6) WHEREAS it is desirable to lay down clear and detailed rules on the calculation of normal value; whereas in particular such value should in all cases be based on repre-

---

1   OJ 1996 L 56 p. 1, as amended by Council Regulation 2331/96 of 2 December 1996 and by Council Regulation 905/98 of 27 April 1998.

sentative sales in the ordinary course of trade in the exporting country; whereas, it is expedient to define the circumstances in which domestic sales may be considered to be made at a loss and may be disregarded, and in which recourse may be had to remaining sales, or to constructed normal value, or to sales to a third country; whereas it is also desirable to provide for a proper allocation of costs, even in start-up situations; whereas it is also appropriate to lay down guidance as to definition of start-up and the extent and method of allocation; whereas it is also necessary, when constructing normal value, to indicate the methodology that is to be applied in determining the amounts for selling, general and administrative costs and the profit margin that should be included in such value;

(7) WHEREAS when determining normal value for non-market economy countries, it appears prudent to set out rules for choosing the appropriate market-economy third country that is to be used for such purpose and, where it is not possible to find a suitable third country, to provide that normal value may be established on any other reasonable basis;

(8) WHEREAS it is expedient to define the export price and to enumerate the adjustments which are to be made in those cases where a reconstruction of this price from the first open-market price is deemed necessary;

(9) WHEREAS, for the purpose of ensuring a fair comparison between export price and normal value, it is advisable to list the factors which may affect prices and price comparability and to lay down specific rules as to when and how the adjustments should be made, including the fact that any duplication of adjustments should be avoided; whereas it is also necessary to provide that comparison may be made using average prices although individual export prices may be compared to an average normal value where the former vary by customer, region or time period;

(10) WHEREAS it is desirable to lay down clear and detailed guidance as to the factors which may be relevant for the determination of whether the dumped imports have caused material injury or are threatening to cause injury; whereas, in demonstrating that the volume and price levels of the imports concerned are responsible for injury sustained by a Community industry, attention should be given to the effect of other factors and in particular prevailing market conditions in the Community;

(11) WHEREAS it is advisable to define the term "Community industry" and to provide that parties related to exporters may be excluded from such industry and to define the term "related"; whereas, it is also necessary to provide for anti-dumping action to be taken on behalf of producers in a region of the Community and to lay down guidelines on the definition of such region;

(12) WHEREAS it is necessary to lay down who may lodge an anti-dumping complaint, including the extent to which it should be supported by the Community industry, and the information on dumping, injury and causation which such complaint should contain; whereas it is also expedient to specify the procedures for the rejection of complaints or the initiation of proceedings;

(13) WHEREAS it is necessary to lay down the manner in which interested parties should be given notice of the information which the authorities require, and should have ample opportunity to present all relevant evidence and to defend their interests; whereas it is also desirable to set out clearly the rules and procedures to be followed during the investigation, in particular the rules whereby interested parties are to make themselves known, present their views and submit information within specified time limits, if such views and information are to be taken into account; whereas it is also appropriate to set out the conditions under which an interested party may have access to, and comment on, information presented by other interested parties; whereas there should also be cooperation between the Member States and the Commission in the collection of information;

(14) WHEREAS it is necessary to lay down the conditions under which provisional duties may be imposed, including the condition that they may be imposed no earlier than 60 days from initiation and not later than nine months thereafter; whereas, for administrative reasons, it is also necessary to provide that such duties may in all cases be imposed by the Commission, either directly for a nine-month period or in two stages of six and three months;

(15) WHEREAS it is necessary to specify procedures for accepting undertakings which eliminate dumping and injury instead of imposing provisional or definitive duties; whereas it is also appropriate to lay down the consequences of breach or withdrawal of undertakings and that provisional duties may be imposed in cases of suspected violation or where further investigation is necessary to supplement the findings; whereas, in accepting undertakings, care should be taken that the proposed undertakings, and their enforcement, do not lead to anti-competitive behaviour;

(16) WHEREAS it is necessary to provide that the termination of cases should, irrespective of whether definitive measures are adopted or not, normally take place within 12 months, and in no case later than 15 months, from the initiation of the investigation; whereas investigations or proceedings should be terminated where the dumping is de minimis or the injury is negligible, and it is appropriate to define those terms; whereas, where measures are to be imposed, it is necessary to provide for the termination of investigations and to lay down that measures should be less than the margin of dumping if such lesser amount would remove the injury, as well as to specify the method of calculating the level of measures in cases of sampling;

(17) WHEREAS it is necessary to provide for retroactive collection of provisional duties if that is deemed appropriate and to define the circumstances which may trigger the retroactive application of duties to avoid the undermining of the definitive measures to be applied; whereas it is also necessary to provide that duties may be applied retroactively in cases of breach or withdrawal of undertakings;

(18) WHEREAS it is necessary to provide that measures are to lapse after five years unless a review indicates that they should be maintained; whereas it is also necessary to provide, in cases where sufficient evidence is submitted of changed circumstances, for interim reviews or for investigations to determine whether refunds of anti-dumping duties are warranted; whereas it is also appropriate to lay down that in any recalculation of dumping which necessitates a reconstruction of export prices, duties are not to be treated as a cost incurred between importation and resale where the said duty is being reflected in the prices of the products subject to measures in the Community;

(19) WHEREAS it is necessary to provide specifically for the reassessment of export prices and dumping margins where the duty is being absorbed by the exporter through a form of compensatory arrangement and the measures are not being reflected in the prices of the products subject to measures in the Community;

(20) WHEREAS the 1994 Anti-Dumping Agreement does not contain provisions regarding the circumvention of anti-dumping measures, though a separate GATT Ministerial Decision recognizes circumvention as a problem and has referred it to the GATT Antidumping Committee for resolution; whereas given the failure of the multilateral negotiations so far and pending the outcome of the referral to the GATT Anti-Dumping Committee, it is necessary to introduce new provisions into Community legislation to deal with practices, including mere assembly of goods in the Community or a third country, which have as their main aim the circumvention of anti- dumping measures;

(21) WHEREAS it is expedient to permit suspension of anti-dumping measures where there is a temporary change in market conditions which makes the continued imposition of such measures temporarily inappropriate;

(22) WHEREAS it is necessary to provide that imports under investigation may be made subject to registration upon importation in order to enable measures to be applied subsequently against such imports;

(23) WHEREAS in order to ensure proper enforcement of measures, it is necessary that Member States monitor, and report to the Commission, the import trade of products subject to investigation or subject to measures, and also the amount of duties collected under this Regulation;

(24) WHEREAS it is necessary to provide for consultation of an Advisory Committee at regular and specified stages of the investigation; whereas, the Committee should consist of representatives of Member States with a representative of the Commission as chairman;

(25) WHEREAS it is expedient to provide for verification visits to check information submitted on dumping and injury, such visits being, however, conditional on proper replies to questionnaires being received;

(26) WHEREAS it is essential to provide for sampling in cases where the number of parties or transactions is large in order to permit completion of investigations within the appointed time limits;

(27) WHEREAS it is necessary to provide that where parties do not cooperate satisfactorily other information may be used to establish findings and that such information may be less favourable to the parties than if they had cooperated;

(28) WHEREAS provision should be made for the treatment of confidential information so that business secrets are not divulged;

(29) WHEREAS it is essential that provision be made for proper disclosure of essential facts and considerations to parties which qualify for such treatment and that such disclosure be made, with due regard to the decision-making process in the Community, within a time period which permits parties to defend their interests;

(30) WHEREAS it is prudent to provide for an administrative system under which arguments can be presented as to whether measures are in the Community interest, including the consumers' interest, and to lay down the time periods within which such information has to be presented as well as the disclosure rights of the parties concerned;

(31) WHEREAS, by Regulation 3283/94 of 22 December 1994 on protection against dumped imports from countries not members of the European Community, the Council repealed Regulation 2423/88 and instituted a new common system of defence against dumped imports from countries not members of the European Community;

(32) WHEREAS significant errors in the text of Regulation 3283/94 became apparent on publication;

(33) WHEREAS, moreover, that Regulation has already been twice amended;

(34) WHEREAS, in the interests of clarity, transparency and legal certainty, that Regulation should therefore be repealed and replaced, without prejudice to the anti-dumping proceedings already initiated under it or under Regulation 2423/88,

HAS ADOPTED THIS REGULATION:

Article 1 Principles

1.   An anti-dumping duty may be applied to any dumped product whose release for free circulation in the Community causes injury.

2.   A product is to be considered as being dumped if its export price to the Community is less than a comparable price for the like product, in the ordinary course of trade, as established for the exporting country.

3.   The exporting country shall normally be the country of origin. However, it may be an intermediate country, except where, for example, the products are merely tranship-

ped through that country, or the products concerned are not produced in that country, or there is no comparable price for them in that country.

4.   For the purpose of this Regulation, the term "like product" shall be interpreted to mean a product which is identical, that is to say, alike in all respects, to the product under consideration, or in the absence of such a product, another product which although not alike in all respects, has characteristics closely resembling those of the product under consideration.

Article 2 Determination of dumping

A. NORMAL VALUE

1.   The normal value shall normally be based on the prices paid or payable, in the ordinary course of trade, by independent customers in the exporting country.

However, where the exporter in the exporting country does not produce or does not sell the like product, the normal value may be established on the basis of prices of other sellers or producers.

Prices between parties which appear to be associated or to have a compensatory arrangement with each other may not be considered to be in the ordinary course of trade and may not be used to establish normal value unless it is determined that they are unaffected by the relationship.

2.   Sales of the like product intended for domestic consumption shall normally be used to determine normal value if such sales volume constitutes 5% or more of the sales volume of the product under consideration to the Community. However, a lower volume of sales may be used when, for example, the prices charged are considered representative for the market concerned.

3.   When there are no or insufficient sales of the like product in the ordinary course of trade, or where because of the particular market situation such sales do not permit a proper comparison, the normal value of the like product shall be calculated on the basis of the cost of production in the country of origin plus a reasonable amount for selling, general and administrative costs and for profits, or on the basis of the export prices, in the ordinary course of trade, to an appropriate third country, provided that those prices are representative.

4.   Sales of the like product in the domestic market of the exporting country, or export sales to a third country, at prices below unit production costs (fixed and variable) plus selling, general and administrative costs may be treated as not being in the ordinary course of trade by reason of price, and may be disregarded in determining normal value, only if it is determined that such sales are made within an extended period in substantial quantities, and are at prices which do not provide for the recovery of all costs within a reasonable period of time.

If prices which are below costs at the time of sale are above weighted average costs for the period of investigation, such prices shall be considered to provide for recovery of costs within a reasonable period of time.

The extended period of time shall normally be one year but shall in no case be less than six months, and sales below unit cost shall be considered to be made in substantial quantities within such a period when it is established that the weighted average selling price is below the weighted average unit cost, or that the volume of sales below unit cost is not less than 20% of sales being used to determine normal value.

5.   Costs shall normally be calculated on the basis of records kept by the party under investigation, provided that such records are in accordance with the generally accepted accounting principles of the country concerned and that it is shown that the records reasonably reflect the costs associated with the production and sale of the product under consideration.

Consideration shall be given to evidence submitted on the proper allocation of costs, provided that it is shown that such allocations have been historically utilized. In the absence of a more appropriate method, preference shall be given to the allocation of costs on the basis of turnover. Unless already reflected in the cost allocations under this subparagraph, costs shall be adjusted appropriately for those non-recurring items of cost which benefit future and/or current production.

Where the costs for part of the period for cost recovery are affected by the use of new production facilities requiring substantial additional investment and by low capacity utilization rates, which are the result of start-up operations which take place within or during part of the investigation period, the average costs for the start-up phase shall be those applicable, under the abovementioned allocation rules, at the end of such a phase, and shall be included at that level, for the period concerned, in the weighted average costs referred to in the second sub-paragraph of paragraph 4. The length of a start-up phase shall be determined in relation to the circumstances of the producer or exporter concerned, but shall not exceed an appropriate initial portion of the period for cost recovery. For this adjustment to costs applicable during the investigation period, information relating to a start-up phase which extends beyond that period shall be taken into account where it is submitted prior to verification visits and within three months of the initiation of the investigation.

6.   The amounts for selling, for general and administrative costs and for profits shall be based on actual data pertaining to production and sales, in the ordinary course of trade, of the like product, by the exporter or producer under investigation. When such amounts cannot be determined on this basis, the amounts may be determined on the basis of:

(a) the weighted average of the actual amounts determined for other exporters or producers subject to investigation in respect of production and sales of the like product in the domestic market of the country of origin;

(b) the actual amounts applicable to production and sales, in the ordinary course of trade, of the same general category of products for the exporter or producer in question in the domestic market of the country of origin;

(c) any other reasonable method, provided that the amount for profit so established shall not exceed the profit normally realized by other exporters or producers on sales of products of the same general category in the domestic market of the country of origin.

7.   (a) In the case of imports from non-market economy countries,[1] normal value shall be determined on the basis of the price or constructed value in a market economy third country, or the price from such a third country to other countries, including the Community, or where those are not possible, on any other reasonable basis, including the price actually paid or payable in the Community for the like product, duly adjusted if necessary to include a reasonable profit margin. An appropriate market economy third country shall be selected in a not unreasonable manner, due account being taken of any reliable information made available at the time of selection. Account shall also be taken of time limits; where appropriate, a market economy third country which is subject to the same investigation shall be used.

The parties to the investigation shall be informed shortly after its initiation of the market economy third country envisaged and shall be given 10 days to comment.

---

1   Including Albania, Armenia, Azerbaijan, Belarus, Georgia, Kazakhstan, North Korea, Kyrgyzstan, Moldavia, Mongolia, Tajikistan, Turkmenistan, Ukraine, Uzbekistan, Vietnam.

(b) In anti-dumping investigations concerning imports from the Russian Federation and the People's Republic of China, normal value will be determined in accordance with paragraphs 1 to 6, if it is shown, on the basis of properly substantiated claims by one or more producers subject to the investigation and in accordance with the criteria and procedures set out in subparagraph (c) that market economy conditions prevail for this producer or producers in respect of the manufacture and sale of the like product concerned. When this is not the case, the rules set out under subparagraph (a) shall apply.

(c) A claim under subparagraph (b) must be made in writing and contain sufficient evidence that the producer operates under market economy conditions, that is if:
   — decisions of firms regarding prices, costs and inputs, including for instance raw materials, cost of technology and labour, output, sales and investment, are made in response to market signals reflecting supply and demand, and without significant State interference in this regard, and costs of major inputs substantially reflect market values,
   — firms have one clear set of basic accounting records which are independently audited in line with international accounting standards and are applied for all purposes,
   — the production costs and financial situation of firms are not subject to significant distortions carried over from the former non-market economy system, in particular in relation to depreciation of assets, other write-offs, barter trade and payment via compensation of debts,
   — the firms concerned are subject to bankruptcy and property laws which guarantee legal certainty and stability for the operation of firms, and
   — exchange rate conversions are carried out at the market rate.

A determination whether the producer meets the abovementioned criteria shall be made within three months of the initiation of the investigation, after specific consultation of the Advisory Committee and after the Community industry has been given an opportunity to comment. This determination shall remain in force throughout the investigation.

B. EXPORT PRICE

8. The export price shall be the price actually paid or payable for the product when sold for export from the exporting country to the Community.

9. In cases where there is no export price or where it appears that the export price is unreliable because of an association or a compensatory arrangement between the exporter and the importer or a third party, the export price may be constructed on the basis of the price at which the imported products are first resold to an independent buyer, or, if the products are not resold to an independent buyer, or are not resold in the condition in which they were imported, on any reasonable basis.

In these cases, adjustment for all costs, including duties and taxes, incurred between importation and resale, and for profits accruing, shall be made so as to establish a reliable export price, at the Community frontier level.

The items for which adjustment shall be made shall include those normally borne by an importer but paid by any party, either inside or outside the Community, which appears to be associated or to have a compensatory arrangement with the importer or exporter, including usual transport, insurance, handling, loading and ancillary costs; customs duties, any anti-dumping duties, and other taxes payable in the importing country by reason of the importation or sale of the goods; and a reasonable margin for selling, general and administrative costs and profit.

C. COMPARISON

10. A fair comparison shall be made between the export price and the normal value. This comparison shall be made at the same level of trade and in respect of sales made at as nearly as possible the same time and with due account taken of other differences which affect price comparability. Where the normal value and the export price as established are not on such a comparable basis due allowance, in the form of adjustments, shall be made in each case, on its merits, for differences in factors which are claimed, and demonstrated, to affect prices and price comparability. Any duplication when making adjustments shall be avoided, in particular in relation to discounts, rebates, quantities and level of trade. When the specified conditions are met, the factors for which adjustment can be made are listed as follows:

(a) Physical characteristics

An adjustment shall be made for differences in the physical characteristics of the product concerned. The amount of the adjustment shall correspond to a reasonable estimate of the market value of the difference.

(b) Import charges and indirect taxes

An adjustment shall be made to normal value for an amount corresponding to any import charges or indirect taxes borne by the like product and by materials physically incorporated therein, when intended for consumption in the exporting country and not collected or refunded in respect of the product exported to the Community.

(c) Discounts, rebates and quantities

An adjustment shall be made for differences in discounts and rebates, including those given for differences in quantities, if these are properly quantified and are directly linked to the sales under consideration. An adjustment may also be made for deferred discounts and rebates if the claim is based on consistent practice in prior periods, including compliance with the conditions required to qualify for the discount or rebates.

(d) Level of trade

(i) An adjustment for differences in levels of trade, including any differences which may arise in OEM (Original Equipment Manufacturer) sales, shall be made where, in relation to the distribution chain in both markets, it is shown that the export price, including a constructed export price, is at a different level of trade from the normal value and the difference has affected price comparability which is demonstrated by consistent and distinct differences in functions and prices of the seller for the different levels of trade in the domestic market of the exporting country. The amount of the adjustment shall be based on the market value of the difference.

(ii) However, in circumstances not envisaged under (i), when an existing difference in level of trade cannot be quantified because of the absence of the relevant levels on the domestic market of the exporting countries, or where certain functions are shown clearly to relate to levels of trade other than the one which is to be used in the comparison, a special adjustment may be granted.

(e) Transport, insurance, handling, loading and ancillary costs

An adjustment shall be made for differences in the directly related costs incurred for conveying the product concerned from the premises of the exporter to an independent buyer, where such costs are included in the prices charged. Those costs shall include transport, insurance, handling, loading and ancillary costs.

(f) Packing

An adjustment shall be made for differences in the directly related packing costs for the product concerned.

(g) Credit
   An adjustment shall be made for differences in the cost of any credit granted for the
   sales under consideration, provided that it is a factor taken into account in the determination of the prices charged.
(h) After-sales costs
   An adjustment shall be made for differences in the direct costs of providing warran-
   ties, guarantees, technical assistance and services, as provided for by law and/or
   in the sales contract.
(i) Commissions
   An adjustment shall be made for differences in commissions paid in respect of the
   sales under consideration.
(j) Currency conversions
   When the price comparison requires a conversion of currencies, such conversion
   shall be made using the rate of exchange on the date of sale, except that when a
   sale of foreign currency on forward markets is directly linked to the export sale involved, the rate of exchange in the forward sale shall be used. Normally, the date
   of sale shall be the date of invoice but the date of contract, purchase order or order
   confirmation may be used if these more appropriately establish the material terms
   of sale. Fluctuations in exchange rates shall be ignored and exporters shall be
   granted 60 days to reflect a sustained movement in exchange rates during the investigation period.
(k) Other factors
   An adjustment may also be made for differences in other factors not provided for
   under subparagraphs (a) to (j) if it is demonstrated that they affect price comparability as required under this paragraph, in particular that customers consistently pay
   different prices on the domestic market because of the difference in such factors.

D. DUMPING MARGIN
11. Subject to the relevant provisions governing fair comparison, the existence of
margins of dumping during the investigation period shall normally be established on the
basis of a comparison of a weighted average normal value with a weighted average
of prices of all export transactions to the Community, or by a comparison of individual
normal values and individual export prices to the Community on a transaction-to-trans-
action basis. However, a normal value established on a weighted average basis may
be compared to prices of all individual export transactions to the Community, if there
is a pattern of export prices which differs significantly among different purchasers, regions or time periods, and if the methods specified in the first sentence of this paragraph would not reflect the full degree of dumping being practised. This paragraph shall
not preclude the use of sampling in accordance with Article 17.
12. The dumping margin shall be the amount by which the normal value exceeds the
export price. Where dumping margins vary, a weighted average dumping margin may
be established.

Article 3 Determination of injury
1.   Pursuant to this Regulation, the term "injury" shall, unless otherwise specified, be
taken to mean material injury to the Community industry, threat of material injury to the
Community industry or material retardation of the establishment of such an industry
and shall be interpreted in accordance with the provisions of this Article.
2.   A determination of injury shall be based on positive evidence and shall involve an
objective examination of both
(a) the volume of the dumped imports and the effect of the dumped imports on prices
   in the Community market for like products; and

(b) the consequent impact of those imports on the Community industry.

3.   With regard to the volume of the dumped imports, consideration shall be given to whether there has been a significant increase in dumped imports, either in absolute terms or relative to production or consumption in the Community. With regard to the effect of the dumped imports on prices, consideration shall be given to whether there has been significant price undercutting by the dumped imports as compared with the price of a like product of the Community industry, or whether the effect of such imports is otherwise to depress prices to a significant degree or prevent price increases, which would otherwise have occurred, to a significant degree. No one or more of these factors can necessarily give decisive guidance.

4.   Where imports of a product from more than one country are simultaneously subject to anti-dumping investigations, the effects of such imports shall be cumulatively assessed only if it is determined that

(a) the margin of dumping established in relation to the imports from each country is more than *de minimis* as defined in Article 9 (3) and that the volume of imports from each country is not negligible; and

(b) a cumulative assessment of the effects of the imports is appropriate in light of the conditions of competition between imported products and the conditions of competition between the imported products and the like Community product.

5.   The examination of the impact of the dumped imports on the Community industry concerned shall include an evaluation of all relevant economic factors and indices having a bearing on the state of the industry, including the fact that an industry is still in the process of recovering from the effects of past dumping or subsidization, the magnitude of the actual margin of dumping, actual and potential decline in sales, profits, output, market share, productivity, return on investments, utilization of capacity; factors affecting Community prices; actual and potential negative effects on cash flow, inventories, employment, wages, growth, ability to raise capital or investments. This list is not exhaustive, nor can any one or more of these factors necessarily give decisive guidance.

6.   It must be demonstrated, from all the relevant evidence presented in relation to paragraph 2, that the dumped imports are causing injury within the meaning of this Regulation. Specifically, this shall entail a demonstration that the volume and/or price levels identified pursuant to paragraph 3 are responsible for an impact on the Community industry as provided for in paragraph 5, and that this impact exists to a degree which enables it to be classified as material.

7.   Known factors other than the dumped imports which at the same time are injuring the Community industry shall also be examined to ensure that injury caused by these other factors is not attributed to the dumped imports under paragraph 6. Factors which may be considered in this respect include the volume and prices of imports not sold at dumping prices, contraction in demand or changes in the patterns of consumption, restrictive trade practices of, and competition between, third country and Community producers, developments in technology and the export performance and productivity of the Community industry.

8.   The effect of the dumped imports shall be assessed in relation to the production of the Community industry of the like product when available data permit the separate identification of that production on the basis of such criteria as the production process, producers' sales and profits. If such separate identification of that production is not possible, the effects of the dumped imports shall be assessed by examination of the production of the narrowest group or range of products, which includes the like product, for which the necessary information can be provided.

9.   A determination of a threat of material injury shall be based on facts and not merely on allegation, conjecture or remote possibility. The change in circumstances which

would create a situation in which the dumping would cause injury must be clearly foreseen and imminent.

In making a determination regarding the existence of a threat of material injury, consideration should be given to such factors as:

(a) a significant rate of increase of dumped imports into the Community market indicating the likelihood of substantially increased imports;

(b) sufficient freely disposable capacity of the exporter or an imminent and substantial increase in such capacity indicating the likelihood of substantially increased dumped exports to the Community, account being taken of the availability of other export markets to absorb any additional exports;

(c) whether imports are entering at prices that would, to a significant degree, depress prices or prevent price increases which otherwise would have occurred, and would probably increase demand for further imports; and

(d) inventories of the product being investigated.

No one of the factors listed above by itself can necessarily give decisive guidance but the totality of the factors considered must lead to the conclusion that further dumped exports are imminent and that, unless protective action is taken, material injury will occur.

Article 4 Definition of Community industry

1. For the purposes of this Regulation, the term "Community industry" shall be interpreted as referring to the Community producers as a whole of the like products or to those of them whose collective output of the products constitutes a major proportion, as defined in Article 5 (4), of the total Community production of those products, except that:

(a) when producers are related to the exporters or importers or are themselves importers of the allegedly dumped product, the term "Community industry" may be interpreted as referring to the rest of the producers;

(b) in exceptional circumstances the territory of the Community may, for the production in question, be divided into two or more competitive markets and the producers within each market may be regarded as a separate industry if (i) the producers within such a market sell all or almost all of their production of the product in question in that market; and (ii) the demand in that market is not to any substantial degree supplied by producers of the product in question located elsewhere in the Community. In such circumstances, injury may be found to exist even where a major portion of the total Community industry is not injured, provided there is a concentration of dumped imports into such an isolated market and provided further that the dumped imports are causing injury to the producers of all or almost all of the production within such a market.

2. For the purpose of paragraph 1, producers shall be considered to be related to exporters or importers only if

(a) one of them directly or indirectly controls the other; or

(b) both of them are directly or indirectly controlled by a third person; or

(c) together they directly or indirectly control a third person provided that there are grounds for believing or suspecting that the effect of the relationship is such as to cause the producer concerned to behave differently from non-related producers.

For the purpose of this paragraph, one shall be deemed to control another when the former is legally or operationally in a position to exercise restraint or direction over the latter.

3. Where the Community industry has been interpreted as referring to the producers in a certain region, the exporters shall be given an opportunity to offer undertakings pursuant to Article 8 in respect of the region concerned. In such cases, when evalua-

ting the Community interest of the measures, special account shall be taken of the interest of the region. If an adequate undertaking is not offered promptly or the situations set out in Article 8 (9) and (10) apply, a provisional or definitive duty may be imposed in respect of the Community as a whole. In such cases, the duties may, if practicable, be limited to specific producers or exporters.

4.   The provisions of Article 3 (8) shall be applicable to this Article.

Article 5 Initiation of proceedings

1.   Except as provided for in paragraph 6, an investigation to determine the existence, degree and effect of any alleged dumping shall be initiated upon a written complaint by any natural or legal person, or any association not having legal personality, acting on behalf of the Community industry.

The complaint may be submitted to the Commission, or to a Member State, which shall forward it to the Commission. The Commission shall send Member States a copy of any complaint it receives. The complaint shall be deemed to have been lodged on the first working day following its delivery to the Commission by registered mail or the issuing of an acknowledgement of receipt by the Commission.

Where, in the absence of any complaint, a Member State is in possession of sufficient evidence of dumping and of resultant injury to the Community industry, it shall immediately communicate such evidence to the Commission.

2.   A complaint under paragraph 1 shall include evidence of dumping, injury and a causal link between the allegedly dumped imports and the alleged injury. The complaint shall contain such information as is reasonably available to the complainant on the following:

(a) identity of the complainant and a description of the volume and value of the Community production of the like product by the complainant. Where a written complaint is made on behalf of the Community industry, the complaint shall identify the industry on behalf of which the complaint is made by a list of all known Community producers of the like product (or associations of Community producers of the like product) and, to the extent possible, a description of the volume and value of Community production of the like product accounted for by such producers;

(b) a complete description of the allegedly dumped product, the names of the country or countries of origin or export in question, the identity of each known exporter or foreign producer and a list of known persons importing the product in question;

(c) information on prices at which the product in question is sold when destined for consumption in the domestic markets of the country or countries of origin or export (or, where appropriate, information on the prices at which the product is sold from the country or countries of origin or export to a third country or countries or on the constructed value of the product) and information on export prices or, where appropriate, on the prices at which the product is first resold to an independent buyer in the Community;

(d) information on changes in the volume of the allegedly dumped imports, the effect of those imports on prices of the like product on the Community market and the consequent impact of the imports on the Community industry, as demonstrated by relevant factors and indices having a bearing on the state of the Community industry, such as those listed in Article 3 (3) and (5).

3.   The Commission shall, as far as possible, examine the accuracy and adequacy of the evidence provided in the complaint to determine whether there is sufficient evidence to justify the initiation of an investigation.

4.   An investigation shall not be initiated pursuant to paragraph 1 unless it has been determined, on the basis of an examination as to the degree of support for, or opposition to, the complaint expressed by Community producers of the like product, that the

complaint has been made by or on behalf of the Community industry. The complaint shall be considered to have been made by or on behalf of the Community industry if it is supported by those Community producers whose collective output constitutes more than 50% of the total production of the like product produced by that portion of the Community industry expressing either support for or opposition to the complaint. However, no investigation shall be initiated when Community producers expressly supporting the complaint account for less than 25% of total production of the like product produced by the Community industry.

5.   The authorities shall avoid, unless a decision has been made to initiate an investigation, any publicising of the complaint seeking the initiation of an investigation. However, after receipt of a properly documented complaint and before proceeding to initiate an investigation, the government of the exporting country concerned shall be notified.

6.   If in special circumstances, it is decided to initiate an investigation without having received a written complaint by or on behalf of the Community industry for the initiation of such investigation, this shall be done on the basis of sufficient evidence of dumping, injury and a causal link, as described in paragraph 2, to justify such initiation.

7.   The evidence of both dumping and injury shall be considered simultaneously in the decision on whether or not to initiate an investigation. A complaint shall be rejected where there is insufficient evidence of either dumping or of injury to justify proceeding with the case. Proceedings shall not be initiated against countries whose imports represent a market share of below 1%, unless such countries collectively account for 3% or more of Community consumption.

8.   The complaint may be withdrawn prior to initiation, in which case it shall be considered not to have been lodged.

9.   Where, after consultation, it is apparent that there is sufficient evidence to justify initiating a proceeding, the Commission shall do so within 45 days of the lodging of the complaint and shall publish a notice in the Official Journal of the European Communities. Where insufficient evidence has been presented, the complainant shall, after consultation, be so informed within 45 days of the date on which the complaint is lodged with the Commission.

10. The notice of initiation of the proceedings shall announce the initiation of an investigation, indicate the product and countries concerned, give a summary of the information received, and provide that all relevant information is to be communicated to the Commission it shall state the periods within which interested parties may make themselves known, present their views in writing and submit information if such views and information are to be taken into account during the investigation; it shall also state the period within which interested parties may apply to be heard by the Commission in accordance with Article 6 (5).

11. The Commission shall advise the exporters, importers and representative associations of importers or exporters known to it to be concerned, as well as representatives of the exporting country and the complainants, of the initiation of the proceedings and, with due regard to the protection of confidential information, provide the full text of the written complaint received pursuant to paragraph 1 to the known exporters and to the authorities of the exporting country, and make it available upon request to other interested parties involved. Where the number of exporters involved is particularly high, the full text of the written complaint may instead be provided only to the authorities of the exporting country or to the relevant trade association.

12. An anti-dumping investigation shall not hinder the procedures of customs clearance.

Article 6 The investigation

1.   Following the initiation of the proceeding, the Commission, acting in cooperation with the Member States, shall commence an investigation at Community level. Such investigation shall cover both dumping and injury and these shall be investigated simultaneously. For the purpose of a representative finding, an investigation period shall be selected which, in the case of dumping shall, normally, cover a period of not less than six months immediately prior to the initiation of the proceeding. Information relating to a period subsequent to the investigation period shall, normally, not be taken into account.

2.   Parties receiving questionnaires used in an anti-dumping investigation shall be given at least 30 days to reply. The time limit for exporters shall be counted from the date of receipt of the questionnaire, which for this purpose shall be deemed to have been received one week from the day on which it was sent to the exporter or transmitted to the appropriate diplomatic representative of the exporting country. An extension to the 30 day period may be granted, due account being taken of the time limits of the investigation, provided that the party shows due cause for such extension, in terms of its particular circumstances.

3.   The Commission may request Member States to supply information, and Member States shall take whatever steps are necessary in order to give effect to such requests. They shall send to the Commission the information requested together within the results of all inspections, checks or investigations carried out. Where this information is of general interest or where its transmission has been requested by a Member State, the Commission shall forward it to the Member States, provided it is not confidential, in which case a non-confidential summary shall be forwarded.

4.   The Commission may request Member States to carry out all necessary checks and inspections, particularly amongst importers, traders and Community producers, and to carry out investigations in third countries, provided that the firms concerned give their consent and that the government of the country in question has been officially notified and raises no objection. Member States shall take whatever steps are necessary in order to give effect to such requests from the Commission. Officials of the Commission shall be authorized, if the Commission or a Member State so requests, to assist the officials of Member States in carrying out their duties.

5.   The interested parties which have made themselves known in accordance with Article 5 (10) shall be heard if they have, within the period prescribed in the notice published in the Official Journal of the European Communities, made a written request for a hearing showing that they are an interested party likely to be affected by the result of the proceeding and that there are particular reasons why they should be heard.

6.   Opportunities shall, on request, be provided for the importers, exporters, representatives of the government of the exporting country and the complainants, which have made themselves known in accordance with Article 5 (10), to meet those parties with adverse interests, so that opposing views may be presented and rebuttal arguments offered. Provision of such opportunities must take account of the need to preserve confidentiality and of the convenience to the parties. There shall be no obligation on any party to attend a meeting, and failure to do so shall not be prejudicial to that party's case. Oral information provided under this paragraph shall be taken into account in so far as it is subsequently confirmed in writing.

7.   The complainants, importers and exporters and their representative associations, users and consumer organizations, which have made themselves known in accordance with Article 5 (10), as well as the representatives of the exporting country may, upon written request, inspect all information made available by any party to an investigation, as distinct from internal documents prepared by the authorities of the Community or its Member States, which is relevant to the presentation of their cases and

not confidential within the meaning of Article 19, and that it is used in the investigation. Such parties may respond to such information and their comments shall be taken into consideration, wherever they are sufficiently substantiated in the response.

8. Except in the circumstances provided for in Article 18, the information which is supplied by interested parties and upon which findings are based shall be examined for accuracy as far as possible.

9. For proceedings initiated pursuant to Article 5 (9), an investigation shall, whenever possible, be concluded within one year. In any event, such investigations shall in all cases be concluded within 15 months of initiation, in accordance with the findings made pursuant to Article 8 for undertakings or the findings made pursuant to Article 9 for definitive action.

Article 7 Provisional measures

1. Provisional duties may be imposed if proceedings have been initiated in accordance with Article 5, if a notice has been given to that effect and interested parties have been given adequate opportunities to submit information and make comments in accordance with Article 5 (10), if a provisional affirmative determination has been made of dumping and consequent injury to the Community industry, and if the Community interest calls for intervention to prevent such injury. The provisional duties shall be imposed no earlier than 60 days from the initiation of the proceedings but not later than nine months from the initiation of the proceedings.

2. The amount of the provisional anti-dumping duty shall not exceed the margin of dumping as provisionally established, but it should be less than the margin if such lesser duty would be adequate to remove the injury to the Community industry.

3. Provisional duties shall be secured by a guarantee, and the release of the products concerned for free circulation in the Community shall be conditional upon the provision of such guarantee.

4. The Commission shall take provisional action after consultation or, in cases of extreme urgency, after informing the Member States. In this latter case, consultations shall take place 10 days, at the latest, after notification to the Member States of the action taken by the Commission.

5. Where a Member State requests immediate intervention by the Commission and where the conditions in paragraph 1 are met, the Commission shall within a maximum of five working days of receipt of the request, decide whether a provisional anti-dumping duty shall be imposed.

6. The Commission shall forthwith inform the Council and the Member States of any decision taken under paragraphs 1 to 5. The Council, acting by a qualified majority, may decide differently.

7. Provisional duties may be imposed for six months and extended for a further three months or they may be imposed for nine months. However, they may only be extended, or imposed for a nine-month period, where exporters representing a significant percentage of the trade involved so request or do not object upon notification by the Commission.

Article 8 Undertakings

1. Investigations may be terminated without the imposition of provisional or definitive duties upon receipt of satisfactory voluntary undertakings from any exporter to revise its prices or to cease exports to the area in question at dumped prices, so that the Commission, after consultation, is satisfied that the injurious effect of the dumping is eliminated. Price increases under such undertakings shall not be higher than necessary to eliminate the margin of dumping and they should be less than the margin of dum-

ping if such increases would be adequate to remove the injury to the Community industry.
2.   Undertakings may be suggested by the Commission, but no exporter shall be obliged to enter into such an undertaking. The fact that exporters do not offer such undertakings, or do not accept an invitation to do so, shall in no way prejudice consideration of the case. However, it may be determined that a threat of injury is more likely to be realized if the dumped imports continue. Undertakings shall not be sought or accepted from exporters unless a provisional affirmative determination of dumping and injury caused by such dumping has been made. Save in exceptional circumstances, undertakings may not be offered later than the end of the period during which representations may be made pursuant to Article 20 (5).
3.   Undertakings offered need not be accepted if their acceptance is considered impractical, if such as where the number of actual or potential exporters is too great, or for other reasons, including reasons of general policy. The exporter concerned may be provided with the reasons for which it is proposed to reject the offer of an undertaking and may be given an opportunity to make comments thereon. The reasons for rejection shall be set out in the definitive decision.
4.   Parties which offer an undertaking shall be required to provide a non-confidential version of such undertaking, so that it may be made available to interested parties to the investigation.
5.   Where undertakings are, after consultation, accepted and where there is no objection raised within the Advisory Committee, the investigation shall be terminated. In all other cases, the Commission shall submit to the Council forthwith a report on the results of the consultation, together with a proposal that the investigation be terminated. The investigation shall be deemed terminated if, within one month, the Council, acting by a qualified majority, has not decided otherwise.
6.   If the undertakings are accepted, the investigation of dumping and injury shall normally be completed. In such a case, if a negative determination of dumping or injury is made, the undertaking shall automatically lapse, except in cases where such a determination is due in large part to the existence of an undertaking. In such cases it may be required that an undertaking be maintained for a reasonable period. In the event that an affirmative determination of dumping and injury is made, the undertaking shall continue consistent with its terms and the provisions of this Regulation.
7.   The Commission shall require any exporter from which an undertaking has been accepted to provide, periodically, information relevant to the fulfilment of such undertaking, and to permit verification of pertinent data. Non-compliance with such requirements shall be construed as a breach of the undertaking.
8.   Where undertakings are accepted from certain exporters during the course of an investigation, they shall, for the purpose of Article 11, be deemed to take effect from the date on which the investigation is concluded for the exporting country.
9.   In case of breach or withdrawal of undertakings by any party, a definitive duty shall be imposed in accordance with Article 9, on the basis of the facts established within the context of the investigation which led to the undertaking, provided that such investigation was concluded with a final determination as to dumping and injury and that the exporter concerned has, except where he himself has withdrawn the undertaking, been given an opportunity to comment.
10. A provisional duty may, after consultation, be imposed in accordance with Article 7 on the basis of the best information available, where there is reason to believe that an undertaking is being breached, or in case of breach or withdrawal of an undertaking where the investigation which led to the undertaking has not been concluded.

Article 9 Termination without measures; imposition of definitive duties
1. Where the complaint is withdrawn, the proceeding may be terminated unless such termination would not be in the Community interest.
2. Where, after consultation, protective measures are unnecessary and there is no objection raised within the Advisory Committee, the investigation or proceeding shall be terminated. In all other cases, the Commission shall submit to the Council forthwith a report on the results of the consultation, together with a proposal that the proceeding be terminated. The proceeding shall be deemed terminated if, within one month, the Council, acting by a qualified majority, has not decided otherwise.
3. For a proceeding initiated pursuant to Article 5 (9), injury shall normally be regarded as negligible where the imports concerned represent less than the volumes set out in Article 5 (7). For the same proceeding, there shall be immediate termination where it is determined that the margin of dumping is less than 2%, expressed as a percentage of the export price, provided that it is only the investigation that shall be terminated where the margin is below 2% for individual exporters and they shall remain subject to the proceeding and may be reinvestigated in any subsequent review carried out for the country concerned pursuant to Article 11.
4. Where the facts as finally established show that there is dumping and injury caused thereby, and the Community interest calls for intervention in accordance with Article 21, a definitive anti-dumping duty shall be imposed by the Council, acting by simple majority on a proposal submitted by the Commission after consultation of the Advisory Committee. Where provisional duties are in force, a proposal for definitive action shall be submitted to the Council not later than one month before the expiry of such duties. The amount of the anti-dumping duty shall not exceed the margin of dumping established but it should be less than the margin if such lesser duty would be adequate to remove the injury to the Community industry.
5. An anti-dumping duty shall be imposed in the appropriate amounts in each case, on a non-discriminatory basis on imports of a product from all sources found to be dumped and causing injury, except as to imports from those sources from which undertakings under the terms of this Regulation have been accepted. The Regulation imposing the duty shall specify the duty for each supplier or, if that is impracticable, and as a general rule in the cases referred to in Article 2 (7), the supplying country concerned.
6. When the Commission has limited its examination in accordance with Article 17, any anti-dumping duty applied to imports from exporters or producers which have made themselves known in accordance with Article 17 but were not included in the examination shall not exceed the weighted average margin of dumping established for the parties in the sample. For the purpose of this paragraph, the Commission shall disregard any zero and *de minimis* margins, and margins established in the circumstances referred to in Article 18. Individual duties shall be applied to imports from any exporter or producer which is granted individual treatment, as provided for in Article 17.

Article 10 Retroactivity
1. Provisional measures and definitive anti-dumping duties shall only be applied to products which enter free circulation after the time when the decision taken pursuant to Articles 7 (1) or 9 (4), as the case may be, enters into force, subject to the exceptions set out in this Regulation.
2. Where a provisional duty has been applied and the facts as finally established show that there is dumping and injury, the Council shall decide, irrespective of whether a definitive anti-dumping duty is to be imposed, what proportion of the provisional duty is to be definitively collected. For this purpose, "injury" shall not include material retardation of the establishment of a Community industry, nor threat of material injury, ex-

cept where it is found that this would, in the absence of provisional measures, have developed into material injury. In all other cases involving such threat or retardation, any provisional amounts shall be released and definitive duties can only be imposed from the date that a final determination of threat or material retardation is made.

3.   If the definitive anti-dumping duty is higher than the provisional duty, the difference shall not be collected. If the definitive duty is lower than the provisional duty, the duty shall be recalculated. Where a final determination is negative, the provisional duty shall not be confirmed.

4.   A definitive anti-dumping duty may be levied on products which were entered for consumption not more than 90 days prior to the date of application of provisional measures but not prior to the initiation of the investigation, provided that imports have been registered in accordance with Article 14 (5), the Commission has allowed the importers concerned an opportunity to comment, and:

(a) there is, for the product in question, a history of dumping over an extended period, or the importer was aware of, or should have been aware of, the dumping as regards the extent of the dumping and the injury alleged or found; and

(b) in addition to the level of imports which caused injury during the investigation period, there is a further substantial rise in imports which, in the light of its timing and volume and other circumstances, is likely to seriously undermine the remedial effect of the definitive anti-dumping duty to be applied.

5.   In cases of breach or withdrawal of undertakings, definitive duties may be levied on goods entered for free circulation not more than 90 days before the application of provisional measures, provided that imports have been registered in accordance with Article 14 (5), and that any such retroactive assessment shall not apply to imports entered before the breach or withdrawal of the undertaking.

Article 11 Duration, reviews and refunds

1.   An anti-dumping measure shall remain in force only as long as, and to the extent that, it is necessary to counteract the dumping which is causing injury.

2.   A definitive anti-dumping measure shall expire five years from its imposition or five years from the date of the conclusion of the most recent review which has covered both dumping and injury, unless it is determined in a review that the expiry would be likely to lead to a continuation or recurrence of dumping and injury. Such an expiry review shall be initiated on the initiative of the Commission, or upon request made by or on behalf of Community producers, and the measure shall remain in force pending the outcome of such review.

An expiry review shall be initiated where the request contains sufficient evidence that the expiry of the measures would be likely to result in a continuation or recurrence of dumping and injury. Such a likelihood may, for example, be indicated by evidence of continued dumping and injury or evidence that the removal of injury is partly or solely due to the existence of measures or evidence that the circumstances of the exporters, or market conditions, are such that they would indicate the likelihood of further injurious dumping.

In carrying out investigations under this paragraph, the exporters, importers, the representatives of the exporting country and the Community producers shall be provided with the opportunity to amplify, rebut or comment on the matters set out in the review request, and conclusions shall be reached with due account taken of all relevant and duly documented evidence presented in relation to the question as to whether the expiry of measures would be likely, or unlikely, to lead to the continuation or recurrence of dumping and injury.

A notice of impending expiry shall be published in the Official Journal of the European Communities at an appropriate time in the final year of the period of application of the measures as defined in this paragraph. Thereafter, the Community producers shall, no later than three months before the end of the five-year period, be entitled to lodge a review request in accordance with the second sub-paragraph. A notice announcing the actual expiry of measures pursuant to this paragraph shall also be published.

3.   The need for the continued imposition of measures may also be reviewed, where warranted, on the initiative of the Commission or at the request of a Member State or, provided that a reasonable period of time of at least one year has elapsed since the imposition of the definitive measure, upon a request by any exporter or importer or by the Community producers which contains sufficient evidence substantiating the need for such an interim review.

An interim review shall be initiated where the request contains sufficient evidence that the continued imposition of the measure is no longer necessary to offset dumping and/or that the injury would be unlikely to continue or recur if the measure were removed or varied, or that the existing measure is not, or is no longer, sufficient to counteract the dumping which is causing injury.

In carrying out investigations pursuant to this paragraph, the Commission may, inter alia, consider whether the circumstances with regard to dumping and injury have changed significantly, or whether existing measures are achieving the intended results in removing the injury previously established under Article 3. In these respects, account shall be taken in the final determination of all relevant and duly documented evidence.

4.   A review shall also be carried out for the purpose of determining individual margins of dumping for new exporters in the exporting country in question which have not exported the product during the period of investigation on which the measures were based.

The review shall be initiated where a new exporter or producer can show that it is not related to any of the exporters or producers in the exporting country which are subject to the anti-dumping measures on the product, and that it has actually exported to the Community following the abovementioned investigation period, or where it can demonstrate that it has entered into an irrevocable contractual obligation to export a significant quantity to the Community.

A review for a new exporter shall be initiated, and carried out on an accelerated basis, after consultation of the Advisory Committee and after Community producers have been given an opportunity to comment. The Commission Regulation initiating a review shall repeal the duty in force with regard to the new exporter concerned by amending the Regulation which has imposed such duty, and by making imports subject to registration in accordance with Article 14 (5) in order to ensure that, should the review result in a determination of dumping in respect of such an exporter, anti-dumping duties can be levied retroactively to the date of the initiation of the review.

The provisions of this paragraph shall not apply where duties have been imposed under Article 9 (6).

5.   The relevant provisions of this Regulation with regard to procedures and the conduct of investigations, excluding those relating to time limits, shall apply to any review carried out pursuant to paragraphs 2, 3 and 4. Any such review shall be carried out expeditiously and shall normally be concluded within 12 months of the date of initiation of the review.

6.   Reviews pursuant to this Article shall be initiated by the Commission after consultation of the Advisory Committee. Where warranted by reviews, measures shall be repealed or maintained pursuant to paragraph 2, or repealed, maintained or amended pursuant to paragraphs 3 and 4, by the Community institution responsible for their introduction. Where measures are repealed for individual exporters, but not for the country as a whole, such exporters shall remain subject to the proceeding and may,

automatically, be reinvestigated in any subsequent review carried out for that country pursuant to this Article.

7.   Where a review of measures pursuant to paragraph 3 is in progress at the end of the period of application of measures as defined in paragraph 2, such review shall also cover the circumstances set out in paragraph 2.

8.   Notwithstanding paragraph 2, an importer may request reimbursement of duties collected where it is shown that the dumping margin, on the basis of which duties were paid, has been eliminated, or reduced to a level which is below the level of the duty in force.

In requesting a refund of anti-dumping duties, the importer shall submit an application to the Commission. The application shall be submitted via the Member State of the territory in which the products were released for free circulation, within six months of the date on which the amount of the definitive duties to be levied was duly determined by the competent authorities or of the date on which a decision was made definitively to collect the amounts secured by way of provisional duty. Member States shall forward the request to the Commission forthwith.

An application for refund shall only be considered to be duly supported by evidence where it contains precise information on the amount of refund of anti-dumping duties claimed and all customs documentation relating to the calculation and payment of such amount. It shall also include evidence, for a representative period, of normal values and export prices to the Community for the exporter or producer to which the duty applies. In cases where the importer is not associate with the exporter or producer concerned and such information is not immediately available, or where the exporter or producer is unwilling to release it to the importer, the application shall contain a statement from the exporter or producer that the dumping margin has been reduced or eliminated, as specified in this Article, and that the relevant supporting evidence will be provided to the Commission. Where such evidence is not forthcoming from the exporter or producer within a reasonable period of time the application shall be rejected.

The Commission shall, after consultation of the Advisory Committee, decide whether and to what extent the application should be granted, or it may decide at any time to initiate an interim review, whereupon the information and findings from such review carried out in accordance with the provisions applicable for such reviews, shall be used to determine whether and to what extent a refund is justified. Refunds of duties shall normally take place within 12 months, and in no circumstances more than 18 months after the date on which a request for a refund, duly supported by evidence, has been made by an importer of the product subject to the anti-dumping duty. The payment of any refund authorized should normally be made by Member States within 90 day of the abovementioned decision.

9.   In all review or refund investigations carried out pursuant to this Article, the Commission shall, provided that circumstances have not changed, apply the same methodology as in the investigation which led to the duty, with due account being taken of Article 2, and in particular paragraphs 11 and 12 thereof, and of Article 17.

10. In any investigation carried our pursuant to this Article, the Commission shall examine the reliability of export prices in accordance with Article 2. However, where it is decided to construct the export price in accordance with Article 2 (9), it shall calculate it with no deduction for the amount of anti-dumping duties paid when conclusive evidence is provided that the duty is duly reflected in resale prices and the subsequent selling prices in the Community.

Article 12 [Re-opening of an investigation if prices remain unfairly low]

1.   Where the Community industry submits sufficient information showing that measures have led to no movement, or insufficient movement, in resale prices or subse-

quent selling prices in the Community, the investigation may, after consultation, be re-opened to examine whether the measure has had effects on the abovementioned prices.

2. During a re-investigation pursuant to this Article, exporters, importers and Community producers shall be provided with an opportunity to clarify the situation with regard to resale prices and subsequent selling prices: if it is concluded that the measure should have led to movements in such prices, then, in order to remove the injury previously established in accordance with Article 3, export prices shall be reassessed in accordance with Article 2 and dumping margins shall be recalculated to take account of the reassessed export prices. Where it is considered that a lack of movement in the prices in the Community is due to a fall in export prices which has occurred prior to or following the imposition of measures, dumping margins may be recalculated to take account of such lower export prices.

3. Where a re-investigation pursuant to this Article shows increased dumping the measures in force shall be amended by the Council, by simple majority on a proposal from the Commission, in accordance with the new findings on export prices.

4. The relevant provisions of Articles 5 and 6 shall apply to any review carried out pursuant to this Article, except that such review shall be carried out expeditiously and shall normally be concluded within six months of the date of initiation of the re-investigation.

5. Alleged changes in normal value shall only be taken into account under this Article where complete information on revised normal values, duly substantiated by evidence, is made available to the Commission within the time limits set out in the notice of initiation of an investigation. Where an investigation involves a re-examination of normal values, imports may be made subject to registration in accordance with Article 14 (5) pending the outcome of the re-investigation.

Article 13 Circumvention

1. Anti-dumping duties imposed pursuant to this Regulation may be extended to imports from third countries of like products, or parts thereof, when circumvention of the measures in force is taking place. Circumvention shall be defined as a change in the pattern of trade between third countries and the Community which stems from a practice, process or work for which there is insufficient due cause or economic justification other than the imposition of the duty, and where there is evidence that the remedial effects of the duty are being undermined in terms of the prices and/or quantities of the like products and there is evidence of dumping in relation to the normal values previously established for the like or similar products.

2. An assembly operation in the Community or a third country shall be considered to circumvent the measures in force where:

(a) the operation started or substantially increased since, or just prior to, the initiation of the anti-dumping investigation and the parts concerned are from the country subject to measures; and

(b) the parts constitute 60% or more of the total value of the parts of the assembled product, except that in no case shall circumvention be considered to be taking place where the value added to the parts brought in, during the assembly or completion operation, is greater than 25% of the manufacturing cost, and

(c) the remedial effects of the duty are being undermined in terms of the prices and/or quantities of the assembled like product and there is evidence of dumping in relation to the normal values previously established for the like or similar products.

3. Investigations shall be initiated pursuant to this Article where the request contains sufficient evidence regarding the factors set out in paragraph 1. Initiations shall be made, after consultation of the Advisory Committee, by Commission Regulation which

shall also instruct the customs authorities to make imports subject to registration in accordance with Article 14 (5) or to request guarantees. Investigations shall be carried out by the Commission, which may be assisted by customs authorities and shall be concluded within nine months. When the facts as finally ascertained justify the extension of measures, this shall be done by the Council, acting by simple majority and on a proposal from the Commission, from the date on which registration was imposed pursuant to Article 14 (5) or on which guarantees were requested. The relevant procedural provisions of this Regulation with regard to initiations and the conduct of investigations shall apply pursuant to this Article.

4.   Products shall not be subject to registration pursuant to Article 14 (5) or measures where they are accompanied by a customs certificate declaring that the importation of the goods does not constitute circumvention. These certificates may be issued to importers, upon written application following authorization by decision of the Commission after consultation of the Advisory Committee or decision of the Council imposing measures and they shall remain valid for the period, and under the conditions, set down therein.

5.   Nothing in this Article shall preclude the normal application of the provisions in force concerning customs duties.

Article 14 General provisions

1.   Provisional or definitive anti-dumping duties shall be imposed by Regulation, and collected by Member States in the form, at the rate specified and according to the other criteria laid down in the Regulation imposing such duties. Such duties shall also be collected independently of the customs duties, taxes and other charges normally imposed on imports. No product shall be subject to both anti-dumping and countervailing duties for the purpose of dealing with one and the same situation arising from dumping or from export subsidization.

2.   Regulations imposing provisional or definitive anti-dumping duties, and Regulations or Decisions accepting undertakings or terminating investigations or proceedings, shall be published in the Official Journal of the European Communities. Such Regulations or Decisions shall contain in particular and with due regard to the protection of confidential information, the names of the exporters, if possible, or of the countries involved, a description of the product and a summary of the material facts and considerations relevant to the dumping and injury determinations. In each case, a copy of the Regulation or Decision shall be sent to known interested parties. The provisions of this paragraph shall apply *mutatis mutandis* to reviews.

3.   Special provisions, in particular with regard to the common definition of the concept of origin, as contained in Council Regulation 2913/92,[1] may be adopted pursuant to this Regulation.

4.   In the Community interest, measures imposed pursuant to this Regulation may, after consultation of the Advisory Committee, be suspended by a decision of the Commission for a period of nine months. The suspension may be extended for a further period, not exceeding one year, if the Council so decides, acting by simple majority on a proposal from the Commission. Measures may only be suspended where market conditions have temporarily changed to an extent that injury would be unlikely to resume as a result of the suspension, and provided that the Community industry has been given an opportunity to comment and these comments have been taken into account. Measures may, at any time and after consultation, be reinstated if the reason for suspension is no longer applicable.

---

1   OJ 1992 L 302, p. 1.

5.   The Commission may, after consultation of the Advisory Committee, direct the customs authorities to take the appropriate steps to register imports, so that measures may subsequently be applied against those imports from the date of such registration. Imports may be made subject to registration following a request from the Community industry which contains sufficient evidence to justify such action. Registration shall be introduced by Regulation which shall specify the purpose of the action and, if appropriate, the estimated amount of possible future liability. Imports shall not be made subject to registration for a period longer than nine months.
6.   Member States shall report to the Commission every month, on the import trade in products subject to investigation and to measures, and on the amount of duties collected pursuant to this Regulation.

Article 15 Consultations

1.   Any consultations provided for in this Regulation shall take place within an Advisory Committee, which shall consist of representatives of each Member State, with a representative of the Commission as chairman. Consultations shall be held immediately at the request of a Member State or on the initiative of the Commission and in any event within a period of time which allows the time limits set by this Regulation to be adhered to.
2.   The Committee shall meet when convened by its chairman. He shall provide the Member States, as promptly as possible, with all relevant information.
3.   Where necessary, consultation may be in writing only; in that event, the Commission shall notify the Member States and shall specify a period within which they shall be entitled to express their opinions or to request an oral consultation which the chairman shall arrange, provided that such oral consultation can be held within a period of time which allows the time limits set by this Regulation to be adhered to.
4.   Consultation shall cover, in particular:
(a) the existence of dumping and the methods of establishing the dumping margin;
(b) the existence and extent of injury;
(c) the causal link between the dumped imports and injury;
(d) the measures which, in the circumstances, are appropriate to prevent or remedy the injury caused by dumping and the ways and means of putting such measures into effect.

Article 16 Verification visits

1.   The Commission shall, where it considers it appropriate, carry out visits to examine the records of importers, exporters, traders, agents, producers, trade associations and organizations and to verify information provided on dumping and injury. In the absence of a proper and timely reply, a verification visit may not be carried out.
2.   The Commission may carry out investigations in third countries as required, provided that it obtains the agreement of the firms concerned, that it notifies the representatives of the government of the country in question and that the latter does not object to the investigation. As soon as the agreement of the firms concerned has been obtained the Commission should notify the authorities of the exporting country of the names and addresses of the firms to be visited and the dates agreed.
3.   The firms concerned shall be advised of the nature of the information to be verified during verification visits and of any further information which needs to be provided during such visits, though this should not preclude requests made during the verification for further details to be provided in the light of information obtained.
4.   In investigations carried out pursuant to paragraphs 1, 2 and 3, the Commission shall be assisted by officials of those Member States who so request.

Article 17 Sampling

1.   In cases where the number of complainants, exporters or importers, types of product or transactions is large, the investigation may be limited to a reasonable number of parties, products or transactions by using samples which are statistically valid on the basis of information available at the time of the selection, or to the largest representative volume of production, sales or exports which can reasonably be investigated within the time available.

2.   The final selection of parties, types of products or transactions made under these sampling provisions shall rest with the Commission, though preference shall be given to choosing a sample in consultation with, and with the consent of, the parties concerned, provided such parties make themselves known and make sufficient information available, within three weeks of initiation of the investigation, to enable a representative sample to be chosen.

3.   In cases where the examination has been limited in accordance with this Article, an individual margin of dumping shall, nevertheless, be calculated for any exporter or producer not initially selected who submits the necessary information within the time limits provided for in this Regulation, except where the number of exporters or producers is so large that individual examinations would be unduly burdensome and would prevent completion of the investigation in good time.

4.   Where it is decided to sample and there is a degree of non-cooperation by some or all of the parties selected which is likely to materially affect the outcome of the investigation, a new sample may be selected. However, if a material degree of non-cooperation persists or there is insufficient time to select a new sample, the relevant provisions of Article 18 shall apply.

Article 18 Non-cooperation

1.   In cases in which any interested party refuses access to, or otherwise does not provide, necessary information within the time limits provided in this Regulation, or significantly impedes the investigation, provisional or final findings, affirmative or negative, may be made on the basis of the facts available. Where it is found that any interested party has supplied false or misleading information, the information shall be disregarded and use may be made of facts available. Interested parties should be made aware of the consequences of non-cooperation.

2.   Failure to give a computerized response shall not be deemed to constitute non-cooperation, provided that the interested party shows that presenting the response as requested would result in an unreasonable extra burden or unreasonable additional cost.

3.   Where the information submitted by an interested party is not ideal in all respects it should nevertheless not be disregarded, provided that any deficiencies are not such as to cause undue difficulty in arriving at a reasonably accurate finding and that the information is appropriately submitted in good time and is verifiable, and that the party has acted to the best of its ability.

4.   If evidence or information is not accepted, the supplying party shall be informed forthwith of the reasons therefor and shall be granted an opportunity to provide further explanations within the time limit specified. If the explanations are considered unsatisfactory, the reasons for rejection of such evidence or information shall be disclosed and given in published findings.

5.   If determinations, including those regarding normal value, are based on the provisions of paragraph 1, including the information supplied in the complaint, it shall, where practicable and with due regard to the time limits of the investigation, be checked by reference to information from other independent sources which may be available, such as published price lists, official import statistics and customs returns, or information obtained from other interested parties during the investigation.

6.   If an interested party does not cooperate, or cooperates only partially, so that relevant information is thereby withheld, the result may be less favourable to the party than if it had cooperated.

Article 19 Confidentiality

1.   Any information which is by nature confidential, (for example, because its disclosure would be of significant competitive advantage to a competitor or would have a significantly adverse effect upon a person supplying the information or upon a person from whom he has acquired the information) or which is provided on a confidential basis by parties to an investigation shall, if good cause is shown, be treated as such by the authorities.

2.   Interested parties providing confidential information shall be required to furnish non-confidential summaries thereof. Those summaries shall be in sufficient detail to permit a reasonable understanding of the substance of the information submitted in confidence. In exceptional circumstances, such parties may indicate that such information is not susceptible of summary. In such exceptional circumstances, a statement of the reasons why summarization is not possible must be provided.

3.   If it is considered that a request for confidentiality is not warranted and if the supplier of the information is either unwilling to make the information available or to authorize its disclosure in generalized or summary form, such information may be disregarded unless it can be satisfactorily demonstrated from appropriate sources that the information is correct. Requests for confidentiality shall not be arbitrarily rejected.

4.   This Article shall not preclude the disclosure of general information by the Community authorities and in particular of the reasons on which decisions taken pursuant to this Regulation are based, or disclosure of the evidence relied on by the Community authorities in so far as is necessary to explain those reasons in court proceedings. Such disclosure must take into account the legitimate interests of the parties concerned that their business secrets should not be divulged.

5.   The Council, the Commission and Member States, or the officials of any of these, shall not reveal any information received pursuant to this Regulation for which confidential treatment has been requested by its supplier, without specific permission from the supplier. Exchanges of information between the Commission and Member States, or any information relating to consultations made pursuant to Article 15, or any internal documents prepared by the authorities of the Community or its Member States, shall not be divulged except as specifically provided for in this Regulation.

6.   Information received pursuant to this Regulation shall be used only for the purpose for which it was requested.

Article 20 Disclosure

1.   The complainants, importers and exporters and their representative associations, and representatives of the exporting country, may request disclosure of the details underlying the essential facts and considerations on the basis of which provisional measures have been imposed. Requests for such disclosure shall be made in writing immediately following the imposition of provisional measures, and the disclosure shall be made in writing as soon as possible thereafter.

2.   The parties mentioned in paragraph 1 may request final disclosure of the essential facts and considerations on the basis of which it is intended to recommend the imposition of definitive measures, or the termination of an investigation or proceedings without the imposition of measures, particular attention being paid to the disclosure of any facts or considerations which are different from those used for any provisional measures.

3.   Requests for final disclosure, as defined in paragraph 2, shall be addressed to the Commission in writing and be received, in cases where a provisional duty has been applied, not later than one month after publication of the imposition of that duty. Where a provisional duty has not been applied, parties shall be provided with an opportunity to request final disclosure within time limits set by the Commission.

4.   Final disclosure shall be given in writing. It shall be made, due regard being had to the protection of confidential information, as soon as possible and, normally, not later than one month prior to a definitive decision or the submission by the Commission of any proposal for final action pursuant to Article 9. Where the Commission is not in a position to disclose certain facts or considerations at that time, these shall be disclosed as soon as possible thereafter. Disclosure shall not prejudice any subsequent decision which may be taken by the Commission or the Council but where such decision is based on any different facts and considerations, these shall be disclosed as soon as possible.

5.   Representations made after final disclosure is given shall be taken into consideration only if received within a period to be set by the Commission in each case, which shall be at least 10 days, due consideration being given to the urgency of the matter.

Article 21 Community interest

1.   A determination as to whether the Community interest calls for intervention shall be based on an appreciation of all the various interests taken as a whole, including the interests of the domestic industry and users and consumers; and a determination pursuant to this Article shall only be made where all parties have been given the opportunity to make their views known pursuant to paragraph 2. In such an examination, the need to eliminate the trade distorting effects of injurious dumping and to restore effective competition shall be given special consideration. Measures, as determined on the basis of the dumping and injury found, may not be applied where the authorities, on the basis of all the information submitted, can clearly conclude that it is not in the Community interest to apply such measures.

2.   In order to provide a sound basis on which the authorities can take account of all views and information in the decision as to whether or not the imposition of measures is in the Community interest, the complainants, importers and their representative associations, representative users and representative consumer organizations may, within the time limits specified in the notice of initiation of the anti-dumping investigation, make themselves known and provide information to the Commission. Such information, or appropriate summaries thereof, shall be made available to the other parties specified in this Article, and they shall be entitled to respond to such information.

3.   The parties which have acted in conformity with paragraph 2 may request a hearing. Such requests shall be granted when they are submitted within the time limits set in paragraph 2, and when they set out the reasons, in terms of the Community interest, why the parties should be heard.

4.   The parties which have acted in conformity with paragraph 2 may provide comments on the application of any provisional duties imposed. Such comments shall be received within one month of the application of such measures if they are to be taken into account and they, or appropriate summaries thereof, shall be made available to other parties who shall be entitled to respond to such comments.

5.   The Commission shall examine the information which is properly submitted and the extent to which it is representative and the results of such analysis, together with an opinion on its merits, shall be transmitted to the Advisory Committee. The balance of views expressed in the Committee shall be taken into account by the Commission in any proposal made pursuant to Article 9.

6.   The parties which have acted in conformity with paragraph 2 may request the facts and considerations on which final decisions are likely to be taken to be made available to them. Such information shall be made available to the extent possible and without prejudice to any subsequent decision taken by the Commission or the Council.

7.   Information shall only be taken into account where it is supported by actual evidence which substantiates its validity.

Article 22 Final provisions

This Regulation shall not preclude the application of:
(a) any special rules laid down in agreements concluded between the Community and third countries;
(b) the Community Regulations in the agricultural sector and Council Regulations 3448/93,[1] 2730/75[2] and 2783/75;[3] this Regulation shall operate by way of complement to those Regulations and in derogation from any provisions thereof which preclude the application of anti-dumping duties;
(c) special measures, provided that such action does not run counter to obligations pursuant to the GATT.

Article 23 Repeal of existing legislation and transitional measures

Regulation 3283/94 is hereby repealed, with the exception of the first paragraph of Article 23 thereof.[4]

However, the repeal of Regulation 3283/94 shall not prejudice the validity of proceedings initiated thereunder.

References to Regulation 2423/88 and to Regulation 3283/94 shall be construed as references to this Regulation, where appropriate.

Article 24 Entry into force

This Regulation shall enter into force on the day of its publication in the Official Journal of the European Communities.

However, the time limits provided for in Articles 5 (9), 6 (9) and 7 (1) shall apply to complaints lodged under Article 5 (9) as from 1 September 1995 and investigations initiated pursuant to such complaints.

This Regulation shall be binding in its entirety and directly applicable in all Member States.

Done at Brussels, 22 December 1995.
For the Council: L. ATIENZA SERNA, The President

---

1   OJ 1993 L 318, p. 18.

2   OJ 1975 L 281, p. 20. Regulation as amended by Commission Regulation 222/88, OJ 1988 L 28, p. 1.

3   OJ 1975 L 282, p. 104. Regulation as last amended by Regulation 3290/94, OJ 1994 L 349, p. 105.

4   Art. 23 of that Regulation repealed the preceding Reg. 2423/88; the latter continued to apply to investigations which were pending on 1 September 1994.

Council Regulation 2026/97 of 6 October 1997 on Protection Against Subsidized Imports From Countries Not Members of the European Community[1]

THE COUNCIL OF THE EUROPEAN UNION,

HAVING REGARD to the Treaty establishing the European Community, and in particular Article 113 thereof, [...]
HAVING REGARD to the Regulations establishing the common organization of agricultural markets and the Regulations adopted pursuant to Article 235 of the Treaty applicable to goods manufactured from agricultural products, and in particular the provisions of those Regulations which allow for derogation from the general principle that protective measures at frontiers may be replaced solely by the measures provided for in those Regulations, [...]
(1) WHEREAS, by Regulation 2423/88, the Council adopted common rules for protection against dumped or subsidized imports from countries which are not members of the European Community;
(2) WHEREAS those rules were adopted in accordance with existing international obligations, in particular those arising from Article VI of the General Agreement on Tariffs and Trade ("the GATT"), from the Agreement on Implementation of Article VI of the GATT ("the 1979 Anti-Dumping Code") and from the Agreement on Interpretation and Application of Articles VI, XVI and XXIII of the GATT (Code on Subsidies and Countervailing Duties);
(3) WHEREAS the conclusion of the Uruguay Round of multilateral trade negotiations has led to the establishment of the World Trade Organization ("the WTO");
(4) WHEREAS Annex 1A to the Agreement establishing the WTO ("the WTO Agreement"), approved by Decision 94/800,[2] contains, inter alia, the General Agreement on Tariffs and Trade 1994 ("the GATT 1994"), an Agreement on Agriculture ("the Agreement on Agriculture"), an Agreement on implementation of Article VI of the GATT 1994 (hereinafter referred to as "the 1994 Anti-Dumping Agreement") and a new Agreement on Subsidies and Countervailing Measures ("the Subsidies Agreement");
(5) WHEREAS, in order to reach greater transparency and effectiveness in the application by the Community of the rules laid down in the 1994 Anti-Dumping Agreement and the Subsidies Agreement respectively, it is considered necessary to adopt two separate Regulations which will lay down in sufficient detail the requirements for the application of each of these commercial defence instruments;
(6) WHEREAS it is therefore appropriate to amend Community rules governing the application of countervailing measures in the light of the new multilateral rules, with regard inter alia to the procedures for initiation of proceedings and the conduct of subsequent investigations, including the establishment and treatment of the facts, the imposition of provisional measures, the imposition and collection of countervailing duties, the duration and review of countervailing measures, and the public disclosure of information relating to countervailing investigations;
(7) WHEREAS, in view of the extent of the changes brought about by the new Agreements and to ensure an adequate and transparent implementation of the new rules, it is appropriate to transpose the language of the new Agreements into Community legislation to the extent possible;

---

1   OJ 1997 L 288, p. 1.
2   OJ 1994 L 336, p. 1.

(8) WHEREAS, furthermore, it seems advisable to explain, in adequate detail, when a subsidy shall be deemed to exist, according to which principles it shall be countervailable (in particular whether the subsidy has been granted specifically), and according to which criteria the amount of the countervailable subsidy is to be calculated;

(9) WHEREAS, in determining the existence of a subsidy, it is necessary to demonstrate that there has been a financial contribution by a government or any public body within the territory of a country, or that there has been some form of income or price support within the meaning of Article XVI of the GATT 1994, and that a benefit has thereby been conferred on the recipient enterprise;

(10) WHEREAS it is necessary to explain in sufficient detail which kind of subsidies are not countervailable and which procedure shall be followed if, during an investigation, it is determined that an enterprise undergoing investigation has received non-countervailable subsidies;

(11) WHEREAS the Subsidies Agreement states that the provisions concerning non-countervailable subsidies shall cease to apply five years after the date of entry into force of the WTO Agreement, unless they are extended by mutual agreement of the members of the WTO; whereas it may therefore be necessary to amend this Regulation accordingly if the validity of those provisions is not so extended;

(12) WHEREAS the measures listed in Annex 2 to the Agreement on Agriculture are non-countervailable, to the extent provided for in that Agreement;

(13) WHEREAS it is desirable to lay down clear and detailed guidance as to the factors which may be relevant for the determination of whether the subsidized imports have caused material injury or are threatening to cause injury; whereas, in demonstrating that the volume and price levels of the imports concerned are responsible for injury sustained by a Community industry, attention should be given to the effect of other factors and in particular prevailing market conditions in the Community;

(14) WHEREAS it is advisable to define the term "Community industry" and to provide that parties related to exporters may be excluded from such industry, and to define the term "related"; whereas it is also necessary to provide for countervailing duty action to be taken on behalf of producers in a region of the Community and to lay down guidelines on the definition of such region;

(15) WHEREAS it is necessary to lay down who may lodge a countervailing duty complaint, including the extent to which it should be supported by the Community industry, and the information on countervailable subsidies, injury and causation which such complaint should contain; whereas it is also expedient to specify the procedures for the rejection of complaints or the initiation of proceedings;

(16) WHEREAS it is necessary to lay down the manner in which interested parties should be given notice of the information which the authorities require, and should have ample opportunity to present all relevant evidence and to defend their interests; whereas it is also desirable to set out clearly the rules and procedures to be followed during the investigation, in particular the rules whereby interested parties are to make themselves known, present their views and submit information within specified time limits, if such views and information are to be taken into account; whereas it is also appropriate to set out the conditions under which an interested party may have access to, and comment on, information presented by other interested parties; whereas there should also be cooperation between the Member States and the Commission in the collection of information;

(17) WHEREAS it is necessary to lay down the conditions under which provisional duties may be imposed, including conditions whereby they may be imposed no earlier than 60 days from initiation and not later than nine months thereafter; whereas such duties may in all cases be imposed by the Commission only for a four-month period;

(18) WHEREAS it is necessary to specify procedures for the acceptance of undertakings eliminating or offsetting the countervailable subsidies and injury in lieu of the
imposition of provisional or definitive duties; whereas it is also appropriate to lay down
the consequences of breach or withdrawal of undertakings and that provisional duties
may be imposed in cases of suspected violation or where further investigation is necessary to supplement the findings; whereas, in accepting undertakings, care should
be taken that the proposed undertakings, and their enforcement, do not lead to anti-
competitive behaviour;

(19) WHEREAS it is necessary to provide that the termination of cases should, irrespective of whether definitive measures are adopted or not, normally take place within
12 months, and in no case later than 13 months, from the initiation of the investigation;

(20) WHEREAS an investigation or proceeding should be terminated whenever the
amount of the subsidy is found to be *de minimis* or if, particularly in the case of imports
originating in developing countries, the volume of subsidized imports or the injury is
negligible, and it is appropriate to define those criteria; whereas, where measures are
to be imposed, it is necessary to provide for the termination of investigations and to lay
down that measures should be less than the amount of countervailable subsidies if
such lesser amount would remove the injury, and also to specify the method of calculating the level of measures in cases of sampling;

(21) WHEREAS it is necessary to provide for the retroactive collection of provisional
duties if that is deemed appropriate and to define the circumstances which may trigger
the retroactive application of duties in order to avoid the undermining of the definitive
measures to be applied; whereas it is also necessary to provide that duties may be
applied retroactively in cases of breach or withdrawal of undertakings;

(22) WHEREAS it is necessary to provide that measures are to lapse after five years
unless a review indicates that they should be maintained; whereas it is also necessary
to provide, in cases where sufficient evidence is submitted of changed circumstances,
for interim reviews or for investigations to determine whether refunds of countervailing
duties are warranted;

(23) WHEREAS, even though the Subsidies Agreement does not contain provisions
concerning circumvention of countervailing measures, the possibility of such circumvention exists, in terms similar, albeit not identical, to the circumvention of anti-dumping
measures; whereas it appears therefore appropriate to enact an anti-circumvention
provision in this Regulation;

(24) WHEREAS it is expedient to permit the suspension of countervailing measures
where there is a temporary change in market conditions which makes the continued
imposition of such measures temporarily inappropriate;

(25) WHEREAS it is necessary to provide that imports under investigation may be
made subject to registration upon importation in order to enable measures to be subsequently applied against such imports;

(26) WHEREAS, in order to ensure proper enforcement of measures, it is necessary
that Member States monitor, and report to the Commission, the import trade in products subject to investigation or subject to measures, and also the amount of duties
collected under this Regulation;

(27) WHEREAS it is necessary to provide for consultation of an Advisory Committee
at regular and specified stages of the investigation; whereas the Committee should
consist of representatives of Member States with a representative of the Commission
as chairman;

(28) WHEREAS it is expedient to provide for verification visits to check information
submitted on countervailable subsidies and injury, such visits being, however, conditional on proper replies to questionnaires being received;

(29) WHEREAS it is essential to provide for sampling in cases where the number of parties or transactions is large in order to permit completion of investigations within the appointed time limits;

(30) WHEREAS, it is necessary to provide that, where parties do not cooperate satisfactorily, other information may be used to establish findings and that such information may be less favourable to the parties than if they had cooperated;

(31) WHEREAS provision should be made for the treatment of confidential information so that business or governmental secrets are not divulged;

(32) WHEREAS it is essential that provision be made for proper disclosure of essential facts and considerations to parties which qualify for such treatment and that such disclosure be made, with due regard to the decision-making process in the Community, within a time period which permits parties to defend their interests;

(33) WHEREAS it is prudent to provide for an administrative system under which arguments can be presented as to whether measures are in the Community interest, including the interests of consumers, and to lay down the time periods within which such information has to be presented, together with the disclosure rights of the parties concerned;

(34) WHEREAS in applying the rules of the Subsidies Agreement it is essential, in order to maintain the balance of rights and obligations which this Agreement sought to establish, that the Community take account of their interpretation by the Community's major trading partners, as reflected in legislation or established practice;

(35) WHEREAS, by Regulation 3284/94 of 22 December 1994 on protection against subsidized imports from countries not members of the European Community, the Council replaced Regulation 2423/88 and instituted a new common system of defence against subsidized imports from countries not members of the European Community;

(36) WHEREAS drafting problems in the text of Regulation 3284/94 became apparent on publication; whereas, moreover, the Regulation has already been amended;

(37) WHEREAS, in the interests of clarity, transparency and legal certainty, that Regulation should therefore be repealed and replaced, without prejudice to the countervailing proceedings already initiated under it or under Regulation 2423/88,

HAS ADOPTED THIS REGULATION:

Article 1 Principles

1. A countervailing duty may be imposed for the purpose of offsetting any subsidy granted, directly or indirectly, for the manufacture, production, export or transport of any product whose release for free circulation in the Community causes injury.

2. For the purpose of this Regulation, a product is considered to be subsidized if it benefits from a countervailable subsidy as defined in Articles 2 and 3.

3. Such subsidy may be granted by the government of the country of origin of the imported product, or by the government of an intermediate country from which the product is exported to the Community, known for the purpose of this Regulation as "the country of export".

The term "government" is defined, for the purposes of this Regulation as a government or any public body within the territory of the country of origin or export.

4. Notwithstanding paragraphs 1, 2 and 3, where products are not directly imported from the country of origin but are exported to the Community from an intermediate country, the provisions of this Regulation shall be fully applicable and the transaction or transactions shall, where appropriate, be regarded as having taken place between the country of origin and the Community.

5. For the purpose of this Regulation the term "like product" shall be interpreted to mean a product which is identical, that is to say, alike in all respects, to the product un-

der consideration, or in the absence of such a product, another product which although not alike in all respects, has characteristics closely resembling those of the product under consideration.

Article 2 Definition of a subsidy

A subsidy shall be deemed to exist if:

1. (a) there is a financial contribution by a government in the country of origin or export, that is to say, where:
   (i) a government practice involves a direct transfer of funds (for example, grants, loans, equity infusion), potential direct transfers of funds or liabilities (for example, loan guarantees);
   (ii) government revenue that is otherwise due is forgone or not collected (for example, fiscal incentives such as tax credits); in this regard, the exemption of an exported product from duties or taxes borne by the like product when destined for domestic consumption, or the remission of such duties or taxes in amounts not in excess of those which have been accrued, shall not be deemed to be a subsidy, provided that such an exemption is granted in accordance with the provisions of Annexes I to III;
   (iii) a government provides goods or services other than general infrastructure, or purchases goods;
   (iv) a government:
   — makes payments to a funding mechanism, or
   — entrusts or directs a private body to carry out one or more of the type of functions illustrated in points (i), (ii) and (iii) which would normally be vested in the government, and the practice, in no real sense, differs from practices normally followed by governments; or
   (b) there is any form of income or price support within the meaning of Article XVI of the GATT 1994; and
2. a benefit is thereby conferred.

Article 3 Countervailable subsidies

1. Subsidies shall be subject to countervailing measures only if they are specific, as defined in paragraphs 2, 3 and 4.
2. In order to determine whether a subsidy is specific to an enterprise or industry or group of enterprises or industries (hereinafter referred to as "certain enterprises") within the jurisdiction of the granting authority, the following principles shall apply:
(a) where the granting authority, or the legislation pursuant to which the granting authority operates, explicitly limits access to a subsidy to certain enterprises, such subsidy shall be specific;
(b) where the granting authority, or the legislation pursuant to which the granting authority operates, establishes objective criteria or conditions governing the eligibility for, and the amount of, a subsidy, specificity shall not exist, provided that the eligibility is automatic and that such criteria and conditions are strictly adhered to.

    For the purpose of this Article, objective criteria or conditions mean criteria or conditions which are neutral, which do not favour certain enterprises over others, and which are economic in nature and horizontal in application, such as number of employees or size of enterprise.

    The criteria or conditions must be clearly set out by law, regulation, or other official document, so as to be capable of verification;
(c) if, notwithstanding any appearance of non-specificity resulting from the application of the principles laid down in subparagraphs (a) and (b), there are reasons to believe that the subsidy may in fact be specific, other factors may be considered.

Such factors are: use of a subsidy programme by a limited number of certain enterprises; predominant use by certain enterprises; the granting of disproportionately large amounts of subsidy to certain enterprises; and the manner in which discretion has been exercised by the granting authority in the decision to grant a subsidy. In this regard, information on the frequency with which applications for a subsidy are refused or approved and the reasons for such decisions shall, in particular, be considered.

In applying the first subparagraph, account shall be taken of the extent of diversification of economic activities within the jurisdiction of the granting authority, as well as of the length of time during which the subsidy programme has been in operation.

3. A subsidy which is limited to certain enterprises located within a designated geographical region within the jurisdiction of the granting authority shall be specific. The setting or changing of generally applicable tax rates by all levels of government entitled to do so shall not be deemed to be a specific subsidy for the purposes of this Regulation.

4. Notwithstanding paragraphs 2 and 3, the following subsidies shall be deemed to be specific:

(a) subsidies contingent, in law or in fact, whether solely or as one of several other conditions, upon export performance, including those illustrated in Annex I.

Subsidies shall be considered to be contingent in fact upon export performance when the facts demonstrate that the granting of a subsidy, without having been made legally contingent upon export performance, is in fact tied to actual or anticipated exportation or export earnings. The mere fact that a subsidy is accorded to enterprises which export shall not for that reason alone be considered to be an export subsidy within the meaning of this provision;

(b) subsidies contingent, whether solely or as one of several other conditions, upon the use of domestic over imported goods.

5. Any determination of specificity under the provisions of this Article shall be clearly substantiated on the basis of positive evidence.

Article 4 Non-countervailable subsidies

1. The following subsidies shall not be subjected to countervailing measures:

(a) subsidies which are not specific within the meaning of Article 3 (2) and (3);

(b) subsidies which are specific, within the meaning of Article 3 (2) and (3), but which meet the conditions provided for in paragraphs 2, 3 or 4 of this Article;

(c) the element of subsidy which may exist in any of the measures listed in Annex IV.

2. Subsidies for research activities conducted by firms or by higher education or research establishments on a contract basis with firms shall not be subject to countervailing measures, if the subsidies cover not more than 75% of the costs of industrial research or 50% of the costs of pre-competitive development activity, and provided that such subsidies are limited exclusively to:

(a) personnel costs (researchers, technicians and other supporting staff employed exclusively in the research activity);

(b) costs of instruments, equipment, land and buildings used exclusively and permanently (except when disposed of on a commercial basis) for the research activity;

(c) costs of consultancy and equivalent services used exclusively for the research activity, including bought-in research, technical knowledge, patents, etc.;

(d) additional overhead costs incurred directly as a result of the research activity;

(e) other running costs (such as those of materials, supplies and the like), incurred directly as a result of the research activity.

The first subparagraph shall not apply to civil aircraft (as defined in the 1979 Agreement on Trade in Civil Aircraft, as amended, or in any later Agreement amending or replacing such Agreement).

For the purpose of the first subparagraph:

(a) the allowable levels of non-countervailable subsidy shall be established by reference to the total eligible costs incurred over the duration of an individual project. In the case of programmes which span both "industrial research" and "pre-competitive development activity", the allowable level of non-countervailable subsidy shall not exceed the simple average of the allowable levels of non-countervailable subsidy applicable to the above two categories, calculated on the basis of all eligible costs as set forth in points (a) to (e) of the first subparagraph;

(b) the term "industrial research" means planned search or critical investigation aimed at discovery of new knowledge, with the objective that such knowledge may be useful in developing new products, processes or services, or in bringing about a significant improvement to existing products, processes or services;

(c) the term "pre-competitive development activity" means the translation of industrial research findings into a plan, blueprint or design for new, modified or improved products, processes or services, whether intended for sale or for use, including the creation of a first prototype which would not be capable of commercial use. It may further include the conceptual formulation and design of products, processes or services alternatives and initial demonstration or pilot projects, provided that these same projects cannot be converted or used for industrial application or commercial exploitation. It does not include routine or periodic alterations to existing products, production lines, manufacturing process, services, and other ongoing operations even though those alterations may represent improvements.

3. Subsidies to disadvantaged regions within the territory of the country of origin and/ or export, given pursuant to a general framework of regional development, which would be non-specific if the criteria laid down in Article 3 (2) and (3) were applied to each eligible region concerned, shall not be subject to countervailing measures, provided that:

(a) each disadvantaged region is a clearly designated contiguous geographical area with a definable economic and administrative identity;

(b) the region is regarded as disadvantaged on the basis of neutral and objective criteria, indicating that the region's difficulties arise out of more than temporary circumstances; such criteria must be clearly spelled out by law, regulation, or other official document, so as to be capable of verification;

(c) the criteria mentioned under (b) include a measurement of economic development which shall be based on at least one of the following factors:
— either income per capita, or household income per capita, or GDP per capita, which must not be above 85% of the average for the territory of the country of origin or export concerned,
— unemployment rate, which must be at least 110% of the average for the territory of the country of origin or export concerned;

as measured over a three-year period; such measurement, however, may be a composite one and may include other factors.

For the purpose of the first subparagraph:

(a) a "general framework of regional development" means that regional subsidy programmes are part of an internally consistent and generally applicable regional development policy and that regional development subsidies are not granted in isolated geographical points having no, or virtually no, influence on the development of a region;

(b) "neutral and objective criteria" means criteria which do not favour certain regions beyond what is appropriate for the elimination or reduction of regional disparities within the framework of the regional development policy. In this regard, regional subsidy programmes shall include ceilings on the amount of subsidy which can be granted to each subsidized project. Such ceilings must be differentiated according to the different levels of development of eligible regions and must be expressed in terms of investment costs or the cost of job creation. Within such ceilings, the distribution of subsidy shall be sufficiently broad and even to avoid the predominant use of a subsidy by, or the granting of disproportionately large amounts of subsidy to, certain enterprises.

This provision shall be applied in the light of the criteria set out in Article 3 (2) and (3).

4. Subsidies to promote adaptation of existing facilities to new environmental requirements imposed by law and/or regulation which result in greater constraints and financial burden on firms shall not be subject to countervailing measures, provided that the subsidy:

(a) is a one-off non-recurring measure; and
(b) is limited to 20% of the cost of adaptation; and
(c) does not cover the cost of replacing and operating the subsidized investment, which must be fully borne by the firms; and
(d) is directly linked to and proportionate to a firm's planned reduction of nuisances and pollution, and does not cover any manufacturing cost savings which may be achieved; and
(e) is available to all firms which can adopt the new equipment and/or production processes.

For the purpose of the first subparagraph the term "existing facilities" means facilities having been in operation for at least two years at the time when new environmental requirements are imposed.

Article 5 Calculation of the amount of the countervailable subsidy

The amount of countervailable subsidies, for the purposes of this Regulation, shall be calculated in terms of the benefit conferred on the recipient which is found to exist during the investigation period for subsidization. Normally this period shall be the most recent accounting year of the beneficiary, but may be any other period of at least six months prior to the initiation of the investigation for which reliable financial and other relevant data are available.

Article 6 Calculation of benefit to the recipient

As regards the calculation of benefit to the recipient, the following rules shall apply:

(a) government provision of equity capital shall not be considered to confer a benefit, unless the investment can be regarded as inconsistent with the usual investment practice (including for the provision of risk capital) of private investors in the territory of the country of origin and/or export;
(b) a loan by a government shall not be considered to confer a benefit, unless there is a difference between the amount that the firm receiving the loan pays on the government loan and the amount that the firm would pay for a comparable commercial loan which the firm could actually obtain on the market. In that event the benefit shall be the difference between these two amounts;
(c) a loan guarantee by a government shall not be considered to confer a benefit, unless there is a difference between the amount that the firm receiving the guarantee pays on a loan guaranteed by the government and the amount that the firm would pay for a comparable commercial loan in the absence of the government guarantee. In this case the benefit shall be the difference between these two amounts, adjusted for any differences in fees;

(d) the provision of goods or services or purchase of goods by a government shall not
     be considered to confer a benefit, unless the provision is made for less than ade-
     quate remuneration or the purchase is made for more than adequate remunera-
     tion. The adequacy of remuneration shall be determined in relation to prevailing
     market conditions for the product or service in question in the country of provision
     or purchase (including price, quality, availability, marketability, transportation and
     other conditions of purchase or sale).

Article 7 General provisions on calculation

1.   The amount of the countervailable subsidies shall be determined per unit of the
subsidized product exported to the Community.
     In establishing this amount the following elements may be deducted from the total
subsidy:
(a) any application fee, or other costs necessarily incurred in order to qualify for, or to
     obtain, the subsidy;
(b) export taxes, duties or other charges levied on the export of the product to the
     Community specifically intended to offset the subsidy.
Where an interested party claims a deduction, it must prove that the claim is justified.
2.   Where the subsidy is not granted by reference to the quantities manufactured, produced, exported or transported, the amount of countervailable subsidy shall be determined by allocating the value of the total subsidy, as appropriate, over the level of production, sales or exports of the products concerned during the investigation period for
subsidization.
3.   Where the subsidy can be linked to the acquisition or future acquisition of fixed
assets, the amount of the countervailable subsidy shall be calculated by spreading the
subsidy across a period which reflects the normal depreciation of such assets in the
industry concerned. The amount so calculated which is attributable to the investigation
period, including that which derives from fixed assets acquired before this period, shall
be allocated as described in paragraph 2.
     Where the assets are non-depreciating, the subsidy shall be valued as an interest-
free loan, and be treated in accordance with Article 6 (b).
4.   Where a subsidy cannot be linked to the acquisition of fixed assets, the amount of
the benefit received during the investigation period shall in principle be attributed to this
period, and allocated as described in paragraph 2, unless special circumstances arise
justifying attribution over a different period.

Article 8 Determination of injury

1.   For the purposes of this Regulation, the term "injury" shall, unless otherwise specified, be taken to mean material injury to the Community industry, threat of material
injury to the Community industry or material retardation of the establishment of such
an industry and shall be interpreted in accordance with the provisions of this Article.
2.   A determination of injury shall be based on positive evidence and shall involve an
objective examination of both:
(a) the volume of the subsidized imports and the effect of the subsidized imports on
     prices in the Community market for like products; and
(b) the consequent impact of those imports on the Community industry.
3.   With regard to the volume of the subsidized imports, consideration shall be given
to whether there has been a significant increase in subsidized imports, either in absolute terms or relative to production or consumption in the Community. With regard to
the effect of the subsidized imports on prices, consideration shall be given to whether
there has been significant price undercutting by the subsidized imports as compared
with the price of a like product of the Community industry, or whether the effect of such

imports is otherwise to depress prices to a significant degree or prevent price increases which would otherwise have occurred, to a significant degree. No one or more of these factors can necessarily give decisive guidance.

4.   Where imports of a product from more than one country are simultaneously subject to countervailing duty investigations, the effects of such imports shall be cumulatively assessed only if it is determined that:

(a) the amount of countervailable subsidies established in relation to the imports from each country is more than *de minimis* as defined in Article 14 (5) and that the volume of imports from each country is not negligible; and

(b) a cumulative assessment of the effects of the imports is appropriate in light of the conditions of competition between imported products and the conditions of competition between the imported products and the like Community product.

5.   The examination of the impact of the subsidized imports on the Community industry concerned shall include an evaluation of all relevant economic factors and indices having a bearing on the state of the industry, including: the fact that an industry is still in the process of recovering from the effects of past subsidization or dumping, the magnitude of the amount of countervailable subsidies, actual and potential decline in sales, profits, output, market share, productivity, return on investments, utilization of capacity; factors affecting Community prices; actual and potential negative effects on cash flow, inventories, employment, wages, growth, ability to raise capital or investments and, in the case of agriculture, whether there has been an increased burden on government support programmes. This list is not exhaustive, nor can any one or more of these factors necessarily give decisive guidance.

6.   It must be demonstrated, from all the relevant evidence presented in relation to paragraph 2, that the subsidized imports are causing injury within the meaning of this Regulation. Specifically, this shall entail a demonstration that the volume and/or price levels identified pursuant to paragraph 3 are responsible for an impact on the Community industry as provided for in paragraph 5, and that this impact exists to a degree which enables it to be classified as material.

7.   Known factors other than the subsidized imports which are injuring the Community industry at the same time shall also be examined to ensure that injury caused by these other factors is not attributed to the subsidized imports pursuant to paragraph 6. Factors which may be considered in this respect include the volume and prices of non-subsidized imports, contraction in demand or changes in the patterns of consumption, restrictive trade practices of, and competition between, third country and Community producers, developments in technology and the export performance and productivity of the Community industry.

8.   The effect of the subsidized imports shall be assessed in relation to the production of the Community industry of the like product when available data permit the separate identification of that production on the basis of such criteria as the production process, producers' sales and profits. If such separate identification of that production is not possible, the effects of the subsidized imports shall be assessed by examination of the production of the narrowest group or range of products including the like product, for which the necessary information can be provided.

9.   A determination of a threat of material injury shall be based on facts and not merely on allegation, conjecture or remote possibility. The change in circumstances which would create a situation in which the subsidy would cause injury must be clearly foreseen and imminent.

In making a determination regarding the existence of a threat of material injury, consideration should be given to, inter alia, such factors as:

(a) the nature of the subsidy or subsidies in question and the trade effects likely to arise therefrom;

(b) a significant rate of increase of subsidized imports into the Community market indicating the likelihood of substantially increased imports;

(c) sufficient freely disposable capacity of the exporter or an imminent substantial increase in such capacity indicating the likelihood of substantially increased subsidized exports to the Community, account being taken of the availability of other export markets to absorb any additional exports;

(d) whether imports are entering at prices that would, to a significant degree, depress prices or prevent price increases which otherwise would have occurred, and would probably increase demand for further imports; and

(e) inventories of the product being investigated.

No one of the factors listed above by itself can necessarily give decisive guidance but the totality of the factors considered must lead to the conclusion that further subsidized exports are imminent and that, unless protective action is taken, material injury will occur.

Article 9 Definition of Community industry

1. For the purposes of this Regulation, the term "Community industry" shall be interpreted as referring to the Community producers as a whole of the like products or to those of them whose collective output of the products constitutes a major proportion, as defined in Article 10 (8), of the total Community production of those products, except that:

(a) when producers are related to the exporters or importers or are themselves importers of the allegedly subsidized product, the term "Community industry" may be interpreted as referring to the rest of the producers;

(b) in exceptional circumstances the territory of the Community may, for the production in question, be divided into two or more competitive markets and the producers within each market may be regarded as a separate industry if:

   (i)   the producers within such a market sell all or almost all of their production of the product in question in that market, and

   (ii) the demand in that market is not to any substantial degree met by producers of the product in question located elsewhere in the Community.

In such circumstances, injury may be found to exist even where a major portion of the total Community industry is not injured, provided that there is a concentration of subsidized imports into such an isolated market and provided further that the subsidized imports are causing injury to the producers of all or almost all of the production within such a market.

2. For the purpose of paragraph 1, producers shall be considered to be related to exporters or importers only if:

(a) one of them directly or indirectly controls the other; or

(b) both of them are directly or indirectly controlled by a third person; or

(c) together they directly or indirectly control a third person, provided that there are grounds for believing or suspecting that the effect of the relationship is such as to cause the producer concerned to behave differently from non-related producers.

For the purpose of this paragraph, one shall be deemed to control another when the former is legally or operationally in a position to exercise restraint or direction over the latter.

3. Where the Community industry has been interpreted as referring to the producers in a certain region, the exporters or the government granting countervailable subsidies shall be given an opportunity to offer undertakings pursuant to Article 13 in respect of the region concerned. In such cases, when evaluating the Community interest of the measures, special account shall be taken of the interest of the region. If an adequate undertaking is not offered promptly or if the situations set out in Article 13 (9) and (10)

apply, a provisional or definitive countervailing duty may be imposed in respect of the Community as a whole. In such cases the duties may, if practicable, be limited to specific producers or exporters.

4.   The provisions of Article 8 (8) shall apply to this Article.

Article 10 Initiation of proceedings

1.   Except as provided for in paragraph 10, an investigation to determine the existence, degree and effect of any alleged subsidy shall be initiated upon a written complaint by any natural or legal person, or any association not having legal personality, acting on behalf of the Community industry.

The complaint may be submitted to the Commission, or to a Member State, which shall forward it to the Commission. The Commission shall send Member States a copy of any complaint it receives. The complaint shall be deemed to have been lodged on the first working day following its delivery to the Commission by registered mail or the issuing of an acknowledgement of receipt by the Commission.

Where, in the absence of any complaint, a Member State is in possession of sufficient evidence of subsidization and of resultant injury to the Community industry, it shall immediately communicate such evidence to the Commission.

2.   A complaint as referred to in paragraph 1 shall include sufficient evidence of the existence of countervailable subsidies (including, if possible, of their amount), injury and a causal link between the allegedly subsidized imports and the alleged injury. The complaint shall contain such information as is reasonably available to the complainant on the following:

(a) identity of the complainant and a description of the volume and value of the Community production of the like product by the complainant. Where a written complaint is made on behalf of the Community industry, the complaint shall identify the industry on behalf of which the complaint is made by a list of all known Community producers of the like product (or associations of Community producers of the like product) and, to the extent possible, a description of the volume and value of Community production of the like product accounted for by such producers;

(b) a complete description of the allegedly subsidized product, the names of the country or countries of origin and/or export in question, the identity of each known exporter or foreign producer and a list of known persons importing the product in question;

(c) evidence with regard to the existence, amount, nature and countervailability of the subsidies in question;

(d) information on changes in the volume of the allegedly subsidized imports, the effect of those imports on prices of the like product in the Community market and the consequent impact of the imports on the Community industry, as demonstrated by relevant factors and indices having a bearing on the state of the Community industry, such as those listed in Article 8 (3) and (5).

3.   The Commission shall, as far as possible, examine the accuracy and adequacy of the evidence provided in the complaint, in order to determine whether there is sufficient evidence to justify the initiation of an investigation.

4.   An investigation may be initiated in order to determine whether or not the alleged subsidies are "specific" within the meaning of Article 3 (2) and (3).

5.   An investigation may also be initiated in respect of subsidies which are non-countervailable according to Article 4 (2), (3) or (4), in order to determine whether or not the conditions laid down in those paragraphs have been met.

6.   If a subsidy is granted pursuant to a subsidy programme which has been notified in advance of its implementation to the WTO Committee on Subsidies and Countervailing Measures in accordance with Article 8 of the Subsidies Agreement, and in re-

spect of which the Committee has failed to determine that the relevant conditions laid down in Article 8 of the Subsidies Agreement have not been met, an investigation shall not be initiated in respect of a subsidy granted pursuant to such a programme, unless an infringement of Article 8 of the Subsidies Agreement has been ascertained by the competent WTO Dispute Settlement Body or through arbitration as provided in Article 8 (5) of the Subsidies Agreement.

7. An investigation may also be initiated in respect of measures of the type listed in Annex IV, to the extent that they contain an element of subsidy as defined by Article 2, in order to determine whether the measures in question fully conform to the provisions of that Annex.

8. An investigation shall not be initiated pursuant to paragraph 1 unless it has been determined, on the basis of an examination as to the degree of support for, or opposition to, the complaint expressed by Community producers of the like product, that the complaint has ben made by or on behalf of the Community industry. The complaint shall be considered to have been made by or on behalf of the Community industry if it is supported by those Community producers whose collective output constitutes more than 50% of the total production of the like product produced by that portion of the Community industry expressing either support for or opposition to the complaint. However, no investigation shall be initiated when Community producers expressly supporting the complaint account for less than 25% of total production of the like product produced by the Community industry.

9. The authorities shall, unless a decision has been made to initiate an investigation, avoid any publicizing of the complaint seeking the initiation of an investigation. However, as soon as possible after receipt of a properly documented complaint pursuant to this Article, and in any event before the initiation of an investigation, the Commission shall notify the country of origin and/or export concerned, which shall be invited for consultations with the aim of clarifying the situation as to matters referred to in paragraph 2 and arriving at a mutually agreed solution.

10. If, in special circumstances, the Commission decides to initiate an investigation without having received a written complaint by or on behalf of the Community industry for the initiation of such investigation, this shall be done on the basis of sufficient evidence of the existence of countervailable subsidies, injury and causal link, as described in paragraph 2, to justify such initiation.

11. The evidence both of subsidies and of injury shall be considered simultaneously in the decision on whether or not to initiate an investigation. A complaint shall be rejected where there is insufficient evidence of either countervailable subsidies or of injury to justify proceeding with the case. Proceedings shall not be initiated against countries whose imports represent a market share of below 1%, unless such countries collectively account for 3% or more of Community consumption.

12. The complaint may be withdrawn prior to initiation, in which case it shall be considered not to have been lodged.

13. Where, after consultation, it is apparent that there is sufficient evidence to justify initiating a proceeding, the Commission shall do so within 45 days of the lodging of the complaint and shall publish a notice in the Official Journal of the European Communities. Where insufficient evidence has been presented, the complainant shall, after consultation, be so informed within 45 days of the date on which the complaint is lodged with the Commission.

14. The notice of initiation of the proceedings shall announce the initiation of an investigation, indicate the product and countries concerned, give a summary of the information received, and provide that all relevant information is to be communicated to the Commission it shall state the periods within which interested parties may make themselves known, present their views in writing and submit information, if such views

and information are to be taken into account during the investigation; it shall also state the period within which interested parties may apply to be heard by the Commission in accordance with Article 11 (5).

15. The Commission shall advise the exporters, importers and representative associations of importers or exporters known to it to be concerned, as well as the country of origin and/or export and the complainants, of the initiation of the proceedings and, with due regard to the protection of confidential information, provide the full text of the written complaint referred to in paragraph 1 to the known exporters and to the authorities of the country of origin and/or export, and make it available upon request to other interested parties involved. Where the number of exporters involved is particularly high, the full text of the written complaint may instead be provided only to the authorities of the country of origin and/or export or to the relevant trade association.

16. A countervailing duty investigation shall not hinder the procedures of customs clearance.

Article 11 The investigation

1. Following the initiation of the proceeding, the Commission, acting in cooperation with the Member States, shall commence an investigation at Community level. Such investigation shall cover both subsidization and injury, and these shall be investigated simultaneously. For the purpose of a representative finding, an investigation period shall be selected which, in the case of subsidization shall, normally, cover the investigation period provided for in Article 5. Information relating to a period subsequent to the investigation period shall not, normally, be taken into account.

2. Parties receiving questionnaires used in a countervailing duty investigation shall be given at least 30 days to reply. The time limit for exporters shall be counted from the date of receipt of the questionnaire, which for this purpose shall be deemed to have been received one week from the day on which it was sent to the respondent or transmitted to the appropriate diplomatic representative of the country of origin and/or export. An extension to the 30-day period may be granted, due account being taken of the time limits of the investigation, provided that the party shows due cause for such extension, in terms of its particular circumstances.

3. The Commission may request Member States to supply information, and Member States shall take whatever steps are necessary in order to give effect to such requests. They shall send to the Commission the information requested together with the results of all inspections, checks or investigations carried out. Where this information is of general interest or where its transmission has been requested by a Member State, the Commission shall forward it to the Member States, provided it is not confidential, in which case a non-confidential summary shall be forwarded.

4. The Commission may request Member States to carry out all necessary checks and inspections, particularly amongst importers, traders and Community producers, and to carry out investigations in third countries, provided that the firms concerned give their consent and that the government of the country in question has been officially notified and raises no objection. Member States shall take whatever steps are necessary in order to give effect to such requests from the Commission. Officials of the Commission shall be authorized, if the Commission or a Member State so requests, to assist the officials of Member States in carrying out their duties.

5. The interested parties which have made themselves known in accordance with Article 10 (14), shall be heard if they have, within the period prescribed in the notice published in the Official Journal of the European Communities, made a written request for a hearing showing that they are an interested party likely to be affected by the result of the proceeding and that there are particular reasons why they should be heard.

6.   Opportunities shall, on request, be provided for the importers, exporters and the complainants, which have made themselves known in accordance with Article 10 (14), and the government of the country of origin and/or export, to meet those parties having adverse interests, so that opposing views may be presented and rebuttal arguments offered. Provision of such opportunities must take account of the need to preserve confidentiality and of the convenience to the parties. There shall be no obligation on any party to attend a meeting, and failure to do so shall not be prejudicial to that party's case. Oral information provided under this paragraph shall be taken into account by the Commission in so far as it is subsequently confirmed in writing.

7.   The complainants, the government of the country of origin and/or export, importers and exporters and their representative associations, users and consumer organizations, which have made themselves known in accordance with Article 10 (14), may, upon written request, inspect all information made available to the Commission by any party to an investigation, as distinct from internal documents prepared by the authorities of the Community or its Member States, which is relevant to the presentation of their cases and is not confidential within the meaning of Article 29, and that it is used in the investigation. Such parties may respond to such information and their comments shall be taken into consideration wherever they are sufficiently substantiated in the response.

8.   Except in circumstances provided for in Article 28, the information which is supplied by interested parties and upon which findings are based shall be examined for accuracy as far as possible.

9.   For proceedings initiated pursuant to Article 10 (13), an investigation shall, whenever possible, be concluded within one year. In any event, such investigations shall in all cases be concluded within 13 months of initiation, in accordance with the findings made pursuant to Article 13 for undertakings or the findings made pursuant to Article 15 for definitive action.

10. Throughout the investigation, the Commission shall afford the country of origin and/ or export a reasonable opportunity to continue consultations with a view to clarifying the factual situation and arriving at a mutually agreed solution.

Article 12 Provisional measures

1.   Provisional duties may be imposed if:

(a) proceedings have been initiated in accordance with Article 10;

(b) a notice has been given to that effect and interested parties have been given adequate opportunities to submit information and make comments in accordance with Article 10 (14);

(c) a provisional affirmative determination has been made that the imported product benefits from countervailable subsidies and of consequent injury to the Community industry; and

(d) the Community interest calls for intervention to prevent such injury.

The provisional duties shall be imposed no earlier than 60 days from the initiation of the proceedings but no later than nine months from the initiation of the proceedings.

    The amount of the provisional countervailing duty shall not exceed the total amount of countervailable subsidies as provisionally established but it should be less than this amount, if such lesser duty would be adequate to remove the injury to the Community industry.

2.   Provisional duties shall be secured by a guarantee and the release of the products concerned for free circulation in the Community shall be conditional upon the provision of such guarantee.

3.   The Commission shall take provisional action after consultation or, in cases of extreme urgency, after informing the Member States. In this latter case, consultations

shall take place 10 days, at the latest, after notification to the Member States of the action taken by the Commission.

4. Where a Member State requests immediate intervention by the Commission and where the conditions of the first and second subparagraphs of paragraph 1 are met, the Commission shall, within a maximum of five working days from receipt of the request, decide whether a provisional countervailing duty shall be imposed.

5. The Commission shall forthwith inform the Council and the Member States of any decision taken under paragraphs 1 to 4. The Council, acting by a qualified majority, may decide differently.

6. Provisional countervailing duties shall be imposed for a maximum period of four months.

Article 13 Undertakings

1. Investigations may be terminated without the imposition of provisional or definitive duties upon receipt of satisfactory voluntary undertakings under which:

(a) the country of origin and/or export agrees to eliminate or limit the subsidy or take other measures concerning its effects; or

(b) any exporter undertakes to revise its prices or to cease exports to the area in question as long as such exports benefit from countervailable subsidies, so that the Commission, after consultation, is satisfied that the injurious effect of the subsidies is eliminated. Price increases under such undertakings shall not be higher than is necessary to offset the amount of countervailable subsidies, and should be less than the amount of countervailable subsidies if such increases would be adequate to remove the injury to the Community industry.

2. Undertakings may be suggested by the Commission, but no country or exporter shall be obliged to enter into such an undertaking. The fact that countries or exporters do not offer such undertakings, or do not accept an invitation to do so, shall in no way prejudice consideration of the case. However, it may be determined that a threat of injury is more likely to be realized if the subsidized imports continue. Undertakings shall not be sought or accepted from countries or exporters unless a provisional affirmative determination of subsidization and injury caused by such subsidization has been made. Save in exceptional circumstances, undertakings may not be offered later than the end of the period during which representations may be made pursuant to Article 30 (5).

3. Undertakings offered need not be accepted if their acceptance is considered impractical, such as where the number of actual or potential exporters is too great, or for other reasons, including reasons of general policy. The exporter and/or the country of origin and/or export concerned may be provided with the reasons for which it is proposed to reject the offer of an undertaking and may be given an opportunity to make comments thereon. The reasons for rejection shall be set out in the definitive decision.

4. Parties which offer an undertaking shall be required to provide a non-confidential version of such undertaking, so that it may be made available to interested parties to the investigation.

5. Where undertakings are, after consultation, accepted, and where there is no objection raised within the Advisory Committee, the investigation shall be terminated. In all other cases, the Commission shall submit to the Council forthwith a report on the results of the consultation, together with a proposal that the investigation be terminated. The investigation shall be deemed terminated if, within one month, the Council, acting by qualified majority, has not decided otherwise.

6. If the undertakings are accepted, the investigation of subsidization and injury shall normally be completed. In such a case, if a negative determination of subsidization or injury is made, the undertaking shall automatically lapse, except in cases where such a determination is due in large part to the existence of an undertaking. In such cases,

it may be required that an undertaking be maintained for a reasonable period. In the event that an affirmative determination of subsidization and injury is made, the undertaking shall continue consistent with its terms and the provisions of this Regulation.

7.   The Commission shall require any country or exporter from whom undertakings have been accepted to provide, periodically, information relevant to the fulfilment of such undertaking, and to permit verification of pertinent data. Non-compliance with such requirements shall be construed as a breach of the undertaking.

8.   Where undertakings are accepted from certain exporters during the course of an investigation, they shall, for the purpose of Articles 18, 19, 20 and 22, be deemed to take effect from the date on which the investigation is concluded for the country of origin and/or export.

9.   In case of breach or withdrawal of undertakings by any party, a definitive duty shall be imposed in accordance with Article 15, on the basis of the facts established within the context of the investigation which led to the undertaking, provided that such investigation was concluded with a final determination as to subsidization and injury, and that the exporter concerned, or the country of origin and/or export, has, except in the case of withdrawal of the undertaking by the exporter or such country, been given an opportunity to comment.

10. A provisional duty may, after consultation, be imposed in accordance with Article 12 on the basis of the best information available, where there is reason to believe that an undertaking is being breached, or in case of breach or withdrawal of an undertaking where the investigation which led to the undertaking has not been concluded.

Article 14 Termination without measures

1.   Where the complaint is withdrawn, the proceeding may be terminated unless such termination would not be in the Community interest.

2.   Where, after consultation, protective measures are unnecessary and there is no objection raised within the Advisory Committee, the investigation or proceeding shall be terminated. In all other cases, the Commission shall submit to the Council forthwith a report on the results of the consultation, together with a proposal that the proceeding be terminated. The proceeding shall be deemed terminated if, within one month, the Council, acting by a qualified majority, has not decided otherwise.

3.   There shall be immediate termination of the proceeding where it is determined that the amount of countervailable subsidies is *de minimis*, in accordance with paragraph 5, or where the volume of subsidized imports, actual or potential, or the injury, is negligible.

4.   For a proceeding initiated pursuant to Article 10 (13), injury shall normally be regarded as negligible where the market share of the imports is less than the amounts set out in Article 10 (11). With regard to investigations concerning imports from developing countries, the volume of subsidized imports shall also be considered negligible if it represents less than 4% of the total imports of the like product in the Community, unless imports from developing countries whose individual shares of total imports represent less than 4% collectively account for more than 9% of the total imports of the like product in the Community.

5.   The amount of the countervailable subsidies shall be considered to be *de minimis* if such amount is less than 1% *ad valorem*, except that:

(a) as regards investigations concerning imports from developing countries the *de minimis* threshold shall be 2% *ad valorem*, and

(b) for those developing countries Members of the WTO referred to in Annex VII to the Subsidies Agreement as well as for developing countries Members of the WTO which have completely eliminated export subsidies as defined in Article 3 (4) (a) of this Regulation, the *de minimis* subsidy threshold shall be 3% *ad valorem*; where the application of this provision depends on the elimination of export subsidies, it shall apply from the date on which the elimination of export subsidies is notified to the WTO Committee on Subsidies and Countervailing Measures, and for so long as export subsidies are not granted by the developing country concerned; this provision shall expire eight years from the date of entry into force of the WTO Agreement, provided that it is only the investigation that shall be terminated where the amount of the countervailable subsidies is below the relevant *de minimis* level for individual exporters, who shall remain subject to the proceedings and may be re-investigated in any subsequent review carried out for the country concerned pursuant to Articles 18 and 19.

Article 15 Imposition of definitive duties

1.   Where the facts as finally established show the existence of countervailable subsidies and injury caused thereby, and the Community interest calls for intervention in accordance with Article 31, a definitive countervailing duty shall be imposed by the Council, acting by simple majority on a proposal submitted by the Commission after consultation of the Advisory Committee, unless the subsidy or subsidies are withdrawn or it has been demonstrated that the subsidies no longer confer any benefit on the exporters involved. Where provisional duties are in force, a proposal for definitive action shall be submitted to the Council not later than one month before the expiry of such duties. The amount of the countervailing duty shall not exceed the amount of countervailable subsidies from which the exporters have been found to benefit, established pursuant to this Regulation, but should be less than the total amount of countervailable subsidies, if such lesser duty were to be adequate to remove the injury to the Community industry.

2.   A countervailing duty shall be imposed in the appropriate amounts in each case, on a non-discriminatory basis, on imports of a product from all sources found to benefit from countervailable subsidies and causing injury, except as to imports from those sources from which undertakings under the terms of this Regulation have been accepted. The regulation imposing the duty shall specify the duty for each supplier, or, if that is impracticable, the supplying country concerned.

3.   When the Commission has limited its examination in accordance with Article 27, any countervailing duty applied to imports from exporters or producers which have made themselves known in accordance with Article 27 but were not included in the examination shall not exceed the weighted average amount of countervailable subsidies established for the parties in the sample. For the purpose of this paragraph, the Commission shall disregard any zero and *de minimis* amounts of countervailable subsidies and amounts of countervailable subsidies established in the circumstances referred to in Article 28. Individual duties shall be applied to imports from any exporter or producer for which an individual amount of subsidization has been calculated as provided for in Article 27.

Article 16 Retroactivity

1.   Provisional measures and definitive countervailing duties shall only be applied to products which enter free circulation after the time when the measure taken pursuant to Article 12 (1) or Article 15 (1), as the case may be, enters into force, subject to the exceptions set out in this Regulation.

2.   Where a provisional duty has been applied and the facts as finally established show the existence of countervailable subsidies and injury, the Council shall decide, irrespective of whether a definitive countervailing duty is to be imposed, what proportion of the provisional duty is to be definitively collected. For this purpose, "injury" shall not include material retardation of the establishment of a Community industry, not

threat of material injury, except where it is found that this would, in the absence of provisional measures, have developed into material injury. In all other cases involving such threat or retardation, any provisional amounts shall be released and definitive duties can only be imposed from the date on which a final determination of threat or material retardation is made.

3.   If the definitive countervailing duty is higher than the provisional duty, the difference shall not be collected. If the definitive duty is lower than the provisional duty, the duty shall be recalculated. Where a final determination is negative, the provisional duty shall not be confirmed.

4.   A definitive countervailing duty may be levied on products which were entered for consumption not more than 90 days prior to the date of application of provisional measures but not prior to the initiation of the investigation, provided that the imports have been registered in accordance with Article 24 (5), the importers concerned have been given an opportunity to comment by the Commission, and:

(a) there are critical circumstances where for the subsidized product in question injury which is difficult to repair is caused by massive imports in a relatively short period of a product benefiting from countervailable subsidies under the terms of this Regulation; and,

(b) it is deemed necessary, in order to preclude the recurrence of such injury, to assess countervailing duties retroactively on those imports.

5.   In cases of breach or withdrawal of undertakings, definitive duties may be levied on goods entered for free circulation not more than 90 days before the application of provisional measures, provided that the imports have been registered in accordance with Article 24 (5) and that any such retroactive assessment shall not apply to imports entered before the breach or withdrawal of the undertaking.

Article 17 Duration

A countervailing measure shall remain in force only as long as, and to the extent that, it is necessary to counteract the countervailable subsidies which are causing injury.

Article 18 Expiry reviews

1.   A definitive countervailing measure shall expire five years from its imposition or five years from the date of the most recent review which has covered both subsidization and injury, unless it is determined in a review that the expiry would be likely to lead to a continuation or recurrence of subsidization and injury. Such an expiry review shall be initiated on the initiative of the Commission, or upon a request made by or on behalf of Community producers, and the measure shall remain in force pending the outcome of such review.

2.   An expiry review shall be initiated where the request contains sufficient evidence that the expiry of the measures would be likely to result in a continuation or recurrence of subsidization and injury. Such a likelihood may, for example, be indicated by evidence of continued subsidization and injury or evidence that the removal of injury is partly or solely due to the existence of measures or evidence that the circumstances of the exporters, or market conditions, are such that they would indicate the likelihood of further injurious subsidization.

3.   In carrying out investigations under this Article, the exporters, importers, the country of origin and/or export and the Community producers shall be provided with the opportunity to amplify, rebut or comment on the matters set out in the review request, and conclusions shall be reached with due account taken of all relevant and duly documented evidence presented in relation to the question as to whether the expiry of measures would be likely, or unlikely, to lead to the continuation or recurrence of subsidization and injury.

4.   A notice of impending expiry shall be published in the Official Journal of the European Communities at an appropriate time in the final year of the period of application of the measures as defined in this Article. Thereafter, the Community producers shall, no later than three months before the end of the five-year period, be entitled to lodge a review request in accordance with paragraph 2. A notice announcing the actual expiry of measures under this Article shall also be published.

Article 19 Interim reviews

1.   The need for the continued imposition of measures may also be reviewed, where warranted, on the initiative of the Commission or at the request of a Member State or, provided that a reasonable period of time of at least one year has elapsed since the imposition of the definitive measure, upon a request by any exporter, importer or by the Community producers or the country of origin and/or export which contains sufficient evidence substantiating the need for such an interim review.
2.   An interim review shall be initiated where the request contains sufficient evidence that the continued imposition of the measure is no longer necessary to offset the countervailable subsidy and/or that the injury would be unlikely to continue or recur if the measure were removed or varied, or that the existing measure is not, or is no longer, sufficient to counteract the countervailable subsidy which is causing injury.
3.   Where the countervailing duties imposed are less than the amount of countervailable subsidies found, an interim review shall be initiated if the Community producers provide sufficient evidence that the duties have led to no movement, or insufficient movement, of resale prices of the imported product in the Community. If the investigation proves the allegations to be correct, countervailing duties may be increased to achieve the price increase required to remove injury; however, the increased duty level shall not exceed the amount of the countervailable subsidies.
4.   In carrying out investigations pursuant to this Article, the Commission may inter alia consider whether the circumstances with regard to subsidization and injury have changed significantly, or whether existing measures are achieving the intended results in removing the injury previously established under Article 8. In these respects, account shall be taken in the final determination of all relevant and duly documented evidence.

Article 20 Accelerated reviews

Any exporter whose exports are subject to a definitive countervailing duty but who was not individually investigated during the original investigation for reasons other than a refusal to cooperate with the Commission, shall be entitled, upon request, to an accelerated review in order that the Commission may promptly establish an individual countervailing duty rate for that exporter. Such a review shall be initiated after consultation of the Advisory Committee and after Community producers have been given an opportunity to comment.

Article 21 Refunds

1.   Notwithstanding Article 18, an importer may request reimbursement of duties collected where it is shown that the amount of countervailable subsidies, on the basis of which duties were paid, has been either eliminated or reduced to a level which is below the level of the duty in force.
2.   In requesting a refund of countervailing duties, the importer shall submit an application to the Commission. The application shall be submitted via the Member State in the territory of which the products were released for free circulation, within six months of the date on which the amount of the definitive duties to be levied was duly determined by the competent authorities or of the date on which a decision was made definiti-

vely to collect the amounts secured by way of provisional duty. Member States shall forward the request to the Commission forthwith.

3.   An application for refund shall be considered to be duly supported by evidence only where it contains precise information on the amount of refund of countervailing duties claimed and all customs documentation relating to the calculation and payment of such amount. It shall also include evidence, for a representative period, of the amount of countervailable subsidies for the exporter or producer to which the duty applies. In cases where the importer is not associated with the exporter or producer concerned and such information is not immediately available, or where the exporter or producer is unwilling to release it to the importer, the application shall contain a statement from the exporter or producer that the amount of countervailable subsidies has been reduced or eliminated, as specified in this Article, and that the relevant supporting evidence will be provided to the Commission. Where such evidence is not forthcoming from the exporter or producer within a reasonable period of time the application shall be rejected.

4.   The Commission shall, after consultation of the Advisory Committee, decide whether and to what extent the application should be granted, or it may decide at any time to initiate an interim review, whereupon the information and findings from such review, carried out in accordance with the provisions applicable for such reviews, shall be used to determine whether and to what extent a refund is justified. Refunds of duties shall normally take place within 12 months, and in no circumstances more than 18 months after the date on which a request for a refund, duly supported by evidence, has been made by an importer of the product subject to the countervailing duty. The payment of any refund authorized should normally be made by Member States within 90 days of the abovementioned decision.

Article 22 General provisions on reviews and refunds

1.   The relevant provisions of Articles 10 and 11, excluding those relating to time limits, shall apply to any review carried out pursuant to Articles 18, 19 and 20. Any such review shall be carried out expeditiously and shall normally be concluded within 12 months of the date of initiation of the review.

2.   Reviews pursuant to Articles 18, 19 and 20 shall be initiated by the Commission after consultation of the Advisory Committee. Where warranted by reviews, measures shall be repealed or maintained pursuant to Article 18, or repealed, maintained or amended pursuant to Articles 19 and 20, by the Community institution responsible for their introduction. Where measures are repealed for individual exporters, but not for the country as a whole, such exporters shall remain subject to the proceeding and may be re-investigated in any subsequent review carried out for that country pursuant to this Article.

3.   Where a review of measures pursuant to Article 19 is in progress at the end of the period of application of measures as defined in Article 18, the measures shall also be investigated under the provisions of Article 18.

4.   In all review or refund investigations carried out pursuant to Articles 18 to 21, the Commission shall, provided that circumstances have not changed, apply the same methodology as in the investigation which led to the duty, with due account being taken of Articles 5, 6, 7 and 27.

Article 23 Circumvention

1.   Countervailing duties imposed pursuant to this Regulation may be extended to imports from third countries of like products, or parts thereof, when circumvention of the measures in force is taking place. Circumvention shall be defined as a change in the pattern of trade between third countries and the Community which stems from a

practice, process or work for which there is insufficient cause or economic justification other than the imposition of the duty, and where there is evidence that the remedial effects of the duty are being undermined in terms of the prices and/or quantities of the like products and that the imported like product and/or parts thereof still benefit from the subsidy.

2.   Investigations shall be initiated pursuant to this Article where the request contains sufficient evidence regarding the factors set out in paragraph 1. Initiations shall be made, after consultation of the Advisory Committee, by Commission Regulation which shall also instruct the customs authorities to make imports subject to registration in accordance with Article 24 (5) or to request guarantees. Investigations shall be carried out by the Commission, which may be assisted by customs authorities, and shall be concluded within nine months. When the facts as finally ascertained justify the extension of measures, this shall be done by the Council, acting by simple majority and on a proposal from the Commission, from the date on which registration was imposed pursuant to Article 24 (5) or on which guarantees were requested. The relevant procedural provisions of this Regulation with regard to initiations and the conduct of investigations shall apply pursuant to this Article.

3.   Products shall not be subject to registration pursuant to Article 24 (5) or measures where they are accompanied by a customs certificate declaring that the importation of the goods does not constitute circumvention. Such certificates may be issued to importers, upon written application following authorization by decision of the Commission after consultation of the Advisory Committee, or decision of the Council imposing measures, and they shall remain valid for the period, and under the conditions, set down therein.

4.   Nothing in this Article shall preclude the normal application of the provisions in force concerning customs duties.

Article 24 General provisions

1.   Provisional or definitive countervailing duties shall be imposed by Regulation, and collected by Member States in the form, at the rate specified and according to the other criteria laid down in the Regulation imposing such duties. Such duties shall also be collected independently of the customs duties, taxes and other charges normally imposed on imports. No product shall be subject to both anti-dumping and countervailing duties for the purpose of dealing with one and the same situation arising from dumping or from export subsidization.

2.   Regulations imposing provisional or definitive countervailing duties, and Regulations or Decisions accepting undertakings or terminating investigations or proceedings, shall be published in the Official Journal of the European Communities. Such Regulations or Decisions shall contain in particular, and with due regard to the protection of confidential information, the names of the exporters, if possible, or of the countries involved, a description of the product and a summary of the facts and considerations relevant to the subsidy and injury determinations. In each case, a copy of the Regulation or Decision shall be sent to known interested parties. The provisions of this paragraph shall apply mutatis mutandis to reviews.

3.   Special provisions, in particular with regard to the common definition of the concept of origin, as contained in Council Regulation 2913/92 of 12 October 1992 establishing the Community Customs Code,[1] may be adopted pursuant to this Regulation.

4.   In the Community interest, measures imposed pursuant to this Regulation may, after consultation of the Advisory Committee, be suspended by a decision of the Com-

1   OJ 1992 L 302, p. 1, [as amended].

mission for a period of nine months. The suspension may be extended for a further period, not exceeding one year, if the Council so decides, acting by simple majority on a proposal from the Commission. Measures may only be suspended where market conditions have temporarily changed to such an extent that injury would be unlikely to resume as a result of the suspension, and provided that the Community industry has been given an opportunity to comment and that those comments have been taken into account. Measures may, at any time and after consultation, be reinstated if the reason for suspension is no longer applicable.

5. The Commission may, after consultation of the Advisory Committee, direct the customs authorities to take the appropriate steps to register imports, so that measures may subsequently be applied against those imports from the date of such registration. Imports may be made subject to registration following a request from the Community industry which contains sufficient evidence to justify such action. Registration shall be introduced by Regulation which shall specify the purpose of the action and, if appropriate, the estimated amount of possible future liability. Imports shall not be made subject to registration for a period longer than nine months.

6. Member States shall report to the Commission every month on the import trade of products subject to investigation and to measures, and on the amount of duties collected pursuant to this Regulation.

Article 25 Consultations

1. Any consultations provided for in this Regulation, except those referred to in Articles 10 (9) and 11 (10), shall take place within an Advisory Committee, which shall consist of representatives of each Member State, with a representative of the Commission as chairman. Consultations shall be held immediately on request by a Member State or on the initiative of the Commission, and in any event within a period of time which allows the time limits set by this Regulation to be adhered to.

2. The Committee shall meet when convened by its chairman. He shall provide the Member States, as promptly as possible, with all relevant information.

3. Where necessary, consultation may be in writing only; in that event, the Commission shall notify the Member States and shall specify a period within which they shall be entitled to express their opinions or to request an oral consultation which the chairman shall arrange, provided that such oral consultation can be held within a period of time which allows the time limits set by this Regulation to be adhered to.

4. Consultation shall cover, in particular:

(a) the existence of countervailable subsidies and the methods of establishing their amount;

(b) the existence and extent of injury;

(c) the causal link between the subsidized imports and injury;

(d) the measures which, in the circumstances, are appropriate to prevent or remedy the injury caused by the countervailable subsidies and the ways and means of putting such measures into effect.

Article 26 Verification visits

1. The Commission shall, where it considers it appropriate, carry out visits to examine the records of importers, exporters, traders, agents, producers, trade associations and organizations, to verify information provided on subsidization and injury. In the absence of a proper and timely reply a verification visit may not be carried out.

2. The Commission may carry out investigations in third countries as required, provided that it obtains the agreement of the firms concerned, that it notifies the country in question and that the latter does not object to the investigation. As soon as the agreement of the firms concerned has been obtained the Commission should notify the

country of origin and/or export of the names and addresses of the firms to be visited and the dates agreed.

3.   The firms concerned shall be advised of the nature of the information to be verified during verification visits and of any further information which needs to be provided during such visits, though this should not preclude requests made during the verification for further details to be provided in the light of information obtained.

4.   In investigations carried out pursuant to paragraphs 1, 2 and 3, the Commission shall be assisted by officials of those Member States who so request.

Article 27 Sampling

1.   In cases there the number of complainants, exporters or importers, types of product or transactions is large, the investigation may be limited to:

(a) a reasonable number of parties, products or transactions by using samples which are statistically valid on the basis of information available at the time of the selection; or

(b) to the largest representative volume of the production, sales or exports which can reasonably be investigated within the time available.

2.   The selection of parties, types of products or transactions made under this Article shall rest with the Commission, though preference shall be given to choosing a sample in consultation with, and with the consent of, the parties concerned, provided that such parties make themselves known and make sufficient information available, within three weeks of initiation of the investigation, to enable a representative sample to be chosen.

3.   In cases where the examination has been limited in accordance with this Article, an individual amount of countervailable subsidization shall, nevertheless, be calculated for any exporter or producer not initially selected who submits the necessary information within the time limits provided for in this Regulation, except where the number of exporters or producers is so large that individual examinations would be unduly burdensome and would prevent completion of the investigation in good time.

4.   Where it is decided to sample and there is a degree of non-cooperation by some or all of the parties selected which is likely to materially affect the outcome of the investigation, a new sample may be selected. However, if a material degree of non-cooperation persists or there is insufficient time to select a new sample, the relevant provisions of Article 28 shall apply.

Article 28 Non-cooperation

1.   In cases in which any interested party refuses access to, or otherwise does not provide, necessary information within the time limits provided in this Regulation, or significantly impedes the investigation, provisional or final findings, affirmative or negative, may be made on the basis of the facts available.

Where it is found that any interested party has supplied false or misleading information, the information shall be disregarded and use may be made of the facts available.

Interested parties should be made aware of the consequences of non-cooperation.

2.   Failure to give a computerized response shall not be deemed to constitute non-cooperation, provided that the interested party shows that presenting the response as requested would result in an unreasonable extra burden or unreasonable additional cost.

3.   Where the information submitted by an interested party is not ideal in all respects it should nevertheless not be disregarded, provided that any deficiencies are not such as to cause undue difficulty in arriving at a reasonably accurate finding and that the information is appropriately submitted in good time and is verifiable, and that the party has acted to the best of its ability.

4.   If evidence or information is not accepted, the supplying party shall be informed
forthwith of the reasons therefor and shall be granted an opportunity to provide further
explanations within the time limit specified. If the explanations are considered unsatisfactory, the reasons for rejection of such evidence or information shall be disclosed and
given in published findings.
5.   If determinations, including those regarding the amount of countervailable subsidies, are based on the provisions of paragraph 1, including the information supplied in
the complaint, it shall, where practicable and with due regard to the time limits of the
investigation, be checked by reference to information from other independent sources
which may be available, such as published price lists, official import statistics and
customs returns, or information obtained from other interested parties during the investigation.
6.   If an interested party does not cooperate, or cooperates only partially, so that relevant information is thereby withheld, the result may be less favourable to the party than
if it had cooperated.

Article 29 Confidentiality
1.   Any information which is by nature confidential (for example, because its disclosure
would be of significant competitive advantage to a competitor or would have a significantly adverse effect upon a person supplying the information or upon a person from
whom he has acquired the information), or which is provided on a confidential basis by
parties to an investigation shall, if good cause is shown, be treated as such by the
authorities.
2.   Interested parties providing confidential information shall be required to furnish
non-confidential summaries thereof. Those summaries shall be in sufficient detail to
permit a reasonable understanding of the substance of the information submitted in
confidence. In exceptional circumstances, such parties may indicate that such information is not susceptible of summary. In such exceptional circumstances, a statement of
the reasons why summarization is not possible must be provided.
3.   If it is considered that a request for confidentiality is not warranted and if the supplier of the information is either unwilling to make the information available or to authorize its disclosure in generalized or summary form, such information may be disregarded unless it can be satisfactorily demonstrated from appropriate sources that the
information is correct. Requests for confidentiality shall not be arbitrarily rejected.
4.   This Article shall not preclude the disclosure of general information by the Community authorities, and in particular of the reasons on which decisions taken pursuant
to this Regulation are based, nor disclosure of the evidence relied on by the Community authorities in so far as is necessary to explain those reasons in court proceedings.
Such disclosure must take into account the legitimate interests of the parties concerned
that their business or governmental secrets should not be divulged.
5.   The Council, the Commission and the Member States, or the officials of any of
these, shall not reveal any information received pursuant to this Regulation for which
confidential treatment has been requested by its supplier, without specific permission
from the supplier. Exchanges of information between the Commission and Member
States, or any information relating to consultations made pursuant to Article 25, or consultations described in Articles 10 (9) an 11 (10), or any internal documents prepared
by the authorities of the Community or its Member States, shall not be divulged except
as specifically provided for in this Regulation.
6.   Information received pursuant to this Regulation shall be used only for the purpose
for which it was requested.

Article 30 Disclosure

1.   The complainants, importers and exporters and their representative associations, and the country of origin and/or export, may request disclosure of the details underlying the essential facts and considerations on the basis of which provisional measures have been imposed. Requests for such disclosure shall be made in writing immediately following the imposition of provisional measures, and the disclosure shall be made in writing as soon as possible thereafter.

2.   The parties mentioned in paragraph 1 may request final disclosure of the essential facts and considerations on the basis of which it is intended to recommend the imposition of definitive measures, or the termination of an investigation or proceedings without the imposition of measures, particular attention being paid to the disclosure of any facts or considerations which are different from those used for any provisional measures.

3.   Requests for final disclosure shall be addressed to the Commission in writing and be received, in cases where a provisional duty has been applied, not later than one month after publication of the imposition of that duty. Where a provisional duty has not been imposed, parties shall be provided with an opportunity to request final disclosure within time limits set by the Commission.

4.   Final disclosure shall be given in writing. It shall be made, due regard being had to the protection of confidential information, as soon as possible and, normally, not later than one month prior to a definitive decision or the submission by the Commission of any proposal for final action pursuant to Articles 14 and 15. Where the Commission is not in a position to disclose certain facts or considerations at that time, these shall be disclosed as soon as possible thereafter. Disclosure shall not prejudice any subsequent decision which may be taken by the Commission or the Council but where such decision is based on any different facts and considerations these shall be disclosed as soon as possible.

5.   Representations made after final disclosure is given shall be taken into consideration only if received within a period to be set by the Commission in each case, which shall be at least 10 days, due consideration being given to the urgency of the matter.

Article 31 Community interest

1.   A determination as to whether the Community interest calls for intervention should be based on an appraisal of all the various interests taken as a whole, including the interests of the domestic industry and users and consumers; a determination pursuant to this Article shall be made only where all parties have been given the opportunity to make their views known pursuant to paragraph 2. In such an examination, the need to eliminate the trade-distorting effects of injurious subsidization and to restore effective competition shall be given special consideration. Measures, as determined on the basis of subsidization and injury found, may not be applied where the authorities, on the basis of all the information submitted, can clearly conclude that it is not in the Community interest to apply such measures.

2.   In order to provide a sound basis on which the authorities can take account of all views and information in the decision as to whether or not the imposition of measures is in the Community interest, the complainants, importers and their representative associations, representative users and representative consumer organizations may, within the time limits specified in the notice of initiation of the countervailing duty investigation, make themselves known and provide information to the Commission. Such information, or appropriate summaries thereof, shall be made available to the other parties specified in this paragraph, and they shall be entitled to respond to such information.

3.   The parties which have acted in conformity with paragraph 2 may request a hearing. Such requests shall be granted when they are submitted within the time limits

set in paragraph 2, and when they set out the reasons, in terms of the Community interest, why the parties should be heard.

4.   The parties which have acted in conformity with paragraph 2 may provide comments on the application of any provisional duties imposed. Such comments shall be received within one month of the application of such measures if they are to be taken into account and they, or appropriate summaries thereof, shall be made available to other parties who shall be entitled to respond to such comments.

5.   The Commission shall examine the information which is properly submitted and the extent to which it is representative, and the results of such analysis, together with an opinion on its merits, shall be transmitted to the Advisory Committee. The balance of views expressed in the Committee shall be taken into account by the Commission in any proposal made pursuant to Articles 14 and 15.

6.   The parties which have acted in conformity with paragraph 2 may request that the facts and considerations on which final decisions are likely to be taken be made available to them. Such information shall be made available to the extent possible and without prejudice to any subsequent decision taken by the Commission or the Council.

7.   Information shall be taken into account only where it is supported by actual evidence which substantiates its validity.

Article 32 Relationships between countervailing duty measures and multilateral remedies

If an imported product is made subject to any countermeasures imposed following recourse to the dispute settlement procedures of the Subsidies Agreement, and such measures are appropriate to remove the injury caused by the countervailable subsidies, any countervailing duty imposed with regard to that product shall immediately be suspended, or repealed, as appropriate.

Article 33 Final provisions

This Regulation shall not preclude the application of:

(a) any special rules laid down in agreements concluded between the Community and third countries;

(b) the Community regulations in the agricultural sector and Council Regulations 3448/93 of 6 December 1993 laying down the trade arrangements applicable to certain goods resulting from the processing of agricultural products[1] [...]; this Regulation shall operate by way of complement to those regulations and in derogation from any provisions thereof which preclude the application of countervailing duties;

(c) special measures, provided that such action does not run counter to obligations under the GATT.

Article 34 Repeal of existing legislation and transitional measures

Regulation 3284/94 is hereby repealed.

However, the repeal of Regulation 3284/94 shall not prejudice the validity of proceedings initiated thereunder.

References to Regulations 2423/88 and 3284/94 shall be construed as references to this Regulation, where appropriate.

Article 35 Entry into force

This Regulation shall enter into force on the day of its publication in the Official Journal of the European Communities.

---

1   OJ 1993 L 318, p. 18.

This Regulation shall be binding in its entirety and directly applicable in all Member States.

Done at Luxembourg, 6 October 1997.
For the Council: The President, J. POOS

ANNEX I: ILLUSTRATIVE LIST OF EXPORT SUBSIDIES[1]
(a) The provision by governments of direct subsidies to a firm or an industry contingent upon export performance.
(b) Currency retention schemes or any similar practices which involve a bonus on exports.
(c) Internal transport and freight charges on export shipments, provided or mandated by governments, on terms more favourable than for domestic shipments.
(d) The provision by governments or their agencies either directly or indirectly through government-mandated schemes, of imported or domestic products or services for use in the production of exported goods, on terms or conditions more favourable than for provision of like or directly competitive products or services for use in the production of goods for domestic consumption, if (in the case of products) such terms or conditions are more favourable than those commercially available on world markets to their exporters.
(e) The full or partial exemption, remission, or deferral specifically related to exports, of direct taxes or social welfare charges paid or payable by industrial or commercial enterprises.
(f) The allowance of special deductions directly related to exports or export performance, over and above those granted in respect of production for domestic consumption, in the calculation of the base on which direct taxes are charged.
(g) The exemption or remission, in respect of the production and distribution of exported products, of indirect taxes in excess of those levied in respect of the production and distribution of like products when sold for domestic consumption.
(h) The exemption, remission or deferral of prior-stage cumulative indirect taxes on goods or services used in the production of exported products in excess of the exemption, remission or deferral of like prior-stage cumulative indirect taxes on goods or services used in the production of like products when sold for domestic consumption; provided, however, that prior-stage cumulative indirect taxes may be exempted, remitted or deferred on exported products even when not exempted, remitted or deferred on like products when sold for domestic consumption, if the prior-stage cumulative indirect taxes are levied on inputs that are consumed in the production of the exported product (making normal allowance for waste. This item shall be interpreted in accordance with the guidelines on consumption of inputs in the production process contained in Annex II.
(i) The remission or drawback of import charges in excess of those levied on imported inputs that are consumed in the production of the exported product (making normal allowance for waste); provided, however, that in particular cases a firm may use a quantity of home market inputs equal to, and having the same quality and characteristics as, the imported inputs as a substitute for them in order to benefit from this provision if the import and the corresponding export operations both occur within a reasonable time period, not to exceed two years. This item shall be interpreted in accordance with the guidelines on consumption of inputs in the production process contained in Annex II and the guidelines in the determination of substitution drawback systems as export subsidies contained in Annex III.
(j) The provision by governments (or special institutions controlled by governments) of export credit guarantee or insurance programmes, of insurance or guarantee programmes against increases in the cost of exported products or of exchange risk programmes, at premium rates which are inadequate to cover the long-term operating costs and losses of the programmes.
(k) The grant by governments (or special institutions controlled by and/or acting under the authority of governments) of export credits at rates below those which they actually have to pay for the funds so employed (or would have to pay if they borrowed on international capital markets in order to obtain funds of the same maturity and other credit terms and de-

---

1 Footnotes omitted.

nominated in the same currency as the export credit), or the payment by them of all or part of the costs incurred by exporters or financial institutions in obtaining credits, insofar as they are used to secure a material advantage in the field of export credit terms.

Provided, however, that if a Member of the WTO is a party to an international undertaking on official export credits to which at least 12 original such Members are parties as of 1 January 1979 (or a successor undertaking which has been adopted by those original Members), or if in practice a Member of the WTO applies the interest rates provisions of the relevant undertaking, an export credit practice which is in conformity with those provisions shall not be considered an export subsidy.

(l)   Any other charge on the public account constituting an export subsidy in the sense of Article XVI of GATT 1994.

(1)   The term "commercially available" means that the choice between domestic and imported products is unrestricted and depends only on commercial considerations.

(2)   For the purpose of this Regulation:
—   the term "direct taxes" shall mean taxes on wages, profits, interests, rents, royalties, and all other forms of income, and taxes on the ownership of real property,
—   the term "import charges" shall mean tariffs, duties, and other fiscal charges not elsewhere enumerated in this note that are levied on imports,
—   the term "indirect taxes" shall mean sales, excise, turnover, value added, franchise, stamp, transfer, inventory and equipment taxes, border taxes and all taxes other than direct taxes and import charges,
—   "prior-stage" indirect taxes are those levied on goods or services used directly or indirectly in making the product,
—   "cumulative" indirect taxes are multi-staged taxes levied where there is no mechanism for subsequent crediting of the tax if the goods or services subject to tax at one stage of production are used in a succeeding state of production,
—   "remission" of taxes includes the refund or rebate of taxes,
—   "remission or drawback" includes the full or partial exemption or deferral of import charges.

(3)   Deferral may not amount to an export subsidy where, for example, appropriate interest charges are collected.

(4)   Paragraph (h) does not apply to value-added tax systems and border-tax adjustment in lieu thereof; the problem of the excessive remission of value-added taxes is exclusively covered by paragraph (g).

ANNEX II: GUIDELINES ON CONSUMPTION OF INPUTS IN THE PRODUCTION PROCESS [...]

ANNEX III: GUIDELINES IN THE DETERMINATION OF SUBSTITUTION DRAWBACK SYSTEMS AS EXPORT SUBSIDIES [...]

ANNEX IV: (This Annex reproduces Annex 2 to the Agreement on Agriculture. Any terms or expressions which are not explained herein or which are not self-explanatory are to be interpreted in the context of that Agreement.) [...]

Council Regulation 3286/94 of 22 December 1994 Laying Down Community Procedures in the Field of the Common Commercial Policy in Order to Ensure the Exercise of the Community's Rights Under International Trade Rules, in Particular Those Established Under the Auspices of the World Trade Organization[1]

THE COUNCIL OF THE EUROPEAN UNION,

HAVING REGARD to the Treaty establishing the European Community, and in particular Article 113 thereof,

HAVING REGARD to the rules establishing the common organization of agricultural markets and the rules adopted pursuant to Article 235 of the Treaty, applicable to goods processed from agricultural products, and in particular those provisions thereof, which allow for derogation from the general principle that any quantitative restriction or measure having equivalent effect may be replaced solely by the measures provided for in those instruments, [...]

(1) WHEREAS the common commercial policy must be based on uniform principles, in particular with regard to commercial defence;

(2) WHEREAS Council Regulation 2641/84 of 17 September 1984 on the strengthening of the common commercial policy with regard in particular to protection against illicit commercial practices provided the Community with procedures enabling it:
— to respond to any illicit commercial practice with a view to removing the injury resulting therefrom, and
— to ensure full exercise of the Community's rights with regard to the commercial practices of third countries;

(3) WHEREAS experience in the application of Regulation 2641/84 has shown that the need to deal with obstacles to trade adopted or maintained by third countries remains, and whereas the approach followed in Regulation 2641/84 has not proved to be entirely effective;

(4) WHEREAS it appears necessary, therefore, to establish new and improved Community procedures to ensure the effective exercise of the rights of the Community under international trade rules;

(5) WHEREAS international trade rules are primarily those established under the auspices of the WTO and laid down in the Annexes to the WTO Agreement, but they can also be those laid down in any other agreement to which the Community is a party and which sets out rules applicable to trade between the Community and third countries, and whereas it is appropriate to give a clear idea of the types of agreements to which the term "international trade rules" refers;

(6) WHEREAS the abovementioned Community procedures should be based on a legal mechanism under Community law which would be fully transparent, and would ensure that the decision to invoke the Community's rights under international trade rules is taken on the basis of accurate factual information and legal analysis;

(7) WHEREAS this mechanism aims to provide procedural means to request that the Community institutions react to obstacles to trade adopted or maintained by third countries which cause injury or otherwise adverse trade effects, provided that a right of action exists, in respect of such obstacles, under applicable international trade rules;

(8) WHEREAS the right of Member States to resort to this mechanism should be without prejudice to their possibility to raise the same or similar matters through other exi-

---

1   So-called "New Trade Policy Instrument"; OJ 1994 L 349, p. 71, as amended by Council Regulation 356/95 of 20 February 1995.

sting Community procedures, and in particular before the committee established by Article 113 of the Treaty;

(9) WHEREAS regard should be paid to the institutional role of the committee established by Article 113 of the Treaty in formulating advice for the institutions of the Community on all issues of commercial policy; whereas, therefore, this committee should be kept informed of the development of individual cases, in order to enable it to consider their broader policy implications;

(10) WHEREAS, moreover, to the extent that an agreement with a third country appears to be the most appropriate means to resolve a dispute arising from an obstacle to trade, negotiations to this end shall be conducted according to the procedures established in Article 113 of the Treaty, in particular in consultation with the committee established thereby;

(11) WHEREAS it is appropriate to confirm that the Community must act in compliance with its international obligations and, where such obligations result from agreements, maintain the balance of rights and obligations which it is the purpose of those agreements to establish;

(12) WHEREAS it is also appropriate to confirm that any measures taken under the procedures in question should also be in conformity with the Community's international obligations, as well as being without prejudice to other measures in cases not covered by this Regulation which might be adopted directly pursuant to Article 113 of the Treaty;

(13) WHEREAS the rules of procedures to be followed during the examination procedure provided for in this Regulation should also be confirmed, in particular as regards the rights and obligations of the Community authorities and the parties involved, and the conditions under which interested parties may have access to information and may ask to be informed of the essential facts and considerations resulting from the examination procedure;

(14) WHEREAS in acting pursuant to this Regulation the Community has to bear in mind the need for rapid and effective action, through the application of the decision-making procedures provided for in the Regulation;

(15) WHEREAS it is incumbent on the Commission and the Council to act in respect of obstacles to trade adopted or maintained by third countries, within the framework of the Community's international rights and obligations, only when the interests of the Community call for intervention, and whereas, when assessing such interests, the Commission and the Council should give due consideration to the views by all interested parties in the proceedings;

HAS ADOPTED THIS REGULATION:

Article 1 Aims

This Regulation establishes Community procedures in the field of the common commercial policy in order to ensure the exercise of the Community's rights under international trade rules, in particular those established under the auspices of the World Trade Organization which, subject to compliance with existing international obligations and procedures, are aimed at:

(a) responding to obstacles to trade that have an effect on the market of the Community, with a view to removing the injury resulting therefrom;

(b) responding to obstacles to trade that have an effect on the market of a third country, with a view to removing the adverse trade effects resulting therefrom.

These procedures shall be applied in particular to the initiation and subsequent conduct and termination of international dispute settlement procedures in the area of common commercial policy.

Article 2 Definitions

1.   For the purposes of this Regulation, "obstacles to trade" shall be any trade practice adopted or maintained by a third country in respect of which international trade rules establish a right of action. Such a right of action exists when international trade rules either prohibit a practice outright, or give another party affected by the practice a right to seek elimination of the effect of the practice in question.

2.   For the purposes of this Regulation and subject to paragraph 8, "the Community's rights" shall be those international trade rights of which it may avail itself under international trade rules. In this context, "international trade rules" are primarily those established under the auspices of the WTO and laid down in the Annexes to the WTO Agreement, but they can also be those laid down in any other agreement to which the Community is a party and which sets out rules applicable to trade between the Community and third countries.

3.   For the purposes of this Regulation, "injury" shall be any material injury which an obstacle to trade causes or threatens to cause, in respect of a product or service, to a Community industry on the market of the Community.

4.   For the purposes of this Regulation, "adverse trade effects" shall be those which an obstacle to trade causes or threatens to cause, in respect of a product or service, to Community enterprises on the market of any third country, and which have a material impact on the economy of the Community or of a region of the Community, or on a sector of economic activity therein. The fact that the complainant suffers from such adverse effects shall not be considered sufficient to justify, on its own, that the Community institutions proceed with any action.

5.   The term "Community industry" shall be taken to mean all Community producers or providers, respectively:
—   of products or services identical or similar to the product or service which is the subject of an obstacle to trade, or
—   of products or services competing directly with that product or service, or
—   who are consumers or processors of the product or consumers or users of the service which is the subject of an obstacle to trade,
or all those producers or providers whose combined output constitutes a major proportion of total Community production of the products or services in question; however:
(a)   when producers or providers are related to the exporters or importers or are themselves importers of the product or service alleged to be the subject of obstacles to trade, the term "Community industry" may be interpreted as referring to the rest of the producers or providers;
(b)   in particular circumstances, the producers or providers within a region of the Community may be regarded as the Community industry if their collective output constitutes the major proportion of the output of the product or service in question in the Member State or Member States within which the region is located provided that the effect of the obstacle to trade is concentrated in that Member State or those Member States.

6.   The term "Community enterprise" shall be taken to mean a company or firm formed in accordance with the law of a Member State and having its registered office, central administration or principal place of business within the Community, directly concerned by the production of goods or the provision of services which are the subject of the obstacle to trade.

7.   For the purposes of this Regulation, the notion of "providers of services" in the context of both the term "Community industry" as defined in paragraph 5, and the term "Community enterprises" as defined in paragraph 6, is without prejudice to the non-commercial nature which the provision of any particular service may have according to the legislation or regulation of a Member State.

8.   For the purposes of this Regulation, the term "services" shall be taken to mean those services in respect of which international agreements can be concluded by the Community on the basis of Article 113 of the Treaty.

Article 3 Complaint on behalf of the Community industry
1.   Any natural or legal person, or any association not having legal personality, acting on behalf of a Community industry which considers that it has suffered injury as a result of obstacles to trade that have an effect on the market of the Community may lodge a written complaint.
2.   The complaint must contain sufficient evidence of the existence of the obstacles to trade and of the injury resulting therefrom. Evidence of injury must be given on the basis of the illustrative list of factors indicated in Article 10, where applicable.

Article 4 Complaint on behalf of Community enterprises
1.   Any Community enterprise, or any association, having or not legal personality, acting on behalf of one or more Community enterprises, which considers that such Community enterprises have suffered adverse trade effects as a result of obstacles to trade that have an effect on the market of a third country may lodge a written complaint. Such complaint, however, shall only be admissible if the obstacle to trade alleged therein is the subject of a right of action established under international trade rules laid down in a multilateral or plurilateral trade agreement.
2.   The complaint must contain sufficient evidence of the existence of the obstacles to trade and of the adverse trade effects, resulting therefrom. Evidence of adverse trade effects must be given on the basis of the illustrative list of factors indicated in Article 10, where applicable.

Article 5 Complaint procedures
1.   The complaint shall be submitted to the Commission, which shall send a copy thereof to the Member States.
2.   The complaint may be withdrawn, in which case the procedure may be terminated unless such termination would not be in the interests of the Community.
3.   Where it becomes apparent after consultation that the complaint does not provide sufficient evidence to justify initiating an investigation, then the complainant shall be so informed.
4.   The Commission shall take a decision as soon as possible on the opening of a Community examination procedure following any complaint made in accordance with Articles 3 or 4; the decision shall normally be taken within 45 days of the lodging of the complaint; this period may be suspended at the request, or with the agreement, of the complainant, in order to allow the provision of complementary information which may be needed to fully assess the validity of the complainant's case.

Article 6 Referral by a Member State
1.   Any Member State may ask the Commission to initiate the procedures referred to in Article 1.
2.   It shall supply the Commission with sufficient evidence to support its request, as regards obstacles to trade and of any effects resulting therefrom. Where evidence of injury or of adverse trade effects is appropriate, is must be given on the basis of the illustrative list of factors indicated in Article 10, where applicable.
3.   The Commission shall notify the other Member States of the requests without delay.

4. Where it becomes apparent after consultation that the request does not provide sufficient evidence to justify initiating an investigation, then the Member State shall be so informed.
5. The Commission shall take a decision as soon as possible on the opening of a Community examination procedure following any referral by a Member State made in accordance with Article 6; the decision shall normally be taken with 45 days of the referral; this period may be suspended at the request, or with the agreement, of the referring Member State, in order to allow the provision of complementary information which may be needed to fully assess the validity of the case presented by the referring Member State.

Article 7 Consultation procedure

1. For the purpose of consultations pursuant to this Regulation, an Advisory Committee, hereinafter referred to as "the Committee", is hereby set up and shall consist of representatives of each Member State, with a representative of the Commission as chairman.
2. Consultations shall be held immediately at the request of a Member State or on the initiative of the Commission, and in any event within a time frame which allows the time limits set by this Regulation to be respected. The chairman of the Committee shall provide the Member States, as promptly as possible, with all relevant information in his possession. The Commission shall also refer such information to the committee established by Article 113 of the Treaty so that it can consider any wider implications for the common commercial policy.
3. The Committee shall meet when convened by its chairman.
4. Where necessary, consultations may be in writing. In such case the Commission shall notify in writing the Member States who, within a period of eight working days from such notification, shall be entitled to express their opinions in writing or to request oral consultations which the chairman shall arrange, provided that such oral consultations can be held within a time frame which allows the time limits set by this Regulation to be respected.

Article 8 Community examination procedure

1. Where, after consultation, it is apparent to the Commission that there is sufficient evidence to justify initiating an examination procedure and that it is necessary in the interest of the Community, the Commission shall act as follows:
(a) it shall announce the initiation of an examination procedure in the Official Journal of the European Communities; such announcement shall indicate the product or service and countries concerned, give a summary of the information received, and provide that all relevant information is to be communicated to the Commission; it shall state the period within which interested parties may apply to be heard orally by the Commission in accordance with paragraph 5;
(b) it shall officially notify the representatives of the country or countries which are the subject of the procedure, with whom, where appropriate, consultations may be held;
(c) it shall conduct the examination at Community level, acting in cooperation with the Member States.
2. (a) If necessary the Commission shall seek all the information it deems necessary and attempt to check this information with the importers, traders, agents, producers, trade associations and organizations, provided that the undertakings or organizations concerned give their consent.

(b) Where necessary, the Commission shall carry out investigations in the territory of third countries, provided that the governments of the countries have been officially notified and raise no objection within a reasonable period.

(c) The Commission shall be assisted in its investigation by officials of the Member State in whose territory the checks are carried out, provided that the Member State in question so requests.

3.   Member States shall supply the Commission, upon request, with all information necessary for the examination, in accordance with the detailed arrangements laid down by the Commission.

4.   (a) The complainants and the exporters and importers concerned, as well as the representatives of the country or countries concerned, may inspect all information made available to the Commission except for internal documents for the use of the Commission and the administrations, provided that such information is relevant to the protection of their interests and not confidential within the meaning of Article 9 and that it is used by the Commission in its examination procedure. The persons concerned shall address a reasoned request in writing to the Commission, indicating the information required.

(b) The complainants and the exporters and importers concerned and the representatives of the country or countries concerned may ask to be informed of the principal facts and considerations resulting from the examination procedure.

5.   The Commission may hear the parties concerned. It shall hear them if they have, within the period prescribed in the notice published in the Official Journal of the European Communities, made a written request for a hearing showing that they are a party primarily concerned by the result of the procedure.

6.   Furthermore, the Commission shall, on request, give the parties primarily concerned an opportunity to meet, so that opposing views may be presented and any rebuttal argument put forward. In providing this opportunity the Commission shall take account of the wishes of the parties and of the need to preserve confidentiality. There shall be no obligation on any party to attend a meeting and failure to do so shall not be prejudicial to that party's case.

7.   When the information requested by the Commission is not supplied within a reasonable time or where the investigation is significantly impeded, findings may be made on the basis of the facts available.

8.   When it has concluded its examination the Commission shall report to the Committee. The report should normally be presented within five months of the announcement of initiation of the procedure, unless the complexity of the examination is such that the Commission extends the period to seven months.

Article 9 Confidentiality

1.   Information received pursuant to this Regulation shall be used only for the purpose for which it was requested.

2.   (a) Neither the Council, nor the Commission, nor Member States, nor the officials of any of these, shall reveal any information of a confidential nature received pursuant to this Regulation, or any information provided on a confidential basis by a party to an examination procedure, without specific permission from the party submitting such information.

(b) Each request for confidential treatment shall indicate why the information is confidential and shall be accompanied by a non-confidential summary of the information or a statement of the reasons why the information is not susceptible of such summary.

3. Information will normally be considered to be confidential if its disclosure is likely to have a significantly adverse effect upon the supplier or the source of such information.
4. However, if it appears that a request for confidentiality is not warranted and if the supplier is either unwilling to make the information public or to authorize its disclosure in generalized or summary form, the information in question may be disregarded.
5. This Article shall not preclude the disclosure of general information by the Community authorities and in particular of the reasons on which decisions taken pursuant to this Regulation are based. Such disclosure must take into account the legitimate interest of the parties concerned that their business secrets should not be divulged.

Article 10 Evidence

1. An examination of injury shall involve where applicable the following factors:
(a) the volume of Community imports or exports concerned, notably where there has been a significant increase or decrease, either in absolute terms or relative to production or consumption on the market in question;
(b) the prices of the Community industry's competitors, in particular in order to determine whether there has been, either in the Community or on third country markets, significant undercutting of the prices of the Community industry;
(c) the consequent impact on the Community industry and as indicated by trends in certain economic factors such as: production, utilization of capacity, stocks, sales, market share, prices (that is depression of prices or prevention of price increases which would normally have occurred), profits, return on capital, investment, employment.
2. Where a threat of injury is alleged, the Commission shall also examine whether it is clearly foreseeable that a particular situation is likely to develop into actual injury. In this regard, account may also be taken of factors such as:
(a) the rate of increase of exports to the market where the competition with Community products is taking place;
(b) export capacity in the country of origin or export, which is already in existence or will be operational in the foreseeable future, and the likelihood that the exports resulting from that capacity will be to the market referred to in point (a).
3. Injury caused by other factors which, either individually or in combination, are also adversely affecting Community industry must not be attributed to the practices under consideration.
4. Where adverse trade effects are alleged, the Commission shall examine the impact of such adverse effects on the economy of the Community or of a region of the Community, or on a sector of economic activity therein. To this effect, the Commission may take into account, where relevant, factors of the type listed in paragraphs 1 and 2. Adverse trade effects may arise, inter alia, in situations in which trade flows concerning a product or service are prevented, impeded or diverted as a result of any obstacle to trade, or from situations in which obstacles to trade have materially affected the supply or inputs (e. g. parts and components or raw materials) to Community enterprises. Where a threat of adverse trade effects is alleged, the Commission shall also examine whether it is clearly foreseeable that a particular situation is likely to develop into actual adverse trade effects.
5. The Commission shall also, in examining evidence of adverse trade effects, have regard to the provisions, principles or practice which govern the right of action under relevant international rules referred to in Article 2 (1).
6. The Commission shall further examine any other relevant evidence contained in the complaint or in the referral. In this respect, the list of factors and the indications given in paragraphs 1 to 5 are not exhaustive, nor can one or several of such factors

and indications necessarily give decisive guidance as to the existence of injury or of adverse trade effects.

Article 11 Termination and suspension of the procedure

1.   When it is found as a result of the examination procedure that the interests of the Community do not require any action to be taken, the procedure shall be terminated in accordance with Article 14.

2.   (a) When, after an examination procedure, the third country or countries concerned take(s) measures which are considered satisfactory, and therefore no action by the Community is required, the procedure may be suspended in accordance with the provisions of Article 14.

(b) The Commission shall supervise the application of these measures, where appropriate on the basis of information supplied at intervals, which it may request from the third countries concerned and check as necessary.

(c) Where the measures taken by the third country or countries concerned have been rescinded, suspended or improperly implemented or where the Commission has grounds for believing this to be the case or, finally, where a request for information made by the Commission as provided for by point (b) has not been granted, the Commission shall inform the Member States, and where necessary and justified by the results of the investigation and the new facts available any measures shall be taken in accordance with Article 13 (3).

3.   Where, either after an examination procedure, or at any time before, during and after an international dispute settlement procedure, it appears that the most appropriate means to resolve a dispute arising from an obstacle to trade is the conclusion of an agreement with the third country or countries concerned, which may change the substantive rights of the Community and of the third country or countries concerned, the procedure shall be suspended according to the provisions of Article 14, and negotiations shall be carried out according to the provisions of Article 113 of the Treaty.

Article 12 Adoption of commercial policy measures

1.   Where it is found (as a result of the examination procedure, unless the factual and legal situation is such that an examination procedure may not be required) that action is necessary in the interests of the Community in order to ensure the exercise of the Community's rights under international trade rules, with a view to removing the injury or the adverse trade effects resulting from obstacles to trade adopted or maintained by third countries, the appropriate measures shall be determined in accordance with the procedure set out in Article 13.

2.   Where the Community's international obligations require the prior discharge of an international procedure for consultation or for the settlement of disputes, the measures referred to in paragraph 3 shall only be decided on after that procedure has been terminated, and taking account of the results of the procedure. In particular, where the Community has requested an international dispute settlement body to indicate and authorize the measures which are appropriate for the implementation of the results of an international dispute settlement procedure, the Community commercial policy measures which may be needed in consequence of such authorization shall be in accordance with the recommendation of such international dispute settlement body.

3.   Any commercial policy measures may be taken which are compatible with existing international obligations and procedures, notably:

(a) suspension or withdrawal of any concession resulting from commercial policy negotiations;

(b) the raising of existing customs duties or the introduction of any other charge on imports;

(c) the introduction of quantitative restrictions or any other measures modifying import or export conditions or otherwise affecting trade with the third country concerned.

4. The corresponding decisions shall state the reasons on which they are based and shall be published in the Official Journal of the European Communities. Publication shall also be deemed to constitute notification to the countries and parties primarily concerned.

Article 13 Decision-making procedures

1. The decisions referred to in Article 11 (1) and (2) (a) shall be adopted in accordance with the provisions of Article 14.

2. Where the Community, as a result of a complaint pursuant to Articles 3 or 4, or of a referral pursuant to Article 6, follows formal international consultation or dispute settlement procedures, decisions relating to the initiation, conduct or termination of such procedures shall be taken in accordance with Article 14.

3. Where the Community, having acted in accordance with Article 12 (2), has to take a decision on the measures of commercial policy to be adopted pursuant to Article 11 (2) (c) or pursuant to Article 12 the Council shall act, in accordance with Article 113 of the Treaty, by a qualified majority, not later than 30 working days after receiving the proposal.

Article 14 Committee procedure

1. Should reference be made to the procedure provided for in this Article, the matter shall be brought before the Committee by its chairman.

2. The Commission representative shall submit to the Committee a draft of the decision to be taken. The Committee shall discuss the matter within a period to be fixed by the chairman, depending on the urgency of the matter.

3. The Commission shall adopt a decision which it shall communicate to the Member States and which shall apply after a period of 10 days if during this period no Member State has referred the matter to the Council.

4. The Council may, at the request of a Member State and acting by a qualified majority revise the Commission's decision.

5. The Commission's decision shall apply after a period of 30 days if the Council has not given a ruling within this period, calculated from the day on which the matter was referred to the Council.

Article 15 General provisions

1. This Regulation shall not apply in cases covered by other existing rules in the common commercial policy field. It shall operate by way of complement to:
— the rules establishing the common organization of agricultural markets and their implementing provisions, and
— the specific rules adopted pursuant to Article 235 of the Treaty, applicable to goods processed from agricultural products.

It shall be without prejudice to other measures which may be taken pursuant to Article 113 of the Treaty, as well as to Community procedures for dealing with matters concerning obstacles to trade raised by Member States in the committee established by Article 113 of the Treaty.

2. Regulation 2641/84 is hereby repealed. References to the repealed Regulation shall be construed as references to this Regulation where appropriate.

Article 16 Entry into force

This Regulation shall enter into force on 1 January 1995.

It shall apply to proceedings initiated after that date as well as to proceedings pending at that date and in relation to which Community examination procedures have been completed.

Done at Brussels, 22 December 1994.
For the Council: The President, H. SEEHOFER

EIGHT: OTHER COMMON POLICIES OF THE EUROPEAN UNION

Protection of the Environment

Council Directive 85/337 of 27 June 1985 on the Assessment of the Effects of Certain Public and Private Projects on the Environment[1]

THE COUNCIL OF THE EUROPEAN COMMUNITIES,

HAVING REGARD to the Treaty establishing the European Economic Community, and in particular Articles 100 and 235 thereof, [...]

(1) WHEREAS the 1973[2] and 1977[3] action programmes of the European Communities on the environment, as well as the 1983[4] action programme, the main outlines of which have been approved by the Council of the European Communities and the representatives of the Governments of the Member States, stress that the best environmental policy consists in preventing the creation of pollution or nuisances at source, rather than subsequently trying to counteract their effects; whereas they affirm the need to take effects on the environment into account at the earliest possible stage in all the technical planning and decision-making processes; whereas to that end, they provide for the implementation of procedures to evaluate such effects;

(2) WHEREAS the disparities between the laws in force in the various Member States with regard to the assessment of the environmental effects of public and private projects may create unfavourable competitive conditions and thereby directly affect the functioning of the common market; whereas, therefore, it is necessary to approximate national laws in this field pursuant to Article 100 of the Treaty;

(3) WHEREAS, in addition, it is necessary to achieve one of the Community's objectives in the sphere of the protection of the environment and the quality of life;

(4) WHEREAS, since the Treaty has not provided the powers required for this end, recourse should be had to Article 235 of the Treaty;

(5) WHEREAS general principles for the assessment of environmental effects should be introduced with a view to supplementing and coordinating development consent procedures governing public and private projects likely to have a major effect on the environment;

(6) WHEREAS development consent for public and private projects which are likely to have significant effects on the environment should be granted only after prior assessment of the likely significant environmental effects of these projects has been carried out; whereas this assessment must be conducted on the basis of the appropriate information supplied by the developer, which may be supplemented by the authorities and by the people who may be concerned by the project in question;

(7) WHEREAS the principles of the assessment of environmental effects should be harmonized, in particular with reference to the projects which should be subject to assessment, the main obligations of the developers and the content of the assessment;

(8) WHEREAS projects belonging to certain types have significant effects on the environment and these projects must as a rule be subject to systematic assessment;

---

1   OJ 1985 L 175, p. 40, as amended by Council Directive 97/11 of 3 March 1997.

2   OJ 1973 C 112, p. 1.

3   OJ 1977 C 139, p. 1.

4   OJ 1983 C 46, p. 1.

(9) WHEREAS projects of other types may not have significant effects on the environment in every case and whereas these projects should be assessed where the Member States consider that their characteristics so require;

(10) WHEREAS, for projects which are subject to assessment, a certain minimal amount of information must be supplied, concerning the project and its effects;

(11) WHEREAS the effects of a project on the environment must be assessed in order to take account of concerns to protect human health, to contribute by means of a better environment to the quality of life, to ensure maintenance of the diversity of species and to maintain the reproductive capacity of the ecosystem as a basic resource for life;

(12) WHEREAS, however, this Directive should not be applied to projects the details of which are adopted by a specific act of national legislation, since the objectives of this Directive, including that of supplying information, are achieved through the legislative process;

(13) WHEREAS, furthermore, it may be appropriate in exceptional cases to exempt a specific project from the assessment procedures laid down by this Directive, subject to appropriate information being supplied to the Commission,

HAS ADOPTED THIS DIRECTIVE:

Article 1 [Scope and Definitions]

1.   This Directive shall apply to the assessment of the environmental effects of those public and private projects which are likely to have significant effects on the environment.

2.   For the purposes of this Directive:

— "project" means: the execution of construction works or of other installations or schemes, other interventions in the natural surroundings and landscape including those involving the extraction of mineral resources;

— "developer" means: the applicant for authorization for a private project or the public authority which initiates a project;

— "development consent" means: the decision of the competent authority or authorities which entitles the developer to proceed with the project.

3.   The competent authority or authorities shall be that or those which the Member States designate as responsible for performing the duties arising from this Directive.

4.   Projects serving national defence purposes are not covered by this Directive.

5.   This Directive shall not apply to projects the details of which are adopted by a specific act of national legislation, since the objectives of this Directive, including that of supplying information, are achieved through the legislative process.

Article 2 [National Procedures for the Assessment of Projects]

1.   Member States shall adopt all measures necessary to ensure that, before consent is given, projects likely to have significant effects on the environment by virtue, *inter alia*, of their nature, size or location are made subject to a requirement for development consent and an assessment with regard to their effects. These projects are defined in Article 4.

2.   The environmental impact assessment may be integrated into the existing procedures for consent to projects in the Member States, or, failing this, into other procedures or into procedures to be established to comply with the aims of this Directive.

2a. Member States may provide for a single procedure in order to fulfil the requirements of this Directive and the requirements of Council Directive 96/61 of 24 September 1996 on integrated pollution prevention and control.[1]
3. Without prejudice to Article 7, Member States may, in exceptional cases, exempt a specific project in whole or in part from the provisions laid down in this Directive.
    In this event, the Member States shall:
(a) consider whether another form of assessment would be appropriate and whether the information thus collected should be made available to the public;
(b) make available to the public concerned the information relating to the exemption and the reasons for granting it;
(c) inform the Commission, prior to granting consent, of the reasons justifying the exemption granted, and provide it with the information made available, where applicable, to their own nationals.
The Commission shall immediately forward the documents received to the other Member States.
    The Commission shall report annually to the Council on the application of this paragraph.

Article 3 [Purpose of the Impact Assessment]
The environmental impact assessment shall identify, describe and assess in an appropriate manner, in the light of each individual case and in accordance with Articles 4 to 11, the direct and indirect effects of a project on the following factors:
— human beings, fauna and flora;
— soil, water, air, climate and the landscape;
— material assets and the cultural heritage;
— the interaction between the factors mentioned in the first, second and third indents.

Article 4 [Projects Subject to Impact Assessment]
1. Subject to Article 2 (3), projects listed in Annex I shall be made subject to an assessment in accordance with Articles 5 to 10.
2. Subject to Article 2 (3), for projects listed in Annex II, the Member States shall determine through:
(a) a case-by-case examination, or
(b) thresholds or criteria set by the Member State
whether the project shall be made subject to an assessment in accordance with Articles 5 to 10.
    Member States may decide to apply both procedures referred to in (a) and (b).
3. When a case-by-case examination is carried out or thresholds or criteria are set for the purpose of paragraph 2, the relevant selection criteria set out in Annex III shall be taken into account.
4. Member States shall ensure that the determination made by the competent authorities under paragraph 2 is made available to the public.

Article 5 [Information to be Supplied by Developers]
1. In the case of projects which, pursuant to Article 4, must be subjected to an environmental impact assessment in accordance with Articles 5 to 10, Member States shall adopt the necessary measures to ensure that the developer supplies in an appropriate form the information specified in Annex IV inasmuch as:

---

1   OJ 1996 L 257, p. 26.

(a) the Member States consider that the information is relevant to a given stage of the consent procedure and to the specific characteristics of a particular project or type of project and of the environmental features likely to be affected;

(b) the Member States consider that a developer may reasonably be required to compile this information having regard inter alia to current knowledge and methods of assessment.

2.   Member States shall take the necessary measures to ensure that, if the developer so requests before submitting an application for development consent, the competent authority shall give an opinion on the information to be supplied by the developer in accordance with paragraph 1. The competent authority shall consult the developer and authorities referred to in Article 6 (1) before it gives its opinion. The fact that the authority has given an opinion under this paragraph shall not preclude it from subsequently requiring the developer to submit further information.

Member States may require the competent authorities to give such an opinion, irrespective of whether the developer so requests.

3.   The information to be provided by the developer in accordance with paragraph 1 shall include at least:
— a description of the project comprising information on the site, design and size of the project,
— a description of the measures envisaged in order to avoid, reduce and, if possible, remedy significant adverse effects,
— the data required to identify and assess the main effects which the project is likely to have on the environment,
— an outline of the main alternatives studied by the developer and an indication of the main reasons for his choice, taking into account the environmental effects,
— a non-technical summary of the information mentioned in the previous indents.

4.   Member States shall, if necessary, ensure that any authorities holding relevant information, with particular reference to Article 3, shall make this information available to the developer.

Article 6 [Consultation of Authorities and of the Public]

1.   Member States shall take the measures necessary to ensure that the authorities likely to be concerned by the project by reason of their specific environmental responsibilities are given an opportunity to express their opinion on the information supplied by the developer and on the request for development consent. To this end, Member States shall designate the authorities to be consulted, either in general terms or on a case-by-case basis.

The information gathered pursuant to Article 5 shall be forwarded to those authorities. Detailed arrangements for consultation shall be laid down by the Member States.

2.   Member States shall ensure that any request for development consent and any information gathered pursuant to Article 5 are made available to the public within a reasonable time in order to give the public concerned the opportunity to express an opinion before the development consent is granted.

3.   The detailed arrangements for such information and consultation shall be determined by the Member States, which may in particular, depending on the particular characteristics of the projects or sites concerned:
— determine the public concerned,
— specify the places where the information can be consulted,
— specify the way in which the public may be informed, for example by bill-posting within a certain radius, publication in local newspapers, organization of exhibitions with plans, drawings, tables, graphs, models,

— determine the manner in which the public is to be consulted, for example, by written submissions, by public enquiry,
— fix appropriate time limits for the various stages of the procedure in order to ensure that a decision is taken within a reasonable period.

Article 7 [Consultation of Other Member States]

1. Where a Member State is aware that a project is likely to have significant effects on the environment in another Member State or where a Member State likely to be significantly affected so requests, the Member State in whose territory the project is intended to be carried out shall send to the affected Member State as soon as possible and no later than when informing its own public, inter alia:
(a) a description of the project, together with any available information on its possible transboundary impact;
(b) information on the nature of the decision which may be taken,
and shall give the other Member State a reasonable time in which to indicate whether it wishes to participate in the Environmental Impact Assessment procedure, and may include the information referred to in paragraph 2.
2. If a Member State which receives information pursuant to paragraph 1 indicates that it intends to participate in the Environmental Impact Assessment procedure, the Member State in whose territory the project is intended to be carried out shall, if it has not already done so, send to the affected Member State the information gathered pursuant to Article 5 and relevant information regarding the said procedure, including the request for development consent.
3. The Member States concerned, each insofar as it is concerned, shall also:
(a) arrange for the information referred to in paragraphs 1 and 2 to be made available, within a reasonable time, to the authorities referred to in Article 6 (1) and the public concerned in the territory of the Member State likely to be significantly affected; and
(b) ensure that those authorities and the public concerned are given an opportunity, before development consent for the project is granted, to forward their opinion within a reasonable time on the information supplied to the competent authority in the Member State in whose territory the project is intended to be carried out.
4. The Member States concerned shall enter into consultations regarding, inter alia, the potential transboundary effects of the project and the measures envisaged to reduce or eliminate such effects and shall agree on a reasonable time frame for the duration of the consultation period.
5. The detailed arrangements for implementing the provisions of this Article may be determined by the Member States concerned.

Article 8 [Results of Consultations]

The results of consultations and the information gathered pursuant to Articles 5, 6 and 7 must be taken into consideration in the development consent procedure.

Article 9 [Publication of Decisions]

1. When a decision to grant or refuse development consent has been taken, the competent authority or authorities shall inform the public thereof in accordance with the appropriate procedures and shall make available to the public the following information:
— the content of the decision and any conditions attached thereto,
— the main reasons and considerations on which the decision is based,
— a description, where necessary, of the main measures to avoid, reduce and, if possible, offset the major adverse effects.

2.   The competent authority or authorities shall inform any Member State which has been consulted pursuant to Article 7, forwarding to it the information referred to in paragraph 1.

Article 10 [Confidential Information and Public Interest]
The provisions of this Directive shall not affect the obligation on the competent authorities to respect the limitations imposed by national regulations and administrative provisions and accepted legal practices with regard to commercial and industrial confidentiality, including intellectual property, and the safeguarding of the public interest.

Where Article 7 applies, the transmission of information to another Member State and the receipt of information by another Member State shall be subject to the limitations in force in the Member State in which the project is proposed.

Article 11 [Co-operation with the Commission]
1.   The Member States and the Commission shall exchange information on the experience gained in applying this Directive.
2.   In particular, Member States shall inform the Commission of any criteria and/or thresholds adopted for the selection of the projects in question, in accordance with Article 4 (2).
3.   Five years after notification of this Directive, the Commission shall send the European Parliament and the Council a report on its application and effectiveness. The report shall be based on the aforementioned exchange of information.
4.   On the basis of this exchange of information, the Commission shall submit to the Council additional proposals, should this be necessary, with a view to this Directive's being applied in a sufficiently coordinated manner.

Article 12 [Implementation into National Law]
1.   Member States shall take the measures necessary to comply with this Directive within three years of its notification.[1]
2.   Member States shall communicate to the Commission the texts of the provisions of national law which they adopt in the field covered by this Directive.

Article 13 [deleted]

Article 14 [Addressees]
This Directive is addressed to the Member States.

Done at Luxembourg, 27 June 1985.
For the Council, The President, A. BIONDI

ANNEX I: PROJECTS SUBJECT TO ARTICLE 4 (1)
1.   Crude-oil refineries (excluding undertakings manufacturing only lubricants from crude oil) and installations for the gasification and liquefaction of 500 tonnes or more of coal or bituminous shale per day.
2.   —   Thermal power stations and other combustion installations with a heat output of 300 megawatts or more, and

---

[1]   This Directive was notified to the Member States on 3 July 1985.

— nuclear power stations and other nuclear reactors including the dismantling or decommissioning of such power stations or reactors[1] (except research installations for the production and conversion of fissionable and fertile materials, whose maximum power does not exceed 1 kilowatt continuous thermal load).

3. (a) Installations for the reprocessing of irradiated nuclear fuel.
   (b) Installations designed:
       — for the production or enrichment of nuclear fuel,
       — for the processing of irradiated nuclear fuel or high-level radioactive waste,
       — for the final disposal of irradiated nuclear fuel,
       — solely for the final disposal of radioactive waste,
       — solely for the storage (planned for more than 10 years) of irradiated nuclear fuels or radioactive waste in a different site than the production site.

4. — Integrated works for the initial smelting of cast-iron and steel;
   — Installations for the production of non-ferrous crude metals from ore, concentrates or secondary raw materials by metallurgical, chemical or electrolytic processes.

5. Installations for the extraction of asbestos and for the processing and transformation of asbestos and products containing asbestos: for asbestos-cement products, with an annual production of more than 20.000 tonnes of finished products, for friction material, with an annual production of more than 50 tonnes of finished products, and for other uses of asbestos, utilization of more than 200 tonnes per year.

6. Integrated chemical installations, i.e. those installations for the manufacture on an industrial scale of substances using chemical conversion processes, in which several units are juxtaposed and are functionally linked to one another and which are:
   (i) for the production of basic organic chemicals;
   (ii) for the production of basic inorganic chemicals;
   (iii) for the production of phosphorous-, nitrogen- or potassium-based fertilizers (simple or compound fertilizers);
   (iv) for the production of basic plant health products and of biocides;
   (v) for the production of basic pharmaceutical products using a chemical or biological process;
   (vi) for the production of explosives.

7. (a) Construction of lines for long-distance railway traffic and of airports[2] with a basic runway length of 2.100 m or more;
   (b) Construction of motorways and express roads[3];
   (c) Construction of a new road of four or more lanes, or realignment and/or widening of an existing road of two lanes or less so as to provide four or more lanes, where such new road, or realigned and/or widened section of road would be 10 km or more in a continuous length.

8. (a) Inland waterways and ports for inland-waterway traffic which permit the passage of vessels of over 1.350 tonnes;
   (b) Trading ports, piers for loading and unloading connected to land and outside ports (excluding ferry piers) which can take vessels of over 1.350 tonnes.

---

1   Nuclear power stations and other nuclear reactors cease to be such an installation when all nuclear fuel and other radioactively contaminated elements have been removed permanently from the installation site.

2   For the purposes of this Directive, "airport" means airports which comply with the definition in the 1944 Chicago Convention setting up the International Civil Aviation Organization (Annex 14).

3   For the purposes of the Directive, "express road" means a road which complies with the definition in the European Agreement on Main International Traffic Arteries of 15 November 1975.

9.   Waste disposal installations for the incineration, chemical treatment as defined in Annex IIA to Directive 75/442[1] under heading D9, or landfill of hazardous waste (i.e. waste to which Directive 91/689[2] applies).

10. Waste disposal installations for the incineration or chemical treatment as defined in Annex IIA to Directive 75/442 under heading D9 of non-hazardous waste with a capacity exceeding 100 tonnes per day.

11. Groundwater abstraction or artificial groundwater recharge schemes where the annual volume of water abstracted or recharged is equivalent to or exceeds 10 million cubic metres.

12. (a)   Works for the transfer of water resources between river basins where this transfer aims at preventing possible shortages of water and where the amount of water transferred exceeds 100 million cubic metres/year;

(b)   In all other cases, works for the transfer of water resources between river basins where the multi-annual average flow of the basin of abstraction exceeds 2.000 million cubic metres/year and where the amount of water transferred exceeds 5% of this flow.

In both cases transfers of piped drinking water are excluded.

13. Waste water treatment plants with a capacity exceeding 150.000 population equivalent as defined in Article 2 point (6) of Directive 91/271.[3]

14. Extraction of petroleum and natural gas for commercial purposes where the amount extracted exceeds 500 tonnes/day in the case of petroleum and 500.000 m³/day in the case of gas.

15. Dams and other installations designed for the holding back or permanent storage of water, where a new or additional amount of water held back or stored exceeds 10 million cubic metres.

16. Pipelines for the transport of gas, oil or chemicals with a diameter of more than 800 mm and a length of more than 40 km.

17. Installations for the intensive rearing of poultry or pigs with more than:
(a) 85.000 places for broilers, 60.000 places for hens;
(b) 3.000 places for production pigs (over 30 kg); or
(c) 900 places for sows.

18. Industrial plants for the
(a) production of pulp from timber or similar fibrous materials;
(b) production of paper and board with a production capacity exceeding 200 tonnes per day.

19. Quarries and open-cast mining where the surface of the site exceeds 25 hectares, or peat extraction, where the surface of the site exceeds 150 hectares.

20. Construction of overhead electrical power lines with a voltage of 220 kV or more and a length of more than 15 km.

21. Installations for storage of petroleum, petrochemical, or chemical products with a capacity of 200.000 tonnes or more.

ANNEX II: PROJECTS SUBJECT TO ARTICLE 4 (2)
1.   Agriculture, siviculture and aquaculture
(a) Projects for the restructuring of rural land holdings;
(b) Projects for the use of uncultivated land or semi-natural areas for intensive agricultural purposes;
(c) Water management projects for agriculture, including irrigation and land drainage projects;
(d) Initial afforestation and deforestation for the purposes of conversion to another type of land use;
(e) Intensive livestock installations (projects not included in Annex I);
(f) Intensive fish farming;
(g) Reclamation of land from the sea.
2.   Extractive industry
(a) Quarries, open-cast mining and peat extraction (projects not included in Annex I);
(b) Underground mining;

---

1   OJ 1975 L 194, p. 39, [as amended].

2   OJ 1991 L 377, p. 20, [as amended].

3   OJ 1991 L 135, p. 40. [as amended].

(c) Extraction of minerals by marine or fluvial dredging;
(d) Deep drillings, in particular:
— geothermal drilling,
— drilling for the storage of nuclear waste material,
— drilling for water supplies,
with the exception of drillings for investigating the stability of the soil;
(e) Surface industrial installations for the extraction of coal, petroleum, natural gas and ores, as well as bituminous shale.
3. Energy industry
(a) Industrial installations for the production of electricity, steam and hot water (projects not included in Annex I);
(b) Industrial installations for carrying gas, steam and hot water; transmission of electrical energy by overhead cables (projects not included in Annex I);
(c) Surface storage of natural gas;
(d) Underground storage of combustible gases;
(e) Surface storage of fossil fuels;
(f) Industrial briquetting of coal and lignite;
(g) Installations for the processing and storage of radioactive waste (unless included in Annex I);
(h) Installations for hydroelectric energy production;
(i) Installations for the harnessing of wind power for energy production (wind farms).
4. Production and processing of metals
(a) Installations for the production of pig iron or steel (primary or secondary fusion) including continuous casting;
(b) Installations for the processing of ferrous metals:
(i) hot-rolling mills;
(ii) smitheries with hammers;
(iii) application of protective fused metal coats;
(c) Ferrous metal foundries;
(d) Installations for the smelting, including the alloyage, of non-ferrous metals, excluding precious metals, including recovered products (refining, foundry casting, etc.);
(e) Installations for surface treatment of metals and plastic materials using an electrolytic or chemical process;
(f) Manufacture and assembly of motor vehicles and manufacture of motor-vehicle engines;
(g) Shipyards;
(h) Installations for the construction and repair of aircraft;
(i) Manufacture of railway equipment;
(j) Swaging by explosives;
(k) Installations for the roasting and sintering of metallic ores.
5. Mineral industry
(a) Coke ovens (dry coal distillation);
(b) Installations for the manufacture of cement;
(c) Installations for the production of asbestos and the manufacture of asbestos-products (projects not included in Annex I);
(d) Installations for the manufacture of glass including glass fibre;
(e) Installations for smelting mineral substances including the production of mineral fibres;
(f) Manufacture of ceramic products by burning, in particular roofing tiles, bricks, refractory bricks, tiles, stoneware or porcelain.
6. Chemical industry (Projects not included in Annex I)
(a) Treatment of intermediate products and production of chemicals;
(b) Production of pesticides and pharmaceutical products, paint and varnishes, elastomers and peroxides;
(c) Storage facilities for petroleum, petrochemical and chemical products.
7. Food industry
(a) Manufacture of vegetable and animal oils and fats;
(b) Packing and canning of animal and vegetable products;
(c) Manufacture of dairy products;
(d) Brewing and malting;

(e) Confectionery and syrup manufacture;
(f) Installations for the slaughter of animals;
(g) Industrial starch manufacturing installations;
(h) Fish-meal and fish-oil factories;
(i) Sugar factories.
8.   Textile, leather, wood and paper industries
(a) Industrial plants for the production of paper and board (projects not included in Annex I);
(b) Plants for the pretreatment (operations such as washing, bleaching, mercerization) or dyeing of fibres or textiles;
(c) Plants for the tanning of hides and skins;
(d) Cellulose-processing and production installations.
9.   Rubber industry
Manufacture and treatment of elastomer-based products.
10. Infrastructure projects
(a) Industrial estate development projects;
(b) Urban development projects, including the construction of shopping centres and car parks;
(c) Construction of railways and intermodal transshipment facilities, and of intermodal terminals (projects not included in Annex I);
(d) Construction of airfields (projects not included in Annex I);
(e) Construction of roads, harbours and port installations, including fishing harbours (projects not included in Annex I);
(f) Inland-waterway construction not included in Annex I, canalization and flood-relief works;
(g) Dams and other installations designed to hold water or store it on a long-term basis (projects not included in Annex I);
(h) Tramways, elevated and underground railways, suspended lines or similar lines of a particular type, used exclusively or mainly for passenger transport;
(i) Oil and gas pipeline installations (projects not included in Annex I);
(j) Installations of long-distance aqueducts;
(k) Coastal work to combat erosion and maritime works capable of altering the coast through the construction, for example, of dykes, moles, jetties and other sea defence works, excluding the maintenance and reconstruction of such works;
(l) Groundwater abstraction and artificial groundwater recharge schemes not included in Annex I;
(m) Works for the transfer of water resources between river basins not included in Annex I.
11. Other projects
(a) Permanent racing and test tracks for motorized vehicles;
(b) Installations for the disposal of waste (projects not included in Annex I);
(c) Waste-water treatment plants (projects not included in Annex I);
(d) Sludge-deposition sites;
(e) Storage of scrap iron, including scrap vehicles;
(f) Test benches for engines, turbines or reactors;
(g) Installations for the manufacture of artificial mineral fibres;
(h) Installations for the recovery or destruction of explosive substances;
(i) Knackers' yards.
12. Tourism and leisure
(a) Ski-runs, ski-lifts and cable-cars and associated developments;
(b) Marinas;
(c) Holiday villages and hotel complexes outside urban areas and associated developments;
(d) Permanent camp sites and caravan sites;
(e) Theme parks.
13.
—   Any change or extension of projects listed in Annex I or Annex II, already authorized, executed or in the process of being executed, which may have significant adverse effects on the environment;
—   Projects in Annex I, undertaken exclusively or mainly for the development and testing of new methods or products and not used for more than two years.

ANNEX III: SELECTION CRITERIA REFERRED TO IN ARTICLE 4 (3)
1. Characteristics of projects
The characteristics of projects must be considered having regard, in particular, to:
— the size of the project,
— the cumulation with other projects,
— the use of natural resources,
— the production of waste,
— pollution and nuisances,
— the risk of accidents, having regard in particular to substances or technologies used.
2. Location of projects
The environmental sensitivity of geographical areas likely to be affected by projects must be considered, having regard, in particular, to:
— the existing land use,
— the relative abundance, quality and regenerative capacity of natural resources in the area,
— the absorption capacity of the natural environment, paying particular attention to the following areas:
(a) wetlands;
(b) coastal zones;
(c) mountain and forest areas;
(d) nature reserves and parks;
(e) areas classified or protected under Member States' legislation; special protection areas designated by Member States pursuant to Directive 79/409 and 92/43;
(f) areas in which the environmental quality standards laid down in Community legislation have already been exceeded;
(g) densely populated areas;
(h) landscapes of historical, cultural or archaeological significance.
3. Characteristics of the potential impact
The potential significant effects of projects must be considered in relation to criteria set out under 1 and 2 above, and having regard in particular to:
— the extent of the impact (geographical area and size of the affected population),
— the transfrontier nature of the impact,
— the magnitude and complexity of the impact,
— the probability of the impact,
— the duration, frequency and reversibility of the impact.

ANNEX IV INFORMATION REFERRED TO IN ARTICLE 5 (1)
1. Description of the project, including in particular:
— a description of the physical characteristics of the whole project and the land-use requirements during the construction and operational phases,
— a description of the main characteristics of the production processes, for instance, nature and quantity of the materials used,
— an estimate, by type and quantity, of expected residues and emissions (water, air and soil pollution, noise, vibration, light, heat, radiation, etc.) resulting from the operation of the proposed project.
2. An outline of the main alternatives studied by the developer and an indication of the main reasons for this choice, taking into account the environmental effects.
3. A description of the aspects of the environment likely to be significantly affected by the proposed project, including, in particular, population, fauna, flora, soil, water, air, climatic factors, material assets, including the architectural and archaeological heritage, landscape and the inter-relationship between the above factors.
4. A description[1] of the likely significant effects of the proposed project on the environment resulting from:
— the existence of the project,
— the use of natural resources,

---

1   This description should cover the direct effects and any indirect, secondary, cumulative, short, medium and long-term, permanent and temporary, positive and negative effects of the project.

— the emission of pollutants, the creation of nuisances and the elimination of waste, and the description by the developer of the forecasting methods used to assess the effects on the environment.

5. A description of the measures envisaged to prevent, reduce and where possible offset any significant adverse effects on the environment.

6. A non-technical summary of the information provided under the above headings.

7. An indication of any difficulties (technical deficiencies or lack of know-how) encountered by the developer in compiling the required information.

Council Directive 90/313 of 7 June 1990 on the Freedom of Access to Information on the Environment[1]

THE COUNCIL OF THE EUROPEAN COMMUNITIES,

HAVING REGARD to the Treaty establishing the European Economic Community, and in particular Article 130s thereof, [...]

CONSIDERING the principles and objectives defined by the action programmes of the European Communities on the environment of 1973,[2] 1977[3], and 1983,[4] and more particularly the action programme of 1987,[5] which calls, in particular, for devising "ways of improving public access to information held by environmental authorities";

(1) WHEREAS the Council of the European Communities and the representatives of the Governments of the Member States, meeting within the Council, declared in their resolution of 19 October 1987 on the continuation and implementation of a European Community policy and action programme on the environment (1987 to 1992)[6] that it was important, in compliance with the respective responsibilities of the Community and the Member States, to concentrate Community action on certain priority areas, including better access to information on the environment;

(2) WHEREAS the European Parliament stressed, in its opinion on the fourth action programme of the European Communities on the environment,[7] that "access to information for all must be made possible by a specific Community programme";

(4) WHEREAS access to information on the environment held by public authorities will improve environmental protection;

(5) WHEREAS the disparities between the laws in force in the Member States concerning access to information on the environment held by public authorities can create inequality within the Community as regards access to information and/or as regards conditions of competition;

(6) WHEREAS it is necessary to guarantee to any natural or legal person throughout the Community free access to available information on the environment in written, visual, aural or data-base form held by public authorities, concerning the state of the

1 OJ 1990 L 158 , p. 56.

2 OJ 1973 C 112, p. 1.

3 OJ 1977 C 139, p. 1.

4 OJ 1983 C 46, p. 1.

5 OJ 1987 C 70, p. 3.

6 OJ 1987 C 289, p. 3.

7 OJ 1987 C 156, p. 138.

environment, activities or measures adversely affecting, or likely so to affect the environment, and those designed to protect it;
(7) WHEREAS, in certain specific and clearly defined cases, it may be justified to refuse a request for information relating to the environment; whereas a refusal by a public authority to forward the information requested must be justified;
(8) WHEREAS it must be possible for the applicant to appeal against the public authority's decision;
(9) WHEREAS access to information relating to the environment held by bodies with public responsibilities for the environment and under the control of public authorities should also be ensured;
(10) WHEREAS, as part of an overall strategy to disseminate information on the environment, general information should actively be provided to the public on the state of the environment;
(11) WHEREAS the operation of this Directive should be subject to a review in the light of the experience gained,

HAS ADOPTED THIS DIRECTIVE:

Article 1 [Objective]
The object of this Directive is to ensure freedom of access to, and dissemination of, information on the environment held by public authorities and to set out the basic terms and conditions on which such information should be made available.

Article 2 [Definitions]
For the purposes of this Directive:
(a) "information relating to the environment" shall mean any available information in written, visual, aural or data-base form on the state of water, air, soil, fauna, flora, land and natural sites, and on activities (including those which give rise to nuisances such as noise) or measures adversely affecting, or likely so to affect these, and on activities or measures designed to protect these, including administrative measures and environmental management programmes;
(b) "public authorities" shall mean any public administration at national, regional or local level with responsibilities, and possessing information, relating to the environment with the exception of bodies acting in a judicial or legislative capacity.

Article 3 [Member State Obligations]
1. Save as provided in this Article, Member States shall ensure that public authorities are required to make available information relating to the environment to any natural or legal person at his request and without his having to prove an interest.
    Member States shall define the practical arrangements under which such information is effectively made available.
2. Member States may provide for a request for such information to be refused where it affects:
— the confidentiality of the proceedings of public authorities, international relations and national defence,
— public security,
— matters which are, or have been, sub judice, or under enquiry (including disciplinary enquiries), or which are the subject of preliminary investigation proceedings,
— commercial and industrial confidentiality, including intellectual property,
— the confidentiality of personal data and/or files,

— material supplied by a third party without that party being under a legal obligation to do so,

— material, the disclosure of which would make it more likely that the environment to which such material related would be damaged.

Information held by public authorities shall be supplied in part where it is possible to separate out information on items concerning the interests referred to above.

3. A request for information may be refused where it would involve the supply of unfinished documents or data or internal communications, or where the request is manifestly unreasonable or formulated in too general a manner.

4. A public authority shall respond to a person requesting information as soon as possible and at the latest within two months. The reasons for a refusal to provide the information requested must be given.

Article 4 [Legal Remedies]

A person who considers that his request for information has been unreasonably refused or ignored, or has been inadequately answered by a public authority, may seek a judicial or administrative review of the decision in accordance with the relevant national legal system.

Article 5 [Charges for Information]

Member States may make a charge for supplying the information, but such charge may not exceed a reasonable cost.

Article 6 [Obligations of Private Operators]

Member States shall take the necessary steps to ensure that information relating to the environment held by bodies with public responsibilities for the environment and under the control of public authorities is made available on the same terms and conditions as those set out in Articles 3, 4 and 5 either via the competent public authority or directly by the body itself.

Article 7 [General Information of the Environment]

Member States shall take the necessary steps to provide general information to the public on the state of environment by such means as the periodic publication of descriptive reports.

Article 8 [Monitoring]

Four years after the date referred to in Article 9 (1), the Member States shall report to the Commission on the experience gained in the light of which the Commission shall make a report to the European Parliament and the Council together with any proposal for revision which it may consider appropriate.

Article 9 [Implementation into National Law]

1. Member States shall bring into force the laws, regulations and administrative provisions necessary to comply with this Directive by 31 December 1992 at the latest. They shall forthwith inform the Commission thereof.

2. Member States shall communicate to the Commission the main provisions of national law which they adopt in the field governed by this Directive.

Article 10 [Addressees]

This Directive is addressed to the Member States.

Done at Luxembourg, 7 June 1990.

For the Council, The President, P. FLYNN

Consumer Protection

Council Directive 92/59 of 29 June 1992 on General Product Safety[1]

THE COUNCIL OF THE EUROPEAN COMMUNITIES,

HAVING REGARD to the Treaty establishing the European Economic Community, and in particular Article 100a thereof, [...]
(1) WHEREAS it is important to adopt measures with the aim of progressively establishing the internal market over a period expiring on 31 December 1992; whereas the internal market is to comprise an area without internal frontiers in which the free movement of goods, persons, services and capital is ensured;
(2) WHEREAS some Member States have adopted horizontal legislation on product safety, imposing, in particular, a general obligation on economic operators to market only safe products; whereas those legislations differ in the level of protection afforded to persons; whereas such disparities and the absence of horizontal legislation in other Member States are liable to create barriers to trade and distortions of competition within the internal market;
(3) WHEREAS it is very difficult to adopt Community legislation for every product which exists or may be developed; whereas there is a need for a broadly-based, legislative framework of a horizontal nature to deal with those products, and also to cover lacunae in existing or forthcoming specific legislation, in particular with a view to ensuring a high level of protection of safety and health of persons, as required by Article 100 a (3) of the Treaty;
(4) WHEREAS it is therefore necessary to establish on a Community level a general safety requirement for any product placed on the market that is intended for consumers or likely to be used by consumers; whereas certain second-hand goods should nevertheless be excluded by their nature;
(5) WHEREAS production equipment, capital goods and other products used exclusively in the context of a trade or business are not covered by this Directive;
(6) WHEREAS, in the absence of more specific safety provisions, within the framework of Community regulations, covering the products concerned, the provisions of this Directive are to apply;
(7) WHEREAS when there are specific rules of Community law, of the total harmonization type, and in particular rules adopted on the basis of the new approach, which lay down obligations regarding product safety, further obligations should not be imposed on economic operators as regards the placing on the market of products covered by such rules;
(8) WHEREAS, when the provisions of specific Community regulations cover only certain aspects of safety or categories of risks in respect of the product concerned, the obligations of economic operators in respect of such aspects are determined solely by those provisions;
(9) WHEREAS it is appropriate to supplement the duty to observe the general safety requirement by an obligation on economic operators to supply consumers with relevant information and adopt measures commensurate with the characteristics of the products, enabling them to be informed of the risks that these products might present;
(10) WHEREAS in the absence of specific regulations, criteria should be defined whereby product safety can be assessed;

---

1   OJ 1992 L 228, p. 24.

Whereas Member States must establish authorities responsible for monitoring product safety and with powers to take the appropriate measures;

(11) WHEREAS it is necessary in particular for the appropriate measures to include the power for Member States to organize, immediately and efficiently, the withdrawal of dangerous products already placed on the market;

(12) WHEREAS it is necessary for the preservation of the unity of the market to inform the Commission of any measure restricting the placing on the market of a product or requiring its withdrawal from the market except for those relating to an event which is local in effect and in any case limited to the territory of the Member State concerned; whereas such measures can be taken only in compliance with the provisions of the Treaty, and in particular Articles 30 to 36;

(13) WHEREAS this Directive applies without prejudice to the notification procedures in Council Directive 83/189 of 28 March 1983 laying down a procedure for the provision of information in the field of technical standards and regulations[1] and in Commission Decision 88/383 of 24 February 1988 providing for the improvement of information on safety, hygiene and health at work[2];

(14) WHEREAS effective supervision of product safety requires the setting-up at national and Community levels of a system of rapid exchange of information in emergency situations in respect of the safety of a product and whereas the procedure laid down by Council Decision 89/45 of 21 December 1988 on a Community system for the rapid exchange of information on dangers arising from the use of consumer products[3] should therefore be incorporated into this Directive and the above Decision should be repealed; whereas it is also advisable for this Directive to take over the detailed procedures adopted under the above Decision and to give the Commission, assisted by a committee, power to adapt them;

(15) WHEREAS, moreover, equivalent notification procedures already exist for pharmaceuticals, which come under Directives 75/319[4] and 81/851[5], concerning animal diseases referred to in Directive 82/894[6], for products of animal origin covered by Directive 89/662[7], and in the form of the system for the rapid exchange of information in radiological emergencies under Decision 87/600[8];

(16) WHEREAS it is primarily for Member States, in compliance with the Treaty and in particular with Articles 30 to 36 thereof, to take appropriate measures with regard to dangerous products located within their territory;

(17) WHEREAS in such a situation the decision taken on a particular product could differ from one Member State to another; whereas such a difference may entail unacceptable disparities in consumer protection and constitute a barrier to intra-Community trade;

(18) WHEREAS it may be necessary to cope with serious product-safety problems which affect or could affect, in the immediate future, all or a large part of the Commu-

---

1   This Directive has been replaced in the meantime by Directive 98/34, see above, p. 311.

2   OJ 1988 L 183, p. 34.

3   OJ 1989 L 17, p. 51.

4   OJ 1975 L 147, p. 13.

5   OJ 1981 L 317, p. 1.

6   OJ 1982 L 378, p. 58.

7   OJ 1989 L 395, p. 13.

8   OJ 1987 L 371, p. 76.

nity and which, in view of the nature of the safety problem posed by the product cannot be dealt with effectively in a manner commensurate with the urgency of the problem under the procedures laid down in the specific rules of Community law applicable to the products or category of products in question;

(19) WHEREAS it is therefore necessary to provide for an adequate mechanism allowing, in the last resort, for the adoption of measures applicable throughout the Community, in the form of a decision addressed to the Member States, in order to cope with emergency situations as mentioned above; whereas such a decision is not of direct application to economic operators and must be incorporated into a national instrument; whereas measures adopted under such a procedure can be no more than interim measures that have to be taken by the Commission assisted by a committee of representatives of the Member States; whereas, for reasons of cooperation with the Member States, it is appropriate to provide for a regulatory committee according to procedure III (b) of Decision 87/373[1];

(20) WHEREAS this Directive does not affect victims' rights within the meaning of Council Directive 85/374 of 25 July 1985 on the approximation of the laws, regulations and administrative provisions of the Member States concerning liability for defective products[2];

(21) WHEREAS it is necessary that Member States provide for appropriate means of redress before the competent courts in respect of measures taken by the competent authorities which restrict the placing on the market of a product or require its withdrawal;

(22) WHEREAS it is appropriate to consider, in the light of experience, possible adaptation of this Directive, particularly as regards extension of its scope and provisions on emergency situations and intervention at Community level;

(23) WHEREAS, in addition, the adoption of measures concerning imported products with a view to preventing risks to the safety and health of persons must comply with the Community's international obligations,

HAS ADOPTED THIS DIRECTIVE:

TITLE I
OBJECTIVE - SCOPE - DEFINITIONS

Article 1 [Objective]

1.   The purpose of the provisions of this Directive is to ensure that products placed on the market are safe.

2.   The provisions of this Directive shall apply in so far as there are no specific provisions in rules of Community law governing the safety of the products concerned.

In particular, where specific rules of Community law contain provisions imposing safety requirements on the products which they govern, the provisions of Articles 2 to 4 of this Directive shall not, in any event, apply to those products.

Where specific rules of Community law contain provisions governing only certain aspects of product safety or categories of risks for the products concerned, those are the provisions which shall apply to the products concerned with regard to the relevant safety aspects or risks.

---

1   OJ 1987 L 197, p. 33.

2   See below, p. 596.

Article 2 [Definitions]

For the purposes of this Directive:
(a) product shall mean any product intended for consumers or likely to be used by consumers, supplied whether for consideration or not in the course of a commercial activity and whether new, used or reconditioned.

However, this Directive shall not apply to second-hand products supplied as antiques or as products to be repaired or reconditioned prior to being used, provided that the supplier clearly informs the person to whom he supplies the product to that effect;

(b) safe product shall mean any product which, under normal or reasonably foreseeable conditions of use, including duration, does not present any risk or only the minimum risks compatible with the product's use, considered as acceptable and consistent with a high level of protection for the safety and health of persons, taking into account the following points in particular:
— the characteristics of the product, including its composition, packaging, instructions for assembly and maintenance,
— the effect on other products, where it is reasonably foreseeable that it will be used with other products,
— the presentation of the product, the labelling, any instructions for its use and disposal and any other indication or information provided by the producer,
— the categories of consumers at serious risk when using the product, in particular children.

The feasibility of obtaining higher levels of safety or the availability of other products presenting a lesser degree of risk shall not constitute grounds for considering a product to be "unsafe" or "dangerous";

(c) dangerous product shall mean any product which does not meet the definition of "safe product" according to point (b) hereof;

(d) producer shall mean:
— the manufacturer of the product, when he is established in the Community, and any other person presenting himself as the manufacturer by affixing to the product his name, trade mark or other distinctive mark, or the person who reconditions the product,
— the manufacturer's representative, when the manufacturer is not established in the Community or, if there is no representative established in the Community, the importer of the product,
— other professionals in the supply chain, insofar as their activities may affect the safety properties of a product placed on the market.

(e) distributor shall mean any professional in the supply chain whose activity does not affect the safety properties of a product.

TITLE II
GENERAL SAFETY REQUIREMENT

Article 3 [Producer's Obligations]

1. Producers shall be obliged to place only safe products on the market.
2. Within the limits of their respective activities, producers shall:
— provide consumers with the relevant information to enable them to assess the risks inherent in a product throughout the normal or reasonably foreseeable period of its use, where such risks are not immediately obvious without adequate warnings, and to take precautions against those risks.

Provision of such warnings does not, however, exempt any person from compliance with the other requirements laid down in this Directive,

— adopt measures commensurate with the characteristics of the products which they supply, to enable them to be informed of risks which these products might present and to take appropriate action including, if necessary, withdrawing the product in question from the market to avoid these risks.

The above measures shall for example include, whenever appropriate, marking of the products or product batches in such a way that they can be identified, sample testing of marketed products, investigating complaints made and keeping distributors informed of such monitoring.

3. Distributors shall be required to act with due care in order to help to ensure compliance with the general safety requirement, in particular by not supplying products which they know or should have presumed, on the basis of the information in their possession and as professionals, do not comply with this requirement. In particular, within the limits of their respective activities, they shall participate in monitoring the safety of products placed on the market, especially by passing on information on product risks and cooperating in the action taken to avoid these risks.

Article 4 [National Safety Standards]

1. Where there are no specific Community provisions governing the safety of the products in question, a product shall be deemed safe when it conforms to the specific rules of national law of the Member State in whose territory the product is in circulation, such rules being drawn up in conformity with the Treaty, and in particular Articles 30 and 36 thereof, and laying down the health and safety requirements which the product must satisfy in order to be marketed.

2. In the absence of specific rules as referred to in paragraph 1, the conformity of a product to the general safety requirement shall be assessed having regard to voluntary national standards giving effect to a European standard or, where they exist, to Community technical specifications or, failing these, to standards drawn up in the Member State in which the product is in circulation, or to the codes of good practice in respect of health and safety in the sector concerned or to the state of the art and technology and to the safety which consumers may reasonably expect.

3. Conformity of a product with the provisions mentioned in paragraphs 1 or 2 shall not bar the competent authorities of the Member States from taking appropriate measures to impose restrictions on its being placed on the market or to require its withdrawal from the market where there is evidence that, despite such conformity, it is dangerous to the health and safety of consumers.

TITLE III
OBLIGATIONS AND POWERS OF THE MEMBER STATES

Article 5 [Member State Obligations]

Member States shall adopt the necessary laws, regulations and administrative provisions to make producers and distributors comply with their obligations under this Directive in such a way that products placed on the market are safe.

In particular, Member States shall establish or nominate authorities to monitor the compliance of products with the obligation to place only safe products on the market and arrange for such authorities to have the necessary powers to take the appropriate measures incumbent upon them under this Directive, including the possibility of imposing suitable penalties in the event of failure to comply with the obligations deriving from this Directive. They shall notify the Commission of the said authorities; the Commission shall pass on the information to the other Member States.

Article 6 [Member State Powers]

1.　For the purposes of Article 5, Member States shall have the necessary powers, acting in accordance with the degree or risk and in conformity with the Treaty, and in particular Articles 30 and 36 thereof, to adopt appropriate measures with a view, *inter alia*, to:

(a)　organizing appropriate checks on the safety properties of products, even after their being placed on the market as being safe, on an adequate scale, up to the final stage of use or consumption;

(b)　requiring all necessary information from the parties concerned;

(c)　taking samples of a product or a product line and subjecting them to safety checks;

(d)　subjecting product marketing to prior conditions designed to ensure product safety and requiring that suitable warnings be affixed regarding the risks which the product may present;

(e)　making arrangements to ensure that persons who might be exposed to a risk from a product are informed in good time and in a suitable manner of the said risk by, *inter alia*, the publication of special warnings;

(f)　temporarily prohibiting, for the period required to carry out the various checks, anyone from supplying, offering to supply or exhibiting a product or product batch, whenever there are precise and consistent indications that they are dangerous;

(g)　prohibiting the placing on the market of a product or product batch which has proved dangerous and establishing the accompanying measures needed to ensure that the ban is complied with;

(h)　organizing the effective and immediate withdrawal of a dangerous product or product batch already on the market and, if necessary, its destruction under appropriate conditions.

2.　The measures to be taken by the competent authorities of the Member States under this Article shall be addressed, as appropriate, to:

(a)　the producer;

(b)　within the limits of their respective activities, distributors and in particular the party responsible for the first stage of distribution on the national market;

(c)　any other person, where necessary, with regard to cooperation in action taken to avoid risks arising from a product.

TITLE IV
NOTIFICATION AND EXCHANGES OF INFORMATION

Article 7 [Notification of the Measures to the Commission]

1.　Where a Member State takes measures which restrict the placing of a product or a product batch on the market or require its withdrawal from the market, such as provided for in Article 6 (1) (d) to (h), the Member State shall, to the extent that such notification is not required under any specific Community legislation, inform the Commission of the said measures, specifying its reasons for adopting them. This obligation shall not apply where the measures relate to an event which is local in effect and in any case limited to the territory of the Member State concerned.

2.　The Commission shall enter into consultations with the parties concerned as quickly as possible. Where the Commission concludes, after such consultations, that the measure is justified, it shall immediately inform the Member State which initiated the action and the other Member States. Where the Commission concludes, after such consultations, that the measures is not justified, it shall immediately inform the Member State which initiated the action.

Title V
Emergency Situations and Action At Community Level

Article 8 [Notification of Emergency Measures]

1.   Where a Member State adopts or decides to adopt emergency measures to prevent, restrict or impose specific conditions on the possible marketing or use, within its own territory, of a product or product batch by reason of a serious and immediate risk presented by the said product or product batch to the health and safety of consumers, it shall forthwith inform the Commission thereof, unless provision is made for this obligation in procedures of a similar nature in the context of other Community instruments.

This obligation shall not apply if the effects of the risk do not, or cannot, go beyond the territory of the Member State concerned.

Without prejudice to the provisions of the first subparagraph, Member States may pass on to the Commission any information in their possession regarding the existence of a serious and immediate risk before deciding to adopt the measures in question.

2.   On receiving this information, the Commission shall check to see whether it complies with the provisions of this Directive and shall forward it to the other Member States, which, in turn, shall immediately inform the Commission of any measures adopted.

3.   Detailed procedures for the Community information system described in this Article are set out in the Annex. They shall be adapted by the Commission in accordance with the procedure laid down in Article 11.

Article 9 [Commission Decisions]

If the Commission becomes aware, through notification given by the Member States or through information provided by them, in particular under Article 7 or Article 8, of the existence of a serious and immediate risk from a product to the health and safety of consumers in various Member States and if:

(a)   one or more Member States have adopted measures entailing restrictions on the marketing of the product or requiring its withdrawal from the market, such as those provided for in Article 6 (1) (d) to (h);

(b)   Member States differ on the adoption of measures to deal with the risk in question;

(c)   the risk cannot be dealt with, in view of the nature of the safety issue posed by the product and in a manner compatible with the urgency of the case, under the other procedures laid down by the specific Community legislation applicable to the product or category of products concerned; and

(d)   the risk can be eliminated effectively only by adopting appropriate measures applicable at Community level, in order to ensure the protection of the health and safety of consumers and the proper functioning of the common market.

The Commission, after consulting the Member States and at the request of at least one of them, may adopt a decision, in accordance with the procedure laid down in Article 11, requiring Member States to take temporary measures from among those listed in Article 6 (1) (d) to (h).

Article 10 [Committee on Product Safety Emergencies]

1.   The Commission shall be assisted by a Committee on Product Safety Emergencies, hereinafter referred to as "the Committee", composed of the representatives of the Member States and chaired by a representative of the Commission.

2.   Without prejudice to Article 9 (c), there shall be close cooperation between the Committee referred to in paragraph 1 and the other Committees established by specific rules of Community law to assist the Commission as regards the health and safety aspects of the product concerned.

Article 11 [Committee Procedure]

1.   The Commission representative shall submit to the Committee a draft of the measures to be taken. The Committee, having verified that the conditions listed in Article 9 are fulfilled, shall deliver its opinion on the draft within a time limit which the Chairman may lay down according to the urgency of the matter but which may not exceed one month. The opinion shall be delivered by the majority laid down in Article 148 (2) of the Treaty for adoption of decisions by the Council on a proposal from the Commission. The votes of the representatives of the Member States within the Committee shall be weighted in the manner set out in that Article. The Chairman shall not vote.

The Commission shall adopt the measures in question, if they are in accordance with the opinion of the Committee. If the measures proposed are not in accordance with the Committee's opinion, or in the absence of an opinion, the Commission shall forthwith submit to the Council a proposal regarding the measures to be taken. The Council shall act by a qualified majority.

If the Council has not acted within 15 days of the date on which the proposal was submitted to it, the measures proposed shall be adopted by the Commission unless the Council has decided against them by a simple majority.

2.   Any measure adopted under this procedure shall be valid for no longer than tree months. That period may be prolonged under the dame procedure.

3.   Member States shall take all necessary measures to implement the decisions adopted under this procedures within less than 10 days.

4.   The competent authorities of the Member States responsible for carrying out measures adopted under this procedures shall, within one month, give the parties concerned an opportunity to submit their views and shall inform the Commission accordingly.

Article 12 [Confidentiality]

The Member States and the Commission shall take the steps necessary to ensure that their officials and agents are required not to disclose information obtained for the purposes of this Directive which, by its nature, is covered by professional secrecy, except for information relating to the safety properties of a given product which must be made public if circumstances so require, in order to protect the health and safety of persons.

Title VI
Miscellaneous and Final Provisions

Article 13 [Unaffected Provisions]

This Directive shall be without prejudice to Directive 85/374.

Article 14 [Procedural Guarantees]

1.   Any decision adopted under this Directive and involving restrictions on the placing of a product on the market, or requiring its withdrawal from the market, must state the appropriate reasons on which it is based. It shall be notified as soon as possible to the party concerned and shall indicate the remedies available under the provisions in force in the Member State in question and the time limits applying to such remedies.

The parties concerned shall, whenever feasible, be given an opportunity to submit their views before the adoption of the measure. If this has not been done in advance because of the urgency of the measures to be taken, such opportunity shall be given in due course after the measure has been implemented.

Measures requiring the withdrawal of a product from the market shall take into consideration the need to encourage distributors, users and consumers to contribute to the implementation of such measures.

2. Member States shall ensure that any measure taken by the competent authorities involving restrictions on the placing of a product on the market or requiring its withdrawal from the market can be challenged before the competent courts.
3. Any decision taken by virtue of this Directive and involving restrictions on the placing of a product on the market or requiring its withdrawal from the market shall be entirely without prejudice to assessment of the liability of the party concerned, in the light of the national criminal law applying in the case in question.

Article 15 [Reports to Parliament]
Every two years following the date of adoption, the Commission shall submit a report on the implementation of this Directive to the European Parliament and the Council.

Article 16 [Amendments of the Directive]
Four years from the date referred to in Article 17 (1), on the basis of a Commission report on the experience acquired, together with appropriate proposals, the Council shall decide whether to adjust this Directive, in particular with a view to extending its scope as laid down in Article 1 (1) and Article 2 (a), and whether the provisions of Title V should be amended.

Article 17 [Implementation into National Law]
1. Member States shall adopt the laws, regulations and administrative provisions necessary to comply with this Directive by 29 June 1994 at the latest. They shall forthwith inform the Commission thereof. The provisions adopted shall apply with effect from 29 June 1994.
2. When these measures are adopted by the Member States, they shall contain a reference to this Directive or be accompanied by such a reference on the occasion of their official publication. The methods of making such a reference shall be laid down by the Member States.
3. Member States shall communicate to the Commission the text of the provisions of national law which they adopt in the area covered by this Directive.

Article 18 [Repeals]
Decision 89/45 is hereby repealed on the date referred to in Article 17 (1).

Article 19 [Addressees]
This Directive is addressed to the Member States.

Done at Luxembourg, 29 June 1992.
For the Council, The President, Carlos BORREGO

ANNEX: DETAILED PROCEDURES FOR THE APPLICATION OF THE COMMUNITY SYSTEM FOR THE RAPID EXCHANGE OF INFORMATION PROVIDED FOR IN ARTICLE 8 [omitted]

Council Directive 85/374 of 25 July 1985 on the Approximation of the Laws, Regulations and Administrative Provisions of the Member States Concerning Liability for Defective Products[1]

THE COUNCIL OF THE EUROPEAN COMMUNITIES,

HAVING REGARD to the Treaty establishing the European Economic Community, and in particular Article 100 thereof, [...]

(1) WHEREAS approximation of the laws of the Member States concerning the liability of the producer for damage caused by the defectiveness of his products is necessary because the existing divergences may distort competition and affect the movement of goods within the common market and entail a differing degree of protection of the consumer against damage caused by a defective product to his health or property;

(2) WHEREAS liability without fault on the part of the producer is the sole means of adequately solving the problem, peculiar to our age of increasing technicality, of a fair apportionment of the risks inherent in modern technological production;

(3) WHEREAS liability without fault should apply only to movables which have been industrially produced; whereas, as a result, it is appropriate to exclude liability for agricultural products and game, except where they have undergone a processing of an industrial nature which could cause a defect in these products; whereas the liability provided for in this Directive should also apply to movables which are used in the construction of immovables or are installed in immovables;

(4) WHEREAS protection of the consumer requires that all producers involved in the production process should be made liable, in so far as their finished product, component part or any raw material supplied by them was defective; whereas, for the same reason, liability should extend to importers of products into the Community and to persons who present themselves as producers by affixing their name, trade mark or other distinguishing feature or who supply a product the producer of which cannot be identified;

(5) WHEREAS, in situations where several persons are liable for the same damage, the protection of the consumer requires that the injured person should be able to claim full compensation for the damage from any one of them;

(6) WHEREAS, to protect the physical well-being and property of the consumer, the defectiveness of the product should be determined by reference not to its fitness for use but to the lack of the safety which the public at large is entitled to expect; whereas the safety is assessed by excluding any misuse of the product not reasonable under the circumstances;

(7) WHEREAS a fair apportionment of risk between the injured person and the producer implies that the producer should be able to free himself from liability if he furnishes proof as to the existence of certain exonerating circumstances;

(8) WHEREAS the protection of the consumer requires that the liability of the producer remains unaffected by acts or omissions of other persons having contributed to cause the damage; whereas, however, the contributory negligence of the injured person may be taken into account to reduce or disallow such liability;

(9) WHEREAS the protection of the consumer requires compensation for death and personal injury as well as compensation for damage to property; whereas the latter should nevertheless be limited to goods for private use or consumption and be subject to a deduction of a lower threshold of a fixed amount in order to avoid litigation in an

---

1   OJ 1985 L 210, p. 29.

excessive number of cases; whereas this Directive should not prejudice compensation for pain and suffering and other non-material damages payable, where appropriate, under the law applicable to the case;

(10) WHEREAS a uniform period of limitation for the bringing of action for compensation is in the interests both of the injured person and of the producer;

(11) WHEREAS products age in the course of time, higher safety standards are developed and the state of science and technology progresses; whereas, therefore, it would not be reasonable to make the producer liable for an unlimited period for the defectiveness of his product; whereas, therefore, liability should expire after a reasonable length of time, without prejudice to claims pending at law;

(12) WHEREAS, to achieve effective protection of consumers, no contractual derogation should be permitted as regards the liability of the producer in relation to the injured person;

(13) WHEREAS under the legal systems of the Member States an injured party may have a claim for damages based on grounds of contractual liability or on grounds of non-contractual liability other than that provided for in this Directive; in so far as these provisions also serve to attain the objective of effective protection of consumers, they should remain unaffected by this Directive; whereas, in so far as effective protection of consumers in the sector of pharmaceutical products is already also attained in a Member State under a special liability system, claims based on this system should similarly remain possible;

(14) WHEREAS, to the extent that liability for nuclear injury or damage is already covered in all Member States by adequate special rules, it has been possible to exclude damage of this type from the scope of this Directive;

(15) WHEREAS, since the exclusion of primary agricultural products and game from the scope of this Directive may be felt, in certain Member States, in view of what is expected for the protection of consumers, to restrict unduly such protection, it should be possible for a Member State to extend liability to such products;

(16) WHEREAS, for similar reasons, the possibility offered to a producer to free himself from liability if he proves that the state of scientific and technical knowledge at the time when he put the product into circulation was not such as to enable the existence of a defect to be discovered may be felt in certain Member States to restrict unduly the protection of the consumer; whereas it should therefore be possible for a Member State to maintain in its legislation or to provide by new legislation that this exonerating circumstance is not admitted; whereas, in the case of new legislation, making use of this derogation should, however, be subject to a Community stand-still procedure, in order to raise, if possible, the level of protection in a uniform manner throughout the Community;

(17) WHEREAS, taking into account the legal traditions in most of the Member States, it is inappropriate to set any financial ceiling on the producer's liability without fault; whereas, in so far as there are, however, differing traditions, it seems possible to admit that a Member State may derogate from the principle of unlimited liability by providing a limit for the total liability of the producer for damage resulting from a death or personal injury and caused by identical items with the same defect, provided that this limit is established at a level sufficiently high to guarantee adequate protection of the consumer and the correct functioning of the common market;

(18) WHEREAS the harmonization resulting from this cannot be total at the present stage, but opens the way towards greater harmonization; whereas it is therefore necessary that the Council receive at regular intervals, reports from the Commission on the application of this Directive, accompanied, as the case may be, by appropriate proposals;

(19) WHEREAS it is particularly important in this respect that a re-examination be carried out of those parts of the Directive relating to the derogations open to the Member States, at the expiry of a period of sufficient length to gather practical experience on the effects of these derogations on the protection of consumers and on the functioning of the common market,

HAS ADOPTED THIS DIRECTIVE:

Article 1 [General Priciple]
The producer shall be liable for damage caused by a defect in his product.

Article 2 [Definitions of Product]
For the purpose of this Directive "product" means all movables, with the exception of primary agricultural products and game, even though incorporated into another movable or into an immovable. "Primary agricultural products" means the products of the soil, of stock-farming and of fisheries, excluding products which have undergone initial processing. "Product" includes electricity.

Article 3 [Definiton of Producer]
1. "Producer" means the manufacturer of a finished product, the producer of any raw material or the manufacturer of a component part and any person who, by putting his name, trade mark or other distinguishing feature on the product presents himself as its producer.
2. Without prejudice to the liability of the producer, any person who imports into the Community a product for sale, hire, leasing or any form of distribution in the course of his business shall be deemed to be a producer within the meaning of this Directive and shall be responsible as a producer.
3. Where the producer of the product cannot be identified, each supplier of the product shall be treated as its producer unless he informs the injured person, within a reasonable time, of the identity of the producer or of the person who supplied him with the product. The same shall apply, in the case of an imported product, if this product does not indicate the identity of the importer referred to in paragraph 2, even if the name of the producer is indicated.

Article 4 [Burden on Injured Person]
The injured person shall be required to prove the damage, the defect and the causal relationship between defect and damage.

Article 5 [Joint and Several Liability]
Where, as a result of the provisions of this Directive, two or more persons are liable for the same damage, they shall be liable jointly and severally, without prejudice to the provisions of national law concerning the rights of contribution or recourse.

Article 6 [Defective Products]
1. A product is defective when it does not provide the safety which a person is entitled to expect, taking all circumstances into account, including:
(a) the presentation of the product;
(b) the use to which it could reasonably be expected that the product would be put;
(c) the time when the product was put into circulation.
2. A product shall not be considered defective for the sole reason that a better product is subsequently put into circulation.

Article 7 [Exceptions to Liability]

The producer shall not be liable as a result of this Directive if he proves:
(a) that he did not put the product into circulation; or
(b) that, having regard to the circumstances, it is probable that the defect which caused the damage did not exist at the time when the product was put into circulation by him or that this defect came into being afterwards; or
(c) that the product was neither manufactured by him for sale or any form of distribution for economic purpose nor manufactured or distributed by him in the course of his business; or
(d) that the defect is due to compliance of the product with mandatory regulations issued by the public authorities; or
(e) that the state of scientific and technical knowledge at the time when he put the product into circulation was not such as to enable the existence of the defect to be discovered; or
(f) in the case of a manufacturer of a component, that the defect is attributable to the design of the product in which the component has been fitted or to the instructions given by the manufacturer of the product.

Article 8 [Contributory Negligence]

1. Without prejudice to the provisions of national law concerning the right of contribution or recourse, the liability of the producer shall not be reduced when the damage is caused both by a defect in product and by the act or omission of a third party.
2. The liability of the producer may be reduced or disallowed when, having regard to all the circumstances, the damage is caused both by a defect in the product and by the fault of the injured person or any person for whom the injured person is responsible.

Article 9 [Definition of Damage]

For the purpose of Article 1, "damage" means:
(a) damage caused by death or by personal injuries;
(b) damage to, or destruction of, any item of property other than the defective product itself, with a lower threshold of 500 ECU, provided that the item of property:
    (i) is of a type ordinarily intended for private use or consumption, and
    (ii) was used by the injured person mainly for his own private use or consumption.
This Article shall be without prejudice to national provisions relating to non-material damage.

Article 10 [Limitation Period]

1. Member States shall provide in their legislation that a limitation period of three years shall apply to proceedings for the recovery of damages as provided for in this Directive. The limitation period shall begin to run from the day on which the plaintiff became aware, or should reasonably have become aware, of the damage, the defect and the identity of the producer.
2. The laws of Member States regulating suspension or interruption of the limitation period shall not be affected by this Directive.

Article 11 [Extinction of Rights]

Member States shall provide in their legislation that the rights conferred upon the injured person pursuant to this Directive shall be extinguished upon the expiry of a period of 10 years from the date on which the producer put into circulation the actual product which caused the damage, unless the injured person has in the meantime instituted proceedings against the producer.

Article 12 [Contractual Limitation of Liability]

The liability of the producer arising from this Directive may not, in relation to the injured person, be limited or excluded by a provision limiting his liability or exempting him from liability.

Article 13 [Unaffected Provisions]

This Directive shall not affect any rights which an injured person may have according to the rules of the law of contractual or non-contractual liability or a special liability system existing at the moment when this Directive is notified.

Article 14 [Nuclear Accidents not Covered]

This Directive shall not apply to injury or damage arising from nuclear accidents and covered by international conventions ratified by the Member States.

Article 15 [Stricter Member State Legislation]

1.   Each Member State may:
(a) by way of derogation from Article 2, provide in its legislation that within the meaning of Article 1 of this Directive "product" also means primary agricultural products and game;
(b) by way of derogation from Article 7 (e), maintain or, subject to the procedure set out in paragraph 2 of this Article, provide in this legislation that the producer shall be liable even if he proves that the state of scientific and technical knowledge at the time when he put the product into circulation was not such as to enable the existence of a defect to be discovered.

2.   A Member State wishing to introduce the measure specified in paragraph 1 (b) shall communicate the text of the proposed measure to the Commission. The Commission shall inform the other Member States thereof.

The Member State concerned shall hold the proposed measure in abeyance for nine months after the Commission is informed and provided that in the meantime the Commission has not submitted to the Council a proposal amending this Directive on the relevant matter. However, if within three months of receiving the said information, the Commission does not advise the Member State concerned that it intends submitting such a proposal to the Council, the Member State may take the proposed measure immediately.

If the Commission does submit to the Council such a proposal amending this Directive within the aforementioned nine months, the Member State concerned shall hold the proposed measure in abeyance for a further period of 18 months from the date on which the proposal is submitted.

3.   Ten years after the date of notification of this Directive, the Commission shall submit to the Council a report on the effect that rulings by the courts as to the application of Article 7 (e) and of paragraph 1 (b) of this Article have on consumer protection and the functioning of the common market. In the light of this report the Council, acting on a proposal from the Commission and pursuant to the terms of Article 100 of the Treaty, shall decide whether to repeal Article 7 (e).

Article 16 [Limitation of Liability]

1.   Any Member State may provide that a producer's total liability for damage resulting from a death or personal injury and caused by identical items with the same defect shall be limited to an amount which may not be less than 70 million ECU.

2.   Ten years after the date of notification of this Directive, the Commission shall submit to the Council a report on the effect on consumer protection and the functioning of the common market of the implementation of the financial limit on liability by those

Member States which have used the option provided for in paragraph 1. In the light of this report the Council, acting on a proposal from the Commission and pursuant to the terms of Article 100 of the Treaty, shall decide whether to repeal paragraph 1.

Article 17 [No Retroactivity of the Directive]
This Directive shall not apply to products put into circulation before the date on which the provisions referred to in Article 19 enter into force.

Article 18 [Definition of ECU]
1.   For the purposes of this Directive, the ECU shall be that defined by Regulation 3180/78[1] (1), as amended [...]. The equivalent in national currency shall initially be calculated at the rate obtaining on the date of adoption of this Directive.
2.   Every five years the Council, acting on a proposal from the Commission, shall examine and, if need be, revise the amounts in this Directive, in the light of economic and monetary trends in the Community.

Article 19 [Implementation into National Law]
1.   Member States shall bring into force, not later than three years from the date of notification of this Directive, the laws, regulations and administrative provisions necessary to comply with this Directive.[2]
They shall forthwith inform the Commission thereof.
2.   The procedure set out in Article 15 (2) shall apply from the date of notification of this Directive.

Article 20 [Information of the Commission]
Member States shall communicate to the Commission the texts of the main provisions of national law which they subsequently adopt in the field governed by this Directive.

Article 21 [Monitoring]
Every five years the Commission shall present a report to the Council on the application of this Directive and, if necessary, shall submit appropriate proposals to it.

Article 22 [Addressees]
This Directive is addressed to the Member States.

Done at Brussels, 25 July 1985.
For the Council, The President, J. POOS

Council Directive 93/13 of 5 April 1993 on Unfair Terms in Consumer Contracts[3]

THE COUNCIL OF THE EUROPEAN COMMUNITIES,

HAVING REGARD to the Treaty establishing the European Economic Community, and in particular Article 100 A thereof, [...]

---

1   OJ 1978 L 379, p. 1.
2   This Directive was notified to the Member States on 30 July 1985.
3   OJ 1993 L 95, p. 29.

(1) WHEREAS it is necessary to adopt measures with the aim of progressively establishing the internal market before 31 December 1992; whereas the internal market comprises an area without internal frontiers in which goods, persons, services and capital move freely;

(2) WHEREAS the laws of Member States relating to the terms of contract between the seller of goods or supplier of services, on the one hand, and the consumer of them, on the other hand, show many disparities, with the result that the national markets for the sale of goods and services to consumers differ from each other and that distortions of competition may arise amongst the sellers and suppliers, notably when they sell and supply in other Member States;

(3) WHEREAS, in particular, the laws of Member States relating to unfair terms in consumer contracts show marked divergences;

(4) WHEREAS it is the responsibility of the Member States to ensure that contracts concluded with consumers do not contain unfair terms;

(5) WHEREAS, generally speaking, consumers do not know the rules of law which, in Member States other than their own, govern contracts for the sale of goods or services; whereas this lack of awareness may deter them from direct transactions for the purchase of goods or services in another Member State;

(6) WHEREAS, in order to facilitate the establishment of the internal market and to safeguard the citizen in his role as consumer when acquiring goods and services under contracts which are governed by the laws of Member States other than his own, it is essential to remove unfair terms from those contracts;

(7) WHEREAS sellers of goods and suppliers of services will thereby be helped in their task of selling goods and supplying services, both at home and throughout the internal market; whereas competition will thus be stimulated, so contributing to increased choice for Community citizens as consumers;

(8) WHEREAS the two Community programmes for a consumer protection and information policy[1] underlined the importance of safeguarding consumers in the matter of unfair terms of contract; whereas this protection ought to be provided by laws and regulations which are either harmonized at Community level or adopted directly at that level;

(9) WHEREAS in accordance with the principle laid down under the heading "Protection of the economic interests of the consumers", as stated in those programmes: "acquirers of goods and services should be protected against the abuse of power by the seller or supplier, in particular against one-sided standard contracts and the unfair exclusion of essential rights in contracts";

(10) WHEREAS more effective protection of the consumer can be achieved by adopting uniform rules of law in the matter of unfair terms; whereas those rules should apply to all contracts concluded between sellers or suppliers and consumers; whereas as a result inter alia contracts relating to employment, contracts relating to succession rights, contracts relating to rights under family law and contracts relating to the incorporation and organization of companies or partnership agreements must be excluded from this Directive;

(11) WHEREAS the consumer must receive equal protection under contracts concluded by word of mouth and written contracts regardless, in the latter case, of whether the terms of the contract are contained in one or more documents;

(12) WHEREAS, however, as they now stand, national laws allow only partial harmonization to be envisaged; whereas, in particular, only contractual terms which have not been individually negotiated are covered by this Directive; whereas Member States

---

1   OJ 1975 C 92, p. 1 and OJ 1981 C 133, p. 1.

should have the option, with due regard for the Treaty, to afford consumers a higher level of protection through national provisions that are more stringent than those of this Directive;

(13) WHEREAS the statutory or regulatory provisions of the Member States which directly or indirectly determine the terms of consumer contracts are presumed not to contain unfair terms; whereas, therefore, it does not appear to be necessary to subject the terms which reflect mandatory statutory or regulatory provisions and the principles or provisions of international conventions to which the Member States or the Community are party; whereas in that respect the wording "mandatory statutory or regulatory provisions" in Article 1 (2) also covers rules which, according to the law, shall apply between the contracting parties provided that no other arrangements have been established;

(14) WHEREAS Member States must however ensure that unfair terms are not included, particularly because this Directive also applies to trades, business or professions of a public nature;

(15) WHEREAS it is necessary to fix in a general way the criteria for assessing the unfair character of contract terms;

(16) WHEREAS the assessment, according to the general criteria chosen, of the unfair character of terms, in particular in sale or supply activities of a public nature providing collective services which take account of solidarity among users, must be supplemented by a means of making an overall evaluation of the different interests involved; whereas this constitutes the requirement of good faith; whereas, in making an assessment of good faith, particular regard shall be had to the strength of the bargaining positions of the parties, whether the consumer had an inducement to agree to the term and whether the goods or services were sold or supplied to the special order of the consumer; whereas the requirement of good faith may be satisfied by the seller or supplier where he deals fairly and equitably with the other party whose legitimate interests he has to take into account;

(17) WHEREAS, for the purposes of this Directive, the annexed list of terms can be of indicative value only and, because of the cause of the minimal character of the Directive, the scope of these terms may be the subject of amplification or more restrictive editing by the Member States in their national laws;

(18) WHEREAS the nature of goods or services should have an influence on assessing the unfairness of contractual terms;

(19) WHEREAS, for the purposes of this Directive, assessment of unfair character shall not be made of terms which describe the main subject matter of the contract nor the quality/price ratio of the goods or services supplied; whereas the main subject matter of the contract and the price/quality ratio may nevertheless be taken into account in assessing the fairness of other terms; whereas it follows, inter alia, that in insurance contracts, the terms which clearly define or circumscribe the insured risk and the insurer's liability shall not be subject to such assessment since these restrictions are taken into account in calculating the premium paid by the consumer;

(20) WHEREAS contracts should be drafted in plain, intelligible language, the consumer should actually be given an opportunity to examine all the terms and, if in doubt, the interpretation most favourable to the consumer should prevail;

(21) WHEREAS Member States should ensure that unfair terms are not used in contracts concluded with consumers by a seller or supplier and that if, nevertheless, such terms are so used, they will not bind the consumer, and the contract will continue to bind the parties upon those terms if it is capable of continuing in existence without the unfair provisions;

(22) WHEREAS there is a risk that, in certain cases, the consumer may be deprived of protection under this Directive by designating the law of a non-Member country as

the law applicable to the contract; whereas provisions should therefore be included in this Directive designed to avert this risk;

(23) WHEREAS persons or organizations, if regarded under the law of a Member State as having a legitimate interest in the matter, must have facilities for initiating procee-dings concerning terms of contract drawn up for general use in contracts concluded with consumers, and in particular unfair terms, either before a court or before an admi-nistrative authority competent to decide upon complaints or to initiate appropriate legal proceedings; whereas this possibility does not, however, entail prior verification of the general conditions obtaining in individual economic sectors;

(24) WHEREAS the courts or administrative authorities of the Member States must have at their disposal adequate and effective means of preventing the continued appli-cation of unfair terms in consumer contracts,

HAS ADOPTED THIS DIRECTIVE:

Article 1 [Objective]

1. The purpose of this Directive is to approximate the laws, regulations and admini-strative provisions of the Member States relating to unfair terms in contracts concluded between a seller or supplier and a consumer.

2. The contractual terms which reflect mandatory statutory or regulatory provisions and the provisions or principles of international conventions to which the Member States or the Community are party, particularly in the transport area, shall not be sub-ject to the provisions of this Directive.

Article 2 [Definitions]

For the purposes of this Directive:

(a) "unfair terms" means the contractual terms defined in Article 3;
(b) "consumer" means any natural person who, in contracts covered by this Directive, is acting for purposes which are outside his trade, business or profession;
(c) "seller or supplier" means any natural or legal person who, in contracts covered by this Directive, is acting for purposes relating to his trade, business or profession, whether publicly owned or privately owned.

Article 3 [Unfair Terms]

1. A contractual term which has not been individually negotiated shall be regarded as unfair if, contrary to the requirement of good faith, it causes a significant imbalance in the parties' rights and obligations arising under the contract, to the detriment of the con-sumer.

2. A term shall always be regarded as not individually negotiated where it has been drafted in advance and the consumer has therefore not been able to influence the sub-stance of the term, particularly in the context of a pre-formulated standard contract.

The fact that certain aspects of a term or one specific term have been individually negotiated shall not exclude the application of this Article to the rest of a contract if an overall assessment of the contract indicates that it is nevertheless a pre-formulated standard contract.

Where any seller or supplier claims that a standard term has been individually ne-gotiated, the burden of proof in this respect shall be incumbent on him.

3. The Annex shall contain an indicative and non-exhaustive list of the terms which may be regarded as unfair.

Article 4 [Assessment of Unfairness]

1. Without prejudice to Article 7, the unfairness of a contractual term shall be assessed, taking into account the nature of the goods or services for which the contract was concluded and by referring, at the time of conclusion of the contract, to all the circumstances attending the conclusion of the contract and to all the other terms of the contract or of another contract on which it is dependent.

2. Assessment of the unfair nature of the terms shall relate neither to the definition of the main subject matter of the contract nor to the adequacy of the price and remuneration, on the one hand, as against the services or goods supplies in exchange, on the other, in so far as these terms are in plain intelligible language.

Article 5 [Ambiguous Written Clauses]

In the case of contracts where all or certain terms offered to the consumer are in writing, these terms must always be drafted in plain, intelligible language. Where there is doubt about the meaning of a term, the interpretation most favourable to the consumer shall prevail. This rule on interpretation shall not apply in the context of the procedures laid down in Article 7 (2).

Article 6 [Survival of Contracts Without the Unfair Terms]

1. Member States shall lay down that unfair terms used in a contract concluded with a consumer by a seller or supplier shall, as provided for under their national law, not be binding on the consumer and that the contract shall continue to bind the parties upon those terms if it is capable of continuing in existence without the unfair terms.

2. Member States shall take the necessary measures to ensure that the consumer does not lose the protection granted by this Directive by virtue of the choice of the law of a non-Member country as the law applicable to the contract if the latter has a close connection with the territory of the Member States.

Article 7 [Preventing Continued Usage of Unfair Terms]

1. Member States shall ensure that, in the interests of consumers and of competitors, adequate and effective means exist to prevent the continued use of unfair terms in contracts concluded with consumers by sellers or suppliers.

2. The means referred to in paragraph 1 shall include provisions whereby persons or organizations, having a legitimate interest under national law in protecting consumers, may take action according to the national law concerned before the courts or before competent administrative bodies for a decision as to whether contractual terms drawn up for general use are unfair, so that they can apply appropriate and effective means to prevent the continued use of such terms.

3. With due regard for national laws, the legal remedies referred to in paragraph 2 may be directed separately or jointly against a number of sellers or suppliers from the same economic sector or their associations which use or recommend the use of the same general contractual terms or similar terms.

Article 8 [Stricter National Laws]

Member States may adopt or retain the most stringent provisions compatible with the Treaty in the area covered by this Directive, to ensure a maximum degree of protection for the consumer.

Article 9 [Reports to Parliament and Council]

The Commission shall present a report to the European Parliament and to the Council concerning the application of this Directive five years at the latest after the date in Article 10 (1).

Article 10 [Implementation into National Law]

1.   Member States shall bring into force the laws, regulations and administrative provisions necessary to comply with this Directive no later than 31 December 1994. They shall forthwith inform the Commission thereof.

These provisions shall be applicable to all contracts concluded after 31 December 1994.

2.   When Member States adopt these measures, they shall contain a reference to this Directive or shall be accompanied by such reference on the occasion of their official publication. The methods of making such a reference shall be laid down by the Member States.

3.   Member States shall communicate the main provisions of national law which they adopt in the field covered by this Directive to the Commission.

Article 11 [Addressees]

This Directive is addressed to the Member States.

Done at Luxembourg, 5 April 1993.
For the Council, The President, N. HELVEG PETERSEN

ANNEX: TERMS REFERRED TO IN ARTICLE 3 (3)

1.   Terms which have the object or effect of:
(a)   excluding or limiting the legal liability of a seller or supplier in the event of the death of a consumer or personal injury to the latter resulting from an act or omission of that seller or supplier;
(b)   inappropriately excluding or limiting the legal rights of the consumer vis-à-vis the seller or supplier or another party in the event of total or partial non-performance or inadequate performance by the seller or supplier of any of the contractual obligations, including the option of offsetting a debt owed to the seller or supplier against any claim which the consumer may have against him;
(c)   making an agreement binding on the consumer whereas provision of services by the seller or supplier is subject to a condition whose realization depends on his own will alone;
(d)   permitting the seller or supplier to retain sums paid by the consumer where the latter decides not to conclude or perform the contract, without providing for the consumer to receive compensation of an equivalent amount from the seller or supplier where the latter is the party cancelling the contract;
(e)   requiring any consumer who fails to fulfil his obligation to pay a disproportionately high sum in compensation;
(f)   authorizing the seller or supplier to dissolve the contract on a discretionary basis where the same facility is not granted to the consumer, or permitting the seller or supplier to retain the sums paid for services not yet supplied by him where it is the seller or supplier himself who dissolves the contract;
(g)   enabling the seller or supplier to terminate a contract of indeterminate duration without reasonable notice except where there are serious grounds for doing so;
(h)   automatically extending a contract of fixed duration where the consumer does not indicate otherwise, when the deadline fixed for the consumer to express this desire not to extend the contract is unreasonably early;
(i)   irrevocably binding the consumer to terms with which he had no real opportunity of becoming acquainted before the conclusion of the contract;
(j)   enabling the seller or supplier to alter the terms of the contract unilaterally without a valid reason which is specified in the contract;
(k)   enabling the seller or supplier to alter unilaterally without a valid reason any characteristics of the product or service to be provided;
(l)   providing for the price of goods to be determined at the time of delivery or allowing a seller of goods or supplier of services to increase their price without in both cases giving the consumer the corresponding right to cancel the contract if the final price is too high in relation to the price agreed when the contract was concluded;

(m) giving the seller or supplier the right to determine whether the goods or services supplied are in conformity with the contract, or giving him the exclusive right to interpret any term of the contract;
(n) limiting the seller's or supplier's obligation to respect commitments undertaken by his agents or making his commitments subject to compliance with a particular formality;
(o) obliging the consumer to fulfil all his obligations where the seller or supplier does not perform his;
(p) giving the seller or supplier the possibility of transferring his rights and obligations under the contract, where this may serve to reduce the guarantees for the consumer, without the latter's agreement;
(q) excluding or hindering the consumer's right to take legal action or exercise any other legal remedy, particularly by requiring the consumer to take disputes exclusively to arbitration not covered by legal provisions, unduly restricting the evidence available to him or imposing on him a burden of proof which, according to the applicable law, should lie with another party to the contract.
2. Scope of subparagraphs (g), (j) and (l)
(a) Subparagraph (g) is without hindrance to terms by which a supplier of financial services reserves the right to terminate unilaterally a contract of indeterminate duration without notice where there is a valid reason, provided that the supplier is required to inform the other contracting party or parties thereof immediately.
(b) Subparagraph (j) is without hindrance to terms under which a supplier of financial services reserves the right to alter the rate of interest payable by the consumer or due to the latter, or the amount of other charges for financial services without notice where there is a valid reason, provided that the supplier is required to inform the other contracting party or parties thereof at the earliest opportunity and that the latter are free to dissolve the contract immediately.
    Subparagraph (j) is also without hindrance to terms under which a seller or supplier reserves the right to alter unilaterally the conditions of a contract of indeterminate duration, provided that he is required to inform the consumer with reasonable notice and that the consumer is free to dissolve the contract.
(c) Subparagraphs (g), (j) and (l) do not apply to:
— transactions in transferable securities, financial instruments and other products or services where the price is linked to fluctuations in a stock exchange quotation or index or a financial market rate that the seller or supplier does not control;
— contracts for the purchase or sale of foreign currency, traveller's cheques or international money orders denominated in foreign currency;
(d) Subparagraph (l) is without hindrance to price-indexation clauses, where lawful, provided that the method by which prices vary is explicitly described.

Directive 98/6 of the European Parliament and of the Council of 16 February 1998 on Consumer Protection in the Indication of the Prices of Products Offered to Consumers[1]

THE EUROPEAN PARLIAMENT AND THE COUNCIL OF THE EUROPEAN UNION,

HAVING REGARD to the Treaty establishing the European Community, and in particular Article 129a(2) thereof, [...]
(1) WHEREAS transparent operation of the market and correct information is of benefit to consumer protection and healthy competition between enterprises and products;
(2) WHEREAS consumers must be guaranteed a high level of protection; whereas the Community should contribute thereto by specific action which supports and supple-

---

1   OJ 1998 L 80, p. 27.

ments the policy pursued by the Member States regarding precise, transparent and unambiguous information for consumers on the prices of products offered to them;

(3) WHEREAS the Council Resolution of 14 April 1975 on a preliminary programme of the European Economic Community for a consumer protection and information policy[1] and the Council Resolution of 19 May 1981 on a second programme of the European Economic Community for a consumer protection and information policy[2] provide for the establishment of common principles for indicating prices;

(4) WHEREAS these principles have been established by Directive 79/581 concerning the indication of prices of certain foodstuffs[3] and Directive 88/314 concerning the indication of prices of non-food products[4];

(5) WHEREAS the link between indication of the unit price of products and their pre-packaging in pre-established quantities or capacities corresponding to the values of the ranges adopted at Community level has proved overly complex to apply; whereas it is thus necessary to abandon this link in favour of a new simplified mechanism and in the interest of the consumer, without prejudice to the rules governing packaging standardisation;

(6) WHEREAS the obligation to indicate the selling price and the unit price contributes substantially to improving consumer information, as this is the easiest way to enable consumers to evaluate and compare the price of products in an optimum manner and hence to make informed choices on the basis of simple comparisons;

(7) WHEREAS, therefore, there should be a general obligation to indicate both the selling price and the unit price for all products except for products sold in bulk, where the selling price cannot be determined until the consumer indicates how much of the product is required;

(8) WHEREAS it is necessary to take into account the fact that certain products are customarily sold in quantities different from one kilogramme, one litre, one metre, one square metre or one cubic metre; whereas it is thus appropriate to allow Member States to authorise that the unit price refer to a different single unit of quantity, taking into account the nature of the product and the quantities in which it is customarily sold in the Member State concerned;

(9) WHEREAS the obligation to indicate the unit price may entail an excessive burden for certain small retail businesses under certain circumstances; whereas Member States should therefore be allowed to refrain from applying this obligation during an appropriate transitional period;

(10) WHEREAS Member States should also remain free to waive the obligation to indicate the unit price in the case of products for which such price indication would not be useful or would be liable to cause confusion for instance when indication of the quantity is not relevant for price comparison purposes, or when different products are marketed in the same packaging;

(11) WHEREAS in the case of non-food products, Member States, with a view to facilitating application of the mechanism implemented, are free to draw up a list of products or categories of products for which the obligation to indicate the unit price remains applicable;

---

1   OJ 1975 C 92, p. 1.

2   OJ 1981 C 133, p. 1.

3   OJ 1979 L 158, p. 19, [as amended].

4   OJ 1988 L 142, p. 19, [as amended].

(12) WHEREAS Community-level rules can ensure homogenous and transparent information that will benefit all consumers in the context of the internal market; whereas the new, simplified approach is both necessary and sufficient to achieve this objective;
(13) WHEREAS Member States must make sure that the system is effective; whereas the transparency of the system should also be maintained when the euro is introduced; whereas, to that end, the maximum number of prices to be indicated should be limited;
(14) WHEREAS particular attention should be paid to small retail businesses; whereas, to this end, the Commission should, in its report on the application of this Directive to be presented no later than three years after the date referred to in Article 11(1), take particular account of the experience gleaned in the application of the Directive by small retail businesses, inter alia, regarding technological developments and the introduction of the single currency; whereas this report, having regard to the transitional period referred to in Article 6, should be accompanied by a proposal,

HAVE ADOPTED THIS DIRECTIVE:

Article 1 [Objective]
The purpose of this Directive is to stipulate indication of the selling price and the price per unit of measurement of products offered by traders to consumers in order to improve consumer information and to facilitate comparison of prices.

Article 2 [Definitions]
For the purposes of this Directive:
(a) selling price shall mean the final price for a unit of the product, or a given quantity of the product, including VAT and all other taxes;
(b) unit price shall mean the final price, including VAT and all other taxes, for one kilogramme, one litre, one metre, one square metre or one cubic metre of the product or a different single unit of quantity which is widely and customarily used in the Member State concerned in the marketing of specific products;
(c) products sold in bulk shall mean products which are not pre-packaged and are measured in the presence of the consumer;
(d) trader shall mean any natural or legal person who sells or offers for sale products which fall within his commercial or professional activity;
(e) consumer shall mean any natural person who buys a product for purposes that do not fall within the sphere of his commercial or professional activity.

Article 3 [Indication of Prices]
1.   The selling price and the unit price shall be indicated for all products referred to in Article 1, the indication of the unit price being subject to the provisions of Article 5. The unit price need not be indicated if it is identical to the sales price.
2.   Member States may decide not to apply paragraph 1 to:
— products supplied in the course of the provision of a service,
— sales by auction and sales of works of art and antiques.
3.   For products sold in bulk, only the unit price must be indicated.
4.   Any advertisement which mentions the selling price of products referred to in Article 1 shall also indicate the unit price subject to Article 5.

Article 4 [Unambiguous Indications]
1.   The selling price and the unit price must be unambiguous, easily identifiable and clearly legible. Member States may provide that the maximum number of prices to be indicated be limited.

2. The unit price shall refer to a quantity declared in accordance with national and Community provisions.

Where national or Community provisions require the indication of the net weight and the net drained weight for certain pre-packed products, it shall be sufficient to indicate the unit price of the net drained weight.

Article 5 [National Derogations]

1. Member States may waive the obligation to indicate the unit price of products for which such indication would not be useful because of the products' nature or purpose or would be liable to create confusion.
2. With a view to implementing paragraph 1, Member States may, in the case of non-food products, establish a list of the products or product categories to which the obligation to indicate the unit price shall remain applicable.

Article 6 [Exceptions for SMEs]

If the obligation to indicate the unit price were to constitute an excessive burden for certain small retail businesses because of the number of products on sale, the sales area, the nature of the place of sale, specific conditions of sale where the product is not directly accessible for the consumer or certain forms of business, such as certain types of itinerant trade, Member States may, for a transitional period following the date referred to in Article 11 (1), provide that the obligation to indicate the unit price of products other than those sold in bulk, which are sold in the said businesses, shall not apply, subject to Article 12.

Article 7 [Information of Affected Persons]

Member States shall provide appropriate measures to inform all persons concerned of the national law transposing this Directive.

Article 8 [Sanctions]

Member States shall lay down penalties for infringements of national provisions adopted in application of this Directive, and shall take all necessary measures to ensure that these are enforced. These penalties must be effective, proportionate and dissuasive.

Article 9 [Transition Period]

1. The transition period of nine years referred to in Article 1 of Directive 95/58 of the European Parliament and of the Council of 29 November 1995 amending Directive 79/581 on consumer protection in the indication of the prices of foodstuffs and Directive 88/314 on consumer protection in the indication of the prices of non-food products[1] shall be extended until the date referred to in Article 11(1) of this Directive.
2. Directives 79/581 and 88/314 shall be repealed with effect from the date referred to in Article 11 (1) of this Directive.

Article 10 [Stricter National Laws]

This Directive shall not prevent Member States from adopting or maintaining provisions which are more favourable as regards consumer information and comparison of prices, without prejudice to their obligations under the Treaty.

---

1   OJ 1995 L 299, p. 11.

Article 11 [Implementation into National Law]

1.   Member States shall bring into force the laws, regulations and administrative provisions necessary to comply with this Directive not later than 18 March 2000. They shall forthwith inform the Commission thereof. The provisions adopted shall be applicable as of that date. When Member States adopt these measures, they shall contain a reference to this Directive or shall be accompanied by such reference at the time of their official publication. The methods of making such reference shall be laid down by Member States.

2.   Member States shall communicate to the Commission the text of the provisions of national law which they adopt in the field governed by this Directive.

3.   Member States shall communicate the provisions governing the penalties provided for in Article 8, and any later amendments thereto.

Article 12 [Monitoring]

The Commission shall, not later than three years after the date referred to in Article 11 (1), submit to the European Parliament and the Council a comprehensive report on the application of this Directive, in particular on the application of Article 6, accompanied by a proposal.

The European Parliament and the Council shall, on this basis, re-examine the provisions of Article 6 and shall act, in accordance with the Treaty, within three years of the presentation by the Commission of the proposal referred to in the first paragraph.

Article 13 [Entry into Force]

This Directive shall enter into force on the day of its publication in the Official Journal of the European Communities.

Article 14 [Addressees]

This Directive is addressed to the Member States.

Done at Brussels, 16 February 1998.
For the European Parliament, The President, J. M. GIL-ROBLES
For the Council, The President, J. CUNNINGHAM

Council Directive 85/577 of 20 December 1985 to Protect the Consumer in Respect of Contracts Negotiated Away From Business Premises[1]

THE COUNCIL OF THE EUROPEAN COMMUNITIES,

HAVING REGARD to the Treaty establishing the European Economic Community, and in particular Article 100 thereof, [...]

(1) WHEREAS it is a common form of commercial practice in the Member States for the conclusion of a contract or a unilateral engagement between a trader and consumer to be made away from the business premises of the trader, and whereas such contracts and engagements are the subject of legislation which differs from one Member State to another;

---

1   OJ 1985 L 372, p. 31.

(2) WHEREAS any disparity between such legislation may directly affect the functio-ning of the common market; whereas it is therefore necessary to approximate laws in this field;
(3) WHEREAS the preliminary programme of the European Economic Community for a consumer protection and information policy[1] provides inter alia, under paragraphs 24 and 25, that appropriate measures be taken to protect consumers against unfair com-mercial practices in respect of doorstep selling; whereas the second programme of the European Economic Community for a consumer protection and information policy[2] con-firmed that the action and priorities defined in the preliminary programme would be pursued;
(4) WHEREAS the special feature of contracts concluded away from the business pre-mises of the trader is that as a rule it is the trader who initiates the contract negotia-tions, for which the consumer is unprepared or which he does not except; whereas the consumer is often unable to compare the quality and price of the offer with other offers; whereas this surprise element generally exists not only in contracts made at the door-step but also in other forms of contract concluded by the trader away from his business premises;
(5) WHEREAS the consumer should be given a right of cancellation over a period of at least seven days in order to enable him to assess the obligations arising under the contract;
(6) WHEREAS appropriate measures should be taken to ensure that the consumer is informed in writing of this period for reflection; Whereas the freedom of Member States to maintain or introduce a total or partial prohibition on the conclusion of contracts away from business premises, inasmuch as they consider this to be in the interest of consu-mers, must not be affected;

HAS ADOPTED THIS DIRECTIVE:

Article 1 [Scope]
1.   This Directive shall apply to contracts under which a trader supplies goods or ser-vices to a consumer and which are concluded:
— during an excursion organized by the trader away from his business premises, or
— during a visit by a trader
    (i)   to the consumer's home or to that of another consumer;
    (ii) to the consumer's place of work;
    where the visit does not take place at the express request of the consumer.
2.   This Directive shall also apply to contracts for the supply of goods or services other than those concerning which the consumer requested the visit of the trader, provided that when he requested the visit the consumer did not know, or could not reasonably have known, that the supply of those other goods or services formed part of the tra-der's commercial or professional activities.
3.   This Directive shall also apply to contracts in respect of which an offer was made by the consumer under conditions similar to those described in paragraph 1 or para-graph 2 although the consumer was not bound by that offer before its acceptance by the trader.

---

1   OJ 1975 C 92, p. 2.

2   OJ 1981 C 133, p. 1.

4.   This Directive shall also apply to offers made contractually by the consumer under conditions similar to those described in paragraph 1 or paragraph 2 where the consumer is bound by his offer.

Article 2 [Definitions]

For the purposes of this Directive:
— "consumer" means a natural person who, in transactions covered by this Directive, is acting for purposes which can be regarded as outside his trade or profession;
— "trader" means a natural or legal person who, for the transaction in question, acts in his commercial or professional capacity, and anyone acting in the name or on behalf of a trader.

Article 3 [Contracts not Covered]

1.   The Member States may decide that this Directive shall apply only to contracts for which the payment to be made by the consumer exceeds a specified amount. This amount may not exceed 60 ECU. The Council, acting on a proposal from the Commission, shall examine and, if necessary, revise this amount for the first time no later than four years after notification of the Directive and thereafter every two years, taking into account economic and monetary developments in the Community.
2.   This Directive shall not apply to:
(a) contracts for the construction, sale and rental of immovable property or contracts concerning other rights relating to immovable property. Contracts for the supply of goods and for their incorporation in immovable property or contracts for repairing immovable property shall fall within the scope of this Directive;
(b) contracts for the supply of foodstuffs or beverages or other goods intended for current consumption in the household and supplied by regular roundsmen;
(c) contracts for the supply of goods or services, provided that all three of the following conditions are met:
  (i)   the contract is concluded on the basis of a trader's catalogue which the consumer has a proper opportunity of reading in the absence of the trader's representative,
  (ii) there is intended to be continuity of contact between the trader's representative and the consumer in relation to that or any subsequent transaction,
  (iii) both the catalogue and the contract clearly inform the consumer of his right to return goods to the supplier within a period of not less than seven days of receipt or otherwise to cancel the contract within that period without obligation of any kind other than to take reasonable care of the goods;
(d) insurance contracts;
(e) contracts for securities.
3.   By way of derogation from Article 1 (2), Member States may refrain from applying this Directive to contracts for the supply of goods or services having a direct connection with the goods or services concerning which the consumer requested the visit of the trader.

Article 4 [Written Notice of the Right of Cancellation]

In the case of transactions within the scope of Article 1, traders shall be required to give consumers written notice of their right of cancellation within the period laid down in Article 5, together with the name and address of a person against whom that right may be exercised. Such notice shall be dated and shall state particulars enabling the contract to be identified. It shall be given to the consumer:
(a) in the case of Article 1 (1), at the time of conclusion of the contract;
(b) in the case of Article 1 (2), not later than the time of conclusion of the contract;

(c) in the case of Article 1 (3) and 1 (4), when the offer is made by the consumer.
Member States shall ensure that their national legislation lays down appropriate consumer protection measures in cases where the information referred to in this Article is not
supplied.

Article 5 [Seven-Day Cancellation Period]
1.   The consumer shall have the right to renounce the effects of his undertaking by
sending notice within a period of not less than seven days from receipt by the consumer of the notice referred to in Article 4, in accordance with the procedure laid down
by national law. It shall be sufficient if the notice is dispatched before the end of such
period.
2.   The giving of the notice shall have the effect of releasing the consumer from any
obligations under the cancelled contract.

Article 6 [Mandatory Rules of the Directive]
The consumer may not waive the rights conferred on him by this Directive.

Article 7 [Effects of Cancellation Governed by National Law]
If the consumer exercises his right of renunciation, the legal effects of such renunciation shall be governed by national laws, particularly regarding the reimbursement of
payments for goods or services provided and the return of goods received.

Article 8 [Stricter National Laws]
This Directive shall not prevent Member States from adopting or maintaining more
favourable provisions to protect consumers in the field which it covers.

Article 9 [Implementation into National Law]
1.   Member States shall take the measures necessary to comply with this Directive
within 24 months of its notification.[1] They shall forthwith inform the Commission thereof.
2.   Member States shall ensure that the texts of the main provisions of national law
which they adopt in the field covered by this Directive are communicated to the Commission.

Article 10 [Addressees]
This Directive is addressed to the Member States.

Done at Brussels, 20 December 1985.
For the Council, The President, R. KRIEPS

Directive 97/7 of the European Parliament and of the Council of 20 May 1997 on the Protection of Consumers in Respect of Distance Contracts[2]

THE EUROPEAN PARLIAMENT AND THE COUNCIL OF THE EUROPEAN UNION,

HAVING REGARD to the Treaty establishing the European Community, and in particular Article 100a thereof, [...]

---

1   This Directive was notified to the Member States on 23 December 1985.

2   OJ 1997 L 144, p. 19.

(1) WHEREAS, in connection with the attainment of the aims of the internal market, measures must be taken for the gradual consolidation of that market;

(2) WHEREAS the free movement of goods and services affects not only the business sector but also private individuals; whereas it means that consumers should be able to have access to the goods and services of another Member State on the same terms as the population of that State;

(3) WHEREAS, for consumers, cross-border distance selling could be one of the main tangible results of the completion of the internal market, as noted, inter alia, in the communication from the Commission to the Council entitled "Towards a single market in distribution"; whereas it is essential to the smooth operation of the internal market for consumers to be able to have dealings with a business outside their country, even if it has a subsidiary in the consumer's country of residence;

(4) WHEREAS the introduction of new technologies is increasing the number of ways for consumers to obtain information about offers anywhere in the Community and to place orders; whereas some Member States have already taken different or diverging measures to protect consumers in respect of distance selling, which has had a detrimental effect on competition between businesses in the internal market; whereas it is therefore necessary to introduce at Community level a minimum set of common rules in this area;

(5) WHEREAS paragraphs 18 and 19 of the Annex to the Council resolution of 14 April 1975 on a preliminary programme of the European Economic Community for a consumer protection and information policy[1] point to the need to protect the purchasers of goods or services from demands for payment for unsolicited goods and from high-pressure selling methods;

(6) WHEREAS paragraph 33 of the communication from the Commission to the Council entitled "A new impetus for consumer protection policy", which was approved by the Council resolution of 23 June 1986[2], states that the Commission will submit proposals regarding the use of new information technologies enabling consumers to place orders with suppliers from their homes;

(7) WHEREAS the Council resolution of 9 November 1989 on future priorities for re-launching consumer protection policy[3] calls upon the Commission to give priority to the areas referred to in the Annex to that resolution; whereas that Annex refers to new technologies involving tele-shopping; whereas the Commission has responded to that resolution by adopting a three-year action plan for consumer protection policy in the European Economic Community (1990-1992); whereas that plan provides for the adoption of a Directive;

(8) WHEREAS the languages used for distance contracts are a matter for the Member States;

(9) WHEREAS contracts negotiated at a distance involve the use of one or more means of distance communication; whereas the various means of communication are used as part of an organized distance sales or service-provision scheme not involving the simultaneous presence of the supplier and the consumer; whereas the constant development of those means of communication does not allow an exhaustive list to be compiled but does require principles to be defined which are valid even for those which are not as yet in widespread use;

---

1   OJ 1975 C 92, p. 1.

2   OJ 1986 C 167, p. 1.

3   OJ 1989 C 294, p. 1.

(10) WHEREAS the same transaction comprising successive operations or a series of separate operations over a period of time may give rise to different legal descriptions depending on the law of the Member States; whereas the provisions of this Directive cannot be applied differently according to the law of the Member States, subject to their recourse to Article 14; whereas, to that end, there is therefore reason to consider that there must at least be compliance with the provisions of this Directive at the time of the first of a series of successive operations or the first of a series of separate operations over a period of time which may be considered as forming a whole, whether that operation or series of operations are the subject of a single contract or successive, separate contracts;

(11) WHEREAS the use of means of distance communication must not lead to a reduction in the information provided to the consumer; whereas the information that is required to be sent to the consumer should therefore be determined, whatever the means of communication used; whereas the information supplied must also comply with the other relevant Community rules, in particular those in Council Directive 84/450 of 10 September 1984 relating to the approximation of the laws, regulations and administrative provisions of the Member States concerning misleading advertising[1]; whereas, if exceptions are made to the obligation to provide information, it is up to the consumer, on a discretionary basis, to request certain basic information such as the identity of the supplier, the main characteristics of the goods or services and their price;

(12) WHEREAS in the case of communication by telephone it is appropriate that the consumer receive enough information at the beginning of the conversation to decide whether or not to continue;

(13) WHEREAS information disseminated by certain electronic technologies is often ephemeral in nature insofar as it is not received on a permanent medium; whereas the consumer must therefore receive written notice in good time of the information necessary for proper performance of the contract;

(14) WHEREAS the consumer is not able actually to see the product or ascertain the nature of the service provided before concluding the contract; whereas provision should be made, unless otherwise specified in this Directive, for a right of withdrawal from the contract; whereas, if this right is to be more than formal, the costs, if any, borne by the consumer when exercising the right of withdrawal must be limited to the direct costs for returning the goods; whereas this right of withdrawal shall be without prejudice to the consumer's rights under national laws, with particular regard to the receipt of damaged products and services or of products and services not corresponding to the description given in the offer of such products or services; whereas it is for the Member States to determine the other conditions and arrangements following exercise of the right of withdrawal;

(15) WHEREAS it is also necessary to prescribe a time limit for performance of the contract if this is not specified at the time of ordering;

(16) WHEREAS the promotional technique involving the dispatch of a product or the provision of a service to the consumer in return for payment without a prior request from, or the explicit agreement of, the consumer cannot be permitted, unless a substitute product or service is involved;

(17) WHEREAS the principles set out in Articles 8 and 10 of the European Convention for the Protection of Human Rights and Fundamental Freedoms of 4 November 1950[2] apply; whereas the consumer's right to privacy, particularly as regards freedom from

---

1   OJ 1984 L 250, p. 17.

2   See above, p. 286.

certain particularly intrusive means of communication, should be recognized; whereas specific limits on the use of such means should therefore be stipulated; whereas Member States should take appropriate measures to protect effectively those consumers, who do not wish to be contacted through certain means of communication, against such contacts, without prejudice to the particular safeguards available to the consumer under Community legislation concerning the protection of personal data and privacy;
(18) WHEREAS it is important for the minimum binding rules contained in this Directive to be supplemented where appropriate by voluntary arrangements among the traders concerned, in line with Commission recommendation 92/295 of 7 April 1992 on codes of practice for the protection of consumers in respect of contracts negotiated at a distance[1];
(19) WHEREAS in the interest of optimum consumer protection it is important for consumers to be satisfactorily informed of the provisions of this Directive and of codes of practice that may exist in this field;
(20) WHEREAS non-compliance with this Directive may harm not only consumers but also competitors; whereas provisions may therefore be laid down enabling public bodies or their representatives, or consumer organizations which, under national legislation, have a legitimate interest in consumer protection, or professional organizations which have a legitimate interest in taking action, to monitor the application thereof;
(21) WHEREAS it is important, with a view to consumer protection, to address the question of cross-border complaints as soon as this is feasible; whereas the Commission published on 14 February 1996 a plan of action on consumer access to justice and the settlement of consumer disputes in the internal market; whereas that plan of action includes specific initiatives to promote out-of-court procedures; whereas objective criteria (Annex II) are suggested to ensure the reliability of those procedures and provision is made for the use of standardized claims forms (Annex III);
(22) WHEREAS in the use of new technologies the consumer is not in control of the means of communication used; whereas it is therefore necessary to provide that the burden of proof may be on the supplier;
(23) WHEREAS there is a risk that, in certain cases, the consumer may be deprived of protection under this Directive through the designation of the law of a non-member country as the law applicable to the contract; whereas provisions should therefore be included in this Directive to avert that risk;
(24) WHEREAS a Member State may ban, in the general interest, the marketing on its territory of certain goods and services through distance contracts; whereas that ban must comply with Community rules; whereas there is already provision for such bans, notably with regard to medicinal products, under Council Directive 89/552 of 3 October 1989 on the coordination of certain provisions laid down by law, regulation or administrative action in Member States concerning the pursuit of television broadcasting activities[2] and Council Directive 92/28 of 31 March 1992 on the advertising of medicinal products for human use[3],

HAVE ADOPTED THIS DIRECTIVE:

---

1 OJ 1992 L 156, p. 21.

2 OJ 1989 L 298, p. 23.

3 OJ 1992 L 113, p. 13.

Article 1 Object

The object of this Directive is to approximate the laws, regulations and administrative provisions of the Member States concerning distance contracts between consumers and suppliers.

Article 2 Definitions

For the purposes of this Directive:

(1) "distance contract" means any contract concerning goods or services concluded between a supplier and a consumer under an organized distance sales or service-provision scheme run by the supplier, who, for the purpose of the contract, makes exclusive use of one or more means of distance communication up to and including the moment at which the contract is concluded;

(2) "consumer" means any natural person who, in contracts covered by this Directive, is acting for purposes which are outside his trade, business or profession;

(3) "supplier" means any natural or legal person who, in contracts covered by this Directive, is acting in his commercial or professional capacity;

(4) "means of distance communication" means any means which, without the simultaneous physical presence of the supplier and the consumer, may be used for the conclusion of a contract between those parties. An indicative list of the means covered by this Directive is contained in Annex I;

(5) "operator of a means of communication" means any public or private natural or legal person whose trade, business or profession involves making one or more means of distance communication available to suppliers.

Article 3 Exemptions

1. This Directive shall not apply to contracts:
— relating to financial services, a non-exhaustive list of which is given in Annex II,
— concluded by means of automatic vending machines or automated commercial premises,
— concluded with telecommunications operators through the use of public pay-phones,
— concluded for the construction and sale of immovable property or relating to other immovable property rights, except for rental,
— concluded at an auction.

2. Articles 4, 5, 6 and 7 (1) shall not apply:
— to contracts for the supply of foodstuffs, beverages or other goods intended for everyday consumption supplied to the home of the consumer, to his residence or to his workplace by regular roundsmen,
— to contracts for the provision of accommodation, transport, catering or leisure services, where the supplier undertakes, when the contract is concluded, to provide these services on a specific date or within a specific period; exceptionally, in the case of outdoor leisure events, the supplier can reserve the right not to apply Article 7 (2) in specific circumstances.

Article 4 Prior Information

1. In good time prior to the conclusion of any distance contract, the consumer shall be provided with the following information:

(a) the identity of the supplier and, in the case of contracts requiring payment in advance, his address;

(b) the main characteristics of the goods or services;

(c) the price of the goods or services including all taxes;

(d) delivery costs, where appropriate;

(e) the arrangements for payment, delivery or performance;
(f) the existence of a right of withdrawal, except in the cases referred to in Article 6
     (3);
(g) the cost of using the means of distance communication, where it is calculated other
     than at the basic rate;
(h) the period for which the offer or the price remains valid;
(i) where appropriate, the minimum duration of the contract in the case of contracts
     for the supply of products or services to be performed permanently or recurrently.
2.   The information referred to in paragraph 1, the commercial purpose of which must
be made clear, shall be provided in a clear and comprehensible manner in any way
appropriate to the means of distance communication used, with due regard, in particular, to the principles of good faith in commercial transactions, and the principles governing the protection of those who are unable, pursuant to the legislation of the Member
States, to give their consent, such as minors.
3.   Moreover, in the case of telephone communications, the identity of the supplier and
the commercial purpose of the call shall be made explicitly clear at the beginning of any
conversation with the consumer.

Article 5 Written Confirmation of Information

1.   The consumer must receive written confirmation or confirmation in another durable
medium available and accessible to him of the information referred to in Article 4 (1)
(a) to (f), in good time during the performance of the contract, and at the latest at the
time of delivery where goods not for delivery to third parties are concerned, unless the
information has already been given to the consumer prior to conclusion of the contract
in writing or on another durable medium available and accessible to him.
     In any event the following must be provided:
— written information on the conditions and procedures for exercising the right of withdrawal, within the meaning of Article 6, including the cases referred to in the first
   indent of Article 6 (3),
— the geographical address of the place of business of the supplier to which the consumer may address any complaints,
— information on after-sales services and guarantees which exist,
— the conclusion for cancelling the contract, where it is of unspecified duration or a
   duration exceeding one year.
2.   Paragraph 1 shall not apply to services which are performed through the use of a
means of distance communication, where they are supplied on only one occasion and
are invoiced by the operator of the means of distance communication. Nevertheless,
the consumer must in all cases be able to obtain the geographical address of the place
of business of the supplier to which he may address any complaints.

Article 6 Right of Withdrawal

1.   For any distance contract the consumer shall have a period of at least seven working days in which to withdraw from the contract without penalty and without giving any
reason. The only charge that may be made to the consumer because of the exercise
of his right of withdrawal is the direct cost of returning the goods.
     The period for exercise of this right shall begin:
— in the case of goods, from the day of receipt by the consumer where the obligations laid down in Article 5 have been fulfilled,
— in the case of services, from the day of conclusion of the contract or from the day
   on which the obligations laid down in Article 5 were fulfilled if they are fulfilled after
   conclusion of the contract, provided that this period does not exceed the three-
   month period referred to in the following subparagraph.

If the supplier has failed to fulfil the obligations laid down in Article 5, the period shall be three months. The period shall begin:
— in the case of goods, from the day of receipt by the consumer,
— in the case of services, from the day of conclusion of the contract.
If the information referred to in Article 5 is supplied within this three-month period, the seven working day period referred to in the first subparagraph shall begin as from that moment.
2.   Where the right of withdrawal has been exercised by the consumer pursuant to this Article, the supplier shall be obliged to reimburse the sums paid by the consumer free of charge. The only charge that may be made to the consumer because of the exercise of his right of withdrawal is the direct cost of returning the goods. Such reimbursement must be carried out as soon as possible and in any case within 30 days.
3.   Unless the parties have agreed otherwise, the consumer may not exercise the right of withdrawal provided for in paragraph 1 in respect of contracts:
— for the provision of services if performance has begun, with the consumer's agreement, before the end of the seven working day period referred to in paragraph 1,
— for the supply of goods or services the price of which is dependent on fluctuations in the financial market which cannot be controlled by the supplier,
— for the supply of goods made to the consumer's specifications or clearly personalized or which, by reason of their nature, cannot be returned or are liable to deteriorate or expire rapidly,
— for the supply of audio or video recordings or computer software which were unsealed by the consumer,
— for the supply of newspapers, periodicals and magazines,
— for gaming and lottery services.
4.   The Member States shall make provision in their legislation to ensure that:
— if the price of goods or services is fully or partly covered by credit granted by the supplier, or
— if that price is fully or partly covered by credit granted to the consumer by a third party on the basis of an agreement between the third party and the supplier, the credit agreement shall be cancelled, without any penalty, if the consumer exercises his right to withdraw from the contract in accordance with paragraph 1.
      Member States shall determine the detailed rules for cancellation of the credit agreement.

Article 7 Performance

1.   Unless the parties have agreed otherwise, the supplier must execute the order within a maximum of 30 days from the day following that on which the consumer forwarded his order to the supplier.
2.   Where a supplier fails to perform his side of the contract on the grounds that the goods or services ordered are unavailable, the consumer must be informed of this situation and must be able to obtain a refund of any sums he has paid as soon as possible and in any case within 30 days.
3.   Nevertheless, Member States may lay down that the supplier may provide the consumer with goods or services of equivalent quality and price provided that this possibility was provided for prior to the conclusion of the contract or in the contract.
The consumer shall be informed of this possibility in a clear and comprehensible manner. The cost of returning the goods following exercise of the right of withdrawal shall, in this case, be borne by the supplier, and the consumer must be informed of this. In such cases the supply of goods or services may not be deemed to constitute inertia selling within the meaning of Article 9.

Article 8 Payment by Card
Member States shall ensure that appropriate measures exist to allow a consumer:
— to request cancellation of a payment where fraudulent use has been made of his payment card in connection with distance contracts covered by this Directive,
— in the event of fraudulent use, to be recredited with the sums paid or have them returned.

Article 9 Inertia Selling
Member States shall take the measures necessary to:
— prohibit the supply of goods or services to a consumer without their being ordered by the consumer beforehand, where such supply involves a demand for payment,
— exempt the consumer from the provision of any consideration in cases of unsolicited supply, the absence of a response not constituting consent.

Article 10 Restrictions on the use of Certain Means of Distance Communication
1. Use by a supplier of the following means requires the prior consent of the consumer:
— automated calling system without human intervention (automatic calling machine),
— facsimile machine (fax).
2. Member States shall ensure that means of distance communication, other than those referred to in paragraph 1, which allow individual communications may be used only where there is no clear objection from the consumer.

Article 11 Judicial or Administrative Redress
1. Member States shall ensure that adequate and effective means exist to ensure compliance with this Directive in the interests of consumers.
2. The means referred to in paragraph 1 shall include provisions whereby one or more of the following bodies, as determined by national law, may take action under national law before the courts or before the competent administrative bodies to ensure that the national provisions for the implementation of this Directive are applied:
(a) public bodies or their representatives;
(b) consumer organizations having a legitimate interest in protecting consumers;
(c) professional organizations having a legitimate interest in acting.
3. (a) Member States may stipulate that the burden of proof concerning the existence of prior information, written confirmation, compliance with time-limits or consumer consent can be placed on the supplier.
(b) Member States shall take the measures needed to ensure that suppliers and operators of means of communication, where they are able to do so, cease practices which do not comply with measures adopted pursuant to this Directive.
4. Member States may provide for voluntary supervision by self-regulatory bodies of compliance with the provisions of this Directive and recourse to such bodies for the settlement of disputes to be added to the means which Member States must provided to ensure compliance with the provisions of this Directive.

Article 12 Binding nature
1. The consumer may not waive the rights conferred on him by the transposition of this Directive into national law.
2. Member States shall take the measures needed to ensure that the consumer does not lose the protection granted by this Directive by virtue of the choice of the law of a non-member country as the law applicable to the contract if the latter has close connection with the territory of one or more Member States.

Article 13 Community rules

Article 13 Community rules

1.   The provisions of this Directive shall apply insofar as there are no particular provisions in rules of Community law governing certain types of distance contracts in their entirety.

2.   Where specific Community rules contain provisions governing only certain aspects of the supply of goods or provision of services, those provisions, rather than the provisions of this Directive, shall apply to these specific aspects of the distance contracts.

Article 14 Minimal clause

Member States may introduce or maintain, in the area covered by this Directive, more stringent provisions compatible with the Treaty, to ensure a higher level of consumer protection. Such provisions shall, where appropriate, include a ban, in the general interest, on the marketing of certain goods or services, particularly medicinal products, within their territory by means of distance contracts, with due regard for the Treaty.

Article 15 Implementation

1.   Member States shall bring into force the laws, regulations and administrative provisions necessary to comply with this Directive no later than three years after it enters into force. They shall forthwith inform the Commission thereof.

2.   When Member States adopt the measures referred to in paragraph 1, these shall contain a reference to this Directive or shall be accompanied by such reference on the occasion of their official publication. The procedure for such reference shall be laid down by Member States.

3.   Member States shall communicate to the Commission the text of the provisions of national law which they adopt in the field governed by this Directive.

4.   No later than four years after the entry into force of this Directive the Commission shall submit a report to the European Parliament and the Council on the implementation of this Directive, accompanied if appropriate by a proposal for the revision thereof.

Article 16 Consumer information

Member States shall take appropriate measures to inform the consumer of the national law transposing this Directive and shall encourage, where appropriate, professional organizations to inform consumers of their codes of practice.

Article 17 Complaints systems

The Commission shall study the feasibility of establishing effective means to deal with consumers' complaints in respect of distance selling. Within two years after the entry into force of this Directive the Commission shall submit a report to the European Parliament and the Council on the results of the studies, accompanied if appropriate by proposals.

Article 18 [Entry into Force]

This Directive shall enter into force on the day of its publication in the Official Journal of the European Communities.

Article 19 [Addressees]

This Directive is addressed to the Member States.

Done at Brussels, 20 May 1997.
For the European Parliament; The President J.M. GIL-ROBLES
For the Council; The President J. VAN AARTSEN

ANNEX I: MEANS OF COMMUNICATION COVERED BY ARTICLE 2 (4)
— Unaddressed printed matter
— Addressed printed matter
— Standard letter
— Press advertising with order form
— Catalogue
— Telephone with human intervention
— Telephone without human intervention (automatic calling machine, audiotext)
— Radio
— Videophone (telephone with screen)
— Videotex (microcomputer and television screen) with keyboard or touch screen
— Electronic mail
— Facsimile machine (fax)
— Television (teleshopping).

ANNEX II: FINANCIAL SERVICES WITHIN THE MEANING OF ARTICLE 3 (1)
— Investment services
— Insurance and reinsurance operations
— Banking services
— Operations relating to dealings in futures or options.
Such services include in particular:
— investment services referred to in the Annex to Directive 93/22[1]; services of collective investment undertakings,
— services covered by the activities subject to mutual recognition referred to in the Annex to Directive 89/646[2];
— operations covered by the insurance and reinsurance activities referred to in:
— Article 1 of Directive 73/239[3],
— the Annex to Directive 79/267[4],
— Directive 64/225[5],
— Directives 92/49[6] and 92/96[7].

Council Directive 87/102 of 22 December 1986 for the Approximation of the Laws, Regulations and Administrative Provisions of the Member States Concerning Consumer Credit[8]

THE COUNCIL OF THE EUROPEAN COMMUNITIES,

HAVING REGARD to the Treaty establishing the European Economic Community, and in particular Article 100 thereof, [...]
(1) WHEREAS wide differences exist in the laws of the Member States in the field of consumer credit;

---

1 OJ 1993 L 141, p. 27.

2 OJ 1989 L 386, p. 1, [as amended].

3 OJ 1973 L 228, p. 3, [as amended].

4 OJ 1979 L 63, p. 1, [as amended].

5 OJ 1964 No 56, p. 878/64, [as amended].

6 OJ 1992 L 228, p. 1.

7 OJ 1992 L 360, p. 1.

8 OJ 1987 L 42, p. 48, as amended by Council Directive 90/88 of 22 February 1990 and by Directive 98/7 of the European Parliament and of the Council of 16 February 1998.

(2) WHEREAS these differences of law can lead to distortions of competition between grantors of credit in the common market;

(3) WHEREAS these differences limit the opportunities the consumer has to obtain credit in other Member States; whereas they affect the volume and the nature of the credit sought, and also the purchase of goods and services;

(4) WHEREAS, as a result, these differences have an influence on the free movement of goods and services obtainable by consumers on credit and thus directly affect the functioning of the common market;

(5) WHEREAS, given the increasing volume of credit granted in the Community to consumers, the establishment of a common market in consumer credit would benefit alike consumers, grantors of credit, manufacturers, wholesalers and retailers of goods and providers of services;

(6) WHEREAS the programmes of the European Economic Community for a consumer protection and information policy[1] provide, *inter alia*, that the consumer should be protected against unfair credit terms and that a harmonization of the general conditions governing consumer credit should be undertaken as a priority;

(7) WHEREAS differences of law and practice result in unequal consumer protection in the field of consumer credit from one Member State to another;

(8) WHEREAS there has been much change in recent years in the types of credit available to and used by consumers; whereas new forms of consumer credit have emerged and continue to develop;

(9) WHEREAS the consumer should receive adequate information on the conditions and cost of credit and on his obligations; whereas this information should include, *inter alia*, the annual percentage rate of charge for credit, or, failing that, the total amount that the consumer must pay for credit; whereas, pending a decision on a Community method or methods of calculating the annual percentage rate of charge, Member States should be able to retain existing methods or practices for calculating this rate, or failing that, should establish provisions for indicating the total cost of the credit to the consumer;

(10) WHEREAS the terms of credit may be disadvantageous to the consumer; whereas better protection of consumers can be achieved by adopting certain requirements which are to apply to all forms of credit;

(11) WHEREAS, having regard to the character of certain credit agreements or types of transaction, these agreements or transactions should be partially or entirely excluded from the field of application of this Directive;

(12) WHEREAS it should be possible for Member States, in consultation with the Commission, to exempt from the Directive certain forms of credit of a non-commercial character granted under particular conditions;

(13) WHEREAS the practices existing in some Member States in respect of authentic acts drawn up before a notary or judge are such as to render the application of certain provisions of this Directive unnecessary in the case of such acts; whereas it should therefore be possible for Member States to exempt such acts from those provisions;

(14) WHEREAS credit agreements for very large financial amounts tend to differ from the usual consumer credit agreements; whereas the application of the provisions of this Directive to agreements for very small amounts could create unnecessary administrative burdens both for consumers and grantors of credit; whereas therefore, agreements above or below specified financial limits should be excluded from the Directive;

1　　OJ 1975 C 92, p. 1 and OJ 1981 C 133, p. 1.

(15) WHEREAS the provision of information on the cost of credit in advertising and at the business premises of the creditor or credit broker can make it easier for the consumer to compare different offers;

(16) WHEREAS consumer protection is further improved if credit agreements are made in writing and contain certain minimum particulars concerning the contractual terms;

(17) WHEREAS, in the case of credit granted for the acquisition of goods, Member States should lay down the conditions in which goods may be repossessed, particularly if the consumer has not given his consent; whereas the account between the parties should upon repossession be made up in such manner as to ensure that the repossession does not entail any unjustified enrichment;

(18) WHEREAS the consumer should be allowed to discharge his obligations before the due date; whereas the consumer should then be entitled to an equitable reduction in the total cost of the credit;

(19) WHEREAS the assignment of the creditor's rights arising under a credit agreement should not be allowed to weaken the position of the consumer;

(20) WHEREAS those Member States which permit consumers to use bills of exchange, promissory notes or cheques in connection with credit agreements should ensure that the consumer is suitably protected when so using such instruments;

(21) WHEREAS, as regards goods or services which the consumer has contracted to acquire on credit, the consumer should, at least in the circumstances defined below, have rights vis-à-vis the grantor of credit which are in addition to his normal contractual rights against him and against the supplier of the goods or services; whereas the circumstances referred to above are those where the grantor of credit and the supplier of goods or services have a pre-existing agreement whereunder credit is made available exclusively by that grantor of credit to customers of that supplier for the purpose of enabling the consumer to acquire goods or services from the latter;

(22) WHEREAS the ECU is as defined in Council Regulation 3180/78[1], as [...] amended [...]; whereas Member States should to a limited extent be at liberty to round off the amounts in national currency resulting from the conversion of amounts of this Directive expressed in ECU; whereas the amounts in this Directive should be periodically re-examined in the light of economic and monetary trends in the Community, and, if need be, revised;

(23) WHEREAS suitable measures should be adopted by Member States for authorizing persons offering credit or offering to arrange credit agreements or for inspecting or monitoring the activities of persons granting credit or arranging for credit to be granted or for enabling consumers to complain about credit agreements or credit conditions;

(24) WHEREAS credit agreements should not derogate, to the detriment of the consumer, from the provisions adopted in implementation of this Directive or corresponding to its provisions; whereas those provisions should not be circumvented as a result of the way in which agreements are formulated;

(25) WHEREAS, since this Directive provides for a certain degree of approximation of the laws, regulations and administrative provisions of the Member States concerning consumer credit and for a certain level of consumer protection, Member States should not be prevented from retaining or adopting more stringent measures to protect the consumer, with due regard for their obligations under the Treaty;

(26) WHEREAS, not later than 1 January 1995, the Commission should present to the Council a report concerning the operation of this Directive,

---

1   OJ 1978 L 379, p. 1.

HAS ADOPTED THIS DIRECTIVE:

Article 1 [Scope and Definitions]
1. This Directive applies to credit agreements.
2. For the purpose of this Directive:
(a) "consumer" means a natural person who, in transactions covered by this Directive, is acting for purposes which can be regarded as outside his trade or profession;
(b) "creditor" means a natural or legal person who grants credit in the course of his trade, business or profession, or a group of such persons;
(c) "credit agreement" means an agreement whereby a creditor grants or promises to grant to a consumer a credit in the form of a deferred payment, a loan or other similar financial accommodation.

     Agreements for the provision on a continuing basis of a service or a utility, where the consumer has the right to pay for them, for the duration of their provision, by means of instalments, are not deemed to be credit agreements for the purpose of this Directive;
(d) "total cost of the credit to the consumer" means all the costs, including interest and other charges, which the consumer has to pay for the credit;
(e) "annual percentage rate of charge" means the total cost of the credit to the consumer, expressed as an annual percentage of the amount of the credit granted and calculated in accordance with Article 1a.

Article 1a [Calculation of Annual Percentage Rate]
1. (a) The annual percentage rate of charge which shall be that rate, on an annual basis which equalizes the present value of all commitments (loans, repayments and charges), future or existing, agreed by the creditor and the borrower, shall be calculated in accordance with the mathematical formula set out in Annex II.
(b) Four examples of the method of calculation are given in Annex III, by way of illustration.
2. For the purpose of calculating the annual percentage rate of charge, the "total cost of the credit to the consumer" as defined in Article 1 (2) (d) shall be determined, with the exception of the following charges:
(i)   charges payable by the borrower for non-compliance with any of his commitments laid down in the credit agreement;
(ii) charges other than the purchase price which, in purchases of goods or services, the consumer is obliged to pay whether the transaction is paid in cash or by credit;
(iii) charges for the transfer of funds and charges for keeping an account intended to receive payments towards the reimbursement of the credit the payment of interest and other charges except where the consumer does not have reasonable freedom of choice in the matter and where such charges are abnormally high; this provision shall not, however, apply to charges for collection of such reimbursements or payments, whether made in cash or otherwise;
(iv) membership subscriptions to associations or groups and arising from agreements separate from the credit agreement, even though such subscriptions have an effect on the credit terms;
(v)   charges for insurance or guarantees; included are, however, those designed to ensure payment to the creditor, in the event of the death, invalidity, illness or unemployment of the consumer, of a sum equal to or less than the total amount of the credit together with relevant interest and other charges which have to be imposed by the creditor as a condition for credit being granted.
3. deleted

4. (a) The annual percentage rate of charge shall be calculated at the time the credit contract is concluded, without prejudice to the provisions of Article 3 concerning advertisements and special offers.

(b) The calculation shall be made on the assumption that the credit contract is valid for the period agreed and that the creditor and the consumer fulfil their obligations under the terms and by the dates agreed.

5. deleted

6. In the case of credit contracts containing clauses allowing variations in the rate of interest and the amount or level of other charges contained in the annual percentage rate of charge but unquantifiable at the time when it is calculated, the annual percentage rate of charge shall be calculated on the assumption that interest and other charges remain fixed and will apply until the end of the credit contract.

7. Where necessary, the following assumptions may be made in calculating the annual percentage rate of charge:

— if the contract does not specify a credit limit, the amount of credit granted shall be equal to the amount fixed by the relevant Member State, without exceeding a figure equivalent to ECU 2.000;

— if there is no fixed timetable for repayment, and one cannot be deduced from the terms of the agreement and the means for repaying the credit granted, the duration of the credit shall be deemed to be one year;

— unless otherwise specified, where the contract provides for more than one repayment date, the credit will be made available and the repayments made at the earliest time provided for in the agreement.

Article 2 [Exemptions]

1. This Directive shall not apply to:

(a) credit agreements or agreements promising to grant credit:
— intended primarily for the purpose of acquiring or retaining property rights in land or in an existing or projected building,
— intended for the purpose of renovating or improving a building as such;

(b) hiring agreements except where these provide that the title will pass ultimately to the hirer;

(c) credit granted or made available without payment of interest or any other charge;

(d) credit agreements under which no interest is charged provided the consumer agrees to repay the credit in a single payment;

(e) credit in the form of advances on a current account granted by a credit institution or financial institution other than on credit card accounts.
Nevertheless, the provisions of Article 6 shall apply to such credits;

(f) credit agreements involving amounts less than 200 ECU or more than 20.000 ECU;

(g) credit agreements under which the consumer is required to repay the credit:
— either, within a period not exceeding three months,
— or, by a maximum number of four payments within a period not exceeding 12 months.

2. A Member State may, in consultation with the Commission, exempt from the application of this Directive certain types of credit which fulfil the following conditions:
— they are granted at rates of charge below those prevailing in the market, and
— they are not offered to the public generally.

3. The provisions of Article 1a and of Articles 4 to 12 shall not apply to credit agreements or agreements promising to grant credit, secured by mortgage on immovable property, insofar as these are not already excluded from the Directive under paragraph 1 (a).

4.   Member States may exempt from the provisions of Articles 6 to 12 credit agreements in the form of an authentic act signed before a notary or judge.

Article 3 [Application to Advertisements]

Without prejudice to Council Directive 84/450 of 10 September 1984 relating to the approximation of the laws, regulations and administrative provisions of the Member States concerning misleading advertising[1], and to the rules and principles applicable to unfair advertising, any advertisement, or any offer which is displayed at business premises, in which a person offers credit or offers to arrange a credit agreement and in which a rate of interest or any figures relating to the cost of the credit are indicated, shall also include a statement of the annual percentage rate of charge, by means of a representative example if no other means is practicable.

Article 4 [Mandatory Written Form]

1.   Credit agreements shall be made in writing. The consumer shall receive a copy of the written agreement.
2.   The written agreement shall include:
(a) a statement of the annual percentage rate of charge;
(b) a statement of the conditions under which the annual percentage rate of charge may be amended.
        In cases where it is not possible to state the annual percentage rate of charge, the consumer shall be provided with adequate information in the written agreement. This information shall at least include the information provided for in the second indent of Article 6 (1).
(c) a statement of the amount, number and frequency or dates of the payments which the consumer must make to repay the credit, as well as of the payments for interest and other charges; the total amount of these payments should also be indicated where possible;
(d) a statement of the cost items referred to in Article 1a (2) with the exception of expenditure related to the breach of contractual obligations which were not included in the calculation of the annual percentage rate of charge but which have to be paid by the consumer in given circumstances, together with a statement identifying such circumstances. Where the exact amount of those items is known, that sum is to be indicated; if that is not the case, either a method of calculation or as accurate an estimate as possible is to be provided where possible.
3.   The written agreement shall further include the other essential terms of the contract.
        By way of illustration, the Annex to this Directive contains a list of terms which Member States may require to be included in the written agreement as being essential.

Article 5 deleted

Article 6 [Credit on Current Accounts]

1.   Notwithstanding the exclusion provided for in Article 2 (1) (e), where there is an agreement between a credit institution or financial institution and a consumer for the granting of credit in the form of an advance on a current account, other than on credit card accounts, the consumer shall be informed at the time or before the agreement is concluded:
— of the credit limit, if any,

---

1   OJ 1984 L 250, p. 17, [as amended].

— of the annual rate of interest and the charges applicable from the time the agreement is concluded and the conditions under which these may be amended,
— of the procedure for terminating the agreement.
This information shall be confirmed in writing.

2. Furthermore, during the period of the agreement, the consumer shall be informed of any change in the annual rate of interest or in the relevant charges at the time it occurs. Such information may be given in a statement of account or in any other manner acceptable to Member States.

3. In Member States where tacitly accepted overdrafts are permissible, the Member States concerned shall ensure that the consumer is informed of the annual rate of interest and the charges applicable, and of any amendment thereof, where the overdraft extends beyond a period of three months.

Article 7 [Repossession of Goods]
In the case of credit granted for the acquisition of goods, Member States shall lay down the conditions under which goods may be repossessed, in particular if the consumer has not given his consent. They shall further ensure that where the creditor recovers possession of the goods the account between the parties shall be made up so as to ensure that the repossession does not entail any unjustified enrichment.

Article 8 [Early Termination of Credit Agreements]
The consumer shall be entitled to discharge his obligations under a credit agreement before the time fixed by the agreement. In this event, in accordance with the rules laid down by the Member States, the consumer shall be entitled to an equitable reduction in the total cost of the credit.

Article 9 [Consumer Rights Against Third Persons]
Where the creditor's rights under a credit agreement are assigned to a third person, the consumer shall be entitled to plead against that third person any defence which was available to him against the original creditor, including set-off where the latter is permitted in the Member State concerned.

Article 10 [Bills of Exchange]
The Member States which, in connection with credit agreements, permit the consumer:
(a) to make payment by means of bills of exchange including promissory notes;
(b) to give security by means of bills of exchange including promissory notes and cheques,
shall ensure that the consumer is suitably protected when using these instruments in those ways.

Article 11 [Non-Performance with Regard to Services or Goods]
1. Member States shall ensure that the existence of a credit agreement shall not in any way affect the rights of the consumer against the supplier of goods or services purchased by means of such an agreement in cases where the goods or services are not supplied or are otherwise not in conformity with the contract for their supply.
2. Where:
(a) in order to buy goods or obtain services the consumer enters into a credit agreement with a person other than the supplier of them; and
(b) the grantor of the credit and the supplier of the goods or services have a pre-existing agreement whereunder credit is made available exclusively by that grantor of credit to customers of that supplier for the acquisition of goods or services from that supplier; and

(c) the consumer referred to in subparagraph (a) obtains his credit pursuant to that preexisting agreement; and
(d) the goods or services covered by the credit agreement are not supplied, or are supplied only in part, or are not in conformity with the contract for supply of them; and
(e) the consumer has pursued his remedies against the supplier but has failed to obtain the satisfaction to which he is entitled, the consumer shall have the right to pursue remedies against the grantor of credit. Member States shall determine to what extent and under what conditions these remedies shall be exercisable.
3.   Paragraph 2 shall not apply where the individual transaction in question is for an amount less than the equivalent of 200 ECU.

Article 12 [Member State Obligations]
1.   Member States shall:
(a) ensure that persons offering credit or offering to arrange credit agreements shall obtain official authorization to do so, either specifically or as suppliers of goods and services; or
(b) ensure that persons granting credit or arranging for credit to be granted shall be subject to inspection or monitoring of their activities by an institution or official body; or
(c) promote the establishment of appropriate bodies to receive complaints concerning credit agreements or credit conditions and to provide relevant information or advice to consumers regarding them.
2.   Member States may provide that the authorization referred to in paragraph 1 (a) shall not be required where persons offering to conclude or arrange credit agreements satisfy the definition in Article 1 of the first Council Directive of 12 December 1977 on the coordination of laws, regulations and administrative provisions relating to the taking up and pursuit of the business of credit institutions[1] and are authorized in accordance with the provisions of that Directive.
    Where persons granting credit or arranging for credit to be granted have been authorized both specifically, under the provisions of paragraph 1 (a) and also under the provisions of the aforementioned Directive, but the latter authorization is subsequently withdrawn, the competent authority responsible for issuing the specific authorization to grant credit under paragraph 1 (a) shall be informed and shall decide whether the persons concerned may continue to grant credit, or arrange for credit to be granted, or whether the specific authorization granted under paragraph 1 (a) should be withdrawn.

Article 13 [Definitions of the ECU]
1.   For the purposes of this Directive, the ECU shall be that defined by Regulation 3180/78, as amended [...]. The equivalent in national currency shall initially be calculated at the rate obtaining on the date of adoption of this Directive.
    Member States may round off the amounts in national currency resulting from the conversion of the amounts in ECU provided such rounding off does not exceed 10 ECU.
2.   Every five years, and for the first time in 1995, the Council, acting on a proposal from the Commission, shall examine and, if need be, revise the amounts in this Directive, in the light of economic and monetary trends in the Community.

---

1   OJ 1977 L 322, p. 30.

Article 14 [Mandatory Rules of the Directive]
1.   Member States shall ensure that credit agreements shall not derogate, to the detriment of the consumer, from the provisions of national law implementing or corresponding to this Directive.
2.   Member States shall further ensure that the provisions which they adopt in implementation of this directive are not circumvented as a result of the way in which agreements are formulated, in particular by the device of distributing the amount of credit over several agreements.

Article 15 [Stricter National Laws]
This Directive shall not preclude Member States from retaining or adopting more stringent provisions to protect consumers consistent with their obligations under the Treaty.

Article 16 [Implementation into National Law]
1.   Member States shall bring into force the measures necessary to comply with this Directive not later than 1 January 1990 and shall forthwith inform the Commission thereof.
2.   Member States shall communicate to the Commission the texts of the main provisions of national law which they adopt in the field covered by this Directive.

Article 17 [Reports to the Council]
Not later than 1 January 1995 the Commission shall present a report to the Council concerning the operation of this Directive.

Article 18 [Addressees]
This Directive is addressed to the Member States.

Done at Brussels, 22 December 1986.
For the Council, The President, G. SHAW

ANNEX I: LIST OF TERMS REFERRED TO IN ARTICLE 4 (3)
1.   Credit agreements for financing the supply of particular goods or services:
(i)   a description of the goods or services covered by the agreement;
(ii)   the cash price and the price payable under the credit agreement;
(iii)   the amount of the deposit, if any, the number and amount of instalments and the dates on which they fall due, or the method of ascertaining any of the same if unknown at the time the agreement is concluded;
(iv)   an indication that the consumer will be entitled, as provided in Article 8, to a reduction if he repays early;
(v)   who owns the goods (if ownership does not pass immediately to the consumer) and the terms on which the consumer becomes the owner of them;
(vi)   a description of the security required, if any;
(vii)   the cooling-off period, if any;
(viii)   an indication of the insurance(s) required, if any, and, when the choice of insurer is not left to the consumer, an indication of the cost thereof;
(ix)   the obligation on the consumer to save a certain amount of money which must be placed in a special account.
2.   Credit agreements operated by credit cards:
(i)   the amount of the credit limit, if any;
(ii)   the terms of repayment or the means of determining them;
(iii)   the cooling-off period, if any.
3.   Credit agreements operated by running account which are not otherwise covered by the Directive:
(i)   the amount of the credit limit, if any, or the method of determining it;
(ii)   the terms of use and repayment;

(iii)   the cooling-off period, if any.
4.   Other credit agreements covered by the Directive:
(i)   the amount of the credit limit, if any;
(ii)   an indication of the security required, if any;
(iii)   the terms of repayment;
(iv)   the cooling-off period, if any;
(v)   an indication that the consumer will be entitled, as provided in Article 8, to a reduction if
        he repays early.

ANNEX II: THE BASIC EQUATION EXPRESSING THE EQUIVALENCE OF LOANS ON THE
ONE HAND, AND REPAYMENTS AND CHARGES ON THE OTHER [omitted]

ANNEX III: EXAMPLES OF CALCULATIONS [omitted]

Council Directive 90/314 of 13 June 1990 on Package Travel, Package Holidays and Package Tours[1]

THE COUNCIL OF THE EUROPEAN COMMUNITIES,

HAVING REGARD to the Treaty establishing the European Economic Community, and in particular Article 100a thereof, [...]
(1) WHEREAS one of the main objectives of the Community is to complete the internal market, of which the tourist sector is an essential part;
(2) WHEREAS the national laws of Member States concerning package travel, package holidays and package tours, hereinafter referred to as "packages", show many disparities and national practices in this field are markedly different, which gives rise to obstacles to the freedom to provide services in respect of packages and distortions of competition amongst operators established in different Member States;
(3) WHEREAS the establishment of common rules on packages will contribute to the elimination of these obstacles and thereby to the achievement of a common market in services, thus enabling operators established in one Member State to offer their services in other Member States and Community consumers to benefit from comparable conditions when buying a package in any Member State;
(4) WHEREAS paragraph 36 (b) of the Annex to the Council resolution of 19 May 1981 on a second programme of the European Economic Community for a consumer protection and information policy[2] invites the Commission to study, *inter alia*, tourism and, if appropriate, to put forward suitable proposals, with due regard for their significance for consumer protection and the effects of differences in Member States' legislation on the proper functioning of the common market;
(5) WHEREAS in the resolution on a Community policy on tourism on 10 April 1984[3] the Council welcomed the Commission's initiative in drawing attention to the importance of tourism and took note of the Commission's initial guidelines for a Community policy on tourism;
(6) WHEREAS the Commission communication to the Council entitled "A New Impetus for Consumer Protection Policy", which was approved by resolution of the Council on

---

1   OJ 1990 L158, p. 59.

2   OJ 1981 C 165, p. 24.

3   OJ 1984 C 115, p. 1.

6 May 1986[1], lists in paragraph 37, among the measures proposed by the Commission, the harmonization of legislation on packages;

(7) WHEREAS tourism plays an increasingly important role in the economies of the Member States; whereas the package system is a fundamental part of tourism; whereas the package travel industry in Member States would be stimulated to greater growth and productivity if at least a minimum of common rules were adopted in order to give it a Community dimension; whereas this would not only produce benefits for Community citizens buying packages organized on the basis of those rules, but would attract tourists from outside the Community seeking the advantages of guaranteed standards in packages;

(8) WHEREAS disparities in the rules protecting consumers in different Member States are a disincentive to consumers in one Member State from buying packages in another Member State;

(9) WHEREAS this disincentive is particularly effective in deterring consumers from buying packages outside their own Member State, and more effective than it would be in relation to the acquisition of other services, having regard to the special nature of the services supplied in a package which generally involve the expenditure of substantial amounts of money in advance and the supply of the services in a State other than that in which the consumer is resident;

(10) WHEREAS the consumer should have the benefit of the protection introduced by this Directive irrespective of whether he is a direct contracting party, a transferee or a member of a group on whose behalf another person has concluded a contract in respect of a package;

(11) WHEREAS the organizer of the package and/or the retailer of it should be under obligation to ensure that in descriptive matter relating to packages which they respectively organize and sell, the information which is given is not misleading and brochures made available to consumers contain information which is comprehensible and accurate;

(12) WHEREAS the consumer needs to have a record of the terms of contract applicable to the package; whereas this can conveniently be achieved by requiring that all the terms of the contract be stated in writing of such other documentary form as shall be comprehensible and accessible to him, and that he be given a copy thereof;

(13) WHEREAS the consumer should be at liberty in certain circumstances to transfer to a willing third person a booking made by him for a package;

(14) WHEREAS the price established under the contract should not in principle be subject to revision except where the possibility of upward or downward revision is expressly provided for in the contract; whereas that possibility should nonetheless be subject to certain conditions;

(15) WHEREAS the consumer should in certain circumstances be free to withdraw before departure from a package travel contract;

(16) WHEREAS there should be a clear definition of the rights available to the consumer in circumstances where the organizer of the package cancels it before the agreed date of departure;

(17) WHEREAS if, after the consumer has departed, there occurs a significant failure of performance of the services for which he has contracted or the organizer perceives that he will be unable to procure a significant part of the services to be provided; the organizer should have certain obligations towards the consumer;

(18) WHEREAS the organizer and/or retailer party to the contract should be liable to the consumer for the proper performance of the obligations arising from the contract;

---

1   OJ 1986 C 118, p. 28.

whereas, moreover, the organizer and/or retailer should be liable for the damage re-sulting for the consumer from failure to perform or improper performance of the con-tract unless the defects in the performance of the contract are attributable neither to any fault of theirs nor to that of another supplier of services;

(19) WHEREAS in cases where the organizer and/or retailer is liable for failure to per-form or improper performance of the services involved in the package, such liability should be limited in accordance with the international conventions governing such ser-vices, in particular the Warsaw Convention of 1929 in International Carriage by Air, the Berne Convention of 1961 on Carriage by Rail, the Athens Convention of 1974 on Car-riage by Sea and the Paris Convention of 1962 on the Liability of Hotel-keepers; where-as, moreover, with regard to damage other than personal injury, it should be possible for liability also to be limited under the package contract provided, however, that such limits are not unreasonable;

(20) WHEREAS certain arrangements should be made for the information of consu-mers and the handling of complaints;

(21) WHEREAS both the consumer and the package travel industry would benefit if organizers and/or retailers were placed under an obligation to provide sufficient evi-dence of security in the event of insolvency;

(22) WHEREAS Member States should be at liberty to adopt, or retain, more stringent provisions relating to package travel for the purpose of protecting the consumer,

HAS ADOPTED THIS DIRECTIVE:

Article 1 [Objective]
The purpose of this Directive is to approximate the laws, regulations and administrative provisions of the Member States relating to packages sold or offered for sale in the ter-ritory of the Community.

Article 2 [Definitions]
For the purposes of this Directive:

1. "package" means the pre-arranged combination of not fewer than two of the follo-wing when sold or offered for sale at an inclusive price and when the service covers a period of more than twenty-four hours or includes overnight accommodation:
(a) transport;
(b) accommodation;
(c) other tourist services not ancillary to transport or accommodation and accounting for a significant proportion of the package.
The separate billing of various components of the same package shall not absolve the organizer or retailer from the obligations under this Directive;

2. "organize" means the person who, other than occasionally, organizes packages and sells or offers them for sale, whether directly or through a retailer;

3. "retailer" means the person who sells or offers for sale the package put together by the organizer;

4. "consumer" means the person who takes or agrees to take the package ("the prin-cipal contractor"), or any person on whose behalf the principal contractor agrees to purchase the package ("the other beneficiaries") or any person to whom the principal contractor or any of the other beneficiaries transfers the package ("the transferee");

5. "contract" means the agreement linking the consumer to the organizer and/or the retailer.

Article 3 [Duty to Provide Clear Information]

1. Any descriptive matter concerning a package and supplied by the organizer or the retailer to the consumer, the price of the package and any other conditions applying to the contract must not contain any misleading information.

2. When a brochure is made available to the consumer, it shall indicate in a legible, comprehensible and accurate manner both the price and adequate information concerning:

(a) the destination and the means, characteristics and categories of transport used;

(b) the type of accommodation, its location, category or degree of comfort and its main features, its approval and tourist classification under the rules of the host Member State concerned;

(c) the meal plan;

(d) the itinerary;

(e) general information on passport and visa requirements for nationals of the Member State or States concerned and health formalities required for the journey and the stay;

(f) either the monetary amount or the percentage of the price which is to be paid on account, and the timetable for payment of the balance;

(g) whether a minimum number of persons is required for the package to take place and, if so, the deadline for informing the consumer in the event of cancellation.

The particulars contained in the brochure are binding on the organizer or retailer, unless:

— changes in such particulars have been clearly communicated to the consumer before conclusion of the contract, in which case the brochure shall expressly state so,

— changes are made later following an agreement between the parties to the contract.

Article 4 [Minimum Information to be Provided]

1. (a) The organizer and/or the retailer shall provide the consumer, in writing or any other appropriate form, before the contract is concluded, with general information on passport and visa requirements applicable to nationals of the Member State or States concerned and in particular on the periods for obtaining them, as well as with information on the health formalities required for the journey and the stay;

(b) The organizer and/or retailer shall also provide the consumer, in writing or any other appropriate form, with the following information in good time before the start of the journey:

(i) the times and places of intermediate stops and transport connections as well as details of the place to be occupied by the traveller, e.g. cabin or berth on ship, sleeper compartment on train;

(ii) the name, address and telephone number of the organizer's and/or retailer's local representative or, failing that, of local agencies on whose assistance a consumer in difficulty could call. Where no such representatives or agencies exist, the consumer must in any case be provided with an emergency telephone number or any other information that will enable him to contract the organizer and/or the retailer;

(iii) in the case of journeys or stays abroad by minors, information enabling direct contact to be established with the child or the person responsible at the child's place of stay;

(iv) information on the optional conclusion of an insurance policy to cover the cost of cancellation by the consumer or the cost of assistance, including repatriation, in the event of accident or illness.

2.   Member States shall ensure that in relation to the contract the following principles apply:
(a) depending on the particular package, the contract shall contain at least the elements listed in the Annex;
(b) all the terms of the contract are set out in writing or such other form as is comprehensible and accessible to the consumer and must be communicated to him before the conclusion of the contract; the consumer is given a copy of these terms;
(c) the provision under (b) shall not preclude the belated conclusion of last-minute reservations or contracts.
3.   Where the consumer is prevented from proceeding with the package, he may transfer his booking, having first given the organizer or the retailer reasonable notice of his intention before departure, to a person who satisfies all the conditions applicable to the package. The transferor of the package and the transferee shall be jointly and severally liable to the organizer or retailer party to the contract for payment of the balance due and for any additional costs arising from such transfer.
4.   (a) The prices laid down in the contract shall not be subject to revision unless the contract expressly provides for the possibility of upward or downward revision and states precisely how the revised price is to be calculated, and solely to allow for variations in:
—   transportation costs, including the cost of fuel,
—   dues, taxes or fees chargeable for certain services, such as landing taxes or embarkation or disembarkation fees at ports and airports,
—   the exchange rates applied to the particular package.
(b) During the twenty days prior to the departure date stipulated, the price stated in the contract shall not be increased.
5.   If the organizer finds that before the departure he is constrained to alter significantly any of the essential terms, such as the price, he shall notify the consumer as quickly as possible in order to enable him to take appropriate decisions and in particular:
—   either to withdraw from the contract without penalty,
—   or to accept a rider to the contract specifying the alterations made and their impact on the price.
The consumer shall inform the organizer or the retailer of his decision as soon as possible.
6.   If the consumer withdraws from the contract pursuant to paragraph 5, or if, for whatever cause, other than the fault of the consumer, the organizer cancels the package before the agreed date of departure, the consumer shall be entitled:
(a) either to take a substitute package of equivalent or higher quality where the organizer and/or retailer is able to offer him such a substitute. If the replacement package offered is of lower quality, the organizer shall refund the difference in price to the consumer;
(b) or to be repaid as soon as possible all sums paid by him under the contract.
       In such a case, he shall be entitled, if appropriate, to be compensated by either the organizer or the retailer, whichever the relevant Member State's law requires, for non-performance of the contract, except where:
(i)   cancellation is on the grounds that the number of persons enrolled for the package is less than the minimum number required and the consumer is informed of the cancellation, in writing, within the period indicated in the package description; or
(ii) cancellation, excluding overbooking, is for reasons of force majeure, i.e. unusual and unforeseeable circumstances beyond the control of the party by whom it is pleaded, the consequences of which could not have been avoided even if all due care had been exercised.

7. Where, after departure, a significant proportion of the services contracted for is not provided or the organizer perceives that he will be unable to procure a significant proportion of the services to be provided, the organizer shall make suitable alter-native arrangements, at no extra cost to the consumer, for the continuation of the package, and where appropriate compensate the consumer for the difference between the services offered and those supplied.

If it is impossible to make such arrangements or these are not accepted by the consumer for good reasons, the organizer shall, where appropriate, provide the consumer, at no extra cost, with equivalent transport back to the place of departure, or to another return-point to which the consumer has agreed and shall, where appropriate, compensate the consumer.

Article 5 [Liability of Organizers and Retailers]

1. Member States shall take the necessary steps to ensure that the organizer and/or retailer party to the contract is liable to the consumer for the proper performance of the obligations arising from the contract, irrespective of whether such obligations are to be performed by that organizer and/or retailer or by other suppliers of services without prejudice to the right of the organizer and/or retailer to pursue those other suppliers of services.

2. With regard to the damage resulting for the consumer from the failure to perform or the improper performance of the contract, Member States shall take the necessary steps to ensure that the organizer and/or retailer is/are liable unless such failure to perform or improper performance is attributable neither to any fault of theirs nor to that of another supplier of services, because:
— the failures which occur in the performance of the contract are attributable to the consumer,
— such failures are attributable to a third party unconnected with the provision of the services contracted for, and are unforeseeable or unavoidable,
— such failures are due to a case of force majeure such as that defined in Article 4 (6), second subparagraph (ii), or to an event which the organizer and/or retailer or the supplier of services, even with all due care, could not foresee or forestall.
In the cases referred to in the second and third indents, the organizer and/or retailer party to the contract shall be required to give prompt assistance to a consumer in difficulty.

In the matter of damages arising from the non-performance or improper performance of the services involved in the package, the Member States may allow compensation to be limited in accordance with the international conventions governing such services.

In the matter of damage other than personal injury resulting from the non-performance or improper performance of the services involved in the package, the Member States may allow compensation to be limited under the contract. Such limitation shall not be unreasonable.

3. Without prejudice to the fourth subparagraph of paragraph 2, there may be no exclusion by means of a contractual clause from the provisions of paragraphs 1 and 2.

4. The consumer must communicate any failure in the performance of a contract which he perceives on the spot to the supplier of the services concerned and to the organizer and/or retailer in writing or any other appropriate form at the earliest opportunity.

This obligation must be stated clearly and explicitly in the contract.

Article 6 [Prompt Reaction to Complaints]
In cases of complaint, the organizer and/or retailer or his local representative, if there is one, must make prompt efforts to find appropriate solutions.

Article 7 [Precautions Against Insolvency]
The organizer and/or retailer party to the contract shall provide sufficient evidence of security for the refund of money paid over and for the repatriation of the consumer in the event of insolvency.

Article 8 [Stricter National Laws]
Member States may adopt or return more stringent provisions in the field covered by this Directive to protect the consumer.

Article 9 [Implementation into National Laws]
1.   Member States shall bring into force the measures necessary to comply with this Directive before 31 December 1992. They shall forthwith inform the Commission thereof.
2.   Member States shall communicate to the Commission the texts of the main provisions of national law which they adopt in the field governed by this Directive. The Commission shall inform the other Member States thereof.

Article 10 [Addressees]
This Directive is addressed to the Member States.

Done at Luxembourg, 13 June 1990.
For the Council, The President, D. J. O'MALLEY

ANNEX: ELEMENTS TO BE INCLUDED IN THE CONTRACT IF RELEVANT TO THE PARTICULAR PACKAGE
(a)   the travel destination(s) and, where periods of stay are involved, the relevant periods, with dates;
(b)   the means, characteristics and categories of transport to be used, the dates, times and points of departure and return;
(c)   where the package includes accommodation, its location, its tourist category or degree of comfort, its main features, its compliance with the rules of the host Member State concerned and the meal plan;
(d)   whether a minimum number of persons is required for the package to take place and, if so, the deadline for informing the consumer in the event of cancellation;
(e)   the itinerary;
(f)   visits, excursions or other services which are included in the total price agreed for the package;
(g)   the name and address of the organizer, the retailer and, where appropriate, the insurer;
(h)   the price of the package, an indication of the possibility of price revisions under Article 4 (4) and an indication of any dues, taxes or fees chargeable for certain services (landing, embarkation or disembarkation fees at ports and airports, tourist taxes) where such costs are not included in the package;
(i)   the payment schedule and method of payment;
(j)   special requirements which the consumer has communicated to the organizer or retailer when making the booking, and which both have accepted;
(k)   periods within which the consumer must make any complaint concerning failure to perform or improper performance of the contract.

Directive 98/27 of the European Parliament and of the Council of 19 May 1998 on Injunctions for the Protection of Consumers' Interests[1]

THE EUROPEAN PARLIAMENT AND THE COUNCIL OF THE EUROPEAN UNION,

HAVING REGARD to the Treaty establishing the European Community, and in particular Article 100a thereof, [...]

(1) WHEREAS certain Directives, listed in the schedule annexed to this Directive, lay down rules with regard to the protection of consumers' interests;

(2) WHEREAS current mechanisms available both at national and at Community level for ensuring compliance with those Directives do not always allow infringements harmful to the collective interests of consumers to be terminated in good time; whereas collective interests mean interests which do not include the cumulation of interests of individuals who have been harmed by an infringement; whereas this is without prejudice to individual actions brought by individuals who have been harmed by an infringement;

(3) WHEREAS, as far as the purpose of bringing about the cessation of practices that are unlawful under the national provisions applicable is concerned, the effectiveness of national measures transposing the above Directives including protective measures that go beyond the level required by those Directives, provided they are compatible with the Treaty and allowed by those Directives, may be thwarted where those practices produce effects in a Member State other than that in which they originate;

(4) WHEREAS those difficulties can disrupt the smooth functioning of the internal market, their consequence being that it is sufficient to move the source of an unlawful practice to another country in order to place it out of reach of all forms of enforcement; whereas this constitutes a distortion of competition;

(5) WHEREAS those difficulties are likely to diminish consumer confidence in the internal market and may limit the scope for action by organisations representing the collective interests of consumers or independent public bodies responsible for protecting the collective interests of consumers, adversely affected by practices that infringe Community law;

(6) WHEREAS those practices often extend beyond the frontiers between the Member States; whereas there is an urgent need for some degree of approximation of national provisions designed to enjoin the cessation of the abovementioned unlawful practices irrespective of the country in which the unlawful practice has produced its effects; whereas, with regard to jurisdiction, this is without prejudice to the rules of private international law and the Conventions in force between Member States, while respecting the general obligations of the Member States deriving from the Treaty, in particular those related to the smooth functioning of the internal market;

(7) WHEREAS the objective of the action envisaged can only be attained by the Community; whereas it is therefore incumbent on the Community to act;

(8) Whereas the third paragraph of Article 3b of the Treaty makes it incumbent on the Community not to go beyond what is necessary to achieve the objectives of the Treaty; whereas, in accordance with that Article, the specific features of national legal systems must be taken into account to every extent possible by leaving Member States free to choose between different options having equivalent effect; whereas the courts or administrative authorities competent to rule on the proceedings referred to in Article 2 of this Directive should have the right to examine the effects of previous decisions;

---

1   OJ 1998 L 166, p. 51.

(9) WHEREAS one option should consist in requiring one or more independent public bodies, specifically responsible for the protection of the collective interests of consumers, to exercise the rights of action set out in this Directive; whereas another option should provide for the exercise of those rights by organisations whose purpose is to protect the collective interests of consumers, in accordance with criteria laid down by national law;

(10) WHEREAS Member States should be able to choose between or combine these two options in designating at national level the bodies and/or organisations qualified for the purposes of this Directive;

(11) WHEREAS for the purposes of intra-Community infringements the principle of mutual recognition should apply to these bodies and/or organisations; whereas the Member States should, at the request of their national entities, communicate to the Commission the name and purpose of their national entities which are qualified to bring an action in their own country according to the provisions of this Directive;

(12) WHEREAS it is the business of the Commission to ensure the publication of a list of these qualified entities in the Official Journal of the European Communities; whereas, until a statement to the contrary is published, a qualified entity is assumed to have legal capacity if its name is included in that list;

(13) WHEREAS Member States should be able to require that a prior consultation be undertaken by the party that intends to bring an action for an injunction, in order to give the defendant an opportunity to bring the contested infringement to an end; whereas Member States should be able to require that this prior consultation take place jointly with an independent public body designated by those Member States;

(14) WHEREAS, where the Member States have established that there should be prior consultation, a deadline of two weeks after the request for consultation is received should be set after which, should the cessation of the infringement not be achieved, the applicant shall be entitled to bring an action before the competent court or administrative authority without any further delay;

(15) WHEREAS it is appropriate that the Commission report on the functioning of this Directive and in particular on its scope and the operation of prior consultation;

(16) WHEREAS the application of this Directive should not prejudice the application of Community competition rules,

HAVE ADOPTED THIS DIRECTIVE:

Article 1 Scope

1.   The purpose of this Directive is to approximate the laws, regulations and administrative provisions of the Member States relating to actions for an injunction referred to in Article 2 aimed at the protection of the collective interests of consumers included in the Directives listed in the Annex, with a view to ensuring the smooth functioning of the internal market.

2.   For the purpose of this Directive, an infringement shall mean any act contrary to the Directives listed in the Annex as transposed into the internal legal order of the Member States which harms the collective interests referred to in paragraph 1.

Article 2 Actions for an injunction

1.   Member States shall designate the courts or administrative authorities competent to rule on proceedings commenced by qualified entities within the meaning of Article 3 seeking:

(a) an order with all due expediency, where appropriate by way of summary procedure, requiring the cessation or prohibition of any infringement;

(b) where appropriate, measures such as the publication of the decision, in full or in part, in such form as deemed adequate and/or the publication of a corrective statement with a view to eliminating the continuing effects of the infringement;

(c) insofar as the legal system of the Member State concerned so permits, an order against the losing defendant for payments into the public purse or to any beneficiary designated in or under national legislation, in the event of failure to comply with the decision within a time-limit specified by the courts or administrative authorities, of a fixed amount for each day's delay or any other amount provided for in national legislation, with a view to ensuring compliance with the decisions.

2.   This Directive shall be without prejudice to the rules of private international law, with respect to the applicable law, thus leading normally to the application of either the law of the Member State where the infringement originated or the law of the Member State where the infringement has its effects.

Article 3 Entities qualified to bring an action

For the purposes of this Directive, a "qualified entity" means any body or organisation which, being properly constituted according to the law of a Member State, has a legitimate interest in ensuring that the provisions referred to in Article 1 are complied with, in particular:

(a) one or more independent public bodies, specifically responsible for protecting the interests referred to in Article 1, in Member States in which such bodies exist and/ or

(b) organisations whose purpose is to protect the interests referred to in Article 1, in accordance with the criteria laid down by their national law.

Article 4 Intra-Community infringements

1.   Each Member State shall take the measures necessary to ensure that, in the event of an infringement originating in that Member State, any qualified entity from another Member State where the interests protected by that qualified entity are affected by the infringement, may seize the court or administrative authority referred to in Article 2, on presentation of the list provided for in paragraph 3. The courts or administrative authorities shall accept this list as proof of the legal capacity of the qualified entity without prejudice to their right to examine whether the purpose of the qualified entity justifies its taking action in a specific case.

2.   For the purposes of intra-Community infringements, and without prejudice to the rights granted to other entities under national legislation, the Member States shall, at the request of their qualified entities, communicate to the Commission that these entities are qualified to bring an action under Article 2. The Member States shall inform the Commission of the name and purpose of these qualified entities.

3.   The Commission shall draw up a list of the qualified entities referred to in paragraph 2, with the specification of their purpose. This list shall be published in the Official Journal of the European Communities; changes to this list shall be published without delay, the updated list shall be published every six months.

Article 5 Prior consultation

1.   Member States may introduce or maintain in force provisions whereby the party that intends to seek an injunction can only start this procedure after it has tried to achieve the cessation of the infringement in consultation with either the defendant or with both the defendant and a qualified entity within the meaning of Article 3(a) of the Member State in which the injunction is sought. It shall be for the Member State to decide whether the party seeking the injunction must consult the qualified entity. If the cessation of the infringement is not achieved within two weeks after the request for

consultation is received, the party concerned may bring an action for an injunction without any further delay.

2.   The rules governing prior consultation adopted by Member States shall be notified to the Commission and shall be published in the Official Journal of the European Communities.

Article 6 Reports

1.   Every three years and for the first time no later than five years after the entry into force of this Directive the Commission shall submit to the European Parliament and the Council a report on the application of this Directive.

2.   In its first report the Commission shall examine in particular:
— the scope of this Directive in relation to the protection of the collective interests of persons exercising a commercial, industrial, craft or professional activity;
— the scope of this Directive as determined by the Directives listed in the Annex;
— whether the prior consultation in Article 5 has contributed to the effective protection of consumers.

Where appropriate, this report shall be accompanied by proposals with a view to amending this Directive.

Article 7 Provisions for wider action

This Directive shall not prevent Member States from adopting or maintaining in force provisions designed to grant qualified entities and any other person concerned more extensive rights to bring action at national level.

Article 8 Implementation

1.   Member States shall bring into force the laws, regulations and administrative provisions necessary to comply with this Directive no later than 30 months after its entry into force. They shall immediately inform the Commission thereof.

When Member States adopt these measures, they shall contain a reference to this Directive or shall be accompanied by such reference on the occasion of their official publication. The methods of making such reference shall be adopted by Member States.

2.   Member States shall communicate to the Commission the provisions of national law which they adopt in the field covered by this Directive.

Article 9 Entry into force

This Directive shall enter into force on the twentieth day following that of its publication in the Official Journal of the European Communities.

Article 10 Addressees

This Directive is addressed to the Member States.

Done at Brussels, 19 May 1998.
For the European Parliament, The President, J.M. GIL-ROBLES
For the Council, The President, G. BROWN

ANNEX: LIST OF DIRECTIVES COVERED BY ARTICLE 1
1.   Council Directive 84/450 of 10 September 1984 relating to the approximation of the laws, regulations and administrative provisions of the Member States concerning misleading advertising, OJ 1984 L 250, p. 17.
2.   Council Directive 85/577 of 20 December 1985 to protect the consumer in respect of contracts negotiated away from business premises, see above, p. 611.

3.   Council Directive 87/102 of 22 December 1986 for the approximation of the laws, regulations and administrative provisions of the Member States concerning consumer credit, see above, p. 623.

4.   Council Directive 89/552 of 3 October 1989 on the coordination of certain provisions laid down by law, regulation or administrative action in Member States concerning the pursuit of television broadcasting activities: Articles 10 to 21, OJ 1989 L 298, p. 23, as amended [...].

5.   Council Directive 90/314 of 13 June 1990 on package travel, package holidays and package tours, see above, p. 632.

6.   Council Directive 92/28 of 31 March 1992 on the advertising of medicinal products for human use, OJ 1992 L 113, p. 13.

7.   Council Directive 93/13 of 5 April 1993 on unfair terms in consumer contracts, see above, p. 601.

8.   Directive 94/47 of the European Parliament and of the Council of 26 October 1994 on the protection of purchasers in respect of certain aspects of contracts relating to the purchase of the right to use immovable properties on a timeshare basis, OJ 1994 L 280, p. 83.

9.   Directive 97/7 of the European Parliament and of the Council of 20 May 1997 on the protection of consumers in respect of distance contracts, OJ 1997 L 144, p. 19.

Labour Law and Social Policy

Council Directive 75/117 of 10 February 1975 on the Approximation of the Laws of the Member States Relating to the Application of the Principle of Equal Pay for Men and Women[1]

THE COUNCIL OF THE EUROPEAN COMMUNITIES,

HAVING REGARD to the Treaty establishing the European Economic Community, an in particular Article 100 thereof; [...]
WHEREAS implementation of the principle that men and women should receive equal pay contained in Article 119 of the Treaty is an integral part of the establishment and functioning of the common market;
WHEREAS it is primarily the responsibility of the Member States to ensure the application of this principle by means of appropriate laws, regulations and administrative provisions;
WHEREAS the Council Resolution of 21 January 1974 concerning a social action programme, aimed at making it possible to harmonize living and working conditions while the improvement is being maintained and at achieving a balanced social and economic development of the Community, recognized that priority should be given to action taken on behalf of women as regards access to employment and vocational training and advancement, and as regards working conditions, including pay;
WHEREAS it is desirable to reinforce the basic laws by standards aimed at facilitating the practical application of the principle of equality in such a way that all employees in the Community can be protected in these matters;
WHEREAS differences continue to exist in the various Member States despite the efforts made to apply the Resolution of the conference of the Member states of 30 December 1961 on equal pay for men and women and whereas, therefore, the national provisions should be approximated as regards application of the principle of equal pay,

HAS ADOPTED THIS DIRECTIVE:

Article 1 [General Principles]
The principle of equal pay for men and women outlined in Article 119 of the Treaty, hereinafter called "principle of equal pay", means, for the same work or for work to which equal value is attributed, the elimination of all discrimination on grounds of sex with regard to all aspects and conditions of remuneration.

In particular, where a job classification system is used for determining pay, it must be based on the same criteria for both men and women and so drawn up as to exclude any discrimination on grounds of sex.

Article 2 [Legal Remedies for Employees]
Member States shall introduce into their national legal systems such measures as are necessary to enable all employees who consider themselves wronged by failure to apply the principle of equal pay to pursue their claims by judicial process after possible recourse to other competent authorities.

---

1   OJ 1975 L 45, p. 19.

Article 3 [Equal Pay Under Public Law]
Member States shall abolish all discrimination between men and women arising from laws, regulations or administrative provisions which is contrary to the principle of equal pay.

Article 4 [Collective and Individual Agreements]
Member States shall take the necessary measures to ensure that provisions appearing in collective agreements, wage scales, wage agreements or individual contracts of employment which are contrary to the principle of equal pay shall be, or may be declared, null and void or may be amended.

Article 5 [Protection against Dismissal]
Member States shall take the necessary measures to protect employees against dismissal by the employer as a reaction to a complaint within the undertaking or to any legal proceedings aimed at enforcing compliance with the principle of equal pay.

Article 6 [Effective Implementation]
Member States shall, in accordance with their national circumstances and legal systems, take the measures necessary to ensure that the principle of equal pay is applied. They shall see that effective means are available to take care that this principle is observed.

Article 7 [Dissemination of Information]
Member States shall take care that the provisions adopted pursuant to this Directive, together with the relevant provisions already in force, are brought to the attention of employees by all appropriate means, for example at their place of employment.

Article 8 [Implementation into National Law]
1.   Member States shall put into force the laws, Regulations and administrative provisions necessary in order to comply with this Directive within one year of its notification and shall immediately inform the Commission thereof.
2.   Member States shall communicate to the Commission the texts of the laws, regulations and administrative provisions which they adopt in the field covered by this Directive.

Article 9 [Reports]
Within two years of the expiry of the one-year period referred to in Article 8, Member States shall forward all necessary information to the Commission to enable it to draw up a report on the application of this Directive for submission to the Council.

Article 10 [Addressees]
This Directive is addressed to the Member States.

Done at Brussels, 10 February 1975.
For the Council, The President, G. Fitzgerald

Council Directive 76/207 of 9 February 1976 on the Implementation of the Principle of Equal Treatment for Men and Women as Regards Access to Employment, Vocational Training and Promotion, and Working Conditions[1]

THE COUNCIL OF THE EUROPEAN COMMUNITIES,

HAVING REGARD to the Treaty establishing the European Economic Community, and in particular Article 235 thereof, [...]
(1) WHEREAS the Council, in its Resolution of 21 January 1974 concerning a social action programme, included among the priorities action for the purpose of achieving equality between men and women as regards access to employment and vocational training and promotion and as regards working conditions, including pay;
(2) WHEREAS, with regard to pay, the Council adopted on 10 February 1975 Directive 75/117 on the approximation of the laws of the Member States relating to the application of the principle of equal pay for men and women;[2]
(3) WHEREAS Community action to achieve the principle of equal treatment for men and women in respect of access to employment and vocational training and promotion and in respect of other working conditions also appears to be necessary;
(4) WHEREAS, equal treatment for male and female workers constitutes one of the objectives of the Community, in so far as the harmonization of living and working conditions while maintaining their improvement are inter alia to be furthered;
(5) WHEREAS the Treaty does not confer the necessary specific powers for this purpose;
(6) WHEREAS the definition and progressive implementation of the principle of equal treatment in matters of social security should be ensured by means of subsequent instruments,

HAS ADOPTED THIS DIRECTIVE:

Article 1 [Objective]
1. The purpose of this directive is to put into effect in the Member States the principle of equal treatment for men and women as regards access to employment, including promotion, and to vocational training and as regards working conditions and, on the conditions referred to in paragraph 2, social security. This principle is hereinafter referred to as "the principle of equal treatment".
2. With a view to ensuring the progressive implementation of the principle of equal treatment in matters of social security, the Council, acting on a proposal from the Commission, will adopt provisions defining its substance, its scope and the arrangements for its application.

Article 2 [The Principle of Equal Treatment]
1. For the purposes of the following provisions, the principle of equal treatment shall mean that there shall be no discrimination whatsoever on grounds of sex either directly or indirectly by reference in particular to marital or family status.
2. This directive shall be without prejudice to the right of Member States to exclude from its field of application those occupational activities and, where appropriate, the

---

1 OJ 1976 L 39, p. 40.

2 See above, p. 644.

training leading thereto, for which, by reason of their nature or the context in which they are carried out, the sex of the worker constitutes a determining factor.
3. This directive shall be without prejudice to provision concerning the protection of women, particularly as regards pregnancy and maternity.
4. This directive shall be without prejudice to measures to promote equal opportunity for men and women, in particular by removing existing inequalities which affect women's opportunities in the areas referred to in Article 1 (1).

Article 3 [Abolition of Discrimination in the Access to Jobs]
1. Application of the principle of equal treatment means that there shall be no discrimination whatsoever on grounds of sex in the conditions, including selection criteria, for access to all jobs or posts, whatever the sector or branch of activity, and to all levels of the occupational hierarchy.
2. To this end, Member States shall take the measures necessary to ensure that:
(a) any laws, regulations and administrative provisions contrary to the principle of equal treatment shall be abolished;
(b) any provisions contrary to the principle of equal treatment which are included in collective agreements, individual contracts of employment, internal rules of undertakings or in rules governing the independent occupations and professions shall be, or may be declared, null and void or may be amended;
(c) those laws, regulations and administrative provisions contrary to the principle of equal treatment when the concern for protection which originally inspired them is no longer well founded shall be revised; and that where similar provisions are included in collective agreements, labour and management shall be requested to undertake the desired revision.

Article 4 [Abolition of Discrimination in Training]
Application of the principle of equal treatment with regard to access to all types and to all levels of vocational guidance, vocational training, advanced vocational training and retraining, means that Member States shall take all necessary measures to ensure that:
(a) any laws, regulations and administrative provisions contrary to the principle of equal treatment shall be abolished;
(b) any provisions contrary to the principle of equal treatment which are included in collective agreements, individual contracts of employment, internal rules of undertakings or in rules governing the independent occupations and professions shall be, or may be declared, null and void or may be amended;
(c) without prejudice to the freedom granted in certain Member States to certain private training establishments, vocational guidance, vocational training, advanced vocational training and retraining shall be accessible on the basis of the same criteria and at the same levels without any discrimination on grounds of sex.

Article 5 [Abolition of Discrimination Concerning Working Conditions]
1. Application of the principle of equal treatment with regard to working conditions, including the conditions governing dismissal, means that men and women shall be guaranteed the same conditions without discrimination on grounds of sex.
2. To this end, Member States shall take the measures necessary to ensure that:
(a) any laws, regulations and administrative provisions contrary to the principle of equal treatment shall be abolished;
(b) any provisions contrary to the principle of equal treatment which are included in collective agreements, individual contracts of employment, internal rules of under-

takings or in rules governing the independent occupations and professions shall be, or may be declared, null and void or may be amended;
(c) those laws, regulations and administrative provisions contrary to the principle of equal treatment when the concern for protection which originally inspired them is no longer well founded shall be revised; and that where similar provisions are included in collective agreements labour, and management shall be requested to undertake the desired revision.

Article 6 [Legal Remedies]
Member States shall introduce into their national legal systems such measures as are necessary to enable all persons who consider themselves wronged by failure to apply to them the principle of equal treatment within the meaning of Articles 3, 4 and 5 to pursue their claims by judicial process after possible recourse to other competent authorities.

Article 7 [Protection Against Dismissal]
Member States shall take the necessary measures to protect employees against dismissal by the employer as a reaction to a complaint within the undertaking or to any legal proceedings aimed at enforcing compliance with the principle of equal treatment.

Article 8 [Dissemination of Information]
Member States shall take care that the provisions adopted pursuant to this directive, together with the relevant provisions already in force, are brought to the attention of employees by all appropriate means, for example at their place of employment.

Article 9 [Implementation into National Law]
1.   Member States shall put into force the laws, regulations and administrative provisions necessary in order to comply with this directive within 30 months of its notification and shall immediately inform the Commission thereof.
    However, as regards the first part of Article 3 (2)(c) and the first part of Article 5 (2)(c), Member States shall carry out a first examination and if necessary a first revision of the laws, regulations and administrative provisions referred to therein within four years of notification of this directive.
2.   Member States shall periodically assess the occupational activities referred to in Article 2 (2) in order to decide, in the light of social developments, whether there is justification for maintaining the exclusions concerned. They shall notify the Commission of the results of this assessment.
3.   Member States shall also communicate to the Commission the texts of laws, regulations and administrative provisions which they adopt in the field covered by this directive.

Article 10 [Reports]
Within two years following expiry of the 30-month period laid down in the first subparagraph of Article 9 (1), Member States shall forward all necessary information to the Commission to enable it to draw up a report on the application of this Directive for submission to the Council.

Article 11 [Addressees]
This Directive is addressed to the Member States.

Done at Brussels, 9 February 1976.
For the Council, The President, G. Thorn

Council Directive 79/7 of 19 December 1978 on the Progressive Implementation of the Principle of Equal Treatment for Men and Women in Matters of Social Security[1]

THE COUNCIL OF THE EUROPEAN COMMUNITIES,

HAVING REGARD to the Treaty establishing the European Economic Community, and in particular Article 235 thereof, [...]
WHEREAS Article 1 (2) of Council Directive 76/207 of 9 February 1976 on the implementation of the principle of equal treatment for men and women as regards access to employment, vocational training and promotion, and working conditions[2] provides that, with a view to ensuring the progressive implementation of the principle of equal treatment in matters of social security, the Council, acting on a proposal from the Commission, will adopt provisions defining its substance, its scope and the arrangements for its application;
WHEREAS the Treaty does not confer the specific powers required for this purpose;
WHEREAS the principle of equal treatment in matters of social security should be implemented in the first place in the statutory schemes which provide protection against the risks of sickness, invalidity, old age, accidents at work, occupational diseases and unemployment, and in social assistance in so far as it is intended to supplement or replace the abovementioned schemes;
WHEREAS the implementation of the principle of equal treatment in matters of social security does not prejudice the provisions relating to the protection of women on the ground of maternity;
WHEREAS, in this respect, Member States may adopt specific provisions for women to remove existing instances of unequal treatment,

HAS ADOPTED THIS DIRECTIVE:

Article 1 [Objective]
The purpose of this Directive is the progressive implementation, in the field of social security and other elements of social protection provided for in Article 3, of the principle of equal treatment for men and women in matters of social security, hereinafter referred to as "the principle of equal treatment".

Article 2 [Covered Persons]
This Directive shall apply to the working population - including self-employed persons, workers and self-employed persons whose activity is interrupted by illness, accident or involuntary unemployment and persons seeking employment - and to retired or invalided workers and self-employed persons.

Article 3 [Covered Schemes]
1. This Directive shall apply to:
(a) statutory schemes which provide protection against the following risks:
— sickness,

---

1   OJ 1979 L 6, p. 24. See also Council Directive 86/378 of 24 July 1986 on the Implementation of the Principle of Equal Treatment for Men and Women in Occupational Social Security Schemes, OJ 1986 L 225, p. 40.

2   See above, p. 646.

— invalidity,
— old age,
— accidents at work and occupational diseases,
— unemployment
(b) social assistance, in so far as it is intended to supplement or replace the schemes referred to in (a).
2. This Directive shall not apply to the provisions concerning survivors´ benefits nor to those concerning family benefits, except in the case of family benefits granted by way of increases of benefits due in respect of the risks referred to in paragraph 1 (a).
3. With a view to ensuring implementation of the principle of equal treatment in occupational schemes, the Council, acting on a proposal from the Commission, will adopt provisions defining its substance, its scope and the arrangements for its application.

Article 4 [Principle of Equal Treatment]
1. The principle of equal treatment means that there shall be no discrimination whatsoever on ground of sex either directly, or indirectly by reference in particular to marital or family status, in particular as concerns:
— the scope of the schemes and the conditions of access thereto,
— the obligation to contribute and the calculation of contributions,
— the calculation of benefits including increases due in respect of a spouse and for dependants and the conditions governing the duration and retention of entitlement to benefits.
2. The principle of equal treatment shall be without prejudice to the provisions relating to the protection of women on the grounds of maternity.

Article 5 [Abolition of Discriminatory Rules]
Member States shall take the measures necessary to ensure that any laws, regulations and administrative provisions contrary to the principle of equal treatment are abolished.

Article 6 [Legal Remedies]
Member States shall introduce into their national legal systems such measures as are necessary to enable all persons who consider themselves wronged by failure to apply the principle of equal treatment to pursue their claims by judicial process, possibly after recourse to other competent authorities.

Article 7 [Exemptions]
1. This Directive shall be without prejudice to the right of Member States to exclude from its scope:
(a) the determination of pensionable age for the purposes of granting old-age and retirement pensions and the possible consequences thereof for other benefits
(b) advantages in respect of old-age pension schemes granted to persons who have brought up children; the acquisition of benefit entitlements following periods of interruption of employment due to the bringing up of children
(c) the granting of old-age or invalidity benefit entitlements by virtue of the derived entitlements of a wife
(d) the granting of increases of long-term invalidity, old-age, accidents at work and occupational disease benefits for a dependent wife
(e) the consequences of the exercise, before the adoption of this Directive, of a right of option not to acquire rights or incur obligations under a statutory scheme.
2. Member States shall periodically examine matters excluded under paragraph 1 in order to ascertain, in the light of social developments in the matter concerned, whether there is justification for maintaining the exclusions concerned.

Article 8 [Implementation into National Law]

1. Member States shall bring into force the laws, regulations and administrative provisions necessary to comply with this Directive within six years of its notification. They shall immediately inform the Commission thereof.
2. Member States shall communicate to the Commission the text of laws, regulations and administrative provisions which they adopt in the field covered by this Directive, including measures adopted pursuant to Article 7 (2).

They shall inform the Commission of their reasons for maintaining any existing provisions on the matters referred to in Article 7 (1) and of the possibilities for reviewing them at a later date.

Article 9 [Reports]

Within seven years of notification of this Directive, Member States shall forward all information necessary to the Commission to enable it to draw up a report on the application of this Directive for submission to the Council and to propose such further measures as may be required for the implementation of the principle of equal treatment.

Article 10 [Addressees]

This Directive is addressed to the Member States.

Done at Brussels, 19 December 1978.
For the Council, The President, H.-D. Genscher

Council Directive 97/80 of 15 December 1997 on the Burden of Proof in Cases of Discrimination Based on Sex[1]

THE COUNCIL OF THE EUROPEAN UNION,

HAVING REGARD to the Agreement on social policy annexed to the Protocol (No 14) on social policy annexed to the Treaty establishing the European Community, and in particular Article 2(2) thereof, [...]
(1) WHEREAS, on the basis of the Protocol on social policy annexed to the Treaty, the Member States, with the exception of the United Kingdom of Great Britain and Northern Ireland (hereinafter called "the Member States"), wishing to implement the 1989 Social Charter, have concluded an Agreement on social policy;
(2) WHEREAS the Community Charter of the Fundamental Social Rights of Workers recognizes the importance of combatting every form of discrimination, including discrimination on grounds of sex, colour, race, opinions and beliefs;
(3) WHEREAS paragraph 16 of the Community Charter of the Fundamental Social Rights of Workers on equal treatment for men and women, provides, *inter alia*, that "action should be intensified to ensure the implementation of the principle of equality for men and women as regards, in particular, access to employment, remuneration, working conditions, social protection, education, vocational training and career development";
(4) WHEREAS, in accordance with Article 3(2) of the Agreement on social policy, the Commission has consulted management and labour at Community level on the pos-

---

1   OJ 1998 L 14, p. 6, as amended by Council Directive 98/52 of 13 July 1998 on the extension of Directive 97/80 on the burden of proof in cases of discrimination based on sex to the United Kingdom of Great Britain and Northern Ireland.

sible direction of Community action on the burden of proof in cases of discrimination based on sex;

(5) WHEREAS the Commission, considering Community action advisable after such consultation, once again consulted management and labour on the content of the proposal contemplated in accordance with Article 3(3) of the same Agreement; whereas the latter have sent their opinions to the Commission;

(6) WHEREAS, after the second round of consultation, neither management nor labour have informed the Commission of their wish to initiate the process - possibly leading to an agreement - provided for in Article 4 of the same Agreement;

(7) WHEREAS, in accordance with Article 1 of the Agreement, the Community and the Member States have set themselves the objective, inter alia, of improving living and working conditions; whereas effective implementation of the principle of equal treatment for men and women would contribute to the achievement of that aim;

(8) WHEREAS the principle of equal treatment was stated in Article 119 of the Treaty, in Council Directive 75/117 of 10 February 1975 on the approximation of the laws of the Member States relating to the application of the principle of equal pay for men and women[1] and in Council Directive 76/207 of 9 February 1976 on the implementation of the principle of equal treatment for men and women as regards access to employment, vocational training and promotion and working conditions;[2]

(9) WHEREAS Council Directive 92/85 of 19 October 1992 on the introduction of measures to encourage improvements in the safety and health at work of pregnant workers and workers who have recently given birth or are breastfeeding[3] also contributes to the effective implementation of the principle of equal treatment for men and women; whereas that Directive should not work to the detriment of the aforementioned Directives on equal treatment; whereas, therefore, female workers covered by that Directive should likewise benefit from the adaptation of the rules on the burden of proof;

(10) WHEREAS Council Directive 96/34 of 3 June 1996 on the framework agreement on parental leave concluded by UNICE, CEEP and the ETUC[4], is also based on the principle of equal treatment for men and women;

(11) WHEREAS the references to "judicial process" and "court" cover mechanisms by means of which disputes may be submitted for examination and decision to independent bodies which may hand down decisions that are binding on the parties to those disputes;

(12) WHEREAS the expression "out-of-court procedures" means in particular procedures such as conciliation and mediation;

(13) WHEREAS the appreciation of the facts from which it may be presumed that there has been direct or indirect discrimination is a matter for national judicial or other competent bodies, in accordance with national law or practice;

(14) WHEREAS it is for the Member States to introduce, at any appropriate stage of the proceedings, rules of evidence which are more favourable to plaintiffs;

(15) WHEREAS it is necessary to take account of the specific features of certain Member States' legal systems, inter alia where an inference of discrimination is drawn if the respondent fails to produce evidence that satisfies the court or other competent authority that there has been no breach of the principle of equal treatment;

---

1   See above, p. 644.

2   See above, p. 646.

3   OJ L 348, 28. 11. 1992, p. 1.

4   OJ L 145, 19. 6. 1996, p. 4.

(16) WHEREAS Member States need not apply the rules on the burden of proof to proceedings in which it is for the court or other competent body to investigate the facts of the case; whereas the procedures thus referred to are those in which the plaintiff is not required to prove the facts, which it is for the court or competent body to investigate;

(17) WHEREAS plaintiffs could be deprived of any effective means of enforcing the principle of equal treatment before the national courts if the effect of introducing evidence of an apparent discrimination were not to impose upon the respondent the burden of proving that his practice is not in fact discriminatory;

(18) WHEREAS the Court of Justice of the European Communities has therefore held that the rules on the burden of proof must be adapted when there is a *prima facie* case of discrimination and that, for the principle of equal treatment to be applied effectively, the burden of proof must shift back to the respondent when evidence of such discrimination is brought;

(19) WHEREAS it is all the more difficult to prove discrimination when it is indirect; whereas it is therefore important to define indirect discrimination;

(20)WHEREAS the aim of adequately adapting the rules on the burden of proof has not been achieved satisfactorily in all Member States and, in accordance with the principle of subsidiarity stated in Article 3b of the Treaty and with that of proportionality, that aim must be attained at Community level; whereas this Directive confines itself to the minimum action required and does not go beyond what is necessary for that purpose,

HAS ADOPTED THIS DIRECTIVE:

Article 1 Aim

The aim of this Directive shall be to ensure that the measures taken by the Member States to implement the principle of equal treatment are made more effective, in order to enable all persons who consider themselves wronged because the principle of equal treatment has not been applied to them to have their rights asserted by judicial process after possible recourse to other competent bodies.

Article 2 Definitions

1.   For the purposes of this Directive, the principle of equal treatment shall mean that there shall be no discrimination whatsoever based on sex, either directly or indirectly.

2.   For purposes of the principle of equal treatment referred to in paragraph 1, indirect discrimination shall exist where an apparently neutral provision, criterion or practice disadvantages a substantially higher proportion of the members of one sex unless that provision, criterion or practice is appropriate and necessary and can be justified by objective factors unrelated to sex.

Article 3 Scope

1.   This Directive shall apply to:
(a) the situations covered by Article 119 of the Treaty and by Directives 75/117, 76/207 and, insofar as discrimination based on sex is concerned, 92/85 and 96/34;
(b) any civil or administrative procedure concerning the public or private sector which provides for means of redress under national law pursuant to the measures referred to in (a) with the exception of out-of-court procedures of a voluntary nature or provided for in national law.

2.   This Directive shall not apply to criminal procedures, unless otherwise provided by the Member States.

Article 4 Burden of proof

1.   Member States shall take such measures as are necessary, in accordance with their national judicial systems, to ensure that, when persons who consider themselves wronged because the principle of equal treatment has not been applied to them establish, before a court or other competent authority, facts from which it may be presumed that there has been direct or indirect discrimination, it shall be for the respondent to prove that there has been no breach of the principle of equal treatment.

2.   This Directive shall not prevent Member States from introducing rules of evidence which are more favourable to plaintiffs.

3.   Member States need not apply paragraph 1 to proceedings in which it is for the court or competent body to investigate the facts of the case.

Article 5 Information

Member States shall ensure that measures taken pursuant to this Directive, together with the provisions already in force, are brought to the attention of all the persons concerned by all appropriate means.

Article 6 Non-regression

Implementation of this Directive shall under no circumstances be sufficient grounds for a reduction in the general level of protection of workers in the areas to which it applies, without prejudice to the Member States' right to respond to changes in the situation by introducing laws, regulations and administrative provisions which differ from those in force on the notification of this Directive, provided that the minimum requirements of this Directive are complied with.

Article 7 Implementation

The Member States shall bring into force the laws, regulations and administrative provisions necessary for them to comply with this Directive by 1 January 2001. They shall immediately inform the Commission thereof.

As regards the United Kingdom of Great Britain and Northern Ireland, the date of 1 January 2001 in paragraph 1 shall be replaced by 22 July 2001.

When the Member States adopt those measures they shall contain a reference to this Directive or shall be accompanied by such a reference on the occasion of their official publication. The methods of making such references shall be laid down by the Member States.

The Member States shall communicate to the Commission, within two years of the entry into force of this Directive, all the information necessary for the Commission to draw up a report to the European Parliament and the Council on the application of this Directive.

Article 8 [Addressee]

This Directive is addressed to the Member States.

Done at Brussels, 15 December 1997.
For the Council, The President, J.-C. JUNCKER

Council Directive 77/187 of 14 February 1977 on the Approximation of the Laws of the Member States Relating to the Safeguarding of Employees' Rights in the Event of Transfers of Undertakings, Businesses or Parts of Undertakings or Businesses[1]

THE COUNCIL OF THE EUROPEAN COMMUNITIES,

HAVING REGARD to the Treaty establishing the European Economic Community, and in particular Article 100 thereof, [...]
Whereas economic trends are bringing in their wake, at both national and Community level, changes in the structure of undertakings, through transfers of undertakings, businesses or parts of businesses to other employers as a result of legal transfers or mergers;
WHEREAS it is necessary to provide for the protection of employees in the event of a change of employer, in particular, to ensure that their rights are safeguarded;
Whereas differences still remain in the Member States as regards the extent of the protection of employees in this respect and these differences should be reduced;
Whereas these differences can have a direct effect on the functioning of the Common Market;
WHEREAS it is therefore necessary to promote the approximation of laws in this field while maintaining the improvement described in Article 117 of the Treaty,

HAS ADOPTED THIS DIRECTIVE:

Section I Scope and definitions
Article 1 [Scope]
1. (a) This Directive shall apply to any transfer of an undertaking, business, or part of an undertaking or business to another employer as a result of a legal transfer or merger.
(b) Subject to subparagraph (a) and the following provisions of this Article, there is a transfer within the meaning of this Directive where there is a transfer of an economic entity which retains its identity, meaning an organised grouping of resources which has the objective of pursuing an economic activity, whether or not that activity is central or ancillary.
(c) This Directive shall apply to public and private undertakings engaged in economic activities whether or not they are operating for gain. An administrative reorganisation of public administrative authorities, or the transfer of administrative functions between public administrative authorities, is not a transfer within the meaning of this Directive.
2. This Directive shall apply where and insofar as the undertaking, business or part of the undertaking or business to be transferred is situated within the territorial scope of the Treaty.
3. This Directive shall not apply to sea-going vessels.

---

1   OJ 1977 L 61, p. 26, as amended by Council Directive 98/50 of 29 June 1998.

Article 2 [Definitions]
1.   For the purposes of this Directive:
(a) "transferor" shall mean any natural or legal person who, by reason of a transfer within the meaning of Article 1(1), ceases to be the employer in respect of the undertaking, business or part of the undertaking or business;
(b) "transferee" shall mean any natural or legal person who, by reason of a transfer within the meaning of Article 1(1), becomes the employer in respect of the undertaking, business or part of the undertaking or business;
(c) "representatives of employees" and related expressions shall mean the representatives of the employees provided for by the laws or practices of the Member States;
(d) "employee" shall mean any person who, in the Member State concerned, is protected as an employee under national employment law.
2.   This Directive shall be without prejudice to national law as regards the definition of contract of employment or employment relationship.

However, Member States shall not exclude from the scope of this Directive contracts of employment or employment relationships solely because:
(a) of the number of working hours performed or to be performed,
(b) they are employment relationships governed by a fixed-duration contract of employment within the meaning of Article 1(1) of Council Directive 91/383 of 25 June 1991 supplementing the measures to encourage improvements in the safety and health at work of workers with a fixed-duration employment relationship or a temporary employment relationship[1], or
(c) they are temporary employment relationships within the meaning of Article 1(2) of Directive 91/383, and the undertaking, business or part of the undertaking or business transferred is, or is part of, the temporary employment business which is the employer.

Section II Safeguarding of employees' rights
Article 3 [General Principle]
1.   The transferor's rights and obligations arising from a contract of employment or from an employment relationship existing on the date of a transfer shall, by reason of such transfer, be transferred to the transferee.

Member States may provide that, after the date of transfer, the transferor and the transferee shall be jointly and severally liable in respect of obligations which arose before the date of transfer from a contract of employment or an employment relationship existing on the date of the transfer.
2.   Member States may adopt appropriate measures to ensure that the transferor notifies the transferee of all the rights and obligations which will be transferred to the transferee under this Article, so far as those rights and obligations are or ought to have been known to the transferor at the time of the transfer. A failure by the transferor to notify the transferee of any such right or obligation shall not affect the transfer of that right or obligation and the rights of any employees against the transferee and/or transferor in respect of that right or obligation.
3.   Following the transfer, the transferee shall continue to observe the terms and conditions agreed in any collective agreement on the same terms applicable to the transferor under that agreement, until the date of termination or expiry of the collective agreement or the entry into force or application of another collective agreement.

---

1   OJ 1991 L 206, p. 19.

Member States may limit the period for observing such terms and conditions with the proviso that it shall not be less than one year.
4. (a) Unless Member States provide otherwise, paragraphs 1 and 3 shall not apply in relation to employees' rights to old-age, invalidity or survivors' benefits under supplementary company or inter-company pension schemes outside the statutory social security schemes in Member States.
(b) Even where they do not provide in accordance with subparagraph (a) that paragraphs 1 and 3 apply in relation to such rights, Member States shall adopt the measures necessary to protect the interests of employees and of persons no longer employed in the transferor's business at the time of the transfer in respect of rights conferring on them immediate or prospective entitlement to old age benefits, including survivors' benefits, under supplementary schemes referred to in subparagraph (a).

Article 4 [No Dismissal Because of Transfer]
1. The transfer of the undertaking, business or part of the undertaking or business shall not in itself constitute grounds for dismissal by the transferor or the transferee. This provision shall not stand in the way of dismissals that may take place for economic, technical or organisational reasons entailing changes in the workforce.
Member States may provide that the first subparagraph shall not apply to certain specific categories of employees who are not covered by the laws or practice of the Member States in respect of protection against dismissal.
2. If the contract of employment or the employment relationship is terminated because the transfer involves a substantial change in working conditions to the detriment of the employee, the employer shall be regarded as having been responsible for termination of the contract of employment or of the employment relationship.

Article 4a [Insolvency of Employer]
1. Unless Member States provide otherwise, Articles 3 and 4 shall not apply to any transfer of an undertaking, business or part of an undertaking or business where the transferor is the subject of bankruptcy proceedings or any analogous insolvency proceedings which have been instituted with a view to the liquidation of the assets of the transferor and are under the supervision of a competent public authority (which may be an insolvency practitioner authorised by a competent public authority).
2. Where Articles 3 and 4 apply to a transfer during insolvency proceedings which have been opened in relation to a transferor (whether or not those proceedings have been instituted with a view to the liquidation of the assets of the transferor) and provided that such proceedings are under the supervision of a competent public authority (which may be an insolvency practitioner determined by national law) a Member State may provide that:
(a) notwithstanding Article 3(1), the transferor's debts arising from any contracts of employment or employment relationships and payable before the transfer or before the opening of the insolvency proceedings shall not be transferred to the transferee, provided that such proceedings give rise, under the law of that Member State, to protection at least equivalent to that provided for in situations covered by Council Directive 80/987 of 20 October 1980 on the approximation of the laws of the Member States relating to the protection of employees in the event of the insolvency of their employer[1]; and, or alternatively, that

---

1   OJ 1980 L 283, p. 23, [as amended].

(b) the transferee, transferor, or person or persons exercising the transferor's functions, on the one hand, and the representatives of the employees on the other hand may agree alterations, insofar as current law or practice permits, to the employees' terms and conditions of employment designed to safeguard employment opportunities by ensuring the survival of the undertaking, business or part of the undertaking or business.

3.   A Member State may apply paragraph 2(b) to any transfers where the transferor is in a situation of serious economic crisis, as defined by national law, provided that the situation is declared by a competent public authority and open to judicial supervision, on condition that such provisions already exist in national law by 17 July 1998.

The Commission shall present a report on the effects of this provision before 17 July 2003 and shall submit any appropriate proposals to the Council.

4.   Member States shall take appropriate measures with a view to preventing misuse of insolvency proceedings in such a way as to deprive employees of the rights provided for in this Directive.

Article 5 [Preservation of Employees Rights]

1.   If the undertaking, business or part of an undertaking or business preserves its autonomy, the status and function of the representatives or of the representation of the employees affected by the transfer shall be preserved on the same terms and subject to the same conditions as existed before the date of the transfer by virtue of law, regulation, administrative provision or agreement, provided that the conditions necessary for the constitution of the employees' representation are fulfilled.

The first subparagraph shall not apply if, under the laws, regulations, administrative provisions or practice in the Member States, or by agreement with the representatives of the employees, the conditions necessary for the reappointment of the representatives of the employees or for the reconstitution of the representation of the employees are fulfilled.

Where the transferor is the subject of bankruptcy proceedings or any analogous insolvency proceedings which have been instituted with a view to the liquidation of the assets of the transferor and are under the supervision of a competent public authority (which may be an insolvency practitioner authorised by a competent public authority), Member States may take the necessary measures to ensure that the transferred employees are properly represented until the new election or designation of representatives of the employees.

If the undertaking, business or part of an undertaking or business does not preserve its autonomy, the Member States shall take the necessary measures to ensure that the employees transferred who were represented before the transfer continue to be properly represented during the period necessary for the reconstitution or reappointment of the representation of employees in accordance with national law or practice.

2.   If the term of office of the representatives of the employees affected by the transfer expires as a result of the transfer, the representatives shall continue to enjoy the protection provided by the laws, regulations, administrative provisions or practice of the Member States.

Section III Information and consultation
Article 6 [Pre-Transfer Information Duties]

1.   The transferor and transferee shall be required to inform the representatives of their respective employees affected by the transfer of the following:
—   the date or proposed date of the transfer,
—   the reasons for the transfer,
—   the legal, economic and social implications of the transfer for the employees,

— any measures envisaged in relation to the employees.

The transferor must give such information to the representatives of his employees in good time before the transfer is carried out.

The transferee must give such information to the representatives of his employees in good time, and in any event before his employees are directly affected by the transfer as regards their conditions of work and employment.

2. Where the transferor or the transferee envisages measures in relation to his employees, he shall consult the representatives of his employees in good time on such measures with a view to reaching an agreement.

3. Member States whose laws, regulations or administrative provisions provide that representatives of the employees may have recourse to an arbitration board to obtain a decision on the measures to be taken in relation to employees may limit the obligations laid down in paragraphs 1 and 2 to cases where the transfer carried out gives rise to a change in the business likely to entail serious disadvantages for a considerable number of the employees.

The information and consultations shall cover at least the measures envisaged in relation to the employees. The information must be provided and consultations taken place in good time before the change in the business as referred to in the first subparagraph is effected.

4. The obligations laid down in this Article shall apply irrespective of whether the decision resulting in the transfer is taken by the employer or an undertaking controlling the employer.

In considering alleged breaches of the information and consultation requirements laid down by this Directive, the argument that such a breach occurred because the information was not provided by an undertaking controlling the employer shall not be accepted as an excuse.

5. Member States may limit the obligations laid down in paragraphs 1, 2 and 3 to undertakings or businesses which, in terms of the number of employees, meet the conditions for the election or nomination of a collegiate body representing the employees.

6. Member States shall provide that, where there are no representatives of the employees in an undertaking or business through no fault of their own, the employees concerned must be informed in advance of:

— the date or proposed date of the transfer,
— the reason for the transfer,
— the legal, economic and social implications of the transfer for the employees,
— any measures envisaged in relation to the employees.

Section IV Final provisions
Article 7 [Stricter national Laws]

This Directive shall not affect the right of Member States to apply or introduce laws, regulations or administrative provisions which are more favourable to employees or to promote or permit collective agreements or agreements between social partners more favourable to employees.

Article 7a [Legal Remedies]

Member States shall introduce into their national legal systems such measures as are necessary to enable all employees and representatives of employees who consider themselves wronged by failure to comply with the obligations arising from this Directive to pursue their claims by judicial process after possible recourse to other competent authorities.

Article 7b [Amendments of the Directive]
The Commission shall submit to the Council an analysis of the effects of the provisions of this Directive before 17 July 2006. It shall propose any amendment which may seem necessary.

Article 8 [Implementation into National Law]
1.   Member States shall bring into force the laws, regulations and administrative provisions needed to comply with this Directive within two years of its notification and shall forthwith inform the Commission thereof.
2.   Member States shall communicate to the Commission the texts of the laws, regulations and administrative provisions which they adopt in the field covered by this Directive.

Article 9 [Reports]
Within two years following expiry of the two-year period laid down in Article 8, Member States shall forward all relevant information to the Commission in order to enable it to draw up a report on the application of this Directive for submission to the Council.

Article 10 [Addressees]
This Directive is addressed to the Member States.

Done at Brussels, 14 February 1977.
For the Council, The President, J. Silkin

1992 Agreement on Social Policy Concluded Between the Member States of the European Community

The undersigned 11 HIGH CONTRACTING PARTIES, that is to say the Kingdom of Belgium, the Kingdom of Denmark, the Federal Republic of Germany, the Hellenic Republic, the Kingdom of Spain, the French Republic, Ireland, the Italian Republic, the Grand Duchy of Luxembourg, the Kingdom of the Netherlands and the Portuguese Republic (hereinafter referred to as "the Member States"),[1]

WISHING to implement the 1989 Social Charter on the basis of the *acquis communautaire*,
CONSIDERING the Protocol on Social Policy,
HAVE AGREED as follows:

Article 1 [Objectives]
The Community and the Member States shall have as their objectives the promotion of employment, improved living and working conditions, proper social protection, dialogue between management and labour, the development of human resources with a view to lasting high employment and the combatting of exclusion. To this end the Community and the Member States shall implement measures which take account of the diverse forms of national practices, in particular in the field of contractual relations, and the need to maintain the competitiveness of the Community economy.

---

1   The United Kingdom, Austria, Finland and Sweden have subsequently ratified this protocol.

Article 2 [Community Powers]

1. With a view to achieving the objectives of Article I, the Community shall support and complement the activities of the Member States in the following fields:
— improvement in particular of the working environment to protect workers' health and safety;
— working conditions;
— the information and consultation of workers;
— equality between men and women with regard to labour market opportunities and treatment at work;
— the integration of persons excluded from the labour market, without prejudice to Article 127 of the Treaty establishing the European Community (hereinafter referred to as "the Treaty").

2. To this end, the Council may adopt, by means of directives, minimum requirements for gradual implementation, having regard to the conditions and technical rules obtaining in each of the Member States. Such directives shall avoid imposing administrative, financial and legal constraints in a way which would hold back the creation and development of small and medium-sized undertakings.

The Council shall act in accordance with the procedure referred to in Article 189c of the Treaty after consulting the Economic and Social Committee.

3. However, the Council shall act unanimously on a proposal from the Commission, after consulting the European Parliament and the Economic and Social Committee, in the following areas:
— social security and social protection of workers;
— protection of workers where their employment contract is terminated;
— representation and collective defence of the interests of workers and employers, including co-determination, subject to paragraph 6;
— conditions of employment for third-country nationals legally residing in Community territory;
— financial contributions for promotion of employment and job-creation, without prejudice to the provisions relating to the Social Fund.

4. A Member State may entrust management and labour, at their joint request, with the implementation of directives adopted pursuant to paragraphs 2 and 3.

In this case, it shall ensure that, no later than the date on which a directive must be transposed in accordance with Article 189, management and labour have introduced the necessary measures by agreement, the Member State concerned being required to take any necessary measure enabling it at any time to be in a position to guarantee the results imposed by that directive.

5. The provisions adopted pursuant to this Article shall not prevent any Member State from maintaining or introducing more stringent protective measures compatible with the Treaty.

6. The provisions of this Article shall not apply to pay, the right of association, the right to strike or the right to impose lock-outs.

Article 3 [Commission Action]

1. The Commission shall have the task of promoting the consultation of management and labour at Community level and shall take any relevant measure to facilitate their dialogue by ensuring balanced support for the parties.

2. To this end, before submitting proposals in the social policy field, the Commission shall consult management and labour on the possible direction of Community action.

3. If, after such consultation, the Commission considers Community action advisable, it shall consult management and labour on the content of the envisaged proposal.

Management and labour shall forward to the Commission an opinion or, where appropriate, a recommendation.

4.	On the occasion of such consultation, management and labour may inform the Commission of their wish to initiate the process provided for in Article 4. The duration of the procedure shall not exceed nine months, unless the management and labour concerned and the Commission decide jointly to extend it.

Article 4 ["Legislative Powers" of the Social Partners]

1.	Should management and labour so desire, the dialogue between them at Community level may lead to contractual relations, including agreements.

2.	Agreements concluded at Community level shall be implemented either in accordance with the procedures and practices specific to management and labour and the Member States or, in matters covered by Article 2, at the joint request of the signatory parties, by a Council decision on a proposal from the Commission.

The Council shall act by qualified majority, except where the agreement in question contains one or more provisions relating to one of the areas referred to in Article 2(3), in which case it shall act unanimously.

Article 5 [Cooperation Between Member States]

With a view to achieving the objectives of Article 1 and without prejudice to the other provisions of the Treaty, the Commission shall encourage cooperation between the Member States and facilitate the coordination of their action in all social policy fields under this Agreement.

Article 6 [The Principle of Equal Pay]

1.	Each Member State shall ensure that the principle of equal pay for male and female workers for equal work is applied.

2.	For the purpose of this Article, "pay" means the ordinary basic or minimum wage or salary and any other consideration, whether in cash or in kind, which the worker receives directly or indirectly, in respect of his employment, from his employer.

Equal pay without discrimination based on sex means:

(a)	that pay for the same work at piece rates shall be calculated on the basis of the same unit of measurement;

(b)	that pay for work at time rates shall be the same for the same job.

3.	This Article shall not prevent any Member State from maintaining or adopting measures providing for specific advantages in order to make it easier for women to pursue a vocational activity or to prevent or compensate for disadvantages in their professional careers.

Article 7 [Reports]

The Commission shall draw up a report each year on progress in achieving the objectives of Article 1, including the demographic situation in the Community. It shall forward the report to the European Parliament, the Council and the Economic and Social Committee.

The European Parliament may invite the Commission to draw up reports on particular problems concerning the social situation.

INDEX